CHRISTOPHER ANDREW
and
JULIUS GREEN

Stars and Spies

Intelligence Operations and the
Entertainment Business

VINTAGE

1 3 5 7 9 10 8 6 4 2

Vintage is part of the Penguin Random House group of companies
whose addresses can be found at global.penguinrandomhouse.com

Penguin
Random House
UK

Copyright © Christopher Andrew and Julius Green 2021

Christopher Andrew and Julius Green have asserted their
right to be identified as the authors of this Work in accordance
with the Copyright, Designs and Patents Act 1988

First published in Vintage in 2022
First published in hardback by The Bodley Head in 2021

penguin.co.uk/vintage

A CIP catalogue record for this book is available from the British Library

ISBN 9781784708719

Printed and bound in Great Britain by Clays Ltd, Elcograf S.p.A.

The authorised representative in the EEA is Penguin Random House Ireland,
Morrison Chambers, 32 Nassau Street, Dublin D02 YH68

Penguin Random House is committed to a sustainable future
for our business, our readers and our planet. This book is made
from Forest Stewardship Council® certified paper.

CHRISTOPHER ANDREW

Christopher Andrew is Emeritus Professor of Modern and Contemporary History at Cambridge University, Fellow and former President of Corpus Christi College, Honorary Professor at Queen's University, Belfast, former Official Historian of MI5, and former Visiting Professor at Harvard, Toronto and the Australian National University. He has presented numerous BBC documentaries, including, for twelve years, the Radio 4 series *What If?* His many books include a number which have appeared on bestseller lists on four continents. His most recent book, *The Secret World*, won the Airey Neave Book Prize, was a *Times* and *Daily Telegraph* Book of the Year, and was selected by Ben Macintyre as one of the five best books ever written on espionage. Professor Andrew has visited the Lubyanka, Russian intelligence HQ in Moscow, as well as lectured in the main auditorium of the CIA HQ in Langley, Virginia.

JULIUS GREEN

Julius Green is an entertainment historian. He received an MA in History from Cambridge University, where he attended Corpus Christi College, and was awarded his PhD by Goldsmiths, University of London. He is a Fellow of the Birkbeck Centre for Contemporary Theatre, and a lecturer at the Central School of Speech and Drama and the National Film and Television School. In 2014 he was Fellow Commoner at Corpus Christi. He is also an award-winning theatre producer and circus director, with over 250 productions to his credit, and has been a member of the Board of Management of the Society of London Theatre and the Board of Directors of the Edinburgh Festival Fringe Society. His books include *How to Produce a West End Show* and *Agatha Christie: A Life in Theatre*, and he is a regular columnist for *The Stage* newspaper.

For Dianne and Jenny

Contents

Introduction: The Art of Deception · 1

1 Golden Age: Theatre and Intelligence
   in the Reign of Elizabeth I · 11
2 'Our Revels Now are Ended': Stars and Spies
   under the Early Stuarts · 33
3 'Astrea Wants Money': Stars and Spies
   after the Restoration · 57
4 British Theatre, the 'Golden Rump'
   and the Ancien Régime · 76
5 The Age of Revolution · 94
6 From Counter-Revolution in Europe
   to Civil War in America · 115
7 The Late Nineteenth Century:
   From the Fenians to 'J'Accuse!' · 141
8 Spies and German Spy Scares · 159
9 The First World War: From Mistinguett
   to the Hush-Hush Revue · 176
10 Between the Wars: From Tallulah Bankhead
   to Secret Agent Ronald Reagan · 208
11 The Second World War: Soviet Penetration
   and British Deception · 241
12 Shaken not Stirred: The 'Special
   Relationship' and the Founding of the
   Central Intelligence Agency · 270
13 Cold War Intelligence and the
   Entertainment Business · 300
14 Spies in the Limelight · 339

Notes   383
Bibliography of Publications   449
Picture Credits   477
Acknowledgements   479
Index   481

Introduction

The Art of Deception

Interplay between the worlds of entertainment and espionage goes back at least 2,500 years. The fact that one relies on publicity and the other on secrecy, that stars live in the spotlight and spies in the shadows, might seem to rule out successful symbiosis between the two professions. A famous entertainer is generally a successful entertainer, while a famous spy is most often either a failed spy or an ex-spy. Both professions, however, often require similar skills and sometimes attract similar personalities. This book investigates the affinities between these two worlds of smoke and mirrors, and examines the overlapping expertise of some of their leading players.

The adoption of a fictional persona, the learning of scripts and the ability to improvise are central to both professions, and undercover agents often find themselves engaged in what is effectively an exercise in long-form role play. In the early twentieth century, Mansfield Cumming, the first chief of Britain's foreign intelligence service, SIS (also known as MI6), purchased his disguises from the same theatrical costumier as the leading West End theatres. His heads of station abroad included a number of leading theatricals. 'We like your poetical reports immensely', Cumming wrote to one of them. 'Please send us some more.' Role play remains compulsory for today's recruits to SIS and the Security Service MI5, all of whom pretend to have other jobs. During his thirty-three-year career in SIS before becoming its chief in 1999, Richard Dearlove 'used to travel the world extensively in different identities ... well supported with bank accounts, credit cards, everything you needed'.

A number of entertainment industry luminaries – performers, writers, directors and other creative practitioners – have at one time or another tried their hands at espionage. The transitory lifestyle of itinerant entertainers is often not dissimilar to that of many spies, and this can make them peculiarly well suited to undercover work – a fact which intelligence services have sometimes been able to exploit to good effect. France's most internationally renowned playwright at the end of the Ancien Régime was also its leading spy, whose operations led to Britain's first defeat in the American War of Independence. Some enthusiastic entertainer-spies, however, proved out of their depth. Those executed for German espionage during the First World War ranged from the manager of the Bijou Picture Theatre in Finchley Road, London, to the upmarket international exotic dancer, Mata Hari.

While the roles of both stars and spies have evolved over the centuries, their priorities have changed little. Though the primary responsibility of spies remains to 'steal secrets', they have also been used for a variety of other covert activities. From Elizabethan times onwards, talented entertainers have been involved in a diverse series of influence operations. The most successful – and outrageous – attempt ever made by a British intelligence agency to deceive a US president came not from an intelligence professional but from a professional entertainer recruited for the purpose, who later became head of BBC TV Light Entertainment. Given the colourful dramatis personae involved over the centuries in both espionage and show business, it is unsurprising that the lines between fantasy and reality have sometimes been blurred. It now seems that the foreign intelligence reports sent by Britain's first successful female dramatist in the mid 1660s were probably invented – though they provide remarkable evidence of her creative imagination.

Some of the most successful deceptions in intelligence history have drawn on the skills more commonly found in a film studio's scenery, props and make-up departments. There is a strong argument that an intelligence agency which shows the creative imagination of a successful film studio will have a clear advantage over less imaginative opponents – as in Operation MINCEMEAT during the Second World War when German intelligence was deceived by the British into believing that the corpse of a homeless Welshman carrying fake documents was that of a Royal Marine officer bearing genuine top-secret plans for an Allied invasion. One of the CIA's most successful deceptions, the 'Canadian Caper' in Iran, was based on the creation of a bogus film studio. The leader of the operation, who was also chief of Agency disguise, graphics and (false) authentication, later entitled his memoirs *The Master of Disguise: My Secret Life in the CIA*.[1] Operation TROJAN SHIELD, probably the largest-scale and most wide-ranging post-Cold War intelligence deception mounted by the 'Five Eyes' (the US, UK, Canada, Australia and New Zealand), owed its success to a creative imagination reminiscent of the highly successful wartime Double-Cross system. Criminal gangs around the world were duped into using a compromised messaging app which enabled 27 million of their messages to be intercepted.[2]

The best known assassination by a twentieth-century intelligence agency, the killing of Leon Trotsky by Stalin's NKVD in Mexico City in 1940, was also a triumph of role play and deception. The Spanish assassin, Ramón Mercader, a Soviet 'illegal' agent, posed successively as the Belgian Jacques Mornard and the Canadian Frank Jacson. He gained access to Trotsky by seducing his confidante Sylvia Ageloff, an American Trotskyist. Ageloff said later that until Mercader struck Trotsky a fatal blow on the back of his head with a concealed ice pick, she had never doubted the sincerity of Mercader's love for her.[3] Some less homicidal twenty-first-century Russian illegals in the United States have posed so successfully as Americans or Canadians that even their own children had no idea they were either Russian or spies.

Some spies, however, have not found it necessary to play anyone other than themselves. As with the old cliché of the murder weapon displayed on the mantelpiece, undercover operators can sometimes find it most effective to conceal themselves in plain sight. A celebrity performer is uniquely placed to do this, and, like the famous American actor who assassinated Abraham Lincoln in the president's theatre box, enjoys 'access all areas' privileges which any professional spy would envy – rubbing shoulders with politicians and royalty, and sometimes sharing their confidences. While it may well have been possible for England's first playwright-spy, Christopher Marlowe, to work undercover for some years without being identified, despite the popularity of his plays, the development of modern mass media meant that by the time Noël Coward found himself undertaking minor but colourful intelligence-gathering missions in America during the Second World War, he was an instantly recognisable figure and had no option but to 'play' himself. What is interesting in this case is that, in the performance of his duties, he appears to have adopted an exaggerated portrayal of his own persona – almost as if he was consciously playing the character of a spy.

The relationship between stars and spies has never run entirely smoothly. Some entertainers are by nature subversive of established regimes. Ben Jonson raged against the 'vile spies' of early Jacobean

Dame Judi Dench as 'M' in *Skyfall*, with Daniel Craig as Bond.

England, and by the mid nineteenth century, detailed intelligence files were being kept on some of Europe's leading writers and playwrights. The archives of intelligence agencies around the globe contain numerous dossiers on creative practitioners working across the entertainment media of theatre, film, music and broadcasting, mostly as the subjects of state surveillance and (in some countries) censorship.

The entertainment media have always found the ambivalent role of the spy popular with audiences. Their fictionalised portrayals of the world of espionage, a necessarily secretive profession which until very recently has done little to engage with public perceptions of its activities, has led to a glamorisation of its work which often bears little relation to reality. The fictional character of James Bond, who has effectively become a global ambassador for the British secret service (whether it likes it or not) is far better known than any real spy has ever been. The current chief of SIS has publicly suggested that his agency should have a voice in the choice of the next actor to play Bond.[4]

In 1995, for the first time, 'M' in the Bond films was played by a woman, Dame Judi Dench, who continued as chief for a total of seven films. Though assassinated in *Skyfall* (2012), Dench is still probably better known than any of the growing minority of real twenty-first-century female intelligence chiefs.

The inspiration for Dench's fictional role as 'M' was the appointment in 1992 of Stella Rimington as both MI5's first female director general and the first woman to head any of the world's major intelligence agencies. Many in Whitehall believed that, unlike her male predecessors, Rimington, a keen amateur actor, 'enjoyed being in the limelight'. The first generation of female recruits to MI5 had taken the lead role after victory in the First World War in an affectionately irreverent in-house revue, *Hush-Hush*, in which women writers and performers outnumbered men. The programme cover showed the director, Vernon Kell, being tied up and taken away for questioning on suspicion of being a German spy.

In recent years a majority of Western, as well as some non-Western, intelligence agencies have devised often entertaining posts on social media both to promote what they consider less fanciful depictions of themselves than those in spy films and to encourage new recruits. Since the CIA enigmatically opened a twitter account in 2014 ('We can neither confirm nor deny that this is our first tweet'),[5] it has posted items on the entertainment business ranging from the film *Black Panther* to the cult TV series *Game of Thrones*. Like a number of other intelligence agencies, it also sends Valentine's Day greetings each year to its social media followers.[6]

*

The first books to argue the case for the importance of intelligence operations were written not in classical Greece or Rome[7] but in ancient China and the Indian subcontinent: *The Art of War*, traditionally ascribed to Confucius's contemporary, the Chinese general Sun Tzu (c.544–c.496 BC); and the *Arthashastra*, a manual on statecraft attributed to Kautilya, a senior adviser to the Maurya dynasty which was at the peak of its power in India between about 350 and 283 BC.

According to *The Art of War*, governments and commanders 'who are able to use the most intelligent people as agents are certain to achieve great things'. Their achievements, especially in wartime, usually depend on deceiving the enemy. 'All warfare is based on deception', wrote Sun Tzu. 'Therefore, when capable, feign incapacity. When active, inactivity.'[8] The ability to deceive is a key skill for actors as well as for spies. Entertainers have historically played key roles in some strategic, as well as tactical, deceptions, though, as we are reminded

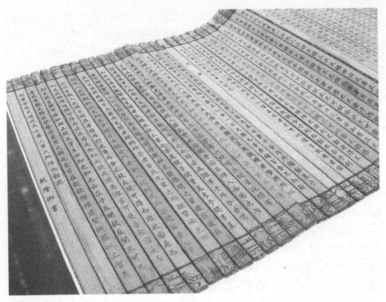

Bamboo edition of *The Art of War*.

by Leo Rosten, probably the only twentieth-century political scientist who was also a successful screen writer during the golden age of Hollywood: 'Acting is a form of deception, and actors can mesmerize themselves almost as easily as an audience.'[9]

Kautilya's *Arthashastra* discussed in enormous detail the recruitment, uses and cover occupations of the huge espionage network which he urged the king to establish under his personal control, both to collect intelligence and to conduct covert operations. Those recommended by the *Arthashastra* for working undercover in enemy courts without arousing suspicion include hunchbacks and dwarfs (both likely to have been engaged as court entertainers) and 'women skilled in various arts' (chiefly singers and dancers).[10] Amongst those listed as useful for smuggling out hostages held by the enemy were actors, dancers, singers, musicians, storytellers, acrobats and conjurers.[11] Kautilya was also a pioneer in devising what were later called 'honey-traps': ' … acrobats, actors and actresses, dancers and conjurers shall make chiefs [of ruling oligarchies] infatuated with young women of great beauty'[12]; 'women secret agents may pose as a rich widow, one with a secret income, a singer, a dancer or an expert in abetting love affairs'.[13]

European 'courtesans' were also originally to be found – as the word suggests – at court, where their responsibilities, like those of the court jester, would sometimes include both entertainment (usually as singers or dancers) and intelligence gathering. Catherine de' Medici, queen consort of France (1547–1559) and a notable sponsor of the arts, retained a troupe of dancers (later dubbed 'the Flying Squadron' in recognition of their balletic skills) whose members, if legend is to be believed, both seduced and spied upon visitors to the French court.[14] As members of a profession (some would say the oldest) which regularly engages in role play in the course of its work, courtesans unsurprisingly make a number of notable guest appearances in the history of stars and spies. Spies are said to be the second-oldest profession.

While both performers and spies often owed their living to the court, there is only one known example of a monarch who, reputedly, was personally proficient in both spheres. The most celebrated act of espionage in Anglo-Saxon England was the alleged eavesdropping by King Alfred the Great during his wars against the Danish invaders led by Guthrum the Old. In 878, at a low point during the conflict, Alfred left his island refuge of Athelney in the Somerset marshes and entered Guthrum's camp disguised as a minstrel. According to the great twelfth-century English historian, William of Malmesbury: 'Taking a harp in his hand, he proceeded to the king's tent. Singing before the entrance, and at times touching the trembling strings in harmonious cadence, he was readily admitted.'[15] The

King Alfred the Great: probably the first and most successful English royal spy. The only contemporary images of him are on coins like this and the small 'Alfred Jewel'. All show him as clean-shaven, not, as was later imagined, bearded.

intelligence Alfred obtained while posing as a minstrel is said to have enabled him to win the decisive battle of Ethandun over the Danes.[16] No other monarch in English history has been credited with an espionage operation of comparable importance. His choice of disguise was significant – no one thought twice about letting in a travelling entertainer.

The early troubadours were 'stars' in a way that no earlier musicians had been, 'creating the first "modern" European examples of the individual artist, a genius set apart from the common folk'.[17] They were also, observes David Boyle, 'stateless wanderers who often provided valuable intelligence to princes': 'They would be there by the fire as the local lord and his family and servants discussed their hopes, plans and local events ... All they needed to do was listen ... '[18]

The most famous minstrel said to have been involved in espionage during the high Middle Ages was the twelfth-century troubadour[19] Blondel de Nesle, whose music was performed at the coronation in Reims Cathedral in 1179 of the 14-year-old Philip II Augustus, the first French ruler to style himself 'King of France'. It was probably at the coronation that Blondel first met the heir to the English throne, Richard the Lionheart, who was also a talented musician. According to folklore, when Richard (by now the English king) was captured while returning from the Third Crusade in 1192, it was Blondel who discovered the castle where he was being secretly held captive. Blondel made his way through Germany and Austria, stopping beneath a succession of castle walls, playing his lute and singing verses he and Richard had composed together. There was no response until he reached the castle of Dürnstein, high above the Danube, forty miles west of Vienna. Here, when Blondel had finished the first verse, Richard's voice from within the castle tower joined in the second. Though this (once widely believed) account of the discovery of the captured King of England is now known to be fictitious,[20] it is interestingly reminiscent of the *Arthashastra*'s advocacy 1,500 years before of using singers and musicians to secure the release of hostages.

The most talented musical star to spy for an English monarch was the Bavarian Petrus Alamire, a singer and instrumentalist who performed regularly at royal courts. From 1515 to 1518 Henry VIII and his chief adviser, Cardinal Thomas Wolsey, used him to spy on the pretender to the English throne, Richard de la Pole, who had sought refuge in Metz; Alamire signed his reports with the musical notation, 'La Mi Re'. To show his loyalty to Henry, Alamire presented him with a sumptuously illustrated choirbook which included motets by leading French and Flemish composers. When it was recorded for the first time in 2014 under the title *The Spy's Choirbook: Petrus Alamire and the Court of Henry VIII*,[21] the CD quickly rose to number two in the classical music charts. Alamire, however, was a double agent who transferred his main allegiance to de la Pole. When the king and Wolsey discovered his treachery, Alamire wisely decided not to return to England.[22] In Elizabethan and early Stuart England, musicians and travelling players continued to play occasional roles as spies and confidential couriers.[23]

Stars and Spies explores the historic link between espionage and entertainment in a great variety of manifestations. As we consider the history of intelligence operations from a new perspective, by interweaving it with that of the entertainment business, we hope that the multi-faceted and sometimes complex relationship between the two will become apparent. The starting point of our detailed investigation is the reign of Queen Elizabeth I, which saw England emerge as the world leader in both intelligence operations and theatre: a combination which we believe to be no coincidence. Both thrive on the wit and dramatic ability of their practitioners – qualities which arguably typified the best of the Elizabethan age itself. Since Shakespeare's day, the pantheon of stars and spies – whether working in collaboration or in opposition – has been populated by a cast-list of sometimes eccentric personalities, who have contributed to a series of remarkable dramas and deceptions.

I

Golden Age: Theatre and Intelligence in the Reign of Elizabeth I

Elizabeth I's long reign from 1558 to 1603, though glorious in retrospect, was at the time a period of intense insecurity. The Catholic powers of Europe regarded her as both a bastard and a heretic. The loyalty of English Catholics, unreconciled to her Protestant Church settlement, was always in doubt.

The main threats to English security came from invasion plans by the most powerful ruler of the time, Philip II of Spain, and from plots backed by him, with papal blessing, to depose Elizabeth and put Mary, Queen of Scots on the throne to return England to the Catholic faith. Elizabeth faced a serious threat of assassination. Rulers assassinated on the continent included both Henry III and Henry IV of France. The combined menace of foreign invasion and a Catholic fifth column at home led the Elizabethan state to create what was then the world's most sophisticated intelligence system. Sir Francis Walsingham, who from 1573 to 1590 combined the roles of foreign minister ('principal Secretary of State') and intelligence chief, had daily access to the queen. The intelligence he reported to Elizabeth came from domestic surveillance, foreign espionage and – for the first time in English history – from codebreaking. Walsingham told his chief codebreaker, Thomas Phelippes, that he would 'not believe in how good part [the queen] accepteth of your service'.

Unlike many later intelligence chiefs around the world, Walsingham did not hesitate to 'speak truth to power'. The truth was sometimes unwelcome. On one occasion, exasperated by what Walsingham told her, Elizabeth took off one of her slippers and threw it at his head. But the queen also gave Walsingham a portrait of her and the three previous Tudor monarchs as a 'mark of her people's and her own content' with him.[1] What Walsingham told Elizabeth about the plots to assassinate her made, unsurprisingly, a deep impression. In 1586 she asked that the execution of Sir Anthony Babington and his fellow plotters be made particularly painful. She was told that the existing method of 'protracting' their public execution by hanging, drawing and quartering was as terrible as could be devised.[2]

As well as being the first English monarch to have daily meetings with her intelligence chief, Elizabeth also had an unprecedented interest in drama. During her reign, far more plays were performed at court than under any of her predecessors. She followed most of them with close attention and became well known for helping confused foreign ambassadors understand what was happening on stage.[3]

'The Theatre', which opened in Shoreditch in 1576, was the first purpose-built venue in London since Roman rule ended over a millennium earlier. It was one of at least ten commercial theatres, all open-air, which sprung up in various locations in and around the capital between 1574 and 1578. 'Nothing of the kind', writes the theatre historian, Herbert Berry, 'had happened anywhere or would happen again in London for centuries.'[4] Elizabethan playhouses were the greatest innovation in the entertainment business until twentieth-century cinemas and television.

By the mid 1580s, the best actors worked for the queen. In 1583, on behalf of the Privy Council, Walsingham instructed Elizabeth's Master of the Revels, Edmund Tilney, to found her own acting company, the Queen's Men. Tilney picked the best actors from other companies. Twice the size of any of their rivals, the Queen's Men had a monopoly for the next five years of performances at court, as well as performing in London theatres and on tour.[5] Their undoubted star – the first in the history of the English theatre – was the comedian Richard Tarlton, who, despite his humble, probably rural, origins, was given the right to describe himself in his will as 'one of the Groomes of the Queenes maiesties chamber'. According to the playwright Thomas Nashe, Tarlton had only to appear on stage to have the audience – Elizabeth included – in fits of laughter. If Walsingham was the queen's favourite spy, Tarlton, until his death in 1588, was her favourite star. According to the seventeenth-century historian and cleric, Thomas Fuller:

> When Queen Elizabeth was serious, I dare not say sullen, and out of good humour, he could un-dumpish her at his pleasure. Her highest

favourites would, in some cases, go to Tarlton before they would go to the queen, and he was their usher to prepare their advantageous access unto her. In a word, he told the queen more of her faults than most of her chaplains, and cured her melancholy better than all of her physicians.[6]

Will Kemp, Tarlton's successor as London's most popular clown and 'jesting player', was probably the inspiration for Shakespeare's Yorick, remembered by Hamlet as 'a fellow of infinite jest, of most excellent fancy'. For a time Kemp was used as a confidential courier between England and the Low Countries, where he sometimes performed, but he proved unreliable and absent-minded. On one occasion, Sir Philip Sidney complained to Walsingham that letters he had written to his wife Frances (Walsingham's daughter) containing frank criticism of Robert Dudley, Earl of Leicester, had been mistakenly delivered by Kemp to the Countess of Leicester.[7]

Though Walsingham had little personal enthusiasm for drama, he was a strong supporter of the Queen's Men, whose pro-Tudor history plays and other performances were intended to reinforce popular loyalty to Elizabeth and her Church. Some of the Queen's Men were spies as well as stars. Their provincial tours helped Walsingham to monitor regional support for Roman Catholicism. An Act of 1584 commanded all Catholic priests to leave the country within forty days or to swear an oath of loyalty to the queen – failing which they would be guilty of high treason.[8] Between 1582 and 1595 thirty Catholic priests were hanged, drawn and quartered in the north of England,[9] most at the Knavesmire gallows near York, a city which was one of the most profitable venues for the Queen's Men.[10] As a result of the destruction of all Walsingham's papers, no records survive of reports by the Queen's Men on signs of sedition in the areas where they performed. But intelligence on York's small but tenacious Catholic minority, which secretly sheltered priests, must have been of particular interest to him.[11]

Walsingham regarded acting ability as a key skill for his intelligence recruits. Probably his most successful spy abroad was Anthony Standen, an English Catholic loyal to Elizabeth I who posed as 'Pompeo Pellegrini' and provided vital intelligence on Philip II's preparations for an invasion of England by the Spanish Armada. In 1587 intelligence from Standen enabled Elizabeth's favourite privateer, Sir Francis Drake, to 'singe the King of Spain's beard' and delay the departure of the Armada for England by attacking the Spanish fleet in Cadiz harbour – thus demonstrating, Walsingham boasted to Standen, 'how little we did fear them'.[12]

Some of Walsingham's other spies at home and abroad were Protestants who pretended to be Catholics in order to penetrate Catholic institutions and suspected conspiracies. In February 1579, Anthony Munday, a 19-year-old actor[13] and later a leading playwright, began a three-month stay in Rome at the Jesuit-controlled Collegium Anglorum (English College), almost certainly as one of Walsingham's spies.[14] Using the alias 'Anthony Hawley', Munday was the first significant English writer to visit Rome since the Reformation. (The next to do so was John Milton sixty years later).[15] To penetrate the English College, Munday had to pretend to be a devout Catholic, serve at mass, go to confession and join in denunciations of Anglican heresy. He later justified what, for a loyal Anglican, was blasphemous behaviour by claiming that he had no option:

> my adversaries object against me, that I went to mass, and helped the priest myself to say mass: so that (say they) who is worst, I am as evil as he. I answer, I did indeed, for he that is in Rome, especially in the College among the scholars, must live as he may, not as he will; favour comes by conformity, and death by obstinacy.[16]

Munday was so successful in acting the part of a committed Catholic that two English Jesuit novices, Luke Kirby (later canonised) and Henry Orton, lent him money and entrusted to him letters for delivery to their friends and family in England.[17] Though the letters do not survive, they were doubtless passed on to Walsingham and probably revealed their plans to return secretly to England as Catholic missionaries. Kirby was arrested as soon as he landed at Dover in June 1580.[18]

On Ash Wednesday 1579, Munday, alongside other novices from the English College, had been present at an audience with Pope Gregory XIII in the Apostolic Palace – a unique moment in the history of post-Reformation English espionage. According to Munday, tears trickled down the Pope's white beard as he told the novices:

> As I am your refuge when persecution dealeth straitly with you in your country by reason of the heretical religion there used, so I will be your

bulwark to defend you, your guide to protect you, your father to
nourish you, and your friend with my heart blood to do you any profit.

Munday dismissed the Pope's concern for the fate of Jesuit missionaries
in England as hypocrisy – 'deceites the devil hath to accomplish his
desire'.[19] He also mocked the self-imposed suffering of some of the
novices as they prepared for their dangerous missions:

> The Jesuits have, some of them, to whip themselves, whips with cords
> of wire, wherewith they will beat themselves till with too much effuse
> of blood they be ready to give up the ghost.[20]

By twenty-first-century standards, some of Walsingham's spies were
remarkably young. His use of the 19-year-old Munday as a spy in
Rome was paralleled by his recruitment of several Cambridge
University students to penetrate the Rheims seminary.

On Munday's return to London, as well as resuming his career as
an actor, he helped to track down the members of Jesuit missions to
England, and published a series of savage anti-Catholic pamphlets.[21]
Though Munday had never met Edmund Campion (later canonised),
a leader of the first mission, he was one of the chief witnesses at
Campion's trial in Westminster Hall in November 1581. Part of
Munday's tract, *A Discouerie of Edmund Campion, and his Confederates*,
which accused them of 'the most horrible and traitorous practises
against Her Maiesties most royall person and the realme', was read
aloud from the scaffold at Tyburn, when Campion and other Jesuits
were executed on 1 December. Munday described himself on the title
page as 'sometime the Popes Scholler, allowed in the Seminarie
[English College] at Roome'.

Some of the priests executed that day showed extraordinary bravery
and religious devotion on the scaffold as they were first hanged, cut
down while still alive, castrated, disembowelled and beheaded before
their bodies were cut in four. The (admittedly sympathetic) Thomas
Alfield, who stood 'very near' the scaffold, reported that Campion
'meekly and sweetly yielded his soul unto his Saviour, protesting that
he died a perfect catholic'.[22]

From Elizabethan England onwards, playwrights and others in the
entertainment business were used for what a modern intelligence
agency would call 'influence operations', as well as to collect

¶ A Difcouerie of *Edmund*
Campion , and his Confederates, their moſt horrible and traite-
rous practiſes,againſt her Maieſties moſt
royall perſon , and the Realme.

Wherein may be ſeene , how
thorowe the whole courſe of their
Araignement: they were notably
conuicted of euery cauſe.

VVhereto is added , the Execution of
Edmund Campion,Raphe Sherwin,*and*
Alexander Brian , *executed at Ti-*
borne the 1. of *December.*

Publiſhed by *A. M.* ſometime the
Popes Scholler, allowed in the Seminarie
at *Roome* amongſt them : a Diſcourſe
needefull to be read of euery man,
to beware how they deale with
ſuch ſecret ſeducers.

Seene ,and allowed.

↵ Imprinted at London for *Edwarde*
VVhite, dwelling at the little North
doore of Paules,at the ſigne of
the Gunne,the 29.of Ianua.1581.

intelligence. Munday was one of the first, publicly denigrating all the condemned missionary priests as contemptible cowards:

> These are the Martyrs of the Romish Church, not one of them patient, penitent, nor endued with courage unto the extremitie of death: but dismaying, trembling & fearful as the eye witnesses can beare me record.[23]

Luke Kirby, against whom Munday had testified at his trial, showed, on the contrary, conspicuous courage on the scaffold, declaring his innocence and claiming that Munday had no evidence against him. The Sheriff then summoned Munday from the crowd of onlookers to respond to Kirby's claims. Even by Munday's account, Kirby seems to have had the better of their exchange, reminding Munday

> what freendshippe he had shewed unto me [in Rome], and had done the lyke unto a number of English men, whom he knew well not to be of their Religion, bothe out of his own purse, as also be freending

them to some of the Popes Chamber, he made conveyance for them thence, some tyme going fortie miles with them …[24]

During the hunt for priests and other hidden papists, Munday worked closely with the most brutal of Walsingham's interrogators, Richard Topcliffe, notorious for his use of a variety of tortures – 'Topcliffian customs', as they were euphemistically termed at court.[25] Munday even dedicated a book to Topcliffe. Published in 1588, its title was curiously at odds with Topcliffe's fearsome reputation: *A Banquet of Daintie Conceits. Furnished with Verie Delicate and Choyse Inuentions, to Delight Their Mindes, who Take Pleasure in Musique, and There-withall to Sing Sweete Ditties* … A promised second volume failed to appear.

In 1584, Munday found fame as a playwright with *Fedele and Fortunio*, his adaptation of the Italian romantic comedy *Il Fedele*, written eight years earlier by Luigi Pasqualigo. In the play Fedele returns from a journey abroad to find that his friend Fortunio has fallen in love with his lover Victoria. Wrongly believing that Victoria has betrayed him, Fedele turns his attentions to Virginia. Espionage, combined with an element of sorcery, reveals the two women's true feelings, and, after a number of entanglements and misadventures, the play ends happily with Fedele marrying Victoria and Fortunio marrying Virginia. The popularity of the play at court in 1584 did much to ensure its success. The printed version of the play, published in the following year, recorded on the title page that it had been 'presented before the Queenes most excellent Majestie', and included both a 'Prologue before the Queen' and an 'Epilogue at the Court'. Munday's reputation at court was heightened by his hunt for hidden papists. In 1587, as a reward for his good service, Elizabeth granted Munday leases in reversion of eight Crown properties. From 1588 to 1596 Munday signed his publications 'Anthony Munday, Messenger of Her Majesties Chamber'.[26]

*

In contrast to the light entertainment provided by *Fedele and Fortunio*, the dramatic sensation of the mid 1580s was the first production in 1587 of *Tamburlaine*, a blood-soaked tragedy in blank verse loosely based on the life of the Central Asian tyrant, Timur. *Tamburlaine* established its 23-year-old author, Christopher ('Kit') Marlowe, as the greatest playwright of the era. The play's popular appeal led to a

Marlowe in Corpus Christi's
Buttery Book for Easter term
1581. 'Marlen', at the bottom
of the list, has spent 5s. 4d.

proliferation of Asian tyrants ('Tamerlanes and Tamer-chams', as Ben
Jonson called them) in the drama of the next decade.

What makes Marlowe's precocious success as a playwright even
more extraordinary is that, like Munday, he was also a spy, probably
recruited to Walsingham's secret service in 1585 while studying for
his MA at Corpus Christi College, Cambridge.[27]

The Corpus Christi Buttery Book, which recorded students' expenditure on food and drink, shows that from 1585, when Marlowe began
his intelligence career, his presence at the College became irregular
and his expenditure while there considerably higher.[28]

An anonymous portrait in Corpus painted in 1585,[29] widely believed
to be of Marlowe, shows a flamboyantly-dressed 21-year-old and carries
the Latin inscription *Quod me nutrit me destruit*: 'What nourishes me
destroys me'. The inscription arguably proved prophetic. The personal
passions which came to consume Marlowe generated enmities which
help to explain his murder in 1593 at the age of 29.[30]

In June 1587, the Privy Council sent a letter to Cambridge University
authorities designed to ensure that Marlowe's absences abroad did

not delay the award of his MA: 'in all his actions he had behaved himself orderly and discreetly whereby he had done her Majesty good service, & deserved to be rewarded for his faithful dealing'. Though the Privy Council did not, of course, refer directly to Marlowe's espionage, it acknowledged rumours that, like other of Walsingham's recruits, he had visited the Catholic seminary in Rheims, successor to the English College in Rome as the main source of missionary priests trained to travel secretly to England. The Privy Council, however, denounced claims by 'those who are ignorant in th'affaires he went about' that Marlowe intended to take up residence in Rheims:

> Whereas it was reported that Christopher Morley [Marlowe] was determined to have gone beyond the seas to Reames [Rheims] and there to remain, Their L[ordshi]ps thought good to certify that he had no such intent ...[31]

Few clues survive of how Marlowe's experience of espionage influenced his writing. But, when describing how Faustus sold his soul to

the Devil in *The Tragical History of the Life and Death of Doctor Faustus*,
written in 1588, he must have had in mind how his fellow Cambridge
recruit to the Elizabethan secret service, Richard Baines from Christ's
College, had blasphemously taken vows as a Catholic priest at the
Rheims seminary in 1581, swearing 'on the Bible that I believed in all
the articles of the Catholic faith', before trying unsuccessfully to poison
his fellow seminarians.[32] In the longer version of *Doctor Faustus*, Faustus
and Mephistopheles improve on Baines' deception and visit the Pope
disguised as cardinals. The Pope is completely deceived and blesses
Mephistopheles, who tells Faustus, 'was never devil thus bless'd
before.'[33]

The most successful spy used by Walsingham against extremist
Catholic conspirators in England was Robert Poley, graduate of Clare
College, Cambridge, and – initially – a friend of Marlowe. Poley
penetrated the entourage of Anthony Babington, leader of probably
the most dangerous plot to assassinate the queen, by posing as a
committed Catholic supporter of Mary, Queen of Scots. Babington
gave him a diamond ring as a token of close friendship. After his arrest
Babington suspected that he had been betrayed by Poley but could
not quite believe him capable of such treachery. He wrote to Poley:
'Farewell sweet Robyn, if as I take thee, true to me. If not adieu,
omnium bipedum nequissimus [vilest of all two-footed creatures].'
Marlowe was to find the devious Poley, like the obnoxious Baines, an
untrustworthy friend.[34]

Unlike Marlowe, the even more talented but less precocious
William Shakespeare was an actor before he became a playwright.
Will probably had a good grammar school education in Stratford-
upon-Avon until the age of 15 but did not go on to university. Though
born only about a month after Marlowe,[35] he did not have his
first play performed until a few months before Marlowe's murder in
1593.

Shakespeare's first serious contact with the acting profession probably came at the age of 5 in 1569, when two troupes of travelling
actors, the Queen's Players and Worcester's Men, the first companies
known to have played in Stratford, came successively to his father
John's house in Henley Street (now, as 'Shakespeare's Birthplace', a
major tourist attraction).[36] Will would have seen them parade through
Stratford, dressed in colourful liveries, to the rattle of drums and the
blare of trumpets. John Shakespeare was then high bailiff (mayor),

and the troupes needed his permission to perform in Stratford at the Guildhall and post bills advertising their performances. John may well have taken his son, free of charge, to see one of their plays. Another young boy named R. (possibly Robert) Willis, whose father took him to a performance by travelling players, later recalled: 'This sight tooke such impression in me that when I came towards mans estate, it was as fresh in my memory, as if I had seen it newly acted.'[37] Will Shakespeare probably had equally vivid memories.

Shakespeare's name appears in no written records between 1585 and 1592. In 1585 he was living in Stratford with his wife and three children. Seven years later he was working as a playwright and an actor in London. Though there is no proof, it has been plausibly suggested that, at some point during the seven 'missing years', Shakespeare began an acting career with the Queen's Men (not to be confused with the earlier Queen's Players).[38] He later drew on their repertoire when writing his own history plays, taking plots, characters, and occasionally phrases from, for example, The True Tragedy of Richard III and The Famous Victories of Henry V.[39]

Marlowe was an important influence on Shakespeare's early career as a playwright. Shakespeare's first major experience of Marlowe's work was probably watching Tamburlaine in London in 1587. 'The fingerprints of Tamburlaine', writes Stephen Greenblatt, 'are all over the plays that are among Shakespeare's earliest known ventures as playwright.'[40] Shakespeare allows himself an occasional in-joke when drawing on Marlowe's work. He improves on one of Tamburlaine's insults:

> Holla, ye pampered jades of Asia!
> What can ye draw but twenty miles a day?[41]

In Shakespeare's Henry IV, Part 2, the swaggering soldier, Ancient Pistol, adds a further ten miles:

> Hollow pampered jades of Asia,
> Which cannot go but thirty miles a day.[42]

It is probable that Shakespeare and Marlowe actually collaborated, as Elizabethan playwrights often did.[43] On successive days in January 1593, the Rose Theatre on Bankside put on plays which included

Shakespeare's *Titus Andronicus*, Marlowe's *The Jew of Malta*, and *Harry the Sixth* (presumably *Henry VI, Part I*).[44] Suggestions that the two worked together in writing the three parts of *Henry VI* in 1591–2 have been reinforced by recent computer analysis of the text. The editors of the latest edition of the *New Oxford Shakespeare* controversially ascribe authorship of the plays jointly to 'William Shakespeare and Christopher Marlowe'.[45]

During their collaboration, Marlowe may well have talked to Shakespeare about his intelligence career, which entered its most controversial and indiscreet phase in the confused aftermath of Walsingham's death in 1590. In 1592 Nicholas Faunt, formerly one of Walsingham's chief assistants, complained that 'the multitude of servants in this kind [intelligence] ... of late years hath bred much confusion with want of secrecy and dispatch.'[46] His own recruit Marlowe was one of those responsible. Marlowe's fellow spy and former friend, Richard Baines, accused him of blasphemy, telling the Privy Council, probably correctly, that Marlowe had declared 'that Christ was a bastard and his mother dishonest', and that 'Saint John the Evangelist was bedfellow to Christ [who] used him as the sinners of Sodoma.'[47]

In 1587 the Privy Council had certified that Marlowe 'in all his actions had behaved himself orderly and discreetly whereby he had done her Majesty good service'. By the early 1590s, however, his behaviour was far from 'orderly and discreet'. Marlowe was imprisoned in 1589 after a swordfight in Shoreditch which led to the death of an innkeeper's son, and 'bound over to keep the peace' after another fight in 1592. In the same year he was accused of attacking a tailor in Canterbury. Whether or not he started these fights, Marlowe's hot temper had clearly made him an intelligence liability. While in Flushing (now Vlissingen in Holland), then an English possession, early in 1592, he was arrested for counterfeiting.[48] Marlowe's indiscretions left their mark on Shakespeare's *Richard III*, probably written in 1592: it is the first play which uses 'intelligence' to mean secret information.[49] The Lord Chamberlain, Lord Hastings, boasts in the play that, 'Nothing can proceed that toucheth us whereof I shall not have intelligence'. His intelligence, however, turns out to be seriously flawed, and he is executed by the king.

The collaboration between the two greatest Elizabethan playwrights was cut short by Marlowe's violent death on 30 May 1593. Marlowe was killed after dining in Deptford, near London, with three sinister acquaintances: Robert Poley, Nicholas Skeres, a swindler accused in Star Chamber of 'entrapping young gents', and Ingram Frizer, accused of being in league with Skeres' swindles. According to an inquest held next day by the royal coroner with a local jury, Frizer and Marlowe fell out over the bill. 'Moved with anger', Marlowe allegedly snatched Frizer's dagger from him and struck him on the head, possibly with the blunt end. Frizer grabbed his dagger back and stabbed Marlowe above the right eye, fatally wounding him. The jury found that Frizer had acted in self-defence. Much about Marlowe's death, however, remains mysterious. It is quite possible that Marlowe's violent end was related to the rivalries and disruption within Elizabethan intelligence which followed Walsingham's death, but, unless further evidence is discovered, the truth may never emerge.[50]

Shakespeare later made a veiled but unmistakable reference to Marlowe's death in *As You Like It*, performed in 1599. In a tribute to Marlowe, Shakespeare quoted his words in the play:

> Dead shepherd, now I find thy saw [saying] of might:
> 'Who ever loved who loved not at first sight?'

The 'dead shepherd' was Marlowe. 'Who ever loved who loved not at first sight?' was probably then (as it still is) the best-known line from his narrative poem *Hero and Leander*, first published posthumously in the previous year.[51] Though Shakespeare is known to have collaborated with other dramatists, Marlowe is the only one to whom he paid public tribute.[52] The maxim chosen by Marlowe for his (probable) portrait in his Cambridge College, *Quod me nutrit, me destruit*, reappears in Shakespeare's Sonnet 73 as 'Consumed with that which it was nourished by'.[53]

Thanks, initially, to what he had learned from his discussions with Marlowe about Walsingham's secret service, Shakespeare continued to refer intermittently to intelligence operations for the rest of his career.[54] One of the most famous of his plays, *Hamlet*, first performed at the Globe (of which he was a shareholder) in 1600 or 1601, was also the first in which, at some stage, a majority of the characters spy on the others. The battle of wits between Claudius and Prince Hamlet – two 'mighty opposites' – is dominated by spying.[55] Agatha Christie called *Hamlet* 'a detective play'. She took the title of her celebrated detective drama, *The Mousetrap*, the longest-running play in the history of world theatre, from that jokingly given by Hamlet to the play performed at the Danish court by a group of travelling players which, following his own additions to the script, reveals how his father, the king, was murdered by Claudius.[56] Horatio spies on Claudius to observe his shocked reaction to the re-enactment of the murder. Shakespeare thus makes an ingeniously novel contribution to spy fiction, based on his own first-hand experience of travelling players spreading propaganda and engaging in clandestine activities on behalf of their patrons. When Hamlet discusses the script with the 'first player', he asks him:

> You could, for a need,
> study a speech of some dozen or sixteen lines, which
> I would set down and insert in't, could you not?

'Ay, my lord', replies the actor. Travelling players, the Queen's Men among them, were probably used to such requests.

Hamlet also includes the first memorable use of the word 'spy' in any English play. Claudius tells Gertrude, 'When sorrows come, they come not single spies / But in battalions.' Almost four centuries later, Alan Bennett gave the title *Single Spies* to his play about two of the most successful spies ever to work in Britain for a foreign power. Part One (*An Englishman Abroad*) was devoted to Guy Burgess; Part Two (*A Question of Attribution*) to his friend Anthony Blunt.

Shakespeare showed a better conceptual grasp of intelligence issues than any subsequent British writer until Daniel Defoe, who, like Marlowe, had first-hand experience of espionage. He was the first dramatist to dwell on the frustration of policymakers who receive equivocal or uncertain intelligence reports and on the problems of speaking truth to power (exemplified by Macbeth's order: 'Bring me no more reports!').[57] King John's exasperated reaction to intelligence failure resonates with that of Richard Nixon over three and a half centuries later. John famously asks, after being surprised by unexpected news of the advance of a large French army: 'O, where hath our intelligence been drunk?'[58] President Nixon demanded after an intelligence failure in Cambodia, 'What the hell do those clowns do out there at Langley [CIA HQ]?'[59]

Shakespeare also gives some striking examples of SIGINT (intelligence derived from intercepting and, where necessary, decrypting messages). Like Marlowe, he was probably aware of its use to monitor plots to bring Mary, Queen of Scots to the throne. Elizabeth was full of praise for Thomas Phelippes's success in decrypting Mary's correspondence and awarded him an annual pension of 100 marks (worth about £10,000 today) – an unheard-of sign of royal favour to a codebreaker.[60]

Until Mary's 1586 treason trial, which revealed her correspondence with Babington and led to her execution at Fotheringhay Castle the following year, Mary had been blithely unaware that her correspondence had been intercepted and decrypted by Phelippes.[61] Similarly, in Shakespeare's *Henry V*, believed to be the first play performed at the new Globe Theatre in 1599, 'The king hath note of all that they [his enemies] intend,/By interception which they dream not of.' When Hamlet kills Polonius, Claudius sends Rosencrantz and Guildenstern (the names of two real Danish courtiers)[62] to escort the prince on a journey to England, providing them with a secret letter to the King of England asking him to arrange for Hamlet's prompt execution. En route, the rightly distrustful Hamlet opens the letter and replaces it with another, purporting to come from Claudius, requesting the execution of Rosencrantz and Guildenstern instead.[63]

Where Shakespeare differs most from twenty-first-century notions of intelligence is in the role of the supernatural. Intelligence on the murder of King Hamlet comes from his Ghost. According to tradition, in the first performance of *Hamlet*, the Ghost was played by Shakespeare himself. In *Macbeth* three 'secret, black and midnight hags' respond to his request for future intelligence by summoning apparitions. The third famously assures him that

> Macbeth shall never vanquish'd be until
> Great Birnam wood to high Dunsinane hill
> Shall come against him.

When this improbable event begins his downfall, Macbeth blames 'th' equivocation of the fiend,/That lies like truth'.[64]

*

It is possible that Shakespeare's recipe for the brew in the witches' cauldron in *Macbeth* was influenced by that of the witch Medusa in

Munday's *Fedele and Fortunio*.[65] For the remainder of Elizabeth's reign, Munday combined success as a playwright with continuing involvement in intelligence operations. The fragmentary record of his operations provides further evidence of his lack of scruples. As one agent reported shortly before Walsingham's death in 1590, Munday

> hath been in divers places, where I have passed; whose dealing hath been very rigorous and yet done very small good, but rather much hurt; for in one place, in pretence to search for [Catholic] Agnus Deis and hallowed grains, he carried from a widow 40/-, the which he took out of a chest. A few of these matches will either raise a rebellion or cause your officers to be murdered.

Topcliffe, however, retained complete confidence in Munday as 'a man that wants no wytte', and was 'not ... of dull dispocytion towardes Gods trewe relidgion. Or to her majesty his Sovereigne, But Rather well disposed, & dewtyfull.'[66]

Munday was also engaged in covert operations against Puritan critics of the leadership of the Church of England. He took a central part in the hunt for the anonymous author of the 'Martin Marprelate' tracts: six pamphlets and a broadsheet printed on a press which from October 1588 to September 1589 was secretly moved across England from one puritan household to another to escape its pursuers. Witty, rumbustious and outrageously irreverent, the tracts are now widely recognised as 'the finest prose satires of their era'. As the author's pseudonym, 'Mar-prelate', suggests, his main targets were prelates: 'It is not possible that naturally there can be any good bishop.' Chief among the 'proud, popish, presumptuous, profane, paultrie, pestilent, and pernicious prelates' of the Church of England ridiculed by the tracts were Archbishop John Whitgift, the 'Canterbury Caiaphas', and Bishop Thomas Cooper of Winchester, whom Marprelate threatened to 'bumfeg' (spank) vigorously: 'hold my cloak there somebody, that I may go roundly to work.'[67] Munday too was attacked in a Marprelate tract of July 1589: 'Ah, thou Judas! Thou that hast already betrayed the papists, I think meanest to betray us also.'[68] Though the identity of Martin Marprelate remained unknown,[69] Munday and other agents successfully tracked down the printing press and most of those involved in the publication of his tracts.[70]

Privately recognising the ineffectiveness of official ripostes to the tracts, Archbishop Whitgift insisted that accomplished writers be found to 'stop Martin & his fellows mouths' by answering them 'after their own vein of writing'.[71] A group of leading playwrights was covertly commissioned to write anonymous tracts mocking critics of the leadership of the Church of England. Though Munday played some part in the influence operation,[72] the chief role in the attempt to discredit the Marprelate tracts was secretly assigned to the writers and playwrights John Lyly and Thomas Nashe.

John Lyly's *Euphues, the Anatomy of Wit: Very Pleasant for All Gentlemen to Read*, published in 1578, had made him for a time the most fashionable author in England. In 1583–4 his first two plays, *Campaspe* and *Sappho and Phao*, were performed at court.[73] Thomas Nashe's closeness to Whitgift during the Marprelate controversy is shown by the fact that his only surviving play, *Summers Last Will and Testament* (now best known for its poems), was written while staying in the Archbishop's summer palace at Croydon in 1592. His chief contribution to the campaign against Martin Marprelate was the pamphlet, *An Almond for a Parrat*, written under the alias Cuthbert Curry-Knave and probably published in early 1590. To try to ensure its popularity, he dedicated his anonymous attack on 'the knave Martin' to the most popular comic actor of the time:

To that most comical and conceited cavalier, Monsieur du Kempe, Jest-monger and vicegerent general to the ghost of Dick Tarleton, his loving brother Cuthbert Curry-Knave sendeth greeting.

Will Kemp had succeeded Tarlton as London's favourite clown, for whom Shakespeare was to write some of his most famous comic roles. Nashe, however, could not equal the exceptional comic talent either of the 'knave Martin' or of the clown Kemp. *An Almond for a Parrat* was notable more for invective than for wit. It concluded: 'Yours to command as your own for two or three cudgellings at all times. Cuthbert Curry-Knave the younger'.[74]

For those who knew or guessed that Cuthbert Curry-Knave was Thomas Nashe, the notion of him 'cudgelling' Martin Marprelate, who had famously extolled the 'bumfegging' of 'pestilent prelates', was probably the funniest part of *An Almond for a Parrat*. Nashe was well known for his puny physique and for his inability to grow a beard.

In Shakespeare's *Love's Labour's Lost*, the diminutive, impudent page-boy, Moth – a 'halfepennie purse of wit' – is believed to be a caricature of Nashe. Ironically, perhaps, the later development of Nashe's own comic style owed much to what he had learned from the uproarious satire of the Marprelate tracts.[75]

Anthony Munday's career as a playwright during the final years of the sixteenth century continued more smoothly than those of Lyly or Nashe, whose fortunes went into decline. The 1590s, when Munday received regular payments from the Rose Theatre, were his most productive decade. A number of his plays were performed at court.[76] In 1598 the cleric and literary critic Francis Meres named Munday in a list of distinguished playwrights (including Shakespeare) as being one of the best writers of comedies. He called Munday 'our best plotter' – probably a reference to his talent for conspiracy as well as in constructing dramatic plots.[77]

In 1601, however, Munday fell foul of official censorship. The long-serving Master of the Revels, Edmund Tilney, refused to allow the performance of his play, *Sir Thomas More*, fearing that its depiction of London riots against foreigners in 1517 might provoke more civil unrest. Shakespeare was one of several playwrights asked by Tilney in 1603 to revise the text. The 147 lines produced by Shakespeare for the revised version are now the only ones in his handwriting to survive in the manuscript of any play – his own included. Shakespeare added a passionate plea by Sir Thomas More for tolerance of foreign refugees in the capital. 'More', writes the Shakespearian scholar, Jonathan Bate, 'asks the on-stage crowd, and by extension the theatre audience, to imagine what it would be like to be an asylum-seeker undergoing forced repatriation.'[78]

The revised *Sir Thomas More* seems never to have been performed or printed. Though Munday was responsible for a series of successful civic pageants, he gave up writing for the theatre. For the next decade, however, he continued to take an active part in intelligence operations against Catholic recusants, who refused to attend Anglican services. Some recusants accused of treachery by Munday and others were so fearful of execution that they agreed to become informers or spies to prove their loyalty. Among them was the celebrated lutenist and composer, John Dowland, the most famous English musician of his time. When his contacts with English Catholic émigrés were reported to Sir Robert Cecil (who in 1598 would succeed his father, Lord

If a portrait was painted of John Dowland, it was probably this mysterious miniature of 1590 by Isaac Oliver. Though the sitter is not identified, his age is given as 27 – the same as Dowland's. The portrait also resembles that of an unidentified lutenist in an engraving of Christian IV's court.

Burghley, as the queen's chief minister), Dowland sent Cecil a grovelling letter of apology, assuring him that he had ceased to be an 'obstinate papist':

> Wherefore I have reformed myself to live according to her Majesty's laws, as I was born under her Highness, and that, most humbly, I do crave pardon, protesting if there were any ability in me I would be most ready to make amends.[79]

The 'amends' made by Dowland included providing intelligence on English Catholics allegedly plotting abroad – chief among them some in Rome who, he claimed, were planning to assassinate the queen. He ended his letter to Cecil by reporting that

> the Kinge of Spain is making gret preparation to com for England this next somer [1596], wher if it pleasde yo. honor to advise me by my poore wyff I wolde most willingly lose my lyffe against them.[80]

Dowland's intelligence on Philip II's preparations for an invasion of England proved correct, though the departure of the new Spanish Armada was delayed until 1597. Like the better-known Armada of 1588, it was scattered by storms when it reached the English Channel. Some ships were wrecked, others captured, and the rest returned to Spain.[81]

Thereafter, Dowland's most valuable intelligence probably came from Copenhagen. On becoming the leading lutenist of Christian IV of Denmark in 1598, Dowland volunteered to provide intelligence from the Danish court to London.[82] Ironically, it was while he was in Copenhagen that *Hamlet*, set in the Danish court and with spying as a major theme, was first staged in London. Unlike most court musicians, Dowland was often able, as Christian's personal lutenist, to move around the king's private chambers, sometimes while he was discussing matters of state or confidential court gossip with his councillors. Though few details of Dowland's intelligence survive, the English diplomat Sir Stephen Lesieur wrote to him in 1602:

> I shalbe very glad from tyme to tyme to heere from yow of as muche as may concerne her ma.stie or her subjects, yt shall come to yr knoledge ... spare not any reasonable charge to do it for I will see yow repaid.

Though this letter was intercepted by the Danes,[83] no action was taken against Dowland.[84] Christian IV was probably too fond of his music to banish him from court.

★

Elizabeth I's fascination with both stars and spies continued until the end of her reign. Among the plays performed at court, Shakespeare's *The Merry Wives of Windsor* is believed to have been a particular favourite of the queen.

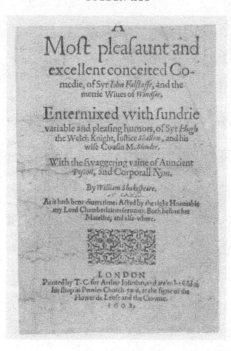

A
Most pleasaunt and
excellent conceited Co-
medie, of Syr *Iohn Falstaffe*, and the
merrie Wiues of *Windsor*.

Entermixed with sundrie
variable and pleasing humors, of Syr *Hugh*
the Welch Knight, Iustice *Shallow*, and his
wise Cousin M. *Slender*.

With the swaggering vaine of Auncient
Pistoll, and Corporall *Nym*.

By *William Shakespeare*.

As it hath bene diuers times Acted by the right Honorable
my Lord Chamberlaines seruants. Both before her
Maiestie, and else-where.

LONDON
Printed by T. C. for Arthur Iohnson, and are to be sold at
his shop in Powles Church-yard, at the signe of the
Flower de Leufe and the Crowne.
1602.

The title page of 'A pleasant conceited comedie called, Loues labors lost' similarly records that it was 'presented before her Highnes this last Christmas. Newly corrected and augmented by W. Shakespere.'

Less well known than the queen's love of drama is her strong support for the intelligence service, vividly portrayed in the last portrait of her reign, the 'Rainbow Portrait', attributed to the painter Isaac Oliver. The portrait was presented to Elizabeth in 1602, a year before her death, by Sir Robert Cecil, now the queen's chief minister (though without the formal title). The painting, to which she undoubtedly gave her approval, is full of the symbolism which appealed to Elizabeth as well as to Cecil. In one hand she holds a rainbow with the motto *non sine sole iris* ('no rainbow without the sun'), reminding the viewer that only the queen can ensure the peace and prosperity of her realm. Embroidered on one arm is the serpent of wisdom with a heart-shaped ruby in its mouth, showing that the queen's wisdom controls her emotions. With the hand of her other arm, she draws attention to the eyes and ears which cover her cloak, symbolising the members of her supposedly all-seeing and all-hearing intelligence service.

Nowhere in the world is there another portrait of a ruler that pays such tribute to the quality of her spies.

Elizabeth's intelligence service, however, had declined since the death of Walsingham. In the mid 1590s, the great codebreaker, Thomas Phelippes, spent several years in debtors' prison. The network of 'false' priests – informants who were, or pretended to be, Catholic priests – was less effective than Cecil believed in providing intelligence on Catholic plotters.[85] Within a few years of succeeding Elizabeth, James I was to come much closer than she had ever been to assassination by Catholic extremists.

2

'Our Revels Now Are Ended': Stars and Spies under the Early Stuarts

The entertainment business, as well as providing recruits and auxiliaries for the intelligence services, has also produced some of their most eloquent critics. Ben Jonson, nine years younger than Shakespeare and second only to him as the most successful Elizabethan and Jacobean dramatist, loathed espionage:

> Spies, you are lights in state, but of base stuff,
> Who, when you've burnt yourselves down to the snuff,
> Stink and are thrown away. End fair enough.[1]

Jonson's denunciation of late Elizabethan spies reflected anger at the banning of his satirical play, *The Isle of Dogs*, written in collaboration with Thomas Nashe, which opened, and then quickly closed, at the Swan Theatre in July 1597. An informer 'of base stuff' in the audience reported to the fearsome Richard Topcliffe that the play was seditious. Since the scripts were seized and no copy survives, the nature of the sedition remains unclear. The title suggests, however, that Jonson and Nashe had dared to mock the Privy Council, which met on the Isle of Dogs. On 28 July the Privy Council ordered, but failed to enforce, the closure of all London theatres, claiming that 'great disorders' had been caused 'by lewd matters that are handled on the stages, and by resort and confluence of bad people'. On 15 August the Council instructed Topcliffe to 'peruse soch papers as were fownd in Nash his lodgings'. Nashe fled to Great Yarmouth, but Jonson and two actors appearing in the play were arrested, charged at Greenwich with 'lewd and mutinous behaviour', and interrogated by Topcliffe.[2]

Woodcut mocking Nashe as a jailbird after the banning of *The Isle of Dogs*, though he seems to have escaped arrest. From Richard Lichfield's *The Trimming of Thomas Nashe, Gentleman* (1597).

Though Topcliffe did not torture Jonson, he placed in his cell two 'damn'd Villains' to act as stool pigeons. The villains, almost certainly, were Robert Poley and Henry Parrot. A decade earlier, Poley had won Babington's confidence through deception, obtaining some of the evidence leading to his conviction for treason in 1586, and as we have seen he may well have been implicated in the death of Marlowe in 1593. Parrot was a more recent intelligence recruit, with a background as clerk in the Court of Exchequer.[3] By 1606 he was writing short volumes of epigrams and satire. The first, 'The Mous-trap' (again taking its title from *Hamlet*), dismissed Jonson as a dramatist past his prime, whose plays appealed to 'few or none'.[4]

Fortunately for Jonson, he was warned about Poley and Parrot by his jailer and gave nothing away. On 2 October 1597, he and the two actors in *The Isle of Dogs* were released from jail.[5] In a poem written to invite a friend to dinner after his release, Jonson promised him the evening would not be spoiled by the presence of informers:

> And we shall have no Poley or Parrot by,
> Nor shall our cups make any guilty men:
> But, at our parting, we will be as when
> We innocently met. No simple word
> That shall be uttered at our mirthful board
> Shall make us sad next morning, or affright
> The liberty that we'll enjoy tonight.[6]

Jonson called himself a 'huge overgrown play-maker'. He was larger than life in both personality and physique. In middle age, he gave his weight as 'twenty stone within two pound', lamenting that ladies 'cannot embrace my mountain belly'.[7] Heavy consumption of 'rich Canary wine' was partly to blame for both his girth and some of his quarrels.

Only a year after his release from Winchelsea, Jonson was back in prison at Newgate, convicted of manslaughter after killing an opponent in a duel. As well as forfeiting his 'goods and chattels', he was branded with a T on the left thumb – a reminder that a second conviction for manslaughter might lead to the Tyburn scaffold. While in Newgate, he was received into the Catholic Church, probably by the jailed priest, Father Thomas Wright, a former Jesuit who had studied in Rome and Milan, and seems to have been greatly admired by Jonson for both his bravery and learning.[8]

Jonson did not join the chorus of loyal poets lamenting the death of Elizabeth I in March 1603. He had much higher hopes of her successor, King James VI of Scotland, who became James I of England, and of his queen, Anne of Denmark (sister of Christian IV). Jonson devised a three-day entertainment to welcome Anne and the new heir apparent, 9-year-old Prince Henry (elder brother of the future Charles I), at Althorp House during their progress to London. Jonson was also commissioned to prepare speeches and one of the triumphal arches for James I's arrival in his new capital. Because of an outbreak of plague, however, the new king's triumphant entry had to be postponed until March 1604. An actor personifying the 'Genius of the City' declaimed an obsequious eulogy composed by Jonson:

> Never came man more longed for, more desired,
> And being come, more reverenced, loved, admired.[9]

James declared himself the chief patron of English theatre. Great nobles were no longer allowed, as under Elizabeth, to have their own acting companies. In May 1603 the Lord Chamberlain's Men became the King's Men.[10] Shakespeare and the other eight members were henceforth part of the royal household; each received four and a half yards of red cloth for the livery they were to wear on state occasions. Probably at least two-thirds of the plays performed at court by the King's Men over the next few years were Shakespeare's.[11]

Despite Ben Jonson's sycophantic welcome to both King James and Queen Anne, he soon antagonised the new regime. In 1604 he was

Ben Jonson (*c*.1617) by Abraham van
Blyenberch.

accused of promoting 'popery and treason' in his tragedy *Sejanus His
Fall*,[12] which told the story of the tyrannical rule and overthrow of the
favourite of the Roman Emperor Tiberius. Sejanus's tyranny depends
on a vast network of what his heroic opponent Sabinus calls 'vile
spies, / That first transfix us with their murdering eyes'. In describing
surveillance in imperial Rome, Jonson had in mind the less homicidal
surveillance to which he was subjected by 'vile spies' in Jacobean
London:

> Every second guest your tables take,
> Is a fee'd spy, t'observe who goes, who comes,
> What conference you have, with whom, where, when.[13]

'Fee'd spies' continued to report on Jonson's controversial career as
a playwright. In the summer of 1605, *Eastward Ho!*, written jointly by
Jonson, John Marston and George Chapman, caused even greater
controversy than *Sejanus* because of its mockery of allegedly uncouth
Scots who had arrived in London. King James was personally offended.
All three playwrights were imprisoned for about a month.[14]

Jonson's militant Catholic friends put him in much greater danger
than his early Jacobean plays. On or about 9 October 1605, soon
after Jonson's latest release from prison, surveillance revealed his
presence at a supper party in the Strand with many of the leading
conspirators in the Gunpowder Plot, then in its final stages of

preparation. Among them was the chief plotter, Robert Catesby, described by two Jesuits who knew him well as 'more than ordinarily well proportioned, some six feet tall, of good carriage and handsome countenance' – an easy surveillance target.[15] Though proof is lacking, during supper Catesby probably mentioned the plot at least in outline. He made the fatal mistake of spreading knowledge of it beyond the original conspirators in order to persuade wealthy Catholics to support and finance the rising in the Midlands which he hoped would follow the assassination of the king and his ministers. One of the wealthy Catholics at the supper party in the Strand was Francis Tresham. Though sworn to secrecy, Tresham sent an anonymous letter to his Catholic brother-in-law, Lord Monteagle, on 26 October warning him not to attend Parliament, where a 'terrible blow' was planned for 5 November. Monteagle took the letter to the secretary of state, Robert Cecil, newly promoted Earl of Salisbury, who showed it to the king.[16]

On 4 November 1605, thirty-six barrels containing almost a ton of gunpowder were discovered under a large pile of firewood in a cellar beneath the House of Lords. According to modern calculations, the explosion of the gunpowder during the state opening of Parliament on 5 November would have destroyed much of Westminster as well as killing the king, his ministers and many others. The fact that what would have been the worst terrorist attack in British history came so close to success was the result of what, several centuries later, would be called 'intelligence failure'. None of the 'false priests', government agents who were – or pretended to be – Catholic clergy, had wind of it. Standards of interrogation, as well as of agent penetration, had declined dramatically since the Walsingham era. When arrested on 4 November, the man found in charge of the gunpowder hidden in the cellar gave his name as 'John Johnson'. It was not until 7 November, the third day of questioning, that it occurred to his inexpert interrogators to look in his pockets. A letter found in one of them instantly revealed that his real name was Guido ('Guy') Fawkes.[17]

Immediately after Fawkes' identification, Ben Jonson was served with a Privy Council warrant instructing him to find a Catholic priest – probably Father Thomas Wright who had converted him in Newgate – who was to persuade Fawkes to name his fellow conspirators and reveal details of their conspiracy. The warrant was the most terrifying communication Jonson ever received. Aware that his links with the plotters had been discovered, he knew that, if found guilty of assisting their treason, he would be hanged, drawn and quartered. Next day, he sent a cringingly obsequious reply to Robert Cecil, whom he privately loathed:[18]

> My most honourable Lord.
>   May it please yo[u]ʳ Lo[rdship] to understand, there hath been no want in me, either of labour or sincerity in the discharge of this business, to the satisfaction of yo[u]ʳ Lo[rdship] and the state. [...]

All Jonson's efforts to contact the priest, either directly or via intermediaries, had so far come to nothing.

> If it shall please yo[u]ʳ Lordsh[ip] I shall yet make further trial [...]
> I do not only w[i]th all readiness offer my service, but will p[er]form it w[i]th as much integrity, as yo[u]ʳ particular Favour, or his Majesty Right in any subject he hath, can exalt.

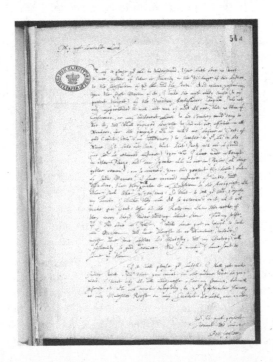

Yo[u]ʳ Ho[nour's] most perfect
servant and Lover
Ben Jonson

On 8 November, the day Jonson wrote to Cecil, Catesby and three other conspirators were killed in Staffordshire by a posse led by the Sheriff of Worcestershire. But all attempts to discover Father Thomas Wright failed. Guy Fawkes and the other surviving conspirators were tortured in the Tower, tried in Westminster Hall, and sentenced to be hanged, drawn and quartered at Tyburn.

In public, Ben Jonson continued to condemn the plotters (some of whom he probably privately admired) and to proclaim his own unconditional loyalty to James I by methods which included publishing a sycophantic poetic eulogy of Lord Monteagle, 'saver of my country':

> Lo what my country should have done (have raised
> An obelisk, or column to thy name,
> Or, if she would but modestly have praised
> Thy fact, in brass or marble writ the same)
> I, that am glad of thy great chance, here do!
> And proud, my works shall out-last common deeds,
> Durst think it great, and worthy wonder too,
> But thine, for which I do't, so much exceeds!
> My country's parents I have many known;
> But, saver of my country, THEE alone.[19]

While eulogising the 'savers of my country' from the Gunpowder Plot, however, Jonson continued to ridicule the espionage mania of the official 'fee'd spies' who kept him and other Catholics under surveillance. Jonson was the inventor of the spy farce. *Volpone*, the most successful of all his plays, first performed at the Globe in March 1606, contains a comic sub-plot in which Sir Politic Would-be ('Sir Pol') expounds a number of paranoid espionage fantasies. The French, he claims had been using baboons as spies, one of whom had told him that they were preparing further secret missions. On being told of the death of 'Stone the Fool', who was habitually drunk, Sir Pol claims that Stone had actually run a sophisticated spy ring, receiving weekly intelligence reports hidden in cabbages, which he passed on concealed in other fruit and vegetables. Sir Pol had also personally

witnessed Stone receive intelligence in 'a trencher of meat' from a
'statesman' in disguise

> And instantly, before the meal was done,
> Convey an answer in a toothpick.

Because Jonson remained a Catholic, he continued to be intermittently accused of disloyalty to the Church of England. In the aftermath
of the Gunpowder Plot, the playwright-spy, Anthony Munday, was
'zealous in tracking down recusants'. Among those on whom he
compiled reports was Hugh Holland,[20] a lifelong Catholic friend of
Jonson, who had written a poem in praise of his unpopular play
Sejanus.[21] Though Jonson loathed Munday, he dared not publicly attack
him for pursuing papist recusants. Instead, he ridiculed Munday's plays,
portraying him as the hack-writer Antonio Balladino in *The Case is
Altered*, first published in 1609. Balladino boasts in Act I: 'I do use as
much stale stuff, though I say it myself, as any man does in that kind,
I am sure.' When reminded that he had been nominated as 'the best
plotter' in the English theatre (a reference to Francis Meres' published
praise of Munday), Balladino replies: 'I might as well have been put
in for a dumb shew too.'[22] Munday, by this time, had given up writing
plays in order to concentrate on pageants and masques.[23] Jonson
continued work on both.

The most lavish theatrical productions in early Stuart England,
especially during the Christmas season, were not stage plays but elaborate court masques, closed to the public, which were far more extravagant than Elizabeth I's relatively modest entertainments. Actors and
singers performed a written text, accompanied by consorts of lutes,
viols and wind instruments. Jonson wrote twenty-one Christmas
masques for the Jacobean court, far more than any other writer, usually
in creative but often acrimonious collaboration with Inigo Jones, who
designed sumptuous costumes and scenery. Masques brought
performers and royalty closer together than plays staged at court
because royals were among the actors. Though King James stopped
dancing after leaving Scotland, Queen Anne had a starring role in six
masques between 1604 and 1611, four of them written by Jonson.[24]
In the first of Jonson's masques, the *Masque of Blacknesse* in 1605,
commissioned by the queen, she and her ladies appeared as Africans,
dancing with blacked-up faces.[25] At a time when all female roles in

theatres had to be played by boys, Anne of Denmark thus became – though not in public – Britain's first prominent actress. Prince Charles, second in line to the throne until the death of his elder brother Henry, also took part in numerous masques and royal entertainments. Even as a toddler, Charles amused courtiers by acting and dancing in elaborate costume with his mother. His early enjoyment of masques and disguise helps to explain why he later became the first heir to the throne to go in disguise on a secret mission abroad.[26]

At the height of Jonson's success as a writer of court masques, he faced a personal religious crisis. In May 1610 Henri IV of France was assassinated by a Catholic fanatic, François Ravaillac. Though Ravaillac acted alone, there were persistent rumours that he was part of a wider Catholic conspiracy. On 2 June James I forbade Catholics access to court. All Catholics were required to renounce allegiance to the pope and pledge allegiance to James. The recusant Jonson gave in to pressure to return to the Church of England. He told a friend that, 'in token of true Reconciliation' at his first Anglican communion and in a typically flamboyant gesture, he drained the whole communion cup.[27]

Jonson's proximity to court had made it impossible to conceal his Catholicism. In some remote Catholic strongholds in the North of England, however, where there was no organised surveillance of recusants, actors and playwrights continued to use drama to denounce the Church of England. One such stronghold was Netherdale (now Nidderdale) in north Yorkshire, where almost all the Gunpowder plotters had relatives. William Stubbes, the 'godly' (Anglican) minister of Pateley Bridge, called Netherdale 'one of the most obscure p[ar]tes' of Yorkshire. Separated from the rest of the country by high moors and 'great wastes', it was a 'fitt place for secrett' activities; 'a great nomber' of the people were 'evillye affected to the true religion established' and 'increasinge daylie in their irreligious courses'.

Among the opponents of 'the true religion established' was a group of Yorkshire players led by the recusant shoemakers, Robert and Christopher Simpson. Though few details survive about the Simpson players, they are known to have performed Shakespeare's *Pericles* a year after the publication of the 1609 quarto edition, which they may have purchased from a York bookseller. But their repertoire also included Catholic plays which condemned the Church of England as heretical. Among them was a version of the play *St Christopher*, which included a religious debate in which a Catholic priest defeats a Protestant minister, who is then carried off to hell 'wth thundering & lightning' and 'flasheings of fire'. Other special effects, probably involving fireworks, included the arrival on stage of Lucifer with 'flaunt of fyre'.[28]

St Christopher was included in a well-received performance by the Simpson players at Christmas 1609 in Gouthwaite Hall, the mansion of the recusant Sir John Yorke at the head of Netherdale, who welcomed the audience with seasonal hospitality.[29] One 'godly' preacher, Mr Mawson, shocked by news of the performance, claimed that a churchwarden whom he sent to summon parishioners to prayer at church was told 'that it woulde hinder the ale wife.' When Mawson went to Gouthwaite Hall to complain in person about the behaviour of Yorke's tenants, the household servants took him to an alehouse and tried to get him drunk. On another occasion, Mawson entered his ill-attended church to find a dummy in the pulpit dressed as a Protestant preacher.[30]

Probably the most prominent of the Simpsons' Yorkshire patrons, Sir Richard Cholmley, had begun acting while at Cambridge University. Despite his 'naturally choleric' temperament, he 'acted the part of a woman in a comedy at Trinity College, in Cambridge ... with great applause, and was esteemed beautiful'. In 1609, Cholmley was summoned before the Star Chamber of privy councillors and judges, which sat in the royal palace of Westminster, accused of 'bearing inward love and affection to such as are obstinate popish recusants and having many obstinate popish recusants that depend on him', as well as licensing a company of actors whose plays contained 'much popery and abuse of the law and justice'. The charges were dropped for lack of evidence.[31]

Theatrical subversion continued in north Yorkshire. In 1616 five 'armigers' (men entitled to heraldic arms), three 'gentlemen' and two yeomen were fined for hosting performances by the recusant Simpson players.[32] Cholmley, the Simpsons' chief early supporter, was briefly MP for Scarborough in 1621 and Sheriff of Yorkshire in 1624–5;[33] Sir John Yorke, though, despite being fined and possibly imprisoned for recusancy offences in 1611, continued his support for popish drama. In 1628 the travelling player, Christopher Malloy (of whom little is known), was prosecuted in Star Chamber for playing the devil in a play at Gouthwaite Hall, during which he carried an actor playing the part of King James I to hell, proclaiming that all Protestants were damned.[34]

*

Jacobean theatre suffered irreparable loss when William Shakespeare retired to Stratford. His last sole-authored play,[35] *The Tempest*, first performed before James I and his court at the Palace of Whitehall on Hallowmas night, 1 November 1611, begins with Prospero, the former Duke of Milan, marooned on an 'enchanted island' after being ousted from Milan by Antonio, his villainous brother. Prospero's mastery of intelligence and covert operations are the secret of his victory over Antonio and the recovery of his duchy. As in *Macbeth*, the intelligence is supernatural.

Shakespeare drew much of the inspiration for the character of Prospero from the extraordinary career of Dr John Dee, England's only home-grown Renaissance magus, a mixture of scientist and magician at a time when there were no clear boundaries between the two. Early in Elizabeth's reign, Dee had won 'her Majestie's great contentment and delight' by casting her horoscope, performing alchemical experiments and demonstrating optical illusions.[36] Dee was both a star and a spy, 'the prototype of the controversial celebrity',[37] who also claimed supernatural access to intelligence.[38] He communed with angels by a variety of 'show-stones' of which the most remarkable was an Aztec mirror made from polished black obsidian sometime before the Spanish conquest of the Aztec Empire,[39] probably originating from what is now the mountain city of Pachuca in central Mexico. If Shakespeare had been able to read the secret 'angelic diaries', in which, with help from a fraudulent medium, Dee recorded the heavenly beings' revelations, he would have been less impressed. One angel, who claimed to have assisted the Israelites' crossing of the Red Sea during their escape from Egypt, reportedly told him: 'I am Prince of the Seas: My power is upon the water. I drowned Pharaoh ... My name was known to Moses.' The medium, Edward Kelley, claimed that another angel, Uriel, had ordered him and Dee to share their wives and all their possessions.[40]

Prospero's spirit world was put to better use than Dee's. At the beginning of *The Tempest*, using his supernatural powers, Prospero arranges for a boat carrying his brother Antonio, along with the King of Naples and others, to be wrecked off his enchanted island. Once ashore, the group are kept under secret surveillance by Prospero's obedient (if sometimes resentful) agent, Ariel, who is able, at times invisibly, 'to fly,/To swim, to dive into the fire, to ride/On the curl'd clouds' during his intelligence missions.[41] Prospero's magical mastery of intelligence finally puts Antonio at his mercy:

> For you, most wicked sir, whom to call brother
> Would even infect my mouth, I do forgive
> Thy rankest fault, all of them, and require
> My dukedom of thee, which perforce I know
> Thou must restore.[42]

Antonio says nothing but surrenders the dukedom. Prospero then winds up his intelligence operations and grants Ariel his freedom. Before the enchantment ends and Prospero returns to Milan, he delivers what Shakespeare probably intended as his own farewell to the audience before leaving London for Stratford:

> Our revels now are ended. These our actors,
> As I foretold you, were all spirits and
> Are melted into air, into thin air;
> … We are such stuff
> As dreams are made on, and our little life
> Is rounded with a sleep.[43]

Ben Jonson's classical tragedy, *Catiline His Conspiracy*, was first performed at almost the same time as *The Tempest*. Though deeply suspicious of all forms of surveillance of Catholics in Jacobean England, Jonson believed the Roman Republic, which he admired, had been justified in using both espionage and SIGINT to defend itself against its enemies. In the final act of *Catiline*, his conspiracy to overthrow the Roman Republic is exposed by Cicero's spies who intercept his correspondence with the rebellious general, Aulus Gabinius. The staunch Republican, Cato the Younger, responds to Gabinius's initial claim that he knows nothing about the correspondence in indignant, if rather clumsy, blank verse:

> Impudent head!
> Stick it in his throat. Were I the Consul,
> I'd make thee eat the mischief thou has vented.

Gabinius soon owns up:

> Stay,
> I will confess. All's true your spies have told you.
> Make much of 'em.[44]

Catiline's plot is defeated by Cicero, whose almost 300-line speech in the Senate sends the traitors, and probably some of Jonson's audience, packing. The play was a flop. Even Jonson's supporter and fellow dramatist, Francis Beaumont, acknowledged that, though displaying Jonson's classical learning, *Catiline* had not 'itched after the wild applause of common people'.[45] Jonson's comedies, by contrast, most recently *The Alchemist* in 1610, were among the most popular plays of the early seventeenth century.

Shakespeare's retirement to Stratford after *The Tempest* left Jonson as the leading playwright in Jacobean London, though by now he was more occupied with court masques than plays for the theatre.[46] Soon after Shakespeare's death in 1616, Jonson was given a royal pension, becoming Britain's first Poet Laureate, though without the formal title. One of his masques was a key component in what the CIA later called a 'covert action' (or, in KGB jargon, an 'active measure') to persuade James I to dismiss the royal favourite, the Scot Robert Carr, Earl of Somerset, whose intimacy with the king gave him great political power. Even when talking to others, James could not stop himself giving Carr adoring glances, pinching his cheek, and occasionally stroking his clothes.[47]

Jonson became closely involved with a court faction opposed to Carr which was seeking, at first with little success, to replace him as royal favourite with the youthful, dashing and remarkably handsome George Villiers, whom they calculated would have even greater erotic appeal to James.[48] On Twelfth Night, 6 January 1615, Villiers took the lead role in *Mercury Vindicated from the Alchemists at Court*, a masque written by Jonson, as usual with Inigo Jones as set designer. James was so captivated by the masque – and Villiers' performance in particular – that he ordered it to be repeated two days later.[49] Soon afterwards, Villiers succeeded Carr as the new royal favourite. James made him successively Earl (1617), Marquess (1618) and Duke (1623) of Buckingham. In his correspondence with the king, Buckingham commonly signed himself 'Your Majesty's humble slave and dog'. James was besotted with him.[50]

Though Buckingham had little grasp of affairs of state, he became the king's chief policy adviser. Buckingham was not remotely equal to the huge foreign policy and intelligence challenge posed by the outbreak in 1618 of the Thirty Years War – a long-drawn-out struggle over the ascendancy of the Habsburg dynasty and the Catholic religion in continental Europe. His malign influence on foreign policy was all the greater because of the death in 1612 of James's secretary of state and ablest administrator, Robert Cecil, Earl of Salisbury. Buckingham's basic ignorance of intelligence operations was evident in the comic-opera scheme which he devised for a secret visit to Madrid in 1623 to enable the heir to the English and Scottish thrones, Prince Charles, to seek the hand in marriage of the Infanta Maria Anna, sister of the King of Spain, Philip IV. So far from seeking intelligence before the trip on the likely reaction of the Spanish court, Buckingham did not even warn the English ambassador of his and Charles's imminent arrival.[51]

Preparations for their supposedly incognito journey to Madrid resembled the court masques, in which Charles had appeared since early childhood. Wearing false beards and periwigs, and posing as the brothers Thomas and John Smith, Buckingham and Charles set off on horseback from London in 1623 on their supposedly secret mission to Madrid. Their disguise (though not their true identity) was so obvious, however, that they were suspected of going illegally to France to fight a duel and pursued all the way to Dover. Once in Madrid, further comic opera followed. Charles climbed over a garden wall in an attempt to meet Maria Anna face-to-face. The infanta and her entourage fled in terror. The mission to Madrid ended in failure.[52]

In 1624, an ailing James I declared war on Spain, thus bringing to an end twenty years of peace. Simultaneously, with his father's and Buckingham's approval, Charles set out to woo another Catholic princess – Henrietta Maria, younger sister of Louis XIII of France. Some lessons had been learned from the Madrid fiasco. Instead of travelling to Paris, Charles and Buckingham stayed in England and sent Buckingham's youthful protégé, the aspiring playwright, Walter ('Wat') Montagu, French-speaking son of the Earl of Manchester and graduate of Sidney Sussex College, Cambridge, on a secret mission to make initial contact with the French court and Henrietta Maria. Though officially only a letter-bearer, Montagu was expected to use his dramatic talents to elaborate on the contents of the correspondence entrusted to him and emphasise both the ardour of Charles' marriage proposal and his many fine qualities. In March 1625 Montagu returned to London with the good news that the French court had agreed to the marriage: 'All is forward, and the lady should be delivered in thirty days'.

'Delivery' of Henrietta Maria, however, was delayed by the terminal illness of James I, who died on 27 March with both Charles and Buckingham by his bedside. On 1 May, a week before James's funeral, Henrietta Maria married King Charles, as he now was, by proxy at the Cathedral of Notre Dame in Paris, with a French courtier representing Charles. Six weeks later, on 13 June, Charles and Henrietta Maria spent their first night together at the royal palace of St Augustine's, Canterbury. On 16 June, they arrived in London. Montagu was paid £200 as a reward for his mission.[53]

Montagu's success in the marriage negotiations led to further, less successful secret missions to the continent. Though few details survive, in 1627 he was imprisoned for several months in the Paris Bastille.[54] By now English intelligence was a shadow of what it had been under Walsingham, and there was no organised espionage service. As in the case of Montagu, secret agents were selected as the need arose. The need was mainly determined by Buckingham until he was assassinated by an English soldier with a personal grievance against him in 1628.

In 1629 Montagu wrote the first version of a pastoral comedy, *The Shepherd's Paradise*, which he later presented to the queen. His interest in drama and the arts helped to bring him closer than any other English courtier to Henrietta Maria. From the winter of 1630–31 onwards the king and queen regularly presented elaborate and expensive masques to each other, staged by Inigo Jones. On Twelfth Night 1633, Henrietta Maria took the starring role in Montagu's *The Shepherd's Paradise*, which portrayed a rural idyll ruled by a queen elected annually by shepherdesses.[55] The king did 'highly congratulate and extoll' to the Earl of Manchester 'the rare and excellent parts of his son Mr Walter Montague [*sic*] appearing in the Pastoral which he hath penned for her Majesty[,] her ladies, and maids to act'.[56] *The Shepherd's Paradise* was a landmark in the history of English drama – the first play (as opposed to masque) known to have been acted by women.[57] Montagu's conversion to Catholicism brought him closer still to the devout Henrietta Maria. In 1637, after his secret ordination in Rome, she made him her chamberlain.[58]

Like Montagu, the poet and dramatist William Davenant also engaged in secret missions. Born in Oxford in 1606, the year of *King Lear*, Davenant enjoyed boasting (truthfully) that he was Shakespeare's godson, sometimes hinting (untruthfully) that their relationship was closer still. He devised his first, characteristically grandiose, plan for a major secret operation in 1628, at the age of only 22. Soon after the performance of his first play, *The Cruel Brother: A Tragedy*, Davenant wrote to the Privy Council offering to blow up the French arsenal at Dunkirk to avenge an English defeat by France the previous year. Claiming to have a friend inside the arsenal and access to an explosive device, Davenant grandly announced: 'I shall perform this service, though with the loss of my life.' The Privy Council failed to take up his offer and the Dunkirk arsenal remained intact.[59] He was later to engage in other, less preposterous secret missions for the Crown in the Civil War.

During the 1630s, Davenant had greater success in winning the literary patronage of Charles I and Henrietta Maria than in intelligence operations. His first court masque in 1635, *The Temple of Love*, featured the establishment in Britain of a Temple of Chaste Love by Queen Indamore, a role played by Henrietta Maria in an exotic costume with feather headdress designed by Inigo Jones. The queen successfully banished Lust, personified by three lecherous Asian magicians, from Britain. Though the success of the masque led to other commissions at court, Davenant had little personal interest in 'chaste love'. He caught the 'French disease' (syphilis) from a prostitute and destroyed much of his nose by misusing mercury in hope of a cure. These misadventures, however, failed to prevent him succeeding Jonson as poet laureate in 1638, a year after the latter's death. Davenant styled himself 'Sweet Swan of Isis' in pretentious imitation of Jonson's tribute to Shakespeare as 'Sweet Swan of Avon'.[60]

*

The most serious threat to the theatre since the Elizabethan golden age was a by-product of the greatest political crisis in modern British history: the Civil War of 1642–9, the unexpected outcome of a conflict between Charles I and Parliament which had run of control. In September 1642, a month after the outbreak of the Civil War, the Puritan-dominated Parliament ordered the closure of the London theatres during the current 'times of humiliation', denouncing 'public stage-plays' for their 'lascivious Mirth and Levity'.[61] Most drama was driven underground to private performances in royalist houses and taverns.[62]

French theatre, by contrast, was beginning a golden age, thanks in large part to the patronage of Louis XIII's chief minister, Cardinal Richelieu, who saw it as central to royal prestige and political propaganda. In January 1641 France's leading theatre, the Théâtre du Palais-Royal, opened in the east wing of the Palais-Royal with a performance of Jean Desmarets' tragicomedy *Mirame*.[63]

Like Elizabeth I, Richelieu was fascinated by both theatre and intelligence. Under his direction, both eclipsed their English rivals. The most productive espionage network in Europe was probably that run for Richelieu by François Leclerc du Tremblay, a Capuchin friar better known by his religious name, Père Joseph de Paris. Dressed in his grey habit, Père Joseph was the original *éminence grise*, a phrase which passed into the English as well as the French language. He combined a deeply mystical Catholicism with passionate loyalty to the French monarchy.[64] Père Joseph had well-placed informants within his and other religious orders, probably including Capuchins in the entourage of Henrietta Maria.[65]

Richelieu's France was even further ahead of early Stuart England in SIGINT than in HUMINT (intelligence from human sources). The fifty-year career of Thomas Phelippes, who had been personally congratulated by Elizabeth I for breaking the ciphers of James I's mother, Mary, Queen of Scots, came to a wretched end when, for reasons which remain obscure, he incurred the enmity of Buckingham at the end of James' reign. Phelippes was placed in solitary confinement in King's Bench Prison and died there (or possibly shortly after his release) early in 1627. The demise of codebreaking in Britain with the death of Phelippes coincided with its dramatic revival in France. Richelieu's intelligence system owed even more to his newly founded SIGINT agency, the *cabinet noir* (black chamber), and its presiding genius, Antoine Rossignol, one of the greatest codebreakers in the history of intelligence, than to Père Joseph.

Charles Perrault of the forty-member Académie française (founded by Richelieu) later included Rossignol in his book on the forty most 'illustrious' Frenchmen of the seventeenth century. According to Perrault, though the usually inscrutable Richelieu rarely displayed visible enthusiasm, at their first meeting Rossignol 'gave such astonishing proof of his ability that this great Cardinal ... was unable to conceal his astonishment'.[66] The ease with which Rossignol broke the ciphers of the Protestant Huguenots accelerated Richelieu's victory over them.[67] Rossignol was so well rewarded for his work in the *cabinet noir* that he was able to purchase the chateau de Juvisy, not far from Paris, where he was paid the extraordinary honour of visits not merely by Richelieu but also by Louis XIII and, later, Louis XIV – an honour bestowed on no other codebreaker in the history of the French monarchy.[68]

By contrast, Charles I entered the Civil War without any SIGINT and with only disorganised sources of information in the enemy camp. Charles' and Henrietta Maria's most important secret contact with the French court was through Walter Montagu, who had been banished from England by Parliament before the outbreak of the Civil War. In 1643, Montagu returned secretly to England disguised as a member of the entourage of the French ambassador in London, bearing sealed letters to both the king and queen from the French court, but was captured in Rochester and taken to London. The House of Commons ordered his imprisonment in the Tower, where he remained for the next four years.[69]

Though Parliament had no centrally organised intelligence system, it revived English cryptanalysis for the first time since the death of Phelippes. The key to the revival was the discovery early in the Civil War of a codebreaker of genius: John Wallis, a Cambridge-educated cleric and mathematician. Wallis's most celebrated SIGINT success came after the decisive parliamentary victory at the battle of Naseby in June 1645, which led to the capture of the king's personal baggage and secret correspondence files, which, when decrypted by Wallis, revealed Charles's plans to seek the support of Catholic forces both in Ireland and on the Continent. Recognising the propaganda value of the captured correspondence, Parliament published the most compromising letters, 'written with the King's own hand', in a volume entitled *The Kings Cabinet Opened*, which included decrypted correspondence with Henrietta Maria, who had taken refuge in France.[70] Never before in British history had SIGINT been publicly used to such dramatic effect. A commentary in *The Kings Cabinet Opened* claimed that the letters revealed Charles as a henpecked husband dominated by his French Catholic wife:

> It is plain here, first, that the King's Counsels are wholly managed by the Queen, though she be of the weaker sex, born an Alien, bred up

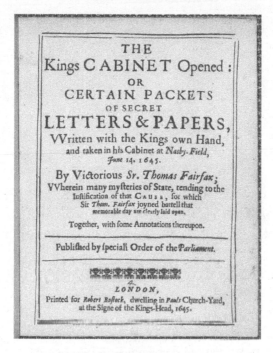

THE
Kings C A B I N E T Opened :
OR
CERTAIN PACKETS
OF SECRET
LETTERS & PAPERS,
VVritten with the Kings own Hand,
and taken in his Cabinet at *Nasby*. *Field*,
June 14. 1 6 4 5.

By Victorious *Sr. Thomas Fairfax*;
VVherein many myfteries of State, tending to the
Iuftification of that C A U S E, for which
Sir *Thom. Fairfax* joyned battell that
memorable day are clearly laid open,

Together, with fome Annotations thereupon.

Publifhed by fpeciall Order of the *Parliament*.

A
LONDON,
Printed for *Robert Boftock*, dwelling in *Pauls* Church-Yard,
at the Signe of the Kings-Head, 1645.

in a contrary Religion, yet nothing great or small is transacted without
her privity & consent ...[71]

No other British king or queen has ever had such compromising
private letters published in their lifetime.[72]

When Montagu was released from the Tower in 1647, he went to
Paris to become Henrietta Maria's chaplain and lord almoner at the
Palais-Royal in Paris.[73] Two years later, after Charles' execution,
Montagu and two other exiled royalists were sentenced by the
Commons to 'perpetual banishment'.

Despite this, in 1655 Montagu succeeded in publishing in London
an extraordinary response to *The Kings Cabinet Opened*, entitled *The
Queens Closet Opened*. By claiming to reveal 'Incomparable Secrets in
Physick, Chirurgery, Preserving, Candying, and Cookery as they were
presented to the Queen By the most Experienced Persons of our
times ... ', he sought to counter the charge that she had been 'harsh
and imperious' towards her henpecked husband by showing that her
interests were essentially domestic, English rather than French, and

devoted to the welfare of her family and household. Some of the 'Incomparable Secrets' were relatively straightforward. A mixture of white wine and rosemary, either taken orally or used as a face wash, could be used 'To make the face fair, and for [stopping] a stinking breath', while the root of bryony 'cleanseth the skin wonderfully from all black and blue spots, freckles, morphew, Leprosy, foul scars, or other deformity'. Cures for plague, however, involved plucking a live 'cock chick' and making open sores on its rump until the bird 'gapes', 'labours' and 'dies'.[74]

The most popular parts of the book were probably its recipes. *The Queens Closet Opened*, published in 1655, was 'arguably the most popular recipe book of the century', and went through at least thirteen further editions.[75] By portraying the French-born Henrietta Maria as a queen with traditional Englishwomen's interests, *The Queen's Closet Opened* was intended to recast her image. Its remarkable sales suggest that it had some success in doing so. Probably no other influence operation in intelligence history has been based on a cookbook.

Sir William Davenant, the poet laureate, who joined royalist forces during the Civil War, was knighted by the king in 1643 for his combination of 'loyalty and poetry'. Thereafter, until the queen finally went into exile in France two years later, Davenant helped to maintain confidential contact between the royal couple while Charles was on campaign, though his capacity to run secret missions was diminished by his distinctively disfigured nose. After the royalist defeat at Naseby in 1645, he left Britain to join the queen's court-in-exile at Saint-Germain-en-Laye and converted to Catholicism.

In 1650, a year after Charles I's execution, Davenant was captured on the high seas by a parliamentary frigate and brought back to England, accused of 'having been an active enemy of the Commonwealth'. The Commons were initially undecided on whether to put him on trial. During a sometimes satirical debate, 'some *Gentlemen*, out of pitty, were pleased to let him have the Noes of the House, because he had [no nose] of his own.' A majority of MPs, however, decided to send Davenant to the Tower, where he remained until released on bail in 1652. He was formally pardoned by Cromwell two years later.[76]

Portrait of Sir William Davenant, with cosmetic enhancement by the artist of his nose, disfigured by treatment for syphilis.

Soon after his release, Davenant began secret preparations for the revival of the London theatre, initially by organising musical performances. Though music lacked the status it had achieved in much of Europe, it survived the Interregnum better than any other part of the English entertainment business. Music in places of worship was anathema to Puritans. But Cromwell, among others, approved of music in other settings; he ordered the organ in Magdalen College Chapel, Oxford, to be moved, for his enjoyment, to his palace at Hampton Court.[77] SIGINT as well as agent and informer reports allowed John Thurloe, Cromwell's intelligence chief, secretary of state and most influential adviser in the mid 1650s, to gauge the appeal of musical entertainment both on state occasions and in private gatherings. At the end of the first Anglo-Dutch War in 1654, a Dutch diplomat wrote in a decrypted despatch, which Thurloe kept in his intelligence papers, that he and other guests had been 'nobly entertained' at dinner with Cromwell. After a welcome in Whitehall by twelve trumpeters, 'The music played all the while we were at dinner. [Afterwards] the Lord Protector had us in another room where we had also music, and voices and a psalm sung ... '[78]

As well as winning a reputation as Cromwell's 'all seeing little secretary', Thurloe was one of the few senior figures with whom he felt fully at ease. According to Cromwell's foreign-policy adviser, Bulstrode Whitelocke, in Thurloe's company the Lord Protector would sometimes 'lay aside his greatness', relax and smoke a pipe.[79] Thurloe did not share hard-line Puritans' hostility to popular entertainment, exemplified by their attempts to eradicate Christmas celebrations. A trusted informant wrote confidentially from York on 29 December 1657 with an irony he knew Thurloe would appreciate:

> You will give me leave so far to observe Christmas, as to send you this letter for a new-year's gift; and I shall therein give you some account of the Christmas spirit, that I perceive stirring in this and other places.[80]

Thurloe's tolerance of some parts of the entertainment business enabled Sir William Davenant to promote 'operatic drama, as a first step towards restoring drama proper'. In May 1656 he put on an 'entertainment', with 'declamations' and music but no dialogue, props or elaborate costumes, which ran for ten days in his home, Rutland House, near the site of today's Barbican Centre. A prologue apologised for the cramped conditions but asked the audience to see it as leading the way 'to our Elyzian field, the *Opera*' – the first use of the word in English.[81] Davenant prudently arranged, as reported to Thurloe by a spy who attended the performance, for the evening to end with new songs in praise of Cromwell as 'Victor' and 'Protector'. The evening came at a fractious moment in Anglo-French relations, and Thurloe's spy also reported a song 'deriding Paris', which mocked the silver sailing ship on its coat of arms:

> And though a ship her scutcheon be,
> Yet Paris hath no ship at sea.

The new songs were composed by the musicians Henry Lawes, England's leading mid seventeenth-century songwriter, and Edward Coleman,[82] best known for setting to music the most famous poem by the dramatist James Shirley, 'The glories of our blood and state', which is believed to have made a deep impression on Cromwell:

> Sceptre and Crown
> Must tumble down,
> And in the dust be equal made
> With the poor crooked scythe and spade.[83]

To judge from the report of Thurloe's spy, neither Lawes nor Coleman gave any hint during Davenant's 'entertainment' of their true loyalties. Both, however, were committed royalists.

Having escaped official censure for his 'entertainment' in May 1656, a few months later Davenant staged Part One of *The Siege of Rhodes*. Though later regarded as the first English opera, the title page describes it as a 'Representation by the Art of Prospective [*sic*] in Scenes, And the Story sung in *Recitative* Musick'; the music was composed by Lawes, Coleman and others. Aware that he had been under surveillance ever since his release from the Tower, Davenant sent a franker statement of his aims to Thurloe. His 'entertainments', he argued, served an important purpose by diverting people's minds from the 'melancholy that breeds sedition'.[84]

If Thurloe, as intelligence chief, had not sympathised with Davenant's argument that entertainment tended to diminish, rather than promote, sedition, he would not have tolerated Davenant's decision to move the two parts of *The Siege of Rhodes* from Rutland House to the refurbished Cockpit Theatre in Drury Lane, and to stage two more 'operas' there.[85] Some stars emerged from the performances at the Cockpit. Particularly notable was the appearance in the lead female role in *The Siege of Rhodes* of England's first professional actress, Catherine Coleman, daughter of the composer, Alfonso Ferrabosco II, and wife of Edward Coleman, who was also one of the singers. The diarist Samuel Pepys later found the Colemans 'the best company for Musique I ever was in in my life', though he preferred Catherine's conversation and singing voice to her husband's: 'When he begins to be drunk, he is excellent company, but afterward troublesome and impertinent.'[86] Other notable performers at the Cockpit included the singers Henry Purcell (father of the more famous composer), Henry Cooke, Henry Lawes and George Hudson; the lutenist and composer William Webb; the organist Christopher Gibbons; and the violinists, Thomas Baltzar and John Banister.[87] All the musicians went on to serve in the Chapel Royal of Charles II or the associated 'Four and Twenty Fiddlers'.[88]

Davenant's fascination with covert operations went back thirty years to the beginning of his dramatic career, when he had tried to persuade the Privy Council to approve his improbable scheme to blow up the Dunkirk Arsenal. His influence operation in the final years of the Interregnum, exploiting Cromwell's and Thurloe's willingness to tolerate the expansion of musical performances as a means of preparing the way for the return of drama, was far more original and practicable. It was threatened, however, by Cromwell's death and the accession of his son Richard as Lord Protector in 1658, followed by Thurloe's dismissal a year later. Some members of both Parliament and the Council of State claimed that Davenant's productions at the Cockpit were 'to the scandal of Religion and the Government'. The decline and fall of republican rule, followed by Charles II's triumphant return to London from exile in 1660, however, ended the threat to the Cockpit.[89] Like Davenant, its performers revealed themselves as royalists. Henry Lawes, who a few years earlier had composed songs in praise of Cromwell, composed the anthem *Zadok the Priest* for the coronation of Charles II.[90]

3

'Astrea Wants Money': Stars and Spies after the Restoration

The restoration of the monarchy by Charles II in 1660 brought with it the restoration of the theatre after its closure during the Civil War and Interregnum. The poet laureate and dramatist, Sir William Davenant, celebrated both restorations in his welcome to Charles at the Cockpit Theatre in Drury Lane:

> This truth we can to our Advantage say,
> They that would have no KING, would have no Play:
> The Laurel and the Crown together went,
> Had the same Foes, and the same Banishment.[1]

Charles II was Britain's most theatregoing monarch. Though his father, Charles I, never visited a public theatre, Charles II often went twice a week during the early years of his reign, and his presence increased the number of other theatregoers. Many enjoyed the opportunity to see the king's mistress, Barbara Palmer (later Duchess of Cleveland), who often accompanied him.[2] Samuel Pepys recorded in his diary a visit to the theatre with his wife in 1661: 'and there saw "The Joviall Crew", where the King, Duke and Duchess [of York], and Madame Palmer were; and my wife, to her great content, had a full sight of them all the while.'[3] It was not until December 1666 that Charles took the queen, Catherine of Braganza, rather than a mistress, to the theatre for the first time.[4]

The second key figure in the revival of Restoration drama, the rather plodding playwright Thomas Killigrew, six years younger than Davenant, had also established himself at court before the Civil War by winning the confidence of Henrietta Maria. He had accompanied

Thomas Killigrew, portrait by Sir Anthony van Dyck, c.1635.

Walter Montagu, the queen's favourite and a fellow playwright, on at least one of his secret missions to the Continent. Further missions as confidential messenger between Charles I and the queen followed during the Civil War.[5]

Shortly after the execution of Charles I in 1649, Killigrew joined the household in Paris of Prince Charles, now recognised by royalists as Charles II. During the 1650s he went on confidential missions to several continental states, either by himself or as Charles's aide. In Venice, increasingly notorious for sex tourism, Killigrew was accused of 'corruption and general debauchery'.[6] His chief asset in keeping the confidence of Charles was his wit rather than his competence. Pepys, who was on board the *Royal Charles* when it brought Charles II back from exile in May 1660, enjoyed 'much mirth, all the day', thanks mainly to Killigrew – 'a merry droll, but a gentleman of great esteem with the King, who told us many merry stories'. When Killigrew sang a bawdy song he had composed about the cutpurse Moll Frith, tears of laughter ran down Charles's cheeks.[7]

But vengeance was also on the merry monarch's mind. Almost the only intelligence operations he followed with close attention were those to track down signatories of his father's death warrant who had fled to the Continent.[8] According to Pepys's fellow diarist, John Evelyn, who had good connections at court, Charles watched, from an inconspicuous vantage point, the first hanging, drawing and quartering of a group of captured regicides on 16 October 1660:

> I saw not the execution, but met their quarters, mangled and cut, and reeking, as they were brought from the gallows in baskets on the hurdle. Oh, the miraculous providence of God!

The mangled remains included those of Cromwell's first intelligence chief, Thomas Scott, who had also been one of the judges who sentenced Charles I to death.[9] Scott was the first, and so far the only, British intelligence chief executed for treason. Because of Charles II's search for vengeance against other regicides living in exile, kidnap and assassination operations abroad were a higher priority during the early Restoration than at any other moment in the history of British intelligence.

In August 1660 Charles II issued letters patent to Killigrew and Davenant, giving them a monopoly of theatrical productions. Killigrew's company of actors, under royal patronage, was known as the King's Men; that of Davenant, under the patronage of the Duke of York (the

Sir William Davenant's grave in Poets' Corner, Westminster Abbey. The vainglorious wording imitates the misspelt inscription of his far more talented predecessor as Poet Laureate, Ben Jonson: 'O Rare Ben Johnson'.

future James II), as the Duke's Men. Both companies initially performed in converted real tennis courts, later replaced by custom-built theatres: the Theatre Royal in Drury Lane for the King's Men, and the Dorset Garden Theatre, on the Thames, for the Duke's Men.[10]

The main innovation in Restoration drama was the introduction of actresses.[11] During their Paris exile, Charles, Killigrew and many other courtiers had seen women perform on stage. A royal grant of 1662 declared that the replacement of boys by women for female roles would be 'useful and instructive', and produce 'harmless delight'. In reality, it also led to sexual exploitation.[12] The king made a series of English actresses, most famously Nell Gwyn, his mistresses. She was painted naked by Sir Peter Lely 'at the express command of King Charles 2nd. Nay he came to Sir Peter Lillys house to see it painted when she was naked on purpose.'[13]

Restoration drama also provided opportunities for a small but talented group of female dramatists, of whom the most remarkable was Aphra Behn, the first British woman to make a living as a writer. Born in 1640, she was probably the daughter of a barber and a wet nurse. As a young woman, Behn is believed to have travelled to Surinam, a Dutch plantation colony in South America – an experience which later inspired her *Oroonoko, or the Royal Slave*, the first work of fiction to argue for the abolition of slavery. In 1666, before she became a dramatist, Behn was recruited as a spy (codenamed ASTREA and 'agent 160') – the first female spy ever officially employed by a British government. Still in her mid twenties, Behn described her intelligence mission as 'unusual with my sex, or to my years'. She was personally recommended by Killigrew, who had probably employed her to copy literary manuscripts and learned of her foreign adventures.[14]

As her biographer, Janet Todd, concludes: 'What is securely known about Aphra Behn outside her works could be summed up in a page.'[15] The main exceptions to our lack of knowledge of Behn's non-literary career are her intelligence reports from Antwerp between July 1666 and April 1667, many of which survive.[16] The choice of a 'she-spy', as a rival called her, for intelligence operations in Antwerp was remarkable. All the paid foreign 'intelligencers' employed during the first two years of the Restoration – around twenty in number – had been men.[17] The most likely explanation for the choice in 1666 of the attractive Aphra Behn, rather than a male intelligencer, is that she was intended to be a honey-trap. Her target was Thomas Scott's son William, one

Aphra Behn, portrait by the court painter Sir Peter Lely, c.1670.

of Behn's former lovers, who began working as a Dutch agent in Antwerp soon after the outbreak of the Second Anglo-Dutch War in 1665. Behn's mission was to turn Scott into a double agent operating against the Dutch.[18]

While not the kind of operation which the godfearing Walsingham and Thurloe would have countenanced, honey-traps caused no moral qualms to Henry Bennet, who became secretary of state in 1662 and was responsible for foreign intelligence, or to Sir Joseph Williamson, his unofficial spy chief. Though supposedly a practising Catholic, Bennet had no compunction in pimping for the king. Pepys noted in his diary in November 1663 that Bennet was part of a small committee for 'the getting ... for the King' of one of the queen's maids of honour, Frances Stuart.[19] A few days later, Pepys noted 'how the King is now become besotted upon [Frances Stuart], that he gets into corners, and will be with her half an houre together kissing her to the observation of all the world'.[20] Frances Stuart later recalled how, before her

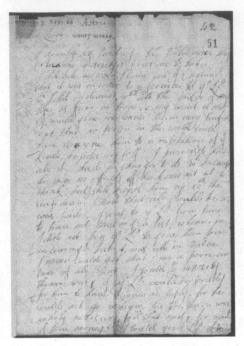

'Astrea wants money': Behn appeals for money in November 1666 during her espionage mission in Antwerp.

seduction by Charles II, Bennet had encouraged her with 'a great number of fine maxims and some historical anecdotes'.[21]

Lord Arlington, as Bennet became in 1665, had no more moral scruples about Aphra Behn than about Frances Stuart. Since Behn had insufficient money to bribe William Scott, her only realistic recruitment method was seduction. She reported to London that Scott (code-named CELADON) had agreed to change sides: 'Though at first shy, he became by arguments extremely willing to undertake the service ...'[22] But the regular intelligence reports from Scott which Behn forwarded to London, all but one in her own hand, contained little significant information or evidence that Scott had become an 'extremely willing' double agent. She regularly explained the paucity of the intelligence he provided by phrases such 'it is att present out of his head', 'according to the best information he can gain', 'as neare as he can remember', and 'he cannot recall'.[23] The intelligence reports attributed to Scott are unlikely to be genuine. He continued to be employed by

Henry Bennet, 1st Earl of Arlington, after Sir Peter Lely, c.1665–70.

the Dutch and, save for the reports sent by Behn, there is no evidence that he had become a double agent. There is no credible reason why Behn would have copied Scott's reports in her own hand, rather than sending the original reports to London – if they existed. Behn probably made them up – remarkable evidence of the creative writing skills which were later to make her such a successful dramatist.[24]

Doubts about the authenticity of Behn's intelligence from Antwerp probably explain why payments to her from London dried up, despite her personal appeals to Lord Arlington. On her return to London, she narrowly avoided debtors' prison.[25]

The Second Anglo-Dutch War demonstrated how little Dutch intelligence Arlington and Williamson had obtained. The decisive English defeat in August 1667 was marked by the deeply humilating spectacle of the Dutch sailing up the river Medway and attacking the Royal Navy at its anchorages in Chatham. In October 1667 the Commons appointed a committee to enquire into the war's 'miscarriages', the first to investigate what was later called 'warning failure'. The committee reported to the House in February 1668 that there had been 'want of intelligence from abroad'. The poet, satirist and MP, Andrew Marvell, complained that 'the money allowed for intelligence [was] so small [that] the intelligence was accordingly'.[26] Behn was, presumably, one of the victims of the small intelligence budget.

In 1670 Behn took satirical revenge on Arlington in her first play, *The Forc'd Marriage*. Arlington was sensitive to the fact that his only military action during the Civil War had been a skirmish at Andover in 1644, from which he emerged with a small scar on the bridge of his nose which he was later prone to cover with black plaster to exaggerate the extent of his injury.[27] In *The Forc'd Marriage*, Behn satirises Arlington as the cowardly Falatius, who tries to fabricate a heroic war record by wearing patches over bogus 'wounds' on his face. The play is also notable for including the line 'The Poetess, too, they say, has spies abroad': a reference to Behn's own past career in intelligence as well as to masked ('vizarded') women in the audience, some of them prostitutes, who acted as her informers.

Behn's mockery of the secretary of state did nothing to diminish her growing popularity with the king. Four of her plays were presented at court, more than any other writer's except John Dryden, who had become Poet Laureate on Davenant's death in 1668. Behn owed much of the popularity of her plays with both the king and other theatregoers to a bawdy dramatic style of which she was a leading exponent.[28] *The Rover* (1677) features a whore with a heart of gold who solicits custom by hanging her portrait outside her house. The play was so popular at court that it was performed twice. In 1679 Behn dedicated *The Feign'd Courtesans* to the King's mistress Nell Gwyn – 'pretty, witty Nell', as Pepys called her.[29] She also dared to raise a wide range of sexual issues from male impotence to female orgasm, and nine of her plays include rape or attempted rape. 'All women together', Virginia Woolf said later, 'ought to let flowers fall upon the tomb of Aphra Behn, for it was she who earned them the right to speak their minds.'[30]

When accused by her critics of bawdiness or worse, Behn replied that she was writing 'for Bread and not ashamed to own it'.[31] Like some male playwrights, Behn was expert at devising 'breeches scenes' in which attractive young women wear men's clothes, usually on the pretext of evading detection, thus exposing shapely legs and ankles

normally concealed under long skirts.[32] As the actress Elizabeth Boutell declared:

> 'Tis worth Money that such Legs appear,
> These are not to be seen so cheap elsewhere.[33]

Behn combined a willingness to use sexual titillation to earn her 'Bread' with extraordinary literary talent. In her 'Epistle dedicatory' to Nell Gwyn at the beginning of *The Feign'd Courtesans*, she denounced 'the malicious world that will allow a woman no wit'. Behn was both the first female dramatist and the first former female spy to be buried in Westminster Abbey. Her gravestone reads:

> Here lies a Proof that Wit can never be
> Defence enough against Mortality.

With few exceptions, however, Behn's wit was considered too rude for public consumption over the next two and a half centuries.

Among the poets and playwrights who most influenced Behn was the Restoration's leading literary libertine, John Wilmot, Earl of Rochester, who, as she acknowledged, 'School'd' her 'loose Neglect' and 'rais'd her fame'.[34] Rochester combined the roles of actor and spy in an extraordinary way. His friend and biographer, Bishop Gilbert Burnet, records that, because his noble rank prevented Rochester fulfilling his ambition to become a professional actor, he appeared on and off stage in disguise: 'Meerly for diversion, he would go about in odd shapes, in which he acted his part so naturally, that even those who were [in] on the secret ... could perceive nothing by which he might be discovered.' Rochester became notorious off-stage for appearing in public disguised, from time to time, as porter, beggar, merchant, landlord of an inn or matronly woman, either for personal amusement to 'follow mean amours' (encounters with prostitutes and women from humble backgrounds) or to spy unobserved on those around him – sometimes in the hope of picking up compromising information on them.[35]

Rochester also employed spies of his own. Behn's biographer, Janet Todd, concludes that 'stories of Rochester posting his spies disguised as sentries at the bedroom doors of those he wished to lampoon did not shock her'.[36] As the following couplet reveals, he was less tolerant of those who informed on him:

> An Epitaph. Stay Reader! and Piss here,
> For it is said Under this Dirt there's an Informer laid.[37]

The nearest Rochester came to mounting a major theatrical production was to secure the commission for Charles II's most expensive court masque for his protégé, the playwright John Crowne,[38] in preference to the far better-known John Dryden, the Poet Laureate. Crowne's elaborate five-act masque *Calisto*, first performed on Shrove Tuesday 1675, cost the enormous sum of over £3,000 and spent almost six months in rehearsal. In the Greek myth on which the masque was based, the Arcadian nymph Calisto is raped by Zeus. Crowne, however, removed the rape from his version of the story in order to allow the lead roles, Calisto and her fellow-nymph Nyphe, to be played by the two royal princesses, 12-year-old Mary and 10-year-old Anne (both future queens of England and Scotland). The masque idealises Stuart Britain as a land of peace and plenty, receiving offerings from 'the four Parts of the World'.[39]

Rochester, who had a Whitehall apartment, probably had some influence on the masque during its lengthy rehearsals. Afterwards, he wrote a comic, pornographic poem which, though not published, probably came to the attention of the king whom it lampooned. All those who saw *Calisto* would have recognised Rochester's reference in the poem to Charles's seduction of Mary Knight, who spoke the prologue, playing the role of Peace:[40]

Rochester's most infamous dramatic deception was to star as a quack-doctor, Alexander Bendo, on an open-air stage in Tower (later

John Wilmot, 2nd Earl of Rochester, portrait by unknown artist, *c.*1665–70. Rochester, manuscript in hand, bestows poet's laurels on a chattering monkey who is tearing
and crumpling pages from a book, possibly by the Poet Laureate, John Dryden.

Great Tower) Street in the City of London. According to Bishop
Burnet, he 'disguised himself, so that his nearest Friends could not
have known him'. Wearing a green gown, 'lyned through with
exotick furrs of diverse colours, an antique Cap, a great Reverend
Beard', and 'a Magnificent false Medal', Rochester made bogus
diagnoses, cast horoscopes, and dispensed worthless medicaments
and charms which, he claimed, were 'rare secrets … for help, conser-
vation, and augmentation of beauty'. He also recruited and
rehearsed a cast of fraudulent assistants, dressed, one of them later
recalled,

> like the old Witches in Mackbeth … We of the Fraternity kept a
> perpetual Jangling to one another … in a Jargon of damn'd unintelli-
> gible Gybberish all the while, & indeed we judged it not convenient,
> in our Circumstances, to do any thing in plain English but Laugh.

Whenever a female client required intimate physical examination, Bendo arranged for his wife to visit her at home in order 'to be admitted into the Bed Chamber, to View and report the matter'. Bendo's wife, however, was Rochester in another disguise. Reports of such deceptions greatly amused Charles II, who summoned Rochester back to court, after banishing him for other, less amusing bad behaviour.[41]

There was no French equivalent at the court of Louis XIV either of Rochester as exhibitionist court libertine or of Aphra Behn as official female spy and dramatist. The Sun King, self-proclaimed star of European royalty, did, however, involve himself in at least one major espionage honey-trap. Its target was Charles II, with whom Louis signed in 1670 the secret Treaty of Dover, containing two top-secret clauses which would have caused public fury in Britain if they had become known. Charles promised both to suspend anti-Catholic penal laws and to announce his own conversion to Catholicism at an opportune moment.[42] Charles revealed these clauses only to his Catholic brother, the Duke of York, and to two Catholic ministers, Arlington and the Lord Treasurer, Sir Thomas Clifford. To cover his tracks, the king perfidiously instructed two leading anti-Catholics, the Duke of Buckingham (son of the former royal favourite) and the Earl of Shaftesbury, who were unaware of the secret treaty, to negotiate another treaty (also secret) with Louis XIV which omitted the religious clauses. No other British monarch has gone to greater or more devious pains to mislead most of his ministers.[43] Understandably, Louis XIV did not trust him.

Louis XIV and his advisers believed that what was needed to help persuade Charles II to keep his secret commitments was to plant on him a loyal French *maîtresse en titre* (official chief mistress). The woman chosen for the honey-trap in 1671 was the beautiful 21-year-old Louise de Kéroualle, former maid of honour to Charles' sister Henrietta Anne, Duchess of Orleans. After Henrietta Anne's death, Charles made de Kéroualle maid of honour to his wife, Queen Catherine. The Catholic Arlington, who knew the secret pro-Catholic clauses of the Treaty of Dover and also had experience as a royal pimp, was quick to see the opportunity. The French ambassador, Colbert de Croissy, reported that, according to Arlington,

> although his Majesty [Charles II] is not disposed to communicate his
> affairs to women, nevertheless as they can on occasion injure those
> whom they hate, and in that way ruin many affairs, it was much better,

for all good servants of the King that he was attracted to [Louise de Kéroualle], whose humour is not mischievous, and who is a lady, rather than to comediennes and the like ...[44]

Arlington provided the opportunity for the royal seduction in November 1671 at a magnificent party on his estate at Euston Hall in the Suffolk countryside. Charles was in ebullient mood, having just ridden one of his own horses to victory at Newmarket. According to the diarist John Evelyn, immediately after his arrival at Euston Hall, the King set about 'toying' with the 'young wanton'.[45]

Louis XIV's personal congratulations to de Kéroualle on the success of the honey-trap were delivered to her by Colbert de Croissy. The ambassador informed Louis, 'I have made that young lady joyful by assuring her of the pleasure with which His Majesty learned of her brilliant conquest. There is every prospect that she will long hold on to what she has conquered.'[46] Croissy's forecast proved correct. The Catholic de Kéroualle, whom Charles made Duchess of Portsmouth

Portrait of Louise de Kéroualle, Duchess of Portsmouth, by Sir Peter Lely, c.1671–4.

in 1673, remained *maîtresse en titre* until his death in 1685, far longer
than any of her predecessors, and a regular informant of the French
embassy. She also became fabulously wealthy. According to the latest
study of her, in the final years of Charles's reign, she was receiving
from him the modern equivalent of £59 million per year.[47] The last
service de Kéroualle performed for Louis XIV was to ensure that, on
his deathbed in 1685, Charles II, as he had promised, was received
into the Catholic Church.[48]

Like previous mistresses, de Kéroualle accompanied Charles II to
the London theatre far more frequently than did the queen. Many in
the audience went to see her as well as the performance. In an era
of anti-Catholic conspiracy theories, however, she became an off-stage
villain. Though the information she passed to Colbert de Croissy and
his successors remained secret, rumours circulated that she was spying
for Louis XIV. Nell Gwyn famously pacified a mob attacking her
carriage, mistakenly believing de Kéroualle to be inside, by shouting,
'Pray good people be civil, I am the *Protestant* whore!'[49]

*

Louis XIV's court was, in many ways, a gigantic stage set. Drama was
only part of its pervasive theatricality. At his new chateau of Versailles,
Louis's whole day was organised around elaborate rituals. The
celebrated memoirist, the duc de Saint-Simon, wrote of his godfather,
Louis XIV: 'With an almanach and a watch, one could, from 300
leagues away, say accurately what he was doing.' At 8.30 a.m. the first
valet de chambre entered the King's bedchamber to inform him, 'Sire,
it's time to get up.' In summer months, Louis had quite often already
spent several hours hunting but returned to bed in order to be ceremo-
nially woken. The *petit lever du roi* then began, during which select
courtiers and intimates were privileged to witness the king being
washed, shaved and having his hair combed. There followed the *grand
lever*, during which about 100 courtiers (all male) saw Louis being
dressed and given soup for breakfast.

At 10 a.m. a crowd which had gathered in the Hall of Mirrors
witnessed the royal entourage proceed through the state apartments
on the way to mass in the Royal Chapel. A fortunate few were able
to speak briefly to Louis or pass him a note. During mass, which lasted
half an hour, the internationally celebrated choir sang a new piece

every day by leading composers such as Jean-Baptiste Lully and Michel-Richard Delalande. God at Versailles was confined to the chapel. The rest of the largest and grandest palace in Europe was devoted to the cult of the Sun King, celebrated daily through court ritual, devotional art and magnificent architecture. By the end of his reign, resident devotees of his cult numbered about 10,000 nobles, soldiers, priests, officials, musicians, performers, tradesmen and servants. Versailles was second only to the army as France's largest employer.[50]

The intelligence official whom Louis held in highest regard was the great codebreaker Antoine Rossignol, one of the very few advisers personally recommended to him in his father Louis XIII's will. Louis XIV took a personal interest in the work of the *cabinet noir*. Neither of the two great seventeenth-century English codebreakers, Thomas Phelippes and John Wallis, received any sign of royal appreciation from the Stuart kings, none of whom displayed any interest in SIGINT. By contrast, like his father Louis XIII, Louis XIV honoured Antoine Rossignol by visiting his chateau at Juvisy-sur-Orge. Though few details survive, some of the SIGINT of greatest interest to Louis XIV was British. In 1665, Lord Holles, the English ambassador in Paris, complained that despatches from the Foreign Office were always

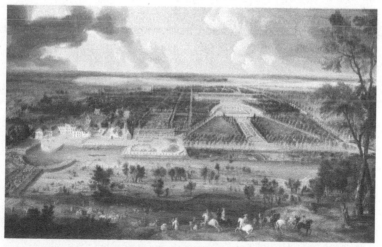

Detail from Pierre-Denis Martin, *La visite de Louis XIV au château de Juvisy*, c.1700, probably commissioned by Antoine Rossignol's son, Bonaventure. Louis, wearing a riding coat, is on the pale horse in the foreground, approaching the chateau from the other side of the river Orge.

opened and read before he received them. His successor, Ralph (later Duke of) Montagu made the same complaint in 1669.[51] The handsome remuneration and royal patronage bestowed on Rossignol enabled him to employ André Le Nôtre, the king's landscape architect and principal gardener, to turn the park at Juvisy into one of the great formal gardens of seventeenth-century France.[52] According to Charles Perrault, Rossignol received the Sun King with extraordinary enthusiasm (*un tel excès de zèle*)[53] at Juvisy – no doubt including a ceremonial welcome. His 'excess of zeal' was doubtless reflected in the cost of hiring singers for the welcome, probably accompanied by viol music of the kind which Marin Marais, *ordinaire de la chambre du roy pour la viole* for almost half a century, made well known at Versailles.[54]

Rossignol and his son Bonaventure also had an office in Versailles.[55] A devout Catholic who read scripture every day, he continued as royal codebreaker until his death in 1682, a total period of over half a century[56] – the longest term of office of any important official during the Ancien Régime.

Drama played its part in the glorification of the Sun King. Louis XIV put his favourite playwright, Jean-Baptiste Poquelin, better known by his stage name Molière, in charge of his most extravagant royal fête, the week-long *Plaisirs de l'île enchantée* ('Delights of the enchanted island'). Held at the unfinished chateau of Versailles in May 1664, the 'delights' included four plays and ballet-comedies by Molière. Chief among them was *Tartuffe*, the most celebrated, if initially controversial, comedy in the history of the French theatre. Spying plays a part in the exposure of Tartuffe's bogus piety, which is the main theme of the play. Elmire, whom Tartuffe hopes to seduce, tells him in Act IV:

> I have secrets for your ear alone.
> But first shut the door, and look everywhere
> For fear of spies.

Confident there are no spies to overhear him, Tartuffe then seeks to seduce Elmire and so reveals his hypocrisy, as she had hoped he would. Unlike Tartuffe, however, the audience has observed that a spy, in the person of Elmire's husband, Orgon, is hiding under the table.[57]

The references to surveillance must have resonated with courtiers who attended the première of *Tartuffe* in ways that may not have occurred to Molière. Most knew, or at least suspected, that their correspondence was opened by the *cabinet noir*. The celebrated wit and letter-writer, the marquise de Sévigné (better known as Madame de Sévigné), sometimes made personal appeals in her letters to the officials charged with opening her correspondence:

> Alas! I beseech those who take this trouble to consider the little pleasure which they gain from reading it and the sorrow they cause to us. Messieurs, at least take the trouble to put [the letters] back in their envelopes so that, sooner or later, they reach their destination.[58]

The king found *Tartuffe* 'highly amusing'. Catholic hardliners did not; the official *Gazette de France* called the play 'wholly injurious to religion'. Though *Tartuffe* was to become the most successful of all Molière's plays, Louis XIV, on the advice of the Archbishop of Paris, initially refused to grant permission for a public performance. Molière, however, retained his reputation as France's leading playwright. When the Comédie-Française was founded as the state theatre by decree of Louis XIV in 1680, seven years after Molière's death, it was popularly known as 'La maison de Molière'.[59]

Molière's reputation stands higher now than at the end of the seventeenth century, when his plays ran foul of the fervently Catholic Madame de Maintenon, whom Louis XIV married in secret after the death of Queen Marie-Thérèse in 1683. At Maintenon's insistence, fig leaves were placed over the private parts of statues at Versailles. She was not amused by *Tartuffe*.[60] Under her influence, Louis lost most of his previous interest in plays.[61]

*

For different reasons, there was a simultaneous decline in royal patronage of the theatre in Britain. None of Charles II's successors matched his interest in the stage. As Duke of York, his Catholic brother James had been patron of the Duke's Men, founded by Davenant, and went frequently to the theatre, usually with the Duchess. Most of the plays seen by either or both of them during his three-year reign as James II, however, were presented at court rather than in a theatre. In the 'Glorious Revolution' of 1688, the unpopular James II was overthrown by an invasion led by the Dutch Stadtholder and Protestant hero William of Orange. In 1689, as William III, he became joint ruler with his wife, James's daughter Mary. The new king had no interest in the theatre. After Queen Mary's death in 1694, William III attended a play only once – to celebrate his forty-seventh birthday in 1697.[62] He had, however, a much greater interest in intelligence than any of his Stuart predecessors.

The most successful dramatist during the reign of William III (1689–1702), John Vanbrugh, was, like Aphra Behn, involved in intelligence operations before he became a playwright. Though few details of the operations survive, from 1686 he worked undercover to bring about the overthrow of James II and William's accession.[63] In September 1688, two months before William invaded England at the invitation of his English Protestant supporters, Vanbrugh was arrested in Calais, charged with espionage on William's behalf. He spent over four years in French prisons during the first half of the Nine Years War (1688–97), which was fought between France and a European coalition effectively led by William. In 1691 Vanbrugh sent letters to James II at his court in exile at Saint-Germain-en-Laye, falsely claiming to be his loyal supporter in the hope that James would secure his release by the French. The last ten months of his imprisonment were spent in the Bastille before his family arranged his exchange for a spy working for James II in November 1692. Though he was able to purchase food and plentiful wine from outside, the prison made such an impression on him that Vanbrugh later called the house which he built for himself on the eastern edge of Greenwich Park 'Bastille House'.[64]

Claims that, while in the Bastille, Vanbrugh wrote one of his most successful comedies, *The Provok'd Wife*, are probably exaggerated.[65] It is likely, however, that during his years in prison and three further months in Paris after his release before he was able to return to England, Vanbrugh had some of the ideas which were later to make him such a successful dramatist. The idea of the French maid, Mademoiselle, spying on the seduction of the 'provok'd wife', Lady Brute, may well have occurred to Vanbrugh while he was imprisoned for alleged espionage.[66] It was almost certainly while in Paris, also, that Vanbrugh became an admirer of the work of the youthful playwright, Florent Carton Dancourt, whose comedies of manners at the Comédie-Française established him as the successor to Molière. Vanbrugh would have known the romantic story of how Dancourt, previously a barrister, had begun his career as a dramatist after eloping with Thérèse de La Thorillière, an actress at the Comédie-Française.

Dancourt's *La Maison de campagne*, written when he was only 26, was first performed shortly before Vanbrugh's imprisonment began in 1688.[67] A decade later, Vanbrugh's adaptation, *The Country House*, was one of the first of his plays to be performed in London.

At what point in the mid 1690s Vanbrugh decided to try to make a living as a playwright remains unknown. Success, however, came remarkably quickly. Two plays in quick succession, both in the tradition of Restoration comedy, made him the most popular playwright of the time: *The Relapse: Or, Virtue in Danger* in 1696, a comedy about a libertine and his long-suffering wife, followed by *The Provok'd Wife* in 1697. Both were revived and reprinted frequently (sometimes in bowdlerised form) over the next half-century. Six further successful plays followed over the next decade.[68]

Though Vanbrugh's mostly unsuccessful intelligence operations seem to have served only to give him some ideas for his future career as a playwright, William III had two major intelligence advantages over the exiled James II and his 'Jacobite' followers. First, unlike all three of his Stuart predecessors, he understood the importance of SIGINT. Decrypted despatches produced by the veteran codebreaker, John Wallis, enabled William to follow the landing in Ireland in 1689 of Jacobite and French forces at the beginning of a campaign which ended in humiliating defeat for James II at the Battle of the Boyne in 1690. Secondly, William was well supplied with intelligence from James II's court in exile at Saint-Germain-en-Laye.[69] Agent penetration of Saint-Germain became so notorious that the Abbé Renaudot, its French liaison with Versailles, mistakenly concluded that James's secretary of state, Lord Melfort, must be in the pay of William III.[70]

Keeping track of Jacobite conspiracies in Britain, however, was complicated by the diffuse nature of William III's domestic intelligence system. William himself was partly responsible. He appointed no Scott or Thurloe to coordinate intelligence operations at home and abroad, as Cromwell had done during the Interregnum. He and his ministers were guilty of a classic failure to learn from past intelligence experience. In the mid 1650s the exiled Charles II had gloomily concluded that Cromwell's spymasters supplied him with 'perfect intelligence of whatsoever His Majesty resolved to do'.[71] The disorganised surveillance of Jacobites in Britain after the Glorious Revolution never approached in efficiency Cromwellian penetration of Royalist opposition a generation earlier.

4

British Theatre, the 'Golden Rump' and the Ancien Régime

The last of the Stuart monarchs, Queen Anne, though only 37 when she succeeded William III in 1702, was prematurely aged by a succession of miscarriages and still births. Her twelve-year reign, however, was the most successful of the Stuart dynasty.[1] While Anne, unlike William III, had little, if any, personal understanding of intelligence, it played a key role both in British victories over France during the War of the Spanish Succession (1702–14) and in the negotiation of the Acts of Union passed by the English and Scottish Parliaments which led to the creation of the United Kingdom of Great Britain on 1 May 1707.

The Battle of Blenheim in Bavaria in 1704 was both the first great English land victory on the Continent since the Hundred Years War and Louis XIV's first decisive defeat. This and later victories by Britain and its allies owed much not merely to the inspired generalship of the Duke of Marlborough, the British commander-in-chief ('captain-general'), but also to the fact that his intelligence from both agents and SIGINT outclassed that available to the French.[2] After Blenheim, Marlborough was given Queen Anne's estate at Woodstock and a blank cheque to construct on it a great palace named in honour of his victory. The architect was none other than the remarkably versatile Sir John Vanbrugh. 'Van's genius without thought or lecture', wrote Jonathan Swift in 1706, 'is hugely turnd to architecture.' Within a few years, the former spy and playwright turned himself into one of Britain's leading architects.[3]

Gaining the consent of the Scottish Parliament in Edinburgh to its own abolition and the creation of the United Kingdom owed much to intelligence operations run by Queen Anne's Northern Secretary of

State, Robert Harley (later Tory first minister), who had acknowledged his own ignorance of 'Scotch business'.[4] Chief among the agents sent to report on, and seek to manipulate, Scottish opinion was the great writer and polemicist, Daniel Defoe, whom Harley instructed:

> 1. You are to use the utmost caution that it may not be supposed you are employed by any person in England: but that you came there upon your own business, & out of love to the Country.

> 2. You are to write constantly the true State how you find things, at least once a week, & you need not subscribe any name, but direct for me under Cover to Mrs Collins at the Posthouse, Middle Temple Gate, London. For variety you may direct under Cover to Michael Read in York Buildings.

'Mrs Collins' has yet to be identified and may not have existed. Michael Read was Harley's porter, described by Jonathan Swift as 'an old Scotch fanatick, and the damn'dest liar in his office alive'.[5]

The first civilian head of the CIA, Allen W. Dulles, would later call Defoe 'one of the greatest author-spies in history'. But, though often considered the 'father of the English novel' as well as a committed spy, Defoe did not write spy novels. Dulles wrote in *The Craft of Intelligence*:

> I have always been intrigued by the fact that ... Defoe never wrote a word about espionage in his major novels ... I cannot dispel the conviction altogether that he never did this because, having the inside view, he felt that for security reasons he could not give a true and full story of espionage as it was really practised in his day, and as a novelist Defoe was above inventing something at variance with the craft.[6]

Defoe, who arrived in Edinburgh early in October 1706, on his Scottish intelligence mission 'to Dispose peoples' minds' to the Act of Union and prevent 'Partys forming Against the Union',[7] was later described by a contemporary as 'a Spy amongst us, but not known to be such, otherways the Mob of Edinburgh had pulled him to pieces'. When the draft Act of Union was published in October, a 'villainous and outragious mobb' threatened members of the Scottish Parliament and judiciary. Despite the street protests, Defoe acquired informers in the Scottish Parliament, the Church of Scotland, business and civic groups, as well as gaining control of much of the press. Though Defoe publicly denied being a spy, writes Professor John Kerrigan, 'he so liked to cut a dash in coffee houses that he couldn't resist hinting at his role. This mixture of concealment and showing off is typical of the man ... '[8] Financial 'inducements' played a major part in Harley's and Defoe's strategy for winning a majority for the Union in the Scottish Parliament. Harley said cynically of the negotiations which won Scottish support for the Act: 'We bought them.'[9] Thereafter the new United Kingdom could lay claim to being the greatest commercial and financial centre in the world.[10]

Though Defoe left espionage out of his novels, he regarded intelligence as a central part of government; it was, he said, 'the soul of public business'. In 1704, he had submitted to Harley a grandiose 'Scheme of General Intelligence', based on a large and expensive network of spies and agents both at home and abroad. Once this network was established, 'a Correspondence may be Effectually Settled with Every Part of England, and all the World beside.' Defoe's proposal was followed by a document entitled 'Maxims and Instructions for Ministers of State' – a Machiavellian scheme for Harley to use his position as secretary of state to take over the government. It would then be the role of the domestic intelligence network to warn Harley of any threats to his popularity which threatened his hold on power. 'A Man Can Never Be Great That Is Not Popular', Defoe declared. Abroad, during the War of the Spanish Succession, Defoe placed particular emphasis on the threat from France despite Marlborough's victories, and on the need for agents in Paris, Toulon, Brest and Dunkirk. His main priority was for 'a Settl'd Person of Sense and Penetration, of Dexterity and Courage, To Reside Constantly in Paris ... As tis a Dangerous Post', the Paris agent would need 'a Larger Allowance than Ordinary', but 'might by One happy Turn, Earn all the money and the charge be Well bestow'd'.[11] As Harley no doubt knew, as in his 'Scheme of General Intelligence', Defoe's budgeting was frequently fanciful. In 1692 he had gone bankrupt with debts of £17,000 (the equivalent today of about £700,000) and spent some time in debtors' prison. In 1706 he went bankrupt again and narrowly escaped jail. Despite his regular literary and intermittent business successes, Defoe was rarely free from debt.[12]

Defoe probably expected his hugely ambitious 'Scheme of General Intelligence' to be financed by the Secret Service Fund, set up under

Charles II and never scrutinised by Parliament. But, as well as paying agents (Defoe included) and financing secret operations, the fund was sometimes diverted to other purposes such as relieving distress among Charles's former mistresses.[13] There was never any prospect of secret government finance for the great intelligence network at home and abroad proposed by Defoe.

*

Most other leading English writers in the reign of Queen Anne looked down on Daniel Defoe as a writer willing to sell himself to the highest bidder. Joseph Addison, celebrity essayist, co-founder of *The Spectator* and leading dramatist, dismissed Defoe as 'a false, shuffling, prevaricating rascal'.[14] Addison's tragedy *Cato*, which ends with its hero, Cato the Younger, committing suicide rather than submit to the tyranny of Julius Caesar, was one of the most popular plays of the eighteenth century. During its uproarious première at Drury Lane on 14 April 1713, rival groups of Tories and Whigs in the audience, intent on denouncing each other as defenders of tyranny, cheered and jeered at key moments during the play.[15]

As Whig under-secretary of state from 1705 to 1709, Addison had gained some experience of secret missions and intelligence operations. In 1706 he accompanied the Earl of Halifax on a mission to Hanover, officially to invest the young Prince George (the future King George I) with the Order of the Garter, but primarily to brief the Hanoverian court secretly on subterranean political manoeuvres over who should succeed to the English throne when the childless Queen Anne died – the main political issue of the time.[16] The fragmentary records of the Secret Service Fund illustrate the kind of intelligence operations which would have come to Addison's attention during his years as under-secretary of state. In 1706 Antoine de Guiscard, abbé de la Bourlie and marquis de Guiscard, became the best-paid English agent of the time, when he received four payments from the Secret Service Fund totalling £1,300 (and one further probable payment of £181) to enable him to 'raise a revolt in Dauphine and Languedoc'.[17] The revolt, however, never took place.

Unlike Defoe, Addison became sceptical of the value of espionage. In his essay 'Of the Infamy of a SPY, and the Caution that is necessary in trusting him', he accepted, no doubt because of the need to monitor the Jacobite threat to the Hanoverian succession after Queen Anne's death,[18] that 'it is absolutely necessary for Rulers to make Use of other Peoples Eyes and Ears' for intelligence collection. But they should 'take particular Care' when doing so:

> A Man who is capable of so infamous a Calling as that of a SPY, is not very much to be relied upon. He can have no great Ties of Honour, or Checks of Conscience, to restrain him in those covert Evidences, where the Person accused has no Opportunity of vindicating himself. He will be more industrious to carry that which is grateful, than that which is true. There will be no Occasion for him, if he does not hear and see Things worth Discovery; so that he naturally inflames every Word and Circumstance, aggravates what is faulty, perverts what is good, and misrepresents what is indifferent. Nor is it to be doubted but that such ignominious Wretches let their private Passions into these their clandestine Informations, and often wreak their particular Spite or Malice against the Person whom they are set to watch.[19]

Addison probably had two particular 'ignominious Wretches' in mind. The first was Guiscard, who ended his woeful career as a British agent by stabbing and almost killing Harley when confronted at a Cabinet meeting on 8 March 1711 with intercepted correspondence which exposed him as a fraud.[20] He died in Newgate Prison on 17 March from wounds sustained after his attack on Harley. The news of the first minister's attempted assassination by a French spy greatly increased his popularity among a public which, unlike Addison, was unaware of Guiscard's earlier career as a fraudulent British agent. Public interest in the failed assassin was so great that the Newgate jailer pickled Guiscard's corpse in a barrel, put it on display, and charged a penny for admission. His remains were eventually interred at Newgate and the jailer, somewhat undeservedly, given £5 'to repair the damages done to the floor and ceilings of 2 rooms by the salt water that ran out of [Guiscard's] coffin'.[21] Though what were later called 'freak shows' had been part of the entertainment business since the sixteenth century, this was the first occasion when the freak on display had been the corpse of a foreign spy.[22]

The second, perhaps less ignominious 'Wretch' Addison would have thought of when writing 'On the Infamy of a SPY' was Daniel Defoe himself. Secret Service Fund records reveal that, during the Harley

Satirical print of the marquis de Guiscard (1711), folded in the middle so that, when closed, the Devil appears wearing a highly embroidered skirt; when open, he is naked, apart from a flaming fringe around the loins, with horns, wings, flaming breasts and a burning globe at his navel. In his right hand, the Devil holds the knife with which Guiscard attempted to assassinate Robert Harley, Earl of Oxford.

ministry of 1710–14, Defoe, using the pseudonym Claude Guilot, received £100 a quarter.[23] For the past decade Defoe had been jealous of Addison's publishing success. In 1704, after the much greater popularity of Addison's poem than his own on Marlborough's great victory at Blenheim, the debt-ridden Defoe ridiculed Addison as 'our modern *Virgil*', sneering that 'he had never sung' without pay – 'till he had 200 [pounds] per Annum secur'd to him'.[24] Six years later, if not earlier, Defoe was receiving twice that amount from the Secret Service Fund.

When Harley fell from power in July 1714, a few days before the death of Queen Anne and the succession of George I of Hanover, Defoe's Secret Service income dried up. Forced to turn to his pen to survive, in 1719 he published what proved to be the century's greatest best-seller: *The Life and Strange Surprizing Adventures of Robinson Crusoe, Of York, Mariner: Who lived Eight and Twenty Years, all alone in an un-inhabited Island … With An Account how he was at last as strangely deliver'd by Pyrates*. The first edition identified Robinson Crusoe himself as the author, leading many readers to believe he was a real person, telling a true story. Thanks to the huge success of the book, which ran to five editions by the end of the year, Defoe was said to have 'cleared over a thousand guineas' and become prosperous for the first time in his career.

Unlike his fellow literary celebrities, Addison and Vanbrugh, Defoe was a lifelong opponent of all things theatrical. In 1705 he responded to the much-trumpeted opening of Vanbrugh's new theatre in the Haymarket, built on the site of former stables and privies ('jakes'), with the crudely satirical verse:

> *Alay'st all this, Apollo spoke the word*,
> And straight arose a playhouse from a T[urd]
> Here *Whores in Hogstyes*, vilely blended lay,
> Just as *in Boxes*, at our *Lewder Play*;
> The Stables have been Cleans'd, the Jakes made Clear,
> Herculean *Labours*, ne'r will Purge us here.

In his periodical *The Review*, Defoe ridiculed the idea that the theatre could benefit society: 'To reform the stage, would not be to build it up, but to pull it down.'[25] It is difficult not to see personal envy, as well as nonconformist principle, in Defoe's denunciation of the celebrated dramatist-architect Vanbrugh's new theatre. The prominent nonconformist minister John How publicly reminded Defoe that the heart of dissent was the individual conscience, and that he ought not to set himself up as 'the Conscience-general of Mankind'.[26] Had How known that Defoe was happy to accept Secret Service money 'to dispose peoples' minds' in favour of government policy, his attack on the writer's moralising pretentiousness would doubtless have been sterner still.

Although Defoe refused to allow any of his work to be adapted for the stage in his own lifetime, after his death theatrical adaptations of *Robinson Crusoe* went on to attract larger audiences than the plays of his *bêtes noires*, Vanbrugh and Addison. The most popular stage versions were for pantomime. The first, performed at Drury Lane in 1781, was 'compiled and adapted to the stage representation by R. B. SHERIDAN, Esq.: author of The SCHOOL for SCANDAL'. It subsequently toured in an evening of entertainment that, remarkably, also included both Shakespeare's *Hamlet* and 'bird imitations' by the improbably named 'Signior Rosigniole'. *Robinson Crusoe, or Harlequin Friday*, 'a Grand Pantomime Entertainment', was notable for including the characters of Pantaloon and Pierrot as well as an allegedly celebrated 'Dance of the Savages'.[27] *Robinson Crusoe* went on to become Britain's most popular pantomime.

*

In his celebrated *Lettres philosophiques*, written during his two years in England (1726–8), François-Marie d'Arouet, better known by his pen-name Voltaire, the most famous writer and dramatist of the Ancien Régime, omitted Defoe from his discussions of English writers and playwrights – despite the popularity of *Robinson Crusoe*.[28] By contrast, Voltaire eulogised the 'illustrious Mr Addison', whose Cato 'seems to me the most noble character to be seen on any stage.'[29] Voltaire would have been unaware that both Defoe and Addison shared with him first-hand experience of intelligence operations.

Voltaire was the leading celebrity of eighteenth-century France.[30] The court and many others who were fascinated by his plays, however, regarded his pleas for toleration and freedom of religion as dangerously subversive. He was twice imprisoned in the Bastille and three times sent into exile. Voltaire's first imprisonment came while he was writing the tragedy *Œdipe*. Verses written to amuse his friends accused the regent, Philippe, Duke of Orleans, of incest with his daughter:

> It is not the son, it is the father;
> It is the daughter, not the mother;
> So far, so good.
> They have already made Eteocles [son of Oedipus and his mother, Jocasta];
> If he were to lose his two eyes [like Oedipus who blinded himself];
> That would really be a story for Sophocles.

After being taken to the Bastille on 16 May 1717, Voltaire tried to pretend he had not written the verse, unaware that two friends to whom he had repeated the lines were government informers. After being freed almost a year later, on Holy Thursday, 14 April 1718, Voltaire wrote a cringing letter of apology to the regent's secretary:

> The only favour I dare ask of you is to please assure His Highness that I am as much obliged to him for my imprisonment as for my liberty, and that I have greatly benefited from the one and shall never abuse the latter.

In November that year, Voltaire had his first great dramatic success with the staging of Œdipe at the Comédie-Française.[31]

Through his links with leading English Jacobite opponents of the Hanoverian succession, Voltaire also attracted the attentions of the intelligence services of Britain's first prime minister, the Whig Sir Robert Walpole (1721–42). In 1722 Voltaire visited the Jacobite Tory leader, Lord Bolingbroke, then living in temporary French exile at the Château de la Source. Bolingbroke was full of praise for both Voltaire and his newly completed epic poem, La Henriade, shortly to be banned in France. Later, during his two-year stay in England, Voltaire gave Bolingbroke's house in Pall Mall as his London address. Some of his letters to and from this address were probably opened on Walpole's orders. It was partly through Bolingbroke that Voltaire met the poet Alexander Pope, who greatly impressed him, and gained introductions to Jonathan Swift and other leading writers.[32] Bolingbroke, wrote Voltaire, 'had the gift of speaking extemporaneously in Parliament with as much purity of language as Swift demonstrated in his writing.'[33]

Though no records survive, Walpole's intelligence services would also have monitored Voltaire's contacts with the Bishop of Rochester, Francis Atterbury, secret leader of Jacobites in England until his exile to France. By 1723 Walpole and his advisers had concluded that the evidence against Atterbury, much of which was obtained from cipher messages decrypted by the British Deciphering Branch (the ancestor of today's GCHQ), was inadequate for a treason trial, since it included nothing written in Atterbury's own hand. They decided instead to opt for a 'bill of pains and penalties', which simply required Parliament to agree that Atterbury was a danger to the state, who should be deprived of all his ecclesiastical offices and exiled for life.[34] Among the most reluctant witnesses to give evidence in the Lords against Atterbury was Edward Willes, head of the Deciphering Branch and the only codebreaker ever to appear before Parliament. No doubt with Walpole's full support, Willes refused to answer any questions on codebreaking as 'disserviceable to the Government' and helpful to its enemies — the position taken by successive British governments ever since.[35]

Jonathan Swift, like many of Atterbury's supporters, mistakenly believed that the codebreakers manufactured evidence on Walpole's instructions. His *Gulliver's Travels* contains the only satire on codebreaking by a major British writer. Gulliver explains that he has spent many years 'in the kingdom of Tribunia by the natives called Langden' (thinly disguised anagrams for 'Britain' and 'England'), where

By their mastery of acrostics and anagrams, the most skilled decipherers can discover 'the deepest designs of a discontented party':

So, for example, if I should say in a letter to a friend, Our brother Tom has just got the piles, a man of skill in this art would discover how the same letters which compose that sentence may be analysed into the following [anagram]: Resist – a plot is brought home – [signed] The Tour.[36]

'The Tour' was Voltaire's Jacobite friend, Lord Bolingbroke, who during his French exile became known as *La Tour*.[37] As a great admirer of Swift,[38] Voltaire probably accepted his claim that Walpole used 'skilled decipherers' to manufacture evidence against Atterbury and other opponents. In 1728–9 Voltaire used Atterbury's former secretary, Thomas Carte, to smuggle banned copies of his *La Henriade* into

France. In 1731 he included a glowing reference to 'the learned bishop of Rochester' in his play *Brutus*, which he dedicated to Bolingbroke.[39]

As Prime Minister, Walpole was much more discreet about SIGINT operations than the previous Whig ministry, which in 1717 had published – in English, French, Dutch and German – decrypted Swedish diplomatic despatches on their assistance to the Jacobites.[40] After Atterbury's expulsion, there was no further public SIGINT controversy during Walpole's premiership. There were, however, regular protests about his network of spies and informers, some of them on the stage. Henry Fielding's play, *Rape upon Rape*, written when he was only twenty-three and first performed at the Haymarket Theatre on 23 June 1730,[41] was largely inspired by probably the most notorious member of Walpole's network: Colonel Francis Charteris, who had become known as 'The Rape-Master General of Britain'.[42] In February 1730 Charteris was sentenced to death for raping his maid, Anne Bond, 'a virtuous and religious young woman', three months earlier. Charteris's chief defence was a letter from Anne Bond, which was exposed as a forgery during his trial.[43]

On 18 April 1730, however, the *London Journal* reported:

> We hear that Anne Bond, on whose oath Col. Charteris was convicted of a rape, has received 800 [pounds] in consideration of her having joined in the petition for his pardon. 'Tis said she was soon to be married to a drawer in Westminster, and that they design to open a tavern with the sign of Col. Charteris's Head.

Walpole no doubt played a central part in securing Charteris's pardon, which required use of the royal prerogative.[44]

John Gay, along with Fielding the most talented new dramatist of the Walpole era, mocked the prime minister's dependence on a network of spies and informers – without mentioning him by name:

> His doors are never closed to spies,
> Who cheer his heart with double lies;
> They natter him, his foes defame,
> So lull the pangs of guilt and shame.[45]

To ensure the Commons had a supportive Whig majority during his record twenty-one years in office, Walpole and his staff regularly rigged elections with money from the Secret Service Fund.[46] The prime minister boasted that bribes by the Tory opposition could never match those of his Whig administration, 'for 100,000 [pounds] a year spent by the Crown will in a little time drain the gentry's pockets'.[47]

Walpole also assembled a team to promote his public image, whose activities were partly paid for by the Secret Service Fund. The actor Tom Davies later recalled that Walpole was in the habit of asking a friend to invite writers who attacked him to dinner so that the prime minister might be 'of the party, as if by chance', and able to 'effect the conversion of the patriotic author[s]' to support the government 'by the powerful eloquence of a bank note'.[48] The key figure in Walpole's literary influence operations, which were kept as inconspicuous as possible, was the classicist and pamphleteer, Thomas Gordon, who from 1723 held the misleading official title of First Commissioner of Wine Licences.[49] Though not an unqualified admirer of Walpole, Gordon had unequivocal views about the Tory opposition:

> A Tory is a Monster, with English Face, a Popish Heart, and an Irish Conscience … In a Word, a Tory is a Tool of Rome, an Emissary of the [Jacobite] Pretender's, a Friend to Priestcraft, an Enemy to his King and Country, and an Underminer of our happy Constitution, both in Church and State.[50]

Walpole, however, was much less successful at controlling the theatre than at controlling the Commons.[51]

The prime minister and his inner circle had no answer to John Gay's mockery in particular. Gay was the inventor of the 'ballad opera', the precursor of the modern musical. His *The Beggar's Opera*, first staged in 1728, was a theatrical sensation which ridiculed Walpole in various dramatic guises – notably that of Jonathan Jeremiah Peachum, a supposedly respectable citizen who was really a ruthless gang-leader as well as a government spy. 'Peaching' was a slang term for being an informer. Peachum complains that the government is in arrears with payments for his services:

> This long arrear of the government is very hard upon us! … In one respect, indeed, our employment may be reckoned dishonest, because, like great statesmen, we encourage those who betray their friends … We must punctually pay our spies or we will have no information.

Walpole also appears in the guise of the rapacious criminal 'Bob Booty', a well-known nickname for him. The prime minister himself attended a performance of *The Beggar's Opera*, and tried to win over the audience by calling for an encore in an effort to show that he had a sense of humour. In reality, he clearly held a grudge. The performance of Gay's sequel, entitled *Polly* (the name of Peachum's daughter), was cancelled, probably on Walpole's instructions.[52]

During the mid 1730s it became increasingly clear that Walpole's preferred methods of covert influence and bribery to end the growing theatrical ridicule and criticism of his administration had failed. The plays performed in the official London theatres were predominantly hostile to the prime minister – revealing a greater level of opposition to the government than at any previous time in the history of the English theatre.

The last straw for Walpole probably came in April 1737 with Henry Fielding's play, *The Historical Register for 1736*. The 'fiddler' Quidam, who bribed his way to power (albeit in Corsica) and then betrayed those he had corrupted, was instantly recognisable to the audience as the prime minister. In a further obvious reference to Walpole, Fielding wrote in the *Dedication to the Publick* at the beginning of the print version:

> Corruption hath the same Influence on all Societies, all Bodies, which it hath on Corporeal Bodies, where we see it always produce an entire Destruction and total Change: For which Reason, whoever attempteth to introduce Corruption into any Community, doth much the same thing, and ought to be treated in much the same manner with him who poisoneth a Fountain in order to disperse a Contagion, which he is sure everyone will drink of.[53]

While Walpole was now determined to introduce theatrical censorship, he was anxious not to expose himself to further ridicule by using Fielding's plays as the explicit justification for doing so. Instead, he embarked on a covert influence operation designed to make it appear that the ultimate target of the theatrical campaign of ridicule was the Crown rather than the prime minister. The basis of the 'active measure' was an offensively satirical two-part article published (and possibly planted) anonymously in the opposition journal *Common Sense* on 19 and 26 March 1737, in which 'the Noblesse of the Kingdom' celebrate the 'Festival of the Golden Rump'. The Rump was easily identifiable

THE FESTIVAL OF THE GOLDEN RUMP.
Rumpatur, quisquis Rumpitur invidia.

UNA EURUS
NOTUSQ.RUUNT
CERBERQ.PROCELLIS
AFRICUS.

Designed by the Author of Common Sense.   Published according to Act of Parliament 1737.   Price 1s.

as the famously large and allegedly flatulent posterior of George II.
A satirical print in *The Craftsman* on 7 May gave a pornographic
portrayal of the Festival.

George II (above, centre) appears as a naked satyr standing on an
altar, kicking his left leg and farting to his right.[54] Queen Caroline,
dressed as a priestess, administers an enema of 'Aurum potabile'
(flavoured brandy – literally, 'drinkable gold'). A royal chaplain, Bishop
Hoadly, stands behind the queen, with men carrying on their heads
gold vessels, several of which have been deposited at the foot of the
altar. On the left, a rotund Robert Walpole acts as master of ceremonies, dressed as Chief Magician in a coat embroidered with dragons.
Behind him is a procession of courtiers with the insignia of the golden
rump embroidered on their shoulders. Walpole's son Horatio (Horace)
holds out a pair of scales, symbol of his father's determination to
preserve the European balance of power which earned him the nickname, 'Balance Master'. Hanging over the festival is a stage curtain
embroidered with golden rumps.

Walpole informed the Commons that the *Festival of the Golden Rump*
was about to be performed as a play – an unprecedented insult to the
royal family which required the introduction of theatrical censorship

to prevent it. Fielding was rightly suspicious. Walpole, he claimed, based his demand for censorship on an '*obscure piece* which was never exhibited upon the Stage, and pretended to be suppress'd; so that it may have been written on purpose, for aught we know with such a particular design'.[55] The implausible official version of events was that the script had been brought to Walpole by a shocked Henry Giffard, manager of the Goodman's Fields Theatre.[56] The text no longer exists and probably never did. The only 'performance' the play ever received was given by the prime minister, when he cited alleged extracts from it in the Commons on 24 May 1737. The bogus 'script' of *The Golden Rump* gave Walpole exactly the ammunition he needed in order to push a hastily drafted Theatrical Licensing Bill through parliament. The Bill, which received Royal Assent on 6 June 1737, stipulated that all new plays must be submitted for licence to the Lord Chamberlain, and gave him absolute statutory powers to reject or censor them. Spoken plays were to be performed only in the 'patent' theatres of Covent Garden and Drury Lane; opera was restricted to the Royal Opera House.[57]

As Noel Annan put it when he launched a campaign against theatrical censorship over two centuries later, 'There began for the English stage a melancholy epoch of over a hundred years of sterility, which was broken only by the comedies of Sheridan and Goldsmith.'[58] The most talented playwrights, including Fielding, turned to writing novels. Fielding himself also became a magistrate and founded the Bow Street Runners – a poacher turned gamekeeper. Remarkably, despite stage censorship, obscene caricatures of members of the royal family by such celebrated artists as James Gillray and the Cruikshanks continued on public sale until the early nineteenth century.[59]

*

In France theatre censorship had existed since 1701, when Louis XIV, influenced by, among others, Madame de Maintenon, decreed that all plays be submitted in advance to the Paris police to ensure that they were 'of the highest purity' – or, as the theatre historian Glynne Wickham put it, to prevent 'any public utterance thought to be critical of the monarchy or suspect to the Church'. Save for brief intervals after the revolutions of 1789, 1830, 1848 and the overthrow of the Second Empire in 1870, French theatre censorship continued for over two centuries. With censorship inevitably came surveillance to ensure that theatres submitted to it.[60]

The long reign of Louis XV (1715–74)[61] was a period of decline for French intelligence as well as for the monarchy. In 1737 British espionage achieved one of its greatest eighteenth-century triumphs over France with the posting of a mercenary British agent, François de Bussy (codenamed 101), recruited two years earlier, to the French embassy in London. In 1744 he provided the entire plan for a French invasion of England in support of the 'Young Pretender', Charles Edward Stuart, better known to posterity as 'Bonnie Prince Charlie', together wiith the names of the English Jacobites involved, who were then arrested. Louis XV cancelled the compromised invasion plan.[62]

While Fielding was abandoning drama for novels, Voltaire was at the height of his success as a playwright. At the première of his tragedy *Mérope* in February 1743, he became the first dramatist to be called onto the stage of the Comédie-Française to be cheered by the audience. 'I cannot appear at the theatre without being applauded', he wrote two months later. At the same time, Voltaire embarked on a much less successful career as a spy. In August 1742 he had written to Louis XV's chief minister, the 89-year-old Cardinal Fleury, offering to provide diplomatic intelligence via his contacts with Frederick II ('the Great') of Prussia, who had invited him to his court. Fleury replied enthusiastically:

> Your words are golden, Sir ... I think like you, and you have entered perfectly into the spirit of the King. I had the honour to read him your letter, with which he was very pleased.[63]

Subsequently, Voltaire sent a number of secret reports in cipher. On 21 July 1743, after a meeting with Frederick II in Amsterdam, he wrote:

> The King of Prussia is having a loan of 400,000 florins secretly negotiated at Amsterdam at 3½ per cent interest. I conclude that his treasury is not as large as people say or that he wishes to borrow at low interest.[64]

Voltaire's ciphers would have caused little difficulty to British or Austrian codebreakers if any of his despatches had been intercepted.

The French *cabinet noir*, a world leader for much of the seventeenth century, was in decline under Louis XV. The French foreign affairs secretariat was unaware that its ciphers had been broken by both the British Deciphering Branch and the even more skilful Austrian 'black chamber', the Geheime Kabinets-Kanzlei in Vienna. In 1744 the French foreign affairs secretariat was alerted to (but seems to have done little to remedy) the weakness of French diplomatic ciphers such as Voltaire's by the humiliating expulsion from St Petersburg of the French ambassador, the marquis de La Chétardie. Before his expulsion, the Russian grand chancellor read out to La Chétardie despatches decrypted by the Russian *cabinet noir* in which the ambassador described the Tsarina Elizabeth as 'so frivolous and so dissipated' that she was 'given entirely to her pleasures'. Whether this episode caused Voltaire to doubt the security of his own cipher will probably never be known. But he was almost certainly aware of La Chétardie's humiliation. The British ambassador in St Petersburg gleefully reported to London, 'I never saw a pickpocket drummed out of a garrison with more infamy than La Chétardie was *culbuté* out of this Empire.'[65]

Though Voltaire was the most famous writer of his time, as a spy he was not in the same class as François de Bussy. He did, however, bequeath to posterity a celebrated intelligence conundrum: the identity of the late seventeenth-century Man in the Iron Mask, which later preoccupied a number of France's leading writers and cryptographers.

Voltaire had first heard the story of the Man in the Iron Mask when imprisoned in the Bastille in 1717. He returned to it in his history, *Le Siècle de Louis XIV*, published in 1751:

> An unknown prisoner, of height above the ordinary, young, and of an extremely handsome and noble figure, was conveyed [in 1661] under the greatest secrecy to the castle of the island of Sainte-Marguerite, lying in the Mediterranean, off Provence. On the journey the prisoner wore a mask, the chin-piece of which had steel springs to enable him to eat while still wearing it, and his guards had orders to kill him if he uncovered his face. He remained in the island until an officer of the secret service, by name Saint-Mars ... who was made warden of the Bastille in 1690, went in that year to Sainte-Marguerite, and brought him to the Bastille, still wearing his mask. The Marquis de Louvois [minister of war] visited him on the island before his removal, evidently regarding him with respect. [In the Bastille] he was refused nothing that he asked for ... The unknown man died in 1703 and was buried by night in the parish church of St Paul.

In the second edition of his *Questions sur l'Encyclopédie* (1771), Voltaire claimed that he had solved the conundrum: the Man in the Iron Mask was the the son of Cardinal Mazarin and Anne of Austria, and so an illegitimate half-brother of Louis XIV. Over a hundred years later, after breaking what he described as 'the Great Cipher of Louis XIV', the leading nineteenth-century French codebreaker, Etienne Bazeries, announced that decrypted military despatches proved that the real identity of the Man in the Iron Mask was General de Bulonde, whom Louis XIV had ordered to be imprisoned for cowardice. Two First World War French cryptographers later confirmed Bazeries' finding. In 1935, however, new evidence proved that they and Bazeries had been mistaken. Equally so were the speculations of a series of French writers from Alexandre Dumas to Marcel Pagnol. The conundrum remains and may never be solved.[66]

5

The Age of Revolution

After Voltaire's death in 1778, his complete works were purchased by a fellow playwright, Pierre-Augustin Caron de Beaumarchais, who published 70 volumes of them over the next twelve years. Like Voltaire, Beaumarchais became the leading French writer of his generation. No other dramatist, apart from Shakespeare, has been so successful in capturing the imagination of opera composers and librettists. Beaumarchais's *Le Barbier de Séville*, which had its première at the Comédie-Française in 1775, inspired a series of comic operas from Giovanni Paisiello's in 1782 to, most famously, Gioachino Rossini's in 1816. Figaro, the barber of Seville who becomes a quick-witted valet, remains one of the best-known characters created by an eighteenth-century playwright. Beaumarchais's *Le Mariage de Figaro*, written in 1778, was banned by French censors until 1784 because of its socially subversive portrayal of a nobleman outwitted by his servant, but was the inspiration for probably the greatest of all comic operas: Mozart's *Le Nozze de Figaro*.[1]

While at the height of his powers as a writer, Beaumarchais, unlike Voltaire, also became the most successful French spy of his generation. Until the death of Louis XV in 1774, he had worked for Louis's personal intelligence agency, the *Secret du roi* ('King's Secret'), which was often at odds with the Foreign Ministry.[2] French envoys sometimes received two sets of instructions, both signed by the king, which contradicted each other.[3] Policy towards Britain was notably confused by the flamboyantly unpredictable chevalier d'Éon de Beaumont, like Beaumarchais an agent of the *Secret du roi*, who was appointed temporary minister plenipotentiary to the Court of St James in the spring of 1763, pending the arrival of the new French ambassador, the comte de Guerchy. When Guerchy arrived in London, d'Éon ignored letters of recall to France and published a book containing official diplomatic correspondence designed to embarrass the new ambassador. Horace

MADEMOISELLE de BEAUMONT, or the
CHEVALIER D'EON.
Female Minifter Plenipo. Capt of Dragoons &c &c.

Split portrait of the chevalier d'Éon shortly before his return to France in 1777: the female half holds a fan and wears an embroidered dress with hair powdered and curled;
the male half is in uniform with a sword at his side.

Walpole pronounced it 'full of wit' with 'a thousand curious circumstances'.[4] The most curious, which caused a sensation in both London
and Paris, were claims that Guerchy was involved in a plot to assassinate d'Éon. Newspaper articles written or inspired by d'Éon also
ridiculed the ambassador's alleged meanness, claiming that he allowed
his staff to smuggle contraband to compensate for their miserly salaries
but insisted that, when travelling, they avoid the expense of dining
at inns by having picnics in the countryside.[5]

D'Éon remained in London, threatening to publish more secret documents, including French plans to invade the south of England. The

stand-off continued for a decade, complicated by widespread rumours from 1770 onwards, encouraged by d'Éon, that he was really a woman. In 1775, however, Beaumarchais, fresh from his dramatic success with *The Barber of Seville*, succeeded in reaching a settlement ('transaction') by which d'Éon agreed to return official documents in his possession and received payment for the substantial expenses he had allegedly incurred in the king's service. Signed by d'Éon on 4 November 1775, the agreement also required him to 'readopt' women's clothing, thus implying that his real gender was female and disqualifying him from any future official position. At one point, Beaumarchais claimed in a letter to Louis XVI's foreign minister, the comte de Vergennes, that 'this crazy woman is insanely in love with me'.[6]

D'Éon so enjoyed life in London as 'Britain's first openly transvestite male'[7] that he did not return to France for almost two years after signing the 'transaction' with Beaumarchais. On 21 November 1777, following a four-hour toilette supervised by Marie-Antoinette's *modiste*, the 49-year-old d'Éon was at last presented in female dress to Louis XVI and his queen at court. Most courtiers probably agreed with the vicomtesse de Fars, who complained: 'She had nothing of our sex except the petticoats and the curls.' A fortnight later, d'Éon was banished from Versailles.[8]

While the chevalier languished in the French provinces, Beaumarchais continued a highly successful career in both drama and intelligence. When negotiating the 'transaction' with d'Éon in 1775, he had written from London: 'All sensible people are convinced in England that the English colonies are lost to the mother country. I agree with them.' So did Vergennes.[9] In May 1776, two months before the American Declaration of Independence, he authorised Beaumarchais to found a company, 'at your own risk', to supply arms as covertly as possible to the American rebels: 'It is important that the operation should have in the eyes of the British government and even the Americans the character of a private speculation of which we know nothing.' With secret financial support from both the French and Spanish crowns, using the pseudonym 'M. Durand', Beaumarchais founded a Spanish front company, Roderigue Hortalez et Compagnie, and worked in secret with an agent of Congress, Silas Deane, who became a personal friend. Beaumarchais's fame as a playwright, however, made it difficult to preserve his alias. While arranging transatlantic arms shipments from Le Havre, he could not resist attending rehearsals of his *Barber of Seville* at the city's main theatre and giving advice to the director and cast. By April 1777, despite such distractions, Hortalez et Cie had sent the American rebels nine vital shiploads of military supplies, only one of which was intercepted by the British. Indeed, until early 1778, Beaumarchais's front company remained almost the only source of supply for the Continental Army commanded by George Washington. 'It is perhaps not too much to say', the CIA's Center for the Study of Intelligence has concluded, 'that Beaumarchais and Deane, by their own efforts, brought the infant United States through the most critical period of its birth.'[10]

'First in war, first in peace, first in the hearts of his countrymen', as Henry Lee famously described him, George Washington also ranks first in the early history of US intelligence. 'The necessity of procuring good intelligence is apparent & need not be further urged,' he wrote to one of his senior officers in July 1777.

> All that remains for me to add is, that you keep the whole matter as secret as possible. For upon Secrecy, success depends in most Enterprises of this kind, & for want of it, they are generally defeated, however well planned ...[11]

Washington's correspondence with officers of the Continental Army contains frequent requests for 'the earliest Advises of every piece of intelligence which you shall judge of importance'.[12] He was also deeply concerned about the threat posed by British espionage: 'There is one evil that I dread & that is their Spies ... I think it is a matter of some importance to prevent them from obtaining Intelligence of our Situation.'[13]

The most famous, though far from the most talented, of Washington's own spies was a 21-year-old Yale graduate, Nathan Hale, who was sent to collect intelligence on British forces on Long Island in September 1776. Hale operated under his own name and was badly prepared for his first mission. His cover as a schoolteacher looking for work after the start of the academic year was unconvincing, and he had never previously been to Long Island. All that is known with certainty about Hale's mission after his landing on the morning of 16 September is an entry in the daybook of the commander of the British forces, General Sir William Howe, four days later: 'A spy from the Enemy (by his own full confession) apprehended last night, was this day Executed at 11

Statue of Nathan Hale in front of CIA headquarters at Langley, Virginia, hands trussed behind his back as he awaits execution: a copy of the original statue on Yale's Old Campus.

o'Clock in front of the Artillery Park.'[14] According to patriotic but plausible tradition, Nathan Hale declared just before he was hanged: 'I only regret that I have but one life to lose for my country.' Some of his British executioners, impressed by his bravery, may have recognised this quotation from Joseph Addison's popular tragedy, *Cato*.[15]

Addison's tragedy was also Washington's favourite play. After seeing it performed and reading it as a teenager, he would regularly quote from *Cato* in letters and speeches for the rest of his life.[16] Like Elizabeth I and Richelieu, he combined fascination with intelligence and a deep love of the theatre.

Most members of the First Continental Congress, however, strongly disapproved of the stage. In October 1774 Congress banned 'every Species of Extravagance and Dissipation ... especially Exhibitions of Shews [*sic*], Plays, Exhibitions and other expensive Diversions and Entertainments'.[17] Boston, remembered today as 'the birthplace of the American Revolution', was particularly hostile to drama. In 1750 the Puritan-dominated Massachusetts General Court had passed an 'Act for preventing Stage-Plays, and other Theatrical Entertainments', in order to stop 'the many and great mischiefs which arise from public stage-plays' that 'tend to increase immorality, impiety, and a contempt for religion'.[18] Washington undoubtedly deplored the ban.[19]

Against this background, the decision by the British authorities to stage plays in Boston, New York and Philadelphia early in the Revolutionary War was a calculated affront to the rebels. The lead was taken by General John Burgoyne, the only British general ever to establish himself as a successful playwright. Before leaving for America, his two-act comedy, *The Maid of the Oaks*, written to celebrate the marriage of a fellow officer in 1774, had been expanded to five acts by his friend, the actor-manager David Garrick, and became a popular part of the Drury Lane repertory.[20] On arriving in Boston in May 1775, a few weeks after the first shots had been fired in the war, 'Gentleman Johnny' Burgoyne turned Boston's main meeting place, Faneuil Hall, into a theatre, where his troops staged a series of plays. In December 1775, in the midst of the siege of Boston by the rebels, Burgoyne put on a performance of the tragedy *Zara* – an adaptation of Voltaire's *Zaïre* by the English dramatist Aaron Hill – for which he wrote a prologue comparing the rebel ban on theatre to that imposed by Cromwell and the English Puritans:

> Amidst the groans sunk every liberal art.
> That polish'd life, or humanized the heart;
> Then fell the stage, quelled by the bigot's roar
> Truth fell with sense, and Shakespere charm'd no more
> To soothe the times too much resembling those,
> And lull the care-tired thought this stage arose;
> Proud if you hear, rewarded if you're pleased,
> We come to minister to minds diseased.

For Boston Puritans, the fact that all female parts in plays at Faneuil Hall were actually played by women and that a 10-year-old girl declaimed an epilogue to *Zara* written by Burgoyne were particular provocations.[21] Theatre was used by Burgoyne in an influence operation designed to show the rebels as kill-joys rather than freedom-fighters.

During the siege of Boston, Burgoyne also used drama to mock both Washington – 'an uncouth figure, awkward in gait, wearing a large wig and a rusty sword' – and the Continental Army as comic bunglers.[22] He wrote a farce ridiculing the Yankee rebels, *The Blockade of Boston*, which was performed by his fellow officers at Faneuil Hall. Its opening night, 8 January 1776, spectacularly misfired, however, when rebels attacked nearby British barracks during the performance. When one of the actors came on stage to give news of the attack, he was applauded by much of the audience, who wrongly assumed that the news was a scripted part of the play.[23]

The ridiculed Continental Army went on to win the siege of Boston.[24] By the time British forces evacuated the city in March 1776, Burgoyne had already left for England by sea to care for his seriously ill wife. Following his return to America later in the year, the nadir of Burgoyne's military career came with his surrender to American forces after the battle of Saratoga on 17 October 1777.[25]

Burgoyne's fellow playwright and French spy, Beaumarchais, had played a crucial part in his defeat by providing most of the arms on which the Continental Army depended. Saratoga proved to be the turning point in the Revolutionary War. After the British defeat, both France and Spain entered the war on the American side.

Burgoyne's first theatrical venture after his defeat at Saratoga and return to England was to assist the leading English playwright of the

'The surrender of General Burgoyne' by John Trumbull (1821).

time, Richard Brinsley Sheridan, in writing *The Camp: A Musical Entertainment*, which satirised British preparations to meet the threat of invasion by America's new allies, France and Spain. *The Camp* was the most performed work at the Drury Lane Theatre during the 1778–9 season, where it was even more popular than Sheridan's now much better-known *School for Scandal*.[26] The characters include an Irish painter called O'Daub, who was suspected of being a French spy working for 'Mr Leatherbag, the great painter'. Many in the audience would have recognised 'Leatherbag' as a satirical reference to Philippe de Loutherbourg, former *peintre du roy* of the French Académie royale, who was revolutionising set design at Drury Lane.[27] The cast included 'the pretty Miss Walpole', better known by her married name, Charlotte Atkyns, who appeared in a 'breeches' role disguised as a male soldier.[28]

*

For George Washington, the most difficult moment of the Revolutionary war was the terrible winter of 1777–8, spent at his headquarters in Valley Forge, Pennsylvania. Deception was central to Washington's survival strategy. He prepared fake documents in his own hand, full of references to non-existent regiments under his command, which were then passed to the enemy by double agents. The forgeries worked. The British credited Washington with over 8,000 troops he did not have and mistakenly concluded he was too strong to be attacked when he was, in reality, at his most vulnerable. But for his successful deception operation, the Continental Army might not have survived the winter.[29] To revive the morale of his troops in the spring of 1778, Washington put on a series of plays at Valley Forge, despite the Continental Congress's earlier attempted ban. They included Addison's *Cato* with its repeated appeals to continue the fight against tyranny: 'Do thou, great Liberty, inspire our souls / And make our lives in thy possession happy / Or our deaths glorious in thy just defence.'[30]

Open French assistance to the Continental Army in the final stages of the Revolutionary War was as vital as Beaumarchais's secret arms supplies at the beginning. Admirals de Grasse and de Barras were able to evade British naval surveillance and reinforce French land forces in the Chesapeake Bay area, thus isolating the British commander, Lord Cornwallis, and his 7,000-strong army on the Yorktown peninsula in Virginia in the autumn of 1781. The 11,000 American forces under

Washington's command were reinforced by 9,000 French troops and French artillery from Rhode Island. The British prime minister, Lord North, famously remarked on hearing the news of the defeat at Yorktown in October: 'Oh God, it is all over.' Yet, although Cornwallis's surrender had settled the outcome of the war, pointless skirmishing continued for almost a year. A peace treaty with Britain recognising American independence was not concluded until September 1783.[31]

Burgoyne enjoyed far more success as a dramatist after the Revolutionary War than he had ever achieved as a military commander. As well as writing political satire, his comedy on upper-class society, *The Heiress*, which opened at the Theatre Royal, Drury Lane in 1786, remained popular on both sides of the Channel for the next half-century. Burgoyne's success, however, did not compare with that of his nemesis, Beaumarchais. At the 1784 Paris première of *The Marriage of Figaro*, crowds were so large that three people were reportedly crushed to death. Box-office receipts were higher than those for any other eighteenth-century French play. The English translation of Beaumarchais's play opened at the Theatre Royal, Covent Garden, late in 1784.[32] The London audience had no idea that its author had operated against England more successfully than any other foreign spy in Ancien Régime Europe.

Nor had they any idea that both Beaumarchais and the chevalier d'Éon de Beaumont, who returned to London in 1785, had originally come to England as spies working for Louis XV's *Secret du roi*. D'Éon's motives for returning in 1785 were quite different, however. Life dressed as a woman in London was far more agreeable than it had been in France. His social circle included the leading radical MP and journalist John Wilkes and his daughter, with whom he dined frequently, as well as the Duke of Dorset, later ambassador in Paris at the outbreak of the revolution in France, who invited d'Éon to stay at the family seat, Knole, near Sevenoaks. Though aged 57 on his return to London, d'Éon added to his annuity by performing fencing demonstrations in a black dress. Speculation continued about the chevalier's gender. It was even the subject of a court case in which the judge declared d'Éon to be a woman (though a post-mortem later concluded that he was male). Today's British support group for transgender people, the Beaumont Society, is named in honour of the chevalier d'Éon de Beaumont.[33]

*

As this print shows, in April 1787 the chevalier d'Éon was invited to stage a fencing match at Carlton House, the newly constructed mansion on Pall Mall of the Prince of Wales (the future George IV). D'Éon toured English and Irish theatres giving further fencing performances in female dress with the actress Mrs Bateman.

Like London theatregoers, Wolfgang Amadeus Mozart was probably unaware of Beaumarchais's double life as a spy when he asked the Venetian exile, Lorenzo Da Ponte, to write the libretto for an opera based on *The Marriage of Figaro*. He is also unlikely to have known that Da Ponte was a lapsed Catholic priest.[34] Since Mozart got to know Da Ponte well, however, he was probably at least vaguely aware that the librettist had fallen foul of the Venetian State Inquisition and been banished from Venice.[35] Da Ponte's friend and fellow libertine, Giacomo Casanova, had also incurred the wrath of the inquisitors and been sentenced to five years' imprisonment. In 1756, after serving only a year of his sentence, Casanova made a dramatic roof-top escape from his cell in the Doge's Palace and fled abroad.

In exile, he tried to ingratiate himself with the State Inquisitors by repeatedly sending them intelligence reports and offering his services

Casanova called his escape from the Doge's Palace 'A wonder if not a miracle. I admit that I am proud of it.'

as a spy across much of Europe. Eventually, in 1780 Casanova was secretly appointed an official spy (*confidente attuale*) with a monthly salary of fifteen ducats. There is scarcely any mention of his espionage in the several thousand pages of his memoirs, which were mainly devoted to boasting of more than 120 sexual conquests. Casanova feared that any suggestion that he was a spy would damage his reputation as well as making espionage more difficult. 'Please remember', he wrote to the Venetian consul in Trieste, to whom he also offered his services, 'that one of my major concerns has to be that no one ever manages to find out that I am one of your secret agents ... ' Casanova was probably the first spy to describe himself as a 'secret agent' – a term which became widely used only in the nineteenth century.[36]

Casanova was a performed playwright as well as a spy. His parents were actors, and he himself had a life-long passion for theatre, especially for opera. He records in his unfinished memoirs an early affair with a female opera singer who was masquerading as a castrato. Casanova's ambition in the 1780s was to become a theatrical impresario and establish a Comédie-Française in Venice for which, however, he found it impossible to raise the funds required. Paolo Preto, a leading authority on the complex Venetian intelligence archives and Casanova's mostly unpublished intelligence reports, considers it 'highly likely' that, while staying in Vienna in 1784–5, he 'lent a hand to Lorenzo Da Ponte', as he began work on the libretto for Mozart's opera, *Don Giovanni*: 'Who better than Casanova to provide lively ideas from lived experience about a successful womanizer and impenitent libertine?' There is also written evidence which suggests, but does not prove, that Casanova had at least a minor part in putting the frantic final touches to the libretto on the night before the première of *Don Giovanni* in Prague on 29 October 1787.[37] Da Ponte was not in Prague at the time, but Casanova was, and it is quite possible that Mozart sought his last minute assistance.[38] Casanova's papers in the Czech state archive include two pages of handwritten notes on Act II, scene 5.

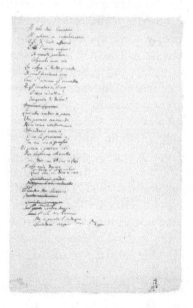

During the première, which was followed by an enormous standing ovation, Casanova watched from a box seat in the wings. When asked by a friend whether he had seen the opera, he allegedly replied, 'Seen it? I practically lived it!'[39]

*

On 14 July 1789, the storming of the Bastille in Paris changed both intelligence priorities and French theatrical production in ways no one could have anticipated.[40] Even a well-organised security service, which the Ancien Régime did not possess, could not have foreseen the subsequent course of the French Revolution. The immediate reaction of d'Éon's friend, the Duke of Dorset, the British ambassador, was to cancel what would have been the first English cricket tour of France. The government of William Pitt the Younger, who had been prime minister for the past six years and was still only 30 years of age, believed that the Revolution would make France weaker and war less likely.[41]

The values of the Revolution were enshrined in the 'Declaration of the Rights of Man and of the Citizen', passed by France's National Constituent Assembly on 26 August 1789. It began by declaring, 'Men are born and remain free and equal in rights.' The theatrical censorship introduced by Louis XIV disintegrated and was formally abolished in 1791.[42] All restrictions on the popular Paris boulevard theatres were lifted.[43]

Revolutionary rituals and celebrations gave rise to a new and unprecedented form of popular, often open-air, theatre. A fête in Paris on 20 June 1790, for example, culminated with a banquet for 300 in the bois de Boulogne 'served by young patriotic nymphs on tables decorated with busts of the friends of humanity, Rousseau, Mably, Benjamin Franklin'. Grace consisted of the first two articles of the Declaration of the Rights of Man and of the Citizen, after which the great revolutionary orator Georges Danton proposed a toast to the liberty and happiness of the whole world. Maximilien Robespierre, later the chief organiser of the Terror of 1793–4, and other prominent revolutionaries followed with further idealistic toasts. The climax came when four of those who had stormed the Bastille a year earlier placed a model of it on a table, destroyed it with their swords and revealed in its midst a baby dressed in white, symbol of innocence and new-born liberty. Amid applause, the red Phrygian cap of the freed slave was placed on the baby's head.[44]

The great romantic poet (and less successful dramatist) William Wordsworth, who witnessed such revolutionary euphoria on his first visit to France a year after the fall of the Bastille, understood it far better than most official British observers:

> Bliss was it in that dawn to be alive,
> But to be young was very Heaven!

By the summer of 1791, however, France was a divided country. A year to the day after the joyful fête in the bois de Boulogne, Louis XVI attempted to escape from Paris to Montmédy, close to the Belgian border, where he planned to put himself at the head of a counter-revolutionary army. When the king was captured en route and escorted back to the capital, republicanism, which had had little support at the time of the storming of the Bastille, began to emerge as a serious political force. Pitt remained determinedly optimistic, assuring the Commons in February 1792: 'Unquestionably there never was a time in the history of this country, when, from the situation of Europe, we might reasonably expect fifteen years of peace, than we might at the present moment.'[45] Only a year later, Britain and France were at war, France was a republic, and Louis XVI had gone to the guillotine. Though he later changed his mind, at the time Wordsworth defended Louis's execution, dismissing 'the idle cry of modish lamentation which has resounded from the court to the cottage' over 'the personal sufferings of the late royal martyr'.[46]

The violence of the early First Republic reached its peak in the Terror from September 1793 to July 1794, an obsessional hunt for often imaginary counter-revolutionaries and foreign spies. Theatrical censorship was reintroduced in 1794.[47] Among the foreign spies supposedly at work in Paris during the Terror was the well-known British actress, Charlotte Atkyns, who had appeared in Sheridan's *The Camp*, but had moved with her husband to France, probably to escape English debtors, and became involved with royalist counter-revolutionaries.[48]

Atkyns was a fantasist rather than an actual royalist spy. The memorial to her in St Peter's Church, Ketteringham, Norfolk, repeats her claim to have been 'the friend of Marie Antoinette and made several brave attempts to rescue her from prison and after that Queen's death strove to save the Dauphin of France'. There is no reliable evidence that Atkyns ever visited Marie Antoinette in prison.[49]

Pitt's main anxiety as the French Republic became increasingly violent and radical was how far it would gain support in Britain. Its most active British supporters were believed to be the members of the London Corresponding Society (LCS), founded in January 1792 in a tavern off the Strand by nine 'well meaning, sober and industrious men'. Six months later, it claimed to have 1,000 members committed to the principle of universal male suffrage, introduced by the French Revolution. In historical hindsight, however, the prospect of a British

NANCY

Charlotte Atkyns as the cross-dressing Nancy in *The Camp*. Her military uniform was probably the source of the legend, which she later promoted, that during an adventurous (but probably fictitious) career as a royalist spy in revolutionary Paris, she dressed as a National Guardsman to gain access to the imprisoned Marie Antoinette.

republic never had any real chance of generating mass enthusiasm. There were eventually about 2,000 Loyalist societies in England, their members many times as numerous as those who wanted to follow the French example.[50] During the early years of the French Republic, however, given the speed with which republicanism had taken hold in France, Pitt could not afford to disregard the threat from English republican sympathisers. The tiny existing 'secret service', headed by one of the Home Office undersecretaries, Evan Nepean, expanded into the Alien Office, which was made responsible for monitoring immigration and subversion after the passage of the Aliens Act in January 1793.[51]

Probably the most eloquent critic of the Pitt government's surveillance of revolutionary sympathisers was Richard Brinsley Sheridan, who also succeeded Garrick as manager of the Drury Lane Theatre in 1776. Elected as a Whig MP in 1780, he initially welcomed news of the Revolution with even greater enthusiasm than the Whig leader, Charles James Fox. It was Sheridan who toasted the 'establishment and confirmation of liberty in France' at a dinner in 1790 to commemorate the first anniversary of the fall of the Bastille, attended by over 500 'friends of liberty' – not including Fox, who went to Ascot instead. The Lord Chamberlain, the Marquess of Salisbury, held Sheridan responsible for several occasions on which the audience at the Haymarket Theatre (which provided a temporary home for his company during the construction of the new Drury Lane) had sung the French revolutionary anthem, *Ça ira*. *The Times* reported on 24 March 1792 that members of the audience had demanded that the orchestra 'play the "foreign notes" of "Ça Ira" in place of "God Save the King".' A week later the Lord Chamberlain wrote to warn Sheridan:

> Information having been given, at this office, that the Tune of Ça ira has been recently, and repeatedly Called for from several Parts of the Theatre in St. James' Haymarket under your direction, I think it my Duty as Chamberlain of the King's Household to acquaint you that [I] Expect you [to] take the Proper Measures to prevent that Tune being Played[. I]n case it shall be called for in future, the Theatre will be shut up.[52]

The fury with which Sheridan later denounced in the Commons the use of government agents provocateurs as well as spies in the LCS and other radical societies strongly suggests that he believed informers had also been present in the Haymarket. All the supposed revolutionary plots discovered in Britain, he declared in 1795, were the responsibility of Pitt's government: 'He would not shrink from what he had said on a former occasion, that he considered Ministers as the sole fabricators of these plots':[53]

> I will not say that there is no government in Europe which does not stand in need of the assistance of spies; but I will affirm that the government which avails itself of such support does not exist for the happiness of the people. It is a system which is calculated to engender suspicion and to beget hostility; it not only destroys all confidence between man and man, but between the governors and the governed; where it does not find sedition it creates it ... The spy, in order to avoid

THE LONG-WINDED SPEECH,
Or the oratorical organ harmonized with
sublime and beautiful inflation.

The Whig leader, Charles James Fox, uses the head of John Wilkes as a bellows to inflate Sheridan's prolix but often spell-binding oratory.

suspicion, is obliged to assume an appearance of zeal and activity; he is the first to disseminate the doctrines of sedition, or to countenance the designs of violence; he deludes the weak by the speciousness of his arguments, and inflames the turbulent by the fury of his zeal. It must have made a man's heart burn to hear the sort of evidence brought forward by these spies on the late trials.

Sheridan cited the case of 'a wretch of the name of [George] Lynam', who had infiltrated the LCS and gave evidence against its leading members at their treason trial in November 1794.[54] All were acquitted and Lynam exposed as a dishonest government spy. As he complained to his controller in the Alien Office: 'My name is wrote as a Spye every night in Wallbrook, I have been personaly threatened by a person of one of the Societys at Aldgate, and yesterday received a threatening letter from another quarter ... '[55]

Sheridan was entirely unaware that one of the most successful Alien Office spies and agents provocateurs was the playwright, James Powell, some of whose plays were later performed at Sheridan's Drury Lane Theatre. During the 1790s Powell penetrated successively three 'subversive' groups: the London Corresponding Society, of which he became assistant secretary;[56] the Society of United Englishmen, a more radical offshoot of the LCS; and the United Irishmen. Fragmentary evidence such as his extravagant expenses claim of £27 7s 2d for a trip from London to Yarmouth indicates that he was very well paid. Powell was also an active agent provocateur who successfully planted on a leading militant of the United Englishmen, Thomas Evans, an incriminating written oath which cast doubt on his allegiance to the Crown and led to his arrest in 1798.[57]

One of James Powell's plays, *The Venetian Outlaw*, performed at Drury Lane in 1805, apparently 'to unbounded applause',[58] draws on his own experience in intelligence. The hero, Vivaldi, infiltrates Count Orsano's conspiracy against the Venetian head of state, the Doge, much as Powell had infiltrated Evans's United Englishmen. The scene where the conspirators swear an incriminating oath is reminiscent of that planted by Powell on Thomas Evans. Vivaldi has to be constantly on his guard against discovery by the real conspirators. His servant warns him, 'Speak softly, my dear unfortunate master. Have you forgot that we are surrounded everywhere by spies and informers? That the walls themselves are evidence to indiscreet actions?' At the climax of the play, Vivaldi throws off his disguise and rounds on the conspirators he has successfully deceived: 'Well, worthy friends, ... you shall now receive the reward due to your valour. Solders, seize [them]!'[59]

During the later 1790s, faced with the threat of French invasion of both England and Ireland, Sheridan began to rally round the government. In February 1797, 1,400 Frenchmen, some freed from prison on condition they took part in an invasion of England, set off under the command of the American pirate William Tate to burn Bristol, but were forced by gales to land further north, at Fishguard in Pembrokeshire, where they gave up military operations and spent most of their time hunting for food before being captured. Farcical though the episode was, news of the invasion caused financial panic in London and a run on the Bank of England which forced a British government for the first time to end the convertibility of paper money into gold. There were periodic scares over the following months, exacerbated by spring mutinies in the Royal Navy, that French spies in England were preparing another invasion.[60]

One of the scares briefly involved Wordsworth and his friend, Samuel Taylor Coleridge – coincidentally at a time when both had plays, which they read aloud to each other,[61] turned down by Sheridan. After the rejection in 1797 of his only play *The Borderers*, Wordsworth did not publish it until 1842.[62] Coleridge's drama *Osorio*, turned down by Sheridan at almost the same time, was eventually performed at Drury Lane sixteen years later under the new title *Remorse*.[63] During the summer of 1797 a Somerset doctor reported to the Home Secretary 'a very suspicious business concerning an emigrant family who have contrived to get possession of a mansion house at Alfoxden' and were, he suspected, 'under-agents' working for a French spy in Bristol. James Walsh of the Aliens Office, who was sent to investigate, discovered that what the doctor suspected was a spy ring at Alfoxden were in reality Wordsworth, Coleridge and Wordsworth's sister, Dorothy. 'I think', Walsh reported, 'this will turn out no French affair but a mischievous gang of disaffected Englishmen.' Wordsworth, he added, was already known to the Aliens Office. Coleridge later wrongly claimed that the ignorant Walsh had overheard him discussing Spinoza with his friends but had mistaken the Dutch philosopher for a sinister figure called 'Spy Nozy'.[64] By 1797 Wordsworth was no longer, as Walsh believed, a 'disaffected' supporter of the French Republic. 'I abandoned France and her Rulers,' he wrote later, 'when they abandoned the struggle for Liberty, gave themselves up to Tyranny, and attempted to enslave the entire World.'[65]

The most dramatic expression of Sheridan's loyalty to the British Crown came during the visit by George III to a performance at his Drury Lane Theatre on 15 May 1800.

A contemporary etching shows the 'Horrid Assassin', James Hadfield, a mentally ill former army officer, standing in the pit as he attempts, unsuccessfully, to shoot the king, who calmly turns to reassure a group of alarmed princesses (left), while the queen enters the box (right). Sheridan bravely grabs Hadfield's right arm and another man seizes him from behind.

Hadfield was then dragged across the orchestra onto the stage and taken to a room in the theatre to be questioned by Sheridan and a

The *HORRID ASSASIN, I. HATFIELD, attempting to Shoot the* KING *in Drury Lane Theatre on the 15 of May 1800.*

Bow Street magistrate.[66] The Drury Lane musical director, Michael Kelly, later recalled:

> 'God save the King' was then called for, and received with shouts of applause, waving of hats, &c. During the whole of the play, the Queen and Princesses were absorbed in tears; – it was a sight never to be forgotten by those present.

At the end of the play, the audience again insisted on singing 'God save the King'. Kelly sang an extra verse written by Sheridan 'on the spur of the moment', which appears on the stage curtain in the etching. It received 'the most rapturous approbation':

> From every latent foe,
> From the assassin's blow.
> God save the King.
> O'er him thine arm extend,
> For Britain's sake defend
> Our father, prince, and friend,
> God save the King.[67]

In February 1806, Sheridan became Treasurer of the Navy in the 'Ministry of All The Talents' (including Fox) formed after the death of Pitt. Its main achievement, shortly before it collapsed only a year later, was to abolish the slave trade in Britain and its empire. Abolition, which had long been one of Sheridan's ambitions, helped to inspire James Powell's most remarkable play, *Furibond or Harlequin Negro*, which opened at Drury Lane in December 1807. A black slave who is about to commit suicide is magically transformed into Harlequin and marries Columbine, the white plantation owner's daughter – the most remarkable representation in an English play since *Othello* two centuries earlier of a white woman's love for a black man. Before departing for England, Harlequin 'supplicates for the emancipation of his brother slaves', who appear on stage in chains. Though willing to betray his radical colleagues for money, Powell seems to have shared some of their ambitions.[68]

6

From Counter-Revolution in Europe to Civil War in America

At the beginning of the nineteenth century, Europe's most prolific and successful dramatist was the German August von Kotzebue, author of – incredibly – over 200 plays, mostly melodramas, which were performed more frequently than those of his nowadays far more famous contemporaries, Goethe and Schiller. His German admirers included Beethoven, who composed incidental music for two of Kotzebue's plays, *The Ruins of Athens* (Beethoven's opus 113) and *King Stephen* (opus 117). Beethoven also proposed that Kotzebue collaborate with him on an opera about Attila, which was never written.[1]

An English critic in 1802 blamed '*Kotzebue-mania*' for the proliferation of ghosts, 'mouldering castles, sulphurous flames, bloody daggers, and other terrific images of a distempered imagination' on the London stage.[2] Unusually for such a popular writer, Kotzebue wrote an essay entitled, 'Why do I have so many enemies?' Though he claimed his enemies were merely jealous of his success, German radicals feared Kotzebue's Russian connections. After beginning his career in Weimar, in the 1780s he became head of the magistracy of the Russian province of Estonia and acquired noble status. Thereafter his career alternated between Germany and the Russian Empire. As Russian consul general in Königsberg in 1817, Kotzebue acted as a pro-Russian propagandist and sent Tsar Alexander I secret monthly reports on politics and public affairs. He was widely regarded by the German student nationalist associations, the *Burschenschaften*, as a Russian spy.[3]

The *Burschenschaften*, who were among the first to campaign for the unification of the fragmented German-speaking states, were also outraged by Kotzebue's opposition to their nationalism. At their Wartburg conference in 1817, they threw his history of Germany on to a bonfire. On 23 March 1819 Karl Sand, a 24-year-old *Burschenschaft* member, called at Kotzebue's house in Mannheim, told him he was a 'traitor to the fatherland', and stabbed him to death. Sand then attempted, but failed, to commit suicide.[4] The charge that Kotzebue was a Russian spy in the service of the reactionary Tsar Alexander I remained the belief of most German patriots for the remainder of the nineteenth century.[5]

Though Sand was a fanatic acting alone, Prince Klemens von Metternich, Austrian foreign minister and (from 1821) chancellor, who made it his mission across Europe to root out all signs of revolution (some of them imaginary), declared himself 'absolutely certain' that Kotzebue's murder had been ordered by a secret student tribunal at Jena University. The counter-revolutionary Carlsbad decrees, drafted by Metternich with Prussian support, which heightened surveillance and censorship in German universities, were ratified by the entire German Confederation in 1819.[6] Most plays and operas dealing with themes of insurrection and national liberation were banned by Austrian and Prussian censors. Among their victims were Friedrich Schiller's play *William Tell* and the opera of the same title by Rossini, which portrayed a Swiss uprising against tyrannical Austrian rule.[7] Plays were believed to possess greater subversive

On the scaffold in May 1820, before being decapitated, Sand repeated his claim that Kotzebue was a Russian spy.

potential than the printed word. In an era of mass illiteracy when no newspaper sold more than a few thousand copies, authoritarian regimes feared the ability of theatres, which played to much larger audiences, to rouse the uneducated 'dark masses' as well as revolutionary students.[8]

*

Alexander Pushkin, Russia's greatest poet, was allowed to publish a censored version of his most famous play, *Boris Godunov*, the first modern Russian historical drama, in 1830,[9] but no performance was permitted until 1866. Though he was closely involved with theatre in St Petersburg and planned numerous plays, he completed few of them. Pushkin's extraordinary burst of dramatic energy in 1830 when, in only three months he wrote four 'little tragedies', masterpieces of Russian blank verse, as well as completing the verse novel *Eugene Onegin* and composing more than thirty lyric poems, shows how much he might have achieved as a playwright under a less intolerant regime.[10] Only the 'little tragedy', *Mozart and Salieri*, premiered in 1832, was allowed on stage during his lifetime.[11]

In Russia, censorship and surveillance went hand in hand. After his accession in December 1825, Tsar Nicholas I established a new Third Section of his chancellery, headed by General Alexander von Benckendorff, to take charge of political policing.[12] It was also given the lead role in theatre censorship.[13] Despite his own notoriously promiscuous past, Benckendorff was quick to criticise the moral failings of Russia's writers and artists. Pushkin, he claimed, was 'undoubtedly pretty much a good-for-nothing but, if one is successful in directing his pen, this will be advantageous'.[14] The Third Section became notorious for its pervasive surveillance. Benckendorff's executive director, Maxim von Fock, who supervised a network of 5,000 informers, reported, with apparent pride, the widespread belief that it was 'impossible to sneeze in one's home ... without the Sovereign finding out about it within the hour'.[15] The Third Section was so intrusive that even some police forces felt threatened by it. Only two months after the founding of the Section, Fock complained to Benckendorff that the St Petersburg city police followed him wherever he went: 'Surveillance itself is being made the object of surveillance, in defiance of all sense and propriety.'[16]

Pushkin's banishment from St Petersburg in 1820 because of the allegedly subversive tendencies of his *Ode to Liberty* and other poems made surveillance of him in exile on his family estates more difficult than it would have been in the capital. In February 1826, two months after the failed Decembrist Revolt against the new tsar, Benckendorff received an alarming report on Pushkin from the Third Section agent, Stepan Viskovatov, a minor poet and prolific playwright:

> Some persons worthy of trust from the Pskov province, attest that ... Aleksandr Pushkin, known for his freethinking, harmful and depraved poems, ... is now with violent and depraved behaviour openly preaching atheism and disobedience.

Viskovatov's denunciation of probably the finest poetry in the Russian language as 'depraved' leaves little doubt that he was deeply jealous of Pushkin's success. He himself is now remembered (if at all) not for his own work but for a translation of *Hamlet*.[17] His aim was clearly the punishment of Pushkin, whom he falsely accused of greeting the death of Alexander I by 'vomiting forth the following hellish words: "Finally the Tyrant has gone, and the rest of his family will not be alive for long".'[18]

Less alarmist reports led some Third Section officials to suspect that Pushkin, though in internal exile, had some part in the origins of the Decembrist rebellion. Some of his friends had taken part; others admitted during interrogation that they had been inspired by the *Ode to Liberty*.[19] To conduct an urgent 'secret investigation of the well-known versifier' in the area around his provincial estates, Benckendorff sent Alexander Boshnyak, one of the Section's most successful spies and agents provocateurs. For his success in 'adopting the guise of the vilest Jacobinism' and penetrating a supposedly dangerous revolutionary society early in 1825, Boshnyak had been personally congratulated by Tsar Alexander I and given a 3,000-rouble reward. Later in the year, he was awarded the Order of St Anne and had his annual salary raised to 5,000 roubles. Adam Mickiewicz, the Polish national poet who, like Pushkin, was spied on by Boshnyak, remembered him as 'a more cunning spy' than any he had encountered in novels. With Boshnyak on his mission in the summer of 1826 went a military courier carrying an open warrant for Pushkin's arrest if the allegations against him were upheld. Unlike the

Alexander Pushkin aged 28. Push-kin's maternal great-grandfather, Abram Ganibal (Hannibal), was a black African general at the court of Peter the Great.

embittered Viskovatov, however, Boshnyak seems to have admired Pushkin's work. He reported in August that Pushkin was innocent of all charges.[20]

Following the favourable Third Section report on Pushkin, Nicholas I summoned him to St Petersburg, believing that he could win him over. At a meeting with the tsar on 8 September 1826, Pushkin frankly admitted his past sympathies with the Decembrists, but promised 'to become different'. Nicholas ended his exile and announced that he personally would act as censor of all the writer's work. 'The advantage is, of course, immense,' Pushkin wrote to a friend. It proved to be less advantageous than he had hoped. He was required to submit his work to Benckendorff for transmission to the tsar, and it was Benckendorff who informed him of Nicholas's censorship decisions.[21] Absurdly, the tsar gave Pushkin advice on writing as well as on respect for authority, often making notes and corrections on both content and style in the margins of his drafts – some of which Pushkin prudently accepted.[22]

Pushkin's courtship of the beautiful Natalya Goncharova was complicated by rumours that he was high on the Third Section's watch list. He wrote to Benckendorff: 'Mme Goncharova is afraid to give her daughter to a man who could have the misfortune of being in the Emperor's disfavour.' Benckendorff sent back a letter, falsely

denying that Pushkin was under surveillance, which he was authorised
to show to Natalya's mother:

> His Majesty the Emperor, in wholly paternal solicitude for you, sir,
> deigned to charge me, General Benckendorff, not as head of the gendar-
> merie, but as the person in whom he places his confidence, to observe
> you and guide you by my counsel; no police have ever been ordered
> to keep a watch on you.

Mme Goncharova was sufficiently reassured, and Pushkin married her
18-year-old daughter in 1831.[23]

*

'Do me a favour', Pushkin's friend, Nikolai Gogol, wrote to him in
October 1835:

> Send me some subject, comical or not, but an authentically Russian
> anecdote. My hand is itching to write a comedy ... Give me a subject
> and I'll knock off a comedy in five acts – I promise, funnier than hell.

The 'anecdote' Pushkin provided became the basis of Gogol's *The
Government Inspector*, probably the greatest comedy of Russian theatre.
Two years earlier, Pushkin had been mistaken in a remote part of
Russia for a government inspector. The same happens to Ivan Khlestakov,
the loquacious minor St Petersburg official in Gogol's play, who is bribed
and fêted by town officials anxious to divert his attention from their
corrupt maladministration.[24] Among the ways in which Khlestakov
impresses his victims is by posing as an intimate friend of Pushkin: 'I
often say to him: "Well, Pushkin, old boy, how goes it?" "So, so," he'd
reply ... He's a great original.' Khlestakov also claims to have written
far more plays than Pushkin – chief among them Beaumarchais'
Marriage of Figaro, of which he pretends to be the real author.[25]

Modern commentaries on *The Government Inspector* often overlook
its intelligence dimension. Khlestakov's deception is so successful
largely because the town authorities are expecting a real government
inspector. They believe that the main purpose of the inspector's
'secret instructions' is 'to find out if there is treasonable activity
anywhere' on the eve of what is expected to be another war with

Turkey.[26] *The Government Inspector* is also the first play to break the taboo on mentioning official letter-opening, one of the main forms of intelligence gathering on, among others, Gogol and Pushkin. The Third Section's operations included letter-interception on an industrial scale throughout the Russian Empire, assisted – according to Benckendorff – by postmasters 'known for their meticulousness and zeal'.[27] The postmaster in *The Government Inspector* tells the governor that he opens letters for pleasure as well as duty: 'I just itch to know what's doing in the world. And it's very interesting reading, I tell you. Some letters are fascinating – parts of them written grand – more edifying than the *Moscow Gazette*.'[28] At the end of the play, the postmaster reads aloud to the horrified governor an intercepted letter sent by Khlestakov which reveals that, 'thanks to my St Petersburg appearance and dress, the whole town took me for a governor-general. Now I am staying at the governor's home. I am having a grand time and I am flirting desperately with his wife and daughter.'[29] In the final scene, a gendarme announces the arrival of the real government inspector.[30]

Without Nicholas I's intervention, the censors would undoubtedly have banned *The Government Inspector*. The tsar, however, so enjoyed reading Gogol's mockery of corrupt and self-important minor provincial officials that he allowed the play to be staged in 1836, subject only to the removal of a few lines he judged disrespectful of religion, such as 'Oh God!' and 'My sainted mother'. Thereafter, Gogol's imperial patronage ensured that the censors of the Third Section handled his other comedies with kid gloves.[31]

Among the intercepted correspondence which the tsar read with greatest personal interest was that between Pushkin and his wife, Natalya. In a letter that particularly annoyed Nicholas, Pushkin told his wife he was not going to present his personal congratulations at the celebrations to mark the coming of age of Tsarevich Alexander. Pushkin wrote to Natalya in a letter which he no doubt expected to be intercepted:

What profound immorality there is in the usages of our government! The police unseal a husband's letters to his wife and take them to the Tsar (a well-brought-up and honorable man) and the Tsar is not ashamed to admit this and put in motion an intrigue worthy of Vidocq [a head of the French Sûreté].[32]

Pushkin was also disturbed to find that the tsar, who, he noted, ran 'a harem of budding actresses' and married noblewomen, showed signs of wishing to add Natalya to his conquests – 'dangling after her like some stripling officer'. At court balls, as well as dancing quadrilles with Natalya, Nicholas was apt to sit next to her at supper: 'Of a morning', complained Pushkin, 'he purposefully drives past her windows several times and in the evening, at a ball, asks why her blinds are always down.'[33] As both the would-be seducer of Natalya and the personal censor of Pushkin's work, Nicholas would have been particularly struck by a remarkable poem on how Natalya, initially 'demurely cold', came to 'share [Pushkin's] flame' during their lovemaking.[34]

However, Pushkin's most dangerous rival for his wife's affection was not the tsar but a French exile in St Petersburg, the Baron Georges d'Anthès, who became an obsessional stalker of Natalya and deluded himself into believing they had had an affair. On 27 January 1837, Pushkin was fatally injured in a duel with d'Anthès. 'If God ordains that we are not to meet again in this world,' Nicholas wrote to the poet on his deathbed, 'then accept my forgiveness and do not worry about your wife and children. They will be my children and I will take them into my care.' Pushkin's death on 29 January caused the postponement of the premiere of his romantic 'little tragedy', The Stone Guest, only the second of his plays whose performance the tsar had so far permitted.

After Pushkin's death, Nicholas ordered the court poet, Vasily Zhukovsky, to go through his papers, in case they contained evidence of treason. Zhukovsky found none, but was horrified by documents recording Pushkin's harassment by the Third Section. As he wrote bitterly to Benckendorff: 'These reprimands of such little account to you coloured his whole life. You turned this protection into police control.' Huge crowds attended Pushkin's funeral in St Isaac's Cathedral, St Petersburg. The final indignity inflicted by the Third Section on the greatest poet in Russian history was to ban all mention of the funeral in the press.[35]

*

In the United States, because of the role of intelligence in the Revolutionary War, it was possible to portray spies like Nathan Hale as fighters for freedom rather than, as in most of Europe, a threat to liberty. Of the three recipients of the United States' first award for military bravery, the Badge of Military Merit, instituted by George Washington during the last year of the Revolutionary War, one was a spy.[36] In August 1781, Daniel Bissell had been despatched on Washington's orders to pose as a deserter and gather intelligence on British military strength in New York, which could be used in planning an attack on the city. Bissell succeeded in joining a unit commanded by the former US military hero, General Benedict Arnold, who had defected to the British. He spent the next thirteen months collecting remarkably detailed (and probably reliable) intelligence before rejoining the Continental Army in September 1782, where he was initially arrested as a deserter until Washington confirmed his story.[37]

Bissell's bravery during his secret mission probably helped to inspire the first major American espionage novel, James Fenimore Cooper's *The Spy*, published in December 1821.[38] The central character is Harvey Birch, whom the Americans believe to be an English spy 'possessed of a coolness and presence of mind that nothing seemed to disturb'.

James Fenimore Cooper, originator of the spy novel.

After being killed in action, however, he is revealed to have been a patriotic American double agent working in the enemy camp for Washington. Clasped to Birch's dying breast is 'a tin box, through which the fatal lead had gone'. Inside the box is a secret document whose contents, though not revealed until the last page of the novel, will have been guessed by attentive readers much earlier:

> Circumstances of a political nature, which involve the lives and fortunes of many, have hitherto kept secret what this paper now reveals. Harvey Birch has for years been a faithful and unrequited servant of his country. Though man does not, may God reward him for his conduct!
>   Geo. Washington

The Spy was the first American novel to be dramatised – though not by Cooper. On 1 March 1822, less than ten weeks after the publication of the book, a play with the same title opened in New York at the New Park Theater. The author was a government official and part-time writer, Charles Powell Clinch. His play, most of which followed the novel quite closely, toured the eastern seaboard for the next thirty years. Though since criticised for its 'melodramatic qualities, stiffness of dialog, and formal soliloquies', for much of the nineteenth century the play proved as popular as Cooper's book.[39] While Cooper himself is now best remembered as the author of *The Last of the Mohicans* and *The Leatherstocking Tales*, it was *The Spy* which made his reputation, going through fifteen editions in the United States alone before his death in 1851.[40] No other American spy novel achieved such popularity prior to the Cold War a century later. The film version in 1914 was to be one of the first American spy films.

When Cooper's novel was first published in the United States, there was still no market in Britain for any form of fiction whose hero was a spy. At the expense of George III, a monument to the British spy, Major John André, had been erected in Westminster Abbey after his execution on Washington's orders during the Revolutionary War.[41] But there was no post-war appetite for stories about British espionage during a war which had ended in ignominious defeat. The one British intelligence success which perhaps would have been capable of capturing the public imagination was the breaking of Napoleon's main cipher, which had hastened Wellington's victory in the Peninsular War, culminating in his decisive defeat of French forces at the battle

of Vitoria in June 1813. But, like Bletchley Park's success against German ciphers in the Second World War, the breaking of the French *grand chiffre* remained a closely guarded secret. Even most twentieth-century historians of the Napoleonic Wars failed to discover it.[42]

The most common images of spies in early nineteenth-century Britain were as Home Office informers or agents provocateurs inside radical movements. Some were publicly exposed. A popular print by George Cruikshank in 1817 showed two villainous-looking agents provocateurs – John Castle and William Oliver, sitting either side of a table presided over by the home and foreign secretaries, Lords Sidmouth and Castlereagh. On the floor beside Sidmouth are 'Instructions for Entrap[in]g the poor & needy'. A horrified John Bull exclaims through an open window (far right): 'Oh! Oh I have found out the Conspirators at last, poor Starving John is to be ensnared into Criminal acts & then the Projectors & perpetrators are brought forward as principal evidences!'[43] Castle was later exposed in court as a bigamist and former brothel-keeper.[44]

As well as trying to penetrate radical movements, successive governments, until a change in the law in 1843, made greater use of spies and informers to monitor London theatres than at any other time in British history. The chief targets were 'illegitimate' theatres and other venues which challenged the monopoly of the two London patent theatres, Drury Lane and Covent Garden, for spoken drama and of the Royal Opera House for opera, conferred on them by the Theatrical Licensing Act of 1737. As we have seen, the same act required all new plays to be submitted to the Lord Chamberlain, whose Examiner of Plays had absolute power to censor or reject them. Paradoxically, notes the historian David Worrall:

> In the age of Blake, Byron, the Shelleys, Keats, and Wordsworth, during a period notable for the way in which its poetry and novels reflected with exceeding complexity the period's considerable political controversies resulting from the French Revolution, a long and divisive war, an unprecedented industrial revolution coupled to sporadic social unrest, stage drama was the only literary form continuously under Government regulation.[45]

Challenges to official censorship and attempts to evade the monopoly of the patent theatres and Royal Opera House took diverse forms: among them song and supper clubs, 'where theatre, literature, and the popular culture of the street met together in clouds of speech, song, alcohol, and tobacco'; tavern 'spouting clubs'; the growth of unregulated private theatres in the 1820s; and penny theatres popular with young working-class audiences from the 1830s.[46]

The climax to intelligence surveillance of 'illegitimate' theatre followed the purchase in 1830 by the radical writer and publisher, Richard Carlile, of the London Rotunda, a rambling building in Southwark which, in addition to a large bar and separate coffee room, included a circular theatre with a gallery previously used for equestrian displays. Though Carlile had served six years in prison for seditious libel (1819–26), his tongue-in-cheek description of the Rotunda as a dissenting chapel enabled him to claim that he did not need to apply for the licence required for theatres or other public meeting places.[47] Soon after Carlile took over, an informer warned the Home Office that

> a gang of Ruffians at night assemble at a Place called the Rotunda in Blackfriars Road for the avowed purpose of political discussions. The exaggerated statements put forth at these meetings, together with the inflammatory nature of their harangues, have gone far, I fear, towards creating that spirit of disaffection now so prevalent among the lower orders.[48]

Much of what we know of performances in the Rotunda theatre comes from the reports of Home Office spies.[49] The most provocative performances were sacrilegious sermons and mock services by Carlile's friend, Robert Taylor, a Cambridge graduate and former Anglican priest, who had earlier served a two-year prison sentence for blasphemy.[50] Dressed in full Anglican clerical vestments, Taylor appeared before a six-foot crucifix and communion table laden with bread and wine. With the theatre in darkness, he would begin some 'services' by chanting, 'Satan, Beelzebub, Baal, Peor, Belial, Lucifer, Abaddon, Apollyon, thou King of the Bottomless Pit, thou King of Scorpions ... to whom it is given to hurt the earth ... Appear.' A large globe on the stage promptly lit up, showing an image of Satan. Then, with a flick of Taylor's wrist, Satan was transformed into an angel of light. In the communion service which followed, Taylor broke bread and drank wine, declaring 'Now I drink in my Saviour's health.' He then pretended to be drunk. 'The result', according to one Home Office spy, 'was continued roars of laughter' from the audience. Taylor ended the 'service' by saying 'Gammon' (a lie) instead of 'Amen'. He regularly attracted crowds of 700 to 1,000; at times hundreds were turned away.[51]

During widespread rural riots in the winter of 1830–31, Carlile and Taylor took the side of agricultural labourers protesting against falling wages and job losses. Farmers and landowners were sent letters, signed by a mythical 'Captain Swing', who threatened them with arson if they failed to meet the labourers' demands. By December 1830, nearly 2,000 people involved in the riots were awaiting trial; nineteen were subsequently executed and over 500 transported. In flagrant breach of the law limiting spoken drama to the patent theatres, Carlile put on a play by Taylor entitled *Swing: Or, Who are the Incendiarists?* Save for the first night in February 1831, a Home Office spy filed a report on every performance.[52] The villains of *Swing* were not the rioters but

> Our proud and haughty lords
> That make the laws only to serve themselves,
> And hire the clergy, like the gospel dogs
> That likt the beggars sores, to slobber us
> Into patience ...

Carlile claimed that *Swing*'s 'plot beats that of any other popular tragedy; for here an injured people finally triumphs; hitherto all dramatic

Robert Taylor on the frontispiece of his
unsuccessful defence against the charge of
blasphemy in 1827.

efforts to exhibit a resistance to tyranny have represented that resistance
as unsuccessful'. By the time the play opened, however, Carlile was
already in prison, beginning a two-year jail sentence for publishing a
letter to 'Insurgent Agricultural Labourers' which was officially interpreted as encouraging arson and machine-breaking. In July 1831 Taylor
was convicted of blasphemous libel for his Easter lectures when he
claimed that Jesus had not really been crucified and called God a 'GOUTY
OLD MAN IN AN ARMCHAIR'. Like Carlile, he was sentenced to two years
imprisonment.[53] Even an unemployed Irishman, who was caught trying
to sell *Swing* playbills in the street, was fined £5.[54]

Early in 1832, with both Carlile and Taylor still in prison, Carlile's
common-law wife, Eliza Sharples, replaced him as manager of the
Rotunda. Brought up in a prosperous Bolton manufacturing family,
Sharples was billed as the 'Lady of the Rotunda' – the first English
woman to lecture on politics and religion, in a 'style unparalleled in
this country'. The Home Office spy, Abel Hall, reported that, though
'no interruptions took place in her proceedings, which were listened to
with great attention and much applause ... I never saw or heard a more
abusive or inflammatory language made of in any assembly and in
which she takes a most Vulgar Pride in delivering.' Sharples' main targets

were 'Religion, Priests and all institutions'.[55] A report in *The Times*, though dismissing the content of her lectures as the 'sorriest rubbish' and deploring her Lancashire accent (which pronounced 'animal' as 'hanimal'), found her rather attractive: her 'figure is good, her appearance and manner rather genteel than otherwise, and she is much more like a pretty woman rather than an ugly one'.[56] With both Carlile and Taylor in prison, however, Sharples was unable to make ends meet. Carlile was forced to sell the Rotunda in 1832.

*

Subversive entertainers reported by spies and informers to have used 'abusive or inflammatory language' were more harshly treated in Ireland than in Britain. The subversive performances which most concerned the British authorities were not in theatres but by nationalist ballad singers in the streets.[57] Though most were male, a minority were women: among them Anne Rooney, arrested in 1831 in County Carlow for 'singing Ballads of an inflammatory nature' calculated to 'excite the minds of the lower orders'.[58] Some singers had large audiences and made a living by selling copies of their ballads. According to a report in 1833 from Cork to the chief secretary for Ireland:

> A mob is attracted by the song, and in whatever part of the street the ballad singer pleases to take his stand, business must be suspended and the shops shut up during his stay.[59]

The penalties for singing and selling subversive ballads could be severe. In 1827 Denis Ring of County Cork was sentenced to seven years' transportation to Botany Bay in New South Wales for 'vending and singing Ballads of the most mischievous and evil tendency'.[60]

The chief villains in these ballads were informers, spies and traitors – three overlapping categories – who for centuries past had betrayed the Irish people to their British rulers in Dublin Castle. During its victorious election campaign in 1918, Sinn Féin would publish a list of traitors and spies who had betrayed Irish independence that went back to Dermot McMurrough, who had invited the English into Ireland in the twelfth century. Other leading villains denounced on Sinn Féin election posters included 'Armstrong the Spy' and 'Reynolds the Spy', who had betrayed the 1798 Irish Rebellion to the British.[61] Among the early nineteenth-century ballads which commemorate the 1798 Rebellion is *Dunlavin Green*, which denounces Colonel Saunders, the leader of a local militia, for deliberately leading his men into an ambush where they were captured and executed:

> Bad luck to you, Saunders, may bad luck never you shun!
> That the widow's curse may melt you like the snow in the sun
> The cries of the orphans whose murmurs you cannot screen,
> For the murder of their dear fathers, on Dunlavin Green.

Ironically, many 'seditious' Irish ballads of the early and mid nineteenth century survive only because some of the informers they denounced, along with the British forces of law and order, sent copies of them to Dublin Castle, claiming that the ballads were corrupting the lower orders.[62] The blinkered, though well-intentioned, assistant secretary to the Treasury, Charles Trevelyan, who implemented – but did not, as often claimed, devise – the Peel and Russell governments' disastrous Irish famine policies in the late 1840s,[63] shared this belief. 'The greatest evil we have to face is not the physical evil of the famine,' he wrote, 'but the moral evil of the selfish, perverse and turbulent character of the Irish people.'[64] Among the anonymous subversive ballads obtained by Dublin Castle and passed to Trevelyan was *The Irish Emigrant's Address to His Irish Landlord*:

> You know you'd like to *stop me*,
> So I'll do it on *the sly*,
> With Me I'll take a half year's Rent,
> Your Honor – Won't you *cry*?

Trevelyan minuted that, ironically, 'the landlords will be ultimately benefited' by the emigration of such small farmer tenants, even 'on the sly', because it enabled them to consolidate and thus increase the value of their holdings.[65]

A majority of Dublin balladeers, however 'turbulent' in Trevelyan's view, seem to have enjoyed poking fun at the British rulers and institutions rather than deliberately setting out to incite rebellion. The most popular in Dublin during the first decade of Queen Victoria's reign was the blind street rhymer, Michael J. Moran, better known as

Zozimus. Mild though his mockery of the monarchy was, it would not have been tolerated in an English music hall:

> O long life to the man who invented potheen –
> Sure the Pope ought to make him a martyr –
> If myself was this moment Victoria, the Queen,
> I'd drink nothing but whiskey and wather.[66]

But other ballads were intentionally seditious. Some of the most enduring were written in the early 1840s by Thomas Osborne Davis, the main founder of Young Ireland, which campaigned for national independence. Its mouthpiece, the weekly *Nation*, founded in 1842, quickly became Ireland's best-selling newspaper. 'Music', wrote Davis, 'is the first faculty of the Irish'; 'A song is worth a thousand harangues.'[67]

Among the ballads published in the *Nation* which outraged Dublin Castle was *The Memory of the Dead*, commemorating the 1798 rebellion, which was included in the evidence used to convict the nationalist 'Liberator', Daniel O'Connell, of sedition in 1844.[68] Davis's own ballads included *Tone's Grave*, now better-known as *Bodenstown Churchyard*, after the burial place of the hero of the 1798 rebellion and founder of Irish republican nationalism, Theobald Wolfe Tone,[69] who is commemorated there annually. This song went on to become part of the repertoire of the best-known contemporary stars of Irish folk and rebel music, the Wolfe Tones, named in his honour.[70]

The most famous of Davis's subversive ballads was, and remains, *A Nation Once Again*, also written in the early 1840s:

> When boyhood's fire was in my blood
> I read of ancient freemen,
> For Greece and Rome who bravely stood,
> Three hundred men and three men;
> And then I prayed I yet might see
> Our fetters rent in twain,
> And Ireland, long a province, be
> A Nation once again!

Over a century and a half later, a recording by the Wolfe Tones of *A Nation Once Again* was to be voted the world's most popular song in a 2002 BBC World Service poll of its global listeners.[71]

★

The largest and best organised popular protest movement in Europe before the 1848 revolutions was that of the Chartists in un-revolutionary Britain. Their People's Charter demanded the vote for all adult males, secret ballots, annual general elections, equal constituencies, salaries and the end of property qualifications for MPs. Chartist demonstrations, rallies and marches were full of dramatic display: music, songs, plays, costumes and torch-lit night-time processions.[72] Their charismatic leader, Feargus O'Connor, wrote two plays and had an intermittent twenty-year affair with one of Britain's best-known and most glamorous actresses, Louisa Nisbett. Ernest Jones, who succeeded O'Connor as the most influential Chartist politician, was the author of eight plays; he published the full text of his Gothic melodrama, St John's Eve, in the Chartist journal, Labourer, which he edited with O'Connor.[73] The most popular Chartist play, performed by three touring groups in the early 1840s, was a re-enactment of the treason trial of the Irish revolutionary, Robert Emmet, after the failed Dublin rising of 1803. One of the ways in which Emmet shows his moral superiority over Ireland's British oppressors was by saving the life of a government spy whom his followers wanted to shoot.[74]

Chartist dramatic performances benefited from the 1843 Act for Regulating Theatres (the 'Theatres Act'), which ended the century-old London monopoly of the Covent Garden and Drury Lane 'patent' theatres for spoken plays and gave additional powers to local authorities to license local theatres as well as popular entertainment venues such as music halls and saloon theatres attached to pubs.[75] The Act, however, reinforced existing censorship by giving the Lord Chamberlain authority to forbid performances 'whenever he shall be of opinion that it is fitting for the Preservation of good Manners, Decorum, or of the public Peace so to do'.[76] Chartist producers of plays and entertainments dealt with censorship simply by ignoring it and refusing to submit scripts to the Lord Chamberlain. Probably fearful of provoking riots, the authorities rarely intervened during unauthorised productions. An unsuccessful police attempt to persuade the Milton Street Theatre in London to cancel a benefit performance for the wife of an imprisoned Chartist militant was hissed by the audience. The main

Chartist newspaper, the *Northern Star*, called on supporters to 'show their love of principle, and detestation of espionage and tyranny, by making the benefit a bumper'. Though the government brought troops into London streets to prevent the delivery of a Chartist petition to parliament in 1848, it did not use force to disrupt Chartist performances.[77] The *Northern Star*, however, regularly warned its readers that spies and informers – 'the scoundrel minions of a tyrant government' – were present at all Chartist gatherings.[78]

As Chartism declined after 1848, so did the numbers of government informers. The end of the patent theatres' monopoly also greatly reduced the number of spies sent to report on unauthorised performances. Britain, unlike the main continental powers, had no centralised system of political intelligence. 'We have no political police, no police over opinion', boasted Charles Dickens's *Household Words* in the 1850s, 'The most rabid demagogue can say in this free country what he chooses ... He speaks not under the terror of an organised spy system.' The Metropolitan Police Force ('Met'), founded by Sir Robert Peel in 1829, originally contained no plain-clothes officers at all. Its detective department, established in 1842, still had only fifteen men a quarter of a century later.[79]

Most informers worked freelance, and in London their main employers were the Met Commissioners. In 1850, a year after beginning a long exile in the capital, Karl Marx wrote a letter to *The Spectator*, mocking the poor quality of the 'Prussian spies and English informers' involved in the surveillance of him and other revolutionary exiles:

Really, Sir, we should have never thought that there existed in this country so many police-spies as we have had the good fortune of making the acquaintance of in the short space of a week. Not only that the doors of the houses where we live are closely watched by individuals of a more than doubtful look, who take down their notes very coolly every time any one enters the house or leaves it; we cannot make a single step without being followed by them wherever we go. We cannot get into an omnibus or enter a coffee-house without being favoured with the company of at least one of these unknown friends. We do not know whether the gentlemen engaged in this grateful occupation are so 'on her Majesty's service'; but we know this, that the majority of them look anything but clean and respectable.[80]

Outside London, informers were used in varying numbers by magistrates, lords lieutenant, military commanders, chief constables and local notables.

Since 1837, Europe's most charismatic revolutionary, the Italian nationalist Giuseppe Mazzini, had also lived in exile in London. Though Metternich called him the most dangerous man in Europe, Mazzini was in reality an incompetent insurgent. During his first decade in London, he planned or inspired eight attempted revolts in Italian states. All ended in fiasco.[81] Of greater concern to Whitehall was the inspiration which Mazzini provided to Irish nationalism. The newspaper of Young Ireland, the *Nation*, declared:

> Ireland has been called the Italy of the west, her land so fair, her soul so fiery, her glories so remote, her sorrow so deep, and her slavery so enduring. A tyrant neighbour [Britain] and a young race full of hope complete the resemblance.[82]

To monitor Mazzini's links with alleged revolutionaries in Ireland, Italy and elsewhere, Sir Robert Peel's Conservative government, which came to power in 1841, decided to intercept Mazzini's correspondence. In 1844, suspecting that his letters were being opened, the Italian exile placed inside the envelopes grains of sand and poppy seeds which had disappeared by the time they reached their destination. Thomas Carlyle thundered his protest in a letter to *The Times*:

> It is a question vital to us that sealed letters in an English post-office be, as we all fancied they were, respected as things sacred; that opening of men's letters, a practice near of kin to picking men's pockets, and to others still viler and far fataler forms of scoundrelism, be not resorted to in England, except in cases of the very last extremity.

The *Times* leader-writer agreed: 'the proceeding cannot be English, any more than masks, poisons, sword-sticks, secret signs and associations, and other such dark inventions.' Parliament also sided with Mazzini. After a scathing report from a Commons committee, in 1844 the Peel government closed down both the Deciphering Branch and the Secret Office of the Post Office.[83] As a result, seventy years later Britain entered the First World War, unlike any of the major wars of the seventeenth and eighteenth centuries, with no codebreakers.

*

The French Second Empire (1852–70) had no such inhibitions about SIGINT. Among the intercepted correspondence which Napoleon III read with most attention was that of his Spanish wife, the Empress Eugénie, with the court in Madrid. He destroyed those of Eugénie's letters which displeased him.[84] Napoleon III also took a personal interest in intelligence on the exiled Victor Hugo, then the world's best-known writer and playwright whose works included ten published plays and nine novels. More successfully than anyone else, Hugo exposed the Emperor to public ridicule. His pamphlet *Napoléon le petit* ('Napoleon the Little'), published in 1852, called him 'vulgar, puerile, theatrical and vain ... Lying comes as easily to him as breathing.' Hugo's attack a year later in the poems of *Les Châtiments* ('Punishments') was still more excoriating, contrasting the pompous grandeur of the emperor with the miserable lives of the poor. Though both books were banned in France, many copies were smuggled in from abroad.

Hugo avoided direct condemnation of Napoleon III in his huge historical novel, *Les Misérables*, in order to secure its publication in France in 1862, but made veiled references to the Second Empire as the 'resuscitation of a corpse' (the empire of Napoleon I). The main character in *Les Misérables*, Jean Valjean, was inspired by the career of Eugène-François Vidocq, an ex-convict and informer who had become head of the Sûreté – the detective department of the Paris police. Valjean's former jailer, Javert, who shows up at his door, was also partly based on Vidocq's later career. Vidocq's ghostwritten memoirs made such an impression on English dramatists that, within a year of their publication in 1828, two separate plays based on them had appeared on the London stage. In both productions Vidocq was portrayed as a master of disguise, who takes the audience by surprise, as well as the criminals he is pursuing, when he reveals his true identity.[85]

While in exile in the Channel Islands, Victor Hugo taunted the *cabinet noir*, which he knew opened his letters to French addresses, by using envelopes printed with the article of the penal code prohibiting letter-opening. He also sometimes wrote satirical comments on the envelope such as 'Family matters – not worth reading'.[86] Surveillance of Hugo continued when he returned to France, temporarily after the overthrow of the Second Empire in 1870 and permanently in 1873. Though the chief concern of the conservative governments of the early Third Republic was his campaign for an amnesty for survivors of the revolutionary Paris Commune of 1871, no aspect of the great writer's private life, as well as his political activities, seems to have escaped the Sûreté's attention. A friend of Hugo, an unidentified police informer codenamed PAMPHILE, even supplied the menu after having dinner with him: 'potage bisque, soles grillées, côtelettes de chevreuil sauce piquante'. Informer JACK reported: 'Victor Hugo keeps all his money in England so that, as soon as he faces any kind of danger, he'll be able to leave France and get it all back.' Hugo's vanity was a regular theme in the reports. So were his many affairs.[87]

*

During the later nineteenth century, European intelligence agencies had to deal with a new threat – an unprecedented number of assassination attempts against rulers and senior politicians, prompted in part by the invention of gelignite, a boon to bomb-makers, and the improved handguns available to assassins. Those assassinated by the end of the century included Tsar Alexander II of Russia (1881), President Sadi Carnot of France (1894), Prime Minister Antonio Cánovas del Castillo of Spain (1897) and the Empress Elisabeth of Austria (1898).[88] Because of woeful security, heads of state were at greatest risk in the United States. Three presidents – Abraham Lincoln, James A. Garfield and William McKinley – were assassinated between 1865 and 1898.[89]

On the evening of 14 April 1865, less than a week after the end of the Civil War, the actor John Wilkes Booth was able to enter President Lincoln's box at Ford's Theatre in Washington and shoot him at point-blank range. Lincoln's bodyguard for the evening, Patrolman John F. Parker, had been instructed to stand guard outside his box, but wandered off to watch the play, was bored by it, and left the theatre to drink in a nearby saloon.[90]

During the Civil War Booth's fame and popularity on both sides had allowed him to move freely across military borders, appearing on stage in 33 cities. In Brooklyn, theatregoers were 'pushing, crowding and jamming' to see him; in Louisville, Kentucky, there was an 'unprecedented' rush for the box office. Unionist audiences, however, had no idea that Booth was a fervent supporter of the Confederate cause, secretly committed to ending Lincoln's 'tyranny'. He was also a

John Wilkes Booth (left) with his brothers Edwin (centre) and Junius, Jr, during a much-praised benefit performance of Shakespeare's *Julius Caesar* in New York in 1864. The proceeds helped to pay for the statue of Shakespeare in Central Park Mall. There is still a Broadway theatre named after Edwin Booth.

Shakespearean enthusiast and claimed to draw inspiration for the assassination of Lincoln from the role of Brutus, 'noblest Roman of them all', in *Julius Caesar*. Ironically, Lincoln shared his enthusiasm for Shakespeare and kept his complete works on his White House desk.

Booth's status as a well-known actor allowed him, unlike the rest of the audience, access to all areas of Ford's Theatre and enabled him to find his way to Lincoln's box unchallenged to carry out the assassination. Despite fracturing his leg when jumping from the box onto the stage, Booth escaped from the theatre amid the pandemonium which followed. He wrote while in hiding after his escape:

> With every man's hand against me, I am here in despair. And why? For doing what Brutus was honored for ... And yet I for striking down a greater tyrant than they ever knew am looked upon as a common cutthroat.

Booth leaps onto the stage of Ford's Theatre after assassinating President Lincoln.

A fortnight after the assassination, Booth was tracked down and shot dead in a tobacco barn near Port Royal, Virginia. He had written in his diary, which was found in his pocket: 'Our country owed all her troubles to [Lincoln], and God simply made me the instrument of his punishment.'[91]

The Civil War left behind a greater legacy of spy stories than the Revolutionary War – some of the best known involving female protagonists.[92] Probably the best Union intelligence of the conflict came from a spy network in Richmond, Virginia, run by a wealthy spinster, Elizabeth Van Lew, who was mainly motivated by her horror of slavery. Financing the network, which seems to have included agents in the Confederate war and navy departments, as well as a slave in the house of Confederate President Jefferson Davis, cost 'Miss Lizzie' most of her fortune. Her messages to the Union commanding general, Ulysses S. Grant, always sent in code or invisible ink, were sometimes accompanied by a rose picked from her garden. 'From her', said Grant, 'I received the most valuable intelligence that ever came from Richmond throughout the entire conflict.'[93]

Though less effective than Van Lew, the actress-turned spy, Pauline Cushman, became far better known. In May 1864, the *New York Times* declared her one of the 'women of America who have made themselves famous since the opening of the rebellion'. It published Cushman's improbable story of how, after being captured by Confederate scouts, she had escaped by surreptitiously paying a bystander $10 to disappear down the road and bring back bogus news that Union forces were advancing. According to Cushman, 'The scouts at this believed his story, mounted their horses, and "skedaddled" for the woods.'[94] Historians have since found it difficult to separate fact from fiction in her accounts of many other adventures. Cushman's fame, however, was such that she was made an honorary major by President Lincoln, hired after the Civil War by the impresario P. T. Barnum, and toured the country in her officer's uniform for several years lecturing about her adventures. In 1872, when the market for her lectures dried up, she made an unsuccessful attempt to return to the stage.[95]

The best-known Confederate spy, Isabella 'Belle' Boyd, the adventurous daughter of a wealthy tobacco farmer and trader, enjoyed a more successful post-Civil War career than Cushman. Her most celebrated exploit occurred in the spring of 1862 when, at the age of only 18, she took to the Confederate General 'Stonewall' Jackson supposedly crucial intelligence on the movements of Union forces prior to his

Rival publicity photographs: Pauline Cushman (*left*) in her honorary major's uniform and Belle Boyd (*right*) in uniform as honorary captain.

beginning an offensive in the Shenandoah Valley. A study by the CIA Center for the Study of Intelligence concludes, however, that, despite Belle Boyd's bravery, 'her information could have had little or no value' to Jackson, who

> For two weeks ... had been diligently collecting information from cavalry, citizens, prisoners, deserters, and spies. Evidently his conclusion from this was that he could probably strike [Union forces in] Front Royal with complete surprise.[96]

After the Civil War, Boyd completed two volumes of unreliable memoirs, *Belle Boyd in Camp and Prison*, which were published on both sides of the Atlantic. Her career as a spy, she declared, had made her a star: 'From the force of circumstances, and not through any desire of my own, I became a celebrity.'[97] Celebrity enabled her to begin a new career as an actress. Though leaving the stage after her second marriage in 1869, she returned to it after divorce and remarriage to her third husband, the actor Nathaniel High, in 1886. Boyd spent the last years of her life re-enacting her adventures in the Civil War, often drawing large audiences. Because of competition from several enterprising imposters, she took documents with her on tour to prove her identity. Boyd died from a heart attack during a performance in Wisconsin on 11 June 1900, thus becoming the only known spy to die on stage.[98]

7

The Late Nineteenth Century: From the Fenians to 'J'Accuse!'

The American Civil War changed the history of Irish rebellion. The military leaders of the 1867 Rising by the Irish Republican Brotherhood (better known as the Fenians)[1] were Irish veterans of the victorious Union Army. The Fenian insurrection, however, was badly planned, infiltrated by British spies ('informers'), and most of its leaders in Ireland were arrested. Though no Fenians were executed in Ireland, three men in Manchester – William Allen, Michael Larkin and Michael O'Brien (the so-called 'Manchester martyrs') – were hanged for their part in a successful ambush to free two Fenian leaders from a prison van in which a policeman was shot dead. A fourth Manchester Fenian, Edward O'Meagher Condon, who was also sentenced to death but later had his sentence commuted, said from the dock: 'I have nothing to regret, or to retract, or to take back. I can only say "God Save Ireland".'[2] His words were turned by the poet, T. D. Sullivan, later Lord Mayor of Dublin and an MP at Westminster, into the well-known Irish ballad, God Save Ireland. For the next half-century, it became Ireland's unofficial national anthem as well as the Fenian marching song:

> High upon the gallows tree swung the noble-hearted Three.
> By the vengeful tyrant stricken in their bloom;
> But they met him face to face, with the courage of their race,
> And they went with souls undaunted to their doom.
> 'God save Ireland!' said the heroes;
> 'God save Ireland' said they all.
> 'Whether on the scaffold high
> Or the battlefield we die,
> O, what matter when for Erin dear we fall!'

Though the Fenian Brotherhood itself remained a secret society, its heroes were publicly celebrated in some of the best-known songs in Irish history. In April 1885 the Derry Opera House witnessed a memorable musical competition. When a tableau portraying the Prince of Wales, the future Edward VII, appeared on stage, opposing factions in the audience sang *God Save the Queen* and *God Save Ireland*. The queen lost.[3]

After the hanging of the 'noble-hearted Three', there was no prospect, with one remarkable exception, that the Lord Chamberlain and his 'examiner of plays', would allow any play featuring Fenians to appear on the English stage.[4] The exception was the melodrama *The Shaughraun* (meaning wanderer), the theatrical sensation of 1875 by the most successful Irish playwright and actor of his generation on both sides of the Atlantic, Dion Boucicault – his popularity in London unaffected by his decision two years earlier to become a US citizen.[5] The play tells the story of Robert Ffolliott, 'a young Irish gentleman, under sentence as a Fenian', who had been transported to Australia but received a royal pardon – thus making *The Shaughraun* sufficiently wholesome to be licensed by the Lord Chamberlain. The villain of the melodrama is the rascally Irish 'police spy', Harvey Duff, who disguises himself as a head of a Fenian cell by shaving off his 'great red whiskers' and wearing a large black wig, in order to 'trap young Ffolliott' and others into swearing allegedly Fenian oaths to justify their arrest. His aim, in league with a corrupt Irish magistrate and squireen, Corry Kinchela, is 'to chate [cheat] young Ffolliott out of his liberty first, then out of his estate, and now out of his wife!' The Lord Chamberlain would never have permitted any of the informers employed by the London Met to be portrayed on stage in such dastardly ways. Harvey Duff survived the Lord Chamberlain's blue pencil because he was a malevolent stage Irishman who suffers a series of well-deserved comic misadventures. A dog attacks the seat of Duff's trousers while he is peering through a keyhole. He tells Kinchela that, in his Fenian disguise, even his mother failed to recognise him:

The last time I went home she pelted me wid the poker. But if the people round here knew I was Harvey Duff, they would tear me to rags; there wouldn't survive of me a piece as big as the one I left in the mouth of that divil of a dog!

The people do eventually discover Duff's real identity. Boucicault's stage directions explain the sequel: 'Uttering a scream of terror, Harvey Duff leaps over the cliff. The crowd pursue him to the edge and lean over.'[6]

Boucicault had much stronger Fenian sympathies than he thought it prudent to display when submitting *The Shaughraun* for review by the Lord Chamberlain. Emboldened by the play's success, he wrote an open letter to the Conservative Prime Minister, Benjamin Disraeli, appealing for an amnesty for Fenian prisoners in England and Ireland. The address at the top of the letter was 'Theatre Royal, Drury Lane', which had staged *The Shaughraun* with Boucicault and his wife appearing as actors, to great applause. 'Thus', writes his biographer, Deirdre McFeely, 'he was seen to be making his appeal from the centre stage of the English theatrical establishment':

> All the leaders of the Fenian outbreak are at large; a few obscure men still linger in chains, and these are, I believe, the only British citizens now in prison for a political offence … Those who say the time is not come for the exercise of clemency, forget that mercy is not a calcula-tion but a noble impulse – no man keeps a fallen foe under his heel but a coward who dares not let him up.

Despite enormous publicity for the letter on both sides of the Atlantic, Disraeli did not reply.[7]

*

There is no evidence that during the final decades of the nineteenth century any British theatre, playwright or actor was thought suffi-ciently subversive to be placed under surveillance by the Metropolitan Police's intelligence department, the Special Branch – originally the Special Irish Branch, formed in 1883 to deal with the Fenian threat.

In France, by contrast, surveillance of leading playwrights and other writers by the Sûreté remained routine – due partly to the prestige of French intellectuals (a word little used by their mostly less prestig-ious British counterparts) and their greater involvement in political controversy. Louis Andrieux, who from 1879 to 1881 remarkably combined the roles of Paris prefect of police and deputy for Lyon, wrote in his memoirs: 'It is an error to believe that [Sûreté] files are reserved for criminals and those other malefactors known as politicians.' On becoming prefect of police, Andrieux, like his predecessors, was handed his own file (no. 14207) and given the opportunity to destroy it. He decided not to do so: 'I had it bound and keep it in my library, with all the gross calumnies and hateful denunciations which commonly form the basis of such documents.' Andrieux, who went on to become the *doyen* (most senior member) of the Chamber of Deputies in the 1920s, defended the importance of continuing to collect even inaccurate information, as in his own case:

> These files are none the less useful, even indispensable, for police enquiries, but on condition that they remain unknown both to individuals and to the justice system – and are never opened except by experienced senior officials who know how to read them and to disentangle, from the mass of inaccurate and often contradictory allegations, truthful content.[8]

In Andrieux's view, increasingly widespread in secret services, it was for the analyst, not the intelligence collector, to separate fact from fiction. What remains shocking is his insistence, in a republic committed to upholding the 1789 Declaration of the Rights of Man and of the Citizen, that the Sûreté should be free to put on file 'gross calumnies and hateful denunciations' of whomever it chose. The ephemeral governments of the pre-1914 Third Republic, with an average life expectancy of nine months (reduced to six between the wars), were incapable of establishing effective control over any intelligence agency or department, thus making possible the scandalous injustice of the Dreyfus Affair.

During the early Third Republic, France's greatest living writer and dramatist, Victor Hugo, remained under surveillance by the Sûreté. There was no shortage of other French writers, jealous of Hugo's extraordinary global success, who were anxious to denigrate his achievements. Alexandre Dumas *fils* compared the experience of reading *Les Misérables* to wading through mud; Hugo loftily responded that 'genius attracts insult'.[9] A series of Sûreté informers and agents, some inspired by professional jealousy, continued to denigrate Hugo even after his election as a senator in 1876.[10]

On 25 March 1877 Hugo gave a major speech to a largely working-class audience at the théâtre du Château-d'Eau, praising their 'majestic

Victor Hugo after his election as a senator in 1876 – still under Sûreté surveillance.

resistance' to the threat of war by foreign powers. The Paris Exposition Universelle of 1878 would, he declared, mark the triumph of peaceful coexistence over the warmongers. A contemporary record of his speech shows that it was punctuated by 'prolonged applause' and repeated 'bravos', concluding with shouts of: *Vive la république! Vive l'amnistie [des Communards]! Vive Victor Hugo!*[11] But the Sûreté's two informants at the théâtre du Château-d'Eau tried, in contradictory ways, to downplay the impact of his speech. While Agent ANDOCHE claimed mendaciously that 'V. Hugo is furious to have been denied his ovation', Agent PAMPHILE acknowledged that Hugo had been cheered but:

> Nonetheless, those people who are capable of rational thought are saying forcefully that Hugo's speech consists of nothing but words, rhetoric and grandiose metaphors, and that it would not stand up to even the most generous of critiques.[12]

The poet Maurice Coste, a strong supporter of Hugo, later derided 'the covert hostility of most of the leaders of the Third Republic towards the man whom they publicly lauded as one of their official glories'.[13]

Hugo was not greatly concerned by official surveillance of his libidinous private life. On the contrary, he was proud of his continued ability to seduce young women even beyond his seventies. But he did attempt to keep secret both from his family and the Sûreté intimate details of his sexual encounters by recording them in his diary in a private code, much of which has since been decrypted. *Suisses* ('Swiss'), for example, is a codeword for female breasts – because, like Switzerland, they produce milk; *poêle* ('stove') refers to its homophone *poils* ('pubic hair'); *n.* (*nue*) and *t.n.* (*toute nue*) indicate occasions when a woman stripped naked in front of him. Some erotic conundrums in Hugo's diary remain unsolved – among them, the initials S. B., jotted down in November 1875, which may refer to a brief affair with Sarah Bernhardt.[14]

How much of the contents of Hugo's secret diary were known to the Sûreté may never be established. Some sections were discovered by his resident *maîtresse en titre*, Juliette Drouet, who sought help in interpreting some entries in Spanish and other details in the diary. She was particularly disturbed by Hugo's sexual encounters with her maid Blanche, for a time his favourite mistress, who, as Hugo claimed excitedly, 'knew how to be a slave and yet remain a queen'. Drouet wrote to her nephew in 1878, asking him to make enquiries: 'You could ask a policeman. There are some at the Préfecture de Police who offer such services, for a fat fee, of course.' On another occasion, Hugo's son-in-law and political ally, the republican deputy Édouard Lockroy, called in the Sûreté when Blanche's husband attempted to blackmail the writer after discovering a cache of obscene messages allegedly sent her by Hugo. Public scandal was somehow avoided, however. Hugo's leading British biographer, Graham Robb, cites rumours that, on their visits to inspect Paris brothels, policemen carried a photograph enabling them to identify Hugo, whom they were instructed not to arrest for fear of causing political uproar.[15]

The Third Republic continued the theatrical censorship of the Second Empire. Despite Hugo's global reputation, the stage adaptation of his novel *Notre-Dame de Paris*, first published in 1831, was among its victims; it was not allowed to be performed until 1885.[16] Émile

Zola, second only to Hugo as France's most famous writer, suffered a similar fate. In 1885 a play which he based on his novel *Germinal* (with modest assistance from his friend William Busnach) was banned because of what the censors claimed was its 'socialist tendency'. Before it was finally allowed on stage three years later, a scene showing 'troops firing at striking miners' had to be removed, along with all references to class conflict, 'capital', 'property', 'stockholder', 'comrade' and 'strike'. Though best known as a novelist, Zola was also the first playwright to call for 'naturalism' on the stage – before August Strindberg made the term popular – an aim partly frustrated by French and British theatre censorship.[17] His play, *Thérèse Raquin*, based on one of his novels, was first staged in Paris in 1873 but refused a licence in England by the Lord Chamberlain on the grounds of indecency. It would not be performed in London until 1891, under the auspices of the Independent Theatre Society.[18]

On his death in 1885 at the age of 83, Victor Hugo was given the greatest state funeral ever accorded a French writer. Over two million people, more than the entire population of Paris, lined the streets of the capital or followed his funeral procession from the Arc de Triomphe to the Panthéon, where he was buried with other republican heroes.[19]

Surveillance of Hugo was often fed by petty jealousy: there was, however, a much more credible case for keeping Sûreté files on the violent relationship between the celebrated poets Paul Verlaine and Arthur Rimbaud. Their love affair in the early 1870s, fuelled by absinthe, opium and hashish, ended with Verlaine being jailed for two years after shooting and wounding Rimbaud in a drunken rage. An anonymous informant in 1873 denounced Verlaine as 'a person of no value' made 'dangerous by the falseness of his character and the baseness of his sentiments'. Verlaine, he reported, had written to Hugo from prison, claiming to be in love with Rimbaud and asking for the famous writer's help. Hugo had not replied but forwarded the letter to Verlaine's abandoned wife.[20] Further reports were collected by the Sûreté after Verlaine's release from prison on his alcoholism, as well as his 'active and passive pederasty'.[21]

Sûreté surveillance operations in the early Third Republic received little assistance from Scotland Yard.[22] Save for Fenians, the authorities in mid Victorian Britain showed no real interest in revolutionaries. Karl Marx was no longer bothered by the shabbily dressed 'police-spies', of whom he had satirically complained in 1850. After the bloodthirsty suppression of the Paris Commune in 1871, the ill-informed Home Office was faced with urgent requests from the French and other foreign governments for intelligence on alleged 'Communists' who had taken refuge in London. Initially, it had little idea how to respond. The home secretary, Henry Bruce, had the bright idea of asking his secretary to write to Marx, who obligingly replied with literature on the activities of the First International and a copy of his celebrated pamphlet on the Commune, *Civil War in France*.[23] Thereafter, Scotland Yard steadily lost interest in Marx and the few followers he had in London. The 1887 English translation of *Das Kapital*, later to become the bible of international communism, was possibly the least-read masterpiece in Victorian England.

Most British playwrights also showed little interest in domestic or foreign revolutionaries. There was, however, one exception. By the 1880s the London stage had developed a fascination with underground Russian revolutionaries or 'Nihilists', as they were usually, though inaccurately, called.[24] 'Beautiful female revolutionaries stabbing their tormentors or committing suicide instead of assassinating their loved ones', notes the literary historian Anna Vaninskaya, 'were especially in demand.'[25] Also popular on stage were agents of the tsarist secret police in disguise, some of whom turned out to be double agents on the side of the Nihilists.[26]

The main inspiration for the wave of mostly melodramatic British 'Nihilist' drama and novels was the founding in August 1878 of a secret Russian terrorist group, the People's Will (*Narodnaya volya*), the first organisation to use systematic terror for political ends. On 4 August, one of its founder members, the 27-year-old Sergei Kravchinsky, assassinated General Nikolai Mezentsev, head of the Third Section of the Imperial Chancellery, the tsarist secret police founded by Nicholas I. Following a daring escape after killing Mezentsev, Kravchinsky published a pamphlet, entitled *A Death for a Death*, justifying the use of terror by the People's Will against the tsarist autocracy.[27] The following year, the group's executive committee condemned Tsar Alexander II to death for 'crimes against the people'. In 1880 the People's Will succeeded in blowing up the main dining room in the Winter Palace, killing eleven and injuring fifty-five people – not, however, the tsar, who was fortunate to be late for dinner. In March 1881 a bomb was thrown under Alexander's sleigh in St Petersburg. The tsar was unhurt but, as he left the sleigh to inspect the injuries to his Cossack escort, he was fatally injured by a second bomb thrown by another People's Will terrorist.[28]

The Third Section, discredited by its failure both to catch the assassin of its chief and to prevent the assassination of the tsar, was replaced by the Okhrana, a much larger intelligence and security agency within the police department. From its St Petersburg headquarters, the Okhrana ran a network of agents and informers which by the end of the century was about 20,000 strong – four times as numerous as the Third Section network half a century earlier. It also opened tens of thousands of letters in post offices across the Russian Empire in its search for subversive correspondence.[29]

The Okhrana's chief target abroad was Sergei Kravchinsky. Hotly but unsuccessfully pursued across Western Europe by Russian agents, he changed his name in 1881 to Stepniak ('Man of the Steppes') and began writing *Underground Russia*, which was published in London in 1883.[30] His book celebrated the assassination of General Mezentsev as proof that Russian terrorism had come of age:

> On August 16, 1878 ... the Terrorism, by putting to death General [Mezentsev], the head of the police and the entire *camarilla*, boldly threw down its glove in the face of the autocracy. From that day forth, it advanced with giant strides ...

Sergei Stepniak's *Underground Russia* failed to mention, however, that he himself had been Mezentsev's assassin. The book was dismissive of what he saw as British caricatures of Russian terrorists – notably of Vera Zasulich, who had narrowly failed to assassinate the governor of St Petersburg early in 1878. Zasulich, insisted Stepniak, 'has nothing about her of the heroine of a pseudo-Radical tragedy'.[31]

The 'pseudo-Radical tragedy' scorned by Stepniak was *Vera; or, The Nihilists*, the first play written by Oscar Wilde. Though set at the start of the nineteenth century, it was clearly inspired by the Zasulich case. Vera, the leader of the 'Nihilists', falls in love with Alexis, supposedly a fellow Nihilist. Alexis, however, is really heir to the Russian throne. When the Nihilists kill his father, Tsar Ivan, and Alexis succeeds him, the Nihilists decide that he too must die, despite his plans to reform the regime. Vera is chosen as Alexis's assassin but loves him too much. She plunges the dagger meant to kill the new tsar into her own heart.

The response from Oscar Wilde's theatre contacts, to whom he circulated the newly completed text of *Vera* in the summer of 1880, has been fairly described as 'underwhelming'. Dion Boucicault, a family friend, told Wilde that five-sixths of *Vera* was 'not *action* but discussion': 'Your action stops for dialogue, whereas dialogue should be the necessary outcome of action exerting its influence on the characters.'[32] By the autumn of 1880, Wilde may already have been considering the possibility of launching the play in New York rather than London.[33] His hopes of a London production returned, however, after the assassination of Tsar Alexander II in March 1881 made *Vera*'s subject a matter of topical interest. By the autumn he believed he had arranged for the play to be performed at the Adelphi Theatre at the end of the year. The production threatened, however, to become dangerously controversial. Wilde's playbill, describing *Vera* as 'my first attack on Tyranny', aroused – probably justified – suspicions that he had in mind not just Tsarist Russia but also British rule in Ireland. Late in 1881, rehearsals for *Vera* at the Adelphi were suddenly cancelled. Wilde, it was said, showed *Vera* to an unidentified 'committee of literary persons, who have advised him to keep it from the stage. The work ... abounds in revolutionary sentiments, which it is thought might stand in the way of its success with loyal British audiences.'[34]

It is quite possible that the Lord Chamberlain's official reviewer of plays, Edward Pigott, had informally contacted the Adelphi Theatre and advised it to cancel the production. Pigott disliked controversial drama. 'I have studied Ibsen's plays pretty carefully', he had remarked of the Norwegian playwright, 'and all the characters ... seem to me morally deranged.'[35] Though Pigott would have found *Vera* less 'morally deranged', he would certainly have considered its staging highly inappropriate so soon after the murder of Tsar Alexander II the previous March.[36]

Wilde, however, remained determined that *Vera* should be staged. Having abandoned the prospect of a London performance, he had high hopes of the play's première at the Union Square Theatre in New York in August 1883, but it was poorly reviewed and closed after a week. The *New York Daily News* dismissed his first play as 'a foolish, highly peppered story of love, intrigue, and politics, with

BROTHER WILLIE.—"NEVER MIND, OSCAR; OTHER GREAT MEN
HAVE HAD THEIR DRAMATIC FAILURES!"

Oscar's brother Willie comforts him after the failure of *Vera* in New York, cartoon by
Alfred Bryan, 1883.

Russian accessories of fur and dark lanterns, and overlaid with
bantam gabble about freedom and the people.'[37] *Vera* has since
become an almost forgotten footnote to Oscar Wilde's extraordinary
career.

Though Stepniak has been a forgotten figure since his accidental
death in 1895 in London, which he had made his home, in 1883 his
Underground Russia captured far more British imaginations than *Vera*.
His book, unlike Wilde's play, combined first-hand experience of
assassination and the revolutionary underground with fashionably
melodramatic prose. 'The Terrorist', he declared, ' ... is noble, terrible,
irresistibly fascinating, for he combines in himself the two sublimities
of human grandeur: the martyr and the hero.' Stepniak also made
more of an impression on the British public than Karl Marx. Only
thirteen people turned up for Marx's funeral in 1883 at Highgate
cemetery. In an introduction to *Underground Russia*, the Russian revolutionary Pyotr Lavrov, in exile in Paris, dismissed most previous

Sergei Mikhailovich Kravchinsky
aka Stepniak.

books on Russian revolutionaries and socialists as having 'not the
slightest value':

> The authors know nothing of the facts related by them, having taken
> them at second or third hand, without the possibility of verifying the
> authenticity of the sources from which they derive their ideas ...

Stepniak's first-hand experience enabled him to explain for the first
time how the Russian revolutionaries had 'gained the strength to
transform themselves, in these later days, into a party that can call
the future its own'.[38]

The impact of Stepniak's book was heightened by the timing of
its publication. It appeared in the middle of the Irish-American
Fenian 'Dynamite War' of 1881–85, the first terrorist bombing
campaign in British history and – mainly because of the indiscrimi-
nate use of explosives – vastly more threatening than the Fenian
Rising of 1867. The main target was London, where Fenian bombs
exploded at the Local Government Board in Whitehall, the offices
of *The Times*, the Houses of Parliament, New Scotland Yard, the
Tower of London, several main railway stations and the London
underground. Queen Victoria was reported to be 'in a great state
of fuss' about the terrorist campaign and fearful that the royal train
might be bombed on its way to Balmoral. The 'Dynamite War' in
the capital, however, petered out early in 1885. A terrorist attempt
to arrange a spectacular Fenian 'firework display' during Queen

Victoria's golden jubilee in 1887 ended in fiasco after Scotland Yard was forewarned by informers.[39]

Censorship continued to make it impossible for Fenians to appear on the British stage. In the mid 1880s, however, plays featuring Russian terrorists and the tsarist secret police began to be allowed, though no attempts were permitted to portray the assassination of even fictional tsars, as in Wilde's *Vera*. The well-known essayist Max Beerbohm later recalled it as a period

> when the scent of Nihilist gunpowder was being wafted through Europe, and when knouts, knives, and the White Terror were the awful topic of our conversation ... I well remember how deeply I was stirred by such plays as *Lost for Russia*, *The Secret Track*, and *The Red Lamp* ...

The most successful of the plays was *The Red Lamp*, a melodrama by William Outram Tristram, which opened at the Comedy Theatre in April 1887, the first venture in actor-management by Max Beerbohm's 34-year-old half-brother, Herbert Beerbohm Tree. Tree played the part of Demetrius, the bald, bespectacled head of the secret police, whose catchphrase 'I wonder' is said to have swept London theatreland. In the play a Russian princess discovers that her beloved brother is the secret leader of a group of Nihilists and stations a red lamp to warn him against raids by the secret police. It turns out, however, that the prince is really a double agent working for Demetrius. The plot hinges on the discovery of a Nihilist 'cache of dynamite'.[40]

After his failure with *Vera*, Oscar Wilde made no further attempt to put a Nihilist drama on the stage. In 1887, however, he wrote *Lord Arthur Savile's Crime*, a brilliantly witty three-part magazine story which makes fun of both Nihilists and Scotland Yard. The criminally minded Lord Arthur asks Count Rouvaloff, an undercover agent for the Nihilists in London, for help in obtaining a homicidal explosive clock 'for a purely family matter':

> Count Rouvaloff ... wrote an address on a piece of paper, initialled it, and handed it to him across the table.
>
> "Scotland Yard would give a good deal to know this address, my dear fellow."
>
> "They shan't have it," cried Lord Arthur, laughing ...

*

The address was that of a bombmaker, Herr Winckelkopf, who told Lord Arthur he was busy with 'important work ... for some friends of mine in Moscow'. Winckelkopf agreed, however, to supply an explosive clock, provided that it was not for use against Scotland Yard:

> 'The English detectives are really our best friends, and I have always found that by relying on their stupidity, we can do exactly what we like. I could not spare one of them.'
> 'I assure you,' said Lord Arthur, 'that it has nothing to do with the police at all. In fact, the clock is intended for the Dean of Chichester.'

Thus reassured, Winckelkopf handed Lord Arthur an explosive clock. The device, however, malfunctioned, and the Dean of Chichester survived.

Lord Arthur Savile's Crime was the first comic masterpiece devoted to covert intelligence operations. There was no prospect, however, that the Lord Chamberlain would allow Scotland Yard to be ridiculed in a stage version. *Lord Arthur Savile's Crime* was not turned into a play until 1952.[41] Though *The Red Lamp* is nowadays largely forgotten, at the end of the nineteenth century it had greater commercial success than Wilde's story. After a first run in the capital at the Comedy Theatre in the spring of 1887, Tree revived it at the Haymarket Theatre in September of the same year, and again in 1890 and 1894. Beginning in 1897, he also arranged four productions at Her Majesty's Theatre.[42]

Britain's only civilian intelligence chief, William Melville, head of the small late Victorian Special Branch, was usually successful at keeping out of the news. Gustav Steinhauer, bodyguard of Queen Victoria's German grandson, Kaiser Wilhelm II, described Melville as 'a silent, reserved man, never given to talking wildly' who, however, entertained him to dinner, cigars and 'one or two bottles of wine' at Simpson's Grand Cigar Divan in The Strand.[43] Melville, however, received one piece of unwelcome publicity from the celebrated American illusionist and escapologist, Harry Houdini, who claimed that he had a private meeting with Melville during his European tour in 1900, which included six months starring at the London *Alhambra*. At their meeting, Melville allegedly ridiculed the idea that anyone could escape from Scotland Yard handcuffs. To prove his point, he is said to have pulled Houdini's arms round a pillar behind him, handcuffed his wrists, and said he would return to free him in two hours' time. Houdini removed the handcuffs so quickly that he followed him out of the room. Melville's biographer suggests that he was so impressed that he went on to acquire some of his expertise in lock-picking from Houdini.[44] It is more likely, however, that Houdini made up the whole story.[45]

*

After the 'Dynamite War', intelligence-related issues very rarely aroused public interest in late Victorian Britain. In France, by contrast, a controversial espionage case dominated politics and public affairs for almost a decade. The Dreyfus Affair, which began in 1894 with the hunt for an agent of the German military attaché in Paris, who was wrongly identified as Captain Alfred Dreyfus, the only Jewish officer on the French General Staff, had its origins in the incompetence and the antisemitism of the French intelligence system. Dreyfus's conviction for high treason at a secret court martial in January 1895, followed by his deportation to Devil's Island off the coast of French Guiana, led to the greatest cause célèbre in modern French history. Three years later, in defence of the officer, Émile Zola, France's most successful writer since the death of Victor Hugo, led a dramatic public protest.[46]

Like Victor Hugo, Zola has a long Sûreté file. An 1891 report noted that he regularly visited a brothel – not, allegedly, 'to have [sexual] relations with its prostitutes but to collect (no doubt for a forthcoming work) their impressions and recollections'. However, Zola regularly complained that these were insufficiently 'spiced up'. One of Zola's repeated questions to the prostitutes baffled the author of the Sûreté report: 'It appears that he particularly insists on asking them whether they have *maquereaux* and, if so, why?' The agent seems to have been unaware that, in the argot of the Paris underworld, 'mackerels' meant 'pimps'.[47]

The majority of the documents in the eight boxes of Zola's Sûreté file are concerned with his role in the Dreyfus affair, when the writer made sensational use of classified information he had been given by a senior intelligence officer. Zola's source was Georges Picquart, who in July 1895 had succeeded the antisemitic Lieutenant-Colonel Jean Conrad Sandherr as head of military counter-intelligence at the French War Ministry. Within a year, Picquart found proof that the German spy in the General Staff was not Dreyfus but a heavily indebted French major, Ferdinand Esterhazy. When Picquart informed the Chief of the General Staff, General Raoul de Boisdeffre, and the head of the Deuxième Bureau, General Charles-Arthur Gonse, they ordered him not to reopen the Dreyfus case. 'What does it matter to you', Gonse remarked, 'if one Jew stays on Devil's Island?' The feeble, ephemeral governments of the mid 1890s preferred not to become involved.

Left with no other way to ensure justice was done, Picquart became the first major French intelligence officer to turn whistle-blower. Late in 1897, he gave Émile Zola the information he used in his celebrated open letter to the French President, 'J'Accuse … !', published in January 1898, denouncing the official framing of Dreyfus and naming those responsible. The War Ministry immediately sought revenge. After the publication of the letter, Picquart was dismissed from the army, falsely accused of forgery, and kept in solitary confinement in a military prison for more than a year. Zola was charged with criminal libel.[48]

Sûreté informants were quick to blacken Zola's character. The probably female agent Coquette[49] reported on 19 April 1898:

> Because the Zola affair is back in the news, it is perhaps worth noting that the naturalist novelist is no better as a husband than as a patriot.
>
> It is said that he terrorises his wife and, in her presence, embraces her housemaid, whose lover he was.
>
> It is also said that his relationship with a niece goes beyond the familial.
>
> Finally, wagging tongues claim that he has a mistress named Rozerot, aged 30, who lives at 3, rue du Havre [Paris], at an annual rent of 4,000 francs.
>
> She is a tall, blonde woman, very elegant, with a lavish lifestyle.
>
> She has many jewels and her monthly expenditure is estimated at 1,500 francs.[50]

It seems that Coquette's information about Zola's wife and mistress was mostly accurate – though the 30-year-old Jeanne Rozerot was not (usually) blonde. Zola had been married to his wife Alexandrine, a former seamstress, for thirty years. But for the past decade, the writer had been living what he himself called a 'double life' with Rozerot, his wife's former chambermaid.[51]

Zola and Jeanne Rozerot (seated to disguise the fact that she was taller than him), c.1893.

On 18 July 1898, Zola was found guilty of criminal libel for publishing 'J'Accuse ... !', sentenced to a year in prison and fined 3,000 francs. A few hours after the verdict he fled to England, arriving at Victoria station with only a night-shirt wrapped in a newspaper.[52] Fearful that the Sûreté was in hot pursuit to arrange his extradition, Zola adopted a series of pseudonyms and stayed in out-of-the way hotels and suburban houses. As his English exile showed, Zola was ill-suited to life undercover; had it wanted to, the Sûreté could easily have tracked him down. Zola wore no disguise, his photograph was prominently displayed in most of the British press, and crowds flocked to see his waxwork at Madame Tussaud's. By the end of August, Zola believed he was safe. He wrote to Alexandrine that he now believed the Sûreté did not want his extradition from Britain: 'They are too pleased to have got rid of me.'[53]

Zola returned to France the following summer of 1899 after evidence emerged that forged documents had been used to convict

Dreyfus. Though Dreyfus was brought home from Devil's Island and pardoned, he was not yet declared innocent. The charges against Zola were dropped. His death from carbon monoxide poisoning in 1902 was probably accidental, after the chimney in his bedroom had become blocked. In 1908 Zola's remains, originally buried in the cemetery of Montmartre, were reinterred with other republican heroes in the Panthéon, next to those of Victor Hugo, who, like Zola, had spent his entire career in the French Third Republic under intelligence surveillance by the Sûreté.

In 1906 Dreyfus's conviction was finally quashed and the new French prime minister, Georges Clemenceau, who had published 'J'Accuse … !' in his newspaper, *L'Aurore,* made Georges Picquart minister of war. 'Dreyfus was the victim', said Clemenceau, 'but Picquart was the hero.'[54]

8

Spies and German Spy Scares

The Dreyfus Affair in France coincided with the emergence in Britain of a new literary genre. The success of the spy novel was prompted by naval competition with Germany and the dramatic growth of the German High Seas Fleet, which posed the first challenge since Trafalgar to the supremacy of the Royal Navy. Among the many novels on German espionage was one masterpiece: *The Riddle of the Sands: A Record of Secret Service* by Erskine Childers, published in 1903. While yachting off the Frisian coast, the heroes of the novel, Carruthers of the Foreign Office and his companion Davies (modelled on Childers himself), gradually uncover a secret German invasion plan. They discover that German spies have already reconnoitred British landing sites and the disposition of the Royal Navy's Home Fleet. The German spymaster, Herr Dollmann, 'was no ordinary spy'. Carruthers could 'never efface the impression of malignant perfidy and base passion exaggerated to caricature' in his features. The First Lord of the Admiralty, the Earl of Selborne, was sufficiently impressed by the novel to call for a detailed report on whether its invasion plan was feasible. The Naval Intelligence Department convinced him it was not. Childers and many of his readers disagreed.[1]

The Riddle of the Sands has never been out of print. But, despite its success, it was impossible in Edwardian Britain to stage a play on the threat posed by Germany. George Redford, who had succeeded Edward Pigott as the Lord Chamberlain's reviewer of plays, insisted that, 'The stage is not a political arena, and it is not desirable that specially important political questions, perhaps involving diplomatic relations with Foreign Powers, should be touched upon.'[2] This principle was taken so seriously that, to the outrage of W. S. Gilbert, publicly advertised performances of *The Mikado* – licensed for the stage in 1885 – were cancelled during a visit to Britain in 1907 by a Japanese prince.[3]

The most successful Edwardian spy novelist, obsessed with the threat of a German invasion, was the amateur spy-hunter and professional fantasist, William Le Queux, who assumed the role of alarmist-in-chief. Despite his slender literary talent, Le Queux's work was so popular that, at his peak, publishers paid him the same rate per thousand words as Thomas Hardy. Le Queux earned more than Hardy because he wrote more. His best-selling *The Invasion of 1910*, one of no fewer than thirteen books published by him in 1906,[4] described how large numbers of German spies were hard at work in England, preparing the way for future invasion. It was serialised ahead of publication in Britain's first mass-circulation newspaper, the *Daily Mail*, which published daily maps to show which part of Britain the Germans would be invading in the next morning's edition. The *Mail*'s newspaper sellers in Oxford Street added to the sense of menace by dressing as Prussian soldiers with *Pickelhaube* helmets. Le Queux's serial added 80,000 to the *Mail*'s daily readership. Le Queux later claimed, probably with his usual exaggeration, that, in book form, *The Invasion of 1910* sold a million copies. There were also numerous translations – including one into German.[5] By contrast Joseph Conrad's masterpiece, *The Secret Agent*, published in 1907, sold no more than 6,500 copies before the First World War and had no discernible influence on either public or official discussion of the alleged spy menace.[6]

Le Queux's often absurd but bestselling spy stories frequently contained dramatic dialogue which would have adapted easily to the stage. In *Spies of the Kaiser: Plotting the Downfall of Britain*, published in 1909, he and his companion, Ray Raymond ('a typical athletic young Englishman – clean-shaven and clean-limbed'), discover a spy's lair in Beccles. On entering the hideout, Le Queux accidentally knocks over some glass negatives which fall to the floor 'with a loud crash':

> We both stood breathless. There was a quick movement in the room adjoining, and we heard men's voices shouting to each other in German.
>
> 'Stay here', Ray said firmly. 'We must not show the white feather now.'
>
> Almost as the words left his mouth we were confronted by the two men we had seen surveying the railway line.
>
> 'Well', cried Ray, gripping his precious bag [containing evidence of their espionage] and facing them boldly, 'you see we've discovered your

little game, gentlemen! Those notes on the map are particularly interesting.'

'By what right, pray, do you enter here?' asked the bearded man, speaking in fairly good English.

'By the right of an Englishman, Herr Stolberg', was Ray's bold reply. 'You'll find your clever wife tied up to a tree in the field opposite.'

The younger man held a revolver, but from his face I saw that he was a coward.

'What do you mean?' demanded the other.

'I mean that I intend destroying all this excellent espionage work of yours. You've lived here for two years, and have been very busy travelling in your car and gathering information. But', [Ray] said, 'you were a little unwise in putting on your car the new Feldmarck non-skids, the only set, I believe, yet in England. They may be very good tyres, but scarcely adapted for spying purposes.'[7]

The enormous sales of Le Queux's spy novels leave no doubt about the potential market for spy plays. Almost ninety years earlier, the play based on the first American espionage novel by James Fenimore Cooper, *The Spy*, had proved as popular as his bestselling book. The absence of popular spy dramas in early twentieth-century British theatres was due solely to official censorship. There was less espionage in any Edwardian play than there had been in *Hamlet* over three centuries earlier.

The War Office, however, became concerned by reports from the public, prompted by alarmist spy fiction and newspaper stories, of alleged German espionage in Britain.[8] A subcommittee of the Committee of Imperial Defence (CID), the chief defence planning council of the realm, chaired by Viscount Haldane, the secretary of state for war, reported on 24 July 1909:

The evidence which was produced left no doubt in the minds of the subcommittee that an extensive system of German espionage exists in this country and that we have no organisation for keeping in touch with that espionage and for accurately determining its extent or objectives.

In reality, there was no significant German military espionage in Britain and no preparations for a German invasion. As Major James Edmonds, the head of the diminutive counter-espionage department of the War Office, acknowledged, when presenting the reports he had compiled on German spies to the subcommittee, 'We have ... no regular system or organisation to detect and report suspicious cases, and are entirely dependent on casual information.'

After a curiously uncritical consideration of the 'casual information' presented to it, Haldane's subcommittee recommended the founding of a Secret Service Bureau

> to deal both with espionage in this country and with our own foreign agents abroad, and to serve as a screen between the Admiralty and the War Office on the one hand and those employed on secret service, or who have information they wish to sell to the British Government, on the other.

Despite the absence of German military intelligence operations in Britain and the absurdity of the bestselling spy scares whipped up by Le Queux and others, the case for establishing the bureau was none the less a strong one. A German naval espionage network, the Nachrichten-Abteilung ('N'), run by the Kaiser's former bodyguard, Gustav Steinhauer, was at work in British ports spying on the Royal Navy, though it did not operate against any of the inland military and invasion targets which preoccupied Le Queux and his readers.[9]

The Secret Service Bureau, whose foundation was approved by H. H. Asquith's Liberal government, was staffed initially by only two officers: the 50-year-old Commander Mansfield Cumming, RN and an army captain fourteen years his junior, Vernon Kell, who met for the first time on 4 October 1909. Cumming and Kell later parted company to become the first heads of what, respectively, became the Security Service (MI5), which operated on British territory, and the Secret Intelligence Service (SIS or MI6), which collected foreign intelligence. Both agencies were so secret that their existence was known only to a small group of senior Whitehall officials and ministers, who never mentioned them to the uninitiated.[10]

In honour of Cumming, today's Chief of the Secret Intelligence Service is still known as 'C' – not 'M', as in the James Bond novels – and, like Cumming, is the only Whitehall official to sign his name in green ink. Unlike his successors, however, Cumming often carried a swordstick.[11]

During the First World War, Cumming looked back nostalgically to the fun he had had on pre-war espionage expeditions. 'That is when

Mansfield Cumming.

this business was really amusing,' he told the writer and wartime intelligence officer, Compton Mackenzie. 'After the War is over, we'll do some amusing secret service work together. It's capital sport!'[12] Part of the fun was dressing up. Cumming made extensive use of the services of Willy Clarkson, 'Theatrical Costumier and Wig Maker To His Majesty The King' (telegraphic address: Wiggery, London), as well as to most London theatres.

In 1905 Clarkson's new London shop on Wardour Street had been opened by none other than Sarah Bernhardt. Clarkson was a distinctive presence at first nights in the West End: 'his red hair, curly moustaches, and full Edwardian beard ... dyed and crimped, his face patently rouged and powdered'.[13]

Clarkson was also well known for providing the disguises for a series of successful hoaxers. Probably the most remarkable stunt he was involved in enabled Virginia Stephen (soon to be better known by her married name Virginia Woolf), the painter Duncan Grant, and four other members and associates of the Bloomsbury group

of writers and artists to be given a ceremonial welcome on board the battleship HMS *Dreadnought*, flagship of the Home Fleet, on 7 February 1910. Four of them, including Virginia Woolf, had their faces blacked with stage make-up and beards stuck on their chins by Clarkson and his staff, who also fitted them with turbans and costumes to enable them to pose as an Abyssinian prince and his male entourage. The other two hoaxers posed as Foreign Office escorts.

In Victorian and Edwardian England the popularity of blackface entertainers cut across both class and gender lines as 'an acceptable prism through which Englishness could become un-English, and so allow laughter and tears to flow without moral inhibition'.[14]

The Abyssinian Prince (seated right) with his entourage, including the bearded Virginia Woolf (seated left), and two equally bogus Foreign Office escorts and interpreters.

Once on board HMS *Dreadnought*, Virginia Woolf and her blackface friends were given the full red-carpet treatment: a band played, the crew saluted them, and African flags were hoisted to the masthead. Even Woolf's cousin, a naval officer on board the ship, failed to recognise her. Her brother, Adrian Stephen, acted as 'interpreter'. The other 'Foreign Office escort' and main organiser of the hoax, Horace de Vere Cole, told their hosts that the Abyssinian visitors 'were "jolly savages" but ... [he] didn't understand much of what they said'.[15] Apparently impressed by what they saw on board, the visitors repeatedly exclaimed 'Bunga Bunga!' The hoax later inspired a music hall song:

> When I went on board a Dreadnought ship
> I looked like a costermonger;
> They said I was an Abyssinian prince
> 'Cos I shouted 'Bunga Bunga!'

After reports of the stunt had been published, there were calls for the hoaxers to be punished. The Captain of the *Dreadnought*, however, rather admired what he considered a clever prank.[16] Cumming, who had a liking for practical jokes,[17] probably agreed. Among the telegrams of congratulation in 1915 when HMS *Dreadnought* rammed and sank a German submarine – the only British battleship ever to do so – was one that read 'BUNGA BUNGA'.[18]

The *Dreadnought* hoax was so well publicised at the time that Clarkson's highly effective disguises and make-up were likely to have impressed Cumming. Even by the costumier's standards, turning Virginia Woolf into a bearded Abyssinian who was not recognised by her own cousin was a remarkable achievement. Clarkson had discovered what the CIA disguise department would recognise during the Cold War – that women could be more effectively disguised as men than vice versa. Cumming noted in his diary some of the disguises provided by Clarkson for his own early spying missions as head of the foreign department of the Secret Service Bureau. For a secret rendezvous in Paris in July 1910, five months after the *Dreadnought* hoax, he was 'slightly disguised (toupee and moustache) and had on a rather peculiar costume'. Before a meeting in January 1911 with a potential agent who had offered to provide intelligence on Austrian shipbuilding in Trieste, Cumming was made up in Clarkson's shop. The disguise, in Cumming's view, was 'perfect ... its existence not being noticeable even in a good light'. He had a photograph taken so that Clarkson could, if he wished, reproduce exactly the same disguise in future.[19] Cumming kept in his office another photograph of himself, made up to look like a stereotypical German, and was delighted when visitors failed to recognise him. Once, during the First World War, he asked his young niece what she would do if she met that German man in London. The little girl suggested shooting him. 'Well, my dear', replied Cumming, 'in that case you'd have killed your uncle!'[20]

Though Asquith, a former Prize Fellow at Balliol College, Oxford, was well versed in British political history, it never occurred to him (or probably any of his cabinet) that the foreign intelligence available to his government before the First World War did not compare to that received by Elizabeth I before the Armada set sail for England in 1588. Whereas Thomas Phelippes had successfully broken the Spanish ciphers, for seventy years before the First World War, by contrast, Britain – unlike, notably, its future wartime allies, France and Russia – had no SIGINT agency at all.

In August 1909, only a month after the Committee of Imperial Defence approved the foundation of the Secret Service Bureau, Tsar Nicholas II and his family arrived at the Cowes Regatta on board the imperial yacht *Standart*, escorted by a number of Russian cruisers and destroyers, to begin a lavishly organised state visit to Britain. Dressed in the uniform of a British admiral, Nicholas II boarded the royal yacht *Victoria and Albert* to review the Royal Navy, the world's mightiest battle fleet, with King Edward VII. There followed extravagant dinners hosted by the two monarchs on their yachts and meetings with Asquith and the foreign secretary, Sir Edward Grey. In talks with his British hosts, Nicholas II benefited from what Shakespeare had referred to as message 'interception which they dream[ed] not of'. The tsar's British interlocutors were splendidly unaware that he prepared for meetings with them by studying decrypted British diplomatic despatches. Nicholas had brought with him his chief cryptanalyst, Ernst Fetterlein, to whom he presented a ruby ring as a reward for breaking British ciphers.[21]

Despite its innocence about SIGINT, the seriousness with which the Asquith government appeared to take the threat of espionage and invasion led the Lord Chamberlain's Office to modify its previous total ban on plays dealing with these topics. Haldane also found invasion and spy scares a useful recruiting aid for the newly founded Territorial Force, his most important innovation as secretary of state for war. The Lord Chamberlain was thus willing to grant a licence to *An Englishman's Home*, a drama on the invasion of England which opened at Wyndham's Theatre on 27 January 1909.[22] The author, originally identified only as 'A Patriot', was Major Guy du Maurier of the Royal Fusiliers, and the play was directed by his younger brother, the actor-manager Gerald du Maurier.

In the original script submitted to the Lord Chamberlain, all the invaders were identified as German or Prussian. Captain Prince von Littenheim, for example, was a stereotypical tall, blond Prussian, 'thick jowled and thick necked', dressed in cavalry uniform. The Lord Chamberlain's Office insisted that all such references be removed. On 17 December 1908 it licensed *An Englishman's Home* 'subject to the understanding that the scenes, situations etc in the play are kept to a supposed invasion of England by an imaginary enemy of no recognised nationality'. In the original script, which survives in the files of the Lord Chamberlain's Office, all the names of the invaders were crossed out in pencil and all references to Prussia and Germany deleted.[23]

Even before the play opened, a prospective parliamentary candidate, Ashton Jonson – best known as the author of a handbook to the works of Chopin – complained that it would be obvious the invaders were

Germans. Jonson was informed that this was not the case: 'If Germany or any other friendly power had been alluded to, the play would not have received His Lordship's licence.' As an additional precaution, however, the Lord Chamberlain's Office consulted Sir Edward Grey, who raised no objection to the staging of *An Englishman's Home*. The management of Wyndham's Theatre was also warned that the invaders' headdress must not be 'a helmet with a spike', that their uniform 'should be non-distinctive of any particular country', and that 'no moustache [must be] brushed up, as is the custom now so much in Germany'.[24]

Ashton Jonson attended the first night and immediately protested that, contrary to the assurances he had been given, 'the names and make-up of the invaders were unmistakably German'.[25] The German military attaché, Major Ostertag (nicknamed 'Easteregg' by British officers), visited the War Office to register a similar complaint. 'Easteregg', whom Edmonds considered 'really a head spy', had an unsympathetic reception from the head of the German section, Major William Thwaites. According to Edmonds, 'Thwaites put up his eyeglass, looked at him and said, "Bad conscience, Ostertag! Bad conscience".'[26] George Bernard Shaw called *An Englishman's Home* 'the most talked-about play of the present year'.[27] Haldane was amazed at its positive impact on recruitment for the Territorials. On 6 February 1909, he wrote to his mother, 'In London alone 300 recruits came in yesterday.' The War Office quickly installed a recruiting booth in the foyer of Wyndham's Theatre.[28]

There was a curious sequel to the performance of *An Englishman's Home*. When Harry Pelissier submitted his play *Chips*, a one-act 'skit' making fun of Guy du Maurier's play, to the Lord Chamberlain, he was refused a licence. The reviewer of plays, George Redford, wrote to the author, 'No skit will be permitted on "An Englishman's Home"'; he was annoyed when Pelissier published his letter.[29] Despite the German military attaché's official complaint to the War Office, the comptroller of the Lord Chamberlain's Office, Sir Douglas Dawson, absurdly claimed that staging *An Englishman's Home* had been uncontroversial. A skit on it, however, would have caused offence to an unnamed foreign power.[30] It seems more likely that, rather than being concerned about offending the Germans, the Lord Chamberlain's Office was reluctant to authorise theatrical mockery of government preparations to repel invasion and to encourage recruitment to the Territorials.

The response to the production of *An Englishman's Home* at the Theatre Royal, Dublin, in 1909, was markedly different to that in

London. The *Gaelic American*, the newspaper of Clan na Gael, the main Irish republican organisation in the United States, reported that when the invaders arrived on stage, some in the Dublin audience shouted: 'You're welcome, Boys!, Long live the Kaiser!, Three Cheers for our Friends the Germans!, Avenge the Concentration Camps of South Africa!' The German embassy in Washington was sufficiently impressed to send the *Gaelic American* article to Berlin, where the Foreign Ministry underlined the pro-German passages.[31] At another performance at the Theatre Royal, members of the newly founded nationalist youth movement, Fianna Éireann, dressed in green shirts and kilts, stood and sang the German patriotic song, *Die Wacht am Rhein*, when the invaders entered. Members of the British armed forces in the audience countered with 'God Save the King'.[32]

Free from censorship by the Lord Chamberlain, theatre in Dublin enjoyed greater liberty than in London.[33] In December 1904 the Protestant landowner and nationalist playwright Lady Gregory (née Persse) and the Irish poet W. B. Yeats jointly founded the Abbey Theatre 'to bring upon the stage the deeper emotions of Ireland'.[34] Among these 'deeper emotions' was the longing to be 'a nation once again'. Two years earlier, Gregory and Yeats had written the play *Cathleen ni Houlihan*, attributed at the time solely to Yeats, which was performed at the Irish National Theatre Society, starring the great love of Yeats' life, Maud Gonne, in the title role. The spirit of Ireland, personified by Gonne, appears in the play as an old woman asking for the restoration of her 'four green fields' (the four Irish provinces), who is miraculously transformed into a 'young girl with the walk of a queen' when Irishmen offer to take up arms for her.[35] Gonne's own ambition was to take up arms as well. In 1903 she and her new husband travelled to Spain on a hare-brained honeymoon mission to assassinate Edward VII in Gibraltar.[36] Thirty years after the first performance of *Cathleen ni Houlihan*, Yeats wrote in his poem 'Man and the Echo':

> I lie awake night after night
> And never get the answers right.
> Did that play of mine send out
> Certain men the English shot?[37]

The actors at the Abbey during its first year included the future Irish president, Eamon de Valera;[38] Lady Gregory, who was notorious for her attempts to keep a 'firm grip' on the actors and 'tireless in her efforts to keep them in their place', seems to have been unimpressed by his acting.[39] The most frequently performed and some of the most successful plays at the theatre from its foundation to the Easter Rising in 1916 were written by Gregory.[40]

At the heart of her 1906 play, *The Gaol Gate*, is what Gregory called 'the feeling of centuries in this country against an informer' to the British. It opens with the wife and mother of Denis Cahel, a prisoner in Galway Gaol, keeping vigil at the gate. When the gatekeeper brings news that Denis has been executed, they take solace in the fact that he had not tried to save himself by informing on his friends. 'Better for Denis to have killed the whole world than to have become an informer,' says his mother. If Denis had been remembered as an informer, both she and his widow would have been ostracised as punishment for his crime.[41] Censorship by the Lord Chamberlain would have made a London production impossible.

Fear of British spies in their ranks was deeply embedded among Irish nationalists and republicans. 'These creatures of the dark', wrote David Neligan, an early member of the IRA, 'had ever been [Dublin] Castle's last line of defence. In every age an Irish Judas was hidden in the undergrowth.'[42] The role of the informer is at the heart of Thomas MacDonagh's *When the Dawn is Come*, first performed at the Abbey in 1908,[43] in which a future Irish army prepares for a final showdown with its English foe. Its leader, Thurlough MacKieran, devises 'a deep ruse' to turn the tables on the English informers:

> You know there are traitors in the camp and spies … What if a captain feigned to sell himself [to the spies], and so learned all the plans and fears of the enemy, and so crushed them at the last?[44]

The 'deep ruse' almost goes disastrously wrong when MacKieran's comrades suspect he is a real, not feigned, English spy. He is vindicated in the final act, when he dies a hero's death and the Irish win a decisive victory.[45]

Music remained central to all varieties of Irish nationalism. A *Times* report complained, possibly with some exaggeration, after a Home Rule demonstration in Dublin in 1912:

> About one hundred and fifty bands kept a persistent music during the afternoon. Nearly all confined themselves to the tune of 'A Nation

Once Again' which, after a while, even the patriots must have found monotonous. It was intended, perhaps, to represent a sort of shouting round the walls of Jericho, for it was played at least 2000 times in the course of the day.[46]

A series of Irish singing stars produced immensely popular recordings of the nationalist anthem. The first, in 1906, was the great Irish tenor, John McCormack, the Irish Caruso – as Caruso himself called him. By 1914 his passionate Irish nationalism had made him so unpopular in Britain that he did not return for another ten years.[47]

In April 1915, Thomas MacDonagh was secretly sworn into the Irish Republican Brotherhood (IRB), which, with the paramilitary Irish Volunteers, staged the Easter Rising a year later. As the insurrection began, the actor Sean Connolly became the first rebel fatality when he was shot as he tried to raise over the City Hall the rebel flag used in the Abbey production of *When the Dawn is Come*.[48] The socialist revolutionary and writer James Connolly (no relation to Sean) was one of the seven self-styled members of the Irish Provisional Government who led the Rising and were executed afterwards by firing squad. In March 1916, while preparing for the uprising, Connolly had staged his play *Under Which Flag?* in Liberty Hall, the Dublin headquarters of his Irish Citizens Army.

Set during the 1867 Fenian Rebellion, the play was both an incitement to rebellion and a warning to informers. The heroine, Mary O'Neill, is tempted to tell the British authorities about the Fenians' preparations for rebellion, but is dissuaded by a blind veteran of the Irish cause, played by Sean Connolly. Her eyes opened, she denounces the police:

> The polis [police-]man spends his whole life as a spy and a traitor upon his own people, drinks with them, goes to the chapel with them, and sits down in their houses, and all the time busy contriving how he can send them to the prison or the gallows.[49]

Mary tells her suitor, Frank, that she can only love him if he fights for Ireland against the British. Though its message was clear, *Under Which Flag?* was poorly constructed. Seán O'Casey, who watched horrified from the stalls, would make fun of Connolly's play in *The Plough and the Stars* a decade later.[50]

When the Easter Rising began, writes the Irish historian, Roy Foster, 'more than one commentator would point to the choreographed nature of the event, as if the theatre had taken to the streets'. When handed a copy of the rebels' 'Proclamation of the Irish Republic', the Dublin architect and theatrical designer, Joseph Holloway, at first mistook it for a playbill.[51]

*

Though theatre in Dublin was much more politically adventurous than in London, the film industry in Ireland lagged far behind Britain. The first cinema in Dublin, founded by the writer James Joyce, did not open until 1909 and was a financial failure, sold at a loss to an English company only a year later.[52] In London, by contrast, the first cinema had opened in Regent Street in 1896, at almost the same time as the first Scottish cinema in Edinburgh. From then until the First World War the main innovation in the British entertainment industry was the 'picture palaces' which opened in almost every town. By 1914 seven to eight million people went to British cinemas each week – vastly more than were going to theatres.[53]

The cinema was eventually to end the supremacy of the spy novel as the main vehicle for espionage fiction. The mass book-reading public which had emerged in the late nineteenth century was significantly smaller on the eve of the First World War than at the death of Queen Victoria. The *New Statesman*, among others, noticed the connection between the declining – but still substantial – numbers of books borrowed from English and Scottish lending libraries and the exponential growth in cinema audiences: 'There is no question that the invention of the cinematograph has made a more radical change in the habits of civilised and partially civilised peoples than anything since the invention of steam.'[54]

Until the First World War, however, spies were as rare on screen as on stage. The first to appear in a picture palace was not a German but a Boer. The inhibitions which prevented the peacetime portrayal of German spies did not apply to the enemy during the war in South Africa (1899–1902). Late in 1899, the pioneering London film-maker, Robert Paul, had made a series of short films in his Muswell Hill studio, using a nearby golf course as a substitute for the African veldt. All, he claimed, were filmed 'under the supervision of a military officer from the Front' and gave authentic portrayals of Boer barbarism. *Attack on a Picquet*, a 'remarkably natural reproduction of an actual occurrence', showed Boers overrunning a British outpost, clubbing and shooting British soldiers, then making off with their guns and personal possessions. *Shooting the Spy* – like many early films, less than a minute long – was the first British spy film. Robert Paul's catalogue describes it thus:

> Scene outside a guardroom, with sentry on duty. An escort comes up, with captured Boer spy, who is eventually shot.[55]

The first film on foreign espionage in Britain, *The Peril of the Fleet*, six minutes in length, was made by the London Cinematograph Company and Electric Theatres in the summer of 1909, incorporating footage from a characteristically impressive Royal Navy review at Spithead. The hero is a clean-shaven British amateur detective who survives being thrown off a cliff by bearded professional foreign spies, and defeats their attempt to blow up the fleet and leave Britain defenceless against invasion.[56] There was no mention of the foreign spies' nationality.[57]

The most ambitious spy film made before the First World War was the Gaumont Cinematograph Company's *The Raid of 1915*, based on an updated version of Le Queux's *The Invasion of 1910* – the first film to feature German spies and invaders. Gaumont prepared two different endings, giving the option of either a British or a German victory. *Punch* suggested showing the British victory in Britain but allowing Germany to win in German cinemas. Completed in February 1913, *The Raid of 1915* immediately fell foul of the British Board of Film Censors (BBFC), founded a month earlier.[58]

The BBFC was set up with the pious purpose of censoring films 'which may be considered in any way opposed to the better feelings of the general public'. During its first year, it rejected at least twenty-two films – far more than the plays refused a licence by the Lord Chamberlain. So far as is known, *The Raid of 1915* was the only film banned because of its references to German aggression and espionage. By far the commonest reason for imposing a ban was the inclusion of 'indelicate or suggestive sexual situations', though the BBFC also objected to 'holding up a minister of Religion to ridicule', any portrayal of 'Christ or the Almighty', 'cruelty to animals', 'judicial executions', 'excessive drunkenness', and 'native customs in foreign lands abhorrent to British ideas'.[59]

German espionage ceased to be taboo on stage and screen after the British declaration of war on 4 August 1914. Over the next twelve days, police arrested virtually the whole German espionage network in Britain – twenty-two agents of the naval Nachrichten-Abteilung, who had been under surveillance for several years by Vernon Kell's counter-espionage bureau (later renamed MI5) and local police.[60] Gustav Steinhauer, who ran the agent network, had the unenviable task of reporting to the Kaiser the 'wholesale round-up of our secret service agents in England'. Wilhelm, Steinhauer later recalled, was beside himself with fury:

> Apparently unable to believe his ears, the Kaiser raved and stormed for the better part of two hours about the incompetence of his so-called intelligence officers, bellowing: 'Am I surrounded by dolts? Why was I not told? Who is responsible?' and more in the same vein.[61]

British readers of spy novels and other alarmists, however, were wrongly convinced that the arrested spies were merely the tip of an espionage iceberg. When the Home Secretary, Reginald McKenna, publicly announced that the whole German spy network in Britain had very probably been 'crushed at the outbreak of the war' (as indeed it had), even *The Times* was 'more than a little incredulous':

> It does not square with what we know of the German spy system …
> In their eager absorption of the baser side of militarism, the Germans seem to have almost converted themselves into a race of spies.

Basil Thomson, head of the CID at Scotland Yard as well as of the Special Branch, wrote later that spy mania 'assumed a virulent epidemic form accompanied by delusions which defied treatment'. Reports flooded in of German agents planning mayhem across Britain and communicating with enemy spymasters by a variety of improbable means. All were false alarms.[62]

Wartime spy mania gave Le Queux a new lease of life. 'The serious truth', he absurdly declared,

> is that German espionage and treasonable propaganda have, during past years, been allowed by a slothful military administration to take

root so deeply that the authorities today find themselves powerless to eradicate its pernicious growth.[63]

In October 1914, his previously banned film, *The Raid of 1915*, retitled *If England were Invaded*, was released by Gaumont, who paid him the considerable sum of £3,000.[64] Over the next year Le Queux wrote and co-directed three more films.[65]

Probably the most popular spy film prompted by the outbreak of war was *The German Spy Peril*, an updated version of the 1605 Gunpowder Plot, in which the original Catholic plotters were replaced by fictional German spies who also attempted to blow up the Houses of Parliament. The simplistic patriotism of the plot was worthy of Le Queux. The British hero, whose ill-health has prevented him volunteering for the army, overhears the German spies plotting to blow up Parliament, pursues them through a secret tunnel and blows them up instead of Parliament. 'We will die together, you German dogs,' he tells them, 'for my King and my country's sake!'[66]

The German Spy Peril (1914). Well-dressed German spies follow in the footsteps of Guy Fawkes three centuries earlier by planting explosives beneath the Houses of Parliament.

9

The First World War: From Mistinguett to the Hush-Hush Revue

During the autumn of 1914 the popularity of spy films declined.[1] No film on fictional German spies could compare with the real-life drama of the trial and execution of Carl Hans Lody, the first spy sent to Britain by German naval intelligence after the outbreak of war. On 30 October Lody appeared before a military court martial in London at the start of the only public spy trial held in Britain in either World War. The trial, reported *The New York Times*, was a celebrity event, and 'many fashionably dressed women thronged the galleries of the courtroom'. Lody's sentencing to death on 2 November was witnessed by 'many leaders of London society as well as by prominent jurists, politicians, and military and naval men'.[2]

A front-page report in the *Daily Express* called Lody 'a most dangerous spy' but paid 'tribute to his daring resourcefulness and inflexible courage'.[3] Most of the press agreed. Before being shot by a firing squad at dawn on 6 November, Lody said to the assistant provost marshal: 'I suppose you will not shake hands with a spy?' The officer replied: 'No, but I will shake hands with a brave man.'[4] Vernon Kell, whose Counter-Espionage Bureau had tracked down Lody, 'felt it deeply', according to his wife, 'that so brave a man should have to face the death penalty'.[5] Lody was the first person to be executed at the Tower of London for 167 years.

It emerged during the trial that a few of Lody's intelligence reports were as absurd as William Le Queux's pre-war spy novels. While spying in Edinburgh, he was taken in by rumours that large numbers of Russian troops had landed in Scotland – some, it was claimed, with snow still on their boots – en route to the Western

Front. On 3 September, Lody wrote to a German intelligence forwarding address:

> Will you kindly communicate with Berlin at once by wire (code or whatever system at your disposal) and inform them that on Sept. 3rd great masses of Russian soldiers have passed through Edinburgh on their way to London and France.

Like some others in the courtroom, Lody smiled when this report was referred to at his trial.[6]

Four of the captured German spies featured by Sir Basil Thomson in his eccentrically entitled memoir, *Queer People* (1922): Anton Kupferle, dismissed by Thomson as 'grotesque in his inefficiency', who hanged himself in his Brixton prison cell; Robert Rosenthal, 'a young man of excitable temperament and a Jew', executed in 1915; Hans Lody, 'a good example of the patriotic spy' and the first to be executed, in 1914; and the 'music hall artist' Courtenay de Rysbach, who was sentenced to life imprisonment.

Despite the shelling of Scarborough, Whitby and Hartlepool by two German battlecruisers in December,[7] the dominant theme in pre-war British espionage fiction of German spies preparing a surprise invasion of England lost all credibility in the new era of trench warfare which began on the Western Front in France and Belgium at the end of 1914. Wartime German spies achieved less in Britain than the pre-war naval intelligence network that was rounded up on the outbreak of war. The ten other spies, captured after Lody, who were executed after conviction at secret trials also became front-page news but attracted little public sympathy.[8]

Kell praised one of his youngest wartime recruits, the 20-year-old Edward Hinchley Cooke, for being 'largely responsible' for the arrest of several of the spies. Hinchley Cooke, who went on to become the only MI5 officer to serve in both world wars, was the son of a German mother and a British father, and had been to school in Dresden before studying at Leipzig University. He was strongly recommended to Kell by the British minister in Dresden, A. C. Grant Duff, as 'entirely British in sentiment': 'the fact that he speaks English with a foreign accent must not be allowed to militate against him.' To counter suspicions

aroused by his German accent, Kell personally wrote on Hinchley Cooke's War Office pass: 'He is an Englishman.'[9]

Hinchley Cooke had considerable acting ability and sometimes operated in disguise, almost certainly with the assistance of Willy Clarkson's theatrical costumiers and wigmakers.[10] Security Service archives contain photographs of Hinchley Cooke in German army uniform, probably supplied by Clarkson, as well as a 1917 Metropolitan Police Alien Enemy Certificate of Registration card identifying him as the German civilian, Wilhelm Eduard Koch, which used the same photograph as his War Office identity document. His most successful acting role seems to have been in German uniform, posing as a captured German officer in POW camps, collecting intelligence from genuine POWs. Under his other, civilian identity as Wilhelm Koch, he was also able to mix with, and report on, Germans who had registration cards allowing them to remain at liberty.[11] He was helped by his genuine German accent.

German archives show that British counter-espionage operations reduced the number of agents in Britain from twenty-two in January 1915 to only four at the end of the year.[12] Though the declining number of German spies detected in Britain simply reflected the declining number being sent, there were mistaken fears in and beyond Whitehall that the spies were using new forms of cover which MI5 had failed to detect.

The founder of the Boy Scout Movement, Lieutenant General Sir Robert (later Lord) Baden-Powell, claimed that German spies were going undetected because of their disguises. His bestselling but eccentric book, My Adventures as a Spy, first published in 1915 and frequently reprinted,[13] included drawings designed to demonstrate that a 'keen eye' such as Baden-Powell's could spot spies in the street.

Sir Edward Troup, the long-serving permanent secretary at the Home Office, strongly suspected that German spies in Britain were evading detection by working as entertainers – particularly in popular music and music halls, of which there were 300 in London alone. Tickets to music-hall performances, which often included 'speciality acts' ranging from juggling to animal acts, sold in millions.[14] Three of the ten German spies convicted in 1915 had links with the entertainment industry. Two were musicians: Fernando Buschmann, who was executed by firing squad at the Tower of London at dawn on 19 October, was a professional violinist as well as a scientist. He was allowed to spend the whole of the previous night playing his violin

'A man may effect a wonderful disguise in front,' Baden-Powell wrote, 'yet be instantly recognised by a keen eye from behind. This is a point which is frequently forgotten by beginners, and yet is one of the most important. The first and third figures show an effective make-up in front, but the second figure, a back-view, shows how easily the man may be recognised by a person behind him. The fourth and fifth sketches show, by means of dotted lines, how the "back-view" can be altered by change of clothing and gait.'

in his cell.[15] Georg Breeckow, alias Reginald Rowland, who faced the firing squad a week later, had worked for some years as a pianist in the United States. Basil Thomson found it 'curious ... that professional musicians should have formed a respectable proportion of the detected spies.'[16]

The entertainer-spy whose trial attracted most publicity in 1915 was Courtenay de Rysbach, a versatile British music-hall performer of Austrian ancestry who combined some of the skills of comedian, juggler, singer and trick cyclist. He had been arrested while on tour in Germany before the war and released only when he agreed to spy for the Germans. In July 1915, British Postal Censorship intercepted a music score posted by Rysbach to a known German agent who was under surveillance. Written in invisible ink between the lines of music for a song called 'The Ladder of Love' was a request for German funds with which to purchase British naval secrets.[17] Following a trial in October at which the jury appeared remarkably sympathetic to Rysbach's predicament – and where it was established that no secrets had actually been relayed by him to the Germans – he was sentenced to life imprisonment. In the event he served eight years before being released and returning to the music hall.[18]

In May 1916 another versatile music-hall entertainer, the Dutch Leopold Vieyra, was arrested on a charge of spying for Germany.[19]

Courtenay de Rysbach's invisible ink message revealed on sheet music for *The Ladder of Love*.

Though he became known during his trial in November as the 'Spy in the Heart of Filmland', Vieyra had begun his career as a musician. In 1906 he became manager of a Paris group of dwarf acrobats, Royaume de Lilliput, whom he later renamed the 'Midgets' and took on tour in England. The fact that a number of their performances took place near naval and military bases raises suspicions that he was already hoping to collect intelligence on the British armed services.[20] In 1912, under the alias Leo Pickard, he became manager of the Bijou Picture Theatre in Finchley Road, London. After the outbreak of war, this gave him the opportunity to export films to the neutral Netherlands. Just before his arrest in May 1916, for example, he wrote to a cover address in Rotterdam used by German intelligence: 'I have bought a parcel of Keystone Comedy and a few exclusives – all very cheap.' As in the case of Rysbach, Postal Censorship discovered writing in invisible ink on this and other letters from Vieyra which provided proof of espionage.[21]

Probably prompted by the Vieyra case, on 16 July 1916, Sir Edward
Troup sent a warning from the Home Office to all chief constables that

> there is reason to believe that the German Government is endeavouring
> to recruit circus-riders, music-hall performers, and persons on the
> regular stage for purposes of espionage in this country. Two such
> persons, circus-riders, who were of German origin, have recently been
> detected endeavouring to come to this country and have been refused
> permission to land, and a third, who had been touring as a music-hall
> performer with a Dutch passport, is believed to be a German and is
> now in custody.[22] I am therefore to request that special attention may
> be paid to any persons belonging to these professions who may visit
> your area, more particularly if they appear to be in the habit of
> performing at important Naval centres ...

Where there was 'reasonable ground for suspicion', the suspect entertainers were to be detained and all papers found in their possession
forwarded to MI5.[23] In November 1916 Vieyra was found guilty of
espionage and condemned to death – a sentence later commuted to
life imprisonment.[24] No further spies were discovered in the British
entertainment business.

The successful round-up of German spies in Britain had a larger
impact on the First World War than is usually realised. Berlin had
intended to use its agent network on both sides of the Atlantic for
sabotage as well as intelligence collection. In the neutral United States,
Sektion P of German military intelligence succeeded in placing explosives, often disguised as coal briquettes, on a number of ships carrying
supplies to Britain and France. Its most notorious act of sabotage was
at a depot in Black Tom Pier, New Jersey, which contained over two
million pounds of ammunition destined for a Russian offensive on the
Eastern Front. On 30 July 1916 the entire depot was blown up. Had
security and counter-espionage in Britain been as ineffective as in the
United States, German sabotage would probably have operated on at
least the same scale.[25]

*

The most successful entertainer to work for French military intelligence during the war was the singer and dancer Jeanne Bourgeois,

Mistinguett at the Moulin Rouge.

better known by her stage name Mistinguett, star successively of the Moulin Rouge, Folies Bergère and the Casino de Paris. From 1908 to 1928 she also starred in forty-eight silent films. At her peak, Mistinguett was believed to be the best-paid female entertainer in the world.

Soon after the outbreak of war, Mistinguett called on Maurice Gamelin, chef de cabinet of the French commander-in-chief, Marshal Joffre, and offered her services as a spy. Gamelin kept their meeting secret until after her death in 1956, when he wrote a classified report (since declassified) on her wartime intelligence role, revealing that he had accepted an offer from Mistinguett to travel abroad to meet those of her distinguished foreign admirers who might be able to provide wartime intelligence. At the top of her list was the Prussian Prince Johannes zu Hohenlohe-Bartenstein, who had been her lover during his visits to Paris before the war and who had asked her to meet him in Switzerland. Though Hohenlohe had no official position, she believed that 'he learns a great deal' from relatives who did. Gamelin kept the secret of Mistinguett's meetings with Hohenlohe and other foreign informants secret for so long not for reasons of national security but because the subject was 'too delicate'.[26] He plainly suspected that she was willing to sleep with Hohenlohe and perhaps with others who gave her information.

The success which meant most to Mistinguett personally was a meeting in Madrid in 1916 with the neutral but somewhat pro-German King of Spain, Alfonso XIII, at which she gained his good offices in securing the release from a German prisoner-of-war camp of her lover, the famously debonair singer and actor, Maurice Chevalier.[27] Though few other details survive of the intelligence obtained by Mistinguett from her foreign celebrity admirers, Gamelin believed that her most important contribution came in the final summer of the war. She discovered from Hohenlohe in June 1918 that the final German offensive, Operation FRIEDENSTURM, would take place in Champagne and not, as expected, on the Somme. Hohenlohe was at his most indiscreet largely because he was wildly optimistic about the outcome, boasting to Mistinguett: 'You will probably be forced to leave Paris.' The failure of the offensive in July, for which Allied forces were well prepared, ended Germany's last hope of victory. Though there was also intelligence from other sources, Gamelin, who was then the general commanding the 9th division on the Western Front, attached particular importance to Mistinguett's.[28]

By far the best-known entertainer to spy for wartime German intelligence was the Dutch exotic dancer and courtesan, Margaretha Geertruida Zelle, better known by her stage name Mata Hari ('eye of the day' in Malay). Zelle, who had fled to Paris in 1902 to escape an abusive marriage, initially worked as an artists' model and a trick horse rider at the Cirque Molier before settling on a career as an upmarket striptease artiste, which made her an international celebrity, appearing at La Scala and giving private performances for the Paris Rothschilds.[29] Her act capitalised on the popularity of stage interpretations of the biblical character Salome's notorious 'dance of the seven veils', which had first appeared in Oscar Wilde's play *Salome*, published in French in 1891 but banned from the British stage by the Lord Chamberlain a year later. Sarah Bernhardt had agreed, enthusiastically, to play the title role in London and had also hoped to star in a French version.[30]

As part of Zelle's act, in place of her bourgeois origins, she invented an alternative upbringing as, variously, a Javanese princess or the daughter of a priest and a dancer in a Hindu temple on the banks of the river Ganges. The audiences from Parisian high society who attended her semi-nude performances could therefore pretend that they were participating not in the vulgar excitement of the can-can at the Moulin Rouge but in the sacred mysteries of the

Mata Hari performing in 1905.

Orient.[31] According to her MI5 file, the introduction of a large snake into her act, combined with her own 'scanty drapery and sinuous movements', particularly appealed to German and Austrian audiences.[32]

By the outbreak of war, however, the dancing career of the 38-year-old Zelle was in decline, threatened by younger competitors.[33] Heavily indebted and increasingly dependent on earnings as a courtesan, she was attracted by what she expected to be a well-paid career as a spy. In December 1914, the German intelligence officer, Carl Krämer, operating under cover as consul general in The Hague, paid Zelle 30,000 marks to collect intelligence from France. In November 1915, apparently impressed by Zelle's range of contacts with French and allied officers, Krämer paid her 20,000 francs, gave her secret ink to use in writing her reports, and recruited her as Agent H21. Unable to cross German-occupied Belgium, Zelle set sail from Holland for France via England, but threw the secret ink overboard when the ship was stopped at Folkestone,[34] where she was questioned by Captain Stephen Dillon of MI5, who described her as 'handsome, bold ... well and fashionably dressed' in an outfit with 'raccoon fur trimming and hat to match':

> Though she had good answers to every question, she impressed me very unfavourably, but after having her very carefully searched and finding nothing, I considered I hadn't enough grounds to refuse her embarkation.[35]

Zelle was allowed to proceed to Paris, where she spent over five weeks engaging in sexual liaisons and other encounters with a series of allied officers, as well as with a cipher official at the Quai d'Orsay – much of the time while under surveillance by the Sûreté. After some weeks in Spain, she returned to Holland and renewed contact with Krämer. When the head of German military intelligence, Colonel Walter Nicolai, examined her file in April 1916, he found it 'mediocre' and ordered her to be sent on an espionage training course in Frankfurt. Though Zelle passed the course and her female instructor concluded that she had an 'astonishing facility' for adapting to new environments, it was noted that her intelligence reports tended to be superficial and she seemed incapable of mastering the use of ciphers and secret inks.[36] It was probably Zelle's ability to seduce allied army officers and French officials that persuaded Nicolai to fund her second espionage mission to France in the summer of 1916.

While in Paris, Zelle began to play a dangerous double game. At a meeting on 16 September with Georges Ladoux, head of military counter-espionage, without admitting her role as a German spy, she agreed to work as a French agent:

> I shall pay regular visits to German HQ in occupied Belgium. I don't intend to waste my time there for several months on minor matters. I shall achieve a major coup, just one, then leave. I ask for a million [francs].

Ladoux ignored the request for a million francs, but took her on.[37] Her next trip, however, was to Spain rather than Belgium. In November 1916, Zelle had a second brush with British intelligence while travelling by sea from Spain to Holland. She was removed by Ports Police when the steamer called at Falmouth, initially being confused with a known German spy, and taken, with her ten travelling trunks, to be questioned in London by Basil Thomson and MI5. 'Time', in Thomson's view, 'had a little dimmed the charms of which we had heard so much.'[38] As had happened a year earlier, it was decided after questioning Zelle that there was insufficient evidence to justify her arrest.[39] Consulted by MI5, a suspicious Ladoux asked for Zelle to be sent back to Spain.[40]

Ladoux's suspicions were soon confirmed by a telegram to Berlin from the German military attaché in Madrid, Arnold Kalle, intercepted by the French listening post at the Eiffel Tower. Kalle reported that Zelle had told him that she had only pretended to agree to become a French spy at her meeting with Ladoux and continued to work solely for German intelligence. Zelle's willingness to dabble in wartime espionage for both sides showed the degree to which she had become a fantasist. She returned to Paris on 4 January 1917 after taking money from the Germans, with no conception of the risks she was taking. Not long before her arrest on 13 February, she resumed an affair with a former lover who found her obsessed with fantasies (chimères): 'she allowed herself to be guided by her imagination and it was this which led to her downfall.'[41] After being arrested, Zelle was initially so confident that she voluntarily signed a statement (which she later revoked) declining the 'assistance of legal counsel'.[42]

A few weeks later, French military intelligence reported to MI5 that she had confessed to working for the Germans.[43] She claimed, however, that her numerous sexual liaisons with allied military officers had no connection with espionage:

> I love officers. I have loved them all my life. I would rather be the mistress of a poor officer than of a rich banker. My greatest pleasure is to go to bed with them without thinking of money, and then, I like to make comparisons among the different nationalities.[44]

At her trial on 24–5 July, Zelle was found guilty of 'espionage and intelligence with the enemy' and sentenced to death. Appeals to the Supreme Court of Appeals and the president of the Republic failed. On 15 October Zelle was shot at dawn by firing squad at the Chateau de Vincennes, courageously refusing a blindfold and looking her executioners in the face – though not, as often claimed,[45] blowing them a kiss just before they opened fire.

In November MI5's liaison officer at the French War Ministry, Lieutenant Colonel Hercules Pakenham, was allowed to read her file, which contained the transcript of a confession in which she admitted to receiving 5,000 francs per mission from German intelligence to collect Allied secrets. However, Pakenham reported to MI5 headquarters that, though Zelle confessed to sending the Germans 'general information of every kind procurable', she did not admit to passing them military secrets.[46] Remarkably, Zelle's French file, which includes references to her in decrypted German telegrams, was not declassified until the centenary of her execution, in 2017. As the persuasive analysis by the French historian Olivier Lahaie concludes, it shows that, 'even if she was a mediocre spy, she did indeed work for the Germans'. The common claim that French military intelligence deliberately turned the Mata Hari case into a media sensation is untrue. No attempt was made to brief the media before her trial began. On the contrary, military intelligence deplored newspaper fascination with Zelle's trial, reporting to the War Ministry: 'the publicity given to the details of this affair is harming counter-espionage operations.'[47] A century later, the name Mata Hari remains better known than that of any other female spy – one example of how much the popular image of espionage owes to imagination rather than reality.

*

The most sensational intelligence-related trial in wartime Britain, which received even more international publicity than Zelle's, was the treason trial in 1916 of the Irish exile, Sir Roger Casement, formerly a distinguished member of the British consular service, who had sought German support for an Irish rebellion. Arms promised to Casement for the 1916 Easter Rising, however, were intercepted by the Royal Navy shortly beforehand. Casement himself was captured after landing from a German U-boat in Tralee Bay. Before Casement's treason trial was due to begin in London, George Bernard Shaw, Ireland's most famous playwright and London resident, appealed to him to conduct his own defence and wrote a speech for him to deliver from the dock:

> Now as a simple matter of fact, I am neither an Englishman nor a traitor: I am an Irishman, captured in a fair attempt to achieve the independence of my country; and you can no more deprive me of the honours of that position, or destroy the effects of my effort, than the abominable cruelties inflicted six hundred years ago on William Wallace in this city when he met a precisely similar indictment with a precisely similar reply, have prevented that brave and honourable Scot from becoming the national hero of his country.

Shaw's friend Beatrice Webb wrote in her diary that the playwright wanted to turn Casement's defence into 'a national dramatic event'. Shaw told Casement 'to finish with a defiant "Now murder me if you like and be damned".' 'I believed, and still believe,' wrote Shaw later, 'that such a defence would have had at least a chance of disagreement in the jury.' But his lawyers persuaded Casement to allow them, inevitably unsuccessfully, to contest the facts of the prosecution case, and to address the jury himself only after he had been condemned. While awaiting execution in July 1916, Casement regretted that he had not performed Shaw's 'national drama'.[48]

Shortly after Casement's execution, Shaw wrote his only spy play, the one-act *Augustus Does His Bit: A True-to-Life Farce*, about a dim-witted British aristocrat who falls for the flattery of a clever female spy, working for Germany. 'What we women admire in you', the spy tells Augustus, 'is not the politician, but the man of action, the heroic warrior, the *beau sabreur*.' Augustus then hands her a top-secret War Office document.[49]

Neither Shaw nor Casement, however, had any idea that Britain's most important intelligence on Germany came not from spies but from SIGINT. German messages decrypted by the Admiralty SIGINT agency, Room 40 in the Admiralty Old Building on Whitehall, had revealed German plans both to supply arms for the Easter Rising and to send Casement to Tralee Bay by U-boat.[50] Directed until 1916 by the former director of naval education, Sir Alfred Ewing, Room 40 was both the most secret and the most successful intelligence agency of the First World War. By the end of 1914, thanks to the German navy's dependence on radio communications, British naval cryptanalysts were providing operational intelligence on a scale unprecedented in the previous history of SIGINT. Room 40's greatest achievement was to make German surprise attack impossible. Until its cryptanalysts got into their stride, the Grand Fleet, based inconveniently far north at Scapa Flow in the Orkneys, was forced to spend much of its time scouring the North Sea for an enemy it failed to find, continually fearful of being caught off its guard. But from December 1914[51] onwards no major movement by the German High Seas Fleet – save briefly in 1918 – escaped the notice of the cryptanalysts. Room 40 also had a diplomatic codebreaking department, dealing chiefly with German intercepts and reporting directly to the Director of Naval Intelligence (DNI), Captain Reginald 'Blinker' Hall. Ewing recruited to Room 40 (later known as ID25) 'men of the professor type': civilian intellectuals whom most admirals would never have dreamed of involving in naval matters. The single most valuable source of 'professor types' for SIGINT operations in both world wars was Ewing's former Cambridge college, King's, with which he retained strong links. Despite Ewing's own academic background in engineering, however, none of Room 40's academic recruits were professional mathematicians – though some had considerable mathematical talent. Room 40 seems to have shared the arts graduate's traditional suspicion that, whatever their dexterity with numbers, the best mathematicians tend to have withdrawn, uncommunicative personalities which make them unsuitable for the collaborative solution of practical problems.[52]

When the first American codebreaking unit, founded after US entry into the war, later sought advice from its British allies on the right kind of recruit, it was told to beware of mathematicians. What was needed was 'an active, well trained and scholarly mind, not mathematical but classical'.[53] The eccentric King's College classicist, Alfred Dillwyn Knox, recruited by Ewing early in 1915, was just such an individual. Reputed to be Room 40's 'most brilliant member', 'Dilly' Knox did some of his best work lying in a bath in Room 53, claiming that codes were most easily cracked in an atmosphere of soap and steam.[54] A series of other academic recruits, mostly classicists and German linguists, included, in addition to Knox, two other Fellows of King's: Frank Adcock (later Professor of Ancient History at Cambridge University), who joined at about the same time as Dilly; and the Old Etonian King's historian, Frank Birch, who was recruited in 1916.[55] At the end of the war, Birch co-wrote a classified 'contribution to the history of German naval warfare 1914–1918', based on Room 40 decrypts.[56]

No one has ever combined careers in SIGINT and on the stage as successfully and flamboyantly as Frank Birch. Before leaving Cambridge in 1927 for a full-time theatre career, his work as a director had included a lauded 1922 production of *Troilus and Cressida* for the Cambridge University Marlowe Society, which transferred to the Hampstead Everyman Theatre. Birch went on to enjoy a successful career as a pantomime dame, appearing regularly at the Lyric Hammersmith, notably as an acclaimed Widow Twankey in *Aladdin*, as well as making numerous other appearances on the stage. Returning to SIGINT in the Second World War, Birch rose to become deputy director at Bletchley Park before resuming his acting career.[57]

At the end of the First World War, Birch and Dilly Knox, both devotees of Lewis Carroll, produced a pantomime for a private audience – probably mainly composed of their colleagues – at the house they shared in Chelsea. Inspired by *Alice's Adventures in Wonderland*, it was an affectionate parody of the work of ID25, starring Knox as Dilly the Dodo and Frank Adcock as the White Rabbit.[58]

This first comedy ever written and performed about an intelligence agency was later turned into the first classified comic history, *Alice in ID25*, written by Birch with poems by Knox. The poems included this celebration of Knox's bathtime codebreaking brainwaves:

> The sailor in Room 53
> Has never, it's true, been to sea
> But though not in a boat

Room 40 cartoonist G. P. Mackeson's
portrait of Frank Adcock as the White
Rabbit.

He has yet served afloat –
In a bath at the Admiralty.[59]

One of Room 40's German diplomatic decrypts, the so-called
Zimmermann telegram of January 1917, in which the German foreign
minister offered Mexico a wartime military alliance which would allow
it to recover Texas, Arizona and New Mexico from the United States,
became front-page news. The British Foreign Secretary, Arthur Balfour,
whose patrician calm was rarely ruffled by excitement, found handing
the decrypted telegram to the US ambassador, Dr Walter Hines Page,
on 23 February 'as dramatic a moment as I remember in all my life'.
On reading the telegram two days later, US President Woodrow Wilson
was as shocked and angry as Balfour and the DNI, 'Blinker' Hall, had
hoped he would be. At the very moment when he had been negotiating in good faith with Germany on ways to bring the war to an
end, Germany had simultaneously been trying to entice Mexico into
attacking the United States.

Even without the Zimmermann telegram, the Wilson administration would, sooner or later, have declared war on Germany. But Hall
and British codebreakers had accelerated its decision to do so. Shocked
by the revelation of secret German perfidy, Americans went to war
on 2 April as a united nation, without significant public protests from
German-Americans and the neutralist lobby. Thereafter, by decrypting
German naval signals, ID25 made what was probably a crucial contribution to the Allied victory against the U-boats in the North Atlantic

after American entry into the war. Without this success in 1917, the United States could not have transferred the men and materiel to the Western Front which made victory possible in 1918.[60]

It never occurred to President Wilson, however, that Britain was intercepting and decrypting American as well as German diplomatic telegrams.[61] Britain's first and longest-serving cabinet secretary, Maurice Hankey, privately said of the intelligence derived from US decrypts, 'This information is of course priceless' – particularly in enabling the Lloyd George government to monitor American peace plans for the end of the war which somewhat differed from its own.[62] As well as successfully concealing this SIGINT success from his US allies, 'Blinker' Hall went to great lengths to conceal how much of his intelligence on Germany was obtained from SIGINT rather than from HUMINT, for fear that the Americans might suspect that their own ciphers were also being broken. Among those he successfully deceived was the impressionable young assistant secretary of the Navy and future US President, Franklin D. Roosevelt, who was responsible for US naval intelligence. Roosevelt's meeting with Hall during a visit to London in the summer of 1918 made a profound impression on him that would still influence his attitude to British intelligence at the beginning of the Second World War. 'Their intelligence unit is much more developed than ours,' he wrote after the visit, 'and this is because it is a much more integral part of their Office of Operations.'

To impress Roosevelt with the phenomenal success of the Admiralty's (almost non-existent) secret agents in Germany, Hall arranged an astonishing piece of theatre in the Admiralty. As he and Roosevelt discussed German troop movements, Hall – probably blinking furiously as he did at moments of excitement, which had earned him his nickname – said suddenly to his American visitor: 'I am going to ask that youngster at the other end of the room to come over here. I will not introduce him by name. I want you to ask him where he was twenty-four hours ago.' When Roosevelt put the question, the young man, whom Hall had instructed to impersonate a spy, replied, 'I was in Kiel, Sir.' Hall then explained that British spies operating in Germany crossed the German–Danish border each night, went by boat to the island of Sylt, and thence by flying boat to Harwich. Roosevelt was deeply impressed. He would never realise that he had been taken in by one of Hall's deceptions.[63]

Hall was a consummate actor who, from time to time, also deceived the US ambassador, Dr Page, who was spellbound in his presence. Page wrote to President Wilson:

> Neither in fiction nor in fact can you find any such man to match [Hall] ... The man is a genius – a clear case of genius. All other secret service men are amateurs by comparison ... I shall never meet another man like him; that were too much to expect. For Hall can look through you and see the very muscular movements of your immortal soul while he is talking to you. Such eyes as the man has! – which is well, because he hasn't a hair on his head nor a tooth in his mouth ... – My Lord! I do study these men here most diligently who have this vast and appalling War Job. There are most uncommon creatures among them – men about whom our great-grandchildren will read in their school histories; but of them all, the most extraordinary is this naval officer – of whom, probably, they'll never hear.[64]

*

Some of Mansfield Cumming's admirers, who also included a number of Americans, found him equally extraordinary. Thanks to the pre-war links which 'C' had built up with London theatre-land, wartime links between British intelligence and the theatre were strongest in Cumming's MI1c (later to become the Secret Intelligence Service SIS). MI1c's wartime recruits included a number of notable theatricals: among them Britain's then most successful playwright, William Somerset Maugham, who had recently achieved the distinction of having four of his plays running simultaneously in London's West End. Codenamed SOMERVILLE, and hidden in plain sight as a playwright finishing his latest work, he was stationed initially in the espionage hotbed of neutral Geneva, with a brief to flush out enemy spies.

Maugham diligently executed some minor intelligence missions including monitoring the playwright Karl Gustav Vollmoeller, a fellow guest at Geneva's Hotel Angleterre who was at the time working for German intelligence and who would later co-write the screenplay for the 1935 film *The Blue Angel* which made a star of Marlene Dietrich.[65] Like Vollmoeller, Maugham showed a remarkable capacity for combining espionage with playwriting, successfully completing the work which provided the pretext for his presence in Geneva – the comedy *Caroline* premiered at the New Theatre in London's West End on 8 February 1916 and became a huge box-office success.[66]

Maugham's most important MI1c mission, which at first 'staggered' him, was to lead a joint British–American covert operation in Petrograd in 1917. 'The long and short of it', he wrote later, 'was that I should go to Russia and keep the Russians in the war.' As well as organising pro-Allied propaganda in the Russian capital, Maugham succeeded, through his former lover Sasha Kropotkin, in gaining an introduction to Alexander Kerensky, second head of the provisional government which had followed the overthrow of the Romanovs in the February Revolution. With Sasha acting as hostess and interpreter, Maugham entertained Kerensky and members of his government once a week at the Medved, reputedly the best restaurant in Russia, paying for the finest caviar and vodka from the ample funds provided by the British and American governments. The austere Woodrow Wilson can scarcely have imagined that some of the $75,000 'propaganda' budget he had authorised was being used to finance such lavish entertainment. 'I think Kerensky must have supposed that I was more important than I really was', wrote Maugham later, 'for he came to Sasha's apartment on several occasions and, walking up and down the room, harangued me as though I were at a public meeting for two hours at a time.' The overthrow of the Kerensky regime in the Bolsheviks' October Revolution meant, however, that the first joint Anglo-American intelligence operation ended in failure.[67]

After the Bolshevik Revolution, Maugham was offered another MI1c posting, this time to Bucharest, but illness forced him to turn it down. Maugham's biographer Selina Hastings concludes that 'The whole idea of being a spy appealed to him enormously. Long a master of disguise, happiest when he could remain under cover, Maugham had no difficulty with the prospect of playing a part.'[68]

Other theatrical recruits attracted to MI1c by Cumming's engagingly eccentric charisma included the American playwright, Edward Knoblauch, partly educated in Germany and famous for his 1911 London and Broadway hit, *Kismet*, later turned into a film starring Marlene Dietrich. Like many MI1c recruits, Knoblauch was spellbound by Mansfield Cumming.[69] 'We all loved him to a man', Knoblauch would recall.[70] He was deeply impressed by C's theatricality. Cumming told Knoblauch that, 'when interviewing job applicants he would sometimes take his sharp paper-knife and jab it to the hilt through his trousers, concluding, if the applicant winced, "Well, I'm afraid you won't do."[71] The hapless applicant would have been unaware that, following a car accident, Cumming had been fitted with an artificial lower leg. As MI1c (and, later, SIS) officers – unlike agents – had to be British citizens, in 1916 Knoblauch gave up American citizenship and became a British national, changing his name to Knoblock.[72] His first foreign posting was in Greece, where he seems to have found intelligence work even less scrupulous than he had expected. As he wrote later:

> In itself Secret Service is far from reputable. All the things one has been taught as a child as being the essentials of clean living are disregarded. Lying, deception, opening other people's letters, overhearing conversations on the telephone and worming secrets out of others by any methods available, are here the order of the day. No wonder if a spy is caught he is shot. He deserves it. For his code of honour is despicable – if honour can be mentioned in such connection. His motive alone saves him from being detested even by his own

Edward Knoblock, *c.*1918.

countrymen. As we were bound to secrecy, naturally I shall not go into the various methods we employed ...[73]

Somerset Maugham told Knoblock to expect much less 'lying, deception' and secret excitement once the war was over:

It seems incredible that one of these days we shall all settle down again in normal existence and read the fat, peaceful Times every morning and eat porridge for breakfast and marmalade. But, my dear, we shall be broken relics of a dead era, on the shelf all dusty and musty.[74]

Knoblock's head of station in Athens was another playwright, his friend Compton Mackenzie,[75] who had been born into one of Britain's leading theatrical families and travelled with their troupe of players, the Compton Comedy Company. On one memorable occasion he learned leading roles in *the Rivals* and *The School for Scandal* overnight in order to understudy for his indisposed father. His early writing included an unperformed stage adaptation of H. G. Wells' *Kipps* and a Sheridan pastiche, *The Gentleman in Grey*, which received favourable reviews on its opening in Edinburgh in 1907.[76]

Incapable of even trying to be inconspicuous, Mackenzie opted instead for theatrical display:

In a city of the size of Athens it would be impossible to achieve secrecy by the usual means of keeping oneself hidden or pretending to be something one was not. Such methods in Athens would be the methods of the ostrich who thinks himself hidden when he buries his own head. I made up my mind to create a focus of publicity, and under cover of that publicity hope to achieve a measure of secrecy.[77]

Mackenzie would travel around Athens in an ostentatious Sunbeam convertible, and ordered his classified code-letter Z to be mono-grammed on his office stationery – thus becoming arguably the least secret secret agent in the whole of Europe.

Cumming warmed to Mackenzie's unconventional reporting style, particularly when he started using blank verse. 'We like your poetical reports immensely', wrote C in February 1917. 'Please send us some more.'[78] Though, sadly, Mackenzie's poetical reports do not survive, the accounts of agent-running in his memoirs, *Greek Memories*, published and promptly banned in 1932,[79] are distinctly, and sometimes implausibly, theatrical. The first involves an agent codenamed CLARENCE, who calls Mackenzie 'Skipper' and is sent on a mission to Larissa to intercept German documents. Mackenzie recalls 'the deeply unctuous tones of his farewell':

> 'Skipper', he breathed hoarsely, 'if they get me, you'll send my old sergeant's uniform, the one I wore at La Bassde, to my old mother ...'
> 'I will, Clarence.'
> He wrung my hand and moved heavily towards the door. Then he came back.
> 'And, Skipper, you'll tell her I died game?'
> 'I will, Clarence.'

Once in Larissa, however, CLARENCE took fright and allegedly spent two days hiding in a lavatory until he was rescued.

Before Greece joined the Allies in June 1917, neutral Athens was a hotbed of espionage with spies from both sides competing against each other. Mackenzie seems to have had the better of the secret intelligence war with Germany. One of his key weapons was bribery. He telegraphed Cumming in June 1916:

> It will be necessary if our control of the [Greek] Police is to be actual as well as theoretical that a special grant ... be telegraphed enabling me at once to supplement the salaries of the new secret police otherwise they will be bought by the Germans or entirely run by the French ...[80]

In 1917, Mackenzie was promoted to Director of Aegean Intelligence, in charge of both espionage and counter-espionage for the entire Mediterranean, in which capacity he conspicuously navigated the Greek islands in a former royal yacht which he had commandeered, dressed in a bespoke white uniform and wielding a swordstick personally presented to him by Cumming. His Aegean Intelligence Service had a staff of thirty-nine officers, far bigger than any SIS station today. For a time, it was rumoured that Cumming had Mackenzie in mind as a possible successor.[81]

The MI1c recruit who most shared Mansfield Cumming's penchant for theatrical disguise and make-up was the talented musician Paul Dukes.[82] After leaving Caterham School, Dukes studied music at the

St Petersburg conservatoire, where he immediately 'felt at home'. He then embarked on a musical career as *répétiteur* at the Mariinsky Imperial Opera, which he left in 1916 to work first for the Anglo-Russian Commission, then for the Foreign Office, to report on conditions in post-revolutionary Russia. For the first six months of 1918 Dukes 'roamed all over Russia', from Samara, where he worked briefly for the YMCA, to the Siberian border, where he was employed for a time by the Boy Scout organisation. Everywhere he found 'a state of indescribable confusion'.[83]

The confusion extended to the first Communist security and intelligence agency, the All-Russian Extraordinary Commission for Combating Counter-Revolution and Sabotage, better known by the Russian abbreviation 'Cheka', founded only six weeks after the Bolshevik Revolution. With its headquarters in Moscow, to which the Bolsheviks moved the capital, the Cheka quickly made clear its distrust of performing arts inherited from the Tsarist regime. Its first victims included Russia's most famous clowns, Bim (Ivan Radunsky, director of Moscow's Salamonsky Circus) and Bom (Polish-born Mechislav Stanevsky, proprietor of the popular artistic café Бом), who performed as the duo Bim-Bom and dared to make fun of the Bolshevik regime. Chekists, who attended a performance at the Salamonsky Circus on 27 March 1918, were outraged by a sketch in which Bim

Bim (Ivan Radunsky, *right*) and Bom (Mechislav Stanevsky).

brandished portraits of Lenin and Trotsky. On being asked by Bom what he was planning to do with them, Bim replied, 'I'll hang one, and put the other up against the wall.' The outraged Chekists leapt into the ring to halt the performance. The audience initially assumed that this was part of the act, but when the clown duo tried to escape and the Chekists began to fire their handguns in the air, the crowd panicked.[84] Next day Bim-Bom were interrogated by the Cheka but seem to have escaped with a warning.[85]

In May 1918 the beginning of civil war between the Bolshevik regime and counter-revolutionary White armies, which had some Western support, made Cumming acutely aware of his lack of Russian intelligence. About two months later, he summoned Paul Dukes to his top-floor office in Whitehall Court (now part of the Royal Horseguards Hotel). Dukes found Cumming seated behind a desk cluttered with six telephones, assorted model aeroplanes and sub-marines, a series of test tubes and a row of coloured bottles. Though initially disoriented by the 'overpowering sense of strangeness and mystery', Dukes agreed to work for MI1c in Russia, and soon formed a deep admiration for Cumming:

'The Chief' was a British officer and English gentleman of the very finest stamp, fearless, gifted with limitless resources of subtle ingenuity, and I counted it one of the great privileges of my life to have been brought within the circle of his acquaintance.[86]

Dukes shared Cumming's passion for disguise, later giving this enthusiastic description of himself as a bedraggled Karelian from the Finnish frontier region:

My outfit consisted of a Russian shirt, black leather breeches, black knee boots, a shabby tunic, an old leather cap with a fur brim and a little tassel on top, of the style worn by the Finns in the district North of Petrograd. With my shaggy black beard, which was by now quite profuse, and long unkempt hair dangling over my ears I looked a sight indeed, and in England or America should doubtless have been regarded as a thoroughly undesirable alien![87]

Dukes later claimed that, during his first ten months in MI1c, code-named ST25, he used at least twenty different given names and twelve

Paul Dukes in various disguises, from the first edition of his book *Red Dusk and the Morrow* (1922).

different surnames, as well as a variety of forged documents. At different times, under various aliases, he succeeded in joining the Red Army, the Communist Party and the Cheka.[88]

Penetrating the Cheka was an extraordinary achievement, made possible both by Dukes' ingenuity and by the Cheka's early disorganisation. So far as is known, no subsequent British intelligence officer ever succeeded in joining Soviet intelligence. Dukes was able to witness at first hand the Cheka's brutal campaign against 'counter-revolution', which was essential to the survival of the Bolshevik regime, 'The terror and the Cheka', Lenin declared, 'are absolutely indispensable.'[89] During the Civil War of 1918–20, Cheka executions may well have exceeded the number of deaths in battle.[90]

Many of Dukes's intelligence reports, which no longer survive even in the inaccessible archives of the Secret Intelligence Service (as MI1c was renamed in 1919), were smuggled by secret couriers out of Russia with the help of a special naval unit headed by Captain Augustus

Agar. Dukes's colourful later accounts of his operations blur the boundaries between fact and romantic fiction:

> I lay full length, my head at the open end of the tomb, recalling the events of the day. I was happy. Klachonka was safe – that she would get off I never doubted. Peter, brave Peter, was at that very moment hidden in the reeds waiting in his skiff, munching the sandwiches Klachonka had prepared, and pulling at his little whisky flask. Sonia, poor Sonia, was still in prison, but with faith – and ingenuity – surely a way would be found? And who, I ask you, could have been gifted with greater ingenuity than my dear friends, who were far more to me than mere collaborators or conspirators? I pondered and wondered much, while the long light hours of the evening faded imperceptibly into a sweet and gentle dusk. I thought no more of the gruesome bones of Michael Semashko outstretched a foot or two beneath me.[91]

*

Morale was high in the British intelligence agencies after victory over Germany. On Armistice Day 1918 GHQ Intelligence in France produced its final 'Order of Battle' report showing the location of the 186 enemy divisions on the Western Front. Only two were shown in the wrong position.[92] MI5, which believed it had protected the Home Front by mopping up the entire German espionage network in Britain, celebrated with the revue *Hush-Hush*, a 'Sententious Stunt' performed by The Barmy Breezies (all from MI5).

The opening sketch featuring Captain Fond O'Fluff and Miss Dickie Bird continued the flirtatious theme of the invitation. Since during the First World War MI5 had recruited several officers from the entertainment business,[93] as well as a number of notable amateur performers, it is perhaps not surprising that its staff wrote and staged an extraordinary theatrical event of their own.

Performed 'for the first and last time' on 24 March 1919 at the Cripplegate Institute in Barbican's Golden Lane, *Hush-Hush* was an evening of song, dance and comedy which wittily, and sometimes mercilessly, parodied the work of MI5 and its contribution to the war effort.[94] The list of writers and performers is testament to the fact that, despite their subordinate positions, women played a more important role in the Security Service than in any other wartime

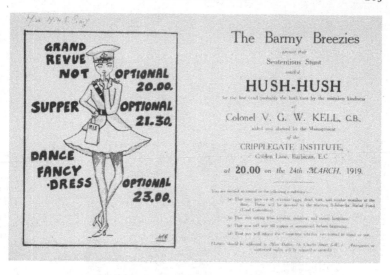

government department – the result of a recruitment strategy which had encouraged candidates for clerical roles from, among others, Oxford's women's colleges, Royal Holloway College (then all female) and Cheltenham Ladies' College. Uniquely in wartime Britain, a minority of MI5's female staff were better educated, and sometimes from higher up the social scale, than a majority of their male superiors.[95]

Amongst the (mostly female) writers of *Hush-Hush* credited in the programme is 'Miss Erskine Hill'. Evelyn Erskine-Hill, who later (as Evelyn Forbes) became beauty editor of *Vogue* magazine, was the superintendent of the numerous Girl Guides who did office duties for MI5 during the war. Mostly aged 14 to 16, they were paid ten shillings a week to fill inkpots and carry messages from floor to floor.[96] As Erskine-Hill later described her work,

> I had the chance of going to Oxford but refused it. Instead, through the influence of an MI5 Colonel I had met on holiday, I gave my age as 21 instead of the true 17, and got into MI5. At MI5 I 'potted' files in the Registry Office, listened at length to my Colonel friend's poems, helped to write the words of a comic opera which MI5 performed, and was in charge of the army of Guide Messengers, engaging, employing them, looking after them and finding them jobs when they left.[97]

Jane Sissmore, *Hush-Hush*'s 'Miss Glibb', after qualifying as a barrister in 1924.

Hush-Hush's numerous female performers included Jane Sissmore playing the role of 'Miss Glibb'. Recruited as an 18-year-old clerk straight from school in 1916, Sissmore would rise rapidly through the ranks to become controller of women staff and eventually MI5's first woman officer. Gaining a degree in law, qualifying as a barrister and awarded the MBE, from 1929 Sissmore would be responsible for Soviet intelligence, also gaining a reputation as a formidable interrogator.[98] Her career is a far cry from the popular myths about female intelligence personnel generated by the Mata Hari case.

MI5's Charles II Street Headquarters were located opposite His Majesty's Theatre on The Haymarket, where the hugely successful musical comedy *Chu Chin Chow* had opened in August 1916. Written by and starring actor-manager Oscar Asche, *Chu Chin Chow* capitalised on the success of SIS officer Edward Knoblock's *Kismet*, another *Arabian Nights* adaptation which Ashe had also produced. *Chu Chin Chow* was a big-budget spectacular and a particular favourite with soldiers on leave. It was particularly notorious for its chorus of scantily clad slave girls;[99] a complaint (not from a soldier) of 'near nudity and non-controlled breast movement' led to an investigation by the Lord Chamberlain's office and an official reprimand to the theatre manager.[100] *Chu Chin Chow* would go on to become London's longest-running musical, playing for five years and 2,238 performances – a record it would hold for almost forty years.[101] Helen Johnson, a member of the MI5 Registry staff, later recalled that MI5 officers' windows 'looked directly into the chorus girls' changing rooms',[102] and there can be no doubt that the staging of the *Hush-Hush* revue was inspired by the success of MI5's cheeky theatrical neighbours; the invitation card shows a female secretary dressed in a male officer's tunic and cap, with a very short skirt and high heels. As a private performance, there was no requirement for the script to be submitted to the Lord Chamberlain, and the writers made the most of the opportunity to poke fun at their superiors.

A bound Vernon Kell portrayed on the cover of the *Hush-Hush* programme.

Wigs for *Hush-Hush*, like those for *Chu Chin Chow*, were supplied by Mansfield Cumming's theatrical costumier of choice, Willy Clarkson, whose Wardour Street emporium was only a five-minute walk from the MI5 offices.[103] By all accounts, the revue was a huge success – the first in a still continuing tradition of occasional in-house entertainments by MI5 staff. Vernon Kell, who was portrayed in a cartoon on the programme cover being tied up and dragged away for questioning, enjoyed the revue; his wife remarked that he

> was very convincingly caricatured and was delighted with the thrusts at him, for they had got him walking with his familiar stoop and with all his tricks of manner. The show was followed by a really good dance, and the whole thing was voted a great success.[104]

The contrast with Cheka officers firing pistols as they chased the clown duo, Bim-Bom, from the circus ring in Moscow could scarcely have been greater.

In the summer of 1919 both Kell and Cumming were awarded knighthoods. Because SIS and its chief were official secrets, Cumming was knighted by King George V at a private ceremony on 29 July in the inner quadrangle of Buckingham Palace.[105] A little later, Dukes's extraordinary adventures as an SIS officer in Russia came to a dramatic end. By August 1919, he was being hunted by the Cheka and, after the failure of a naval rescue mission by Agar, he was forced to make his own escape across the Latvian border. On 18 September Cumming took him to see Winston Churchill, then secretary for war, who gave Dukes a 'long interview over 1½ hours'. Two days later, C accompanied Dukes to a meeting with Lord Curzon, the foreign secretary, at his private residence, 1 Carlton House Terrace.[106]

Dukes's greatest admirer was George V, who summoned him with Agar to Buckingham Palace. The king told Dukes that the spy was the greatest of all soldiers; the enemy detested spies only because he feared them so much. He regretted that, as a civilian, Dukes was not eligible for the Victoria Cross but told him that he would be awarded a knighthood in the 1920 New Year Honours List. George V personally presented Agar with the Victoria Cross. A celebration dinner for the two men followed at the Savoy Hotel with Cumming and his 'top-mates'.[107]

To Cumming's dismay, however, after the award of his KBE in 1920, Sir Paul Dukes became what the official history of the Secret Intelligence Service terms 'an enthusiastic self-publicist'.[108] The existence of SIS was not officially acknowledged until 1992 – past as well as present members were forbidden to mention it. Dukes, however, grandly referred to himself in print as 'Former Chief of the British Secret Intelligence Service in Soviet Russia'.[109] Fortunately for SIS, after moving to the United States, Dukes found quite different interests. Probably in 1922, he joined a tantric community at Nyack, fifteen miles from New York, led by the controversial Dr Pierre Arnold Bernard, known to his devotees as the 'Omnipotent Oom'.[110] Dukes now became a yoga guru.[111] An introduction to his papers in the Hoover Institution begins:

When setting off for your yoga class, take a moment to think about Sir Paul Dukes, British journalist, author, and master of espionage and disguise. Credited for helping introduce yoga to the West ...[112]

Sir Paul Dukes demonstrates yoga positions.

Between the Wars: From Tallulah Bankhead to Secret Agent Ronald Reagan

After the euphoria of its *Hush-Hush* revue and victory in the First World War, MI5 had to fight for its survival, resisting both a takeover bid by SIS and claims that it was no longer needed in peacetime. The main responsibility for monitoring the 'Red Menace' – the alleged subversive threat of pro-Soviet communism – was given not to Sir Vernon Kell but to his rival, Sir Basil Thomson; by 1925, MI5 had only thirty-five staff. Nevertheless, on Kell's instructions, one of its few new recruits, Herbert 'Con' Boddington, succeeded in infiltrating the Communist Party in 1923. On joining MI5 in 1922, despite being wounded in the war, Boddington had listed as his recreations, 'All outdoor games. Principally boxing, rowing and running.' He added: 'Can act. Have played light comedian [*sic*] both at home and abroad.' Boddington's 'literary experience' included writing scripts for silent films. His acting and screenwriting experience was probably of more assistance than outdoor games-playing in passing himself off as a communist.[1] Not until 1931, however, after the discovery of Soviet penetration of the Special Branch at Scotland Yard, was MI5 put in charge of counter-subversion.[2]

Though MI5 had no formal responsibility for doing so during the 1920s, it was asked by the Home Office to investigate the greatest female star of the London stage, Tallulah Bankhead. After arriving from the United States as a 21-year-old in 1923, Tallulah quickly became the West End's most popular actress, instantly recognisable by her husky 'Hello Dahling'. She was beautiful, vivacious, witty and voluble. Her friend Fred Keating once said, 'I've just spent an hour talking to

Tallulah for a few minutes.' In 1928, probably on the initiative of William Joynson-Hicks ('Jix'), the most puritanical home secretary of the twentieth century, who waged a personal crusade against all forms of 'indecency', MI5 was instructed to investigate scandalous rumours that she was seducing boys from Eton College.

The case was politically sensitive. Bankhead came from what was probably Alabama's leading political dynasty. Her paternal grandfather and one of his sons were senators. His other son – Tallulah's father – was a long-serving member, and later Speaker, of the US House of Representatives. MI5 was wrongly told by an unnamed informant that her father had 'turned her out of the house when she was young owing to immoral proclivities'.[3] It seems more likely that, as Tallulah's autobiography claims, her grandfather paid for her to go to New York, aged only 15, with an aunt as ineffectual chaperone, to try to make a career on Broadway: 'Let her go on the stage. She's not worth a damn for anything but acting.' By the time she made her Broadway debut at the age of 17, she was introducing herself at parties in her suite at the Algonquin Hotel by saying, 'I'm a Lesbian. What do you do?' Her father had warned her to avoid men and alcohol. But, according to Tallulah, 'He didn't say anything about women and cocaine.'[4]

In London theatreland Tallulah was notoriously 'ambisextrous' – her self-description – with numerous affairs with both men and women. In 1927 an Old Etonian lover, Tony Wilson, took her to Eton to meet his younger brother and take him and several friends to lunch in a nearby hotel. MI5 reported to Jix in 1928:

> The charge against Miss Tallulah Bankhead (an American aged 26) is quite simply (a) that she is an extremely immoral woman and (b) that in consequence of her association with some Eton boys last term, the latter have had to leave Eton.
>
> As regards (a) according to informant, she is both a Lesbian and immoral with men …
>
> It is also said she 'kept' a negress in America before she came to the country in 1925 and she 'keeps' a girl in London now. As regards her more natural proclivities, informant tells me that she bestows her favours 'generously' without payment. Informant added that her 'circle' is a centre of vice patronised by at least one of the most prominent sodomites in London.

TB was seen at Eton frequently last term. I hear from another master that one or both of Sir M Wilson's older sons used to motor down with her to see the third son who was then smuggled away for the afternoon under a rug in the car. It is said this was the start of a T[allulah] B[ankhead] Eton boys' clique.

It was impossible, however, to take any official action against Tallulah. 'The headmaster', reported MI5, 'is obviously not prepared to assist the Home Office – he wants to do everything possible to keep Eton out of the scandal.'[5]

Though some of the rumours provoked by Tallulah's rendezvous with Eton pupils were wildly exaggerated, Jix was not the only senior member of the Stanley Baldwin government who suspected Eton's headmaster, Cyril Alington, of a cover-up. The Special Branch was ordered to make further investigations and the most devoted Old Etonian in the cabinet, William Bridgeman, First Lord of the Admiralty and a close friend of Baldwin, was sent to see Alington, a firm disciplinarian who had reintroduced birching after it had been dropped by his predecessor. Bridgeman had briefly taught at Eton; each of his three sons had succeeded him as Captain of the Oppidans (the majority of pupils, who lived in houses outside the College); and he was to be elected an Eton Fellow in 1929.[6] The headmaster, however, was unforthcoming, preoccupied by his determination to avoid public scandal. Miss Bankhead, he said, had paid one visit to the school but had been asked not to return. Alington claimed that no boys had been expelled, though several parents had been asked to withdraw their sons for what he described as motoring offences.[7]

Jix's hopes of finding evidence to expel Tallulah from Britain were dashed. In 1931, however, she returned to the United States, where she received the highest salaries paid on Broadway, in Las Vegas, on the road and on radio.[8] MI5 opened no file on her because they did not assess Tallulah as a security risk.[9]

*

Others who left Eton during Alington's headship as the result of sexual scandal included Ian Fleming, who – like several boys whose parents withdrew them in the wake of the Tallulah Bankhead affair – was also accused of motoring offences. The two things tended to go

Tallulah Bankhead, *c.* 1931.

together since cars were often required to take pupils to forbidden rendezvous. Expulsion was avoided in Fleming's case when his mother agreed to remove him voluntarily in 1925 at the age of 17 and enrol him as a cadet at Sandhurst.[10] He departed prematurely from Sandhurst too, after contracting gonorrhoea from a Soho prostitute. Unlike Fleming, his fictional hero, James Bond, was formally expelled from Eton after a sexual liaison with one of the College maids.[11]

The greater part of Bond, who first appeared in print almost thirty years after Fleming's ignominious departure from Eton, came from his creator's imagination. Fleming, however, was also influenced by a handful of individuals with intelligence connections whom he knew or greatly admired. The first was probably T. E. Lawrence,[12] later immortalised in the 1962 film *Lawrence of Arabia*, directed by David Lean with Peter O'Toole in the title role, which won seven Oscars.[13]

Lawrence is now best remembered as a brilliant practitioner of guerrilla warfare. Having gained the trust of Arab nationalists who were seeking freedom from Turkish rule, he became military adviser and trusted confidant of Prince Faisal, son of the leader of the Arab Revolt, Hussein Ibn Ali, Sharif of Mecca, who was an important British ally of convenience. The surprise attack by Lawrence and his Arab allies which took the Red Sea port of Aqaba from the Turks in 1917 allowed Faisal's forces to move north and attack the Turks with British logistical support.

Less well known is the fact that Lawrence was also one of the most brilliantly innovative intelligence officers of the First World War, a pioneer in the use of both SIGINT and aerial photography. Helped by clear skies and the absence of enemy aircraft, overhead reconnaissance was far more effective in the Middle East than on the Western Front. The Arab Bureau in Cairo, of which Lawrence was a member, also contained the war's best intelligence analysts. Its regular *Arab Bulletins*, based on an understanding of the Arab past as well as present, were the most readable as well as the most scholarly intelligence reports of the First World War.[14]

Winston Churchill, then secretary of state for war, wrote of T. E. Lawrence's appearance at the 1919 Paris peace conference:

> He wore his Arab robes, and the full magnificence of his countenance revealed itself. The gravity of his demeanour; the precision of his opinions; the range and quality of his conversation; all seemed enhanced to a remarkable degree by the splendid Arab head-dress and garb. From amid the flowing draperies his noble features, his perfectly-chiseled lips and flashing eyes loaded with fire and comprehension shone forth. He looked what he was, one of Nature's greatest princes.[15]

Lawrence became a media superstar long before Peter O'Toole's legendary portrayal of him on screen. It was the American journalist Lowell Thomas – a showman as well as a newsman – who first captured the public imagination with the heroic image of 'Lawrence of Arabia' at the end of the First World War. Accompanied by his photographer Harry Chase, Thomas arrived in the Middle East early in 1918. There, with the help of the War Office, they covered the campaigns of General Edmund Allenby, commander of the British forces in Palestine, including the Allied capture of Jericho on 21 February. They were then introduced to Lawrence, who invited them to Aqaba to observe his work with the Arabs.

Lawrence (*left*) with Lowell Thomas.

Though Thomas and Chase stayed with Lawrence for only a few days and saw no actual combat, they obtained sufficient film footage, photographs and interview material (mostly from third parties) to construct an extraordinary multimedia entertainment entitled *The Last of the Crusaders: With Allenby in Palestine and Lawrence in Arabia*, which Thomas masterminded after the war with enormous success, playing to capacity audiences on both sides of the Atlantic, including sold-out seasons in 1919 at the Royal Albert Hall and the Royal Opera House, Covent Garden.

The two-hour performance featured special lighting effects, 240 lantern slides, three film projectors and thirty film segments. Audiences witnessed for the first time aerial photographs and film footage of archaeological sites in the Middle East, including the pyramids in Egypt and parts of Arabia previously forbidden to non-Muslims. Thomas augmented his presentation with slides provided by the National Geographic Society in Washington and others borrowed from the War Office in London. It also featured painted scenery, dancers, singers and musicians, and opened with a live performance of the 'Dance of the Seven Veils' – in a less revealing interpretation than that made famous by Mata Hari.[16] Audiences whose appetite for theatrical Arabian exoticism had been whetted by *Kismet* and *Chu Chin Chow* were not disappointed. In one heroic scene during the capture of Aqaba, Lawrence's camel is shot from under him. Audiences were not told that, in reality, Lawrence accidentally shot the camel through the head.[17]

Thomas, wrote Lawrence, 'seems to have realised my "star" quality on the film'.[18] Some of Chase's pictures of Lawrence were posed photographs taken after his return to London. The small number actually shot on location in the Middle East included an iconic picture of the robed Lawrence on the balcony of Fast's Hotel in Jerusalem. His adoption of local costume, effectively a form of role play and a key factor in his assimilation into Arab culture, also enhanced his romantic appeal to Lowell Thomas's audiences. Although Lawrence professed to be embarrassed by the publicity generated by Thomas, he regularly attended the shows and cooperated fully with Thomas's requests for additional material. His celebrity contributed to his influence at the Foreign Office, and subsequently as an advisor to Winston Churchill at the Colonial Office in 1921–2.[19]

Among Lawrence's admirers was Britain's most formidable intelligence adversary of the time, Michael Collins, director of intelligence as well as president of the Irish Republican Brotherhood (IRB) during the Irish War of Independence (1919–21).[20] In the long line of Irish rebels, Collins was the first effective revolutionary. His strategy was twofold: to reduce Ireland to 'a general state of disorder' and to 'put out the eyes of the British', thus making it impossible for them to counter the disruption. Irish history, Collins maintained, had shown that 'Without her spies England was helpless.' At 9 a.m. on 'Bloody Sunday', 21 November 1920, at seven different locations in Dublin, Collins' 'squad' assassinated twelve British officers, most of whom were involved in undercover intelligence operations. 'It's to be done exactly at nine', Collins had insisted, 'neither before nor after. These "hoors", the British, have got to learn that Irishmen can turn up on time.'[21]

No Irish revolutionary had ever been a more passionate theatregoer than Collins, who was also an amateur actor in productions of the Gaelic League. George Bernard Shaw's 1897 play on the early career of Napoleon, *Man of Destiny*, made such a deep impression on the young Collins that he copied an extract from it to keep in his wallet.

Even during the War of Independence, he continued – at some personal risk – to attend the Dublin theatre. One evening, while he was watching a play at the Abbey, the theatre was surrounded by British Auxiliaries. An usherette led Collins to safety out of the backstage door. After the Auxiliaries had left, he is said to have slipped back into the Abbey to watch the rest of the play. Returning to London in 1921 as part of the Irish delegation to negotiate a peace settlement, Collins made straight for the Royal Court to see a production of Shaw's *Heartbreak House*.[22] Given his passion for the theatre, Collins would have been aware of the extraordinary success on both sides of the Atlantic of *The Last of the Crusaders*, which highlighted Lawrence's mastery of guerrilla warfare.

In a private letter to one of his most frequent correspondents, Shaw's wife Charlotte, Lawrence would later claim that he had met Collins during the treaty negotiations with the British government late in 1921 and 'tried to give him confidence that might be wanted' to agree to Lloyd George's terms for the establishment of the Irish Free State.[23] The meeting, however, never took place. Lawrence was away from London at the crucial moment of the negotiations.[24] One recent biographer, Lawrence James, concludes:

> Lawrence's ornamentation of the truth was the exercise of artistic licence. He perplexed rather than deceived and, as his distant kinsman, Lord Vansittart, commented, he may have been a 'show-off', but 'he had something to show'.[25]

After the founding of the Free State in January 1922, Collins was both chairman and charismatic figurehead of the transitional provisional government. When civil war with opponents of the treaty broke out in June, Collins became commander-in-chief of government forces. Whether, as has been suggested, he wanted Lawrence to become adviser to the Free State army will probably never be known. There is no record of Lawrence receiving such an invitation, which he would have been unlikely to accept, before Collins was killed in an ambush by republican extremists in August.

In the same month Lawrence enlisted in the RAF under the alias John Hume Ross. Seeking anonymity, he would spend the rest of his life under various pseudonyms in subordinate roles in the air force, save for two years in the Royal Tank Corps. Lawrence, however,

Photograph by Harry Chase, pur-
portedly showing T. E. Lawrence in
disguise as a Syrian gypsy woman.

continued to write and to correspond with others about his career.
His desire both to celebrate his achievements in print and to repudiate
the fame they generated remains perplexing.[26]

The first significant book about Lawrence after he had left public
life was *With Lawrence in Arabia*, published in 1924 by Lowell Thomas
with photographs by Harry Chase. In the first edition one image was
captioned: 'Lawrence occasionally visited enemy territory disguised
as a gypsy woman of Syria.'[27] Whilst the caption makes no explicit
claim that the picture of a masked figure in female dress is in fact
Lawrence himself, the inference is clear. It is also misleading. Thomas's
original list of glass plate negatives reveals that the picture in question
actually comes from a group of photographs taken by Chase of
Palestinian women and children. In the inventory the print is simply
titled 'Heavily veiled woman'.[28] Lawrence, however, later revealed to
his biographer Robert Graves that, on one – and only one – occasion,
he was 'disguised ... [as] a woman, when I went to Amman with
Farraj [an Arab friend and servant] and some gipsies' in 1917.[29]

In 1926 Lawrence published, in a limited edition for subscribers, his
own account of his role in the Arab Revolt, *Seven Pillars of Wisdom*,
reissued to the public a year later in an abridged edition entitled *Revolt
in the Desert*. *Seven Pillars of Wisdom* had benefited from the considerable editorial input of Lawrence's close friend and mentor George
Bernard Shaw; 'T. E. Shaw' was one of a number of assumed names
adopted by Lawrence in order to conceal his identity after the war.

But, as Shaw wrote in 1937, two years after Lawrence's death, it was to no avail:

> The limelight of history follows the authentic hero as the theatre limelight follows the *prima ballerina assoluta*. It soon concentrated its whitest radiance on Colonel Lawrence ... the mystery man, the wonder man, the man ... who did, when all the lies and all the legends are subtracted, authentically and unquestionably and in his own way and largely with his own hands explode and smash the Turkish dominion in Arabia ... When he was in the middle of the stage with ten lime-lights blazing on him, everybody pointed to him and said: 'See! He is in hiding. He hates publicity.' He was so conspicuous that he was bothered by it and really did make some half-hearted efforts to hide himself; but it was no use: he was the most impish of comedians, and always did something that turned up the lights again.[30]

In 1933 Shaw became the first playwright to put the character of Lawrence on the stage, thinly disguised as Private Napoleon Alexander Trotsky Meek in his play *Too True to be Good*.

The following year, director Alexander Korda secured the film rights for *Seven Pillars of Wisdom* from the author, on condition that 'there would be no departure from historical accuracy' and 'no female char-acters' in the resulting film;[31] Leslie Howard was engaged to play the lead. The project was abandoned when Lawrence suddenly stipulated that no film should be made until after his death. It was revived following his fatal motorbike accident in 1935 and Winston Churchill was engaged by Korda as a script consultant. Despite a positive, detailed report by Churchill, the project was again abandoned on the outbreak of the Second World War.[32]

*

The two most successful playwrights and writers recruited by Mansfield Cumming as wartime heads of station, Somerset Maugham and Compton Mackenzie, both published works of fiction in 1928 which were inspired by their foreign intelligence work in MI1c. Much of Maugham's mission to Petrograd in 1917 reappeared, thinly disguised, in his short story collection *Ashenden: Or, The British Agent*. Ashenden uses Maugham's own codename 'Somerville' and has the same London

address in Chesterfield Street, Mayfair. The British ambassador in Petrograd, Sir George Buchanan, whose welcome to Maugham 'could not have been more frigid', reappears as Sir Herbert Witherspoon, who receives Ashenden 'with a frigidity that would have sent a little shiver down the spine of a polar bear'. David R. Francis, the American ambassador, a political appointee whom Maugham found 'something of a roughneck',[33] is the model for Wilbur Schäfer, whose mobile face looked to Ashenden 'as though it were made out of the red india-rubber from which they make hot-water bottles'. Maugham's former lover, Sasha Kropotkin, hostess at his frequent meetings with Kerensky, is portrayed as Anastasia Alexandrovna, in whose 'dark melancholy eyes Ashenden saw the boundless steppes of Russia, and the Kremlin with its pealing bells, and the solemn ceremonies of Easter at St Isaac's, and forests of silver birches, and the Nevsky Prospekt ... '[34]

On Churchill's advice, Maugham is alleged to have destroyed several Ashenden stories which were more significant breaches of the Official Secrets Act. Maugham, John le Carré has noted, was 'the first person to write about espionage in a mood of disenchantment and almost

prosaic reality'. Even Giulia Lazzari, an exotic dancer in one of the
Ashenden stories working as an undercover agent, who is clearly
inspired by Mata Hari, finds her career rather tedious: 'It is not very
gay, the life one leads in these music halls, all over Europe, never resting
... and men – they are not much, the men who haunt those places.'[35]

Compton Mackenzie's 1928 novel, *Extremes Meet*, published at the
same time as the Ashenden stories, concerns the exploits of a wartime
intelligence officer in a neutral Balkan state. His protagonist, Waterlow,
is in the habit of codenaming his agents after famous English poets, as
Mackenzie himself had done. Mackenzie followed *Extremes Meet* with
two memoirs of his wartime espionage career: *Athenian Memories* (1931)
and the far more indiscreet *Greek Memories* (1932),[36] which led to his
conviction under the Official Secrets Act at the Old Bailey, a trial which
he later described in his autobiography as a 'self-indulgent harlequinade'.
As one study of 'spyography' observes, the term was carefully chosen:

A harlequinade is a theatrical genre featuring masked characters
involved in a comical conspiracy that spirals into a slapstick chase scene.

Significantly, a harlequinade is also a mime act, and its silence – or
speechlessness – therefore makes it an appropriate *genre* to characterise
a case involving government secrets.[37]

Among Mackenzie's alleged breaches of the Official Secrets Act was
revealing the identity of the first chief of SIS, Sir Mansfield Cumming.
When Mackenzie was first stationed in Athens, even he did not know
Cumming's identity and was told to refer to the chief simply as 'C'.
Mackenzie's first clue to C's identity came when the naval attaché in
Athens, Commander William Sells, describes him as a 'funny old boy
with a wooden leg'. Sells then discovers C's real name and tells
Mackenzie that the wooden leg was the result of a car accident in
France early in the War. Cumming's leg had been trapped beneath the
car but, hearing the moans of his dying son who was travelling with
him, he had hacked off the leg with a penknife so that he could crawl
over to him. 'That's the sort of old chap C is', said Sells.[38]

As this account reveals, Mackenzie seems to enjoy adding to the
entertainment value of his memoirs by including unreliably colourful
detail. The basis of most of his stories, however, is probably authentic.
Cumming really did lose the lower part of one leg as the result of a
car accident in which his son was killed, though it is unlikely that C
performed the amputation himself.

The alarm of Cumming's successor, Admiral Sir Hugh Sinclair, at
the publication of *Greek Memories* in 1932 had some rational foundation. As well as publishing top-secret SIS telegrams on such sensitive
subjects as the proposed bribery of the Greek police, Mackenzie had
identified a number of SIS agents and officers, and revealed some of
the covers still used by SIS between the wars. Other claims that
Mackenzie had compromised national security, for example by identifying Cumming, were absurd. During Mackenzie's trial at the Old
Bailey in 1933, the judge asked the attorney general, who led the
prosecution, how recently Cumming had died. The attorney general
did not know; neither did the defence. Mackenzie then told the court
that Cumming had died in 1923.

Mackenzie was persuaded by his counsel to plead guilty, and was
fined £100 with £100 costs. He took a satirical revenge. To pay his
own much more substantial costs, he wrote *Water on the Brain*, a comic
novel about British intelligence set in the Directorate of Extraordinary
Intelligence, known as M.Q.99 (E), mocking an obsession with secrecy

which oscillates between farce and paranoia. Cumming is satirised as N, and Vernon Kell as P. SIS's HQ eventually becomes 'an asylum for the servants of bureaucracy who have been driven mad in the service of the country'.

Mackenzie's MI5 file reveals that he continued to plan further vengeance for at least a decade. In 1942 he told an MI5 informant of his plan to become a whistle-blower and 'blow the roof off' MI5 and SIS. As the informant reported to MI5: 'Mackenzie was fortunately so under the influence of liquor during the conversation that it was able to proceed without any prompting or expression of opinion on my part.' Mackenzie was also later overheard by an agent at a cocktail party declaring 'very emphatically' that 'the IRA were doing exactly the right thing in perpetrating their various outrages, and they should continue to do so until they won their demands'.[39]

Mackenzie continued to dabble in playwriting, but, like Maugham, moved away from his theatrical origins to concentrate on his career as a novelist. He did, however, successfully write his own screenplay for the 1949 film of his novel *Whisky Galore*, and could not resist casting himself in the small role of Captain Buncher. In 1966 he would present five episodes of the children's television programme *Jackanory*, reading, appropriately, stories based on Greek myths.

*

The rise of the talkies in the early 1930s created a new generation of screen stars. The decade would witness a proliferation of films inspired by far less controversial tales of wartime espionage than Mackenzie's, romanticising the role of the undercover agent. In 1931 Greta Garbo immortalised Mata Hari on screen in her biggest box-office success: an erotic re-telling of her story (now available only in a censored version) that would further blur the boundaries between fiction and reality.[40]

Earlier the same year, rival screen siren Marlene Dietrich had starred as 'Marie Kolverer', a character also based on Mata Hari, in Josef von Sternberg's *Dishonored*.

In 1933 Madeleine Carroll joined the growing list of glamorous screen spies, playing the role of Marthe McKenna in the film of McKenna's autobiography, *I Was a Spy*, which recounted her undercover wartime exploits in occupied Belgium. McKenna (née Cnockaert),

spied on the Germans for almost two years from early 1915, using her position as a nurse in a military hospital to gain their trust while passing on information to the British. She was awarded the Iron Cross by the Germans for her nursing work during the war, and subsequently became a member of both the French and Belgian Legions of Honour in recognition of her espionage activities.[41]

I Was a Spy told of harrowing missions and narrow escapes, some in the dubious tradition of Charlotte Atkyns, Belle Boyd and Pauline Cushman. Though parts of Marthe McKenna's account were invented (probably by her British husband and literary collaborator, John 'Jock' McKenna),[42] the story captivated readers – among them Winston Churchill, who wrote in an introduction to her book:

> I believe it to be unquestionably true that the British Secret Service before and during the Great War was more skilfully organised, more daringly pursued and achieved more important results than that of any other country, friend or foe. Marthe McKenna, the heroine of this account, fulfilled in every respect the conditions which make the terrible profession of a spy dignified and honourable ... Her tale is a thrilling one. Having begun it, I could not put out my light till four o'clock in

the morning. I cannot, of course, vouch for the accuracy of every incident; but the main description of her life, intrigues and adventures is undoubtedly authentic.[43]

The rivalry between Greta Garbo, Marlene Dietrich and Madeleine Carroll, among others, for the accolade of most glamorous screen spy was both celebrated and satirised in R. P. Weston and Bert Lee's popular 1935 song, 'Olga Pulloffski, the Beautiful Spy'. Recorded the same year by legendary bandleader, Henry Hall, it rejoiced in the refrain:

> Olga Pulloffski, the beautiful spy!
> The gay continental rapscallion!
> Some say she's Russian and some say she's French
> But her accent is gin and Italian.
> Shame on you! Shame on you! Oh fie fie!
> Olga Pulloffski you beautiful spy![44]

The image of the 'gay continental rapscallion' was a far cry from the tragic end to Mata Hari's life as a spy or the unglamorous pioneering work of MI5's Soviet expert, Jane Sissmore.

MI5's most successful inter-war agent-recruiter Maxwell Knight, later the BBC's first naturalist and a popular broadcaster,[45] was 'no believer in Mata Hari methods':

It is difficult to imagine anything more terrifying than for an [MI5] officer to become landed with a woman agent who suffers from an overdose of sex. What is required is a clever woman who can use her personal attractions wisely. Nothing is easier than for a woman to gain a man's confidence by the showing and expression of a little sympathy ... I am convinced that more information has been obtained by women agents by keeping out of the arms of the man, than was ever obtained by too willingly sinking into them.[46]

A majority of Knight's most successful agents were 'clever women'. Among them was Olga Gray, who gained a job in British Communist Party HQ, working for a time as personal secretary to the general secretary, Harry Pollitt. In 1937 Gray's intelligence led to the detection of a Soviet spy ring in the Woolwich Arsenal. Gray, wrote Knight, 'had attained that very enviable position where an agent becomes a piece of furniture, so to speak: that is, when persons visiting an office do not consciously notice whether the agent is there or not'.[47]

Hollywood, however, had little interest in portraying spies as part of the furniture. During its golden age, both film-makers and filmgoers demanded adventure, glamour and suspense. Films did far more than the documentary record (most of it classified) to shape the popular image of the intelligence services. By the eve of the Second World War, the worlds of espionage and entertainment had become inextricably linked in the public imagination.

The most successful British film director to emerge during the 1930s, Alfred Hitchcock, the 'master of suspense', made a notable contribution to the growing popularity of the spy film. Two of his thrillers, *The 39 Steps* (1935)[48] and *The Lady Vanishes* (1938), both with espionage as a major theme, are commonly ranked among the greatest British films of the twentieth century. The vanishing lady, played by May Whitty, turns out to be a British agent who must deliver critical intelligence to the Foreign Office. Ironically, the male hero who, with the help of Margaret Lockwood, saves Whitty from a pro-Nazi police state, was Michael Redgrave, on whom MI5 was to open a file in 1940 after being informed by the BBC that he had communist connections.[49]

The Lord Chamberlain would never have licensed a stage version of *The Lady Vanishes* because of its hostility to Nazism. Jokes about Hitler, or fictional characters suspiciously like Hitler, were not allowed even in pantomime. The Lord Chamberlain's secretary, George Titman, noted after a performance of *Robinson Crusoe* at the King's Theatre, Hammersmith, in January 1937:

Representations have been made to the Foreign Office by the German Embassy concerning the caricature of Herr Hitler ...

After perusing the script and being assured that no such representation of Herr Hitler or a dictator had been passed, I attended last evening's performance at the theatre.

I found that the German embassy was fully justified in the protest made.

Both the theatre manager and 'the offending Comedian' were prosecuted under the Theatres Act, found guilty and each fined £10.

There was great controversy in the Lord Chamberlain's office in 1938 over *On the Frontier: A Melodrama in Three Acts*, by W. H. Auden and Christopher Isherwood, in which two fictional European countries, Ostnia and Westland, go to war. A licence was eventually granted after the office reader classed the play as 'anti-war', rather than 'anti-German'. Terence Rattigan was less fortunate. His farce, *Follow My Leader*, written with Anthony Maurice, poked fun at both Hitler and Mussolini (though mentioning neither by name) as well as at British appeasers. Major Norman Gwatkin, assistant comptroller of the Lord Chamberlain's Office, wrote during the 1938 Munich crisis:

> At such a time as this the best interests of the country are served by avoiding any unnecessary exasperation to the leaders of the German people – even if this entails a certain muzzling of contemporary playwrights.[50]

The priorities of The British Board of Film Censors (BBFC) were rather different to those of the Lord Chamberlain. While prepared to tolerate some criticism of Nazism, as in *The Lady Vanishes*, it was deeply concerned by the Red Menace. The BBFC, to which most British local authorities deferred, turned down all films which it considered 'Bolshevik propaganda' or 'incitement to class hatred'. Censorship was so severe that, though the Soviet film industry had established itself during the 1920s as one of the most creative in the world, no Soviet feature film between the wars was screened in any licensed British public cinema outside London.

Stalin was outraged. Unknown to the West, he and his daughter Svetlana enjoyed seeing the latest Hollywood films in his private Kremlin cinema. While Svetlana particularly enjoyed comedies, Stalin preferred Westerns. His favourite was John Ford's *Lost Patrol*, which he enjoyed so much that he later ordered a Russian remake.[51]

Stalin also approved a campaign by foreign communists to promote Soviet films in the West. In May 1933, the Moscow Congress of the International Union of Revolutionary Theatres urged its delegates to establish film sections in their national organisations, in order to exploit the propaganda potential of Soviet and pro-Soviet films. Within a few months the British Workers' Theatre Movement had responded by founding a film section known as Kino, not subject to BBFC censorship. It was praised by the communist *Daily Worker* for using film as 'direct propaganda', as well as attempting to establish 'a united front of revolutionary film art together with all interested art, cultural, educational, trade union and professional organisations'.

Kino's General Council included such well-known figures as J. D. Bernal, Aneurin Bevan, the Bishop of Birmingham, Alberto Cavalcanti, Stafford Cripps, Maurice Dobb, Havelock Ellis and Victor Gollancz. The audience for its films grew steadily, reaching an estimated 200,000 in 1938. But Kino could not make ends meet. One letter from Kino to a Communist Party official, intercepted by MI5, complained that collections at a congress where its films were shown had been so 'lousy' that showing them 'nearly broke us financially'. Kino went bankrupt in 1939.[52]

The impact of Soviet films on some left-wing intellectuals, however, was profound. Among them was Cedric Belfrage, probably the most important Cambridge graduate recruited by the Cheka's successor, the NKVD, with the exception of the 'Cambridge Five'. Thanks to a wealthy father, Belfrage began his undergraduate studies at Corpus Christi College in 1922 'with a manservant to wait on me, and many of the trappings and privileges of a gentleman at large'. Though he left without a degree only two years later, he remained long enough to embark on a career as a film critic. By the beginning of the 1930s, he had become Britain's best-paid critic, thanks largely to his success in securing interviews with Hollywood stars.[53] Belfrage was initially attracted to the Soviet Union by its films. Sergei Eisenstein's brilliantly original *Strike* and *Battleship Potemkin* (both released in 1925) and his memorable celebration of the Bolshevik Revolution in *October* (1928) struck Belfrage as vastly superior to the commercialised vulgarity of Tinseltown:

> There are hundreds of females in Hollywood with doll-like youth on their faces. But they wear so much powder, rouge and mascara, not to speak of henna and peroxide, that you can't tell whether underneath it all they are sixteen or thirty-six. You can't – but the camera can. That is why so many of the ravishing things you see prancing up and down Hollywood Boulevard are out of a job.[54]

Belfrage wrote later that, when he visited Russia for the first time in 1936, 'Of Marx, Lenin or Engels I had read not a line, but I had been attracted by Moscow's revolutionary films.'[55] Belfrage returned to California, where he had made his home, a convinced communist. He joined the American Communist Party in 1937.[56] When he was recruited by the NKVD soon afterwards, however, he was told to break off all overt contact with communism and resigned from the Party. What he was not told was that the NKVD already had a well-placed agent in Hollywood. That agent was Russian-born Boris Morros, who received three Oscar nominations as director of music at Paramount Pictures.

Morros was given the rather transparent codename FROST ('moroz' in Russian).[57] His first encounter with the NKVD came in 1934 when he went to the Soviet consulate in New York to arrange the return of his father from the United States to Russia, where four of his sons were members of the Communist Party. The NKVD *rezident*, Peter Gutzeit, reported to Moscow:

> I had the opportunity to meet with M[orros] and his father, who was staying here and left for the [Soviet] Union at the end of May because 'he was disgusted with the capitalist country' ... In conversation with M[orros], I got the impression that he could be used to get our workers jobs at the P[aramount] Company's offices, which exist in every country and major city ... I think M[orro]s could be brilliantly put to use providing our workers with a cover.[58]

Though NKVD contact with Morros in Hollywood proved inter-mittent, he provided Paramount documentation which enabled Vasily Zarubin (later *rezident* in the United States) to operate as an illegal in Nazi Germany from 1934 to 1937, and regularly sent him money. As Zarubin reported to Moscow in 1938:

> F[ROST] can and should be used primarily as someone who can arrange for our people [NKVD personnel] to be legalized – or rather, provide them with documents confirming that this or that worker of ours is associated with his company ... As experience has shown, these doc[ument]s are so good that they are all that is needed to settle down and obtain residency permits under the most difficult conditions of our underground work.[59]

Morros is probably best known nowadays as the producer in 1939 of *Flying Deuces*, starring Laurel and Hardy as new members of the

Morros (centre) with Oliver Hardy.

French Foreign Legion, which was made by his own production company. He complained to his Soviet case officer that the film had been banned in Switzerland at the insistence of the French ambassador in Berne, who complained that Laurel and Hardy made fun of the Foreign Legion. Morros's negotiations with the authorities in Berne were conducted by an NKVD illegal codenamed WEST. 'This', noted NKVD headquarters, 'will be a lengthy affair and will make a good cover, allowing [WEST] to become a representative for F[ROST]'s company in Switzerland.'[60]

It was Morros's success in using Paramount Pictures in the United States to provide cover for Soviet intelligence personnel that probably encouraged the Austrian 'great illegal', Arnold Deutsch to try to secure something similar when he was posted by the NKVD to Britain in the spring of 1934. Deutsch, who went on to recruit the 'Cambridge Five', had obtained a short-term visa as a postgraduate student at London University. While in London, he and his wife Josefine lived at the epicentre of Hampstead's chattering classes in Lawn Road Flats, Britain's first modernist building constructed from reinforced concrete. No fewer than seven Soviet agents lived in the flats at various times between the mid 1930s and the mid 1940s, as well as an extraordinary

Arnold Deutsch, photograph
from MI5 files.

array of writers and artists – among them Britain's greatest detective
novelist and most successful female playwright, Agatha Christie, who
was a regular guest at the flats' Isobar restaurant during the writing
of her only spy novel, *N or M?*, before herself taking up residence.[61]

Soon after arriving in London, Deutsch made contact with his
British cousin, Oscar Deutsch, the millionaire owner of Odeon
Cinemas, whom he had never previously met. Odeon publicists
claimed that the name of the cinemas had originated as an acronym
derived from the slogan, 'Oscar Deutsch Entertains Our Nation'.

Unaware of Arnold's work for the NKVD, Oscar agreed to find him
a job as the first psychologist for his cinema chain, telling the Home
Office that Arnold had 'made an intensive study of Psychology in relation
to the Cinema' and would 'investigate the suitability of sites for cinemas,
popularity of certain types of films, lighting, colour schemes, etc.'[62]

Arnold Deutsch did indeed have remarkable, but rather different,
expertise as a psychologist. After gaining a PhD with distinction[63] at
Vienna University only five years after matriculating as a first-year
undergraduate, he had combined secret work for Soviet intelligence
with open collaboration in Vienna with the German communist
psychologist and sexologist, Wilhelm Reich, who was then engaged
in an attempt to synthesise the works of Marx and Freud. Deutsch
publicly assisted Reich, reputedly 'the prophet of the better orgasm',
in the sexual politics movement, which ran clinics designed to bring
birth control and sexual enlightenment to Viennese workers, and

Oscar Deutsch with film star Mary Pickford at his Park Lane HQ.

founded a small publishing house, Münster Verlag (Dr Arnold Deutsch), to publish Reich's work and 'Sex-Pol' literature. By the time Deutsch moved from Vienna to London in April 1934 to recruit the first of the 'Cambridge Five', Kim Philby, as a Soviet agent, he was under surveillance by the 'anti-pornography' section of the Vienna police.[64]

His cousin, Oscar Deutsch, on the other hand, was an observant Jew, warden and president of the Orthodox Singers Hill Synagogue in Birmingham, where he spent weekends and sometimes invited Arnold, who came from an Orthodox family[65] and fitted in easily at Friday dinners.[66] Had Oscar known of Arnold's close involvement with the sexologist Wilhelm Reich he would have disapproved. So would the British authorities. The proposal to employ him as psychologist for Odeon Cinemas, however, was turned down by the Home Office on the more prosaic grounds that Arnold Deutsch was an alien and 'no effort had been made to obtain a British subject for the post. The Institute of Industrial Psychology would have no difficulty in submitting the names of qualified and experienced psychologists who would be quite capable of the work.'[67]

But Arnold Deutsch did not give up easily. He submitted to the Home Office through his solicitors a more elaborate proposal for the formation of a private limited company, Cinema Research and Development Ltd, with himself and Oscar's best friend, Solomon 'Sol' Joseph, as directors. The proposal claimed that Arnold Deutsch's expertise extended far beyond psychology:

> Dr Deutsch was also interested in the technical development of the Cinema Industry and had invented [a] device designed to increase the volume of light thrown onto the screen when projecting films, an improved means for indicating vacant seats in darkened theatres, more practical ash-trays for Cinemas, etc. It was intended to grant non-exclusive licences in regard to these inventions.

Deutsch named as his referees Professor Cyril Burt, the controversial head of the Psychology Department at University College, London,[68] where Deutsch was taking the postgraduate diploma course for which he had been granted a visa; and Walter Mutch, chief film critic of the *Daily Mail* and *Sunday Pictorial*.[69]

The Home Office was again unimpressed and turned the application down. An official minute reads: 'This looks like an ingenious wangle' (which indeed it was). When Arnold Deutsch finally left England in November 1937 with his wife and small daughter,[70] however, he had recruited – according to KGB records – a total of twenty agents. Among them were the 'Cambridge Five' – Kim Philby, Guy Burgess, Donald Maclean, Anthony Blunt and John Cairncross.[71] Probably the ablest group of British spies ever to work for a foreign power, they were later sometimes privately referred to by Soviet intelligence as 'the Magnificent Five', after the celebrated 1960 Western *The Magnificent Seven*, the highest-grossing Hollywood film ever shown in Soviet cinemas.[72]

Arnold Deutsch's role as a Soviet intelligence officer was not discovered by MI5 until 1940.[73] At the same time, ironically, the Ministry of Information began requesting regular reports from Oscar Deutsch on the morale of his wartime cinema audiences. Suspicions that Oscar shared these reports with Soviet intelligence before his death from cancer in 1941 were probably unfounded.[74]

*

By the mid 1930s, as well as having the world's best SIGINT, the Soviet Union had more foreign agents around the world than any intelligence agency before. Its high-flying Ivy League recruits in the United States – Larry Duggan, Alger Hiss, Harry Dexter White and Duncan Lee chief among them – matched their equally high-flying Cambridge counterparts.[75] During the 1930s, by contrast, neither the United States nor Britain had a single spy in Moscow. Indeed, the first American ambassador to the Soviet Union after the establishment of US–Soviet diplomatic relations, William Christian Bullitt, Jr insisted that none be sent. He wrote naively to the State Department:

> We should never send a spy to the Soviet Union. There is no weapon at once so disarming and effective in relations with the Communists as sheer honesty.[76]

Harpo Marx, however, claimed to have successfully completed one secret intelligence mission during Bullitt's term as ambassador.

A chapter in Harpo's memoirs, entitled 'EXAPNO MAPCASE, SECRET AGENT', gives a hugely entertaining account of the comedian's extensive tour of the USSR in 1933–4.[77] The title was Harpo's eccentric version

Harpo Marx performing at the Moscow Theatre Club, 9 January 1934.

of the Cyrillic spelling of his name (ХАРПО МАРКС) on posters advertising his show. Harpo was the first American artiste to perform in the Soviet Union, and his non-verbal comedy went down a storm with audiences in Moscow, Leningrad and several provincial cities, playing to full houses and standing ovations. Russian border officials were less welcoming when they opened his luggage to discover his theatrical props – according to Harpo's calculations, 'four hundred knives, two revolvers, three stilettos, half a dozen bottles marked POISON, and a collection of red wigs and false beards, moustaches and hands'. Marx was touched by the response of Soviet theatregoers:

> The audiences couldn't have been warmer ... I got a tremendous satis-faction out of going into the hinterlands of the Soviet Union, where no Marx Brothers picture had ever played – where in fact no-one had ever heard of any non-Russian Marx except Karl – and scoring a hit.

At his final performance in Moscow, Stalin's Jewish foreign minister (and later ambassador to the US) Maxim Litvinov came on stage personally to thank the comedian for the pleasure he had brought to Russian audiences, and, to the huge delight of the crowd, improvised a comedy routine – with Marx as the straight man for the first time in his career. As Harpo shook the foreign minister's hand: 'A cascade of steel knives tumbled out of his sleeve and clanked to the stage. The audience exploded with one great shriek [of laughter].'[78]

According to Harpo, just before his departure from Moscow he was summoned by the US ambassador and given a secret mission. Bullitt asked him to transport back to New York 'a thin packet of letters tied with string':

> No one – *no* one must know you have it. It will be strapped to your [right] leg, under your sock ...
> 'Okay', I said. 'Strap me up.' ...
> 'Just forget you're carrying it', said the Ambassador. 'Except', he added, 'when you go in the shower.'

Except for keeping his right leg out of the shower on his transatlantic liner, Harpo told himself, 'There wasn't so much to this cloak and dagger business, once you got the hang of it.'

Just over half an hour before the liner docked in New York harbour, Harpo's door was 'flung open':

> Two hulking, stony-faced bruisers came in the stateroom, slammed the door behind them, and turned the lock ...
> The one with the briefcase said in perfect English, 'Marx, you have something that we want. You probably have it strapped to yourself somewhere under your clothing. You will be good enough to remove it and hand it over.'

The 'bruisers' then identified themselves as agents of the US Secret Service. 'I pulled up my pants, ripped off the tape, unwound the straps, handed over the despatches from Ambassador Bullitt, and gave my leg its first scratch in ten days. It was a beautiful scratch, sheer ecstasy. It was all the reward I wanted for what I had done.'[79]

The story ranks Harpo Marx alongside Shakespeare's favourite comic actor, Will Kemp, as a 'courier clown'. It is, alas, not credible. Bullitt showed little interest in the security either of his embassy or of his correspondence.[80] At least one of his first group of cipher clerks, Tyler G. Kent, was quickly recruited as an active, if somewhat conspicuous, NKVD agent.[81] So far as Soviet intelligence was concerned, Bullitt was conducting – albeit unintentionally – something akin to open diplomacy. He bequeathed both to his successors and to the NKVD a deeply penetrated US embassy and ambassador's official residence.

'Chip' Bohlen, a member of the first Moscow embassy and later ambassador himself, recalled numerous attempts by the NKVD to use ballerinas from the Moscow Ballet to seduce embassy staff:

> There were usually two or three ballerinas running around the Embassy. They would go there for lunch and supper and would sit around talking and drinking until dawn ... Many temporary liaisons were formed.

Attempts to seduce Bullitt, however, were unsuccessful. One of the ballerinas repeatedly expressed 'undying love' for the ambassador, whom she poetically described as her 'sun, moon and stars' – apparently to no effect.[82]

The US embassy was successfully and comprehensively bugged, however. A long-overdue electronic sweep of the building in 1944 by an FBI expert was to find 120 hidden microphones in the first twenty-four hours. Thereafter, according to an eyewitness, 'they kept turning up, in the legs of any new tables or chairs which were delivered, in the plaster of walls, any and everywhere.'[83]

*

The most theatrical innovations pioneered by Stalinist intelligence were the show trials.[84] Because the guilt of the defendants had been secretly determined in advance, none were trials in any accepted sense. Rather, they were dramatic productions in which carefully rehearsed defendants confessed to improbable crimes for which all were found guilty and most were shot. Though they reached their peak during the Great Terror of 1936–8, the first was the Shakhty trial of 1928 at which fifty-three engineers (three of them German) were exposed as 'dastardly saboteurs, plotters and spies'. The long-drawn-out 'trial' took place among the Corinthian columns and immense crystal chandeliers of the pre-revolutionary Nobles' Club, now the Moscow House of Trade Unions. At one end of the main hall, a special stage was constructed for court officials, witnesses, the accused and guards with fixed bayonets. Special stage lighting was installed for film cameramen. There was a new audience on every day of the trial. In all, well over a hundred thousand factory workers, peasants, schoolchildren and other selected spectators witnessed part of the proceedings. Though the US United Press correspondent, Eugene Lyons, dismissed the charges against the engineers as based on 'a melodramatic international plot', he described the trial itself as 'superb drama, bolstered by confessions and documents', imbued with 'a spirit of festival touched with hysteria – a crowd come to see a righteous hanging'.[85]

There was no 'spirit of festival' to temper the much greater hysteria of the Great Terror. In 1937 alone, 353,074 mostly innocent Soviet citizens were sentenced to death by shooting, euphemistically termed 'the Highest Level of Punishment'. Millions feared that they might be next. The key figure in implementing the Terror was Nikolai Yezhov, whom Stalin had made head of the NKVD in September 1936. Yezhov spent more time with Stalin than probably any other intelligence chief has ever spent with any political leader before or since.[86] Though no record of their discussions survives, one of their principal preoccupations must have been Stalin's increasingly paranoid obsession with his great rival Leon Trotsky, who had been expelled from the Soviet Union in 1929 and was thus unavailable for what would have been the most sensational of the show trials. The final revelation of the extent of the imaginary counter-revolutionary conspiracy came in February 1938 with the surreal show trial of twenty-one 'Rightists and Trotskyists', among them most of the surviving Bolshevik leaders as well as Yezhov's predecessor as head of the NKVD, Genrikh Yagoda. They were accused of a catalogue of Trotskyist crimes: espionage, 'wrecking', terrorism, attempting to assassinate both Lenin and Stalin, and making preparations for foreign invasion, the dismemberment of the USSR, the overthrow of the Soviet system and the restoration of capitalism. Previously, the Trotskyists had been allegedly conspiring with the German and Japanese secret services; now they were accused of working for British and Polish intelligence as well.[87]

Among those present at this extraordinary example of what might later have been termed 'immersive theatre' was Fitzroy Maclean, then a young British diplomat at the Moscow embassy. At one point a clumsily manoeuvred arc light illuminated a private box at the back of the hall and Maclean recognised, to his astonishment, the drooping moustache and yellowish complexion of Joseph Stalin.[88] The absurdity of the NKVD's attempt to present its latest dramatic production in the House of Trades Unions as a treason trial was well summed up by an editorial in the *New York Times*:

> It is as if twenty years after Yorktown somebody in power at Washington found it necessary for the safety of the State to send to the scaffold Thomas Jefferson, Madison, John Adams, Hamilton, Jay and most of their associates. The charge against them would be that they conspired to hand over the United States to George III.[89]

Most of the Soviet population, however, accepted the deluded official doctrine that they were threatened by a major conspiracy of spies and saboteurs in the pay of foreign secret services. In every factory, NKVD officers lectured workers on the dangers from non-existent imperialist agents in their midst. Films at Soviet cinemas, comedies included, invariably contained their obligatory quota of spies.[90] On both stage and screen, Felix Dzerzhinsky, the founding head of Soviet intelligence (1917–26), was portrayed as a man whose heroism, meticulous efficiency and selfless idealism continued to inspire the NKVD's victorious struggle against subversion and espionage. Dzerzhinsky's bungles, however, remained a closely guarded secret. No Soviet biography of Lenin was permitted to mention that on several occasions the head of the Cheka's failure to provide basic security had put him at serious personal risk. In 1919, unprotected by the Cheka while being driven in his official limousine to visit his wife Nadezhda Krupskaya, Lenin became the first – and so far the only – head of government to be the victim of a car-jack. The gang who robbed him of his car also took his wallet and Browning pistol. In 1922, after the Cheka had forgotten once gain to provide basic security, Lenin returned home one day to find that his desk and other furniture had been vandalised during the renovation of his flat.[91] In the Stalin era, Dzerzhinsky was posthumously turned into a secular saint. A reviewer of the 1939 play, *The Chekists*, hailed Dzerzhinsky – despite the bloodletting of the Civil War – as:

> the expresser of active, efficacious humanism, which has become the banner of the people of the Revolution, for whom real love for people is expressed not in idle empathy with the sorrows and hardships of human life, but in active struggle with their perpetrators.[92]

By a macabre irony, however, the most (allegedly) dangerous 'enemies of the people' unmasked during the Great Terror were discovered in the higher reaches of three institutions which shared responsibility for defending the Soviet state against them: the Communist Party, the Red Army and the NKVD. In December 1938 Yezhov was sacked as head of the NKVD and later found guilty of the charge of simultaneous conspiracy with Britain, Germany, Japan and Poland – a conviction as preposterous as almost any in the show trials he had stage-managed.[93]

In the midst of the Terror, which was little understood in the United States, the NKVD orchestrated one dramatic public triumph in Hollywood. On 14 July 1937, at a time when almost 1,000 'enemies of the people' were being shot every day, a Soviet long-range experimental aircraft, the Tupolev ANT-25, landed in a cow pasture at San Jacinto, California, after a record-breaking 7,100-mile non-stop flight from Moscow over the North Pole. The three Russian aviators on board, lauded in Moscow as 'Stalin's falcons', were taken to a hero's welcome in Hollywood, hosted by nine-year-old Shirley Temple, the twentieth century's most famous child star.

Shirley Temple poses with Andrei Yumashev, Mikhail Gromov and Sergei Danilin after their record-breaking transpolar flight in 1937.

Shirley Temple's welcome to the Russian aviators had been orchestrated by a Russian graduate of the Massachusetts Institute of Technology (MIT), Stanislav Shumovsky, who was also an NKVD officer codenamed BLÉRIOT and had a gift for public relations as well as espionage. As soon as the aviators landed, he rushed up to the plane with three new suits so that the men should be smartly dressed by the time photographers arrived. From California, the aviators went to Washington, where they were personally congratulated by President Roosevelt in the White House, and to New York, where they became the first Russians to receive a ticker-tape welcome.

As well as being a huge Soviet public relations triumph in the United States, the record-breaking flight of 'Stalin's falcons' was also an intelligence success. The ANT-25, with its 34-metre wingspan, could not have succeeded in its flight without technology secretly obtained by Shumovsky from his MIT agent, Benjamin Smilg. It never occurred to those who cheered the aviators that their flight was made possible by American as well as Soviet technology.[94]

Shirley Temple later recalled how handsome the Soviet aviators had been. However, the FBI director, J. Edgar Hoover, who more than any

previous intelligence chief had a flair for publicity and media manipulation, supplanted the Russians in Temple's affections during a highly
publicised, much photographed tour of FBI headquarters which he
arranged for her in June 1938. As she later recalled: 'My role models
were Amelia Earhart and Eleanor Roosevelt and my major crush was
J. Edgar Hoover.'[95]

*

While 'America's sweetheart', Shirley Temple, then under contract to
Twentieth Century Fox, was boosting the popular image of the FBI,
Warner Brothers were promoting – with less spectacular publicity –
America's first Junior Secret Service Club. Its commander, four decades
before he was elected US President, was Ronald Reagan, then at the
beginning of his Hollywood career. Ten of Reagan's first thirty films
dealt with threats to national security. The Secret Service Club was
founded to publicise a series of films featuring the future president as
Brass Bancroft, Secret Agent J-24; the club gave each of its members
a secret code and a membership card signed by Reagan. Cinema
managers were urged to 'fingerprint new members under the supervision of local police officials', play up the 'spying angle' of the films,
and sponsor school essay competitions with the title, 'What steps do
you think our government must take to combat espionage and spying?'[96]

In the early 1930s Warner Bros had been better known for films
glamorising gangsters. The Brass Bancroft films thus responded to

pressure from Roosevelt's attorney general, Homer Stille Cumming, as well as the author of the movie industry's censorship guidelines, Will H. Hays, for films portraying law enforcement in a positive light.[97] Secret Agent J-24's improbable exploits were advertised as 'thinly disguised dramatizations of actual adventures'. 'I was as brave as Errol [Flynn]', Reagan later recalled, 'but in low-budget fashion.' His last picture before he was drafted in 1942 was *Desperate Journey*, in which he and Flynn played Royal Air Force pilots shot down behind German lines.[98]

Among the British cinemas which screened the second Brass Bancroft film, *Code of the Secret Service*, soon after the outbreak of the Second World War was one in the town of Bletchley. The film was 'well attended' by the first wave of codebreaking recruits to the nearby SIGINT agency at Bletchley Park, who must have been intrigued by the title.[99] They were doubtless less impressed by the improbable plot in which Secret Agent J-24 pursues a counterfeiting ring in Mexico, is wrongly blamed for the death of a fellow Secret Service agent, escapes from jail, captures the leader of the counterfeiters, and wins the heart of Elaine (played by Rosella Towne).[100] Probably none of the codebreakers recognised or later recalled the name of the actor playing Brass Bancroft. Nor could they possibly have guessed that he would go on to become US president. In retrospect, Reagan thought *Code of the Secret Service* possibly the worst film he ever made.[101]

II

The Second World War: Soviet Penetration and British Deception

The first step to Soviet infiltration of the British intelligence community was penetration of the BBC, the newest of Britain's national institutions and a key component of the entertainment business as well as the news industry. When the corporation received its royal charter in 1927, there were fewer than 2.2 million licence holders entitled to listen to its broadcasts. By the outbreak of war they had grown to over nine million, almost three-quarters of British households.[1] Late in 1936, Guy Burgess, who had been recruited as an NKVD agent two years earlier by Arnold Deutsch on the recommendation of his Trinity College contemporary, Kim Philby,[2] began work as a BBC producer. The Talks Department, where he worked, was responsible for most factual content on the BBC's only domestic radio station, the National Programme (later renamed the Home Service). It was Deutsch who guided Burgess to his first important contact in British intelligence. Having discovered from his agent in the Foreign Office, Donald Maclean (also one of the Cambridge Five), that the travel author David Footman was secretly deputy head of the Political Intelligence Department in SIS, Deutsch suggested that Burgess get to know him. After their first meeting in the spring of 1937, Burgess reported to the NKVD: 'F[ootman] is always on his guard. But I think he likes me and this is what I was after.'[3] At Burgess's request, Footman gave several travel talks on the BBC, beginning in August 1937 with *Albania, A Fish and A Motorcar*, which Burgess asked him to write 'in the style of – though, of course, not out of – your book', *Balkan Holiday*.[4] 'Does F[ootman] suspect me?' Burgess wrote to Deutsch. 'I think he doesn't. Why? Class blinkers – Eton, my family, an intellectual.'[5] A year later, Footman helped to get him a job in SIS.[6]

Guy Burgess in his favourite Old Etonian tie, which he wore even after defection to Moscow.

Burgess also produced talks by his friend and former Trinity College tutor, Anthony Blunt, whom Deutsch had recruited as an NKVD agent with Burgess's assistance early in 1937.[7] Blunt made his broadcasting debut with a talk on the Royal Academy Winter Exhibition in January 1938. 'Mr Blunt is a reputable art critic', wrote Burgess on the BBC booking form, 'and should be paid the maximum ... ' There followed further broadcasts on the Sistine Chapel, on modern art (with William Coldstream), and on the rescue of works of art from the Nazis.[8] In the space of less than six months, Burgess had thus produced successful talks by both an SIS officer and an NKVD agent.

Sir John Reith, the first director-general of the BBC from 1922 to 1938, would have been outraged, as well as incredulous, to discover that the corporation had been penetrated by Soviet intelligence. An authoritarian Calvinist, six feet six inches tall and aptly described by Winston Churchill as 'the wuthering height', Reith believed that the BBC's responsibility for public service broadcasting required him to seek MI5 assistance in preventing recruitment of communists and fascists. Initially informal, vetting by MI5 was formally introduced at his request in 1937 and changed little over the next twenty years.[9] Burgess's career was unaffected. Shortly before Burgess joined SIS in 1938, Churchill, from whom he had commissioned talks on the BBC, gave him a published copy of his recent speeches, writing on the flyleaf: 'To Guy Burgess from Winston S. Churchill to confirm his admirable sentiments.' He added that, if war broke out, he would find Burgess a job.[10]

Burgess's main service to Soviet intelligence while in SIS was to help Philby to join the service. In the summer of 1940, Philby tried to find a job at Bletchley Park but was turned down by Frank Birch, the veteran Room 40 codebreaker who, after a successful career on the stage in the 1930s, had returned to SIGINT at the outbreak of war. According to Philby, Birch rejected him, despite his fluent German, 'on the infuriating ground that he could not offer enough money to make it worth my while'.[11] Philby's explanation is unconvincing. The young academics and others from the professions recruited by Birch were paid £600 a year, the same starting salary as Philby's when he joined SIS (though his was tax free).

At this crucial stage in Philby's career, Burgess came to his rescue. Philby was summoned to tea at St Ermin's Hotel near St James's Park to discuss 'war work' with Marjorie Maxse, 'an intensely likeable elderly lady' as well as one of the very few women with a senior post in wartime intelligence, who discussed with him 'the possibilities of political work against the Germans in Europe'. As well as being chief organisation officer of the Conservative Party, Maxse was chief of staff in Section D of SIS, which specialised in sabotage. At Philby's second interview a few days later, Maxse was accompanied by Guy Burgess:

> Encouraged by Guy's presence, I began to show off, namedropping shamelessly, as one does at interviews. From time to time, my interlocutors exchanged glances; Guy would nod gravely and approvingly. It turned out that I was wasting my time, since a decision had already been taken.

Burgess and Philby were briefly members of the Special Operations Executive (SOE), founded in July 1940 to carry out sabotage, espionage and reconnaissance in occupied Europe (and later South East Asia), as well as to aid local resistance movements. In 1941 Philby transferred to SIS, where he remained for the next decade. Burgess, however, was fired after being arrested for drunk driving and other misadventures, and returned to the BBC.

By the time Burgess began his second stint as a BBC producer in January 1941, the Talks Department had considerably expanded its pre-war role. Much the most popular talks were those of the best-selling Yorkshire novelist and playwright, J. B. Priestley. MI5 had responded, somewhat nervously, to a vetting enquiry about him from the Ministry of Information in May 1939: 'Has left wing tendencies but might be used with caution.'[12] Broadcasting House threw caution to the winds. Priestley's 'Afterthoughts', which began in June 1940 immediately after the evacuation from Dunkirk of almost 340,000 British and French soldiers by 'little ships' as well as the Royal Navy, continued intermittently for two years and caught the popular mood more successfully than any previous wartime broadcaster. The first 'Afterthought' told how

> our great-grandchildren, when they learn how we began this War by snatching glory out of defeat, and then swept on to victory, may also learn how the little holiday steamers made an excursion to hell and came back glorious'.[13]

Though Graham Greene disliked Priestley's novels and plays, he claimed at the end of 1940 that his broadcasts had established him as 'a leader second in importance only to Mr Churchill'.[14]

The main inspiration for Guy Burgess as a wartime talks producer was not the Dunkirk evacuation but Hitler's invasion of Russia on 22 June 1941,[15] which transformed his ability to promote the Soviet cause in Broadcasting House. In July, with Britain and Russia now allies, he circulated within the BBC 'Draft Suggestions for Talks on Russia', covering literature, science, culture and politics. Topics included economic planning ('The Soviet Union were the pioneers'), the federal system of the USSR ('one in which the Soviet Union has done some interesting experiments') and Soviet foreign policy ('Carefully handled there should be room for an objective talk'). On art and history, Burgess picked out three possible speakers:

> Dr Klingender, Dr Blunt are possible speakers on art – neither are communists. Christopher Hill (a fellow of All Souls) is a communist, but is also probably the best authority in England on Russian historical studies.[16]

As a member of MI5 since June 1940, Anthony Blunt was officially exempt from any suspicion of loyalty to Moscow. But Burgess must have known that Fred Klingender, a Marxist art historian at the LSE, was an active communist.[17] Christopher Hill first came to MI5's attention when he visited Russia in 1935 while an undergraduate at Oxford. His MI5 file records that, after a second visit to Russia in 1936, he joined the Communist Party.[18]

Burgess was well aware that most BBC management were opposed to broadcasts by communists. In April 1941, for example, the BBC's regional director for the North, John Coatman, acting entirely on his 'own initiative', issued an order barring Joan Littlewood and James Miller (who later took the name Ewan MacColl), two of Britain's most innovative theatre-makers, from broadcasting:

> Miss Littlewood ... and her husband Mr James Miller, are not only well known Communists but are active Communists who have taken a leading part in the organisation of the Communist party and its activities in this area ... Clearly I could not allow people like this to have the use of the microphone or be prominently identified with the BBC.[19]

Though Littlewood remained barred from permanent employment by the BBC, she later became a frequent wartime broadcaster. The police in Hyde, Greater Manchester, reported to MI5 in 1943 that, after a BBC warning to 'discontinue her communist activities, the once frequent visits of communists to [her home in Hyde] have now ceased.'[20]

Ironically, the main MI5 agent within the BBC was Guy Burgess, who was recruited by his friend Blunt as an agent-runner, codenamed VAUXHALL. Blunt reported to MI5 (and, no doubt, to the NKVD): 'Burgess ... has done extremely valuable work – principally the running of two very important agents, whom he discovered and took on.' Though Burgess had 'completely abandoned' his former support for communism, Blunt added that he retained 'an extraordinary knowledge of it', as well as of the work of the Communist Party, which would continue to make him 'very useful'.[21]

The Soviet ambassador, Ivan Maisky, wrote in his diary on 12 October 1941: 'Everything Russian is in vogue today: Russian music, Russian songs, Russian films and books about the USSR.'[22] Russian films, all previously banned by the BBFC, were suddenly showing to full houses in British cinemas. When Maisky and his wife attended a performance of Mussorgsky's opera, *Sorochintsy Fair*, at the Savoy

Cartoon of Stalin drawn
by Guy Burgess.

Theatre on 20 October, they were greeted by thunderous applause
and the playing of the *Internationale*, which had previously been banned
from the airwaves by the BBC.[23]

Burgess, meanwhile, continued to expand his role as the most
influential foreign agent in British broadcasting. In October 1941, he
was given responsibility for the BBC's flagship political talks programme,
The Week in Westminster, then so popular that it was broadcast every
Saturday evening. He became a leading liaison figure between the
BBC and the Commons, with an impressive range of political contacts,
on whom he reported to Soviet intelligence.[24] Burgess's most remarkable coup during his second term as a BBC producer, however, was
to broadcast a talk on the Eastern Front in January 1942 by the Soviet
agent Semyon Rostovsky, who operated under cover as a Russian
journalist in London with the alias Ernst Henri.[25] Henri told his
listeners that the Red Army would be victorious because 'they fight
for the people, for their motherland and for the people's rule'. Then
he had an unprecedented message for other Soviet agents. The Soviet
Union, he told them over the air, had 'an intelligence service which
is among the best in the world'. The Gestapo (and, by implication,
MI5) were powerless against it.[26] The Soviet agents who heard Henri's
remarkable broadcast must have been encouraged by their intelligence
service's ability to advertise its success over the BBC.[27]

No fictional Soviet spies appeared on stage, screen or radio in
wartime Britain. By contrast, the most popular radio comedy of the
war, *It's That Man Again (ITMA)*, starring the Liverpool comedian,
Tommy Handley, included the menacing but comically incompetent
German spy, Funf, played by Jack Train.[28]

Tommy Handley takes a call from Funf.

Funf became BBC radio's best known and most imitated spy. Numerous listeners enjoyed ringing friends and announcing, 'This is Funf speaking!' Funf also made a guest appearance at Windsor Castle as part of an *ITMA* Royal Command Performance to mark Princess Elizabeth's sixteenth birthday in 1942.[29]

The irony of calling the German spy Funf — *fünf* means five – was that, unknown to either *ITMA* or British intelligence, the most active real spies in wartime Britain were the NKVD's 'Cambridge Five'. By 1941 London was the NKVD's most productive intelligence station or 'residency'. According to secret statistics compiled in the Centre, its Moscow headquarters, the residency sent to it in that year 7,867 classified political and diplomatic documents, 715 on military matters, 127 on economic affairs and 51 on British intelligence. In addition, it provided many other reports based on verbal information from the Cambridge Five and other agents.[30] The Soviet Union had more and better intelligence about Britain (as well as the United States, which had entered the war by the end of the year), than any power had ever had before on its wartime allies.

Britain, on the other hand, had better intelligence about Germany than any power had ever had before about a wartime enemy – chiefly because its SIGINT was the best in the world. Soviet intelligence lacked the advanced technology which enabled Bletchley Park to break the German Enigma machine cipher. ULTRA, the SIGINT obtained from successively decrypting Enigma, in several variants, and other high-grade enemy ciphers, began to come on stream in June 1940, the month when Churchill became Prime Minister. By 1943 the UK/ US SIGINT alliance, in which Britain was the senior partner, was decrypting between 3,000 and 4,000 German signals a month as well as a large volume of Italian and Japanese traffic. By contrast, though Germany had as many SIGINT personnel as Britain (about 30,000), it was no longer able to break any significant Allied ciphers. Neither were its Italian and Japanese allies.[31]

As well as having the best SIGINT, Britain also ran the most ingenious and successful programme of wartime deception. Though deception took many forms, at its heart were double agents used to feed disinformation to the Abwehr, the main German foreign intelligence service. The first double agent deployed against Nazi Germany, only a few months after Hitler came to power in 1933, was Major Christopher Draper, a First World War fighter ace who had won both the DSC and the French Croix de Guerre. After a brief post-war career in the RAF, Draper embarked on a career as a jobbing actor. He became far more famous, however, as one of the most successful stunt pilots, nicknamed the 'Mad Major', in air shows, the main outdoor innovation in the early twentieth century entertainment business.[32] On 30 September 1931, Draper, ever the showman, famously flew a

de Havilland Puss Moth under most of London's twenty-four bridges. A plan to film the escapade from the plane's cockpit failed, but strategically placed news photographers took a series of pictures including one of a perfectly executed flight through the central arch of Westminster Bridge.

Following this exploit, Draper enlisted in a lecture tour entitled *Aces of the Air*, featuring leading First World War military pilots from both Britain and Germany. One of the German pilots, Major Eduard Ritter von Schleich, was an old aerial adversary of Draper's; the two struck up a friendship, and in 1932 von Schleich invited Draper to Germany where he was famously introduced to (and photographed with) Hitler at a Munich air show, four months before Hitler became chancellor.

Less than a year after meeting Hitler, Draper was asked by the London correspondent of the official Nazi newspaper, *Völkischer Beobachter*, to provide intelligence on the RAF. As he later recalled:

> The actor in me put on the necessary poker face and I played for time … It is almost unnecessary to say how anxious I was to get in touch with MI5 as quickly as possible, for I realised that here was the most wonderful opportunity to double-cross the Hun.[33]

The 'Mad Major' (left) meets Hitler in 1932. Between them are two German pilots. Draper signed some copies of his memoirs, which included this photo, as 'the not so mad major'.

MI5 agreed and in June 1933 Draper travelled to Hamburg to meet his Abwehr case officer. For the next three years he sent disinformation prepared by MI5, disguised – on Abwehr instructions – as correspondence on stamp collecting, to a cover address in Hamburg. Lacking the interdepartmental system for assembling disinformation that would be developed during the Second World War, however, MI5 began to run out of plausible falsehoods of interest to the Germans. In the mid 1930s Draper did rather better as an actor than as a double agent, culminating in 1938 with a role in a West End production of Thomas Dekker's *The Shoemaker's Holiday*, which became one of the first live television drama broadcasts from Alexandra Palace.

By then Draper's espionage career was over. The Abwehr broke contact with him late in 1937 after expressing 'grave dissatisfaction' with the quality of his intelligence.[34] Then, in October 1938, Draper suffered the embarrassment of being publicly identified as a German spy at a trial in New York,[35] forcing the Air Ministry to issue a statement that 'the loyalty and integrity of Major Christopher Draper ... is not in any way called into question'. 'The official statement by the air ministry,' wrote Draper, 'confirmed any German suspicions that I was a deep-dyed double-crosser.'[36]

Draper's unsuccessful career as a double agent, however, gave the Security Service an important insight into German espionage. By intercepting correspondence between Britain and the Abwehr cover address given to Draper (Box 629, Hamburg), MI5 discovered a letter from Arthur Owens, a Welsh-born electrical engineer who began to work for the Abwehr in 1936. Turned by MI5 and codenamed SNOW, shortly after the outbreak of war, he became the first of the almost 120 double agents run by B1a, MI5's double-agent section.[37] SNOW's case officers found him personally tiresome, with disagreeably plebeian habits which included 'only wearing his false teeth when eating'.[38] His daughter Patricia, by contrast, became a glamorous postwar Hollywood film star, playing opposite – among others – Marlon Brando and James Mason.

B1a was run by Thomas Argyll ('Tar') Robertson, who had begun his career in the Seaforth Highlanders before working in the City in the early 1930s and joining the Security Service in 1933.[39] In MI5 headquarters Robertson continued to wear his tartan Seaforth trews, thus earning the nickname 'passion pants'.[40] Tar's natural air of authority did not suffer from the nickname, however: the historian

Left: Passport photograph of Arthur Owens (SNOW); right: his daughter Patricia Owens.

Sir Michael Howard described him as 'a perfect officer type, who could have been played by Ronald Colman'.[41] He had a remarkable gift for selecting case officers, all previously inexperienced wartime recruits, who had the acting ability to take on the personalities of their double agents. Tar later recalled that 'one golden rule in running an agent was that his personality should be stamped on every message he transmitted' to the Abwehr.[42]

In order to run its double agents successfully, B1a needed a mixture of accurate information and plausible disinformation with which they could impress and deceive German case officers. From January 1941 the selection of both information and disinformation was entrusted to the Twenty Committee, so called because the Roman numeral for twenty (XX) is a double cross. The committee, which included representatives from MI5, SIS, the War Office, the three service intelligence departments, GHQ Home Forces and, when necessary, other interested departments, met weekly for the remainder of the war.[43]

Like Tar Robertson, the MI5 chairman of the Twenty Committee, the Oxford history don, J. C. Masterman, was an inspired choice. Born in 1891, Masterman was considerably older than most other B1a officers.[44] He was, however, probably the best all-round games player ever to join the Security Service. As an undergraduate he had won an athletics blue. Between the wars he played hockey and tennis for England, and, at the age of forty-six, was still a good enough cricketer to tour Canada with the MCC.[45] Masterman was also a successful writer; his *An Oxford Tragedy*, published in 1933, established the tradition of the murder mystery novel set in a (fictional) Oxford college.

But his main literary ambition at the outbreak of the war was as a playwright. In the autumn of 1939, his five-act play *Marshal Ney*, a lengthy drama about events leading up to the execution of Napoleon's loyal general after Waterloo, was about to receive its premiere at the newly built Oxford Playhouse until the war intervened. But, as Masterman wrote later, 'the war came and the play was, with many other things, forgotten.'[46]

Marshal Ney had originally been intended as a collaboration with Masterman's friend, the playwright R. C. Sherriff, whose celebrated First World War drama *Journey's End* had premiered in 1928, starring the 21-year-old Laurence Olivier. 'Just as a dramatist must have a sense of history, a historian, to inspire his pupils, must have a sense of drama,' wrote Sherriff in the introduction to the 1937 published script of *Marshal Ney*:

> It is Mr Masterman's ability to dramatize history that make his lectures so popular … *Marshal Ney* … challenges the modern theory that History, to be accepted by the theatre-going public must be "pepped up".[47]

Despite a glowing review of Masterman's published script of *Marshal Ney* in *The Spectator*[48] and the apparent enthusiasm of Oxford Playhouse director, Eric Dance, the play remained unperformed until a (perhaps wisely) shortened adaptation was broadcast on the BBC Home Service in 1953. Although he failed to become a successful playwright, Masterman's keen 'sense of drama' made him uniquely qualified to oversee the scripts for his 120-strong cast of double agents.

For the first year of the Second World War, as at the beginning of the First, there were numerous spy scares, most based simply on alarmist rumours, which interfered with the hunt for real German spies.[49] Masterman himself suspected – probably mistakenly – that a penniless German theatre company arrested at a British port a few weeks after the outbreak of war had been intended as a cover for enemy espionage, and ordered its internment.[50] By the time the Twenty Committee met for the first time, under his chairmanship, in January 1941, counter-espionage was no longer complicated by baseless spy scares. Thanks to the success of the double agents in deceiving the Abwehr, the Committee began to grasp the astonishing fact that, in Masterman's words, *'we actively ran and controlled the German espionage system in this country'*.[51]

B1a strongly suspected, however, that several of its double agents, if given the opportunity, might return to the German side. Elaborate plans were therefore made to remove most to secret locations in North Wales in the event of a German invasion, which early in 1941 was still regarded as a real possibility. The operation was initially codenamed MR MILLS' CIRCUS in honour of the B1a officer put in charge, the Cambridge engineering graduate and circus impresario, Cyril Bertram Mills, son of Britain's leading circus-owner, Bertram Mills.

Cyril Mills and his brother, Bernard, had taken over management of the circus founded by their father in 1925. Cyril was a keen pilot and, prior to the war, frequently flew his de Havilland Hornet Moth to Europe in search of new circus acts. In the course of these expeditions he became involved in intelligence work, photographing and reporting on the German military build-up, and in 1936 undertook an aerial survey of the Messerschmitt Factory at Regensburg. He was recruited to MI5 B section in 1940.

The officer responsible for the North Wales end of the MR MILLS' CIRCUS operation, Captain P. E. S. Finney, sometimes used circus metaphors in his correspondence with MI5 head office, writing from Colwyn Bay in April 1941:

> I have now completed arrangements for the accommodation of the animals, the young and their keepers, together with accommodation for Mr Mills himself.

All double agents were to be housed in hotels at Betws-y-Coed, Llanrwst and Llandudno, whose owners had been vetted.[52] A majority of them were trusted to make their own way to North Wales, and were to be given car passes, petrol coupons and money for their journeys. Those who were not trusted, including the increasingly unreliable SNOW, were to be put in handcuffs (loaned by Scotland Yard) and taken by car under armed guard to their allocated hotel. So important was preservation of the Double-Cross system that Tar Robertson made clear that 'if there is any danger of the more dangerous cases falling into enemy hands they will be liquidated forcefully'.[53] Sir David Petrie, who became MI5's director general in 1941,[54] reiterated the need to 'take any step necessary' to prevent double agents from being captured, thus becoming the only DG effectively to authorise executions (though in the event none were carried out).[55] As fear of a German invasion receded, MR MILLS' CIRCUS gradually wound down. The untrustworthy SNOW, however, was imprisoned in Dartmoor for the rest of the war.

*

In the summer of 1941 the Twenty Committee began to make its priority the strategic deception of the German high command, rather than – as before – the deception of its forces in the field. Strategic deception began not in the European theatre but in the Middle East, where early in the war the British commander-in-chief, General Sir Archibald Wavell, appointed an intelligence officer, Lieutenant Colonel Dudley Clarke, to devise deception plans.[56] Clarke's 'A Force' set the tone for deception campaigns throughout the Middle East, and ultimately for other theatres of the war. The official historian of British wartime deception, Sir Michael Howard, concludes:

> A small acorn planted by Dudley Clarke in December 1940 in the shape of a few bogus units in the Western Desert was to grow into a massive oak tree whose branches included the non-existent British Twelfth Army in Egypt (and the barely existent Ninth and Tenth Armies in Syria and Iraq) and the First United States Army Group (FUSAG) in the United Kingdom.[57]

Dudley Clarke's capacity for deception extended to his private life, still mysterious today. In November 1941 Kim Philby, who enjoyed retailing personal scandals to Soviet Intelligence, reported that Clarke had been arrested by Spanish police in Madrid, dressed in women's clothing ('down to a brassiere').[58] Philby occasionally perplexed Moscow with some of the reports he sent, most likely after heavy drinking sessions, along with his high-grade intelligence. They could contain bizarrely improbable information such as that Germany was infiltrating cocaine and other hard drugs, probably by parachute, into the Irish Republic; from here they were supposedly smuggled into Britain by Welsh fishermen in motor launches and supplied to London clubs where RAF officers 'under the influence of drugs, alcohol, sexual orgies or Black Mass are induced to part with information'.[59] By contrast, Philby's account of Clarke's transvestite

1941 Spanish police photographs of Dudley Clarke, in and out of women's clothing.

tendencies, which led to his temporary imprisonment in Spain, was quite correct. Clarke's love of pantomime had given him earlier opportunities for cross-dressing. At the staff college in Camberley in 1933–4 he wrote and directed *Alice in Blunderland* and *Al Din and a Wonderful Ramp*.[60]

Clarke's successful deception operations in the Middle East inspired the creation of the London Controlling Section (LCS), headed from May 1942 by Lieutenant Colonel J. H. Bevan, in order to 'prepare deception plans on a world-wide basis with the object of causing the enemy to waste his military resources'. Though given the grand title of Controlling Officer, Bevan lacked executive authority; his role was to plan, coordinate and supervise.[61]

Strategic deception coordinated by the LCS was central to the first major Allied offensive of the war: Operation TORCH, the invasion of French North Africa, for which planning began in July 1942. The two main deception plans devised by Bevan, OVERTHROW and SOLO 1, successfully persuaded the Germans that Allied preparations for landings in, respectively, northern France and Norway were at an advanced stage.[62] Throughout both deception operations, which successfully distracted German attention from the threat to French North Africa, the LCS maintained close contact with the Twenty Committee and B1a.

Bevan's deputy, the RAF representative on LCS, was the best-selling thriller writer Dennis Wheatley, inventor of the supernatural suspense novel. Wheatley was a close friend of MI5's leading agent-runner, Maxwell Knight, who once went with him to a séance conducted by the sinister occultist, Aleister Crowley, and was 'very, very, shaken' by the experience.[63] Wheatley was one of George VI's favourite novelists. His wartime involvement in Whitehall began during the Dunkirk evacuation when he was asked by the Joint Planning Staff (JPS) to imagine himself a member of the German high command and draft their plan for the invasion of England. According to Wheatley, the invasion commander would demand the total humiliation of the defeated British:

> Not until British women lick the boots of German soldiers while British men look on can we be certain that we have achieved our final objective and that Britain can never menace us again.

Somewhat absurd though this and other elements of Wheatley's Nazi invasion plan now appear, some members of the JPS were impressed by its sheer swinishness. 'We've been playing this war like cricket', one commented, 'but Wheatley thinks like a Nazi.' His ability to think out of Whitehall boxes led nineteen more 'war papers' to be commissioned from him by August 1941. These and other contributions to the JPS led to membership of the London Controlling Section. When the LCS moved to a large, bleak basement room in the spring of 1943, Wheatley provided some of his own expensive furniture, including an antique table and Chippendale chairs.

At the centre of the LCS table, also provided by Dennis Wheatley, was a replica of the statuette of a dancing faun found in the House of the Faun at Pompeii. The Roman mythological half-man, half-goat figure of the faun, and its Greek counterpart the satyr, have made regular appearances in ballets and masques through history; but its significance in the context of the LCS is unusual. In 1928 Wheatley had commissioned bookplates for his extensive private library showing him sitting naked at the hooved feet of a faun in the likeness of the adventurer and fraudster, Eric Gordon-Tombe, who had been his friend and mentor. Gordon-Tombe, who had been murdered by an underworld associate in 1922, was the inspiration for Wheatley's debonair fictional spy (and James Bond forerunner) Gregory Sallust who made his best-selling debut in the 1934 novel *Black August*. Wheatley must

London Controlling Section 1943

Major Harold Peteval
Jun Cdr Lady Jane Pleydell-Bouverie
Colonel John Bevan
Wg Cdr Dennis Wheatley
Lt-Col Ronald Wingate
Major Neil Gordon Clark
Cdr James Arbuthnott
Major Derrick Morley
Commander Alec Finter

have relished the presence of the faun statuette at top-secret LCS meetings as they discussed new ways of deceiving the enemy.[64]

Dudley Clarke, noted Wheatley, had 'an uncanny habit of suddenly appearing in a room without anyone having noticed him enter'.[65] Though Clarke declined the offer of a seat on the LCS, he continued to prove highly effective in the field, specialising in operations to mislead the enemy about the size and location of allied forces. Military deception strategies are by their nature intrinsically theatrical, and Clarke's enjoyment of film and role play was evident in his work. Whilst stationed at the Royal Arsenal in Woolwich in 1923, Clarke had revived the pre-war Royal Artillery Officers' Dramatic Club. When asked to direct the Royal Artillery display for the 1925 Royal Tournament at Olympia, he devised a grand historical pageant celebrating artillery firepower from Minden to the Marne and featuring 680 men and 300 animals. For costumes he enlisted the assistance of Willy Clarkson, and persuaded circus impresario Bertram Mills (Cyril's father) to provide two elephants and two camels for the half-hour show, which ran twice daily for thirty performances.[66]

Amongst those working with Clarke's 'A' Force in North Africa was the Oscar-winning film director Geoffrey Barkas, who led an operation before the battle of El Alamein to camouflage military vehicles and create dummy ones for use as decoys; Barkas remembered his role as 'the task of providing props for the biggest "film production" on which I ever expect to be engaged'.[67] The stage magician Jasper Maskelyne also played a role (somewhat exaggerated in his memoirs) in designing dummy tanks and equipment for faking tank tracks, as well as devices aimed at aiding prisoners of war to escape, such as hacksaws concealed in boot heels.[68] Clarke's most celebrated ruse involved parading a bit-part actor, M. E. Clifton James, as a 'double' for Field Marshal Montgomery in Algiers, at a time when Montgomery himself was in England preparing for D-Day. The deception was inspired by a plot twist in the 1943 film *Five Graves to Cairo*. In 1958 James' account of Operation COPPERHEAD would itself become a film, *I was Monty's Double*, starring John Mills and featuring Clifton James as both himself and Montgomery.[69]

*

In Masterman's view, the greatest of all Britain's wartime double agents was the Catalan Juan Pujol García, whose experience of the

Spanish Civil War had left him with a loathing of both fascism and communism. Pujol first offered his services to the British in Madrid in January 1941 but was turned down. He then approached the Abwehr, told them he was travelling to England, and was eventually taken on as Agent ARABEL. Pujol's campaign to deceive the Germans with bogus intelligence showed remarkable acting ability. Though he got no further than Lisbon, Pujol deceived the Abwehr into believing he was in Britain and provided plentiful disinformation on non-existent British troop and naval movements, spiced with details of 'drunken orgies and slack morals at amusement centres' in Liverpool and the surprising revelation that Glasgow dock-workers would 'do anything for a litre of wine'. By February 1942, SIS's Section V had identified Pujol as the author of these colourful reports, which were decrypted by Bletchley Park. A month later SIS recruited him as a double agent with the codename BOVRIL.[70] Though BOVRIL had already established himself as an important channel of disinformation to the Abwehr, it was important to avoid further errors in his fraudulent reports which might arouse German suspicions, such as his description of wine-loving Glaswegian dockers.

After some interdepartmental bickering between SIS and MI5, Pujol was moved from Portugal to England to be run by B1a. He was welcomed at Portsmouth on 25 April 1942 by his first MI5 case officer, Cyril Mills of B1a, who used the alias 'Mr Grey', and the bilingual Tomás (Tommy) Harris of B1g (Spanish counter-espionage), who acted as translator. Mills and Harris spent the next fortnight debriefing Pujol in London, where he was given documents identifying him as a translator working for the BBC and accommodated at a safe house in Hendon, earlier occupied by two Norwegian double agents, John 'Helge' Moe (MUTT)[71] and Tor Glad (JEFF).[72]

The codenames MUTT and JEFF were taken from the well-known characters in a long-running American strip cartoon, which generated numerous film and stage adaptations. Like MUTT, Moe was short and stout; Glad, like JEFF, was tall and lanky. After arriving as German agents by rubber dinghy on a Scottish beach with sabotage equipment in April 1941, they immediately turned themselves in to the local police. JEFF's career as a double agent was quickly compromised by his indiscretions and doubts about his loyalty. He was interned in August 1941 for the remainder of the war, though B1a, with help from MUTT, continued to send the Abwehr misleading radio messages

1920 *Mutt and Jeff* stage show.

in his name. The much more reliable, British-born MUTT was the son of Ida Wade, an English opera singer, and a Norwegian ladies' hairdresser with a salon in Oslo. In 1939 MUTT went to London to become a cinema make-up artist but left for Norway in the following year. MUTT was one of the few double agents permitted to undertake sabotage to enhance his credibility with the Abwehr. Several of his operations involved actual (though not seriously damaging) explosions: among them a staged attack in August 1943 on a generating station at Bury St Edmunds in Suffolk.[73]

Strategic deception coordinated by the London Controlling Section was central to the first major Allied offensive of the war: Operation TORCH, the invasion of French North Africa, for which planning began in July 1942. Deception plans devised by Bevan successfully persuaded the Germans that Allied preparations for landings in northern France and Norway were at an advanced stage, thus distracting them from the real threat to North Africa.[74] MUTT played a key role in persuading the Abwehr of the non-existent Allied preparations for an invasion of Norway.[75]

John Moe (Mutt) and Tor Glad (Jeff).

However, the most inventive disinformation sent to the Abwehr continued to come from the Spanish double agent, Juan Pujol García. Cyril Mills was so impressed by Pujol's success in deceiving the Germans even before he began working for the British that, at Mills' suggestion, his original codename, BOVRIL, was changed to that of 'the best actor in the world'. Thus it was that Pujol became GARBO, in honour of the glamorous Greta Garbo, whose best-known starring roles included that of the exotic Mata Hari.

Because Tomás Harris spoke the same language and arguably boasted an equally vivid imagination, he replaced Mills as GARBO's case officer. Harris had established himself before the war as a wealthy London art dealer, artist and socialite, and had been recommended to MI5 early in 1941 by Anthony Blunt. Throughout the war Harris and his wife kept open house at their Mayfair home, with generous supplies – despite wartime rationing – of champagne and canapés, for friends in the intelligence and art worlds: among them were Blunt,

Guy Burgess and Kim Philby, as well as Bond Street art dealers and Sotheby's auctioneers. Harris's friendship with three leading Soviet agents did not impair – though in hindsight it adds piquancy to – his operational effectiveness in MI5.[76] Blunt doubtless reported to Moscow a private dinner with GARBO and Harris at Garibaldi's restaurant in Jermyn Street. He was later to pay public tribute to Harris as 'one of the principal organisers of what has been described as the greatest Double-Cross operation of the war – 'Operation GARBO'.[77]

The intense collaboration between GARBO and Harris became one of the most extraordinary double-acts in espionage history.[78] Their disinformation output was remarkable. In addition to shorter radio messages, during the last three years of the war they jointly composed 315 intelligence reports in secret writing, each averaging about 2,000 words, which were sent to an Abwehr post office box address in Lisbon. Most of the intelligence supposedly derived from a remarkable cast of sub-agents, eventually numbering no fewer than twenty-seven, all fictional characters with full life stories and credible motivations created with dramatic flair by GARBO and Harris. In Britain they included a US Army sergeant, a Venezuelan living in Glasgow, and a Welsh nationalist in Swansea leading a group of fascists called the 'Brothers of the Aryan World Order' (one of them impersonated by Cyril Mills). Other imaginary sub-agents were stationed as far afield as America and Ceylon.[79]

During GARBO's first year as a double agent, even Churchill was not told about him. MI5 files reveal that, despite the prime minister's daily diet of ULTRA decrypts, he was not informed of the Double-Cross system until March 1943. Unlike Sir Stewart Menzies, chief of SIS, his counterpart in MI5, Sir David Petrie, kept his distance from the prime minister, fearful that Churchill would be so excited by Double-Cross that he would interfere in the running of it. Thanks to Anthony Blunt, until 1943 Stalin was better informed about the use of British double agents against Germany than Churchill. It was typical of the conspiratorial mindset of Stalin and his intelligence chiefs, however, that they should conclude in the middle of the war that the British Double-Cross system was also operating against the Soviet Union. Even the Cambridge Five, later acknowledged as probably the ablest group of foreign agents ever recruited by Soviet intelligence, were for two years believed to be a British deception. In a number of other operations, such as those against imaginary American Trotskyist plots after its assassination of Trotsky himself,[80] the Centre successfully deceived itself.[81]

Recent discoveries in the Security Service archives have shown that, in addition to its double-agent operations, MI5 also ran a successful deception programme targeted against Nazi supporters in Britain, based on the remarkable acting ability of the MI5 officer and former bank clerk, Eric Roberts. From 1942 onwards, under the alias 'Jack King', Roberts posed as the Gestapo's secret representative in wartime Britain, a bogus position that enabled him to identify British Nazi sympathisers, most of them former members of Oswald Mosley's British Union of Fascists who had found it insufficiently extreme. Unlike B1a officers, who never met the Abwehr officers they were deceiving, Roberts had to act the part in person of a secret Gestapo officer.

Some of the pro-Nazis gave 'King' secret information, including details of research into the jet engine, in the mistaken belief that he would pass it on to Germany. None, however, were prosecuted for fear that their defence counsel might convince a jury they were the victims of entrapment by the security authorities.[82]

Hans Kohout, an Austrian-born naturalised Briton working for a firm with secret Admiralty and Air Ministry contracts, gave Roberts classified technical details of the Mosquito fighter-bomber and of the development of WINDOW, an anti-radar 'smokescreen' to protect RAF bombers. He told Roberts that had he not been able to give this information to the Gestapo, he would have passed it to a neutral pro-German embassy in London (possibly Spain's) for onward transmission to Germany. Kohout also stumbled on one of Britain's greatest wartime intelligence secrets. He told Roberts he had learned from a contact that a country house at Bletchley Park had been turned into an intelligence HQ. After taking advice from MI5, Roberts told Kohout that he need make no further enquiries; operations at Bletchley were 'of no interest' to the Gestapo. He presented Kohout with a forged *Kriegsverdienstkreuz* ('War Merit Cross'), supposedly awarded to him by the Gestapo.[83]

The deception which finally persuaded Alfred Duff Cooper, head of the British Security Executive responsible for coordinating security operations, and the leadership of MI5 that the time had come to brief Churchill on Double-Cross was Operation MINCEMEAT in the spring of 1943.[84] The operation epitomised both the creative imagination and the remarkable inter-departmental and civil–military cooperation which characterised the most effective British wartime deception strategies. MINCEMEAT was devised by B1a's Flight Lieutenant Charles Cholmondeley, coordinated by the London Controlling Section, and involved a number of key players from the Twenty Committee, notably its naval representative Lieutenant Commander Ewen Montagu, as well as members from 'A' Force and Bletchley Park. Ironically, Montagu's younger brother, Ivor, a film-producer, writer and loyal Stalinist, had been under intermittent MI5 surveillance for almost twenty years.[85] Ivor Montagu worked on a series of Alfred Hitchcock films and found him 'a joy to work with'.[86] He was recruited as a (somewhat incompetent) agent of Soviet military intelligence, code-named INTELLIGENTSIA, in 1940.[87] He was of less use to Moscow as a spy than as an agent of influence, loyally supporting its policies and denouncing its opponents as well as the victims of show trials. Montagu was later awarded the Lenin Peace Prize.[88] What Moscow learned about MINCEMEAT, however, came not from Ivor Montagu but from Anthony Blunt's penetration of MI5.

An enormously complex piece of role play, notable for the fact that the key player was dead, Operation MINCEMEAT involved the corpse of a homeless Welshman called Glyndwr Michael (who had killed himself) being disguised as that of a Royal Marines officer, Major Martin, and left by submarine to wash up on the nominally neutral Spanish coast at the end of April 1943. Fake top-secret documents concealed on the body gave details of (non-existent) Allied plans for a landing in Greece, codenamed Operation HUSKY, designed to distract the Germans from the forthcoming Allied invasion of Sicily. The controlling officer of the LCS, Colonel Bevan, called on Churchill at 10 a.m. on 15 April to gain his consent to MINCEMEAT. He found the prime minister sitting up in bed, smoking a cigar, surrounded by papers and Cabinet boxes. Churchill quickly gave his enthusiastic support for the deception (subject only to the agreement of Eisenhower, which was also obtained). If the operation did not succeed at the first attempt, said the prime minister, not entirely seriously, 'we shall have to get the body back and give it another swim'.[89]

It is possible that the original idea for the operation came from Ian Fleming. Early in the war, he had included the idea of placing forged douments in the pocket of a corpse dressed in RAF uniform as no. 28 in a list of 51 possible deceptions.[90] Although the implementation of

Operation MINCEMEAT was not MI5's responsibility, it was largely responsible for creating the corpse's fake identity. Ewen Montagu invited secretaries in B Division to audition for the part of Major Martin's fiancée, Pam, by submitting attractive photographs of themselves. The audition was won by Jean Gerard Leslie (later Leigh), then in B1b, and a photograph of her in a swimsuit was placed in Martin's wallet. Other secretaries helped draft love letters from Pam, which were put in his pocket.[91] The photograph in Martin's identity card was of a B1a officer, Ronnie Reed, who bore some resemblance to the unfortunate Glyndwr Michael.[92] Martin's pockets also contained stubs of tickets for Strike a New Note, a popular revue at the Prince of Wales Theatre which made the comedian Sid Field an overnight star. The tickets were for the performance on 22 April, apparent proof that Martin had left England after that date.[93] In reality, the corpse had been loaded several days earlier onto the submarine, HMS Seraph, which took it to the Spanish coast. On 22 April, using the actual tickets whose stubs had been planted on the corpse, Ewen Montagu, Cholmondeley, Leslie and Avril Gordon, one of the the secretaries responsible for the love letters, celebrated 'Bill Martin's farewell' by going to the revue,[94] featuring Field's signature ditty:

> We've seen him on the Panto
> We've heard him on the Air
> And where there's roars of laughter
> You can bet Sid Field is there.[95]

The extraordinary level of involvement by naval intelligence personnel in creating the bogus marine's backstory, and their skilful creation of the faked supporting documentation, were more than worthy of a Pinewood props department. Operation MINCEMEAT was a glorious example of the imaginative penchant for the theatrical which infused many British undercover operations throughout the war and often gave them a notable advantage over the more pedestrian efforts of the enemy.[96] ULTRA decrypts revealed that the Germans had been comprehensively deceived by Major Martin's forged documents. A message sent to Churchill during a visit to Washington said simply: 'MINCEMEAT swallowed whole'. Even when the Allied attack in July 1943 came in Sicily rather than Greece, the Germans did not doubt the authenticity of the MINCEMEAT documents but concluded instead that Allied plans had changed.[97]

The story would become the subject of the 1956 film *The Man Who Never Was*, based on Ewen Montagu's 1953 best-seller of the same title which sold over two million copies.[98] The book, which portrayed Operation MINCEMEAT as a one-off venture and deliberately avoided any reference to the Double-Cross system as a whole, was effectively an official response to the publication in 1950 of the popular spy novel, *Operation Heartbreak* by Duff Cooper, former head of the Security Executive, who clearly based its plot on his inside knowledge of MINCEMEAT. In a surreal moment in the film of *The Man Who Never Was*, Montagu himself makes a brief appearance as an air marshal who is sceptical about the scheme, remarking to American actor Clifton Webb, who played him, 'I suppose you realise, Montagu, that if the Germans see through this it will pinpoint Sicily.'[99]

What Churchill learned about the success of deception and the double agents run by British intelligence during 1943 left him with the conviction that, 'In wartime, truth is so precious that she should always be attended by a bodyguard of lies.' No British military operation had ever been so successfully protected by deception as OVERLORD, the Allied invasion of occupied northern France which began with the D-Day landings on 6 June 1944.[100] The final act of deception prior to D-Day was entrusted, appropriately, to its greatest practitioners, GARBO and Tomás Harris. While continuing to insist that the main attack would come in the Calais region, in order to maintain his credibility with the Abwehr GARBO sent a radio message at 3 a.m. on 6 June – just too late for the Germans to be able to benefit from the warning – that Allied forces were heading towards the Normandy beaches. Though the Abwehr radio station in Madrid had been warned by GARBO to be ready to receive a message at 3 a.m.,[101] it failed to go on air until after 6 a.m.[102] Later on D-Day, GARBO radioed to the Abwehr a withering denunciation of its three-hour delay in receiving his supposedly vital intelligence on imminent Allied landings on the Normandy beaches. On the following morning, after a supposedly sleepless night, GARBO radioed a further self-pitying, melodramatic message of recrimination:

> I am very disgusted as in this struggle for life and death I cannot accept excuses or negligence ... Were it not for my ideals and faith I would abandon this work as having proved myself a failure ... My tiredness and exhaustion due to the excessive work I have had has completely broken me.

The errant Abwehr case officer in Madrid, who had failed to ensure that the radio station came on air at 3 a.m., replied apologetically with a fulsome tribute to the quality of GARBO's intelligence: 'I wish to stress in the clearest terms that your work over the last few weeks has made it possible for our command to be completely forewarned and prepared.'[103] That tribute, which GARBO and Harris must have greeted with hilarity, was quoted in MI5's June report, sent to Churchill on 3 July. Churchill would also have been amused to learn that GARBO had been awarded the Iron Cross.[104]

The climax of GARBO's deception of the Abwehr coincided with the end of the paranoid delusion by Soviet intelligence chiefs that the Cambridge Five were really British double agents. The accuracy of the intelligence sent by Philby (codenamed SÖHNCHEN) in particular before the D-Day landings, which marked the opening of the Second Front long demanded by Moscow, was, the Centre informed its London residency on 24 June 1944, 'a serious confirmation of S[ÖHNCHEN]'s honesty in his work with us, which obliges us to review our attitude towards him and the entire group'. It was now clear, the Centre acknowledged, that intelligence from the Five was 'of great value'.[105]

In December 1944, GARBO became the first British agent (as opposed to intelligence officer) to be awarded the MBE. Since it was thought inappropriate for a double agent to meet the king, the presentation was made instead by the director general of MI5, Sir David Petrie, in a private ceremony attended by Tomás Harris and senior members of B1a. Petrie, noted his deputy, Guy Liddell, 'made a nice little speech': 'Later we lunched at the Savoy when GARBO responded to the toast in halting but not too bad English. I think he was extremely pleased.'[106]

The wartime success of the Double-Cross system initially raised exaggerated expectations about the potential use of deception in the Cold War. Guy Liddell warned in April 1951: 'Our main difficulty may not be so much to persuade senior officers to allow us to run double-agents, but to prevent them from making us run everything in sight as a double-agent.' There was, however, never any prospect that a Double-Cross system directed against Stalin's Soviet Union could achieve anything approaching the level of success attained in the war with Hitler's Germany. 'It would', wrote Liddell, 'be extremely difficult to "do it again" on the Russians.'[107] When his friend Guy Burgess defected to Moscow with the diplomat Donald Maclean in the following month, Liddell must have realised that a Cold War

Double-Cross system would be even more difficult than he had supposed.

Few, if any, of those who knew the secret of the wartime Double-Cross system, however, believed that it would ever be publicly revealed. When Sir John Masterman (who was knighted in 1959) published his now celebrated history of it a quarter of a century after the war, many past and present members of MI5 were deeply shocked. The then director general, Sir Martin Furnival Jones, who had joined a few months after Masterman, wrote to him: 'I consider your action disgraceful and have no doubt that my opinion would have been shared by many of those with whom you worked during the war.'[108]

The even greater codebreaking successes of Bletchley Park also remained top secret for thirty years after the war. But, after the ULTRA secret was declassified in the mid 1970s, the Double-Cross system gradually ceased to be officially taboo. The fortieth anniversary in 1984 of the D-Day landings, to which it had made a notable contribution, marked a turning point. GARBO was invited to Buckingham Palace to be congratulated by the Duke of Edinburgh, made guest of honour at a reception in the Special Forces Club attended by the wartime head of B1a, Tar Robertson, and his first case officer, Cyril Mills, and taken on a guided tour of the Normandy beaches.[109]

GARBO and Cyril Mills (centre left and right) in 1984.

Mills' role in the Double-Cross system was publicly revealed for the first time in 1989 in an edition of the popular Thames Television series, *This is Your Life*, which lured celebrities into a studio where they unexpectedly encountered (sometimes long-lost) friends, family and former colleagues who helped to tell the story of their lives. To celebrate Mills' career, luminaries of the circus world were joined by Tar Robertson and Mills' fellow B1a case officer, Christopher Harmer. 'We double-crossed you!' they gleefully announced as they surprised the clearly dumbfounded Mills. Robertson said of Mills' wartime achievements:

> His job was to look after agents which had been sent to this country and to turn them round and play them back to the Germans. They were in fact double agents. Cyril was a marvellous operator. He was a pretty tough character in every possible way but he was very kind to his agents. He was known by us, with no ill feeling, as 'the old dog'. He had under his control the best agent we ever had – GARBO.[110]

12

Shaken not Stirred: The 'Special Relationship' and the Founding of the Central Intelligence Agency

In defiance of US neutrality, the wartime Anglo-American intelligence 'special relationship' began even before the United States entered the war. Its origins owed much to the appointment in June 1940 as head of the SIS station in New York of William Stephenson, a Canadian First World War fighter ace who had become a wealthy businessman and worked part-time for SIS in the 1930s.

The diminutive 'Little Bill' Stephenson's engaging personality and dry martinis won him many friends in the United States.[1] Among them was the war hero and lawyer, General William 'Big Bill' Donovan (also known as 'Wild Bill' because of his exploits in the First World War). On 3 July 1940 President Franklin D. Roosevelt summoned Donovan to the Oval Office and sent him on a transatlantic mission to investigate British security in the wake of the rapid German conquest of France and the Low Countries. Rightly convinced that Donovan had the ear of the president, Stephenson insisted that he be shown the red carpet, indeed a whole series of red carpets, in London. Donovan was received by Churchill, granted an audience with King George VI, and taken to secret meetings with Stewart Menzies of SIS and other intelligence chiefs. After his return to Washington in August, Donovan urged on Roosevelt 'full intelligence collaboration' with the British. The president's willingness to move in that direction reflected his own admiration for the achievements of Britain's 'wonderful intelligence service' in the First World War, as well as the influence of Donovan and other advisers. At a meeting in London on 31 August 1940 between the British chiefs of staff and the American Observer Mission, the US Army representative,

William Stephenson in 1938.

Brigadier General George V. Strong (later G-2, head of army intelligence), announced that 'the time had come for a free exchange of intelligence'.

To conduct that exchange, Stephenson set up British Security Coordination (BSC) on the 35th and 36th floors of the International Building in Rockefeller Center on New York's Fifth Avenue. For much of the war BSC included officers from SIS, MI5 and the Special Operations Executive (SOE).[2] Among Stephenson's most enthusiastic early supporters in British intelligence were the Director of Naval Intelligence, Admiral John Godfrey, and his assistant, Lieutenant Commander Ian Fleming. 'How much I admire the wonderful set-up you have achieved in New York,' Godfrey wrote to Stephenson after visiting BSC in May 1941. ' ... I consider it beyond praise.' Fleming later called Stephenson 'one of the great secret agents' of the Second World War, a man with 'a magnetic personality and the quality of making anyone ready to follow him to the ends of the earth'. While watching Stephenson mix 'the most powerful martinis in America', Fleming noted that they were 'shaken, not stirred' – a phrase later made famous by James Bond.[3]

Fleming also noted that BSC was located four floors below the Japanese consulate. In the first of his Bond novels, *Casino Royale*, 007 is sent, 'licensed to kill', on a mission to Rockefeller Center to assassinate a Japanese cryptanalyst in the consulate who has been 'cracking our codes'. Bond takes a room on the fortieth floor of a neighbouring skyscraper from which he could see the codebreaker at work and shoot him with a Remington thirty-thirty, equipped with silencer and telescopic sight: 'It was a pretty sound job. Nice and clean too. Three hundred yards away. No personal contact.'[4] Though readers of *Casino Royale* did not realise it, the story was also ironic. While Fleming was in New York in the summer of 1941, US cryptanalysts, having broken the Japanese diplomatic code PURPLE, regularly decrypted telegrams from Tokyo to both its Washington embassy and New York consulate.[5] Japan, by contrast, had no significant success in breaking US and British codes and ciphers. As Admiral Godfrey's assistant, Fleming, unlike most of Churchill's ministers and most senior diplomats, knew the ULTRA secret.[6]

After Godfrey's return to London in June 1941, Fleming stayed on in Washington for another month, remaining in close contact with BSC at the Rockefeller Center, to advise on the establishment of the office of the Coordinator of Information (Intelligence), headed by Donovan; it was to be the forerunner in the following year of America's first civilian intelligence agency, the Office of Strategic Services (OSS), also under Donovan.[7] As well as coordinating Anglo-American HUMINT (though not SIGINT) collaboration, BSC ran the largest influence operation so far run by British intelligence to try to persuade the United States to enter the war.

Stephenson recruited a remarkable range of talents from the entertainment business for the influence operation. All, however, were male. The women at BSC HQ were secretaries – many recruited by Stephenson in Canada, lodged by him in two New York hotels, and bussed to work each day to Rockefeller Center.[8] He overlooked entirely the most successful American-born female entertainer, the charismatic singer, dancer and actor Josephine Baker, a committed supporter of US entry into the war.

★

Baker was recruited not by BSC or OSS but by French intelligence. 'Josephine', as she was usually known on both sides of the Atlantic, was born into poverty in St. Louis, Missouri, in 1906, but succeeded in her later teens in beginning a career as a singer and dancer in Harlem. At 19, she accepted an offer to join an all-black revue in Paris, and was surprised to discover that unlike in America she could sit wherever she wished on French public transport. The turning point

in her career was *La Folie du Jour* at the Folies Bergère, where she caused a sensation by emerging from the jungle wearing little more than a skirt made of sixteen bananas.

Baker became one of Europe's best paid and most popular performers as well as the first black woman to star in a major motion picture, the 1934 French film *Zouzou*.[9] Ernest Hemingway, who met her in Paris, called her 'the most sensational woman anybody ever saw. Or ever will.'[10] Their first meeting, in a fashionable Montparnasse nightclub, was all the more memorable for Hemingway because she was wearing only a fur coat. 'I just threw something on', Josephine explained. 'We don't wear much at the Folies.'[11] In 1937 she took French citizenship.[12]

Soon after the outbreak of the Second World War, like Mistinguett in 1914, Josephine Baker became an unpaid agent ('honorable correspondant') of the Deuxième Bureau. Her recruiter, Captain Maurice Abtey, was impressed by her ability – again, like Mistingett – to persuade well-placed foreign admirers (chief among them the Italian military attaché and the Japanese ambassador in Paris) to talk

indiscreetly about their country's wartime policies. Of particular
interest to the Deuxième Bureau was intelligence on whether Mussolini
planned to declare war on France – which he did in June 1940.[13]
Though none of Josephine's reports survive, it has been claimed that
some were written in invisible ink between the lines of sheet music.[14]
Her role as a secret agent grew in importance after France's humiliating defeat by Germany in the summer of 1940, the establishment
of Marshal Pétain's collaborationist Vichy regime, and General Charles
de Gaulle's broadcast appeal from London as leader of Free French
forces to continue the fight against Germany. As a secret opponent
of Vichy, Abtey sought a way to travel under a false identity to neutral
Lisbon in the autumn of 1940; here he was to pass to the SIS station
important intelligence the Deuxième Bureau had obtained on the
landing craft to be used by Germany during Operation SEALION, its
planned invasion of Britain, and then to make plans to join de Gaulle
in London. The solution was for 'the great artiste Joséphine Baker',
as he described her in a secret report, to accompany him on his intelligence mission.[15] 'It is France who has made me what I am', she told
Abtey. 'I shall remain eternally grateful to her.'[16]

Baker told the Brazilian consulate in Nice that she wished to perform
in Rio de Janeiro and asked for artistes' visas to allow her and her
secretary to travel via Spain and Portugal. The 'secretary', travelling
with a false French passport in the name of Jacques Hebert, was
Maurice Abtey. His visa, which was quickly granted, was marked
'accompanying Mme Joséphine Baker'. At the Spanish and Portuguese
frontiers in November 1940, the customs officials had eyes only for
Josephine; her secretary, wearing thick spectacles, was nodded through.
In Lisbon, Abtey passed the German intelligence to the SIS head of
station and made arrangements for subsequent travel to London,
intending to join de Gaulle's newly established intelligence service,
later named the Bureau central de renseignements et d'action (BCRA).[17]
SIS attached great importance to the reports it received from the Free
French, which in the final months of 1940 amounted to 40 per cent
of all its intelligence on France.[18] Intelligence on Hitler's invasion
plans, in particular, was regarded as 'absolutely vital' by SIS because
most of his invasion fleet would leave from German-occupied French
ports.[19] This intelligence, however, proved to be less important than
expected; it was later learned that by the end of October Hitler had
abandoned plans for Operation SEALION.

Josephine Baker sings US national anthem in the Municipal Theatre, Oran, Algeria, on 17 May 1943.

At the request of the BCRA, Abtey joined the Free French not in London but in French North Africa. So did Josephine Baker. While working in Morocco in the summer of 1941, however, she had an emergency hysterectomy, followed first by peritonitis, then septicaemia. She spent over a year in hospital, fearing for the future of her career, but made a remarkable recovery.[20] After the landing of US troops in Algeria at the end of 1942, Baker became an 'agent of influence' for the Free French in North Africa and the Middle East against the supporters of the Vichy regime for most of the next two years.[21] She ended her performances for French, American and British forces by unfurling a giant Cross of Lorraine, the symbol of de Gaulle and Free France. It cannot have occurred to any of the US troops to whom she sang 'The Star-Spangled Banner' that their national anthem was being sung by an agent of French intelligence.

The troops on whom Josephine had the greatest impact were the Free French. A majority were black, recruited from France's African colonies and protectorates. No better agent of influence could have been found to strengthen their allegiance to de Gaulle and discredit the Vichy collaborationists than the world's most charismatic black francophone singer and female entertainer.

As well as performing in public, Baker continued to carry out secret missions. Though few details survive, a secret post-war report put on record that, for a year, de Gaulle's chief of staff, General Pierre Billotte, had entrusted her with a series of 'particularly delicate missions which she always fulfilled with intelligence and commitment'. She had also done much to 'reinforce France's very precarious position in Morocco' in the winter of 1943–4. Throughout, she had shown herself 'an admirable and great French patriot'.[22] When Baker was awarded the Médaille de la Résistance after the war, de Gaulle wrote to express his personal admiration for 'the enthusiasm with which you have put your magnificent talent at the disposal of our Cause and all who have followed it'. She was later made Chevalier de la Légion d'honneur.[23]

*

The fact that Josephine Baker was black was an even greater obstacle to her employment by Stephenson's BSC than her gender. The US army remained racially segregated throughout the Second World War, with most black troops in non-combat roles. Indeed its generals in Europe insisted that French black soldiers – the majority of de Gaulle's forces – play no part in the liberation of Paris in August 1944.[24]

Though Stephenson's recruits from the entertainment business were limited to white men, however, they included such remarkable talents as the author and screenwriter Roald Dahl (whose film credits later included the screenplay for the 1967 Bond movie *You Only Live Twice* and the 1968 film adaptation of Ian Fleming's *Chitty Chitty Bang Bang*); playwrights Noël Coward and Benn Levy (later a Labour MP and campaigner against stage censorship); radio producer and presenter Giles Playfair (son of the impresario Nigel Playfair, who had produced *Aladdin* at the Lyric, Hammersmith with Frank Birch as Widow Twankey); lyricist and Hollywood screenwriter Eric Maschwitz; *Wizard of Oz* screenwriter Noel Langley; Ian Fleming's close friend, Ivar Bryce, later the producer who commissioned the script for the 1965 Bond film *Thunderball*; Paul Dehn, instructor at Camp X, the Canadian training camp for BSC agents, who became screenwriter of both the 1964 Bond film *Goldfinger* and the 1965 John le Carré adaptation *The Spy Who Came in from the Cold*; and, from December 1941, Hollywood journalist, Cedric Belfrage, a close friend of Maschwitz and brother of actor and news reader Bruce Belfrage, who achieved fame in 1940 by continuing to read the BBC radio news when the studios suffered a direct hit from the Germans.[25]

The most multitalented of Stephenson's recruits was Noël Coward. The actor and director Simon Callow writes of his extraordinary range:

> Certainly his achievements have no parallel in their diversity: revue artist, actor, director (both film and stage), playwright, screenwriter, novelist, composer, lyricist, even – for a couple of hair-raising performances – conductor. In all of these spheres (except perhaps the last) he achieved the utmost distinction. Nor was he confined to any one genre: he wrote sketches, songs, operettas, musical comedies, epics, sentimental comedies, wartime adventure stories; he wrote the songs that rallied Britain during the war; and a half-dozen of his plays rank among the best of the 20th century.[26]

Coward wrote to Winston Churchill after the outbreak of war: 'I am determined to play as much of a part as the powers-that-be allow me ... You may count on my doing whatever I am called upon to do.'[27] At a meeting with Stephenson in London in the summer of 1940, 'He gave me two strong Cuba Libres and waited politely for me to talk a great deal.' Coward accepted a job working for BSC.

Despite his extraordinary theatrical talents, Coward's initial contribution to BSC's influence operation during the London Blitz was undermined by his low boredom threshold and impatience with American politicians:

> In the United States I just talked about Britain under bombing ... I had a terrible time with some of the Senators – one or two who thought we were finished. They were such silly old idiots that I didn't mind very much. In fact, I was rather sharp with them, because they really did talk such unconscionable nonsense. I put them down and pointed out that I was not doing any subversive propaganda of any sort. What I was doing was travelling round the world at the express wishes of my government to talk about the British war effort and, above all, what was happening in Britain during the air raids – to let them know how the British were taking it, etc. So I told them – 'Really calm down, keep your hair on! Nothing really dangerous is going on.' They

suspected me to start with obviously, of being a spy – which, of course, technically I was, as America was a neutral country at the time.[28]

Coward's activities in the United States quickly attracted the attention of the FBI, which opened a file on him, including a series of complaints about his pro-British propaganda. In June 1940 the American Legion in Illinois sent the Bureau a copy of a Communist Party pamphlet attacking him, which had been dropped by plane:

> Noel Coward is one of a whole gang of British agents disguised as actors, novelists, writers, lecturers, etc., who are working to drag the United States into the war ... these war-making agents are adored, entertained, banqueted and welcomed by the 'best society' everywhere ... The recent 'Allied Ball' for relief was organized with Noel Coward as the chief attraction for the 'suckers'. The American people must awaken to this real 'Fifth Column.'[29]

Coward's US mission had critics in Britain as well as America. 'The despatch of Mr Noel Coward to the United States can do nothing but harm ... ', declared the *Sunday Express*,

> Mr Coward is not the man for the job. His flippant England – cocktails, countesses, caviar – has gone. A man of the people, more in tune with the new mood of Britain, would be a better proposition for America.[30]

The *Sunday Express* was wrong. By Pearl Harbor, Coward had learned from some early mistakes. His proudest wartime achievement as a writer was not a play but a screenplay: the 1942 propaganda film *In Which We Serve*, inspired by the naval exploits of Louis Mountbatten and produced with the assistance of the Ministry of Information. As well as scripting the film (with the close cooperation of Mountbatten himself), Coward co-directed it with David Lean and himself played the 'Mountbatten' role of Captain Kinross. The *New York Times* reviewer declared it a triumph:

> The great thing which Mr. Coward has accomplished in this film is a full and complete expression of national fortitude ... Yes, this is truly a picture in which the British may take a wholesome pride and we may regard as an excellent expression of British strength.[31]

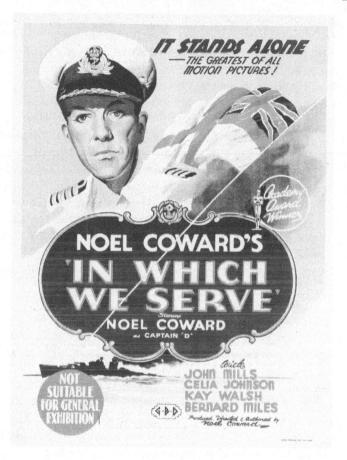

Noël Coward was convinced that he also had a unique talent for intelligence collection:

> I was to go as an entertainer with an accompanist and sing my songs and on the side doing something rather hush-hush ... [Stephenson] saw where my celebrity value would be useful and he seemed to think I ought to be as flamboyant as possible, which was very smart of him. My disguise would be my own reputation as a bit of an idiot ... a merry playboy. It was very disarming. Very clever of him.[32]

Hidden in plain sight like a traditional court jester, Coward believed 'My celebrity value was wonderful cover.' 'I could have made a career in espionage', he claimed, ' ... My life's been full enough of intrigue as it is.' Coward's understanding of espionage, however, was based more on fictional stereotypes than on actual intelligence collection. 'So many career intelligence officers', he wrote, 'went around looking terribly mysterious – long black boots and sinister smiles.'[33] The long black boots and sinister smiles, however, derived from Coward's vivid imagination rather than the reality of SIS operations. When intelligence became dull, he lost interest in it. Copies of confidential reports to BSC, which survive in the Noël Coward archive, of his meetings with leading American industrial and political figures show that his patience was severely tested by, among others, Roosevelt's Republican predecessor as President, Herbert Hoover, who remained active in politics and international relations: 'I am not very favourably impressed by Mr Hoover ... he must have been the hell of a dull President.'[34]

Coward found intelligence collection in Latin America and further afield less tedious:

> I was never terribly good at wearing a jewel in my navel like Mata Hari ... I was the perfect silly ass. Nobody in South America or among other neutrals considered I had a sensible thought in my head, and they would say all kinds of things I would pass along to Bill [Stephenson].[35]

Stephenson, however, became politely uninterested in the 'kinds of things' he passed on. Coward seemed not to notice that 'Little Bill' had ceased to entrust major operations to him. According to his BSC colleague, Roald Dahl:

> Bill would ask him to do the tiny little things, because he passed through New York. And Noel Coward would go all over the place saying 'I'm working for Bill Stephenson.' ... I mean Coward made a huge thing of it. And he'd turn up in the salons in London and say 'Now, shhh. You've heard of this chap Bill Stephenson.'[36]

Coward is not mentioned in the 300-page section on the Second World War of the official history of SIS. His most memorable role in British intelligence came during the Cold War as a star rather than a spy: the satirical portrayal of a fictional SIS officer in the 1959 film *Our Man in Havana*.

The ingenuity of the deceptions devised by BSC for its influence operations in the United States before Pearl Harbor is well illustrated by its use of the German-born celebrity astrologer, novelist and film scriptwriter, Louis de Wohl, who had moved to Britain from Nazi Germany in 1935, probably because of his partly Jewish origins: at the time he claimed to be Hungarian. As well as publishing *Secret Service of the Sky* and other books on astrology, he also developed, according to MI5 reports, 'a widespread trade in horoscopes among highly placed individuals' in Britain.[37] The reports dismissed him as 'a bumptious seeker after notoriety' and 'an exceedingly vain man, with all the German's love of uniform and rank', who also claimed to have frequented cafes in Berlin 'in feminine attire'.[38] De Wohl's friend and fellow astrologer, Dr Felix Jay, later recalled a charity concert 'sometime in 1939 or 1940' at which

> Louis indulged in one of his favourite pleasures, that of dressing up as a woman. And indeed, he looked the part, that is if you like Peter Paul Rubens' corpulent ladies ... To see the 'seer', with a big cigar in his hand, in a flowery silk dressing gown, with eyes raised to Heaven, pronouncing apocalyptic words, walking slowly across his hotel room, was surely something I would not have missed ever ...[39]

Despite his pretentiousness, some intelligence officers, Ian Fleming among them,[40] were impressed by de Wohl's (mistaken) claims that Hitler's strategy was influenced by astrology. His ability to cast horoscopes for Hitler showing that he was doomed to defeat also attracted the attention of SOE.[41] MI5 noted that in the spring of 1941 SOE's sabotage section, SO2, decided to employ de Wohl 'for their own fell purposes'.[42]

De Wohl was sent to the United States in May 1941 to conduct British Intelligence's first astrological propaganda campaign under the covert direction of BSC. In June, the New York *Sun* ran a report, headlined 'Seer Sees Plot to Kill Hitler', in which De Wohl forecast that Hitler was 'doomed' and would be 'done away with within a year'. According to the official history of BSC:[43]

> From this triumphant beginning de Wohl went out on tour, and all the time, at public meetings and over the air, in private assemblies, in interviews, in widely syndicated articles and at an important convention of American astrologers, he declared that Hitler's doom was sealed.[44]

Hitler Will Die Soon, Stars Inform Visiting Astrologer

Hungarian Also Predicts Germans May Try Move Through South America

Adolf Hitler has not long to live.

He is mentally ill.

If Germany wins the Russian campaign it won't be with the help of Hitler's favorite stars.

Germany may well try an invasion of the United States—through South America.

The golden age of peace will start in 1948, although the present world conflict may not last that long.

'NOTHING MYSTIC'

There's absolutely nothing mystic about predictions such as these from Louis De Wohl, Hungarian astro-philosopher now visiting friends in Los Angeles.

As a matter of fact, if you've any illusions about the way an astrologer should look and act, De Wohl will erase them.

Chubby, blue-eyed, curly-headed and bespectacled, De Wohl hopes to see the day when Astrology will be recognized as a science.

COLD LOGIC

Already he has astounded editors and the general public with predictions. A book written in 1938 foresaw many of the things which have followed. Recently he predicted the first clash between German and Italian troops somewhere in Greece, and two days later an item from Athens told of the conflict.

"There's nothing supernatural or uncanny about it," he insists. "It's just cold logic. Stars can affect our doings only 40 per cent and wills of humans affect the remaining 60 per cent. But you can't ignore that 40 per cent."

SECRET OF PREDICTIONS

He explains the whole science by pointing out that the stars, sun and moon are made up of chemical elements and so are the human bodies. Then, he says, is it not logical that the combination of the chemical elements in the heavens in a given position might have certain reactions on the human systems? Therein lies the secret of it, he believes.

Having once been offered a position in the German Geo-Political Institute at Munich, which employs 1000 experts to plot Hitler's stars, De Wohl points out he turned down the offer and told Germany but thus knows that Hitler watches astrological experts.

'HITLER END NEAR'

Hitler's horoscope shows he has not long to live. The mentally ill state explains why he and Mussolini conferred for five days—because Hitler can no long-

Louis De Wohl
Times photo

er engage in lengthy conferences and must limit them to short periods.

The Russian campaign, contrary to other campaigns, was started when the aspects were bad for Hitler and was done by the high command's influence against that of the stars.

After next June 11, the aspects for the United States will turn for the worse and after that date, if Germany is still going, an invasion may be started through Brazil, which already has many German colonists, De Wohl declared.

ICELAND MOVE GOOD

But, meantime, the United States has its best period. The move into Iceland came at a high spot for both the United States and the President and both the nation and Roosevelt will continue in a good position until next spring.

De Wohl declared that between now and June 11, 1942, would be the best time for the United States to enter the war.

FORMERLY AN AUTHOR

De Wohl pointed out that he's really more interested in the psychological aspects of astrology than in predictions. He was an author before he took up astrology 12 years ago and has written several motion-picture scripts.

Incidentally, he won't make any snap predictions. Each one requires weeks of study of horoscopes, birth dates, positions of the stars and other technical points. Then, after lengthy consideration, he'll decide what things are most likely to happen.

De Wohl's case officer, Eric Maschwitz, found him 'a right swindler' personally as well as professionally: 'You never met such a character. He was up to everything and he was paid a lot of money and I know because I used to have to go and pay him once a week.'[45]

De Wohl returned to Britain early in 1942, following the US entry into the war. His diverse ventures over the next few years ranged from Catholic apologetics to a small but sinister role as Hermann Göring in the film Mr. Emmanuel, produced at Teddington Studios.[46] The hero, Isaac Emmanuel, travels secretly to Nazi Germany to try to find the mother of a Jewish refugee in England but discovers that she has married a prominent Nazi and concealed her Jewish identity. Emmanuel returns to England and tells her refugee son that his mother is dead. The film was much praised in The New York Times:

> We would venture the judgment that this simple and stirring little film is the sharpest damnation of Nazi 'kultur' that the screen is likely to show for some time ... They have presented Nazi Germans as coldly monstrous but capable folks, and have shown these polluted people as insensate to human sentiment.[47]

De Wohl's success in concocting bogus horoscopes for Hitler in 1941 prompted Eric Maschwitz to propose that BSC use more fake documents to sway US opinion. 'One thing we haven't got', he complained, 'is a good forgery section.'[48]

Maschwitz was probably both the most creative and the most unscrupulous contributor to BSC's influence operation aimed at bringing the United States into the war. As well as being one of the most successful British lyricists of his generation, whose songs included These Foolish Things Remind Me of You and A Nightingale Sang in Berkeley Square, he received an Oscar nomination in 1939 for the screenplay for Goodbye Mr Chips. Maschwitz considered Stephenson 'a genius'[49] and, after the success of de Wohl's bogus astrology, quickly persuaded him of the need for further forgeries. Convinced that 'Blinker' Hall's brilliantly stage-managed revelation of German intrigues in Mexico early in 1917 had played a critical part in bringing the United States into the First World War, Stephenson planned to use similar evidence of Nazi conspiracies in Latin America to persuade Roosevelt to enter the Second. Since there were no real Nazi conspiracies of sufficient importance, with Maschwitz's help he decided to invent them. By

Eric Maschwitz, head of BSC forgery section, was to become head of BBC TV Light
Entertainment in 1958, joining the rival ITV in 1963.

September 1941 Maschwitz was running Stephenson's new forgery
section, 'Station M' (M for Maschwitz), in a Toronto suburb.[50] His
staff, he later recalled, included 'two splendid ruffians who could
reproduce faultlessly the imprint of any typewriter on earth. I
controlled a chemical laboratory in one place, a photographic studio
in another.'[51]

Station M's most important forgery was a map which claimed to
reveal the Nazi master plan for taking over South America. Though
details of its production remain obscure,[52] one of the BSC forgers
chiefly responsible was Ian Fleming's oldest friend, Ivar Bryce, whom
he had first met when both were pupils at Eton College. Bryce later
found Fleming his Jamaica home 'Goldeneye'; he was one of the
dedicatees of *Diamonds Are Forever*.[53] In October 1941 Stephenson sent
Roosevelt, probably via William Donovan, a copy of the map which,
he claimed, had been obtained by British agents from a German
diplomatic courier in Argentina.

Roosevelt made the map the centrepiece of his 'Navy and Total Defense Day' address broadcast on 27 October:

> I have in my possession a secret map made in Germany by Hitler's government – by planners of the New World Order ... The geographical experts of Berlin have ruthlessly obliterated all the existing boundary lines; they have divided South America into five vassal states, bringing the whole continent under their domination. And they have also so arranged it that the territory of these new puppet states includes the Republic of Panama and our great life-line – the Panama Canal. This map, my friends, makes clear the Nazi design not only against South America but against the United States as well.

Roosevelt went on to denounce another imaginary Nazi masterplan concocted by BSC:

> Your government has, in its possession, another document, made in Germany by Hitler's government ... It is a plan to abolish all existing

religions – Catholic, Protestant, Mohammedan, Hindu, Buddhist and Jewish alike ... The cross and all other symbols of religion are to be forbidden. The clergy are to be forever liquidated.

The basis of Roosevelt's most outspoken attack on Nazi Germany before Pearl Harbor was thus bogus intelligence foisted on him by William Stephenson.[54]

On 26 November Maschwitz proposed following these forged documents with fabricated photographs of German atrocities: 'If asked to do so, my section could quite easily provide a regular supply of atrocity pictures, manufactured by us in Canada.' Station M would arrange 'the buying and hiring of costumes, the manufacture of small pieces of scenery and of dummies', together with the services of 'a first-class make-up man', 'all of which could be carried out under some sort of cover':

> For the sake of accuracy, we should be provided with as complete a library as possible of photographs of German personnel, equipment, vehicles ... also actual specimens of German equipment ... The most obvious setting for atrocity pictures at the moment is Russia, so we should get to work while there is still snow in Canada.[55]

Forged 'atrocity pictures' for the US market, however, proved unnecessary. Only eleven days later Japan attacked Pearl Harbor.

The leading British film producer to take part in the BSC influence operation targeting the United States was the Hungarian-born Alexander Korda, who had collaborated with SIS's shadowy pre-war Z organisation, headed by Claude Dansey, which at the outbreak of war amalgamated with its main espionage network.[56] In May 1940, soon after Churchill became prime minister, Korda was asked by the minister of information, Duff Cooper, to go to Hollywood to make what he termed an 'American' propaganda film. Once in the United States, Korda stayed in close touch with Stephenson and BSC. He also received personal messages of encouragement and advice from Churchill while making *That Hamilton Woman!*, which was released in March 1941. The film starred Laurence Olivier as Admiral Nelson and Vivien Leigh (direct from her Oscar-winning performance in *Gone with the Wind*) as his lover Emma Hamilton. As well as being a box office success in Britain, the United States

and even the Soviet Union, *That Hamilton Woman!* instantly became Churchill's favourite film; he showed it to President Roosevelt on board HMS *Prince of Wales* during their secret mid-Atlantic meeting in August 1941.

For Churchill, as for Stephenson, one of the great merits of the film was its parallel between British resistance to Napoleon and to Hitler – epitomised by the line powerfully delivered by Olivier: 'You cannot make peace with dictators, you have to destroy them, wipe them out!' The best evidence of the propaganda value of *That Hamilton Woman!* was the outraged reaction of the Senate Committee on Foreign Relations, which summoned Korda to appear before it to answer charges of 'inciting the American public to war'. The hearing, scheduled for 12 December, was cancelled after the Japanese attack on Pearl Harbor five days earlier. In the following year, at Churchill's request, Korda became the first film producer or director to receive a knighthood.[57]

★

The complete surprise of both Roosevelt and Churchill at the news from Pearl Harbor reflected a failure of imagination as well as of intelligence collection. It did not occur to either the president or the prime minister that the 'little yellow men', as Churchill sometimes spoke of them and Roosevelt thought of them, were capable of such an astonishing feat of arms. By chance, on 7 December, the day of the Japanese surprise attack, Churchill was dining at Chequers with John Winant, the US ambassador, and Averell Harriman, Roosevelt's special representative, when the BBC broadcast the news. Churchill and his guests were uncertain exactly what the newsreader had reported. 'What did he say?' asked Churchill. 'Pearl Harbor attacked?' Churchill's butler, Sawyers, entered the room. 'It's quite true', he told Churchill and his guests, 'We heard it ourselves [on the BBC]. The Japanese have attacked Pearl Harbor.' Only in a British country house could the news of world war have been announced by the butler.[58]

Pearl Harbor and Hitler's declaration of war on the United States four days later coincided with the final stages of the trial in Brooklyn of the German Duquesne spy ring, the largest ever prosecuted in America. The conclusion of the trial on 13 December brought the total convictions of members of the ring to a record thirty-three and their total prison sentences to over 300 years.[59] The detection of the spies was to inspire the Oscar-winning, FBI-backed film, *House on 92nd Street* (1945), in which Hoover and other FBI personnel appeared alongside Hollywood actors. Probably no other twentieth-century intelligence chief attached as much importance as Hoover to the use of the cinema to burnish his agency's reputation. Even before Pearl Harbor, he had a close relationship with the film producer Louis de Rochemont and collaborated with him on *Men of the F.B.I.* (1941) and *F.B.I. Front* (1942). Hoover wrote to him in October 1942, 'We of the FBI obviously are extremely proud of the manner in which you have portrayed our activities ... It is grand to have such a friend as you.' A month later he awarded de Rochemont the FBI Distinguished Service Cross: 'I hope it will always serve as a constant memento of our feelings toward you.'[60]

After the US entry into the war, BSC continued to promote patriotic anti-Nazi films – among them *Above Suspicion*, based on a best-selling novel by the Scottish writer, Helen MacInnes, then the world's most successful female spy novelist. MacInnes's books sold more than 23 million copies in the United States alone, and were translated into 22 languages. Her British husband, Gilbert Highet, a leading classicist at Columbia University, took wartime leave to work for BSC, later becoming one of its official historians. During their pre-war honeymoon in Bavaria, MacInnes had taken detailed notes on Nazi violence and the Hitler menace which provided the background for *Above Suspicion*, in which a young British couple seek a British anti-Nazi agent during their honeymoon in Germany in the summer of 1939. In 1943 the novel was turned into a popular film, starring Joan Crawford and Fred MacMurray.[61]

Churchill saw the conclusion of a SIGINT alliance with the United States as an even more important intelligence priority than the HUMINT collaboration coordinated by BSC. After the US entry into the war, the rival US military and naval SIGINT agencies established far closer cooperation with Bletchley Park than with each other. The actor and Room 40 veteran, Frank Birch, who had left the stage for Bletchley Park soon after the outbreak of war, played a key role in establishing an alliance with the US naval SIGINT agency. Having initially been in charge of the German naval section, in 1941 he was promoted to head the whole naval section. The 24-year-old German-speaking actress, Pamela Gibson, who, remarkably, had met Hitler during a pre-war visit to Germany, was offered a job by Birch at Bletchley shortly after also being offered a role as understudy in a West End play. She asked Birch 'what he thought I should do. And he said, "Well, I think the stage can wait. The war can't".'[62] That argument, no doubt, explains why both Birch and Gibson gave up their stage careers until after the war.

As in Room 40 during the First World War, when Birch had written and co-produced the first pantomime about a British intelligence agency, he promoted revues and amateur dramatics among the Bletchley staff. The annual dramatic high point was the Christmas/New Year Revue, produced and co-written by Herbert 'Bill' Marchant, former German teacher at Harrow, and somewhat reminiscent of the Cambridge *Footlights* revues he had enjoyed while studying at the Perse School and St John's College.[63]

The composers of the music, Jill Medway and Douglas Jones, both went on to successful post-war musical careers: Medway as a singer, Jones (who changed his name to Craig because of the plethora of musical Joneses) as stage director and assistant general manager at Glyndebourne.[64]

B.P. DRAMA GROUP.

Words by Patrick Wilkinson, Frederick Pickering, Bill Marchant, Nigel de Grey.

Music written and arranged by Douglas Jones and Jill Medway.

Produced by Bill Marchant.

Scenery by Kenneth Gilson.

At the Pianos, Jill Medway, Robert Marchant.

Business Managers, Patrick Wilkinson, Kathleen Parker.

Stage Manager, Dudley Owen.

Stage Staff, Elena Owen, Joyce Fox-Male.

Wardrobe Mistress, Kathleen Parker.

Properties, Marie Contusco.

Lighting Effects by Elwyn Jones.

CHRISTMAS REVUE

HARK ! HARK !
THE PARK !

DEC. 31st, 1941 to JAN. 3rd, 1942,

In aid of the Bletchley "Service of Youth" Recreation Ground Appeal.

Warren, Printer, Bletchley.

Programme.   Threepence.

Edward Travis, who became director of Bletchley Park in February 1942, invited senior officers from the armed services to the revue to strengthen collaboration with those using its SIGINT. Travis's daughter, Valerie, later recalled:

My father always used to have a tremendous party, inviting all the top brass down from London for it. The little man who was the caterer for Bletchley Park had a wonderful line in the black market and he used to produce the most sumptuous feasts.[65]

As head of the naval section, Birch travelled to Washington with Travis to negotiate the first major British SIGINT accord with the United States: the Holden agreement of October 1942, providing for 'full collaboration' between Bletchley's naval section and its US Navy counterpart, OP-20-G, in decrypting German naval ciphers. The agreement was the first step in the creation of a comprehensive UK–US SIGINT alliance which still endures. Birch became a higher-ranking SIGINT officer than any other theatrical before or (so far as is known) since. By the end of the war he was deputy director of Bletchley Park, now known as the Government Communications Headquarters (GCHQ), staying on after the war to write a classified in-house history before returning in 1946 to a career on the stage, in films and at the BBC.[66] In an acting career interrupted by SIGINT operations in both world wars, he appeared in over fifty films, plays and TV dramas.[67]

Like the thousands of other former Bletchley staff, Birch said nothing about his wartime intelligence work to his post-war colleagues. Most veterans did not even tell their spouses. Bletchley remained possibly the best-kept secret in British history. By the time the ULTRA secret was finally declassified thirty years after the war, William Stephenson's memories of BSC had sadly become clouded by self-serving fantasies that he had played a major role in wartime SIGINT. He told his biographer that he had been personally entrusted by Churchill with passing ULTRA decrypts to Roosevelt, thus giving the President 'secret access to Hitler's intentions and plans'. In reality Stephenson had no access to ULTRA.[68]

As well as fantasising in retirement about his non-existent role in ULTRA, Stephenson was also in denial about Soviet penetration, refusing to accept that BSC, like the wartime SIS, MI5 and (more briefly) Bletchley Park, had unwittingly recruited a major Soviet agent. The agent in BSC, codenamed successively CHARLIE and UNC/9, was Cedric Belfrage, recruited by Stephenson after Pearl Harbor largely because, as a successful British writer and journalist in the United States with extensive experience of both print and film media, he was well equipped to carry out influence operations.[69] Belfrage kept the Centre in Moscow well informed about BSC, almost certainly passing on the story of the Nazi map forged by his friend Eric Maschwitz which had deceived Roosevelt. Unlike the Cambridge Five, from the moment he joined BSC Belfrage provided intelligence which confirmed Moscow's belief in the unscrupulousness of British policy. The fact that he had no contact with any of the Five, of whom the Centre had grown suspicious, further enhanced his credibility in Moscow. At almost the moment that Belfrage arrived in Washington, Maschwitz returned to London, initially to take charge of forces broadcasting before moving on to the Political Warfare Executive (as Belfrage was to do in 1944). Though Maschwitz must have had some sense of his Soviet sympathies in the 1930s,[70] Belfrage concealed his involvement with Soviet intelligence from his colleagues in BSC as successfully as Philby and Blunt did from theirs in SIS and MI5.

Belfrage succeeded in becoming Stephenson's main liaison with the FBI as well as his right-hand man in BSC. He later claimed, somewhat improbably, that on a visit to the Bureau's Washington HQ, he was 'turned loose among [the] filing cabinets' and 'took the opportunity to inspect the dossiers of myself and friends'. He was relieved to find, allegedly, that his own dossier was very thin. If Belfrage's claims of virtually unlimited access to FBI filing cabinets might have been exaggerated, there genuinely seem to have been no restrictions on his access to what Soviet intelligence considered 'extremely valuable information from BSC files'. He was also able to pass to the Russians classified documents sent to BSC by the Office of Strategic Services (OSS): among them, for example, a report on the anti-Communist resistance in Yugoslavia led by the royalist General Draža Mihailović which was in competition with the Communist forces of Josip Tito. Because there is no surviving record in British archives that Stephenson was ever, as he later claimed, in personal contact with Churchill, historians have been wrongly inclined to dismiss this as another of Little Bill's postwar fantasies about his wartime role. The best evidence that this contact existed comes from reports to the Centre by Belfrage, such as Stephenson's account of what Churchill had personally told him about British policy on opening a second front.[71]

Belfrage's Soviet case officer, Jacob Golos (codenamed ZVUK, 'Sound'), ran most of his agents, some of them with government jobs in Washington, through a cutout (intermediary). He considered Belfrage so important, however, that he ran him personally.[72] Belfrage aroused no suspicion in British intelligence. When he returned to London in 1944 to take up a job in the Political Warfare Executive, his new employer raised with MI5 the question of his 'alleged Communist connections'. MI5 replied: 'These Communist connections do not amount to anything beyond a mild interest in left-wing affairs.'[73] It discovered its mistake late in 1945 when Golos's leading cutout, Elizabeth Bentley, revealed to the FBI that, while in BSC, Belfrage had been working as a Soviet agent.[74] Belfrage, who had returned to the United States, admitted to the Bureau that he had passed BSC files to a senior American communist but declined to give precise details, since they would make him liable to a five-year jail term and a fine of £10,000 'inasmuch as he had violated his oath under the British [Official] Secrets Act'.[75] The MI5 liaison officer in Washington reported that the FBI did not believe Belfrage could be successfully prosecuted in the United States 'since the documents he handed over were all British, and he had moreover some form of diplomatic immunity. Belfrage was later deported but never prosecuted.[76]

★

William Donovan presents the Medal for Merit to Sir William Stephenson. Looking on (left to right) are Colonel Edward G. Buxton, former assistant director of OSS; the US playwright, Robert Sherwood, friend of Stephenson, winner of four Pulitzer prizes and presidential scriptwriter; and Lady (Mary) Stephenson.

Like BSC, OSS was successfully penetrated by Soviet intelligence – though, as in the case of BSC, not to the apparent detriment of the Allied war effort. Donovan had no idea that his confidential assistant, the former Rhodes Scholar Duncan Chaplin Lee, codenamed KOCH by the NKVD and its successor, the NKGB, was probably the most highly placed Soviet spy ever to penetrate US intelligence.[77] Donovan's satisfaction at the success of wartime HUMINT collaboration with BSC was publicly demonstrated in 1946 with the presentation to Stephenson, who had been knighted in the 1945 New Year Honours List, of the Medal for Merit, the highest US civilian award. On Donovan's recommendation, Stephenson became the first non-American to receive the Medal for his 'valuable assistance to America in the fields of intelligence and special operations'.

By the time the presentation was made, the intelligence careers of both Donovan and Stephenson were at an end. Had Roosevelt not died suddenly on 12 April 1945, it is difficult to believe that he would have closed OSS after victory over Japan without establishing a new peacetime intelligence agency, or that he would have excluded Donovan from any intelligence role. His successor, Harry S. Truman, did both. On becoming Roosevelt's last vice-president in January 1945, he was almost entirely ignorant of intelligence.[78]

By contrast, Truman did have a lifelong passion for musical entertainment. Though he had abandoned teenage ambitions to become a concert pianist, he was the most talented musician to occupy the Oval Office in the twentieth century. He kept a piano by his desk and found it difficult to pass other pianos without playing a tune on them. Truman's most photographed appearance as vice-president was when he played at a concert on 12 February for 800 servicemen in the ballroom of the Washington National Press Club. While he was playing, the glamorous 20-year-old film star, Lauren Bacall, suddenly appeared on stage and perched on top of the vice-president's upright piano. 'I was just a kid,' she said later. 'My press agent made me do it.'

Like the audience, Truman seemed delighted by Bacall's presence on the piano. His wife, Bess was not and tried unsuccessfully to stop him playing in public again.[79] Later that year, Bacall was to star as a British spy in what Warner Bros publicised as a 'scorching' film,

Confidential Agent. The film received mixed reviews; Bacall felt embarrassed by her unconvincing English accent. However, the British author of the novel on which it was based, Graham Greene, was enthusiastic: 'This remains the only good film ever made from one of my books by an American director and Miss Bacall gave an admirable performance, and so did Charles Boyer.'

During his first week as President, Truman was briefed for the first time on ULTRA and the wartime SIGINT alliance with Britain. German and Japanese decrypts gave him a dramatic insight into the last days of the Third Reich and, more importantly, into the final four months of the Pacific War. On 12 September he signed a top-secret one-sentence memorandum authorising peacetime continuation of SIGINT collaboration with Britain.[80]

Truman, however, took much longer to be persuaded of the case for founding the first peacetime US espionage agency, and suspected the ambitious Donovan of wanting to become head of an American 'Gestapo'. On 20 September 1945, he closed down OSS.[81] Donovan responded with a campaign to make the case for the founding of a post-war intelligence agency, using films on the wartime achievements of OSS. The first of these, *O.S.S.*, starring Alan Ladd, was made by Paramount, which ironically had been the first pre-war Hollywood studio penetrated by Soviet intelligence. The film's producer and screenwriter, Richard Maibaum, who had just returned from four years in the army, where he had produced military documentaries, later recalled: 'Every studio in Hollywood was racing to come out with the first OSS film. When I was in Washington I knew some of the OSS people so I had a head start on the subject.' Maibaum, who also narrated the film, later became screenwriter for thirteen of the first sixteen James Bond films.[82] *O.S.S.* had Donovan's personal approval. One scene in the film, the briefing by an OSS instructor to wartime intelligence recruits, was based directly on Donovan's case for the founding of a new peacetime central intelligence agency:

We're late. Four hundred years. That's how long ago the other major powers started their OSS. We've only got months, to build the first central intelligence agency in our history. A world-wide organization that'll beat the enemy at its own game ... Americans aren't brought up to fight the way the enemy fights. We can learn to become intelligence agents and saboteurs, if we have to. But we're too sentimental, too trusting, too easy-going, and what's worse, too self-centered ... Forget everything you've been told about fair play and sportsmanship.[83]

O.S.S. was a box-office success. Bosley Crowther in *The New York Times* called it 'tense, tightly written and swiftly paced'.[84] However, the director, Irving Pichel, a lifelong Christian Socialist, fell victim to the paranoid tendencies of the House Un-American Activities Committee (HUAC) investigation of communist infiltration of Hollywood, and spent most of the rest of his career abroad.[85]

The next film which was intended, with Donovan's blessing, to celebrate the achievements of OSS and demonstrate the need for a peacetime successor, took its title from a 1946 book, *Cloak and Dagger: The Secret Story of O.S.S.* by Corey Ford and Alastair MacBain, to which Donovan had written the introduction. Former OSS agent E. Michael Burke acted as technical adviser. In the first film treatment, Donovan is shown leaving the White House after being asked by Roosevelt to found OSS. When an aide asks him where he is going to find the

Alan Ladd, the first A-List Hollywood star to play a US intelligence officer.

'spies, thieves, murderers, saboteurs' needed by OSS, Donovan points through the car window at the crowds on their way to work: 'There they are. The ordinary people. Those are our spies, our saboteurs, our murderers.' In the original film plot, the OSS hero, played by Gary Cooper, goes on a final (fictional) mission to Germany to destroy a Nazi atomic bomb-factory improbably hidden beneath a Bavarian brewery – thus demonstrating the continuing need for a US intelligence service at the dawn of the nuclear age. At great expense, the director, Fritz Lang, had the brewery and bomb factory constructed in Bronson Canyon, Los Angeles, then spectacularly blown up in the final scene. Production of the film by Warner Bros/United States Pictures, however, was disrupted by bitter conflict between Lang and the producer, Milton Sperling, whom the director banned from both the set and script conferences. Sperling retaliated by cutting the final scene with the destruction of the bomb factory from *Cloak and Dagger* before it was released in September 1946. Unsurprisingly, most reviewers found the film lacked the realistic portrayal of OSS operations promised in advance publicity.[86]

Donovan initially had far higher hopes of *13 Rue Madeleine*, the third and last of the post-war films on OSS. In an attempt to inject greater realism, Twentieth Century Fox chose as the producer Louis de Rochemont, originator of the 'semi-documentary' drama, whose films on the FBI had delighted J. Edgar Hoover. De Rochemont's early draft scripts contained extended depictions of Donovan, including authentic film footage. By July 1946, however, Donovan was outraged by the way the film was developing, writing angrily to de Rochemont:

> The picture is a phony. With all the excellent authentic material which we have sought to make available to you it seems absurd that your company would persist in making a picture that not only lacks reality but [also] plausibility.

Donovan seems to have been particularly indignant about two 'absurdities'. The first was the discovery of a German double-agent in OSS. The second was the decision to parachute the OSS hero, Bob Sharkey (played by James Cagney), into German-occupied France, despite the fact that he possessed top-secret information on plans for the D-Day landings. When Sharkey is captured by the Germans and taken to the Gestapo's Paris headquarters at 13, rue Madeleine, the building is bombed and Sharkey killed to prevent him revealing under torture the secret Allied invasion plans.[87]

Before the film's release in January 1947 all explicit references to OSS were removed. The actor playing Donovan was reduced in rank and renamed 'Abel' – ironically the name of the most notorious Cold War KGB illegal later arrested in the United States. A majority of reviews of 13 Rue Madeleine were positive. Bosley Crowther in The New York Times, however, ridiculed the lack of any reference to OSS:

> In the light of the many fancy stories of the wartime activities of the O.S.S. – you know, the 'cloak and dagger' boys who worked behind the enemy lines – it seems rather odd that any movie pretending to recount such derring-do should have to dissemble in naming the organisation involved.[88]

It is easy to imagine the Schadenfreude of J. Edgar Hoover, a determined opponent of the founding of a new peacetime intelligence service, when he learned of the quarrel between his favourite film-maker, Louis de Rochemont, holder of the FBI Distinguished Service Cross, and General Donovan.

The first step in the creation of a peacetime US foreign intelligence agency was a presidential directive of 22 January 1946, establishing a National Intelligence Authority (NIA) composed of the secretaries of state, war and the navy, with the chairman of the joint chiefs of staff, Admiral William Leahy, representing the president. Truman's directive also established the post of Director of Central Intelligence (DCI), who was to attend the NIA as a non-voting member and direct the work of a new Central Intelligence Group (CIG), a small analytical agency set up to collate and process – but not to collect – all-source intelligence. The chief architect of this reorganisation, Admiral Sidney W. Souers, agreed unenthusiastically to Truman's request that he become the first DCI on condition that he serve no longer than six months. The president celebrated the occasion with probably the most eccentric lunch ever given in the White House, personally presenting each guest with a black cloak, black hat and wooden dagger. He then called Leahy forward and stuck a large black moustache on his upper lip. Souers, Truman announced, had been appointed 'Director of Centralized Snooping'.

As this comic piece of presidential theatre indicates, Truman still found it difficult to take seriously the idea of peacetime American espionage. He also had difficulty in grasping the reality of Soviet espionage in the United States. Not until the summer of 1946 did the president give in to pressure from the Justice Department to authorise wiretapping and bugging of 'persons suspected of subversive activities against the United States, including suspected spies'.[89] By the end of the year, he at last accepted the case for the founding of the Central Intelligence Agency.

The CIA was the first foreign intelligence agency in any major power to be publicly created by act of parliament rather than by (usually secret) executive decision. Congress gave its unqualified approval in July 1947 to the founding of the CIA not because of Donovan's campaign to celebrate the achievements of OSS, or even as a result of the onset of the Cold War, but because of memories of the Pearl Harbor disaster less than six years earlier. Carter Manasco, Democratic Representative for Alabama, summed up the mood of many in Congress: 'If we had had a strong central intelligence organization, in all probability we would never had had the attack on Pearl Harbor; there might not have been a World War II.'[90]

13

Cold War Intelligence and the Entertainment Business

During the Cold War, both the Soviet Union and the United States conducted worldwide intelligence operations on a scale unprecedented in peacetime.[1] In both countries the entertainment business, and the film industry in particular, showed an equally unprecedented interest in espionage (much less in SIGINT).[2] James Bond became a global household name, better known than any real spy, alive or dead.

The first Second World War intelligence officers to star in a post-war film on foreign operations were British: Harry Rée and Jacqueline Nearne, two of the heroes of SOE operations in German-occupied France, who played themselves, slightly disguised, in a 1944 'docu-drama', *School for Danger*, by the RAF Film Production Unit, paid for by the Central Office of Information. Rée was cast as 'Captain Brown', codenamed 'FELIX', in charge of an important secret mission to France; Nearne was his radio operator 'Miss Williams', codenamed 'CAT'. There are few more remarkable examples than Harry Rée of the transformation of a wartime secret agent into a post-war film star. As a student at Cambridge before becoming a language teacher at Bradford Grammar School, he had been a leading light in the Amateur Dramatic Club (ADC), the oldest and one of the most successful of British student drama societies. His wartime role working with the French Resistance was a triumph of dangerously versatile role play. During one nearly fatal encounter with a German military policeman, he was reminded of playing Shakespeare at the ADC: 'I lunged at him and brought him down. I remembered *King Lear* and tried to get one of his eyeballs out by pressing with my thumb. It didn't work ... ' Of the dozen SOE colleagues with whom Rée worked most closely, only six survived the war.[3]

Nearne was one of 39 female SOE secret agents sent to France, who – as the docudrama showed – were given the same operational training as the 431 men.[4] Though officially a courier, she was also made part of a daring and successful sabotage unit. Remarkably, in a country where women did not get the vote until 1944, male *résistants* in her network took orders from her. Like Rée, Nearne had a series of narrow escapes made possible only by a remarkable aptitude for role play:

> Sometimes the Germans helped me as I got off a train and gallantly carried my luggage. That helped me get through the checks without any problems.

After fifteen months in France Nearne had to be evacuated at night in April 1944 by an RAF Westland Lysander, which was able to land on and take off from a grass strip only 300 metres long.[5]

Filming for *Now It Can Be Told* began in Pinewood Studios and on location in the Scottish Highlands in October 1944. Between January and July 1945 there was a total of four months filming in French Savoy and the Midi, followed by Pinewood, London, Brussels and Antwerp.[6] The producer/director and chief scriptwriter was Wing Commander Edward 'Teddy' Baird, who in civilian life was a successful film director. All the parts were played by SOE personnel. Baird commissioned a dramatic score by John Greenwood played by the London Symphony Orchestra. Rée and Nearne had the dramatic ability, good looks and personal charm to justify their star billing.[7]

Wing Commander 'Teddy' Baird's attempt to protect the reputation of the RAF made some of the script painful for both Rée and Nearne. A night attack by RAF bombers in July 1943 on a factory at Sochaux, near Montbéliard, which made armaments for the German armed forces, missed the target but killed hundreds of civilians. On Rée's initiative, the factory was successfully sabotaged by the Resistance, with the secret assistance of its French owners, the Peugeot family, and without causing civilian casualties.[8] In the film version, however, Captain Brown (played by Rée) fails to sabotage the factory and has to call on the RAF for assistance. Rée then had to utter words which must have come close to sticking in his throat: 'The RAF made a marvellous job of it … Very little damage outside the target area.'[9] Nearne also had to swallow hard.[10]

In 1946, to the deep dismay of both Rée and Nearne, a shortened version of the film under the title *School for Danger* was shown in some British cinemas. Nearne complained that the whole film had been dumbed down.[11] The full film under its original title *Now It Can Be Told* was released in 1947 with the opening credits:

> The players are members of the French Resistance and the organisation built up in Great Britain to assist resistance in all occupied countries. Their sabotage culminated on D-Day in insurrections by thousands of armed patriots which helped to paralyse the enemy's communications and hastened their defeat.[12]

The film had greatest impact in the French version, *Maintenant ... on peut le dire,* which had a glittering première at the Théâtre des Champs Élysées in June 1948. Captain Rée DSO OBE had been awarded the Médaille de la Résistance Française and Croix de Guerre, and made Chevalier de la Légion d'honneur. Probably because of her gender and her lowly official status as a courier, Nearne was awarded only an MBE.

THÉATRE DES CHAMPS-ÉLYSÉES
DIRECTEUR : Roger EUDES

MAINTENANT...
ON PEUT LE DIRE

Two months after his triumph on the Champs Élysées, Rée returned to his pre-war job teaching French and German at Bradford Grammar School, later becoming headmaster of Watford Grammar School and first professor of education at York University. As his son later recalled, even when fêted at the Paris première, he had been 'a reluctant film star'.[13] He could not bear basking in public adulation as a war hero turned film star at a time when so many of the Resistance families he had known were overwhelmed with grief. On his return during filming to the Café Grangier in Sochaux, where, as 'Monsieur Henri', he had regularly met local *résistants*:

> Hélène Grangier told me what had happened when Claude was shot. She had denied all knowledge and the [German] officer, in a rage, took her by the hair and led her down the stairs to where Claude was lying in a pool of blood. He pushed her head down into the blood. 'Rub your nose in the blood of this terrorist', he said. 'Perhaps this will make you talk.'[14]

Rée received heartbreaking letters from families he had known in the Resistance who had lost loved ones. Jules Robert wrote to him on 29 July 1945, just as filming was being completed:

> My son Guy was arrested at home on 4 April 1944, condemned to death at Besançon and shot on 9 June. Could you try to get him a medal? He was 18.[15]

For twenty years after his return to a successful career as a teacher, Rée refused to talk about his SOE career. He did not do so until his name and some of his exploits appeared in the official history *SOE in France* by M. R. D. Foot, published in 1966. Even then, so far as is known, he never mentioned his brief but promising career in film.

Now It Can Be Told failed to inspire other British film-makers. SOE was wound up early in 1946 and the three main peacetime intelligence agencies – SIS, MI5 and GCHQ – all loathed the idea of appearing on screen. By contrast, Soviet and, to a lesser extent, American intelligence took a direct interest in film-making. The most popular spy thriller in Soviet cinemas at the start of the Cold War was *The Razvedchik's Feat* (1947). Telling the heroic story of an intelligence officer (*razvedchik*) operating behind the lines in German-occupied Ukraine, the film won the Stalin Prize. Its main scriptwriter was Mikhail Maklyarsky, a former spy with a notably sinister record. During the Second World War he had been a member of Pavel Sudoplatov's Administration of Special Tasks, which was responsible for the assassination of Trotsky and other enemies of the Soviet regime. During his film career, which included another Stalin Prize winner, *The Secret Mission* (1950), Maklyarsky retained close links with Soviet intelligence – and an interest in assassination. His intelligence recruits included the film actor Nikolai Khokhlov, who was trained as an assassin and despatched from Moscow to operate against leading Ukrainian nationalists who had taken refuge in West Germany.[16]

Khokhlov's first target was one of the leaders-in-exile of the Ukrainian Social-Democratic National Labour Union, Georgy Sergeyevich Okolovich. He introduced himself to Okolovich at his flat in Frankfurt on 18 February 1954 with a theatrical flourish: 'Georgy Sergeyevich, I've come to you from Moscow. The Central Committee of the Communist Party of the Soviet Union has ordered your assassination.' Khokhlov then informed the startled Okolovich that he was not going to harm him; soon afterwards he defected to the CIA. At a subsequent press conference the would-be assassin caused a

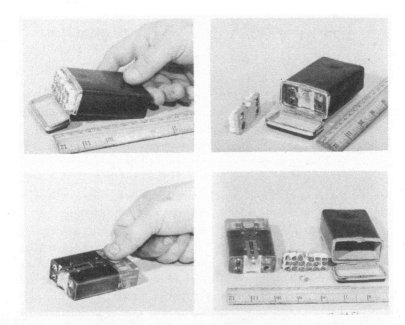

sensation when he displayed the sophisticated murder weapon entrusted to him by the KGB: a miniature electrically operated gun, fitted with a silencer and concealed inside a cigarette packet, which fired cyanide-tipped bullets.

Khokhlov himself now became the target of his former employers. The KGB, in fact, came closer to killing Khokhlov than Okolovich, narrowly failing in 1957 to murder him with radioactive thallium. The public embarrassment to Moscow of the Khokhlov case was compounded by the defection of another KGB assassin, Bogdan Stashinsky, in West Germany in 1961. After confessing to the murder of two exiled Ukrainian nationalist leaders, Stashinsky was sentenced in 1962 to eight years in jail. The judge at his trial, however, declared that the main culprit was the Soviet Union which had institutionalised political murder.[17]

At the time of Stashinsky's defection, the main Moscow film studio, Mosfilm, was producing a major spy film featuring a plot by Western intelligence to assassinate a Soviet scientist. The subject of assassination had become so embarrassing, however, that the KGB insisted that even Western assassins were not to appear on screen.[18] By the early 1960s, secret KGB 'advisers' were attached to the production teams of all films on espionage and other politically sensitive subjects. One of those officers, I. I. Shmelev, insisted that they were committed to making spy films 'more beautiful and more interesting'. In reality, so far as cinemagoers were concerned, they merely made them more boring.[19]

In the early Cold War, the CIA, which as yet attracted little public criticism in the United States, also had some secret influence on the film industry. Its biggest box-office hit was the film version of George Orwell's novel, *Animal Farm*, the first animated feature film made by a British company, Halas and Batchelor, which was probably unaware that the American funding which paid for eighty animators came from the CIA.[20] The man in charge of the US operation was E. Howard Hunt, a prolific author as well as an intelligence officer who would later become notorious for plotting the 1972 Watergate break-in. After Orwell's death in 1950, Hunt sent two agents, Carleton Alsop and Finis Farr, on a mission to England to buy the film rights to *Animal Farm* from the author's widow. As an inducement, they arranged for Sonia Orwell to meet her Hollywood hero, Clark Gable. To produce a more overtly anti-communist film version of *Animal Farm*, Hunt chose J. Edgar Hoover's favourite producer, Louis de Rochemont.[21]

In the film, as in the novel, the pigs Snowball (Trotsky) and Napoleon (Stalin) lead a successful revolution against the owner of Manor Farm, Mr Jones (Tsar Nicholas II). Napoleon then ousts Snowball, falsely accuses him of treason, and sets vicious dogs (the NKVD) on Snowball's supporters and other innocents who are forced to confess to imaginary crimes. The (Stalinist) pigs walk on their hind legs, carry whips and persecute the other animals, while Napoleon allies with human farmers. The novel ends with the other animals watching a dinner party at which pigs and humans eat, drink and play cards acrimoniously together: 'The creatures outside looked from pig to man, and from man to pig, and from pig to man again: but already it was impossible to say which was which.' In the anti-communist ending to the film, however, only the pigs become completely corrupt and the other animals successfully revolt against them.

Though the initiative for the changes in the film version of *Animal Farm* probably came chiefly from de Rochemont rather than the CIA, there is little doubt that Howard Hunt strongly approved of them. The limitations of early Cold War film technology prevented the CIA from smuggling significant numbers of copies behind the Iron Curtain. The Agency attached so much importance to the propaganda value of *Animal Farm*, however, that it filled large containers with condensed editions of the novel, attached them to ten-foot helium balloons at launch sites in West Germany, and waited for following winds to blow them across the border into the communist East.[22]

After a gala launch at the United Nations in New York in 1954, favourable film reviews for *Animal Farm* in the American press included the headline, 'The British out-Disney Disney'. Unlike Disney feature films, however, *Animal Farm* took fifteen years to recoup production costs, and it inspired no other expensive anti-Soviet animated features.[23] Spy films, by contrast, became part of the staple diet of cinema audiences in both East and West. The most successful Western spy films of the early Cold War were based on best-selling novels written by two former British wartime intelligence officers, Graham Greene and Ian Fleming. Some of Greene's three years in SIS were spent working under his friend Kim Philby in the Iberian counter-intelligence section, where he was one of the very few to learn some of the successes of the double agent GARBO. 'No one', Greene wrote later, 'could have been a better chief than Kim Philby ... He worked harder than anyone and never gave the impression of labour. He was always relaxed, completely unflappable.' When Philby later defected to Moscow, Greene remained in touch and wrote a friendly introduction to his memoirs, comparing his work for Soviet intelligence to that of 'many Catholics, who in the reign of Elizabeth, worked for the victory of Spain'.[24]

Greene wrote in the preface to his most famous spy story, *The Third Man*, filmed in 1949, that it 'was never written to be read but only to be seen … The film, in fact, is better than the story.' The most important adviser to both Greene and the director, Carol Reed as they laid the groundwork for the film in post-war, occupied Vienna was Philby's friend, *The Times* correspondent and (as yet unidentified) Soviet agent, Peter Smolka.[25] Greene and Reed learned from Smolka of the black-market trade in watered-down penicillin and police patrols through the sewers of the divided city – both of which feature prominently in the denouement of *The Third Man*.[26] The truth about Harry Lime, the charismatic villain brilliantly played by Orson Welles, is finally revealed in (the fictitious) 'Smolka's Bar' – a tribute to Smolka which passed unnoticed by the film's mostly enthusiastic reviewers.

Having fallen foul of House Un-American Activities Committee (HUAC), the radical (but not communist) Orson Welles left Hollywood to reinvent himself as a wandering European film-maker.[27] The chief victims of the HUAC investigation were ten members of the film industry, the 'Hollywood Ten', who were found guilty in 1948 of obstructing the committee's investigations. After their appeals failed, all began serving one-year jail sentences in 1950, which ended all but one of their Hollywood careers.[28] Though all were current or past members of the Communist Party, there is no reason to believe that any would have been willing to work for Soviet intelligence, which continued to target the US film industry.

Since 1934, the NKVD and its successors had attached great importance to their flamboyant Hollywood agent, Boris Morros (codenamed FROST), originally at Paramount Studios, who had since become an independent producer and entrepreneur in the entertainment business. In 1948, Jack Soble, his current Soviet case officer, reported to Moscow that Morros

> could undoubtedly do a lot of good for our cause in every respect, namely: major connections, getting people jobs, getting entry visas through various channels, transferring funds to various countries, legal-izing people through film divisions in the USA and in Europe.

In both 1948 and 1950, Morros achieved the very rare distinction for an American agent of being summoned to personal meetings with a senior Soviet intelligence officer, Alexander Korotkov, in Switzerland and Moscow.

Though neither Soble nor Korotkov suspected it, Morros had been an FBI double agent since 1947, when the Justice Department had agreed not to prosecute him for his previous work for Soviet intelligence. Morros's role as double agent was finally revealed amid a blaze of publicity in 1957 when he was the key witness at the trial of Soble and other Soviet spies, fourteen of whom were identified in court, thanks chiefly to his evidence. The press, which was unaware of his previous career as a Soviet agent, praised Morros as 'an incredibly brave American'. His 1959 autobiography, *My 10 Years as a Counterspy*, was the basis for the 1960 film, *Man on a String*,[29] produced once again by Louis de Rochemont. The role of Morros, thinly disguised as Boris Mitrov, was played by Ernest Borgnine, who had won an Academy Award for Best Actor a few years earlier. According to the *New York Times* reviewer, 'By a small miracle of Hollywood alchemy, one of the most fantastic and astounding spy careers of them all, that of Boris Morros, has yielded a good movie, "Man on a String".'[30]

In addition to Morros, the FBI had at least eighteen other informants in early Cold War Hollywood. Though most have not been identified, it is known that Source T-10 was Ronald Reagan,[31] who spent seven years as a repeatedly re-elected president of the Screen Actors Guild, to which all Hollywood actors belonged. Reagan was not, however, the fanatical anti-communist crusader his more partisan political opponents have since alleged. In his testimony to HUAC he named no names and said that reports of communist activity in Hollywood were mostly 'hearsay'. Reagan also agreed to sponsor a fundraising concert by Paul Robeson for a local hospital:

> I hesitated for a moment because I don't think that Mr. Robeson's and my political views coincide at all and then I thought I was being a little stupid because, I thought, here is an occasion where Mr. Robeson is perhaps appearing as an artist and certainly the object, raising money, is above any political consideration, it is a hospital supported by everyone … So I felt a little bit as if I had been stuffy for a minute and I said, certainly, you can use my name.[32]

As President of the Screen Actors Guild, Reagan was better known for taking on the Hollywood moguls than the Communist Party.

Reagan led the Guild during its first three strikes and, against strong opposition from the studios, won 'residual' payments for previous films, health and pension benefits for its members.[33]

During the early 1950s HUAC's investigations, which had led to the Hollywood blacklist,[34] were overtaken by the larger anti-communist witch-hunt led by Senator Joseph McCarthy who claimed to have proof that 205 influential communists in the State Department were 'shaping its policy'. President Truman had good reason to claim that 'the greatest asset the Kremlin has is Senator McCarthy'. His self-serving crusade against the 'Red Menace' and wild but newsworthy exaggerations made liberal opinion around the world sceptical of the reality of the intelligence offensive against what Soviet leaders privately called the 'Main Adversary' – the United States.[35]

McCarthyism encouraged Graham Greene to stick what he called his 'feeble twig in the spokes of American foreign policy'. The temptation to do so increased in 1952 when he was refused his usual one-year entry visa to the United States after admitting to brief membership of the Communist Party while an Oxford undergraduate.[36] Greene's novel, *The Quiet American*, published in 1955, was the first major attack on CIA covert action by either a British or American author. The 'Quiet American', Alden Pyle, is an undercover CIA officer in Vietnam,[37] who is ruthlessly determined to create a 'third force' between communism and French colonialism. Pyle supplies a potential leader of this third force with plastic explosive which he uses for a terrorist bombing in Saigon. Pyle's main antagonist is the world-weary British journalist Thomas Fowler, who is engaged in a love triangle with Pyle and a 20-year-old Vietnamese woman. Fowler, like Greene, loathes the Americans in Vietnam 'with their private stores of Coca-Cola and their portable hospitals and their wide cars and their not quite latest guns'.

To Greene's fury, the film version of *The Quiet American*, released in 1958, turned his denunciation of US policy in South East Asia into a sympathetic treatment of American intervention in Vietnam. It has sometimes been assumed that the CIA was behind the changes. It seems more likely that Joseph Mankiewicz, who adapted Greene's novel for the screen, was chiefly responsible.[38] The CIA, however, undoubtedly approved. Its head, Allen Dulles, Director of Central Intelligence, would not otherwise have made it possible for *The Quiet American* to be filmed in Vietnam.

Ironically, Michael Redgrave (later knighted), who played the part of Thomas Fowler in the film, had been under intermittent

Michael Redgrave (*right*) as Thomas Fowler in *The Quiet American*, with Audie Murphy (*left*) as Alden Pyle.

surveillance by MI5 since 1940 when he had signed the manifesto of the pro-communist People's Vigilance Committee; he was later involved, with his wife, in the Unity Theatre Communist Group. Redgrave had been a friend of Guy Burgess since both were students at Cambridge in the 1930s and met him in Moscow in 1958, seven years after Burgess's defection, when Redgrave was playing the role of Hamlet in a touring production by the Shakespeare Memorial Theatre as part of a cultural exchange. MI5 intercepted a letter from Burgess to his mother in England telling her that Redgrave's Hamlet was even better than Olivier's. Burgess did not tell his mother, however, that he was so drunk that he had thrown up in Redgrave's dressing room – an episode which later featured in Alan Bennett's award-winning 1983 TV drama, *An Englishman Abroad*, directed by John Schlesinger.[39]

In his great Cold War espionage parody *Our Man in Havana*, published in 1958 and filmed in Havana a year later, Graham Greene drew on his own wartime experience in SIS. The facility with which the fraudulent Jim Wormold, 'Our Man in Havana' (played in the film by Sir Alec Guinness), invents agents probably owes something to

Greene's knowledge of how GARBO had deceived the Abwehr even before he became a British double agent. Wormold's bogus female agent, Teresa, is modelled on Mata Hari; he reports to London that she 'dances naked', 'quite naked'.[40] Greene gives his own wartime SIS officer number, 59200, to Wormold's SIS superior, Henry Hawthorne (played by Noël Coward).

After the 1962 Cuban Missile Crisis, the most dangerous moment of the Cold War, *Our Man in Havana* began to seem curiously prophetic. Jim Wormold had fraudulently reported to London 'big military installations under construction' in eastern Cuba and sent drawings of them based on hugely enlarged parts of the Atomic Pile vacuum cleaner. After Soviet nuclear missile sites were discovered in Cuba, the British ambassador in Havana, Herbert 'Bill' Marchant, was struck by the coincidence:

> Any record of ... the Cuban Crisis must necessarily read more like a wildly improbable sequel to 'Our Man in Havana' than a Foreign Office

The only communist leader to appear on the set of a Western spy film: Fidel Castro with Sir Alec Guinness (playing the part of Jim Wormold) during the filming of *Our Man in Havana* in 1959. Guinness later called Castro 'a very courageous man and a very impressive one'.

dispatch. Indeed I doubt whether months ago any responsible publisher would have given a moment's consideration to a story in which Soviet Russia was to be credited with shipping some four dozen giant missiles, each one longer than a cricket pitch, across the Atlantic to Cuba, where Russian military technicians disguised as agricultural advisers would set them up in secret on launching sites.[41]

Graham Greene's continuing fascination with intelligence operations was reflected in his willingness to work unofficially for SIS over many years – despite his friendship with Philby. His career as one of Britain's most celebrated authors, for which he was made both a member of the Order of Merit and a Companion of Honour, provided natural cover during his travels. As a Catholic, he was well placed during a visit to Warsaw in 1955 to report on the Soviet-sponsored Catholic Pax movement. During visits to Indochina in the 1950s he worked closely with the SIS head of station in Hanoi, Trevor Wilson.[42] Greene's biographer, Norman Sherry, calls him 'the perfect spy ... an intensely secretive man'.[43]

★

The world's most famous fictional spy could scarcely be described as 'intensely secretive'. James Bond made his first appearance in 1953 in Ian Fleming's novel *Casino Royale*, where he introduces himself as 'Bond – James Bond', a formula repeated in subsequent novels. In retrospect, Fleming believed that the fifth Bond novel, *From Russia, with Love*, published four years later, 'was, in many respects, my best book'. Its ambiguous conclusion, however, which leaves Bond's survival in doubt, indicates that Fleming was undecided at the time whether to carry on with 007. Bond's growing popularity in the United States resolved his doubts. The most powerful endorsement for *From Russia, with Love* came from President John F. Kennedy, who in March 1961 named it as one of his ten favourite books. Later in the year, an advertising campaign by Fleming's US publisher showed the White House at night with a single upstairs light still on, and the caption: 'You can bet on it [the President]'s reading one of those Ian Fleming thrillers.' But it is thanks to the films, more than to Fleming's novels, that Bond has become the world's best-known and most popular fictional spy.

James Bond does not make an appearance in *From Russia, with Love* until one-third of the way through the book. The early part of the novel concentrates instead on the machinations of SMERSH (a contraction of Smert Shpionam, 'Death to Spies'), the most homicidal section of Soviet intelligence. Though SMERSH had been wound up in 1946 and its foreign responsibilities transferred to the future KGB, Fleming insists in a foreword that it still 'exists and remains today the most secret department of the Soviet government'. He also claims that the head of SMERSH, General Grubozaboyschikov, his own fictional creation, was a real individual with two Orders of Lenin: 'My description of his appearance is correct.'[44] In reality, the name 'Grubozaboyschikov' was clearly bogus – a tongue-in-cheek attempt by a non-Russian speaker to invent a gruesome Russian name. Its meaning approximates to 'brutal slaughterers'. The name also begins with a pun: GRU was the acronym for Soviet military intelligence. Fleming knew, however, that, since Soviet intelligence denied carrying out any assassinations, its denials about the existence of SMERSH would carry no credibility.

In *From Russia, with Love*, the leadership of SMERSH is preoccupied by a series of actual humiliations suffered by Soviet foreign intelligence during the mid 1950s, chief among them Khokhlov's defection after refusing to assassinate Okolovich in West Germany. Grubozaboyschikov declares at the outset: 'We cannot have another of those Khokhlov affairs.'[45]

The SMERSH leadership decides to respond to this embarrassment with 'an act of terrorism against the British Secret Service' involving the humiliation and assassination of James Bond. The killer is to be a Northern Irish psychopath, 'Red' Grant (memorably played in the film by Robert Shaw), whose enjoyment of homicide had led him to offer his services to SMERSH. Its decision to use a foreign assassin to kill Bond is not wholly implausible. After the embarrassment of Khokhlov's and Stashinsky's defections, the KGB decided to employ a West German contract killer, Wolfgang Wildprett, to continue the assassination of Ukrainian émigré leaders. In a further humiliation for the KGB, Wildprett then also defected.[46] Grant, by contrast, has no intention of disobeying orders. Like Khokhlov, he warns Bond that he has been instructed to kill him – but only to savour in advance the pleasure of the assassination and the Order of Lenin which he expects as his reward.

Grant's boss, Colonel Rosa Klebb, head of the SMERSH Operations Department, has become the best-known female villain in spy fiction and film, infamous for insisting that 'no torturing take place without her' and breathing in the screams of SMERSH's victims 'as if they were perfume'. In reality, although there had been a number of wartime female colonels in Soviet intelligence, during the Cold War there was a KGB ban on the recruitment of female officers (as opposed to agents) for operational work, which lasted until the Gorbachev era.[47]

It is Klebb who selects the inevitably beautiful Tatiana Romanova (played by Daniela Bianchi) to seduce Bond and lure him to his destruction. Somewhat predictably, Bond first encounters Romanova in his hotel bed in Istanbul, where they perform 'passionate arabesques', secretly filmed by SMERSH photographers through a one-way mirror, before they meet again on the Orient Express. Fleming's biographer, Andrew Lycett, reveals that Fleming had once bribed the attendant on a continental wagon-lit to let him into the compartment of the married film star, Diana Napier, where they made love to 'the hasty metal gallop of the wheels'. A similar phrase is used by Fleming to describe the interrupted love-making of Bond and Romanova aboard the Orient Express, as it 'thunders superbly' over miles of 'glittering steel'.

The bait, apart from Romanova, which is intended to lure Bond to his destruction, is the offer of a Spektor cipher machine (Lektor in the 1963 film version) which will enable British intelligence to decrypt top-secret Soviet communications. Fleming came close at this point to breaking official secrets legislation. He based the Spektor not on any system of Soviet communication but on the Enigma cipher machine used by Nazi Germany. As a Commander in the Naval Intelligence Division during the Second World War, Fleming had been one of the very small group (which included only six of Churchill's ministers) with access to the ULTRA intelligence derived from breaking Enigma and other high-grade enemy ciphers. Yet this most successful British intelligence operation of the war remained a closely guarded secret until 1973. The inspiration for Bond's attempt to acquire the Spektor from Romanova was still a classified operation at the time when Fleming wrote his novel.[48] Even the word SIGINT remained officially classified and was never used in any of the Bond novels and films.[49]

Immensely popular though *From Russia, with Love* proved in print, the film version, starring Sean Connery, is known to many more people around the world. When Connery was first chosen for the role of Bond in 1962, however, Fleming was disappointed: 'He's not what I envisioned of James Bond looks.' Though Fleming later changed his mind, the only physical description of Bond in the novel comes in an extract from his SMERSH file:

> Height: 183 centimetres, weight: 76 kilograms; slim build; eyes: blue; hair: black; scar down right cheek and on left shoulder; signs of plastic surgery on back of right hand (see appendix 'A'); all-round athlete; expert pistol shot, boxer, knife-thrower; does not use disguises. Languages: French and German. Smokes heavily (NB: special cigarettes with three gold bands); vices: drink, but not excess, and women. Not thought to accept bribes.[50]

The only other description of Bond in the novel is Romanova's. Searching for a comparison that would 'give him pleasure', she tells him, 'You are like an American film star', Romanova is startled by his reply: 'For God's sake! That's the worst insult you can pay a man.' The 'film star' insult was removed from the film version.[51]

*

The first Bond novel to be filmed was *Dr No* in 1962. Ironically, the author of the first draft of the screenplay, Wolf Mankowitz, had been under surveillance by MI5 for most of his adult life since his wife, Ann Seligmann, had joined the Communist Party while an undergraduate at Cambridge. In the early Cold War Mankowitz was repeatedly invited to Moscow by the Union of Soviet Writers. MI5, however, noted his opposition to the Soviet invasion of Hungary in 1956 and his call for freedom of expression for Soviet writers. Thereafter MI5 ceased to take an active interest in him.[52]

Mankowitz was one of a number of supposedly subversive stars who were spied upon during the Cold War. By the time it began, the world-famous black American bass-baritone singer, actor and activist, Paul Robeson, was already under close surveillance on both sides of the Atlantic. Robeson had spent most of the pre-war decade in Britain. The director of two plays in which he starred at the Embassy Theatre in Swiss Cottage (now the Central School of Speech and Drama) was André van Gyseghem, a committed Communist Party member and

MI5 surveillance photograph of Wolf Mankowitz (*left*).

regular visitor to the USSR.[53] In 1937, when Robeson was voted Britain's most popular radio singer, the Special Branch reported to MI5 that, at a gala celebration of the twentieth anniversary of the Bolshevik Revolution, Robeson sang 'a number of negro spirituals and two Soviet songs in Russian' to 'tremendous' applause.[54] A decade later, MI5 would still note in his file:

> Has been an enthusiastic supporter of the USSR since he visited that country in January 1935. Is either a member of the Communist Party or a near Communist and has spent a considerable part of his time in Russia where he has had his son and daughter educated.[55]

Russia, Robeson believed, was free from the racism endemic in the West.[56] After spending the war years in the United States, Robeson annoyed both the Colonial Office and MI5 by his support for independence movements in the West Indies and other British colonies – though MI5 regretfully concluded that 'we would not be justified on security grounds in refusing [him] a visa'.[57] During visits to Britain in 1949 and 1950, Robeson was kept under close surveillance, with his correspondence and telephone calls intercepted and his baggage secretly searched on arrival and departure.[58] His most controversial – and misquoted – speech, however, was in 1949 at a conference in Paris, where he was alleged to have said that he could not believe black Americans would ever take part in a war against the Soviet Union. Most of his planned concerts in the United State were cancelled. In 1950 the State Department also cancelled Robeson's passport, thus preventing him from travelling abroad. Hoover promptly sent FBI agents to take his passport from him.[59]

The most controversial black female star in the United States was was the celebrated jazz vocalist Billie Holiday. On 22 January 1949 the Federal Narcotics Bureau arrested Holiday and her abusive husband, Paul Levy, in San Francisco for possession of narcotics; both, it informed Hoover, were habitual drug-users.[60] The Bureau's racist head, Harry Anslinger, chose to make an example of Holiday, rather than a white star who used drugs such as Judy Garland, because Billie was African-American; jazz, Anslinger believed, was the depraved music of 'black junkies'.[61] The flamboyant actor and socialite, Tallulah Bankhead, set out to intercede with the FBI.

Holiday and Bankhead were probably in the middle of an affair begun while both were performing in different Broadway productions. As usual in a crisis, Tallulah believed in going to the top – which, in this case, was J. Edgar Hoover. She told Hoover, 'As my Negro nanny used to say, "When you pray, you pray to God, don't you?"' Hoover took her phone call – chiefly, no doubt, because he and her late father, Speaker of the House of Representatives at the time of his death, had been friends and mutual admirers.[62] Among her own friends, Tallulah took a casual attitude to drug-taking. 'Cocaine isn't habit-forming', she told them, 'and I know because I've been taking it for years.'[63] In talking to Hoover, however, Tallulah made no attempt to defend Billie's use of narcotics. Instead, she wanted him to use his influence to ensure her lover received hospital treatment rather than a jail sentence.

Though Hoover made clear that he could not intervene, Tallulah wrote to thank him 'a thousand times for the kindness, consideration and courtesy, in fact all the nicest adjectives in the book, for the trouble you took re our telephone conversation in connection with Billie

Holiday'. She then made the extraordinary claim, which Hoover probably knew was bogus, that the two women were not personal friends,
let alone lovers:

> I have met Billie Holiday but twice in my life but admire her immensely
> as an artist and feel the most profound compassion for her knowing
> as I do the unfortunate circumstances of her background.[64]

'Unfortunate circumstances' was a considerable understatement.
Growing up in poverty, Holiday had been forced into child prostitu-
tion. She heard her 'first good jazz in a whorehouse'.[65] Her singing
career was an extraordinary triumph over abuse and adversity. Tallulah
optimistically assumed that Hoover sympathised with the ordeals
which Holiday had endured:

> However guilty she may be, whatever penalty she may be required to
> pay for her frailties, poor thing, you I know did everything within the
> law to lighten her burden. Bless you for this.[66]

Hoover replied two days later with a remarkably friendly letter
which, however, made no mention of Billie Holiday:

> Dear Tallulah
>   ... Your kind comments are greatly appreciated, and I trust you will
> not hesitate to call on me at any time you think I might be of assistance
> to you.
>   Hoping to see you in the not too distant future and with kindest
> regards,
>   J. Edgar Hoover[67]

Holiday was not to need the assistance Hoover was unwilling to provide. Thanks to a talented lawyer, she was found not guilty at her trial
in June 1949. Tallulah's best-selling memoirs did not mention Billie
Holiday. By the time they were published in 1952, Tallulah was distancing herself from Holiday's increasingly tumultuous career. By threatening to sue, she forced the removal of all reference to her from Billie's
ghost-written 1955 memoir *Lady Sings the Blues*.[68]
    Just as Billlie Holiday's career went into what proved to be terminal
decline,[69] Paul Robeson began an unexpected but hugely successful

Tallulah Bankhead (*right*) and Billie Holiday with jazz trombonist Dickie Wells, 1951.

comeback at Carnegie Hall in May 1958 – his first advertised New York concert since he had been deprived of his passport eight years earlier. An FBI agent tapped a phone conversation in which he told a close friend that he was 'astounded at the success of the concert and that it opens up entire new vistas' for him. Hoover ordered 'Immediate investigation ... to identify the sponsor of Robeson's Carnegie Hall concert'. The investigation, however, was to no avail. On 16 June the Supreme Court ruled that the passport ban was unconstitutional.[70]

Following the recovery of his passport, Robeson made a triumphant return to Britain, where he sang to an audience of millions on TV and radio, as well as at a packed evensong in St Paul's Cathedral.[71]

In April 1959, Robeson was the first black actor to play the role of Othello at the Shakespeare Memorial Theatre in Stratford-upon-Avon.[72] Playing Iago opposite him was another American who had fallen foul of HUAC and McCarthyism: the Chicago-born theatre director and actor, Sam Wanamaker. Because of his US communist links – including, it was believed, several years as a Party member – when Wanamaker moved to Britain in 1952 he was placed by MI5 on a list of those to be interned 'in the event of an emergency with

Russia'.[73] In the Stratford production of *Othello*, the two male starring roles were thus both taken by actors with lengthy intelligence
files. Wanamaker's MI5 file noted percipiently that he was 'unlike
most US visitors of the theatrical world in that the majority of his
projects do materialise'.[74] The projects included the founding of the
Globe Theatre, for which he was later to be made an honorary CBE.

The most subversive star under MI5 surveillance during the early
Cold War was the brilliant Irish republican poet and playwright,
Brendan Behan, former 'borstal boy' (to quote the title of one of his
books) and IRA bomb-maker. Though never an actor, Behan was an
extrovert, entertaining and heavy-drinking performer in a variety of
public venues; he was once told during a BBC interview that he was
'coming over 100 degrees proof'. No Irish writer of his time was better
known around the world. When he died in 1964 at the age of only 41,
his health ruined by alcoholism, Behan was given a bigger Dublin
funeral than any previous Irish writer.[75] In 1942, only six months after
being released from an English youth prison, Behan was sentenced to
fourteen years' imprisonment in Dublin, of which he served four, for
the attempted murder of two Irish detectives. MI5 believed that his
frequent conversations in Mountjoy Prison with the convicted murderer
Barney Kirwan, 'right up to the day of his execution', had inspired him

to write his first stage play, *The Quare Fellow*,[76] which opened in Dublin in 1954 and in London in 1956, where it was first staged in Joan Littlewood's Theatre Workshop, before transferring to the West End. MI5 probably listened in to the discussion of the Theatre Workshop production at the British Communist Party's bugged headquarters.[77]

Like Godot, the 'quare fellow', a prisoner awaiting execution in Mountjoy Prison, never appears on stage. 'The Free State', says one of the prisoners, echoing Behan's republican beliefs, 'didn't change anything more than the badges on the warders' caps.' As Behan was aware, not even the hangmen changed. The best-known twentieth-century English hangman, Albert Pierrepoint, was put in charge of the execution of Barney Kirwan.[78] The unnamed English hangman in *The Quare Fellow* tells the Mountjoy warders, 'It's nice to get over to old Ireland, you know, a nice bit of steak and a couple of pints as soon as you get off the boat.'[79]

After the success of *The Quare Fellow*, Behan remained an IRA supporter, probably for the rest of his life. An MI5 informant reported in 1958 that 'the playwright has lost none of his sympathy with the IRA and continues to be a contributor to its funds.'[80] Behan was also a supporter of the British Communist Party, which he preferred to its Irish equivalent. He wrote to Barbara Niven at Party HQ after the Soviet suppression of the 1956 Hungarian Rising, in a letter intercepted by MI5: 'God Bless You All. We'll stand firm here for Socialism – Long live the USSR!'[81] Behan's increasingly heavy drinking made life difficult for the MI5 personnel who listened into his phone calls. One wrote after transcribing a telephone call by Behan to Niven in August 1957: 'I assume from the above conversation that Brendan was either a little mad, or drunk.' MI5 seems to have concluded, like one of its sources, that Behan was 'too unstable and too drunken to be particularly dangerous'.[82]

*

The reasons for FBI surveillance of American stars in the 1950s and 1960s were sometimes personal as well as political. J. Edgar Hoover, director of the Bureau from 1924 until his death in 1972 – the longest tenure by any head of a US government department or agency – became increasingly irascible and intolerant of the slightest criticism. In 1961, the FBI opened a file on the famously acerbic writer Gore Vidal, after receiving a report of an 'unnecessary, quite unfunny and certainly unfair jibe at J. Edgar Hoover' during a performance of *The*

Best Man, Vidal's most successful Broadway play. Supervisor Tom King of the FBI's New York Office was sent to investigate and reported that a character in the play, whom he believed to be President Truman, had commented, 'I'll reserve my opinion of J. Edgar Hoover for a posthumous memoir.' King also claimed, reassuringly but perhaps unreliably, that 'the crack came out fast and fell very flat'.[83]

The writer and playwright James Baldwin was one of Hoover's *bêtes noires* and most eloquent critics. An FBI memorandum noted in June 1963:

> We have received information to the effect that Baldwin, an author who has been critical of the Bureau and has been connected with communist front and integration activities, is allegedly preparing a statement concerning the FBI which supposedly 'is going to nail them to the wall' and 'is going to be like an atom bomb when it is dropped.'[84]

Though the memo proved to be alarmist, the FBI's New York office reported to Hoover in December 1963:

> A review of the material in Bureau files ... clearly depicts [Baldwin] as a dangerous individual who could be expected to commit acts inimical to the national defense and public safety of the United States in time of an emergency.[85]

Hoover commented sourly, 'Isn't Baldwin a well known pervert?' An FBI memorandum solemnly responded: 'It is not a matter of official record that he is a pervert; however, the theme of homosexuality has figured prominently in two of his three published novels.'[86]

Among those in the film industry on whom the FBI had lengthy files was the British-born Charlie Chaplin, who had been a Hollywood star since the eve of the First World War. In 1956 Sir Anthony Eden's government dropped its plan to award Chaplin a knighthood for fear of offending the Americans during the Suez crisis. Hoover regarded Chaplin as 'a parlour Bolshevik'. In 1953, after Chaplin had taken his family to London for the première of his latest film, *Limelight*, the US attorney general, James McGranery, denied him a re-entry permit on the grounds that communist connections made him an 'undesirable alien'. Chaplin spent the rest of his life in Switzerland.[87]

MI5 had opened a file on the film star in 1952 in response to an enquiry from the FBI which wrongly suspected that Chaplin was using an alias, and that his real name might well be Israel Thornstein. MI5's security liaison officer in Washington confirmed to the FBI that 'Chaplin has given funds to communist front organisations ... He has [also] been involved in paternity and abortion cases.' However, MI5's search of birth records at Somerset House had drawn a blank: there was 'no trace in our records of Charlie Chaplin' but also 'no evidence that Chaplin's name is or ever has been Israel Thornstein'. Unlike the FBI, MI5 assessed Chaplin as a 'progressive or radical' rather than a communist, and concluded in 1958 that he was not a security risk.[88] He was knighted, belatedly, in 1975.

*

One of the obligations of the KGB was to ensure the ideological orthodoxy of the Soviet entertainment business both at home and abroad. Russian ballet dancers, musicians and others performing in the West were carefully chaperoned by KGB minders. The few who succeeded in fleeing were pursued by the KGB, which attempted to ruin their careers abroad.

During a foreign tour by the Kirov (now Mariinsky) Ballet in 1961, its world-famous star, Rudolf Nureyev, described by *Time* as 'one of the most electrifying male dancers of all time', made a dramatic escape at Le Bourget airport in Paris. He had just been told by one of the Ballet's KGB minders that, instead of continuing to London with the rest of the Kirov Ballet to perform at Covent Garden, he was being sent back to Moscow to perform at a Kremlin gala. Nureyev believed he was being punished for unruly behaviour in Paris and, once back in Russia, would never be allowed to go on foreign tours again. He appealed for help to a Paris friend, Clara Saint, who told Nureyev to approach the French police, who would prevent the KGB forcing him to return to Moscow.[89]

Having failed to prevent his defection, the KGB now began a campaign of intimidation. At Nureyev's first major performance with a Western company, he played the Blue Bird in a Paris production of *Sleeping Beauty*:

I had barely come on to the stage [he later recalled] ... when shouting and whistling broke out, almost drowning Tchaikovsky's music. I went on dancing the Blue Bird, but beyond the haze of the footlights ... I was perfectly aware that some communists were trying to sabotage the performance. I could hardly hear the music and I saw pieces of what looked like glass thrown onto the stage at me but I kept on dancing.[90]

Nureyev refused to be cowed. On 21 February 1962, he made his Covent Garden debut, dancing with Margot Fonteyn in *Giselle*. To those who saw their performance and the twenty-three curtain calls which followed, it was clear that one of ballet's greatest ever partnerships had been born. 'I would have followed her', said Nureyev, 'to the end of the world.' In November a top-secret KGB plan for dealing with defectors proposed 'special action' against Nureyev.[91] Subsequent KGB directives included schemes to break one or both of his legs.[92]

Similar plots were devised by the KGB to injure one of Nureyev's near contemporaries, Natalia Makarova, who defected from the Kirov Ballet in September 1970 during a London season at the Royal Festival Hall. Soon afterwards she began performing with the American Ballet Theatre in New York as well as with the Royal Ballet in London – to the predictable outrage of the KGB:

> Depending on the results of special actions taken with respect to Nureyev, aimed at lessening his professional skills, [the KGB] should consider carrying out a similar action with respect to Makarova, in order to localize the negative effect of her forthcoming performances in Britain and the United States. If the British propaganda organs are activated and information provided by her is used to slander Soviet life, additional measures will be devised.[93]

The threats to Makarova, like those to Nureyev, proved hollow.

The KGB leadership's ideological blinkers prevented it realising that, at least in the West, its campaigns to discredit dissident stars were mostly counterproductive. The international popularity of Boris Pasternak, who had won the Nobel Prize for Literature in 1958, had been visibly increased by official hostility in Moscow. His best-known novel, *Doctor Zhivago*, a love story set in revolutionary Russia, had been officially banned because of its scornful description of Bolshevik leaders as 'men in whom everything alive and human had been driven out by political conceit'. With the help of ingenious covert operations by the CIA, however, the book became an international best-seller in many languages. The 1965 film version, directed by David Lean, the Oscar-winning director of *Lawrence of Arabia*, was more popular still.[94]

By the time the world-class cellist, the dissident Mstislav Rostropovich (codenamed VOYAZHER, 'Traveller', by the KGB), left Russia for the West in 1974, the KGB had ceased to plan operations to cause physical injuries to émigrés in the performing arts. To the outrage of the Centre, Rostropovich received a hero's welcome in the West. Initially, he spent some time at Corpus Christi College, Cambridge, whose Master, Sir Duncan Wilson, was a former ambassador in Moscow; his younger daughter, the cellist Elizabeth Wilson, had been a pupil of Rostropovich at the Moscow conservatoire.[95] When Rostropovich dined in a packed Corpus Hall on his first evening in Cambridge, the students, who had no advance knowledge of his arrival, gave him a standing ovation. During dinner, he went round the hall, engaging in animated conversation with groups of students in mixed fragments of several languages.[96] None of the stars who fled from the Soviet Union had a more extraordinary ability to connect with Westerners. They found him, however, very protective of his Stradivarius cello. On his arrival in Cambridge, when college staff began to carry the cello along with the rest of his luggage to his accommodation in the Master's Lodge, he told them firmly: 'No! Cello I take myself.'

In 1976 Rostropovich and his wife, the singer Galina Vishnevskaya, were stripped of their Soviet citizenship. The Centre appealed to all Soviet Bloc intelligence services for help in finding agents to penetrate his entourage. It was outraged by Rostropovich's appointment in 1977 as director of the National Symphony Orchestra in Washington DC but encouraged by a critical review in the *Washington Post* in May 1979 of his sometimes eccentric behaviour as conductor. The Centre circulated the review to its Western residencies as an example of the kind of criticism they were to encourage, and demanded that they inspire articles attacking Rostropovich's alleged vanity, failure to live up to Western expectations and – especially ironic in view of the KGB's active measures against him – his supposed attempts to manipulate the Western media.[97]

Some of the KGB's Soviet Bloc allies, in particular the Bulgarian Darzhavna Sigurnost (DS), were much less cautious in their pursuit of defectors. The zeal with which the DS hunted down Bulgarian émigrés in the West owed much to the personal outrage with which Todor Zhivkov, against strong competition probably the most grotesque of the communist rulers of Eastern Europe, responded to émigré mockery. The most eloquent ridicule in the 1970s came from Georgi Markov, who for most of the previous decade had been one of Bulgaria's most successful writers and playwrights. Immediately before going into exile in 1969, he was centrally involved in a TV series, *At Every Kilometre*, which told the heroic story of Bulgaria's wartime resistance and liberation, and is still remembered as probably the most popular programme of the communist era. Once Markov had left Bulgaria, however, his name was removed from the list of credits.[98]

Based in London, Markov broadcast regular commentaries on the corruption and brutality of the Zhivkov regime on the Bulgarian-language services of the BBC World Service and Radio Free Europe, ridiculing Zhivkov himself as a man with 'a distastefully mediocre sense of humour', the bullying behaviour of 'a village policeman', a penchant for 'pompous phrases' and the deluded belief that he was a great hunter.

Early in 1978 General Dimitar Stoyanov, Bulgarian interior minister and head of the DS, appealed to the KGB for help in liquidating Markov, accused of 'slandering Comrade Zhivkov' during many radio broadcasts from London. Yuri Andropov, the KGB chairman and future Soviet leader, eventually agreed. 'But', he insisted,

> there is to be no direct participation on our part. Give the Bulgarians what they need, show them how to use it and send someone to Sofia to train their people.

Georgi Markov with his wife Marina and small son in exile in London.

The murder weapon provided by the KGB was a silenced compressed-air gun, concealed in an umbrella, which fired a tiny pellet containing a lethal dose of the highly toxic poison, ricin. While waiting at a bus stop on Waterloo Bridge on 7 September 1978, Markov felt a sudden stinging sensation in his right thigh. A man near him had dropped an umbrella, which Markov thought must have accidentally struck his thigh. The stranger apologised, picked up the umbrella and got into a taxi waiting nearby.

Though Markov felt no immediate effect from the poisoning, he became seriously ill next day and died in hospital on 11 September. During a visit to Sofia soon afterwards Oleg Kalugin, head of KGB foreign counter-intelligence, was presented by Stoyanov with an expensive Browning hunting rifle in gratitude for Soviet technical assistance in the assassination.[99]

*

By the mid 1970s the KGB and CIA had sharply contrasting public images. Unlike the CIA, the KGB remained immune from domestic criticism. The statue of its founder, Felix Dzerzhinsky, outside its headquarters at the Lubyanka near Red Square, was the tallest in Moscow and a prominent landmark. On becoming KGB chairman in 1967, Yuri Andropov commissioned a series of books, songs and films to glorify the work of Soviet foreign intelligence. His greatest success came in 1973 with a TV series written by the novelist Yulian Semyonov and starring Vyacheslav Tikhonov, *Seventeen Moments of Spring*, which tells the heroic story of a fictional Second World War Soviet intelligence illegal, Colonel Maxim Maximovich Isayev, who penetrates the Wehrmacht high command in Berlin. Isayev poses as a Nazi by the name of Max Otto von Stierlitz. Little by little, at great personal risk, he foils Operation SUNRISE, an unscrupulous American plot to negotiate a separate peace with Nazi Germany at the expense of the Soviet Union.

First shown on twelve consecutive nights in August 1973 at 7.30 p.m., the seventy-minute-long episodes each attracted an astonishing 50 to 80 million viewers. Eleonora Shashkova, who played Stierlitz's wife, recalled that 'Every evening the streets were deserted, and people rushed home from work to watch the latest episode.' The Soviet leader, Leonid Brezhnev, is said to have changed the time of Central Committee meetings in order to watch the series.[100] Until the end of

Stierlitz, played by Vyacheslav Tikhonov, at a newspaper kiosk in Nazi Berlin.

the Soviet era, *Seventeen Moments of Spring* was shown again every year throughout the countries of the Warsaw Pact, beginning on 9 May as part of the annual celebrations of victory over Germany.

In 1978, on Andropov's initiative, the Centre began making annual awards to those writers, film-makers, actors, musicians and others in the arts who had done most to promote a positive image of the KGB. The first award-winners included both Yulian Semyonov and Vyacheslav Tikhonov.[101] Like Andropov, Vladimir Putin, who worked for the KGB in East Germany during the 1980s, was a great admirer of *Seventeen Moments of Spring*. While he was a local councillor in St Petersburg in 1991, a short film was made showing him behind the wheel of his GAZ Volga, re-enacting the final episode of the TV series, when Stierlitz drives back to Berlin. The theme song from the series, *Somewhere Far Away*, can be heard playing on Putin's car radio.[102] Putin later became the first person since Andropov to become successively intelligence chief and Russian leader.

At about the same time that Soviet TV began broadcasting *Seventeen Moments*, the Hollywood studio United Artists released the spy thriller, *Scorpio*, the first feature film allowed by the CIA to include footage filmed at its HQ in Langley, Virginia. Despite the Agency's role early in the Cold War in commissioning *Animal Farm* and enabling the filming of *The Quiet American* in Vietnam, it had so far shown little interest in its Hollywood image. Before allowing *Scorpio*'s director, Michael Winner and his crew to film at Langley, it did not even ask to see either the script or a film treatment – both routinely requested by the FBI and the Pentagon. When the film came out, the CIA was appalled. *Scorpio* portrayed the Agency as a deeply sinister organisation willing to deceive and murder US citizens, even its own personnel, in order to achieve its nefarious aims.

Though some TV crews were subsequently allowed at Langley under close supervision, after the experience of *Scorpio* it was to be another two decades before the CIA again cooperated with Hollywood film-makers.[103]

Winner's film also included footage of the Watergate complex in downtown Washington, though he had no idea of its topical significance until the final stages of production. On the evening of 16 June 1972, while staying at the Watergate Hotel during filming, two of *Scorpio*'s stars, Burt Lancaster and Alain Delon, had a chance encounter with five now infamous White House spies, the bungling 'Watergate burglars' who were arrested that night for breaking into the offices of the Democratic National Committee in the Watergate office building.[104] The break-in had been planned by the CIA veteran, Howard Hunt, and a reckless former FBI agent, G. Gordon Liddy, on behalf of the Committee to Re-elect the President [Nixon], derisively known as CREEP. Their aim was to install bugging devices and discover the Democrats' plans for the 1972 presidential election campaign.[105]

The first attempted break-in on 26 May, led by Howard Hunt, had to be aborted, forcing Hunt to spend the night in a liquor closet at the Watergate Hotel. The next morning he advised a fellow conspirator never to order a Scotch at the hotel: 'Last night in that damn closet I had to take a leak ... I was desperate. Finally I found a nearly empty bottle of Johnnie Walker Red. It's now quite full.' During future break-ins, Hunt acted simply as a lookout. On the night of 27 May, the five other burglars (three Cubans, a Cuban–American and a former CIA agent) tried again but discovered that one of them had brought the wrong house-breaking equipment. The following night, the break-in seemed to go according to plan. The burglars photographed Democratic National Committee files and fitted bugs to two of the phones. Next day, however, it was discovered they had failed to photo-graph key documents and to bug the most important phone. On 16 June the team returned to 'get everything sorted out', but in the early hours of 17 June were caught red-handed in possession of a bag of burglary tools, a walkie-talkie, forty rolls of unexposed film, two 35-millimetre cameras, pen-size tear-gas guns, bugging devices, a wig, $2,300 (mostly in new $100-dollar bills), documents linking them to CREEP, and address books containing the name and telephone number of Howard Hunt with the note 'W. House'.[106] The security guard who caught the burglars, Frank Wills, later played himself in the award-winning 1976 film on the Watergate Affair, *All the President's Men*.[107]

The break-in undermined the reputation of both the White House and the intelligence community. By involving the White House in covert action against his 'enemies' and in a complex cover-up after-wards, President Nixon criminalised his administration.[108] Watergate, followed by revelations of past CIA 'dirty tricks', including mostly failed plots to assassinate foreign leaders, persuaded a majority of Americans – mistakenly – that the CIA had somehow been involved in the assassination of President Kennedy.[109]

The main media stars created by the Watergate Affair were the *Washington Post* investigative journalists, Bob Woodward and Carl Bernstein (played in the film based on their book *All The President's Men* by Robert Redford and Dustin Hoffman), who assembled some of the evidence which forced Nixon to resign on 9 August 1974. Their main source, whose identity was known only to Woodward, was an informant, codenamed DEEP THROAT after the title of a notorious recent porno-graphic film. The unsuccessful hunt by the rest of the media for the identity of DEEP THROAT overlooked one important and, in retrospect, rather obvious clue. Initially Woodward had called his source MY FRIEND or 'M. F.' This, he later acknowledged, was 'not very good tradecraft'.[110] M. F. were the initials of Mark Felt, whose experience of intelligence deception went back to the Double-Cross system of the Second World War.[111] After Hoover's death in May 1972 he had become associate director (the second-ranking position) of the FBI. Not until thirty years later did Felt publicly admit that he had been DEEP THROAT; the identi-fication was confirmed by Woodward and the *Washington Post*.[112]

The portrayal of the unidentified DEEP THROAT in the film version of *All The President's Men* is partly misleading. He tells Woodward to 'follow the money' – a now well-known catchphrase which Felt never

uttered – and tells him that his and Bernstein's lives are in danger, which is unlikely. DEEP THROAT also claims that the Watergate cover-up was intended to conceal not simply the break-ins to the Democratic National Committee offices but 'covert operations' involving the CIA, FBI and the entire intelligence community. In reality, it was the CIA's refusal to become involved in the cover-up which made it unsustainable.[113] Nixon took his revenge by summoning the DCI (head of the CIA), Richard Helms, to Camp David and firing him. Helms said privately of Nixon, 'The man is a shit.'[114]

*

By coincidence, the British Double-Cross system, which had remained top secret ever since the War, began to be declassified during the Watergate Affair. So did the ULTRA secret. Bletchley Park, previously hardly heard of, became a tourist site. Its greatest codebreaker, Alan Turing, almost unknown in his lifetime, had committed suicide in 1954 after being convicted of homosexual 'gross indecency'. After a change in the law and the ULTRA revelations, he became a posthumous national hero: the star of the play *Breaking the Code* by Hugh

Whitemore (with Derek Jacobi as Turing both in the West End and on Broadway) and the Hollywood feature film, *The Imitation Game* (starring Benedict Cumberbatch as Turing).[115] In 2012 Turing became the first British intelligence officer to appear on a British postage stamp (though Philby had been honoured by a Russian stamp some years earlier).

The first star to be created by revelations in the mid 1970s of previously classified wartime intelligence operations, however, was Sir William Stephenson, former head of British Security Coordination (BSC) in New York, who had retired to Bermuda soon after the war. Stephenson commissioned the Canadian journalist, William Stevenson (no relation), to write his biography. Published in 1976 with the title *A Man Called Intrepid*, it quickly became the biggest-selling book ever on intelligence history. In 1979, a three-part TV mini-series with the same title, starring David Niven as William Stephenson, was watched by large audiences in the United States and Canada.

Stevenson's publisher, however, was subsequently forced to reclassify the book as fiction when it emerged that much of it was invented.[116] Even the title was fraudulent. Stephenson was never 'INTREPID' – a codename he claimed was personally chosen for him by Churchill but which, in reality, was merely BSC's telegraphic address in New York. In *A Man Called Intrepid*, Stephenson immodestly awarded himself the Légion d'honneur and the Croix de guerre with palms, as well as – even more improbably – the title of world amateur lightweight boxing champion. His fantasies about the Second World War began with the frontispiece, a photograph which purported to show Churchill with Stephenson. In fact, it showed the prime minister with his close friend and minister of information, Brendan Bracken. A series of false claims followed about Stephenson's role as a supposed secret intermediary between Churchill and Roosevelt.

A Man Called Intrepid went on to enumerate the best-known successes of British wartime intelligence, and ascribe to Stephenson a role in them which he did not have: the breaking of the German Enigma machine cipher, the development of nuclear weapons, and the organisation of European resistance. Stephenson supposedly also found time also to invent new petroleum-based weapons[117] and devise the V sign, as well as to help with the production of the Spitfire and the jet engine. He is described as the invisible man directing the work of the whole British intelligence community in North America. In an

The caption in *A Man Called Intrepid* under this picture of Jacqueline Nearne in *Now It Can Be Told* reads 'Here MADELEINE is practicing "blind drops", parachuting from a moving aircraft at night. The figure behind her is the jump master.'

act of forgery worthy of BSC's wartime M Section, stills from *Now It Can be Told*, showing Jacqueline Nearne as fictional agent 'CAT', were misrepresented as genuine archival images of legendary SOE agent MADELEINE (Noor Inyat Khan) in training.[118] The book, despite its success, was strongly criticised by knowledgeable reviewers in Britain who called it 'worthless', 'ludicrous', and 'dishonest', but these views did little to diminish Stephenson's heroic reputation in North America.

Stephenson's fantasies probably have a partly medical explanation. When the Canadian-born former Conservative MP, Sir Ted Leather, became Governor of Bermuda in 1973, he quickly realised that Stephenson's memory had been seriously affected by a massive stroke: 'Sir William believed that he remembered everything and the real tragedy was that he had it all wrong.' A decade later, Stephenson showed the historian, David Stafford what he called 'documentary film about what I did during the war ... You're going to see one of my instructors at [BSC's Canadian] Camp X during the war.' Stafford immediately realised that the 'instructor' was the British actor, Michael York, and that what Stephenson had convinced himself was wartime footage actually came from the 1979 TV adaptation of *A Man Called Intrepid*. Despite his delusions, honours were showered on him. When he received the William J. Donovan award in the United States in 1983, President Reagan sent Stephenson his personal congratulations:

> Your career … adds up to one of the great legends. As long as Americans value courage and freedom, there will be a special place in our hearts, our minds and our history books for the Man called Intrepid.[119]

*

In contrast to the romantic wartime intelligence myths promoted by *A Man Called Intrepid*, another former British intelligence officer, David Cornwell (better known by his pen-name, John le Carré), simultaneously presented a decidedly unheroic image of contemporary British espionage. Le Carré believed he 'was writing for a public hooked on Bond and desperate for an antidote'.[120] In his 1964 global best-seller, *The Spy Who Came in from the Cold* (filmed in 1965), le Carré provided it. At its centre is the SIS officer, Alec Leamas, who believes he is being sent on an undercover revenge mission into Communist East Germany, unaware that he is being cynically deceived by his superiors. Cynicism is at the heart of both the novel and the film.[121] Leamas asks:

> What do you think spies are: priests, saints and martyrs? They are a squalid procession of vain fools, traitors, too, yes; pansies, sadists and drunkards, people who play cowboys and Indians to brighten their rotten lives.

Both the novel and the film, wrote le Carré later, were 'sheer fiction from start to finish':

> This was not, however, the view taken by the world's press, which with one voice, decided that the book was not merely authentic but some kind of revelatory Message From The Other Side, leaving me with nothing to do but sit tight and watch, in a kind of frozen awe, as it climbed the best-seller list and stuck there, while pundit after pundit heralded it as the real thing.[122]

Readers and viewers believed *The Spy Who Came in from the Cold* was 'the real thing' because le Carré wrote realistically as well as brilliantly. Graham Greene called it the 'best spy story I have ever read'.

It was also widely known that, like Greene, le Carré was a former intelligence officer, though he was forbidden to mention it. He was the first spy novelist to have served in both MI5 and SIS, spending a few years in each. In his novels and films, the two are amalgamated into a single fictional secret service, 'The Circus'.

Le Carré was deeply conscious at the beginning of his writing career of following in the footsteps of Christopher Marlowe, the first major English writer-spy. The climax of *Call from the Dead* comes with the assassination of Elsa Fennan by the East German spy Dieter Frey during a performance of Marlowe's *Edward II*. George Smiley, who was in the packed theatre, watched as 'The shouts of soldiers and the screams of the demented king filled the theatre until the dreadful climax of his foul death.' Simultaneously, sitting next to Fennan in the stalls, Frey silently murders her with a 'one-finger carotid touch'.[123]

George Smiley and The Circus were also at the heart of the hugely successful seven-part 1979 BBC TV serial, *Tinker, Tailor, Soldier, Spy*, based on le Carré's most popular novel published four years before. Smiley is made head of The Circus with a mission to track down a long-term Soviet mole inside it.[124] The series achieved viewing figures of eight and a half million, with three million more watching the repeats, and was sold to over thirty countries. It was made even more memorable, only a month after the last episode in the series was aired, when the former Surveyor of the Queen's Pictures, Sir Anthony Blunt (later stripped of his knighthood), was officially exposed as an ex-Soviet agent in a Commons statement by the prime minister, Margaret Thatcher. There were a number of similarities between Blunt and the fictional mole uncovered by Smiley, Bill Haydon, who was also gay and interested in the fine arts. The actor Ian Richardson, who played the part of Haydon, somewhat resembled Blunt in both appearance and manner. Unsurprisingly, a number of reviewers believed that 'life was imitating art'.[125]

Many of le Carré's former intelligence colleagues both enjoyed and disliked his depiction of them. At a lunch hosted by le Carré, Sir Maurice Oldfield, who was SIS chief when *The Spy Who Came in from the Cold* was published and filmed, told Sir Alec Guinness, who played George Smiley in the 1979 TV adaptation of *Tinker, Tailor, Soldier, Spy*: 'It's young David [Cornwell] and his like that make it much harder for the Service to recruit decent officers and sources. They read his books and are put off.'[126] More recently, Sir Richard Dearlove, SIS chief from 1999 to 2004, told a literary festival:

> We've all enjoyed enormously reading the Smiley books ... and he does capture some of the essence of what it was like in the Cold War. However, he is so corrosive in his view of MI6 that most professional SIS officers are pretty angry with him.
>
> Intelligence organisations are based on trust between colleagues. That's how they operate. His books are exclusively about betrayal.[127]

By contrast, the last head of Soviet foreign intelligence, Yevgeny Primakov, was a great admirer of le Carré. At the end of the Cold War, the British Foreign Secretary, Sir Malcolm Rifkind, presented him with a signed copy of *Smiley's People*.[128] 'I identify with George Smiley,' said Primakov later.[129]

The most novel interaction between American intelligence and the entertainment business during the final decade of the Cold War was the CIA's creation of a bogus film studio as part of an extraordinary operation to rescue six US diplomats from Tehran in 1980. When militant student supporters of the Iranian Revolution stormed the US embassy in 1979, they had taken prisoner most of its personnel. Six Americans, however, escaped to the homes of Canadian diplomats. To organise the rescue of the 'Canadian Six', the CIA's main exfiltration expert, Antonio (Tony) Mendez, Chief of Disguise and the Graphics and Authentication Division, set up a supposedly Canadian film company, 'Studio Six Productions', in a former Columbia studio where Michael Douglas had recently completed *The China Syndrome*. With help from an experienced Hollywood consultant, Studio Six concocted the treatment for a complex Middle Eastern sci-fi film glorifying Islam, which persuaded the Iranian authorities to allow filming in Tehran.

The bogus film was given the title *Argo*, after the ship in which Jason and the Argonauts sailed to rescue the Golden Fleece from a hydra-headed dragon. Posing as the *Argo* production team, the six US diplomats, led by Tony Mendez as 'production manager', managed to leave safely on a plane to Zurich from Tehran's chaotic Mehrabad Airport. Everything had been carefully rehearsed by Mendez before their departure. The disguises worked perfectly. One diplomat conformed to what was then a fashionable Hollywood stereotype by wearing a silk shirt unbuttoned to reveal chest hair and medallion on a gold chain.[130] The operation successfully deceived Hollywood as well as the Iranian authorities. 'By the time Studio Six folded several weeks after the rescue,' wrote Tony Mendez, 'we had received twenty-six scripts. One was from Steven Spielberg.'[131] The deception was so well maintained that no word of it leaked out until the operation was revealed by the CIA as part of its fiftieth-birthday celebrations in 1997. In 2012 an Oscar-winning film was made of the operation, entitled *Argo*, starring Ben Affleck (who was also director) as Mendez.[132]

*

In the later Cold War, many in the KGB domestic security directorates were more concerned by the threat from Western pop stars than from Western spies. Despite official attempts to jam foreign broadcasts, more young Russians were able to listen in than ever before. In the mid 1970s in Dnepropetrovsk Oblast, where the Soviet leader, Leonid Brehznev, had begun his career as a party apparatchik, the local KGB calculated, after opening young people's correspondence, that almost 80 per cent of 15-to 20-year-olds 'systematically listened to broadcasts from Western radio stations', especially popular music, and showed other unhealthy signs of interest in Western pop stars, such as asking for their autographs. The KGB's sometimes surreal obsession with musical subversion is a reminder of how the hunt for ideological dissidence frequently destroyed all sense of the absurd among those committed to the holy war against it:

> Even listening to musical programmes gave young people a distorted idea of Soviet reality, and led to incidents of a treasonable nature. Infatuation with trendy Western popular music, musical groups and performers falling under their influence leads to the possibility of these young people embarking on a hostile path. Such infatuation has a negative influence on the interests of society, inflames ambitions and unjustified demands and can encourage the emergence of informal groups with a treasonable tendency.[133]

Remarkably, even Michael Jackson was identified as a potential threat to the Soviet system.[134]

In 1985, the Communist Party youth wing, Komsomol, no doubt in consultation with the KGB, drew up a secret list of thirty-eight 'foreign music groups and artists whose repertoires contain ideologically harmful compositions', which were not be broadcast or played at Soviet discos. Most were American or British. At the top of the blacklist was the English punk rock band, the Sex Pistols, who were chiefly responsible for founding the angry, anti-establishment UK punk movement. The fact that the Sex Pistols had fallen apart amid mutual recriminations and litigation at the end of the 1970s is proof of KGB fears that many of their recordings remained in circulation. The alleged 'type of propaganda' used by the Sex Pistols and the next four groups on the Komsomol blacklist was 'Punk, Violence'.[135] In retrospect, some in the KGB were embarrassed by their fear of punk. One retired KGB officer later falsely claimed on National Russian Television that the KGB had spent 'hundreds of millions of rubles' financing the Sex Pistols and other punk bands in order to 'create utter chaos' in the West and 'pervert Western youth to nihilist, anti-establishment and anti-American ideologies'.[136]

Other Western musicians were banned because of what they had said about the Soviet Union. The English rock band, Pink Floyd, was accused of 'interfering in the foreign policy of the USSR', after recording their 1983 song, 'Get Your Filthy Hands Off My Desert', which began with the line, 'Brezhnev took Afghanistan'. The US rock band, Talking Heads, were similarly blamed for spreading 'the myth of Soviet military danger'. Some others on the blacklist, even if politically uncontroversial, were considered too sexy for Soviet youth. The 'type of propaganda' which led to the banning of the American–Swiss 'Queen of Rock 'n' Roll', Tina Turner, was listed simply as 'Sex'. Donna Summer, the American 'Queen of Disco', was accused of the similar offence of 'Eroticism'.[137]

The fact that the Communist one-party states felt so visibly threatened by Western pop stars further enhanced their status as symbols of youthful rebellion. Even in Albania, after the collapse in 1992 of Europe's last and most isolated Communist regime (isolated even from Moscow), the elegant tree-lined but rubbish-strewn Bulevard in the centre of Tirana was full of young people wearing Michael Jackson (usually spelt 'Mikel Jaksen') T-shirts. The decapitated statue of Stalin was inscribed in large red characters with the words 'Pink Floyd'.[138]

14

Spies in the Limelight

Since the end of the Cold War, most of the world's major intelligence services have revealed more about themselves than ever before. The Queen's Speech at the opening of Parliament in 1992 officially admitted, for the first time, the existence of SIS, Britain's most secretive intelligence agency. Just over a decade later, though many secrets remained, published official reports on intelligence failures in the United States before the terrorist attacks of 9/11 2001 and in Britain before the 2003 war in Iraq proved too detailed and voluminous for all but the most committed Western spywatchers.[1]

The main Chinese intelligence agency, the Ministry of State Security (MSS), founded in 1983, now the biggest and most active in the world, has lifted fewer veils. But it began 2021 with an unusually frank public warning of the dangers ahead, calling itself 'the loyal defender of the Party and the people':

> The world is experiencing a profound change that was never seen in the past century. The unexpected COVID-19 pandemic has triggered a global crisis. Power politics, the Cold War mentality, unilateralism and protectionism have risen. The development of mankind is facing unprecedented challenges and the international situation has entered a period of turbulent changes.[2]

Chinese Communist intelligence successes before the founding of the People's Republic in 1949 – especially those against the nationalist Kuomintang and the Japanese – are publicly celebrated. By the beginning of the twenty-first century, the People's Republic of China had become the world's largest market for spy films and TV serials.[3] The most successful spy novelist and screenwriter to have emerged anywhere in the world since the end of the Cold War is Chinese. All MSS foreign operations, however, are taboo. So is the massacre of pro-democracy protesters in Tiananmen Square in central Beijing and other cities on 4 June 1989. Thanks to whistle-blowers in Beijing, Western readers are now far better informed about the role of the MSS in 1989 than the Chinese public. Leaked official documents, known in the West as the 'Tiananmen Papers', show that Vice-President Wang Zhen, Prime Minister Li Peng, and others in the ruling circle believed that the Communist regime was threatened with overthrow. Alarmist MSS reports to the Party leadership wrongly claimed that US intelligence had penetrated the student pro-democracy movement.[4] Ever since the massacre, the MSS, together with a vast army of online censors, has helped turn China into what one writer calls the 'People's Republic of Amnesia', committed to destroying popular memory of the 1989 democracy movement. As well as removing all search terms related to Tiananmen Square, official censorship even seeks to prevent any online reference to the massacre of 4 June by blocking all combinations of the numbers 4, 6 and 1989.[5]

The Chinese public has also been kept in ignorance of MSS intelligence operations to penetrate foreign embassies in Beijing, even when widely reported abroad – among them one so well publicised in the West that, at the end of the Cold War, it inspired a major Broadway hit. The intelligence target was Bernard Boursicot, a naïve and gauche 20-year-old accountant in the French embassy, nicknamed 'Bouricot' ('donkey') by the typing pool. In 1964 he began an affair with a Beijing Opera diva, Shi Pei Pu. Over twenty years later, a French intelligence investigation concluded that the Chinese intelligence had targeted Boursicot almost as soon as he arrived, 'and threw Shi Pei Pu at him'.[6] Shi appeared to follow the Chinese 'nandan' tradition of male opera singers portraying female characters, but told Boursicot that, unlike others, she really was a woman who had been forced by the circumstances of her upbringing to dress and behave as a man.[7]

During their intermittent affair in various locations for almost two decades, Boursicot handed over more than a hundred classified documents which Shi passed to Chinese intelligence. What made their affair extraordinary was that, even when they were in bed together, Boursicot failed to discover that Shi was male.

Shi Pei Pu in the mid 1960s.

In the summer of 1983 Boursicot and Shi were arrested in Paris. Boursicot is reported to have fainted when he heard the news on the radio that Shi had been medically examined and that 'The Chinese Mata Hari is actually a man.' The only explanation the diplomat could offer for failing to identify Shi's gender was that 'It was dark and Shi was modest', and that he was 'the patron saint of the socially inept'. Shi even produced a baby boy whom she persuaded Boursicot was their son.[8] Both were found guilty and sentenced to six years imprisonment but given presidential pardons and released after only a year.[9]

In 1988, a year after they were freed from prison, their case inspired an extraordinary Broadway hit: *M. Butterfly* ('M' for 'Monsieur') by David Henry Hwang, which ran for 777 performances and won the Tony Best Play award. The end of *M. Butterfly* inverts the tragic climax of Puccini's 1904 opera, *Madame Butterfly*, after which the play was named. Instead of an Asian woman killing herself after being abandoned by her Western lover, René Gallimard (modelled on Boursicot) commits suicide after being deceived by his Chinese 'Butterfly', who turns out to be male. In

Bernard Boursicot and Shi Pei Pu at the opening of their trial for espionage in Paris on 5 May 1986.

1993 Hwang's play was made into a film with the same title, directed by David Cronenberg and starring Jeremy Irons as Gallimard.

The bizarre nature of the Boursicot–Shi case in all its manifestations tended to distract attention in the West from the use by Chinese intelligence of more conventional honey-traps – 'the beautiful person stratagem' (*meiren ji*), as it was known.[10] The MSS was undoubtedly influenced by the KGB's success in using both heterosexual and homosexual honey-traps to blackmail foreign diplomats, spies and cipher clerks, particularly in Moscow, into supplying intelligence. The usual procedure was to confront those seduced by KGB 'swallows' with photographs of their seduction. John Vassall later recalled how, while serving as a clerk in the British embassy in the Soviet capital, after being lured to a gay orgy:

> I was shown a box of photographs of myself at the party ... There I was caught by the camera, enjoying every sexual activity ... with a number of different men.[11]

MSS *meiren ji* successes include the seduction in 1998 of the head of the French foreign intelligence service (DGSE) Beijing station, Henri Manioc, by his female Chinese interpreter, whom he subsequently married. The MSS kept the secret so successfully that it did not become public until Manioc was arrested in Paris twenty years later. In what *Le Monde* called 'a very rare and ultra-sensitive trial behind closed doors' in July 2020, the seventy-three year-old Manioc, named in court only as 'Henri M', was sentenced to eight years' jail for treason.[12]

*

The state whose intelligence community was most transformed by the end of the Cold War was Russia. For the first time the KGB had to face public criticism, some of it on prime-time TV during the 1989 Congress of People's Deputies. As the last leader of the Soviet Union, Mikhail Gorbachev, acknowledged, 'unquestionably the commanding personality' at the Congress was the Nobel-winning dissident scientist, Andrei Sakharov, an uncompromising opponent of the KGB, once described by Andropov as 'Public Enemy Number One'.[13]

The male-dominated KGB made an unintentionally comic attempt to use female glamour to improve its public image after its first ever public mauling. In January 1990 it announced, amid a blaze of Russian press and TV publicity, the appointment of Katya Mayorova as Miss KGB, the world's first holder of a 'security services beauty title'. According to Russia's best-selling newspaper, *Komsomolskaya Pravda*, Ms Mayorova wore her bullet-proof vest 'with an exquisite softness,

International publicity for Miss KGB in 1990.

like a Pierre Cardin model', but had the ability to deliver a well-aimed, lethal karate kick 'to her enemy's head'. The more sceptical *Washington Post* reported that, at press interviews, Miss KGB 'giggled and smiled through all her answers, and when she was asked to pose for a photo, she sidled up to a bust of Dzerzhinsky and positively cooed'.[14]

By 1991 Miss KGB had disappeared from view. The main priority of the leadership of the KGB and its hard-line allies was not public relations but the survival of the Soviet Union which it believed had been put in doubt by Gorbachev's reformist regime. While Gorbachev was on holiday in the Crimea in August, he was put under house arrest. The manifesto of the leaders of the August 1991 coup, of which the KGB chairman, Vladimir Kryuchkov, was the chief organiser, implicitly acknowledged that the relaxation of the campaign against ideological subversion had shaken the foundations of the one-party state:

> Authority at all levels has lost the confidence of the population ... Malicious mockery of all the institutions of state is being implanted. The country has in effect become ungovernable.[15]

What the plotters failed to grasp was that it was too late to turn back the clock. 'If the *coup d'état* had happened a year and a half or two years earlier,' wrote Gorbachev afterwards, 'it might, presumably, have succeeded. But now society was completely changed.'[16]

As soon as he heard news of the attempted coup, the great cellist, Mstislav Rostropovich, who had been forced into exile by the KGB seventeen years earlier,[17] flew to Moscow with his cello but without a visa, somehow talked his way through passport control, and joined Boris Yeltsin, the recently elected first President of the Russian Republic, at the barricades around the White House parliament building.[18] Rostropovich spent the night playing his cello. Yeltsin said later that his presence helped to persuade troops sent by the coup leaders not to shell the White House.[19]

One of the chief targets of popular anger after the failure of the coup was the huge statue of the founder of Soviet intelligence, Felix Dzerzhinsky, outside the Lubyanka, the KGB headquarters. Witnessed by TV viewers around the world, 'Iron Felix' was toppled from his pedestal, trampled underfoot, and taken away in disgrace on the back of a huge lorry. Among those photographed outside the Lubyanka celebrating his downfall was Rostropovich. He was among those later

given the award 'Defender of Free Russia' for his role in resisting the attack on the new Russian democracy.

The best-selling single in the aftermath of the failed August coup, not merely in Russia but across most of Europe, was 'Wind of Change' by the West German hard-rock stars, the Scorpions:

> I follow the Moskva
> Down to Gorky Park
> Listening to the wind of change ...

In the mid 1980s the Scorpions had been on the Komsomol banned list of Western musicians whose 'ideologically harmful compositions' were excluded from Soviet discos and broadcasts.[20] The single sold 14 million copies worldwide. 'Wind of Change', said its composer and the band's lead singer, Klaus Meine, 'blew us into the Kremlin.' The invitation came from Mikhail Gorbachev, who saw his policies of *glasnost* and *perestroika* as the embodiment of the 'Wind of Change'. Among Gorbachev's final acts as president before the Soviet Union disappeared at the end of 1991 was to welcome the Scorpions at the Kremlin. They thus became the first – and last – rock stars to receive the official blessing of a Soviet leader. It was, Meine recalled, 'like the Beatles meeting the Queen'.[21] The event was so remarkable that it generated the improbable conspiracy theory that 'Wind of Change' was the work of the CIA.[22]

Yeltsin declined the opportunity of a photo opportunity with the Scorpions before they left Moscow but remained close to Rostropovich. In September 1993, to rally popular support for Yeltsin against opposition in the Russian parliament, Rostropovich conducted the Washington National Symphony Orchestra in a free concert before a huge crowd in Red Square. The performance included the finale to Prokofiev's *Alexander Nevsky* and Tchaikovsky's *1812 Overture*, complete with cannon fire and Kremlin bells. 'Why is there a concert in Red Square?' asked Rostropovich: 'I want people to feel proud that they are Russian … The Russian people were completely betrayed for 70 years … '[23] A quarter of a century had passed since the KGB had asked its foreign intelligence network to undermine Rostropovich's reputation in the West by spreading stories of his supposedly dismal record in conducting the Washington National Symphony Orchestra.

*

Interaction between British stars and spies after the Cold War was greatly increased by the growing visibility of Britain's intelligence agencies. In February 1992, Stella Rimington became both the first woman to be appointed director general of MI5 and the first British intelligence chief to be publicly identified since soon after the Second World War.[24]

Her appointment followed soon after her first visit to Moscow. 'If I could go back and relive one day', Rimington said later, 'it would be the day I went to meet the men who had so long been our enemies, the KGB.' In December 1991, she led a small delegation to Moscow for what proved to be unproductive talks with the KGB leadership about their post-Cold War relationship:

> I thought the Cold War would last for my lifetime. Yet there I was in the British ambassador's Rolls-Royce with the Union Jack flying on the bonnet, driving through a snowy Moscow night to have dinner with the KGB.

Rimington found it 'difficult to avoid the feeling that we had somehow slipped into a James Bond film'.[25]

The KGB was less surprised than the British media by the announcement two months later of Rimington's appointment as MI5 DG. Unlike the British public, it was aware that since 1990 she had been one of the two deputy DGs. For some years, unknown to the media, the Security Service had been recruiting more women at officer/executive level than probably any other branch of British government. In Rimington's view, 'The fact that I was female had almost ceased to be relevant to the progress of my career ... As far as colleagues in the Service or in Whitehall went, I did not think it was an issue.'[26] For the press, however, it was front-page news. Miss Marple and other female fictional detectives had not prepared it for a woman at the head of MI5. As Rimington recalls:

> The trouble was that Ian Fleming and John le Carré, depending on your taste in reading, had done their jobs too well. They had convinced us that the world of intelligence was full of intrigue and excitement involving men like Alec Guinness or Sean Connery. When a middle-aged woman popped up ... looking, as someone said to me, 'as if you could have been a teacher', no-one knew how to react.[27]

MI5's decision not to release her picture when her appointment was publicly announced, Rimington wrote later,

> was amazingly naïve because it was inevitable that the press would get a photograph. In the end it was me personally who thought, 'Stuff it, I'm going to stand there and let them take a picture because I'm fed up with all this.'

The *Evening Standard* was the first to take a photo and published it with a black band across Rimington's face to conceal her identity. It later used another, unflattering picture of her shopping in old clothes, this time showing her face, to illustrate an article entitled 'Success and the Dowdy Englishwoman', which advised Rimington to visit 'a decent hairdresser on a regular basis' and 'use some subtle make-up'. The *Sun* broke the news that she was divorced from her husband in a front-page story under the sensationalist banner headline 'MI5 Wife In Secret Love Split'.

Rimington soon became something of a household name. In 1994, she also became the first DG to speak in public when she delivered the annual BBC TV Dimbleby Lecture on 'Security and Democracy: Is There a Conflict?' Though Rimington admitted being 'extremely nervous', she was helped on her TV debut by long experience of amateur

Rimington at her desk in MI5.

dramatics. (Her memoirs include photographs of her playing Marcelle in *Hotel Paradiso* in 1968 and celebrating her birthday in 1999 by appearing in Tom Stoppard's *The Fifteen-Minute Hamlet* at a barge theatre in Copenhagen.)[28] The *Guardian*, one of MI5's most frequent critics, reported after the Dimbleby Lecture: 'The first, superficial, impression was of a brilliantly accomplished performance, almost a culture shock.' As usual, Rimington's wardrobe aroused intense media interest:

> Commentators, including fashion editors, have dwelt at length on her powerdressing – her rather severe primrose yellow jacket – offset by her body language with the use of large, unblinking, eyes reminiscent of Princess Diana as she paused to drive a point home, or completed a well-rehearsed delivery of a light-hearted anecdote.[29]

After the Dimbleby Lecture, many in Whitehall believed that Rimington 'enjoyed being in the limelight' – even though she disapproved of public appearances by other members of MI5, past or present.[30] In 1995 she became the inspiration for the first female 'M' in the James Bond films, played by Dame Judi Dench. Despite the outlandish Bond plots, Rimington found Dench's no-nonsense manner 'really very good. Both my daughters said so. One even noted that

she holds her hands the way I do.'[31] The role which secretly most
attracted Rimington herself in the Bond films, however, was not 'M'
but the glamorous jewel smuggler and circus proprietor Octopussy.[32]

*

No late twentieth-century SIS chief was tempted to follow Rimington's
example and become a public figure. In 1990, however, SIS took the
unprecedented step of allowing its most outstanding living agent, the
KGB colonel Oleg Gordievsky, to star, albeit in disguise, in a TV
documentary. His eleven years providing sometimes crucial intelligence from inside the KGB – notably on misplaced Soviet fears that
President Ronald Reagan, with support from Margaret Thatcher and
their NATO allies, was planning a nuclear first strike – had come to
an abrupt and almost fatal conclusion in 1985 when the Centre at last
realised that he was working for the British. With assistance from SIS
in Operation PIMLICO, Gordievsky escaped from Moscow across the
Finnish border in the boot of a car – despite being under KGB surveillance. He spent much of the next three years engaged in what MI5's
head of counter-espionage called 'the longest and most comprehensive
debrief ever undertaken by the Service'.[33] From 1986 one of the authors
of this book, Christopher Andrew, had the good fortune to collaborate
in secret with Gordievsky on a history of KGB foreign operations,
published as KGB: The Inside Story in 1990, which drew on Gordievsky's
inside knowledge and some of the top-secret KGB documents he had
passed to SIS. Since Andrew had for some years been presenting radio
and TV programmes on intelligence history, they also decided to
collaborate on a TV documentary based on their book.[34]

The revelation at the centre of the Granada documentary broadcast
in October 1990 on the eve of the book's publication brought to a public
conclusion Britain's longest modern mole hunt – the search for the Fifth
Man in the KGB's Cambridge 'Ring of Five'. Two of the Five, Guy
Burgess and Donald Maclean, fled to Moscow in 1951, followed by Kim
Philby in 1963. Anthony Blunt confessed secretly in 1964 to having
worked for Soviet intelligence in return for immunity from prosecution.
But, as late as 1977, MI5's director general, Sir Michael Hanley, told
Prime Minister James Callaghan that there was still no sign of success
in the hunt for the Fifth Man. Five years later, the problem was unex-
pectedly solved by intelligence from Oleg Gordievsky which identified

Oleg Gordievsky meets President Reagan in the White House in 1987.

him as John Cairncross, who had worked successively as a Soviet spy in the Foreign Office and the Treasury, as an aide to one of Churchill's ministers, and in SIS. Most importantly, at a crucial moment in the Second World War when the tide was turning on the Eastern Front, he became the only Soviet agent to penetrate Bletchley Park.[35]

Since Cairncross was not publicly named when Gordievsky secretly identified him in 1982, the media mole hunt continued for the rest of the decade. Among those publicly misidentified as the missing Fifth Man were three distinguished scientists: Sir Rudolf Peierls (who denied claims that he was dead and sued successfully for libel), Lord Rothschild (the victim during his lifetime of innuendo rather than open allegation, in case he also sued), and Wilfred Mann (who did not sue but wrote a book to prove his innocence). The best-publicised false allegations, however, concerned Sir Roger Hollis, MI5 DG from 1956 to 1965. Hollis's principal accuser was a maverick former MI5 officer and conspiracy theorist, Peter Wright, who had emigrated to Australia. In a sensational 1984 *World in Action* TV documentary, Wright became the first retired British intelligence officer to accuse his former chief of treason. The British government's bungled attempt to ban the publication of his memoirs, *Spycatcher*, through legal action in Australian courts in 1986–7, turned the book into a global best-seller and Wright himself into a household name.[36]

In the 1990 Granada documentary, entitled *The Fifth Man: The Secrets of the Ring of Five*,[37] Gordievsky publicly identified Cairncross as the

Gordievsky on TV in 1990, disguised in wig and facial hair (after pruning).

Fifth Man for the first time.[38] He also revealed that some of his senior colleagues in the KGB regarded Wright's allegation against Hollis as such nonsense that they suspected it might be part of a bizarre British plot to discredit Soviet intelligence. Granada initially failed to match the standards of disguise set by Willy Clarkson's theatrical outfitters for the infant SIS before the First World War. When filming began, Gordievsky was fitted with a shaggy wig and a false moustache which tilted to one side under the arc lights. Both had to be pruned. The modified disguise, however, worked. After *The Fifth Man* had been broadcast, a neighbour who knew Gordievsky only under his non-Russian alias asked him if he had seen it. Gordievsky in turn asked the neighbour if she had noticed anything familiar about the KGB officer in the documentary. Her jaw dropped as she suddenly realised the true identity of the neighbour with a foreign accent.

Like the identification of John Cairncross as the Fifth Man, the even more dramatic media exposure in 1999 of Melita ('Letty') Norwood as Russia's 'great-granny spy' was made possible by intelligence from a major KGB defector. On 7 November 1992, the seventy-fifth anniversary

of the Bolshevik Revolution, SIS exfiltrated a former senior KGB archivist, Vasili Mitrokhin and his family from Moscow, by way of the Baltic. Mitrokhin brought with him a treasure trove of notes and transcripts from highly classified KGB files which he had secretly assembled over a period of twelve years, ten of them while he was in charge of moving the entire foreign intelligence archive to a new headquarters. The FBI called the Mitrokhin Archive 'the most complete and extensive intelligence ever received from any source'; the CIA described it as 'the biggest counter-intelligence bonanza of the post-war period'.[39] The bonanza included key extracts from Norwood's KGB file, which codenamed her Hola. The high point of her career had been as secretary to the CEO of a company with contracts from 1945 to 1949 for Tube Alloys, the British atomic bomb project. Her file records that the KGB later awarded her the Order of the Red Banner and a life pension.[40]

Though news of Gordievsky's escape in 1985 had been made public within a few months, Mitrokhin's exfiltration with his archive in 1992 and his presence in Britain were successfully kept secret for the next seven years.[41] In 1995 Christopher Andrew began collaborating in secret with Mitrokhin on a book entitled *The Mitrokhin Archive: The KGB in Europe and the West*.[42] Publication was planned for 1999 along with a simultaneous TV documentary and serialisation in *The Times*.

On 11 September 1999 in *The Times*, therefore, Melita Norwood was exposed by Mitrokhin as the longest-serving Russian agent in

Britain and the KGB's most important British female agent. Though offered temporary alternative accommodation before the news broke, Norwood elected to stay put in her end-of-terrace house in Bexleyheath. She was surprisingly unfazed by the massed ranks of reporters who gathered outside her front door after her photograph appeared on the front page of *The Times* with the caption, 'The Spy Who Came in from the Co-op' (where she did most of her shopping). 'Oh dear', she told *The Times* reporter, the only one she allowed inside her house. 'This is so different from my quiet little life. I thought I'd got away with it. But I'm not that surprised it's finally come out.'

At such moments, TV news became a major point of contact between intelligence operations and the entertainment business. The image of the great-granny spy walking down her garden path between well-tended rose bushes to make a televised confession, despite the fact that it was, unsurprisingly, economical with the truth, caught the imagination of millions of viewers and newspaper readers. 'I'm 87', Norwood began,

> and unfortunately my memory is not what it was. I did what I did not to make money, but to help prevent the defeat of a new [Soviet] system which had, at great cost, given ordinary people food and fares which they could afford, given them education and a health service.

No newly identified spy had ever had a larger TV audience around the world.

KGB senior archivist Vasili Mitrokhin at the time of his first meeting with the British in 1992.

Mitrokhin disguised for the 1999 BBC TV documentary.

Shortly afterwards, Vasili Mitrokhin, whose presence in London had previously been undetected by the media, made his first TV appearance in a BBC documentary on Norwood's career. Like Oleg Gordievsky on his TV debut nine years earlier, he appeared in disguise.

*

Before the beginning of the 2003 Iraq War, the George W. Bush administration planned to make even more dramatic use of a global television audience to reveal intelligence from an unnamed defector in order to justify its claim that Saddam Hussein had assembled a secret stockpile of weapons of mass destruction (WMD). The defector was Rafid Ahmed Alwan al-Janabi (later codenamed CURVEBALL), an Iraqi chemical engineer who sought asylum in Germany in December 1999, claiming to have important scientific and technological intelligence (or 'S&T') on Saddam's WMD programme. Over the next two years, the German foreign intelligence service, the Bundesnachrichtendienst (BND), sent some 100 top secret reports on CURVEBALL's intelligence to Washington, as well as to the British, French and Israelis.[43] Though the BND did not allow its allies direct access to al-Janabi, an SIS report in September 2002 concluded that his supposedly 'phenomenal access' to S&T might be the 'key' to understanding Saddam Hussein's biological and chemical weapons programme.

CURVEBALL's revelations were central to the televised presentation at the UN Security Council on 5 February 2003 by the US Secretary of State, Colin Powell, who claimed to have proof that 'Saddam Hussein and his regime are concealing their efforts to produce more weapons of mass destruction':

> We have first-hand descriptions of biological weapons factories on wheels and on rails ... In a matter of months, they can produce a quantity of biological poison equal to the entire amount that Iraq claimed to have produced in the years prior to the [1991] Gulf War.

Powell then displayed diagrams of mobile biological weapons factories based on CURVEBALL's intelligence.[44]

Al-Janabi, however, proved to be simply a more plausible version of 'Our Man in Havana', Jim Wormold, who made a living by

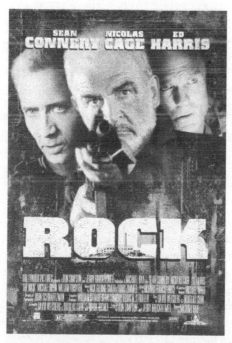

The Rock (1996): A former SAS captain (Sean Connery) and an FBI chemist (Nicholas Cage) have to stop a group of rogue marines who are threatening to launch rockets filled with nerve gas over San Francisco unless they are paid $100 million.

fabricating alarming intelligence. SIS eventually realised that CURVEBALL's description of glass containers (not normally used to store nerve gas) was 'remarkably similar to the fictional chemical weapon portrayed in the film *The Rock*', and that he himself was 'a fabricator who had lied from the outset'.[45]

The British prime minister, Tony Blair, later acknowledged that, like Powell and the Bush administration, he was taken in by bogus intelligence, including CURVEBALL's: 'We thought there was an active WMD programme and there wasn't.'[46] No WMD were discovered during or after the Iraq War for the simple reason that none existed.

*

Beijing and the MSS in particular must have felt a secret sense of *Schadenfreude* after the Iraq War. Whereas American S&T on Iraqi WMD had been publicly exposed as ridiculous, the MSS was running the largest and most successful S&T operations in the world, with the United States as its chief target.[47] The West was slow to grasp the intelligence threat from Huawei and other Chinese hi-tech companies with rapidly expanding international markets.[48]

The People's Republic of China has also produced some of the most original spy fiction of the early twenty-first century. The most successful new spy novelist and screenwriter to have emerged anywhere in the world since the Cold War is the Chinese author Jiang Benhu, better known by his *nom de plume*, Mai Jia. Like a series of Western spy novelists whose books have been turned into even more successful films, Mai is a former intelligence officer. Unlike any of his best-known counterparts in the West, however, his background was in SIGINT as well as HUMINT. The SIGINT agency which features in a number of his novels, Special Unit 701, recaptures some of his own claustro-phobic experiences: 'The strict secrecy that their profession demanded resulted in them losing even the most basic freedoms; they did not have the right to send mail.'[49] He claims that the hero of his first spy novel, *Decoded*, published in 2002, is based far more on Alan Turing than on James Bond. Getting permission to publish the first novel on Chinese SIGINT was, unsurprisingly, a laborious process. According to Mai Jia, *Decoded* was examined in detail by an official committee of no less than twenty-three cryptographers.[50]

Mai may have visited Cambridge while writing his novels. The bril-liant female mathematician 'Abacus Head', founder of his fictional

SIGINT dynasty, studies early in the twentieth century at Cambridge University where she writes a PhD thesis on Sir Isaac Newton's mathematical bridge over the river Cam at Queens' College. (Mai did not realise that Cambridge degrees were not then awarded to women.) *In The Dark* (2003) makes much of ULTRA and KGB codebreaking, with briefer allusions to the East German Stasi, French and Japanese intelligence and even a reference to Mata Hari.

His intelligence novels have been made into major films or TV series, usually with screenplays by Mai Jia himself.[51] During the making of the 2009 spy-thriller, *The Message,* he took the producer to court over whose name should come first in the film credits. Neither Ian Fleming nor le Carré ever rivalled Mai's expertise as a screen writer. In 2013 *Wind Talk* made him China's highest paid author, with a million-dollar advance. As well as selling over three million books in China with translations in over thirty languages, Mai has become a particular favourite of President Xi Jinping, who publicly praised him in 2014 as 'the Number One writer of Communist espionage wars'.[52]

Remarkably, none of Mai's best-selling novels appeared in English translation until *Decoded* was published in the Penguin Modern Classics series in 2014. His British publisher told readers: 'Mai Jia may be the most popular writer in the world you've never heard of.' The *Economist,* among others, declared him 'China's answer to John le Carré'.[53]

Until – and even after – the belated appearance of Mai's novels in English translation, the Chinese work on intelligence which was most studied in the West was also the oldest. By the end of the Cold War,

Mai Jia at the 2019 Frankfurt Book Fair.

Sun Tzu's *The Art of War* had become required reading at West Point and numerous other armed forces academies in the West as well as Asia. When President Hu Jintao became the first Chinese leader to visit the White House in 2006, he presented President George W. Bush with silk copies of it in English and Mandarin.[54] As well as being more frequently quoted on intelligence in the United States than any pre-twentieth-century Western writer, Sun Tzu's teachings on what were later called 'soft power' and influence operations have also been taken up by writers on many other subjects. By 2011 Amazon had on sale no fewer than 1,500 paperbacks based on the lessons of *The Art of War*:[55] among them titles as varied as *Sun Tzu for Women*[56] and *Golf and the Art of War: How the Timeless Strategies of Sun Tzu Can Transform Your Game*.[57] *The Art of War* also penetrated the entertainment business, notably the booming internet strategic games market. 'Sun Tzu Games' promised purchasers of its products 'engaging fun and challenging game experiences'.[58] Among Sun Tzu's celebrity following was the media personality, Paris Hilton, author of the aphorism 'Dress cute wherever you go. Life is too short to blend in', who was photographed, dressed cutely and studying *The Art of War*.[59] Aidan Gillen, one of the stars of *Game of Thrones*, later recorded an audiobook version of Sun Tzu's masterpiece.[60]

*

There is little doubt that Russian 'active measures' in the Putin era have been influenced by the teachings of Sun Tzu.[61] This influence, however, is officially taboo. Vladimir Putin's election as president of the Russian Federation in 2000 in succession to Boris Yeltsin was followed by a multimedia campaign to improve the public image of the KGB's post-Soviet successors, the domestic Federalnaya Sluzhba Bezopasnosti (FSB) and foreign intelligence Sluzhba Vneshney Razvedki (SVR). Though practising Christians had been prohibited in the KGB, Putin and the FSB officially found God. Russia, they claimed, had a unique role to play in defending Christian values. Vasily Stavitsky, head of FSB public relations from 1999 to 2001, published several volumes of poetry with a strong 'spiritual' content, among them *Secrets of the Soul*, *Constellation of Love: Selected Verse* and a book of 'spiritual-patriotic' poetry for children entitled *Light a Candle, Mamma*. Many of Stavitsky's poems were set to music, recorded on CDs, and put on public sale.[62] One of his less obviously spiritual poems became an FSB official hymn:

> Always at the front
> Always at one's post
> Don't touch Russia –
> A Chekist is always vigilant.[63]

To the former director of the CIA, Robert Gates, who has a doctorate in Russian history, 'Putin's policies began to sound very like the ideology of Tsar Nicholas I in the first half of the nineteenth century: "Orthodoxy, Autocracy and Nationality".'[64] In 2002 the FSB founded the world's first spy church. Patriarch Alexy II consecrated a restored Orthodox church in central Moscow, St Sofia, as the FSB's parish church to minister to the previously neglected spiritual needs of its staff. The FSB director, Nikolai Patrushev and the patriarch publicly celebrated the mystical union of the Orthodox Church and the state security apparatus by a solemn exchange of gifts. Patrushev presented a symbolic golden key of the church and an icon of the medieval Moscow metropolitan, St Alexis, 'Wonderworker of All Russia', to the patriarch. In return Alexy II gave the FSB director a Mother of God 'Umilenie'

Putin at midnight Easter services in 2007 with Mikhail Fradkov, head of foreign intelligence (SVR) from 2007 to 2018.

icon and another representing Patrushev's own patron saint, St Nicholas – the possession of which in the Soviet era would have cost a KGB officer his job.[65] The public were – and are – invited to join FSB staff and their families at worship in St Sofia.[66] The patriarch later awarded Patrushev the Order of the Holy Prince Dimitry Donskoi, first class, in recognition of his collaboration with the Orthodox Church.[67]

The greatest obstacle to the official multimedia campaign to improve the public image of Russian intelligence at the start of the Putin presidency was the near collapse of the former Soviet cinema during the Yeltsin era. The mostly state-owned film industry could not cope with competition from the sudden influx of foreign – especially American – films which could be shown in Russian cinemas for the first time, as well as from pirated DVDs of Hollywood blockbusters. In 1996 there were only thirty-four Russian feature films being produced. There was a dramatic increase in the Putin era, however. By 2007 some 250 films were in production, over 100 of them fully or partially funded by the FSB, the defence ministry and other government agencies.[68]

Anxious to encourage a new wave of patriotic spy films, in 2006 the FSB re-established and expanded the annual award scheme introduced by Andropov as KGB chairman almost thirty years earlier for the best 'positive' – or most flattering – portrayals of the Russian intelligence services. The head of FSB public relations, Oleg Matveev, announced:

> At a time when in cinemas, in [TV] serials, in detective stories, a negative image of the staff of the special [intelligence] services frequently manifests itself, we have decided to revive this competition and to decorate those who do not discredit the special services staff, but who are creating a popular image of defenders [of Russia].[69]

The FSB made awards in six artistic categories – literature, broadcasting, cinema, acting, music and visual arts.[70] The music award in 2006 went to Nikolai Rastorguev, lead singer and instrumentalist of the rock group 'Lyube', some of whose repertoire – unusually for rock groups – included 'military-patriotic' songs such as *Through the Tall Grass*, dedicated to the FSB's elite counter-terrorist Alpha Group.[71] In 2007 Putin awarded him 'For Merit to the Fatherland', a combined civilian and military order. Three years later, Rastorguev was elected to the Duma as a deputy for the pro-Putin United Russia party.[72]

The 2007 FSB award-winner in the film category, *Apocalypse Code*, was the most ambitious spy film yet made by Moscow studios, filmed on location in France, Italy, Norway, Malaysia and Ukraine, as well as in Russia. With FSB support, the director, Sergei Bazhenov, intended the film as a Russian response to James Bond. The *Wall Street Journal* called it 'a plot straight out of Hollywood. A sexy female superagent circles the globe in pursuit of a cold-blooded terrorist who has hidden nuclear bombs in four of the world's major cities.'[73] The 'sexy female superagent' (codename Beautiful) is the glamorous Russian film star, Anastasia Zavorotnyuk, who plays the role of FSB Colonel Darya Vyacheslavovna, chasing terrorists in lingerie and stiletto heels, and making crucial phone calls while in the shower. Despite interference from the bungling CIA, Darya successfully deactivates all four of the nuclear bombs. Even US soldiers applaud her as, mission accomplished, she returns by helicopter to FSB HQ, escorted by Russian fighters.

FSB triumphalism, however, failed to appeal to Russian cinemagoers. *Apocalypse Code* was a box-office flop and recovered barely half

its production costs. The FSB was not put off. The judges at its 2007 awards ceremony eulogised the film's 'highly artistic creation of Russian security services' and claimed, absurdly, that it provided a 'most objective depiction of FSB's activity'. Prizes were awarded to both Sergei Bazhenov and Anastasia Zavorotnyuk.[74]

*

Spooks (strapline 'MI5 not 9 to 5'), the first major TV drama series on a current British intelligence agency, was far more popular than *Apocalypse Code* – partly because MI5, unlike the FSB, did not interfere with its production. Broadcast on the BBC from 2002 to 2011, *Spooks* remains Britain's longest-running TV spy series. As well as attracting over 7 million viewers, the first series won numerous awards as 'Best Drama Series'.[75] *Spooks'* exciting, well-constructed plots, however, bore little relation to actual MI5 operations. In only the second episode two MI5 officers, Helen and Tom, are captured by a race riot instigator who tortures Helen in an attempt to make Tom reveal classified information. When Tom refuses, Helen is killed by having her head plunged into a deep-fat fryer. Though BBC switchboards were jammed with complaints, the episode seems only to have increased the popularity of the series. In addition to the regular cast, some of whom, like Helen, suffered untimely deaths, numerous guest stars appeared on *Spooks*; two of them – Hermione Norris and Rupert Penry-Jones – were blown up.[76] 'Characters getting killed in TV spy series is nothing new,' wrote the *Independent* reviewer, 'but has Spooks knocked off too many to be taken seriously?'[77] Viewers did not think so. *Spooks* has been exported to at least twenty-six countries. The series was as popular as ever at the end of its nine-year run. 'We wanted to kill it off in its prime,' said the executive producer, Jane Featherstone.[78]

Among the distinctive MI5 qualities missing from *Spooks* was a sense of humour. In the twenty-first century MI5 maintained the tradition of occasional satirical in-house entertainments established by the 1919 revue *Hush-Hush*. Revue topics now included the unwelcome inroads into MI5 vocabulary by currently fashionable jargon favoured by Whitehall bureaucrats and management consultants with a tin ear for the English language and a passion for performance indicators. There was enthusiastic applause at a 2007 revue for this sketch on the appraisal interview of a Second World War fighter ace, disappointed by his 'overall box marking':

WING-COMMANDER 'TIN-ARSE' FROBISHER: Well, the thing is, Smedley, you've done jolly well on shooting down the Hun. In fact, you've exceeded your target by 953%. Trouble is, you have personal development needs.

FLIGHT LIEUTENANT SMEDLEY: Personal development needs, Sir?

FROBISHER: Yes, Smedley. You have personal development needs in the areas of policy formation, project management and resource planning.

SMEDLEY: But Sir, I'm a Spitfire pilot. Surely, my job is to shoot down Nazi bombers before they obliterate London?

FROBISHER: That's all very well, Smedley, but we senior managers have to ... consider broader issues.

In another sketch, pirates in the Caribbean complain that, despite record levels of booty, their careers are being blighted by the lack of 'a skills-based competency audit framework'.[79] The MI5 Centenary Revue of 2009, in keeping with the precedent set by *Hush-Hush* ninety years earlier, contained a short satirical sketch on the first DG, Sir Vernon Kell,[80] with some of the gentle mockery which he and his wife had claimed to enjoy in 1919.

★

The leading American TV spy series of the twenty-first century so far,[81] launched a decade later than the first episode of *Spooks*, was a direct result of the most successful FBI counter-espionage operation against the Russian SVR. In June 2010, at the climax of its long-running Operation GHOST STORIES, the FBI arrested ten Russian agents. Seven were deep-cover illegals who had adopted bogus names and nationalities. None of the ten, however, had so far obtained any classified information.

Some of the surveillance footage released by the FBI revealed lapses of FSB tradecraft which would not have been permitted in a good spy movie. Anna Chapman, the most glamorous and (largely for that reason) best publicised of the spies, was filmed in a New York Starbucks gratefully handing her laptop for repair to a man she believed to be

an SVR officer, who was in reality a Russian-speaking member of the FBI. Chapman and the other arrested spies were allowed to return to Moscow in exchange for four real or alleged Western agents imprisoned in Russia. The exchange rankled with Putin. In 2018 he authorised an unsuccessful attempt to assassinate one of the freed agents, Sergei Skripal, then living in Salisbury.

SVR spies arrested in Operation Ghost Stories.

Despite the ten spies' slender achievements (other than concealing their identities) in the United States, they were given heroes' welcomes on their return to Russia. After being awarded medals by President Dmitry Medvedev, they were congratulated by Vladimir Putin, then prime minister,[82] and joined him in singing the Soviet patriotic song *Where Does the Motherland Begin?* At a ceremony in Moscow on 22 December 2010, Anna Chapman was appointed a leader of the youth branch of Vladimir Putin's political party, United Russia. She visibly enjoyed her new career as a celebrity, fronting the first episode of a new prime-time TV series and telling viewers (misleadingly): 'I'll reveal all the secrets.'[83] Putin was undeterred by the fact that the January issue of *Playboy*, which was already on sale, contained nude photographs of Chapman, obtained from a former lover.[84] Chapman's response, undoubtedly approved by Putin and the SVR, was to appear as 'Agent 90–60–90' (her 'vital statistics' in centimetres) in Agent Provocateur lingerie, apparently licensed to kill, on the front cover of the Moscow edition of the magazine *Maxim*. Chapman had become an updated version of 'Miss KGB'.

GHOST STORIES inspired the popular, long-running and critically-acclaimed US TV series, *The Americans* (2013 to 2018), devised by the former undercover CIA operations officer, Joe Weisberg. Set during the final decade of the Cold War, it tells the story of two KGB illegals in a Washington suburb who successfully pose as a married American couple, Elizabeth and Philip Jennings. For some years, as in the case of one real illegal couple expelled from the United States in 2010,[85] even their children have no idea that their parents are Russian, let alone KGB officers.

During his CIA training, Joe Weisberg discovered that he had a gift for deception and disguise. For lunch one day, he put on glasses and a false moustache, and changed his hairstyle. None of the twelve people at the table from his training course recognised him. Weisberg made the performances of the leading characters in *The Americans* more convincing by passing on espionage tradecraft as he and the actors walked round Brooklyn. One simple lesson was how to discover if they were being followed, without arousing suspicion, by crossing the road. 'You can look [around] two or three times if you know

KGB illegals Philip and Elizabeth Jennings, played by Keri Russell and Matthew Rhys.

how to do it well,' remembers Matthew Rhys, who played Philip Jennings. More complex tradecraft required longer training, sometimes involving body doubles. The former head of CIA disguise, Jonna Mendez, recalls:

> When I watched Matthew Rhys ... speed in reverse through an FBI roadblock in the final episode of Season 1, well, I have practiced that maneuver countless times, wrecking more than one car while learning the procedure. They did it right.

For the script Weisberg also drew on copious material from the top-secret KGB illegals' files which Mitrokhin had smuggled out of Russia. Every episode he wrote, however, had to be submitted in advance to the CIA Publications Review Board.[86]

A *Guardian* reviewer commented: 'It's hard not to watch *The Americans* and think that if all KGB agents had the energy, ruthlessness and creative acumen of Philip and Elizabeth Jennings, the Soviets should really have won the Cold War.'[87] But, like *Spooks*, the realism – though not the popularity – of *The Americans* was diminished by its intermittent violence, which had no parallel in the actual US careers of the GHOST STORIES Russian spies. The Jennings live next door to an FBI officer, Stan Beaman, who, early in the first series, becomes Philip's best friend, oblivious of his Russian identity. Unknown to Stan, Philip is responsible for killing his FBI colleague, Chris Amador. Stan retaliates by killing Vlad, a young and inexperienced KGB officer. Series 1 ends with Elizabeth being shot and badly injured when she is detected picking up a dead drop. More improbable murders follow in subsequent series. In the final Series 6, the Jennings' cover is blown but Stan allows them to escape to Russia. TV critics as well as viewers suspended their disbelief.[88]

The CIA responded to the success of *The Americans* by organising an unprecedented 'Reel vs Real' public discussion in Los Angeles, chaired by Joe Weisberg, which brought together three of the leading actors with two veteran undercover CIA officers. Perhaps the most striking part of the discussion was the sympathy felt by the CIA officers for the fictional illegals who, like them and the real Russian illegals arrested in 2010, had to conceal their jobs from their children:

> Former CIA operations officer 'Marti' Peterson recounted the time she first told her two teenage children where she worked. They had no

idea growing up that Marti was actually an operations officer with CIA. She asked her kids to meet her at a fast food restaurant near CIA Headquarters in McLean, Virginia, and then brought them onto the CIA Headquarters compound. Her kids were stunned. She brought them to the CIA Memorial wall, where her first husband [killed during an Agency operation] has a star. 'We held hands, and cried ... ' Marti recalled.[89]

By far the most successful French TV espionage series, *Le Bureau des légendes*, broadcast since 2015, is also centred on deep-cover intelligence officers. The *'légendes'* are the bogus identities created for them by a department of France's foreign intelligence agency. The series marked a turning point in relations between French stars and spies. Hitherto most of France's leading directors and producers had shown little interest in the DGSE. The idea for *Le Bureau des légendes* came from one individual, the award-winning film director, Éric Rochant, who approached the DGSE in 2013. After some hesitation, the newly appointed director, Bernard Bajolet, allowed Rochant to use its official emblem and film the exterior of its headquarters, as well as giving his set designer brief access to some of the interior.

In contrast to the equally successful BBC series *Spooks*, whose sets bear no relation to the rooms in MI5 headquarters, the décor of the fictional headquarters of *Le Bureau des légendes* closely resembles some of that in the DGSE. As in the real Service headquarters, known to its members as 'la boîte', the Bureau's walls are lined with the portraits of former heads of French foreign intelligence since the Second World War. Bajolet's successor, Bernard Émié, believes that, though Rochant alone decided the content of the series and all the episodes are fictional, his discussions with the DGSE 'perhaps gave him some ideas'.[90] One of Émié's first acts on his appointment as director in 2017 was to spend an afternoon watching the filming of an episode of *Le Bureau des légendes*. 'This series', he says, 'has had a very positive impact on our staff – a kind of recognition for them after so many caricatures,' emphasising that their work 'has nothing to do with James Bond'. Remarkably, photographs of the leading actors now decorate the walls of one of the DGSE reception rooms.[91] A leading French academic press has published a detailed study of the series by the former DGSE officer, Yves Trotignon.[92]

In 2017 *Le Bureau des légendes* won both the best series and best writing awards from the French TV Critics Association. The reviewer in *Le Monde diplomatique* praised the series for 'revealing with precision what is at stake in the great crises which are shaking the Middle East – in contrast to the fictions propagated by American espionage'.[93] Among the American 'fictions' picked out for particular ridicule was the popular US TV series, *Homeland*, starring Claire Danes as a CIA officer charged with thwarting terrorist attacks, which was well known for being President Obama's favourite TV viewing during its first year in 2011.[94]

It seems likely that Obama enjoyed *Homeland* as a gripping, award-winning thriller series rather than for its insights into intelligence operations. Though Danes is a fine actor, her ill-concealed blonde hair made her rather too conspicuous to operate credibly under cover in the Middle East. The makers of the series, complained *Le Monde diplomatique*, 'do not hesitate to put camels, Bedouins and palm trees in a city intended to be Beirut'. *Homeland*'s lowest moment came when it hired Arab street artists, who loathed the series, to make the set of a Syrian refugee camp more realistic by putting graffiti on the walls. Only after the episode was broadcast was it noticed that one of the slogans read in Arabic, 'Homeland is Racist'. Few spy films have suffered such an embarrassing intelligence failure.[95]

*

In addition to the making of spy films and TV series, twenty-first-century interactions between intelligence and the entertainment business have taken a number of new forms, ranging from interactive spy museums to the release of intelligence files on some of the stars of the Cold War era. The first of the museums, the International Spy Museum in Washington, which opened on 19 July 2002, occupied a building, a few blocks from the FBI, which had formerly housed the headquarters of the Communist Party of the United States. Though one of the few Washington museums with admission charges (despite being not-for-profit), the Spy Museum was an instant success, attracting even more visitors than the White House.[96] The founder was the media magnate, Milton Maltz, who had been fascinated by intelligence ever since serving in the National Security Agency during the Korean War.[97]

The museum's first executive director was Peter Earnest, veteran of the CIA clandestine service, former CIA Director of Media Relations and chairman of the US Association of Former Intelligence Officers (AFIO). Museum board members included a number of other retired senior US intelligence officers. The highest ranking were Judge William Webster, the only man to have served, successively, as both FBI director and Director of Central Intelligence (head of the CIA), and Ambassador James Woolsey, President Clinton's first Director of Central Intelligence.

The opening ceremony on a hot summer day enabled two other board members, Tony and Jonna Mendez, both former CIA chiefs of disguise, to give the first public demonstration of their phenomenal expertise in disguise and deception. The opening, covertly orchestrated by the Mendezes, was performed by Washington's mayor, Anthony A. Williams in his trademark white shirt and colourful bow tie. He then went inside the museum, reappeared on the roof, where there was a staged scuffle with two apparent spies, and abseiled down to music from the museum's hit compilation 'Music to Spy By'. When he reached the ground, a museum security guard ripped off "Williams"' disguise and showed him to be an imposter. The security guard then removed his own disguise and revealed himself to be the real Mayor Williams. Current displays at the International Spy Museum include other examples of the Mendezes' extraordinary virtuosity, among them photographs of Jonna in the Oval Office early in 1993 briefing George H. W. Bush (the only former DCI to be elected president) while convincingly disguised as one of her colleagues, then removing the disguise in mid briefing.[98]

The museum board included two non-Americans: Christopher Andrew[99] and – much more remarkably – Oleg Kalugin, who in 1973 had been made the youngest general in KGB foreign intelligence, chiefly in recognition of successful operations in the United States.[100] In 1990, after falling out with the hard-line leadership of the KGB, Kalugin was stripped of his general's rank, decorations and pension. All were returned after the failure of the Moscow coup of August 1991, but he remained one of the *bêtes noires* of the FSB and SVR. In 1995 he moved to the United States to teach in Washington and write his intelligence memoirs. Just as Kalugin joined the International Spy Museum board, he was tried in absentia in Moscow on trumped-up treason charges and sentenced to a fifteen-year prison term that he was never to serve. He later became a US citizen.

The museum contains the world's largest collection of espionage artefacts on public display, covering intelligence operations 'from the Bible to Bond'. Bond attracts more attention than the Bible. A video shows former CIA officers talking about episodes in their careers when they had a 'Bond' moment. When the media were shown around the Spy Museum on the eve of its opening, they showed particular interest in a replica of Bond's Aston Martin D85.

As well as bringing together senior intelligence professionals on its board and acting as a research centre, the museum is also a novel and successful part of the US entertainment business. Events for children include sleepovers after the museum closes:

> Transform yourself through disguise, make and break secret codes, uncover important secrets, interrogate real spies, and hunt for a mole within your ranks! Operation Secret Slumber is designed for kids – Ages: 9–13. Snacks and breakfast included.[101]

*

To mark their centenaries in 2009 both MI5 and SIS commissioned 'official' or 'authorised' histories, based on their archives.[102] The annual or biennial declassification of many fifty-year-old MI5 (but not SIS) files[103] has also attracted increasing media interest by revealing details of the surveillance, at its peak in the early and mid Cold War, of stars in the entertainment industry who had actual or suspected communist connections. 'REVEALED', ran a headline in the Daily Mail in March 2009, 'MI5 spied on Swedish actress and Vogue photographer as communist sympathisers.'[104] Few stars, it emerged, had been priority surveillance targets. In most cases, from the American harmonica virtuoso, Larry Adler, to the glamorous Swedish film star Mai Zetterling, the files simply reflected MI5 – and government – policy to keep a complete record of Communist Party members and leading fellow travellers.

When Adler sought refuge from McCarthyism in Britain, MI5 thought 'the Communist Party would make every effort to exploit his name as an entertainer'. It did not do so.[105] Mai Zetterling first came to MI5's attention in 1952 as a result of her involvement with a left-wing discussion group believed to have communist links.[106] A note in her file concludes: 'If her present enthusiasm for extreme left-wing politics continues, she may well be led to join the Communist Party.' Zetterling did not do so and her file was closed in 1958. Earlier surveillance had revealed that she was having an affair with Herbert Lom, who became famous for his role in the *Pink Panther* films as the exasperated, ultimately demented boss of Peter Sellers's Inspector Clouseau.[107] During the McCarthy era, Lom was refused a US visa to work in Hollywood because of his alleged 'Communist sympathies'.[108]

More than any other film star of the time, Lom was fascinated by Marlowe's career as both playwright and spy. In Lom's historical novel, *Enter a Spy: The Double Life of Christopher Marlowe*, Marlowe marries the daughter of Elizabeth I's spymaster, Sir Francis Walsingham.[109] By far the best and most credible novel on Marlowe, *A Fine Madness*, was written more recently by the former intelligence officer, Alan Petty, under the *nom de plume* Alan Judd.[110] Petty has put nothing on record about his own intelligence career. Like le Carré, however, he is believed to have worked for both SIS and MI5, and to have begun publishing while still in SIS.

★

Just over four centuries after the 'Rainbow portrait' showed Elizabeth I paying symbolic tribute to her secret service, Elizabeth II chose to open the 2012 London Olympic Games in the company of Britain's – and the world's – most famous fictional spy, James Bond. The queen

Bond escorts the queen to the opening ceremony of the London Olympics.

was filmed greeting Daniel Craig at Buckingham Palace with the words 'Hello, Mr Bond', then accompanying him to a helicopter, from which, at the age of 87, she appeared, with the help of a body double, to make her first parachute jump, landing safely in what is now the O2 Arena. The secret had been so well kept that no one in the royal box, even the Duke of Edinburgh, had any idea that this was how the queen intended to make her entrance at the opening ceremony.[111]

The interaction between Stars and Spies had finally received royal recognition. The queen subsequently received a BAFTA award.[112]

As well as winning royal recognition, Bond was also part of the Special Relationship. For his final Bond film, *No Time to Die*, Daniel Craig is lured out of retirement by his friend and former CIA collaborator, Felix Leiter. On 25 June 2018, while the script for the film was still being written, as part of the Agency's new 'Reel vs Real' initiative, Craig visited CIA HQ at Langley, Virginia, for a briefing and discussion.

According to a statement by the CIA:

> Mr Craig met with our leadership and workforce, who explained that real life espionage is a lot more 'cloak' and a lot less 'dagger' than presented in the entertainment world of spy vs. spy.[113]

Though the 'dagger' reference was a general comment on the violence of the Bond films, Craig had actually used a dagger at the end of *Skyfall* to kill the arch-villain, Raoul Silva (played by Javier Bardem). The director, Sir Sam Mendes, who has a first-class degree in English from Cambridge University, was almost certainly aware of the comparison with Christopher Marlowe, who had been killed by a dagger in a brawl with the villainous Ingram Frizer.[114] While at Cambridge, Mendes had directed several plays for the Marlowe Society.[115]

*

Until recently both the entertainment business and Western intelligence agencies have paid little attention to would-be child and teenage spies.[116] The most successful author in this growing global market is the British novelist and screenwriter, Anthony Horowitz, whose Alex Rider novels follow the adventures of a 14-year-old recruit to SIS. Horowitz was separately commissioned by the Ian Fleming estate to write two James Bond novels, *Trigger Mortis* (2015) and *Forever and a Day* (2018).[117] Well before these were published, the Alex Rider novels were already international best-sellers; by 2020 they had been translated into twenty-eight languages (including Chinese) and sold over 21 million copies. In June 2020 an eight-part Alex Rider series, produced by Sony Pictures Television, began streaming in Britain, followed by broadcasts in many other countries. The *Guardian* reviewer described Alex Rider as a 'teenage James Bond'.[118]

The first significant contribution by the British entertainment business to the understanding of children's aptitude for intelligence was made in 2015 by BBC's *Blue Peter*, which, since its first broadcast in 1958, had become the longest-running TV children's programme in the world.[119] Much of the success of both Walsingham's secret service and Bletchley Park in the Second World War was based on their recruitment of bright university students. Horowitz had long been fascinated by the idea of what schoolchildren could also contribute. Christopher Andrew's research on the intelligence operations of Walsingham's and

Thames House: MI5 HQ.

Bletchley's recruits while some of them were still in their teens had left him with the same fascination. *Blue Peter* made Horowitz and Andrew judges for its Project PETRA (named in honour of the programme's first dog), which aimed to discover Britain's best spies in the age-group 8 to 14.[120] Andrew was asked to ensure that all the challenges set during PETRA 'were based on historical operations of real life' intelligence operatives, and thus found himself once again experiencing at first hand the interplay between espionage and entertainment.[121]

From the moment the final shortlist of eight (selected by *Blue Peter* from several thousand applicants) were put on a blacked-out helicopter near Manchester and flown to a deserted airstrip with a coded clue on a runway (quickly solved by one of the children), it was clear that most had a flair for intelligence and that choosing only three winners would be difficult. The runway and other clues elsewhere led them to a portrait of Christopher Marlowe in Manchester Art Gallery – a copy of the original in his Cambridge College.[122] During the following weekend they also showed skill in working as a team, role play and presenting their findings. Several on the shortlist seemed better suited to intelligence work than some of the fictional MI5 officers in *Spooks*. The *Blue Peter* editor, Ewan Vinnicombe, said later that he had never worked with such individually talented children who were also exceptional as team players.

Sir Andrew Parker (DG, MI5) with Britain's youngest spies.

There was great excitement when the three winners (two aged 13, one only 10) were told they were to receive their certificates as Britain's best young spies in Thames House, MI5 headquarters, from the MI5 DG, Sir Andrew Parker. For the first time, cameras were allowed into the building in order to film the presentation. Ten-year-old Finlay found Thames House 'quite mysterious' but 'way cooler' than he expected. He told the *Guardian* that he and the other winners had enjoyed being shown some spy 'gadgets' but were not allowed to talk about them: 'So I can't really go into detail.'[123]

Project PETRA showed that children sometimes notice things that adult spies do not (and vice-versa, of course). This twenty-first century discovery would have come as no surprise to Shakespeare, who knew that, in an era when women were not allowed on stage, talented boys the age of the PETRA winners could play female roles as demanding as Desdemona and Lady Macbeth.

Possibly encouraged by the success of PETRA, the CIA began an online 'Spy Kids' programme with, it was hoped, wide appeal, combining information about the Agency with entertainment:

We are the Nation's first line of defense. We accomplish what others cannot accomplish and go where others cannot go ... When you're ready for a secret mission of your own, check out our games section. Help us crack codes, solve puzzles, and find secret clues to solve intelligence mysteries.[124]

The French DGSE helped to launch a more academic annual competition to discover France's best 13- to 15-year-old codebreakers. Named in honour of the great ninth-century Muslim codebreaker, Yaqub ibn Ishaq al-Kindi, the competition attracted 18,000 entrants during its first year. The DGSE's declared aim was to persuade the public as well as the competitors and their parents that 'cryptanalysis is essential for the security of our country', and to attract to it some of France's brightest young mathematicians.[125] Bernard Émié believes that France has traditionally been handicapped by lack of what he calls an 'intelligence culture'. In an attempt to implant this culture and enhance its recruitment, DGSE has embarked on a multimedia campaign which extends from the Alkindi competition to Twitter. Émié even uses his personal twitter account (@BernardEmie, the first to be opened by a DGSE director) as part of this campaign. On 19 June 2020, for example, he tweeted the video link to TV interviews on France 3 with three unidentified young foreign intelligence recruits: 'As proud as they are discreet, French secret agents of the DGSE explain their commitment to operations in the shadows.' One of them explains that he is about to begin a three-year mission to the Middle East under a false identity which, in the national interest, will force him to lie about the whole of his past life.[126]

*

Despite the increasing variety of interactions between intelligence operations and the entertainment business, the commonest point of contact between stars and spies remains the spy film, which in the twenty-first century has become an increasingly global phenomenon. Fictional spies have won huge new markets in the world's most populous states, China and India, which over two millennia ago were the first to produce major books on intelligence operations. India's 'Bollywood' has overtaken Hollywood as the biggest film producer, with almost 1,800 titles released in 2018. By contrast, India's great rival, Pakistan, lost most of its once flourishing film industry in the late twentieth century as a result of Islamisation and censorship.

Instead of going to the cinema, many families stayed at home to watch Bollywood movies on VCRs, thus – in the words of Indira Gandhi – enabling 'Indian culture to invade and take over Pakistani culture in their bedrooms'.[127]

Until the twenty-first century, however, hardly any of the Bollywood blockbusters seen in Indian cinemas and Pakistani bedrooms featured the secretive Indian foreign intelligence service, the Research and Analysis Wing (RAW), which was anxious to avoid public reference to operations against its two main targets, Pakistan and China. There were few references also to the domestic Intelligence Branch. Since the Hindu nationalist BJP, led by Narendra Modi, came to power in 2014, these inhibitions have largely disappeared. Modi and his National Security Adviser, Ajit Doval, appear, thinly disguised, in the 2019 box-office hit *Uri: The Surgical Strike*, in which a successful attack on a target in Pakistani-administered Kashmir is assisted by Indian spies in Pakistan. At the end of the credits, a Pakistani minister shouts in frustration and the final scene cuts to the slogan 'Jai Hind' (Victory to India!).[128]

The Indian International Film Award (the Bollywood Oscar) for best picture in 2019 went to the Hindi-language spy-thriller *Raazi*, thought to be the highest-grossing Indian film ever made with a female lead. Raazi, played by Alia Bhatt (who won the Best Actress award), patriotically marries a Pakistani military officer before the 1971 Indo-Pakistani War so that she can obtain intelligence on the threat to India. She hides surveillance equipment in her trousseau.[129]

Bollywood was also the first to produce a Covid-19-inspired spy-thriller, *London Confidential: The Chinese Conspiracy*, released in September 2020. RAW gains intelligence pointing to the spread by China's MSS of another deadly virus along the Indo-Chinese border. Just as RAW's London station is about to obtain the final proof, it is thwarted by an MSS mole in the Indian embassy. Once again, the leading spy is a woman, Uma Kulkarni, head of RAW, played by Mouni Roy. She and her team, ingeniously disguised as Indian grocers in London, uncover the MSS conspiracy just in time to prevent the Chinese virus spreading out of control – without, however, at any stage wearing masks or socially distancing.[130]

The appeal of Bollywood's Hindi-language blockbusters, however, is mainly limited to India, its diaspora and some of its neighbours. The closest non-state-directed collaboration between stars and spies has come with the foundation in 2018 of Spycraft Entertainment,

Mouni Roy (centre) defeats a Chinese pandemic plot.

based in Los Angeles and Washington, which brings together former senior intelligence officers and producers of films, TV and new media formats, aims to 'help retired members of the intelligence community turn their ideas and intellectual property into world-class content':

> We focus on true fiction, emphasizing quality, authenticity, and great storytelling. Our network of 'ordinary people who have done extraordinary things' comprises innumerable untold tales that have the power to inform, inspire, and entertain audiences around the world.[131]

The global gold standard in spy films, however, still remains the entirely fictional James Bond, whose latest and most expensive epic, *No Time To Die*, premiered around the world in autumn 2021, almost sixty years after his first appearance in *Dr No*. As well as being by far the world's best-known intelligence officer, real or fictional, Bond has had the longest career – longer even than J. Edgar Hoover's forty-eight years as director of the FBI. The popularity of Bond's filmed adventures has given SIS what other intelligence services tend to regard as an enviable, if misleading, brand image. One former SIS chief[132] recalls that during a mission to make contact with a tribal elder in deepest South East Asia in the midst of the Cold War, the elder greeted him with the words, 'Hello, Mr Bond!' The current C, Richard Moore, who became chief in October 2020, said after Sean Connery's death soon afterwards that he had been 'My favourite Bond. No question. So sorry he's gone.'[133] Moore is the first chief to open a Twitter account (@ChiefMI6), tweeting a satirical suggestion for 'a vote on who should be the next @007 –we [MI6] get a say right?' In honour of the Bond films, the director of MI6's technical department is nowadays known as Q.[134]

Intelligence agencies, particularly in the West, increasingly use entertaining posts on social media to improve their public image, emphasise the growing diversity of their workforce, and attract new recruits. The Australian SIGINT agency ASD celebrated Harmony Week 2021 with an online cookbook to 'showcase the diversity of ASD's workforce and their cultural backgrounds'.[135] Every Monday its Five Eyes ally, GCHQ, encourages its 130,000 Twitter followers to 'puzzle your way out of those Monday blues with this new #GCHQPuzzle'. Some of its tweets (regularly retweeted by its US allies, CIA and NSA), are closely linked to the entertainment business:

> Fancy yourself as a Jedi #puzzle master? Use the Force and have a go at our special #StarWarsDay puzzle![136]

For Valentine's Day 2021 the CIA tweeted an encrypted poem to its followers, together with some codebreaking clues. The decrypted verse was disappointingly predictable:

> Roses are red,
> Violets are blue,
> Happy Valentine's Day
> From CIA to You[137]

GCHQ was also in romantic mood, though its Valentine's Day verse was not encrypted:

> Roses are red,
> Violets are blue,
> A Top Secret Tale,
> That we can tell You

GCHQ then disclosed for the first time 'a special #ValentinesDay tale of a shy intelligence officer sending a marriage proposal to his girlfriend via top-secret tube messaging service'. She accepted and they 'lived happily ever after'.[138]

@ChiefMI6 has prudently avoided posting similar stories of shy, romantic British spies on social media. Richard Moore has, however, revealed his personal love of cricket (a passion once shared by Kim Philby) and of John le Carré's novels. Following le Carré's death in December 2020, a fortnight after Sean Connery's, he tweeted 'condolences from all at the #RiverHouse' (le Carré's name for MI6 HQ):

> Very sad to hear the news about #JohnLeCarre. A giant of literature who left his mark on #MI6 through his evocative & brilliant novels.[139]

On World Book Day 2021, Moore 'thought a 24 hour poll [on Twitter] to judge his best spy book might be a fun and a fitting memorial to the great man'. *Tinker, Tailor, Soldier, Spy*, one of C's own favourites, was an easy winner – no doubt partly because of the immensely popular TV series and award-winning film based on it, which were seen by many more people than read the book.[140]

Even more unprecedented than MI6's first public quiz was Moore's Twitter video of his meeting in February 2021 with Sir Ian McKellen, whom he called 'one of the nation's most cherished actors' – the first ever recorded conversation between Britain's chief spy and one of its leading stars. A major purpose of the video was to promote MI6's publicly declared aim of 'promoting gender equality [and] enabling an open LGBT+ workplace'.[141] Moore was proud that the campaigning

I'm delighted to be joined today in conversation by Sir Ian McKellen, one of the nation's most cherished actors,

group Stonewall, of which McKellen had been a founder, had named MI6 one of the country's one hundred best LGBT+ employers, but he apologised publicly for past discrimination against LGBT+ applicants and personnel. He told his Twitter followers that he had a 'great discussion with @IanMcKellen talking about all things LGBT+ including the #MI6 and his work campaigning for LGBT+ rights'.[142]

Britain's most famous twentieth-century intelligence officer, the codebreaker Alan Turing, who was subjected to chemical castration after a conviction for 'gross indecency' in 1952, is now hailed by the director of GCHQ, Jeremy Fleming, as 'one of the most iconic LGBT+ figures in the world'. To celebrate Turing's appearance on the new £50 banknote in 2021, GCHQ posted on social media 'the Turing Challenge' – its 'toughest puzzle ever ... put together by some of our intelligence staff, where problem solving and a diverse mix of minds are at the heart of our work'.[143]

'Diversity', declares Richard Moore, 'makes us more effective, inclusion makes us stronger.'[144] James Bond, however, comprehensively fails the MI6 diversity test. In her first film as 'M', Judi Dench told Bond he was 'a sexist, misogynist dinosaur. A relic of the Cold War.'[145] Despite Moore's admiration for Sean Connery's acting and James Bond's undimmed popularity in the global entertainment business, 007 is now officially out of favour at MI6 headquarters. According to the last C, Sir Alex Younger, 'Were Bond to apply to join MI6 now, he would have to change his ways' – but is too reckless and immoral to have much chance of doing so.[146] And while Moore continues to regard John le Carré as a 'giant of literature', George Smiley too is now unwelcome at 'River House'. Younger bridles at the implied 'moral equivalence between us and our opponents that runs through John le Carré's novels'.[147] An earlier C, Sir Richard Dearlove, complains that, while MI6 is based on 'trust between colleagues', the novels are about betrayal.[148]

On his first day as chief, Richard Moore told his Twitter followers, 'I'll ... try to persuade some of you to come and work for #MI6.' But there are two exceptions:

#Bond or #Smiley need not apply. They're (splendid) fiction but actually we're #secretlyjustlikeyou.[149]

Notes

Abbreviations

AN	Archives Nationales, Paris
BL	British Library
BM	British Museum
BN	Bibliothèque Nationale, Paris
CAB	Cabinet Office
CO	Colonial Office
FCO	Foreign and Commonwealth Office
FO	Foreign Office
HO	Home Office
HW	Government Communications Headquarters (GCHQ) files, TNA
IMDB	Internet Movie Database
IWM	Imperial War Museum
KV	MI5 (Security Service) files, TNA
LCP	Lord Chamberlain's plays, BL
LHC	Liddell Hart Centre for Military Archives, King's College London
NAI	National Archives of Ireland, Dublin
MAE	Ministère des Affaires étrangères, Paris, Archives diplomatiques de La Courneuve
NAW	US National Archives, Washington DC
ODNB	*Oxford Dictionary of National Biography*
RG	Record Group, NAW
SP	State Papers, TNA
T	Treasury files, TNA
TNA	The National Archives, Kew
WO	War Office files, TNA

NB: unless otherwise stated, all websites accessed January 2021.

Introduction: The Art of Deception

• **1.** Antonio J. Mendez, *The Master of Disguise: My Secret Life in the CIA* (New York: HarperCollins, 2009) • **2.** The scale and success of TROJAN SHIELD (known in Australia as Operation IRONSIDE), was first revealed by the Australian prime minister, Scott Morrison, on 7 June 2021. • **3.** Christopher Andrew and Oleg Gordievsky, *KGB: The Inside Story of Its Foreign Operations from Lenin to Gorbachev*, paperback edn (London: Sceptre, 1990), pp.181–6. • **4.** The suggestion was not, of course, intended seriously: @ ChiefMI6, 17 March 2021 • **5.**@CIA, 6 June 2014. • **6.** Christopher Andrew and Daniela Richterova, 'Intelligence Services' Use of Social Media: Towards a Global Perspective': presentation to Cambridge Intelligence Seminar on 7 May 2021 and forthcoming publication. • **7.** On the slender interest in intelligence in classical Greece and Rome, see Christopher Andrew, *The Secret World: A History of Intelligence* (London: Allen Lane, 2018), chs 3, 4. • **8.** Sun Tzu, *The Art of War: Bilingual Chinese and English Text*, trans. Lionel Giles with introduction by John Minford (Hong Kong: Tuttle Publishing, 2016). • **9.** Leo Rosten, *Hollywood: The Movie Colony, The Movie Makers* (New York: Harcourt, Brace, 1941). • **10.** Kautilya, *The Arthashastra*, ed. L. N. Rangarajan (Haryana, India: Penguin, 1992), p. 471. Though this edition is the most readable translation of the Sanskrit *Arthashastra*, it is not quite definitive. Rangarajan omits some verses and reorders others. • **11.** Ibid., pp. 563–4. • **12.** Ibid., p. 486. • **13.** Ibid., p. 487. • **14.** Una McIlvenna, 'A "Stable of Whores"? The "Flying Squadron" of Catherine de Medici', in Nadine Akkerman and Brigid Houben (eds), *The Politics of Female Households: Ladies-in-Waiting across Early Modern Europe* (Leiden: Brill, 2013). • **15.** William of Malmesbury, *Gesta regum Anglorum*, 12th-century MS, Cambridge University Library MS Ii.2.3, ff. 33v–34r. According to the Elizabethan historian Holinshed, inside the Danish camp Alfred 'was suffered to go into every part, and play on his instrument, as well afore the king as others, so that there was no secret, but that he understood it'. • **16.** The Radio 4 documentary, 'What if Alfred … ?' (presenter: Christopher Andrew; producer: Ian Bell), first broadcast on 18 March 1999, considered how different English history might have been if Alfred had failed to gain good intelligence on the Danes and had been defeated at Ethandun (where much of the programme was recorded). • **17.** Stephen G. Nichols, 'The early troubadours: Guilhem IX to Bernart de Ventadorn', in Simon Gaunt and Sarah Kay (eds), *The Troubadours: An Introduction* (Cambridge: Cambridge University Press, 1999), pp. 66–82. • **18.** David Boyle, *Blondel's Song: The Capture, Imprisonment and Ransom of Richard the Lionheart* (London: Penguin, 2006), p. 178. There is, however, almost no reliable record of the confidences which troubadours and trouvères heard from their hosts and sometimes passed on. • **19.** More correctly, *trouvère*, the northern French equivalent. • **20.** Boyle, *Blondel's Song.* • **21.** Obsidian Records, CD712, 2014. • **22.***The Spy's Choirbook* (MS Royal 8.g.vii) remains one of the greatest treasures of Renaissance music in the British Library. Beth Rose, 'Henry VIII, the choir book and Alamire the spy', BBC News, 13 December 2014: bbc.co.uk/news/uk-england-london-29693410. • **23.** Musicians in Elizabethan and early Stuart England who sometimes played such roles included John Dowland, Alfonso Ferrabosco, Anthony Holborne, Thomas Morley, Angelo Notari and Peter Philips.

1: Golden Age

• **1.** Andrew, *The Secret World*, ch. 10. • **2.** Stephen Alford, *The Watchers: A Secret History of the Reign of Elizabeth I* (London: Allen Lane, 2012), pp. 219–35. • **3.** W.R. Streitberger, *The Masters of the Revels and Elizabeth I's Court Theatre* (Oxford: Oxford University Press, 2016), p. 124. • **4.** Herbert Berry, 'Playhouses', in Arthur F. Kinney (ed.), *A Companion to Renaissance Drama* (Oxford: Blackwell, 2000), p. 148 • **5.** *Oxford Dictionary of National Biography* (*ODNB*), 'Edmund Tilney'. Scott McMillin and Sally-Beth MacLean, *The Queen's Men and Their Plays* (Cambridge: Cambridge University Press, 1998). • **6.** *ODNB*. Thomas Fuller, *History of the Worthies of England* (1662). Fuller's sources do not survive. His tribute to Tarlton's influence on the Queen may have been too fulsome: Mathew Lyons, 'Richard Tarlton: the greatest star of the Elizabethan theatre'; mathewlyons.co.uk/2012/03/05/richard-tarlton-the-greatest-star-of-the-elizabethan-theatre. • **7.** *ODNB*, 'Will Kemp'. Patrick H. Martin, *Elizabethan Espionage: Plotters and Spies in the Struggle between Catholicism and the Crown* (Jefferson, North Carolina: McFarland & Co., 2016), ch. 23: 'From Intelligence to Entertainment'. Kemp was also known as Kempe. • **8.** 27 Eliz. 1, c. 2. Those who harboured Catholic priests or knew of their presence and failed to inform the authorities were to be fined and imprisoned for felony. Where the authorities wished to make an example of them, they might be executed. • **9.** One of the last Catholic priests in the north to be executed under Elizabeth was Blessed Christopher Robinson, hanged, but (unlike his predecessors) not drawn and quartered, at Carlisle in 1598. The fact that he was was found hiding at Johnby Hall, near Penrith (where a priest hole still survives) strongly suggests – though no records survive – that his discovery was due to intelligence report(s). We are grateful for information on this case to Dr Henry Howard of Johnby Hall. • **10.** In July 1596, for example, the Queen's Men were paid 40 shillings for performances by the

York civic authorities, as compared to the 14 shillings paid by London's Rose Theatre in the same month to the Admiral's Men for performances of *Dr Faustus*. McMillin and MacLean, *The Queen's Men and Their Plays*. • **11.** Other, now celebrated Catholic victims included Margaret Clitheroe (later canonised as one of the 'English Martyrs'), wife of a York butcher, who was 'pressed' (crushed) to death in 1586 after refusing to enter a plea on a charge of sheltering a priest at their house in the Shambles: historyofyork.org.uk/themes/catholic-resistance. • **12.** Andrew, *The Secret World*, pp.180–81. • **13.** In a denunciation of Munday published in 1582, the future Cardinal William Allen, head of the English seminary at Rheims (formerly Douai) wrote that, before going to Rome, Munday 'was first a stage player (no doubt a calling of some credit)'; Andrew Hadfield, *Lying in Early Modern English Culture: From the Oath of Supremacy to the Oath of Allegiance* (Oxford: Oxford University Press, 2017), pp.8–9. • **14.** Among those with whom Munday allied himself in Rome were several of Walsingham's agents. Thomas Merriam, 'The misunderstanding of Munday as author of Sir Thomas More', *The Review of English Studies* (2000), no. 204, p. 549. Only Munday, however, had an audience with the Pope. • **15.** Hadfield, *Lying in Early Modern English Culture*, p. 6. • **16.** Anthony Munday, *The English Roman Life*, ed. Philip J. Ayres (Oxford: Clarendon Press, 1980), p. 66; Hadfield, *Lying in Early Modern English Culture*, pp. 8–10. To defend himself against the accusation of premeditated blasphemy, Munday claimed implausibly that his original decision to visit Rome was prompted by nothing more than 'desire to see strange countries, as also affection to learn the languages'. • **17.** Kristin M. S. Bezio, '"Munday I sweare shalbee a hollidaye": The politics of Anthony Munday, from anti-Catholic spy to civic pageanteer (1579–1630)', *Études Anglaises*, vol. 71 (2018), no. 4. • **18.** The attempt to arrest Orton failed because he was wrongly identified when landing at Dover. Mordechai Feingold, 'The reluctant martyr: John Hart's English mission', *Journal of Jesuit Studies*, vol. 6 (2019). • **19.** Munday, *English Roman Life*, pp. 91–2. • **20.** Ibid., p. 39. • **21.** The Catholic pamphlet, *True Report of the Death of M. Campion Jesuit*, written early in 1582 in response to a hostile tract by Munday, calls Munday 'a stage player' and notes that 'he now begins again to ruffle upon the stage': 'I omit to declare how this scholar new come out of Italy did play extempore, those gentlemen and others which were present can best give witness of his dexterity, who being weary of his folly, hissed him from his stage.' Munday, *The English Roman Life*, ed. Ayres, p. xviii. As with most actors in the 1580s, no details survive of the parts played by Munday. • **22.** *ODNB*, 'Edmund Campion'. • **23.** Munday, *A Discoverie of Edmund Campion and his Confederates* ... (1582). • **24.** Munday, *A breefe and true reporte of the execution of certaine traytours at Tiborne, the xxviii, and xxx days of Maye, 1582*. • **25.** *ODNB*, 'Richard Topcliffe'. • **26.** *ODNB*, 'Anthony Munday'.

• **27.** Marlowe's talent-spotter was probably Nicholas Faunt, who was at Corpus Christi College from 1573 to 1577, became an assistant to Walsingham in 1578, and took part in numerous intelligence operations. Dr Peter Roberts, a former Corpus Fellow, has shown that Faunt, like Marlowe, was a Matthew Parker Scholar from King's School, Canterbury. • **28.** Corpus Christi College, Cambridge, Archives. • **29.** Tests at the National Portrait Gallery have confirmed that the pigment dates from the 1580s. Before the weekly term-time meetings of today's Cambridge University Intelligence Seminar, founded by Christopher Andrew in 1999, the convenors meet for tea beneath Marlowe's portrait in Corpus Christi College Old Combination Room. The portrait serves as a reminder of the importance of long-term perspective in intelligence operations. • **30.** It is very rare in an Elizabethan portrait for the sitter's arms to be folded, as Marlowe's are. The implication perhaps is that he is keeping to himself secrets that he will not share with others. • **31.** Though the testimonial for Marlowe has not survived, a digest of its contents survives in Privy Council minutes: The National Archives (TNA), Privy Council register, Eliz. 6.381b. • **32.** In 1582, after another English priest, whom Baines had tried to recruit 'as associate', reported him to the seminary authorities, he was imprisoned in the Rheims town jail. A year later, he confessed – apparently sincerely – to 'unholy and abominable rebellion against God and the holy Church': 'the devil was in my heart and was compelling me to all crimes with the hope of rewards, honour and advancement in England'. Baines promised to 'make reparation to God's Church as far as I am able', was set at liberty and fled to England. Roy Kendall, *Christopher Marlowe and Richard Baines: Journeys Through the Elizabethan Underworld* (Madison, NJ: Fairleigh Dickinson University Press, 2003), ch. 1. • **33.** David Bevington and Eric Rasmussen (eds), *Christopher Marlowe, Dr Faustus: The A and B Texts (1604, 1616)*, parallel text edition (Manchester: Manchester University Press, 2014). • **34.** Poley was later present at, and may bear some responsibility for, Marlowe's murder. Park Honan, *Christopher Marlowe: Poet and Spy* (Oxford: Oxford University Press, 2005), pp. 145–6; David Riggs, *The World of Christopher Marlowe* (London: Faber & Faber, 2004), pp. 143–5, 150, 154, 257; Charles Nicholl, *The Reckoning:.The Murder of Chtistopher Marlowe*, 2nd edn (London: Viking, 2002), pp. 185–7. • **35.** In both cases, a record survives of the date of baptism, but not of the date of birth. • **36.** Further visits to Stratford followed: Leicester's Men in 1572 and 1576, Warwick's Men in 1574, Worcester's Men in 1574 and 1581, Lord Strange's Men in 1578, Essex's Men in 1578 and 1583, Derby's Men in 1579, Lord Berkeley's Men in 1580 and 1582. ODNB, 'William Shakespeare'. • **37.** Stephen Greenblatt, *Will in the World: How Shakespeare Became Shakespeare* (London: Bodley Head, 2016), ch. 1. Though Willis's exact age is unknown, he was small enough to stand between his seated father's legs.

• **38.** One possibility is that Shakespeare joined the Queen's Men during their visit to Stratford in 1587. • **39.** qme.uvic.ca/Foyer/historyofthequeensmen/index.html. • **40.** Greenblatt, *Will in the World*, p. 193. • **41.** *Tamburlaine*, part 2, Act III. • **42.** *2 Henry IV*, II.4.155. Pistol later reappeared in *The Merry Wives of Windsor* and *Henry V*. • **43.** It is widely accepted that Shakespeare himself collaborated with four other playwrights: on *Titus Andronicus* with George Peele; on *Timon of Athens* with Thomas Middleton; on *Pericles* with George Wilkins; and on *Henry VIII* and *The Two Noble Kinsmen* with John Fletcher. • **44.** Stanley Wells, *Shakespeare and Co.* (London: Allen Lane, 2006), p. 22. The Rose had been the first to stage Shakespeare's plays. • **45.** 'Two households reprise ancient grudge over Shakespeare', *The Times*, 16 April 2020; Letter from Gerald Baker in the *Times Literary Supplement*, 28 April 2020. Cf. John V. Nance, '"We, John Cade": Shakespeare, Marlowe, and the authorship of 4.2.33–189 *2 Henry VI*', *Shakespeare*, vol. 13 (2017), no. 1; Edward Burns (ed.), *King Henry VI, Part 1*, The Arden Shakespeare, Series 3 (London: Bloomsbury, 2000), p. 75. • **46.** Charles Hughes (ed.), 'Nicholas Faunt's Discourse Touching the Office of Principal Secretary of State &c., 1592', *English Historical Review*, vol. 50 (1905), no. 79. • **47.** BL, Harley MS 6848, fols 185–6; MS 6853, fols 307–8. • **48.** *ODNB*, 'Christopher Marlowe'. • **49.** The use of 'intelligence' to mean superior understanding dates from the early fifteenth century. By the mid fifteenth century it was also used to mean news or information – without, as yet, any specific association with spies: etymonline.com/word/intelligence. By the reign of Henry VIII, 'intelligence' was sometimes used in secret despatches, particularly on military matters, to mean information from espionage; Neil Murphy, 'Spies, informers and Thomas Howard's defence of England's northern frontier in 1523', *Historical Research*, vol. 93 (2020), no. 260. • **50.** Andrew, *The Secret World*, pp. 187–8. • **51.** Harold Bloom (ed.), *William Shakespeare's As You Like It* (Philadelphia: Chelsea House, 2004), pp. 2–3,158. Steve Sohmer is the latest in a series of leading Shakespearian scholars to interpret Touchstone's comment, 'it strikes a man more dead than a great reckoning in a little roome', as a reference to the Coroner's Jury's verdict on Marlowe's death. Steve Sohmer, *Reading Shakespeare's Mind* (Manchester: Manchester University Press, 2017), p. 15. • **52.** Wells, *Shakespeare and Co.*, p. 75. Steve Sohmer argues that Shakespeare wrote *As You Like It* as an 'emphatic (if discreet) memorial for Marlowe'; that Shakespeare created the character of Jaques in the image of Marlowe; and that Shakespeare himself may have taken the part of Jaques in a performance of *As You Like It*. Sohmer, *Reading Shakespeare's Mind*. • **53.** And in *Pericles, Prince of Tyre* as 'Quod me alit, me extinguit' ('What feeds me extinguishes me'). • **54.** He made a total of 29 references to intelligence. Vivian Thomas, *Shakespeare's Political and Economic Language*, Arden Shakespeare Dictionaries (London: Bloomsbury, 2008), pp.154–7. • **55.** Richard Angus Smith, 'Spying and Surveillance in Shakespeare's Dramatic Courts', PhD thesis, University of Sydney (2014), ch. 6. • **56.** '*Hamlet* would certainly qualify as a detective drama', Agatha Christie wrote to an admirer named Mrs Fink on 12 June 1969. Kenneth W. Rendell Inc historical manuscript sales catalogue, Massachusetts: kwrendellgallery.com/literature/literature-englishirish/christie-agatha-2. • **57.** *Macbeth*, Act IV, scene 1. • **58.** *King John* (1596), Act IV, scene 2. • **59.** Christopher Andrew, *For The President's Eyes Only*, paperback edn (London: HarperCollins, 1996), p. 538. • **60.** Andrew, *The Secret World*, p. 179. • **61.** Ibid., pp. 176–7. • **62.** A church near Lund in Sweden (formerly part of Christian IV's Denmark) contains a series of tombs of both Rosencrantz and Guildenstern family members in the Christian IV era, as well as a monument recording a marriage alliance between them. • **63.** Ambassadors later arrive at the Danish court to announce that this 'commandment is fulfilled ... Rosencrantz and Guildenstern are dead.' In 1966 Tom Stoppard's Tony-winning absurdist tragicomedy *Rosencrantz and Guildenstern Are Dead*, first staged at the Edinburgh Festival Fringe, launched him on his career as one of the leading contemporary playwrights. • **64.** The Jesuit priest Father Henry Garnet was repeatedly accused of 'equivocation' as a means of disguising the truth during his trial in 1606 for alleged involvement in the Gunpowder Plot. *Macbeth*'s reference to 'th' equivocation of the fiend, That lies like truth' probably refers to Garnet. • **65.** Bezio, '"Munday I sweare shalbee a hollidaye"'. It has also been argued that some elements in *A Midsummer Night's Dream*, *The Merchant of Venice* and *Much Ado About Nothing* were influenced by Munday's plays. hankwhittemore.com/tag/anthony-munday. • **66.** Donna B. Hamilton, *Anthony Munday and the Catholics, 1560–1633* (London: Routledge, 2005). The role of Heneage as spymaster reflects a decline in centralised control of espionage after the death of Walsingham. • **67.** Joseph L. Black, 'The Marprelate Controversy', in Andrew Hadfield (ed.), *The Oxford Handbook of English Prose 1500–1640* (Oxford: Oxford University Press, 2013); Joseph L. Black (ed.) *The Martin Marprelate Tracts* (Cambridge: Cambridge University Press, 2008). • **68.** oxford-shakespeare.com/Marprelate/Just_Censure.pdf. • **69.** Only in the late twentieth century was it established that the main author of the tracts was almost certainly the eloquent Puritan politician and religious pamphleteer, Job Throckmorton: *ODNB*, 'Job Throckmorton'. • **70.** The final tract, *The Protestatyon*, appeared in late September 1589, just under a year after the first: Black, 'The Marprelate Controversy'. • **71.** Whitgift, quoted in A. Peel, *Tracts Ascribed to Richard Bancroft* (Cambridge: Cambridge University Press, 1953), p. xviii. *ODNB*, 'Thomas Nashe'. • **72.** *ODNB*, 'Anthony Munday'. • **73.** As Lyly's biographer, G. K. Hunter, observes, he was 'an unfortunate choice' to take on Martin Marprelate: 'anyone less suited to the cut and thrust of political satire can hardly be imagined.' *ODNB*, 'John Lely'. • **74.** Cuthbert Curry-Knave [Thomas Nashe], *An Almond for a Parrat* (1590). • **75.** In 1594 Nashe's name appeared with that of his Cambridge contemporary, Christopher Marlowe, on the title-page of Marlowe's early drama, *Dido Queene of Carthage*. *ODNB*, Thomas Nashe. • **76.** R. A. Foakes and R. T. Rickert, *Henslowe's Diary* (Cambridge: Cambridge University Press, 1961), pp. 85–7; *ODNB*, 'Anthony Munday'. • **77.** Francis Meres, *Palladis tamia*, 1598; *ODNB*, 'Anthony Munday'. • **78.** 'The Book of Sir Thomas More': Shakespeare's only surviving literary manuscript': bl.uk/collection-items/shakespeares-handwriting-in-the-book-of-sir-thomas-more. • **79.** Lillian M. Ruff and D. Arnold Wilson, 'The madrigal, the lute song and Elizabethan politics', *Past & Present*, no. 44 (August 1969), p. 28; *ODNB* 'John Dowland'. • **80.** Peter Hauge, 'Dowland and his time in Copenhagen, 1598–1606', *Early Music*, vol. 41, no. 2 (2013), pp. 196–7. • **81.** Winston Graham, *The Spanish Armadas* (London: Pan Macmillan, 2003), pp. 212–13. • **82.** We are grateful to Nicholas Howard for alerting us to recent research on Dowland's intelligence from the Danish court. Holinshed's *Chronicles*, a major source for Shakespeare, Marlowe and other Elizabethan writers, told the story, probably also known to Dowland, of how, seven centuries before, Alfred the Great had obtained vital intelligence while playing his harp at the court of a Danish king. • **83.** Kongelige Bibliotek, Copenhagen, MS NKS 1305 in-fol. • **84.** Hauge, 'Dowland and his time in Copenhagen'; idem, 'John Dowland's employment at the royal Danish court: Musician, agent – and spy?', in M. Keblusek and B. V. Noldus (eds) *Double Agents: Cultural and Political Brokerage in Early Modern Europe* (Leyden: Brill, 2011); Neil Kent, *Imperial Denmark: The Danish Colonial Empire and the Modern World* (London & Washington DC: forthcoming). • **85.** Andrew, *The Secret World*, pp. 188–93.

2: 'Our Revels Now Are Ended'

• **1.** Jonson, 'On Spies'. • **2.** *ODNB*, 'Ben Jonson'; ibid., 'Thomas Nashe'. • **3.** Parrot's name – like Marlowe's and Shakespeare's – had variant spellings, among them Parrat and Perrot. He is not named as a spy in surviving official records until 1600; Ian Donaldson, *Ben Jonson: A Life* (Oxford: Oxford University Press, 2011), p.117. 'One *Parrat*' (probably Parrot) is identified in State Papers of 1600 as an informer attempting to extort money from a prisoner in Newgate. The painter John Taylor, who probably painted the only portrait of Shakespeare from life, later claimed that Parrot had been 'in prison'. *ODNB*, 'Henry Parrot'. • **4.** Ibid. • **5.** *ODNB*, 'Ben Jonson'. • **6.** Jonson, 'Inviting a Friend to Supper'. Jonson and Parrot went on to exchange insults in published epigrams. *ODNB*, Henry Parrot. • **7.** Jonson, 'My Picture Left in Scotland'. • **8.** On Wright and Jonson's Catholic conversion, see Donaldson, *Ben Jonson*, pp. 138–43. Some of Jonson's earliest surviving poems, written after his conversion, were addressed to fellow Catholics. Robert S. Miola, 'Ben Jonson, Catholic poet', *Renaissance and Reformation/ Renaissance et Réforme*, vol. 25 (2001), no. 4. • **9.** Donaldson, *Ben Jonson*, pp. 195–8. • **10.** There were three other royal companies of actors: the Queen's Men, Prince Henry's Men and Prince Charles's Men. • **11.** During the holiday period from Hallowmas Day at the start of November 1604 to Shrove Tuesday 1605, the only one for which precise details survive, seven of the ten plays performed at court by the King's Men were by Shakespeare. James Shapiro, *1606: Shakespeare and the Year of Lear* (London: Faber & Faber, 2015), ch. 1. • **12.** The basis of these charges remains unclear. As Jonson acknowledged, the later printed text differs substantially from that used in the controversial original production, which does not survive: universitypublishingonline.org/ cambridge/benjonson/k/essays/Sejanus_textual_essay. • **13.** gutenberg.org/ files/5232/5232-h/5232-h.htm. • **14.** Donaldson, *Ben Jonson*, pp. 206–15. The detailed circumstances of Jonson's imprisonment remain unclear. • **15.** Andrew, *The Secret World*, p. 193. Few records survive on the surveillance of Jonson. • **16.** *ODNB*, 'Robert Catesby'; Anonymous letter delivered to Lord Monteagle, 26 Oct. 1605, TNA, SP 14/21; Andrew, *The Secret World*, pp. 193–4. • **17.** *ODNB*, 'Gunpowder Plot'; ibid., 'Guy Fawkes'; Andrew, *The Secret World*, pp. 193–4. • **18.** bl.uk/collection-items/autograph-letter-by-ben-jonson-concerning-the-gunpowder-plot. • **19.** Jonson, *Epigrams*, 60. • **20.** *ODNB*, 'Anthony Munday'. • **21.** *ODNB*, 'Hugh Holland'. Holland also wrote one of the eulogies of Shakespeare published at the beginning of the First Folio edition of his plays. He remained a Catholic until April 1626, when he was indicted for recusancy and became an Anglican. • **22.** Jonson, *The Case is Altered*, Act I, scene 1. • **23.** *ODNB*, 'Anthony Munday'. • **24.** Martin Butler, 'The court masque' (n. d.): universitypublishingonline.org/cambridge/ benjonson/k/essays/court_msq_essay. • **25.** hrp.org.uk/banqueting-house/ history-and-stories/the-masque/#gs.jp5sue. • **26.** Miranda Garno Nesler, 'Charles I and the act of dying': wondersandmarvels.com/2009/08/charles-i-and-the-act-of-dying.html. • **27.** Donaldson, *Ben Jonson*, pp. 272–4. Jonson seems, however to have retained Catholic friends and sympathies for the rest of his life. Alison Searle, 'Ben Jonson and religion', in Eugene Giddens (ed.), *The Oxford Handbook of Ben Jonson* (Oxford: Oxford University Press, 2015). *ODNB*, 'John Overall'. • **28.** Siobhan Keenan, 'The Simpson Players of Jacobean Yorkshire and the professional stage', *Theatre Notebook*, vol. 67 (2013), no. 1. The text of *St Christopher* does not survive. • **29.** Christopher Howard, *Sir John Yorke of Nidderdale, 1565–1634* (London: Sheed & Ward, 1939); Joanna

Moody, *Traces of Nidderdale in 40 Years and 40 Objects: Stories of the Museum* (Pateley Bridge: Nidderdale History Museum, 2014). The episode was the subject of a well-reviewed performance at Pateley Bridge Playhouse in 2009: pateleyplayhouse.co.uk/pages/past-productions/2009/gouthwaite-hall/gouthwaite-hall-review-feedback.php. • **30.** Andy Wood, 'Subordination, solidarity and the limits of popular agency in a Yorkshire valley *c.* 1596–1615', *Past & Present,* no. 193 (Nov. 2006). The original Gouthwaite Hall is now beneath the waters of the Gouthwaite reservoir. • **31.** Keenan, 'The Simpson Players', p. 31. Cholmley's son acknowledged his father's 'naturally choleric' temperament; histparl.ac.uk/volume/1604–1629/member/cholmley-sir-richard-1580–1631. • **32.** Keenan, 'The Simpson Players', pp. 28–9. • **33.** histparl.ac.uk/volume/1604–1629/member/cholmley-sir-richard-1580–1631. • **34.** Wood, 'Subordination, solidarity and the limits'. Richard Dutton, *Shakespeare's Theatre: A History* (Hoboken, NJ: Wiley-Blackwell, 2018), pp. 58–9. • **35.** John Fletcher subsequently collaborated with Shakespeare in writing *Henry VIII, The Two Noble Kinsmen* and the lost play *Cardenio.* As Shakespeare must have known, Fletcher, like his probable first collaborator, Christopher Marlowe, studied at Corpus Christi College, Cambridge. There is a joint monument in Corpus Old Court to Marlowe and Fletcher, though Fletcher, unlike Marlowe, may have left the college without taking a degree. • **36.** Glyn Parry, *The Arch-Conjuror of England: John Dee and Magic at the Courts of Renaissance Europe* (New Haven and London: Yale University Press, 2012). In 2012 Damon Albarn's opera, *Dr Dee* (director Rufus Norris) had its premiere at the English National Opera. • **37.** Neil MacGregor, *Shakespeare's Restless World* (London: Allen Lane, 2012), ch. 9. • **38.** Dee's guide to summoning angels, *De Heptarchia Mystica,* written in 1582, is in BL Sloane MS 3191. • **39.** The Aztec mirror was an exhibit in the 2012 British Museum exhibition, 'Shakespeare: Staging the World': bl.uk/collection-items/john-dees-spirit-mirror. • **40.** MacGregor, *Shakespeare's Restless World,* p. 120. Parry, *The Arch-Conjuror of England.* • **41.** *The Tempest,* Act I, scene 2.190–91 • **42.** Ibid., Act V, scene.1.132–5 • **43.** Ibid., Act IV, scene 2. • **44.** *Catiline,* Act V, scene 3. • **45.** David Bevington, 'Catiline: Textual essay' (n. d.): university publishingonline.org/cambridge/benjonson/k/essays/Catiline_textual_essay. • **46.** Martin Butler, 'The court masque'. • **47.** *ODNB,* 'Robert Carr'. • **48.** Ibid. • **49.** E. K. Chambers, *The Elizabethan Stage,* 4 vols (Oxford: Clarendon Press, 1923), vol. 3, p. 389; 'The politics of desire: George Villiers, James I and courtly entertainment' (2015): medium.com/@LukeBoneham/the-politics-of-desire-george-villiers-james-i-and-courtly-entertainment-1ba33106b69a courtly entertainment. • **50.** Andrew, *The Secret World,* pp. 203–4. • **51.** Ibid., p. 204 • **52.** Ibid. • **53.** *ODNB,* 'Walter Montagu'; Sarah Poynting, '"The rare and excellent partes of Mr Walter Montague": Henrietta Maria and her playwright', in Erin Grifley (ed.), *Henrietta Maria: Piety, Politics and Patronage* (Aldershot: Ashgate, 2008). Official responsibility for the marriage negotiations was vested in the much older and doubtless less romantic Earls of Carlisle and Holland. • **54.** *ODNB*, Walter Montagu; Poynting, '"The rare and excellent partes"'. • **55.** Sarah Poynting (ed.), *The Shepherds' Paradise, by Walter Montagu*, Malone Society Reprint, vol. 159 (Oxford: Oxford University Press, 1998). • **56.** Poynting, '"The rare and excellent partes"'. • **57.** The Queen's patronage also extended to two professional playwrights, John Shirley and William Davenant (on whom see below) and to Queen Henrietta's Men, who performed successively at the Cockpit Theatre and Salisbury Court. Lucy Munro, 'The queen and the cockpit: Henrietta Maria's theatrical patronage revisited', *Shakespeare Bulletin*, vol. 37 (2019), no.1; Karen Britland, *Drama at the Courts of Queen Henrietta Maria* (Cambridge: Cambridge University Press, 2006). • **58.** *ODNB*, 'Walter Montagu'. • **59.** John Stubbs, *Reprobates: The Cavaliers of the English Civil War* (London: Viking, 2011), p. 94. • **60.** Dawn Lewcock, *Sir William Davenant, the Court Masque, and the English Seventeenth Century Scenic Stage, c1605–c1700* (Amherst, NY: Cambria Press, 2008), pp. 51–2; *ODNB*, 'William Davenant'. • **61.** Jane Milling and Peter Thomson, *The Cambridge History of British Theatre* (Cambridge: Cambridge University Press, 2004), p. 439. • **62.** In 1672 the author, bookseller and publisher, Francis Kirkman, published a collection of short theatrical pieces performed in secret during the Interregnum, many from manuscripts in his possession. Francis Kirkman, *The Wits; or sport upon sport: in selected pieces of drollery, digested into scenes by way of dialogue* (London: Printed by E.C. for Fancis [sic] Kirkman, 1672). Cambridge University Library special collections: classmark SSS.26.19. • **63.** Catherine Guillot, 'Richelieu et le théâtre', *Transversalités*, no. 1 (2011), pp. 85–102. • **64.** Andrew, *The Secret World*, p. 209. • **65.** On the Capuchins in the entourage of Henrietta Maria, see *ODNB*, 'Henrietta Maria'. No evidence has survived on their contact with Père Joseph. • **66.** Charles Perrault, *Les Hommes illustres qui ont paru en France pendant ce siècle avec leurs portraits au naturel* (Paris: Antoine Dezallier, 1696), p. 57. • **67.** Andrew, *The Secret World*, pp. 205–6. Rossignol passes curiously unmentioned in most studies of the reign of Louis XIII. • **68.** Rossignol's reputation was such that in 1696 Charles Perrault of the Académie Française claimed in his book on the most illustrious Frenchmen of the seventeenth century that, in fifty years, Rossignol had almost never encountered a cipher that defeated him. • **69.** *ODNB*, 'Walter Montagu'. • **70.** books.google.co.uk/ books/about/The_king_s_Cabinet_opened.html?id=-kk-AAAAcAAJ&redir_ esc=y. • **71.** *The Kings Cabinet opened.*, pp. 43–4. • **72.** Andrew, *The Secret World*, pp. 216–18 • **73.** Montagu was simultaneously mostly non-resident abbot of St Martin's Benedictine monastery, Pontoise. • **74.** Edith Snook, '"Soveraigne Receipts" and the politics of beauty in *The Queens Closet Opened*', *Early Modern Literary Studies*, Special Issue 15 (August 2007): purl.oclc.org/emls/si-15/snooksov.htm; Polly Russell, 'The history cook: The Queen's Closet Opened', *Financial Times*: ft.com/content/9a5de88c-133c-11e2-ac28-00144feabdco. • **75.** Elizabeth Spiller, 'Printed recipe books in medical, political, and scientific contexts', in Laura Lunger Knoppers (ed.), *The Oxford Handbook of Literature and the English Revolution* (Oxford: Oxford University Press, 2012). • **76.** Stubbs, *Reprobates*, p.426. • **77.** Muriel Zagha, 'The Puritan paradox', *Guardian*, 16 February 2002. • **78.** Decrypted despatch from A. P. Jongestall to Prince of Nassau-Dietz, 28 April 1654; Thomas Birch (ed.), *A Collection of the State Papers of John Thurloe ...*, vol. 2: 1654 (1952–3), p. 257: british-history.ac.uk/search/series/thurloe-papers. • **79.** *ODNB*, 'John Thurloe'. • **80.** Edward Bowles (York) to Thurloe, 29 December 1657; Birch (ed.), *State Papers of John Thurloe*, vol. 7: 1657–1658. • **81.** Timothy Raylor, '"Faire Englands joy is fled"? Visual and performance arts in the 1650s', 2006, available online in *ODNB*; Stephen Watkins, 'The protectorate playhouse: William Davenant's cockpit in the 1650s', *Shakespeare Bulletin*, vol. 37, no. 1 (2019). • **82.** TNA, SP18/128/108. We are grateful for advice on this intelligence report to Dr David L. Smith. • **83.** *ODNB*, 'Edward Coleman'; ibid., 'George Shirley'. • **84.** Ibid., 'William Davenant'; Watkins, 'The protectorate playhouse'. • **85.** Ibid. • **86.** Pepys Diary (pepysdiary.com), 29 October and 8 November 1665. • **87.** The music played does not survive. Raylor, '"Faire Englands joy is fled"?' • **88.** We are indebted for this information to Dr Henry Howard; cf. Peter Holman, *Four and Twenty Fiddlers: The violin at the English court, 1540–1690* (Oxford: Clarendon Press, 1993). • **89.** *ODNB*, 'William Davenant'. Stubbs, *Reprobates*, pp. 437–8. • **90.** Not to be confused with Handel's later anthem; Ian Spink, *Cavalier Songwriter: Henry Lawes* (Oxford: Oxford University Press, 2000).

3: *'Astrea Wants Money'*

• **1.** Sir William Davenant, 'The prologue to His Majesty at the first play presented at the Cock-pit in Whitehall' (1660). • **2.** Allan Richard Botica, 'Audience, Playhouse and Play in Restoration Theatre, 1660–1710', DPhil thesis, Oxford University (1986). • **3.** Pepys Diary, 27 August 1661. • **4.** Botica, 'Audience, Playhouse and Play'. • **5.** *ODNB*, 'Thomas Killigrew'. • **6.** Ibid. Stubbs, *Reprobates*, pp. 438–9. • **7.** Pepys Diary, 24 May 1660; Jenny Uglow, *A Gambling Man: Charles II and the Restoration, 1660–1670* (London: Faber & Faber, 2009), p. 28. • **8.** Andrew, *The Secret World*, pp. 231–5. • **9.** John Evelyn, *Diary*, 17 October 1660. Scott had briefly returned as intelligence chief at the end of the Interregnum after the dismissal of Thurloe. • **10.** *ODNB*, 'Thomas Killigrew'; ibid., 'William Davenant'. • **11.** In early Stuart England, women (Charles's mother, Henrietta Maria, among them) had played roles in court masques, though not on the public stage. • **12.** Abigail Williams and Kate O'Connor, 'Aphra Behn and the Restoration theatre'; writersinspire.org/content/aphra-behn-restoration-theatre. • **13.** A. J. Finberg (ed.), *Vertue Note Books*, *I*, Walpole Society, vol. 18 (Oxford: Oxford University Press, 1930), p. 97. • **14.** Nadine Akkerman, *Invisible Agents: Women and Espionage in Seventeenth-Century Britain* (Oxford: Oxford University Press, 2018), ch. 7. • **15.** Janet Todd, *Aphra Behn: A Secret Life* (London: Bloomsbury Reader, 2017), Introduction. • **16.** Accurate transcriptions of Behn's reports from Antwerp appear in W. J. Cameron (ed.), *New Light on Aphra Behn* (Auckland: Wakefield Press, 1961). • **17.** Akkerman, *Invisible Agents*, p. 25. No similar information on the gender of intelligencers is available for the mid 1660s. • **18.** Alan Marshall, '"Memorialls for Mrs Affora": Aphra Behn and the Restoration intelligence world', *Women's Writing*, vol. 22, no.1 (2015). • **19.** Pepys Diary, 6 November 1663. Pepys's source was another member of the 'committee', Edward Montagu, first Earl of Sandwich. • **20.** Ibid., 9 November 1663. Charles II was much put out when Frances Stuart married the Duke of Richmond in the following year. • **21.** *ODNB*, 'Henry Bennet, Lord Arlington'. Bennet was elevated to the peerage in 1665. • **22.** Andrew, *The Secret World*, p. 235. • **23.** Marshall, '"Memorialls for Mrs Affora"'. • **24.** Akkerman, *Invisible Agents*, ch. 7. A 'computational stylistic analysis', comparing the alleged reports by Scott with Behn's known writings is currently being conducted by the project 'Editing Aphra Behn in the Digital Age' (aphrabehn.online). We are grateful for information on this project from the co-investigator, Dr Mel Evans. • **25.** *ODNB*, 'Aphra Behn'. • **26.** Peter Fraser, *The Intelligence of the Secretaries of State and Their Monopoly of Licensed News, 1660–1688* (Cambridge: Cambridge University Press, 1956), ch. 4; Andrew, *The Secret World*, pp. 235–6. • **27.** *ODNB*, 'Henry Bennet, Lord Arlington'. • **28.** Ann Marie Stewart, *The Ravishing Restoration: Aphra Behn, Violence and Comedy* (Selinsgrove, PA: Susquehanna University Press, 2010). • **29.** *ODNB*, 'Aphra Behn'. • **30.** Janet Todd, *Aphra Behn: A Secret Life*, preface. • **31.** Ibid., ch.17. • **32.** Behn included 'breeches scenes' in *The Rover* I and II, *The Debauchee* and *The Widow Ranter*. • **33.** Williams and O'Connor, 'Aphra Behn and the Restoration theatre'. • **34.** Todd, *Aphra Behn: A Secret Life*, ch. 15. • **35.** G. Burnet, *Some passages of the life and death of the right honourable John earl of Rochester, who died the 26th of July, 1680* (1680). • **36.** Todd, *Aphra Behn: A Secret Life*, ch. 15. • **37.** First published in *Rome rhym'd to death, being a collection of choice poems: in two parts, written by the E[arl] of R[ochester], Dr Wild and others of the best modern wits* (1683). • **38.** On Crowne's relations with Rochester, see *ODNB*, 'John Crowne'. • **39.** David Francis Taylor,

'Rochester, the theatre and Restoration theatricality', in Matthew C. Augustine (ed.), *Lord Rochester in the Restoration World* (Cambridge: Cambridge University Press, 2015). For details of the staging of and expenditure on *Calisto*, see Andrew R. Walkling, 'Masque and Politics at the Restoration Court: John Crowne's "Calisto"', *Early Music*, vol. 24, no. 1 (1996). • **40.** Frank H. Ellis (ed.), *John Wilmot, Earl of Rochester: Selected Works* (London: Penguin, 2004), Introduction. • **41.** V. de S. Pinto (ed.), *The Famous Pathologist, or, The Noble Mountebank, by Thomas Alcock and John Wilmot, Earl of Rochester* (Nottingham: Sisson and Parker, 1961); Kirk Combe, 'Making monkeys of important men: Performance satire and Rochester's "Alexander Bendo's Brochure"', *Journal for Early Modern Cultural Studies*, vol. 12, no. 2 (2012); Todd, *Aphra Behn: A Secret Life*, ch. 20; *ODNB*, 'John Wilmot, Earl of Rochester'. • **42.** Charles's Declaration of Indulgence in 1672 suspending the Penal Laws, which infringed the religious liberty of both Catholics and Nonconformists, produced such a serious anti-Catholic backlash that it had to be withdrawn. Not until Charles was on his deathbed was he received into the Catholic Church. • **43.** Even Arlington's non-Catholic intelligence chief, Sir Joseph Williamson, was probably not informed. Andrew, *The Secret World*, pp. 236–7. • **44.** Despatch from Colby de Croissy, 8 October 1671, Ministère des Affaires étrangères, Paris, Archives diplomatiques de La Courneuve (MAE); Uglow, *A Gambling Man*, p. 509. • **45.** Don Jordan and Michael Walsh, *The King's Bed: Sex, Power and the Court of Charles II* (London: Little, Brown, 2016), ch. 16. • **46.** archive.org/details/louisedekeroualloofornuoft. • **47.** Linda Porter, *Mistresses: Sex and Scandal at the Court of Charles II* (London: Picador, 2020) • **48.** Antonia Fraser, *King Charles II* (London: Weidenfeld and Nicolson, 1979), p. 456. • **49.** Ibid. • **50.** en.chateauversailles.fr/discover/history/key-dates/day-life-louis-xiv#mornings; Andrew, *The Secret World*, p. 242. • **51.** Eugène Vaillé, *Le Cabinet noir* (Paris: Presses Universitaires de France, 1950), pp. 83–4. Montagu later became a paid French agent; *ODNB*, 'Ralph Montagu'. • **52.** Le Nôtre is most famous for the design and construction of the park of the Palace of Versailles. On his work at Juvisy, see: andrelenotre.com/andre-le-notre-et-juvisy. The large (165 cm x 265 cm) painting by Pierre-Denis Martin (Fig. 22) is a rare example of a detailed painting of a seventeenth-century chateau. • **53.** Perrault, *Les Hommes illustres*, pp. 57–8. • **54.** In 1676 Marin Marais was employed as a musician to the royal court of Versailles; in 1679 he was appointed *ordinaire de la chambre du roy pour la viole*, a title he kept until 1725. We are very grateful to Professor Katherine Ellis for advice on the kind of musical welcome likely to have been arranged by Rossignol at Juvisy. • **55.** chateauversailles-recherche.fr/curia/documents/roi1683.pdf. • **56.** Perrault, *Les hommes illustres*, pp. 57–8. • **57.** *Tartuffe*, Act IV, scene 5. Earlier in the play, Damis, son of Orgon and Elmire, also conceals himself in order to overhear a conversation between Elmire and Tartuffe. • **58.** Vaillé, *Le cabinet noir*, p. 76. • **59.** In 1937 the NKVD (forerunner of the KGB) gave the codename MOLIÈRE to one of its most brilliant British agents, the Scot John Cairncross, a graduate of both the Sorbonne and Cambridge. Had Cairncross been told his codename (which agents almost never were), he might well have objected to its transparency but would otherwise have been pleased to take the name of his favourite French writer, on whom he later published two academic works in French notable for their 'strident image of Molière as a bourgeois and libertine forerunner of revolution against all forms of neo-feudal tyranny'. Cairncross must privately have compared the key role of deception in *Tartuffe* (his favourite French play) and in his own career as a Soviet agent. Cairncross was considerably more successful than Tartuffe – deceiving successively the Foreign Office, the Treasury, one of Churchill's ministers, the wartime SIGINT agency at Bletchley Park, and the Secret Intelligence Service (SIS). • **60.** John Conley, *The Suspicion of Virtue: Women Philosophers in Neoclassical France* (Ithaca, NY: Cornell University Press, 2002), pp. 124–56. • **61.** Jean-Pierre Néraudau, *L'Olympe du Roi-Soleil* (Paris: Les Belles-Lettres, 1986). • **62.** Botica, 'Audience, Playhouse and Play'. On William III and intelligence, see Andrew, *The Secret World*, pp. 249–60. • **63.** A recently discovered letter shows that Vanbrugh was closely associated with Robert Bertie, Lord Willoughby d'Eresby, who in 1687 drew up for William of Orange (probably with Vanbrugh's assistance) a secret list of English peers opposed to James II. John Lord, 'Sir John Vanbrugh and the 1st Duke of Ancaster: Newly discovered documents', *Architectural History*, vol. 34 (2016). • **64.** Kerry Downes, *Sir John Vanbrugh: A Biography* (London: Sidgwick & Jackson, 1987); *ODNB*, 'Sir John Vanbrugh'. • **65.** Voltaire, who spent two years in England shortly after Vanbrugh's death in 1726 and admired his comedies, wrote that one of them (*The Provok'd Wife*) had been written in the Bastille: 'what is very strange, to my way of thinking, is that there is in it no criticism of the country which made him suffer this affront.' Voltaire, *Lettres anglaises*, no. 19. • **66.** Lady Brute and her niece Belinda, disguised as Shepherd Market doxies (prostitutes), are also spied on by the envious Lady Fanciful during a secret tryst with their lovers. • **67.** André Blanc, *F. C. Dancourt, 1661–1725: la Comédie française à l'heure du soleil couchant* (Paris: Editions Jean-Michel Place, 1984). • **68.** Throughout Colley Cibber's long acting career, he was much in demand for the role of Lord Foppington in *The Relapse*. Probably the most famous role of the eighteenth century's most famous actor, David Garrick, was that of Sir John Brute, husband of the provoked wife, in *The Provok'd Wife*. • **69.** Andrew, *The Secret World*, pp. 251–6. • **70.** Lucien Bély, *Les Secrets de Louis XIV: Mystères d'État et pouvoir absolu* (Paris: Tallandier, 2013), pp. 454, 457.

• **71.** Philip Aubrey, *Mr Secretary Thurloe: Cromwell's Secretary of State* (London: Athlone Press 1990), p. 101.

4: British Theatre, the 'Golden Rump' and the Ancien Régime

• **1.** Mark Kishlansky, *A Monarchy Transformed: Britain 1630–1714* (London: Penguin, 1997), p. 315. • **2.** The military historian Richard Holmes concludes: 'The acquisition and analysis of intelligence underlay everything he did'; Richard Holmes, *Marlborough: England's Fragile Genius* (London: HarperPress, 2008), p. 479. On SIGINT, see Andrew, *The Secret World*, pp. 262–4. • **3.** Downes, *Sir John Vanbrugh*; *ODNB*, 'Sir John Vanbrugh'. • **4.** Kishlansky, *A Monarchy Transformed*, p. 47. • **5.** Unsigned and unaddressed instructions from Harley to Defoe, (?)Oct. 1706: George Harris Healey (ed.), *The Letters of Daniel Defoe* (Oxford: Oxford University Press, 2016), letter 55 and editor's notes. • **6.** Allen W. Dulles, *The Craft of Intelligence*, paperback edn (New York: Signet, 1965), pp. 187–8. Dulles was Director of Central Intelligence from 1953 to 1961. • **7.** Defoe to Harley, 13 Sept. 1706: Healey (ed.), *Letters of Daniel Defoe*. • **8.** John Kerrigan, 'The secret agent', *Guardian*, 8 March 2008. • **9.** *ODNB*, 'Robert Harley, first Earl of Oxford'. Some have argued the £20,000 paid to Scottish politicians was the overdue payment of salaries and pensions. • **10.** Kishlansky, *A Monarchy Transformed*, p. 315. • **11.** Maximilian E. Novak, *Daniel Defoe: Master of Fictions: His Life and Ideas* (Oxford: Oxford University Press, 2001), pp. 233–5. • **12.** *ODNB*, 'Daniel Defoe'. • **13.** Christopher Andrew, *Secret Service: The Making of the British Intelligence Community* (London: Heinemann, 1985), pp. 2–3; J. A. Downie, 'Secret Service payments to Daniel Defoe, 1710–1714', *The Review of English Studies*, vol. 30 (1979). • **14.** Nicholson Baker, 'The greatest liar?', *Columbia Journalism Review*, July–Aug. 2009. • **15.** *ODNB*, 'Joseph Addison'. • **16.** Peter Smithers, *The Life of Joseph Addison* (Oxford: Clarendon Press, 1954), p. 382. Prince George's mother, Sophia of Hanover, was heiress presumptive to Queen Anne under the 1701 English Act of Settlement. Her death in May 1714, less than three months before Anne's, left George as heir to the throne. Halifax was one of the regents appointed by George I to govern England until his arrival in September 1714. • **17.** *Calendar of State Papers, 1706 Foreign*: entries for 25 March, 15 May, 30 July, 1 August, 9 November; Andrew, *The Secret World*, pp. 265–6. • **18.** James II's son, James Francis Edward (the 'Old Pretender'), was recognised after his father's death in 1701 by the 'Jacobites' and by Louis XIV as James III of England and VIII of Scotland. He led an unsuccessful rising in Scotland in 1715 after George I's accession. • **19.** 'Of the Infamy of a SPY, and the Caution that is necessary in trusting him', *Delphi Complete Works of Joseph Addison* (Hastings: Delphi Classics, 2017). Addison similarly denounces the 'infamy' of 'the faithless spy' in his poem 'The Transformation of Battus to a Touchstone'. • **20.** Only three days later, Guiscard was ridiculed in an early issue of *The Spectator*, co-edited by Addison: *The Spectator*, No. 14, 11 March 1711. • **21.** Andrew, *The Secret World*, pp. 265–7. The best account of the assassination attempt is Clyve Jones, 'Robert Harley and the myth of the golden thread' (2010): bl.uk/eblj/2010articles/pdf/ebljar ticle112010.pdf. • **22.** In a satirical print of Guiscard (fig. 23), a label hanging from the devil's wing-tip identifies the knife with a note referring to *The Spectator* of 11 March 1711. Six satirical lines of verse warn the reader against women in masquerade: https://www.britishmuseum.org/collection/obje ct/P_1850–1109-16. • **23.** The first quarterly payment to 'Claude Guilot' for 'her Majesty's special service' of which record survives was on 9 September 1710; Downie, 'Secret Service Payments to Daniel Defoe'. • **24.** Paula R. Backscheider, *Daniel Defoe: His Life* (Baltimore: Johns Hopkins University Press, 1989), p. 150. • **25.** Calhoun Winton, *John Gay and the London Theatre* (Lexington: University of Kentucky Press, 1993), pp. 4–5. • **26.** Backscheider, *Daniel Defoe*, p. 89. • **27.** Mita Choudhury, *Interculturalism and resistance in the London theater, 1660–1800: Identity, performance, empire* (Lewisburg, PA: Bucknell University Press, 2000), pp. 152–3. • **28.** Voltaire, *Lettres Philosophiques* (1733–4), nos 18–23. Voltaire entitled the English version (1733), *Letters Concerning the English Nation*. • **29.** Ibid., no. 18. • **30.** Antoine Lilti, *The Invention of Celebrity* (Cambridge: Polity, 2017), ch. 1 • **31.** Auriane de Viry, '16 mai 1717: Le jeune Voltaire est embastillé', *Revue des Deux Mondes*, 16 May 2017; Ian Davidson, *Voltaire: A Life* (London: Profile Books, 2010), ch. 2. • **32.** Davidson, *Voltaire*, chs 4, 7. • **33.** Voltaire, *Lettres Philosophiques*, no. 24 • **34.** *ODNB*, 'Robert Walpole, first Earl of Orford'; ibid., 'Francis Atterbury'; Edward Pearce, *The Great Man: Sir Robert Walpole: Scoundrel, Genius and Britain's First Prime Minister* (London: Jonathan Cape, 2017), pp. 169–70. • **35.** Evelyn Cruikshanks and Howard Erskine-Hill, *The Atterbury Plot* (Basingstoke: Palgrave Macmillan, 2004), pp. 208–9. • **36.** Jonathan Swift, *Gulliver's Travels* (1726), part III. • **37.** Andrew, *The Secret World*, p. 276. • **38.** Voltaire called Swift 'Rabelais at his best, living in better company; it is true that he has not the gaiety of the latter, but he has all the elegance, the reason, the discrimination, the good taste lacking in [Rabelais]': Voltaire, *Lettres Philosophiques*, no. 22. • **39.** voltaire.ox.ac.uk/news/blog/voltaire-and-jacobites. • **40.** *Letters which passed between Count Gyllenborg, the Barons Gortz, Sparre, and others: Relating to the design of raising a rebellion in His Majesty's dominions, to be supported by a force from Sweden* (Dublin: Tho. Hume, 1717); Andrew, *The Secret World*, pp. 271–2. • **41.** On Fielding's sometimes jocular treatment of rape, see Simon Dickie, 'Fielding's rape jokes', *The Review of English Studies*, vol. 61, no. 251 (2010). • **42.** Pearce, *The Great Man*, p. 343. •

43. *London Journal*, 28 February 1730. • **44.** Pearce, *The Great Man*, p. 343. • **45.** John Gay, *Fables*, p. 210: https://archive.org/details/fablesofjohngayw-oogayjuoft. • **46.** Andrew Blick and George Jones, 'Prime Ministers and Number Ten' (2013): history.blog.gov.uk/2013/10/17/the-prime-minis ters-people-indispensable-aides-to-three-premiers. • **47.** D. M. Clark, *The Rise of the British Treasury* (New Haven: Yale University Press, 1960), p. 44. • **48.** Tone Sundt Urstad, *Sir Robert Walpole's Poets: The Use of Literature as Pro-Government Propaganda, 1721–1742* (Newark: University of Delaware Press, 1999), pp. 35–6. • **49.** *ODNB*, 'Thomas Gordon'. • **50.** Thomas Gordon, *The true picture of a modern Tory; or a High-Churchman painted to the life* (1722). • **51.** The same was true of the press. No ministerial newspaper could rival the circulation of the main anti-Walpole papers, *The Craftsman* in the late 1720s and early 1730s, and *Common Sense* in the late 1730s. • **52.** David Nokes, *John Gay: A Profession of Friendship* (Oxford: Oxford University Press, 1995), p. 464. • **53.** J. A. Downie, *A Political Biography of Henry Fielding* (London: Routledge, 2009), pp. 80–81. • **54.** For a surprisingly scholarly discussion of 'the popular humour attendant upon farts', see Andrew McRae, 'Farting in the House of Commons: Popular humour and political discourse in Early Modern England', in Mark Knights and Adam Morton (eds), *The Power of Laughter and Satire in Early Modern Britain: Political and Religious Culture, 1500–1820* (Martlesham: Boydell & Brewer, 2017). • **55.** M. C. Battestin and R. R. Battestin, *Henry Fielding: A Life*, new edn (London: Routledge, 1993), p. 229. Recent research shows that there is no foundation for the claim that Fielding wrote the missing play himself; Downie, *A Political Biography of Henry Fielding*. • **56.** Pearce, *The Great Man*, pp. 352–4. • **57.** Joseph Donohue (ed.), *The Cambridge History of British Theatre*, vol. 2 (Cambridge: Cambridge University Press, 2004). In Paris, until the Revolution, the Odéon, Comédie Française and Opéra Comique similarly had a virtual monopoly of dramatic produc-tions. Boulevard theatres were subjected to a series of arcane and sometimes bizarre regulations. Michèle Root-Bernstein, *Boulevard Theater and Revolution in Eighteenth-Century Paris* (Ann Arbor: UMI Research Press, 1981). • **58.** Hansard, HL Deb. 17 February 1966, vol. 272 cols 1151–68. • **59.** Vic Gatrell, *City of Laughter: Sex and Satire in Eighteenth-Century London* (London: Atlantic Books, 2006). • **60.** Robert Justin Goldstein, 'Introduction' and 'France', in Goldstein (ed.), *The Frightful Stage: Political Censorship of the Stage in Nineteenth-Century Europe* (New York: Berghahn Books, 2009). French theatre censorship, though it remained on the statute book, effectively ended when the Chamber of Deputies ceased to fund it in 1906. • **61.** Until Louis XV's thirteenth birthday in 1723, France was ruled by Philippe II, duc d'Orléans, as regent. Thereafter, Louis entrusted most affairs of state to his chief minister, Cardinal Fleury, until Fleury's death in 1743 at the age of almost ninety. • **62.** Stéphane Genêt,

Les Espions des lumières: Actions secrètes et espionnage militaire au temps de Louis XV (Paris: Ministère de la Défense, 2013), pp. 204–5; Andrew, *The Secret World*, pp. 281–2. • **63.** Davidson, *Voltaire*, ch. 15. • **64.** Ciphered despatch by Voltaire, 21 July 1743, MAE, reproduced by Pascale Debert, 'Voltaire, espion secret de Louis XV auprès du roi de Prusse', histoiresgalantes.fr/blog/2018/01/02/voltaire-espion-secret-de-louis-xv-aupres-du-roi-de-prusse. • **65.** Andrew, *The Secret World*, p. 277. • **66.** David Kahn, 'The Man in the Iron Mask – encore et enfin, cryptologically', *Cryptologia*, vol. 29 (2005), no. 1.

5: The Age of Revolution

• **1.** Michael Billington, 'How to stage a revolution', *The Guardian*, 6 January 2006. • **2.** The surviving secret correspondence between the head of the Secret du roi, the comte de Broglie, and Louis XV from 1756 until Louis's death in 1774 is published in Didier Ozanam and Michel Antoine, *Correspondance secrète du Comte de Broglie avec Louis XV*, 2 vols (Paris: Librarie C. Klinksieck, 1956–61). • **3.** H. M. Scott, *The Birth of a Great Power System, 1740–1815* (Harlow: Longman, 2005), p. 82. • **4.** Jonathan Conlin, 'Wilkes, the Chevalier d'Eon and "the dregs of liberty": An Anglo-French perspective on ministerial despotism', *English Historical Review*, vol. 120 (2005); id., 'The Strange Case of the Chevalier d'Eon', *History Today*, vol. 60, no. 4 (2010). Despite his self-proclaimed sexual sophistication, Casanova, who met d'Éon at the French embassy during a visit to London in 1763, 'soon recognised her as a woman … her shape was too rounded to be that of a man'; rbkclocalstudies.wordpress.com/tag/chevalier-deon. • **5.** Simon Burrows, 'The Chevalier d'Éon, media manipulation and the making of an eighteenth-century celebrity', in Simon Burrows, Jonathan Conlin, Russell Goulbourne and Valerie Mainz (eds.), *The Chevalier d'Eon and His Worlds: Gender, Espionage and Politics in the Eighteenth Century* (London: Continuum, 2010). • **6.** Burrows et al., *The Chevalier d'Eon and His Worlds*; Andrew, *The Secret World*, pp. 292–3. Source for Fig. 26: media.britishmuseum.org/media/Repository/Documents/2015_11/13_12/6e3af8a6_a687_440f_b143_a54f00d16d7b/mid_ppa435880. • **7.** Lucy Peltz, curator of eighteenth-century portraits at the National Portrait Gallery, quoted in 'Portrait mistaken for 18th century lady is early painting of tranvestite', *Guardian*, 6 June 2012. • **8.** Conlin, 'Strange case of the Chevalier d'Eon'. D'd'Éon's career has, unsurprisingly, generated a considerable mythology, such as the claim that he penetrated the court of the Russian Empress Elizabeth, dressed as a woman. • **9.** Rick Atkinson, *The British are Coming: The War For America, 1775–1777* (London: William Collins, 2019), pp. 473–4. • **10.** Streeter Bass, 'Beaumarchais and the American Revolution' (1970): cia.

gov/static/27a5b4a0e2c146897adff5415ab24835/Beaumarchais-and-American-Revolution.pdf. • **11.** Washington to Colonel Elias Dayton, 26 July 1777. The original is in the Walter L. Pforzheimer Collection on Intelligence Service (in Washington when consulted by the author, now at Yale). Ironically, Washington's understanding of the importance of military intelligence, and his success in using it, owed much to his ability to learn from his experience as a British army officer in the French and Indian War, operating against the French, who were to become his allies against the British in the Revolutionary War. • **12.** Philander D. Chase (ed.), *Papers of George Washington: Revolutionary War Series*, vol. 1 (Charlottesville and London: University Press of Virginia, 1985), p. 38; cf. pp. 57, 79, 91, 138, 306, 332–3, 399, 410, 421, 437, 458, 459. • **13.** Ibid., vol. 3 (1988), pp. 528–9. Washington's main counter-espionage organiser was the future Chief Justice John Jay, who organized a network of at least ten counterintelligence agents. In 1997 the CIA named him as 'America's first counterintelligence chief': P.K. Rose, The *Founding Fathers of American Intelligence* (Langley, Va: CIA Center for the Study of Intelligence, 1999); Andrew, *The Secret World*, p.303n. • **14.** Streeter Bass, 'Nathan Hale's Mission' (1973): cia.gov/static/d709cbec73f51410da657b2bafc90466/Nathan-Hales-Mission.pdf; Brian Kilmeade and Don Yaeger, *George Washington's Secret Six: The Spy Ring that Saved the American Revolution* (New York: Sentinel, 2013), pp. 20–26. • **15.** The exact quotation was: 'What Pity is it,/That we can die but once to serve our Country!' (*Cato*, Act VI, scene 1). The line also appealed to 'many an English patriot': Susan Staves, 'Tragedy', in Jane Moody and Daniel O'Quinn (eds), *The Cambridge Companion to British Theatre, 1730–1830* (Cambridge: Cambridge University Press, 2007), p. 97. • **16.** Thomas A. Bogar, *American Presidents Attend the Theatre: The Playgoing Experiences of Each Chief Executive* (Jefferson, NC: McFarland & Co., 2006), p. 6. • **17.** Articles of Continental Association, Article 8, 20 October 1774. • **18.** bostonliteraryhistory.com/chapter-6/massachusetts-general-court-%E2%80%9C-act-preventing-stage-plays-and-other-theatrical.html. • **19.** Bogar, *American Presidents Attend the Theatre*, chs 1, 3. • **20.** Gillian Russell, *Women, Sociability and Theatre in Georgian London* (Cambridge: Cambridge University Press, 2007), p. 143. • **21.** George O. Seilhamer, *History of the American Theatre*, vol. 2: *During the Revolution and After* (London: Ardent Media, 1968), pp. 16–19. • **22.** nypl.org/blog/2016/04/21/british-soldiers-theatre-revolutionary-war. • **23.** William Dunlap, *A History of the American Theatre During the Revolution and After* (Champagne: University of Illinois Press, 2005), p. 47 (first published in 1832). • **24.** The senior British commander during the siege of Boston was General William Howe. • **25.** *ODNB*, 'John Burgoyne'. • **26.** David Francis Taylor, *Theatres of Opposition: Empire, Revolution, and Richard Brinsley Sheridan* (Oxford: Oxford University Press, 2012) • **27.** *ODNB*, 'Philippe Jacques [Philip

James] de Loutherbourg'. • **28.** Ibid., 'Charlotte Atkyns'. • **29.** Andrew, *The Secret World*, p. 304. • **30.** Bogar, *American Presidents Attend the Theatre*, p. 11. • **31.** Andrew, *The Secret World*, p. 304. • **32.** William D. Howarth, *Beaumarchais and the Theatre* (London: Routledge, 1995). • **33.** beaumontsociety.org.uk/ documents/Biography.pdf. The print of Beaumont (fig. 29) was based on a painting commissioned by the future George IV, shown in the *George IV: Art and Spectacle* exhibition at the Queen's Gallery, Buckingham Palace, November 2019–May 2020. See also *ODNB*, 'D'Éon de Beaumont, Charles Geneviève Louis Auguste André Timothée, Chevalier D'Éon in the French nobility'. • **34.** Daniel Heartz, 'Mozart and Da Ponte', *The Musical Quarterly*, vol. 79, no. 4 (1995). Even when he was still active in holy orders, Da Ponte fathered at least two children. • **35.** The main biographies of Da Ponte are well reviewed by Joan Acocella, 'Nights at the opera: The life of a man who put words to Mozart', *New Yorker*, 8 January 2007. • **36.** Paolo Preto, 'Giacomo Casanova and the Venetian inquisitors: A domestic espionage system in eighteenth-century Europe', in Daniel Szechi (ed.), *The Dangerous Trade: Spies, Spymasters and the Making of Europe* (Dundee: Dundee University Press, 2010). • **37.** In 1752, two of Casanova's works for the stage enjoyed success in Dresden: his Italian translation of Cahusac's libretto for Rameau's opera *Zoroastre*, in a production starring his mother; and his imaginative reinvention of Racine's tragedy *La Thébaïde* as an Italian comedy entitled *Moluccheide*. On Casanova's works for the stage, see Ian Kelly, *Casanova: Actor, Lover, Priest* (London: Hodder & Stoughton, 2008), p. 157 • **38.** The first written evidence that Casanova helped put some finishing touches to the libretto of *Don Giovanni* was published in 1876 by Alfred Meissner in his book *Rococo Bilder*, based on notes by his grandfather, a Prague professor who knew some of the musicians who performed at the opera's 1787 premiere. • **39.** Tony Perrottet, 'When Casanova met Mozart', *Smithsonian Magazine*, 21 March 2012. • **40.** The first dramatic re-enactment in London of the fall of the Bastille took place only six days later in the amphitheatre near Westminster Bridge of the circus-owner, Philip Astley, who in 1783 had opened the Amphithéâtre Astley in Paris – the first of its kind in France – under the patronage of Queen Marie Antoinette. Astley is now recognised as the founder of the art form of circus. *ODNB*, 'Philip Astley'; philipastley.org.uk. • **41.** Andrew, *The Secret World*, pp. 312–14. • **42.** Goldstein, 'France', in Goldstein (ed.), *The Frightful Stage*. • **43.** In 1790 all restrictions on the previously heavily regulated boulevard theatres were removed. In 1806, however, Napoleon limited performances to only four boulevard theatres. Root-Bernstein, *Boulevard Theater and Revolution*. • **44.** Alfred Cobban, *History of Modern France*, vol. 1, pp. 164–5. • **45.** *ODNB*, 'William Pitt the Younger'. • **46.** 'Letter to the Bishop of Llandaff', probably written in February and March 1793 but not published. Unwilling to make public his support for regicide as a necessary step to the French establishment of 'true Liberty', Wordsworth signed himself simply 'A Republican'. His only play, *The Borderers* (written in 1796–7, but not published until 1842), though set in the thirteenth century, reflected disillusion with republican France. • **47.** Goldstein, 'France', in Goldstein (ed.), *The Frightful Stage*. • **48.** *ODNB*, 'Charlotte Atkyns'. After the restoration of Louis XVIII, his government turned down Atkyns' claim for the enormous sum of between £30,000 and £40,000 which she claimed, unconvincingly, to have spent on the Bourbon cause. • **49.** norfolktalesmyths.com/2018/04/27/norfolks-scarlett-pimpernel-perhaps. Atkyns' claims did, however, convince the French dramatist Victorien Sardou, who included her in his successful 1896 play, *Pamela, marchande de frivolités*. According to Sardou, 'Lady Atkyns suggested that the Queen should escape dressed in [Atkyns'] costume, but the Royal prisoner would not forsake her children': archive.org/details/friendofmarieantoobar brich. There is no mention of Atkyns in the comprehensive, archives-based study by Hugues Marquis, *Agents de l'ennemi: les espions à la solde de l'Angleterre dans une France en Révolution* (Paris: Vendémiaire, 2014). • **50.** Robert Tombs, *The English and Their History* (London: Allen Lane, 2014), pp. 184–5. • **51.** Elizabeth Sparrow, 'The Alien Office, 1792–1806', *The Historical Journal*, vol. 33, no. 2 (1990); *ODNB*, 'Evan Nepean'. • **52.** Taylor, *Theatres of Opposition*, pp. 158–60. • **53.** *The Speeches of the Right Honourable Richard Brinsley Sheridan* ..., vol. 2 (1842), p. 450; speech of 5 January 1795. • **54.** Ibid., p. 451. • **55.** Clive Emsley, 'The Home Office and its sources of information and investigation 1791–1801', *English Historical Review*, vol. 94, no. 372 (1979), p. 559. • **56.** *ODNB*, 'London Corresponding Society'. • **57.** David Worrall, *Theatric Revolution: Drama, Censorship, and the Romantic Period Subcultures 1773–1832* (Oxford: Oxford University Press, 2006), ch. 8. • **58.** James Powell, *The Venetian Outlaw, His Country's Friend. Now performing at the Theatre Royal, Drury-Lane, with unbounded applause* (1805). • **59.** Worrall, *Theatric Revolution*, pp. 287–8. • **60.** Andrew, *The Secret World*, pp. 331–2. • **61.** Jonathan Bate, *Radical Wordsworth: The Poet who Changed the World* (London: William Collins, 2020), pp. 147–8. • **62.** Frederick Burwick, 'The Borderers (1796–1842)', in Richard Gravil and Daniel Robinson (eds), *The Oxford Handbook of William Wordworth* (Oxford: Oxford University Press, 2015). • **63.** *ODNB*, 'Samuel Taylor Coleridge'. • **64.** Andrew, *The Secret World*, pp. 332–3. • **65.** Marjean D. Purinton, 'Wordsworth's "The Borderers" and the ideology of revolution', *The Wordsworth Circle*, vol. 23, no. 2 (1992), p. 97. • **66.** M. Dorothy George, *Catalogue of Political and Personal Satires in the British Museum*', vol. 7 (1942). Hadfield was put on trial for high treason but acquitted on the grounds of insanity: TNA, KB 33/8/3. • **67.** Michael Kelly, *Reminiscences of Michael Kelly of the King's Theatre and Theatre Royal Drury Lane* (London: H. Colburn, 1826). • **68.** Worrall, *Theatric Revolution*, ch. 8.

6: From Counter-Revolution in Europe to Civil War in America

• **1.** Beethoven's correspondence with Kotzebue is published in Emily Anderson (ed. & trans.), *The Letters of Beethoven* (London: Macmillan, 1961), vol. 2. • **2.** Cecil Price, *The Dramatic Works of Richard Brinsley Sheridan* (Oxford: Clarendon Press, 1973), vol. 2, p.637. • **3.** The *Burschenschaften* were not to know that Kotzebue's secret reports probably contained no classified information. 'Kotzebue, August von (russischer Dienstadel 1785)': deutsche-biographie.de/sfz68592.html; G. S. Williamson, 'What killed August von Kotzebue? The temptations of virtue and the political theology of German nationalism, 1789–1819', *Journal of Modern History*, vol.72 (2000), no.4. • **4.** Andrew, *The Secret World*, pp. 372–3. • **5.** The leading Socialist in Wilhelmine Germany, August Bebel, among others, referred to 'Kotzebue, the Russian spy': Bebel, 'Assassinations and socialism', 2 November 1898, slp.org/pdf/others/assass_ab.pdf. • **6.** Andrew, *The Secret World*, pp. 372–3. • **7.** Gary D. Stark, 'Germany', in Goldstein (ed.), *The Frightful Stage*. • **8.** Ibid., pp. 1–2. • **9.** Chester Dunning, 'The Tsar's red pencil: Nicholas I and censorship of Pushkin's "Boris Godunov"', *Slavic and East European Journal*, vol. 54, no. 2 (2010). Chester Dunning et al., *The Uncensored Boris Godunov: The Case for Pushkin's Original Comedy* (Madison: University of Wisconsin Press, 2006). • **10.** Nancy K. Anderson (ed), *Pushkin: The Little Tragedies* (New Haven and London: Yale University Press, 2000). • **11.** Anthony Swift, 'Russia', in Goldstein (ed.), *The Frightful Stage*. *Mozart and Salieri* later became the inspiration for Peter Shaffer's *Amadeus*, whose Broadway production won the 1981 Tony Award for Best Play. The 1984 film adaptation won eight Oscars, including Best Picture. • **12.** Adam Zamoyski, *Phantom Terror: The Threat of Revolution and the Repression of Liberty, 1789–1848* (London: William Collins, 1984), p. 343. • **13.** In 1865 responsibility for theatre and other forms of censorship was moved from the Third Section to the Main Administration for Press Affairs, attached to the Interior ministry. Swift, 'Russia', in Goldstein (ed.), *The Frightful Stage*. • **14.** Simon Sebag-Montefiore, *The Romanovs: 1613–1917* (London: Weidenfeld & Nicolson, 2016), Act III, scene 1. • **15.** On Fock's death from cholera in 1831, he was succeeded by another civilian, A. A. Mordvinov, until 1839. Charles A. Ruud and Sergei A. Stepanov, *Fontanka 16: The Tsars' Secret Police* (Montreal and Kingston, Ont.: McGill–Queen's University Press, 1999), p. 23. • **16.** Zamoyski, *Phantom Terror*, p. 344. • **17.** Daria Chernysheva, 'Transplacing Ophelia: Woman and nation in the earliest Russian *Hamlets*', *Comparative Drama*, vol. 51, no. 2 (2017). • **18.** T. J. Binyon, *Pushkin: A Biography* (London: HarperCollins, 2003), ch. 9. • **19.** Chester Dunning, 'The tragic fate of Pushkin's comedy', in Alexander Dolinin (ed.), *The Uncensored Boris Godunov: The Case for Pushkin's Original Comedy*, with

Annotated Text and Translation (Madison: University of Wisconsin Press, 2006). • **20.** Binyon, *Pushkin*, ch. 9. Dunning, 'The tragic fate of Pushkin's comedy'. • **21.** Binyon, *Pushkin*, ch. 10; Dunning, 'The tragic fate of Pushkin's comedy'. • **22.** E. V. Petrukhov, 'On the relationship of Emperor Nicholas I and A. S. Pushkin', lecture delivered on 12 December 1896, Yeltsin Presidential Library Pushkin collection; prlib.ru/en/news/658859 (with a link to the text in Russian). • **23.** Binyon, *Pushkin*, ch. 11. • **24.** Milton Ehre, *Notes for the Theater of Nikolay Gogol* (Chicago: University of Chicago Press, 1980). • **25.** Nikolai Gogol, *The Government Inspector*, trans. Christopher English (World Classics Kindle edition), Act III, scene 4. • **26.** Ibid., Act I, scene 1. • **27.** Ruud and Stepanov, *Fontanka 16*, p. 21. • **28.** Gogol, *Government Inspector*, Act I, scene 2. • **29.** Ibid., Act V, scene 8. Pushkin had suggested the bogus government inspector flirt with both the wife and daughter of the governor: Ehre, *Notes for the Theater of Nikolay Gogol*. • **30.** Gogol, *Government Inspector*, Act V, unnumbered 'last scene'. • **31.** Swift, 'Russia', in Goldstein (ed.), *The Frightful Stage*. • **32.** Sebag-Montefiore, *The Romanovs*. • **33.** Ibid. • **34.** Binyon, *Pushkin*, ch. 12. • **35.** Sebag-Montefiore, *The Romanovs*. • **36.** John C. Fitzpatrick (ed.), *The Writings of George Washington from the Original Manuscript Sources, 1745–1799*, vol. 26 (Washington DC: Government Printing Office, 1939), p. 481. • **37.** Bissell's key intelligence reports are published in Todd W. Braisted, 'A spy wins a purple heart: The amazing tale of Daniel Bissell and the Military Order of Merit', *Journal of the American Revolution*, 2 June 2015. His intelligence would probably have been invaluable if Washington had gone ahead with his original plan for an attack on New York. Washington, however, decided instead to concentrate his efforts against Cornwallis's forces in Virginia. • **38.** James Fenimore Cooper may also have been influenced by the case of James Rivington, who had posed as a wartime British propagandist and was afterwards hounded by American patriots unaware of what was probably his true role as a double agent working for Washington. • **39.** *American National Biography*, 'Charles Powell Clinch'; jfcoopersociety.org/DRAMA/STAGE.HTML. • **40.** On the publishing history of *The Spy*, see the introduction by J. E. Morpurgo to the Oxford University Press edition, first published in 1988. There were also many foreign editions. • **41.** André's remains were brought from the United States and buried close to the monument in 1821. Andrew, *The Secret World*, p. 303. • **42.** Ibid., pp. 347–52. The first, detailed study of the breaking of Napoleon's *grand chiffre* was Mark Urban, *The Man Who Broke Napoleon's Codes: The Story of George Scovell* (London: Faber & Faber, 2002). • **43.** M. Dorothy George, *Catalogue of Political and Personal Satires in the British Museum*, vol. 9, 1949; media.britishmuseum.org/media/Repository/Documents/2014_9/30_7/9baf4bce_5b70_4945_900c_a3b600749adb/mid_00174465_001.jpg. • **44.** *ODNB*, 'James Watson (1766–1838)'. • **45.** Worrall,

Theatric Revolution, pp. 1–2. • **46.** Ibid., chs 6–8. • **47.** Christina Parolin, *Radical Spaces: Venues of popular politics in London, 1790–c.1845* (Canberra: ANU E Press, 2010), pp. 202–3. • **48.** Worrall, *Theatric Revolution*, p. 342. At least one Home Office spy, Abel Hall, regularly reported on discussions in the Rotunda coffee room; Parolin, *Radical Spaces*, p. 215. • **49.** TNA, HO64/11–13. • **50.** *ODNB*, 'Robert Taylor'. • **51.** Parolin, *Radical Spaces*, pp. 219–21. • **52.** Worrall, *Theatric Revolution*, p. 350. Although the spy's identity is not known, it is clear from his reports that he had known personally (and probably informed on) such prominent revolutionaries as James Watson, one of the leaders of the 1816 Spa Fields rising, and Arthur Thistlewood, a Spa Fields veteran executed for his part in the failed 1820 Cato Street conspiracy to kill the entire cabinet. • **53.** Parolin, *Radical Spaces*, pp. 240–41. • **54.** Worrall, *Theatric Revolution*, p. 354. • **55.** Parolin, *Radical Spaces*, ch. 8. • **56.** *The Times*, 18 February 1832; Parolin, *Radical Spaces*, p. 283. • **57.** There had been complaints since at least the early eighteenth century of ballad singers who were out to 'inflame the spirit of the common people': G. D. Zimmermann, *Songs of Irish Rebellion: Political Street Ballads and Rebel Songs, 1780–1900* (Dublin: Allen Figgis, 1967), p. 35; Richard Parfitt, *Musical Culture and the Spirit of Irish Nationalism, 1848–1972* (London: Routledge, 2020), introduction. • **58.** National Archives of Ireland (NAI), CSO/RP/1831/1499. • **59.** Thomas Sloane, Chief Secretary's Office Registered Papers, Outrage Reports, Cork, 1833, NAI; itma.ie/blog/the-seller-to-the-fair. • **60.** J. Bayley to (?)Dublin Castle, August 1827; NAI, CSO/RP/1827/1465. • **61.** Sinn Féin poster, 'SINN FEIN/THE OTHERS … Which Will You Vote For?', December 1918. We are grateful to Dr Jackie Uí Chionna for drawing this poster to our attention. • **62.** 'Singing Sedition: ballads and verse in the age of O'Connell': nationalarchives.ie/article/singing-sedition-ballads-verse-age-oconnell; Maura Murphy, 'The ballad singer and the role of the seditious ballad in nineteenth-century Ireland: Dublin Castle's view', *Ulster Folklife Magazine*, vol. 25 (1979). • **63.** For a persuasive reassessment of Trevelyan's supposed role in forcing through the implementation of laissez-faire and non-interventionist government policies after 1846, see Charles Read, 'Laissez-faire, the Irish famine, and British financial crisis', *Economic History Review*, vol. 69, no. 2 (2016). • **64.** Robin Haines, *Charles Trevelyan and the Great Irish Famine* (Dublin: Four Courts Press, 2004) • **65.** Treasury note, 2 April 1850, Trevelyan papers, TNA, T64/370C/1; cited by Charles Read, 'British Economic Policy and Ireland, c.1841–53', University of Cambridge, PhD thesis (2016), pp. 259–61. • **66.** Liam O Meara, *Zozimus, The Life and Works of Michael Moran* (Dublin: Riposte Books, 2011). • **67.** Raymond Daly, *Celtic and Ireland in Song and Story* (Kilcock: Studio Print, 2008), p. 84. Davis died in 1845, aged only 31. • **68.** heinonline.org/HOL/LandingPage?handle=hein.trials/irishtri0001&div=1&src=home. O'Connell was sentenced to a year in jail but freed after three months. Others convicted included the editor of the *Nation*, Charles Duffy; Ian McBride (ed.), *History and Memory in Modern Ireland* (Cambridge: Cambridge University Press, 2001), p. 145. • **69.** As a student at Trinity College, Dublin, Tone had been an enthusiastic amateur actor and had an affair with the leading actress, Mrs Elizabeth Martin. A recently discovered fragment of Tone's diary records her influence on 'my taste for theatrical performances'. historyireland.com/volume-25/mrs-martin-endebted. • **70.** youtube.com/watch?v=Gs_D808xmZA. • **71.** The poll may have been influenced by an active email campaign. • **72.** Gregory Vargo, 'Chartist drama: The performance of revolt', *Victorian Studies*, vol. 61, no. 1 (2018). • **73.** The text of *St John's Eve* is reprinted in Gregory Vargo (ed.), *Chartist Drama* (Manchester: Manchester University Press, 2020), pp. 181–226. • **74.** Ibid., pp. 159–63, 169–70. • **75.** Act for Regulating Theatres 1843 (6 & 7 Vict., c. 68); David Thomas, David Carlton and Anne Etienne, *Theatre Censorship from Walpole to Wilson* (Oxford: Oxford University Press, 2007), ch. 2. Repeated applications by new owners of the Rotunda for a theatre licence, however, were turned down in 1844, 1847 and 1858 on the grounds that the premises had previously been used 'for propagating infidel principles and socialism'. • **76.** Act for Regulating Theatres 1843 (6 & 7 Vict., c. 68). • **77.** Vargo, 'Chartist drama: The performance of revolt'. • **78.** Richard Moran, *Knowing Right from Wrong: The Insanity Defense of Daniel McNaughtan* (New York: Simon and Schuster, 2000), p. 58; Andrew, *Secret World*, pp. 379–80. • **79.** Andrew, *Secret Service*, p. 15. • **80.** *The Spectator*, 14 June 1850. Marx's letter was also sent on behalf of Engels and August Willich, another Prussian revolutionary. • **81.** Zamoyski, *Phantom Terror*, p. 403. • **82.** Michael Huggins, 'The "Nation" and Giuseppe Mazzini, 1842–48', *New Hibernia Review*, vol. 17, no. 3 (2013). • **83.** Andrew, *The Secret World*, pp. 382–3. • **84.** Vaillé, *Le cabinet noir*, 2ème partie, ch. 12. • **85.** Douglas Jerrold, *Vidocq! The French Police Spy* (Surrey Theatre, 6 Jan 1829); John Baldwin Buckstone, *Vidocq, The French Police Spy* (Coburg Theatre 6 July 1829); Frederick Burwick, *Romanticism: Keywords* (Hoboken, NJ: Wiley-Blackwell, 2015), p. 45. • **86.** Vaillé, *Le cabinet noir*, 2ème partie, ch. 12; Christopher Andrew, 'Déchiffrement et diplomatie: Le cabinet noir du Quai d'Orsay sous la Troisième République', *Relations Internationales*, vol. 3, no. 5 (1976), p. 39. All Sûreté surveillance records up to 1870 were destroyed during the Paris Commune of 1871. It is highly unlikely, however, that reports on Hugo before 1870 were less intrusive than those which survive for the early Third Republic. • **87.** Extracts from Hugo's Sûreté file are published in Bruno Fuligni, *La Police des écrivains*, 2nd edn (Paris: Editions Horay, 2011). • **88.** Andrew, *The Secret World*, ch. 21. • **89.** The Warren Commission on the assassination of President John F. Kennedy in 1962 later concluded that security failures were largely responsible for the death of all three; *Report of the President's Commission on the Assassination of President Kennedy*, Appendix 7: archives.gov/research/jfk/warren-commission-report/appendix7.html. • **90.** Andrew, *For the President's Eyes Only*, pp. 22–4. • **91.** James L. Swanson, *Manhunt: The 12-Day Chase for Lincoln's Killer* (New York: William Morrow, 2006). On Lincoln's love of Shakespeare, see: folger.edu/men-letters-shakespeares-influence-abraham-lincoln. • **92.** The History Office of today's US Defense Intelligence Agency lists four significant female spies for the Civil War but only one for the Revolutionary War: dia.mil/News/Articles/Article-View/Article/566952/women-in-intelligence-part-1. • **93.** At the end of the war, however, Van Lew was treated as a pariah in her native Virginia. She died almost bankrupt in 1900 and was buried vertically in an unmarked grave. Douglas Waller, *Lincoln's Spies: Their Secret War to Save a Nation* (New York: Simon & Schuster, 2019); David Smith, 'Lincoln's spies: Elizabeth Van Lew, southern sexism and the winning of a secret war', *Guardian*, 17 August 2019; Andrew, *For the President's Eyes Only*, p. 22. • **94.** 'A Thrilling Narrative; Miss Maj. Pauline Cashman, the Federal Scout and Spy', *Detroit Tribune*, 24 May 1864; reprinted in *New York Times*, 28 May 1864. • **95.** William J. Christen, *Pauline Cushman: Spy of the Cumberland* (Edinburgh: Edinburgh University Press, 2006); Emily Toomey, 'The actress who left the stage to become a Civil War spy', *Smithsonian Magazine*, 12 August 2019. • **96.** Edwin C. Fishel, CIA Center for the Study of Intelligence, 'Military Intelligence 1861–63 (Part I)' (1966); cia.gov/resources/csi/studies-in-intelligence/archives/vol-10-no-3/military-intelligence-1861–63-part-i. • **97.** Belle Boyd, *Belle Boyd in Camp and Prison*, 2 vols (London: Saunders, Otley and Co., 1865); quotation from vol. 1, p.291. • **98.** *American National Biography*, 'Belle Boyd'; Debra Michals, 'Isabella "Belle" Boyd' (2015): womenshistory.org/education-resources/biographies/isabelle-boyd.

7: The Late Nineteenth Century

• **1.** Originally a distinct group, the Fenians took their name from Finn MacCool's legendary band of warriors, the Fianna. • **2.** John Ranelagh, *A Short History of Ireland*, 3rd edn (Cambridge: Cambridge University Press, 2012), pp. 135–8. • **3.** Richard Parfitt, '"Oh, what matter, when for Erin dear we fall?": Music and Irish nationalism, 1848–1913', *Irish Studies Review*, vol. 23, no. 4 (2015). • **4.** Fewer than one per cent of plays submitted to the Lord Chamberlain were refused a licence, though it was not uncommon for changes to a play to be required (John Johnston, *The Lord Chancellor's Blue Pencil* (London: Hodder & Stoughton, 1990), p. 35). Since there was no prospect of a play featuring Fenians, with the exception of *The Shaughraun*, receiving a licence after 1867, none were submitted. In the few years before 1867, two plays including Fenians had been licensed, subject to changes which included removal of references to Fenian hangings. Susan Schuyler, 'Crowds, Fenianism and the Victorian stage', *Journal of Victorian Culture*, vol. 16, no. 2 (2011). • **5.** On the enthusiastic reception of *The Shaughraun* at the Theatre Royal, Drury Lane, London's largest theatre, see Deirdre McFeely, *Dion Boucicault : Irish Identity on Stage* (Cambridge: Cambridge University Press, 2012), ch. 6. • **6.** Dion Boucicault, *The Shaughraun*, 'original complete edition' (Kindle). • **7.** McFeely, *Dion Boucicault*, ch. 6. • **8.** Louis Andrieux, *Souvenirs d'un préfet de police* (Paris: J. Rouff, 1885). • **9.** David Bellos, *The Novel of the Century: The Extraordinary Adventure of 'Les Misérables'* (London: Particular Books, 2017). • **10.** See, for example, report by agent BARFOND to the Sûreté, n.d. [1876]: Fuligni, *La police des écrivains*, p. 27. • **11.** fr.wikisource.org/wiki/ Actes_et_paroles/Depuis_l%E2%80%99exil/1877. • **12.** ANDOCHE report to the Sûreté, 27 March 1877; PAMPHILE report to the Sûreté, 27 March 1877: Fuligni, *La police des écrivains*, pp. 29–30. • **13.** Maurice Coste, *Souvenirs d'avant le déluge, 1870–1914* (Paris: Perrin, 1927). • **14.** For an introduction to Hugo's erotic code in his *Carnets* and *Choses vues*, see Victor Hugo, *Choses vues 1870–1885*, ed. Hubert Juin (Paris: Gallimard, 1972), pp. 521–2; further details in Raymond Escholier, *Un amant de génie, Victor Hugo: lettres d'amour et carnets inédits* (Paris: Fayard, 1979) and Henri Guillemin, *Hugo et la sexualité* (Paris: Gallimard, 1954). • **15.** Graham Robb, *Victor Hugo* (London: Picador, 1997), chs 21, 23. • **16.** Odile Krakovitch, *Hugo censuré: La liberté au théâtre au XIXe siècle* (Paris: Calmann-Lévy, 1985). • **17.** Emile Zola, 'Naturalism on the stage' (1881), in Toby Cole (ed.), *Playwrights on Playwriting: From Ibsen to Ionescu* (New York: Cooper Square Press, 2001); Goldstein, 'France', in Goldstein (ed.), *The Frightful Stage*; Martin Kanes, '"Germinal": Drama and dramatic structure', *Modern Philology*, vol. 61, no. 1 (1963). • **18.** Ernest Vizetelly, *With Zola in England: A Story of Exile* (London: Chatto & Windus, 1899); Vizetelly translated the play into English. On the role of British theatre clubs, see Johnston, *The Lord Chancellor's Blue Pencil*, ch. 16. • **19.** Robb, *Victor Hugo*. • **20.** 'Renseignements concernant le nommé Verlaine', 1 August 1873: Fuligni, *La police des écrivains*, pp. 41–3. • **21.** Ibid., pp. 45–9. • **22.** During the 1870s, the Sûreté conducted its own surveillance operations in Britain, where its chief target was the French writer and former Communard, Jules Vallès: Ibid., pp. 51–79. • **23.** Andrew, *Secret Service*, p. 17; Francis Wheen, *Karl Marx* (London: Fourth Estate, 2000), pp. 165–6. • **24.** Russian nihilism originated as a philosophy of moral and epistemological scepticism. Outside Russia, the term 'nihilist' was commonly applied to the whole revolutionary milieu: Kristian Petrov, '"Strike out, right and left!": a conceptual-historical analysis of 1860s Russian nihilism and its notion of negation', *Studies in Eastern European Thought*, vol. 71, no. 2 (2019). • **25.** Anna Vaninskaya, '"Truth about Russia": Russia in Britain at the Fin de Siècle', in Josephine M. Guy (ed.), *Edinburgh Companion to Fin de Siècle Literature, Culture and the Arts* (Edinburgh: Edinburgh University Press, 2017). • **26.** As in Joseph Conrad's 1907 novel, *The Secret Agent*, the only example of the genre to have an enduring reputation. • **27.** Claudia Verhoeven, 'Adventures in terrorism: Sergei Stepniak-Kravchinsky and the literary lives of the Russian revolutionary community', in J. Coy, B. Marschke, I. Poley and G. Verhoeven (eds), *Kinship, Community, and Self: Essays in Honor of David Warren Sabean* (New York: Berghahn Books, 2015); *ODNB*, 'Sergey Mikhailovich Kravchinsky (Stepniak)'. • **28.** Andrew, *The Secret World*, p. 425. • **29.** Ibid., pp. 425–6. Within two years of Alexander II's assassination, the Okhrana had succeeded in disrupting operations of the People's Will. For the remainder of the century there were no further political assassinations or successful bomb attacks in Russia. • **30.** *ODNB*, Sergey Mikhailovich Kravchinsky (Stepniak). • **31.** S. Stepniak, *Underground Russia: Revolutionary Profiles and Sketches from Life* (London: Smith Elder, 1883), Kindle edition • **32.** Matthew Sturgis, *Oscar* (London. Head of Zeus, 2018), part III. • **33.** He wrote from London to the American actress, Clara Morris, 'On account of its avowedly republican sentiments I have not been able to get permission to have it brought out here'; Wilde to Clara Morris, c. Sept. 1880: Merlin Holland (ed) *Oscar Wilde: A Life in Letters* (London: Fourth Estate, 2003), pp. 70–71. • **34.** Michael Newton, '"Nihilists of Castlebar!" Exporting Russian Nihilism in the 1880s and the case of Oscar Wilde's *Vera; or the Nihilists*', in Rebecca Beasley and Philip Ross Bullock (eds), *Russia in Britain, 1880–1940: From Melodrama to Modernism* (Oxford: Oxford University Press, 2013). • **35.** Pigott's words were recalled in evidence to a parliamentary Joint Select Committee on 30 July 1909: parliament.uk/about/living-heritage/transformingsociety/private-lives/relationships/collections1/1968-theatre-censorship/1909-censorship-committee/1909-censorship-committee. • **36.** *ODNB*, 'Oscar Wilde'. • **37.** Jennifer Wilson, 'When Oscar Wilde colluded with the Russians', *The Paris Review*, 18 October 2017. • **38.** Stepniak, *Underground Russia* • **39.** Andrew, *Secret Service*, pp. 18–19. • **40.** Laurence Senelick, '"For God, for Czar, for Fatherland": Russians on the British stage from Napoleon to the Great War', in Beasley and Bullock, *Russia in Britain*, pp. 29–33. • **41.** The playwright was Constance Cox. • **42.** Senelick, '"For God, for Czar, for Fatherland"'. • **43.** Andrew, *The Defence of the Realm*, paperback edn, pp. 5–6. Melville later became MI5's first spy-catcher. • **44.** Andrew Cook, *M: MI5's First Spymaster* (London: Tempus, 2002). • **45.** Joe Posnanski, *The Life and Afterlife of Harry Houdini* (London: Avid Reader, 2019);

'The real story of Houdini at Scotland Yard?': wildabouthoudini.com/2018/05/the-real-story-of-houdini-at-scotland.html. • **46.** Henri Mitterand, *Zola*, 3 vols (Paris: Fayard, 1999–2002). • **47.** 'Au sujet d'Émile Zola', 5 July 1891: Fuligni, *La police des écrivains*, p. 126. • **48.** Andrew, *The Secret World*, pp. 461–2. • **49.** Male agents very rarely had female codenames. • **50.** COQUETTE report to the Sûreté, 19 April 1898: Fuligni, *La police des écrivains*, p. 127. Zola fathered two children by Jeanne Rozerot: Denise in 1889 and Jacques in 1891. After Zola's probably accidental death in 1902, both took his surname. • **51.** Brigitte Émile-Zola and Alain Pagès, *Lettres à Jeanne Rozerot: 1892–1902*, (Paris: Gallimard, 2004). • **52.** Vizetelly, *With Zola in England*. • **53.** Michael Rosen, *The Disappearance of Zola: Love, Literature and the Dreyfus Case* (London: Faber & Faber, 2017); Mitterand, *Zola*, vol. 3. • **54.** Robert Harris, 'The whistle-blower who freed Dreyfus', *New York Times*, 17 January 2014.

8: Spies and German Spy Scares

• **1.** Paul Kennedy, 'Riddle of the Sands', *The Times*, 3 January 1991; Andrew, *Secret Service*, pp. 36–7. Erskine Childers later became an Irish republican. Selborne had started out as assistant private secretary to Erskine's cousin, Hugh Childers, when the latter was First Lord of the Admiralty. • **2.** Evidence to a parliamentary Joint Select Committee on 29 July 1909. The select committee agreed with the principle that the Lord Chamberlain should not license plays 'calculated to impair friendly relations with any foreign power', though some members had reservations about how the principle had been put into practice: parliament.uk/about/living-heritage/transformingsociety/private-lives/relationships/collections1/1968-theatre-censorship/1909-censorship-committee/1909-censorship-committee. • **3.** Johnston, *The Lord Chamberlain's Blue Pencil*, pp. 42–5. • **4.** The other twelve were mainly romantic novels. • **5.** Andrew, *The Secret World*, pp. 472–3. For the most recent research on Le Queux, see the two special issues (ed. Ailise Bulfin and Harry Wood) of *Critical Survey* (Oxford: Berghahn Books), vol. 32, nos 1–2 (2020). • **6.** *The Secret Agent* was inspired by the death of a French anarchist who accidentally blew himself up in 1894, probably while preparing to attack the Greenwich Royal Observatory. By the time Conrad's book was published, anarchist terrorism was no longer regarded as a threat to national security: Maya Jasanoff, *The Dawn Watch: Joseph Conrad in a Global World* (London: William Collins, 2017), ch. 3. • **7.** Le Queux, *Spies of the Kaiser: Plotting the Downfall of England* (London: Hurst & Blackett, 1909); reissued with introduction by Nicholas Hiley (London: Frank Cass, 1996), p. 87. • **8.** *The Invasion of 1910* was published too late to have any impact on the campaign for the 1906 general election, which ended in a landslide victory for the Liberals, on whom Le Queux placed much of the blame for ignoring the threat of German invasion. Christian K. Melby, 'Empire and nation in British future-war and invasion-scare fiction, 1871–1914', *Historical Journal*, vol. 63, no. 2 (2020). • **9.** Andrew, *The Secret World*, pp. 475–7. • **10.** More than half a century later, the main biographers of Asquith and his ministers were still apparently unaware of the Secret Service Bureau's existence and omitted it from their books. Andrew, *The Secret World*, p. 477. • **11.** Christopher Andrew wielded the swordstick, the property of Cumming's niece, Diana Pares, when presenting a BBC2 *Timewatch* documentary on Cumming in 1985. • **12.** Compton Mackenzie, *Greek Memories*, 2nd edn (London: Chatto & Windus, 1939), p. 324. • **13.** Angus McLaren, "Smoke and mirrors: Willy Clarkson and the role of disguises in inter war England," *Journal of Social History*, vol. 40, no. 3 (2007). • **14.** Michael Pickering, *Blackface Minstrelsy in Britain* (Burlington, VT: Ashgate, 2008), p. 105. • **15.** While an undergraduate at Trinity College, Cambridge, in 1905, Horace de Vere Cole had played a similar hoax with the help of his fellow undergraduate, Adrian Stephen. Posing as the uncle of the Sultan of Zanzibar, Cole received a civic reception in Cambridge and toured some of the colleges. Willy Clarkson provided the makeup and costumes: Martyn Downer, *The Sultan of Zanzibar: The Bizarre World and Spectacular Hoaxes of Horace de Vere Cole* (London: Black Spring Press, 2010). • **16.** Kevin Young, *Bunk: The Rise of Hoaxes, Humbug, Plagiarists, Phonies, Post-Facts, and Fake News* (Minneapolis: Graywolf Press, 2017), p. 69. • **17.** Andrew, *Secret Service*, pp. 74–5 • **18.** Young, *Bunk*, pp. 69–70; Moira Marsh, 'Bunga-bunga on the Dreadnought: Hoax, race and Woolf', *Comedy Studies*, vol. 9, no. 2 (2018). • **19.** Keith Jeffery, *MI6: The History of the Secret Intelligence Service, 1909–1949* (London: Bloomsbury, 2010), p. 50. • **20.** Interviews by Christopher Andrew with Diana Pares in 1984. • **21.** Andrew, *The Secret World*, pp. 457–8, 576. • **22.** Andrew, *Secret Service*, p. 53. • **23.** British Library, LCP 1908/28. • **24.** Ibid.; Johnston, *The Lord Chamberlain's Blue Pencil*, pp. 61–2. • **25.** Ibid., p.61. • **26.** Brigadier General Sir James Edmonds, Unpublished Memoirs, ch. 20; Liddell Hart Centre for Military Archives, King's College London, Edmonds MSS III/5. • **27.** Harry Wood, "'The play all London is discussing": The great success of Guy du Maurier's *An Englishman's Home*, 1909', *Theatre Notebook*, vol. 70, no. 3 (2016). • **28.** Andrew, *Secret Service,* p. 53. • **29.** Evidence by Redford to a parliamentary Joint Select Committee on 29 July 1909: parliament.uk/about/living-heritage/transformingsociety/private-lives/relationships/collections1/1968-theatre-censorship/1909-censorship-committee/1909-censorship-committee. • **30.** Johnston, *The Lord Chamberlain's Blue Pencil*, p. 62. • **31.** Jérôme aan de Wiel, 'German invasion and spy scares in Ireland, 1890s–1914: Between fiction and fact', *Études irlandaises*, vol. 37

(2012), no. 1. • **32.** Margaret Skinnider, *Doing my Bit for Ireland* (New York: Century, 1917), p. 4. • **33.** George Bernard Shaw's play, *The Shewing-up of Blanco Posnet*, banned in London, was performed in Dublin at the Abbey Theatre in 1909. His lengthy 'preface on censorship' in the 1909 published edition of the play was a major contribution to the British censorship debate. • **34.** The Irish historian Roy Foster concludes that by 1905 the Abbey had become the 'established church' of Irish theatre. Though there was an overlapping network of small, more radical theatrical groups, 'The trouble was that the political plays mounted by the radicals were manifestly unsuccessful with audiences.' R.F. Foster, *Vivid Faces: The Revolutionary Generation in Ireland 1890–1923*, paperback edn (London: Penguin, 2015), ch. 5. • **35.** James Pethica, 'Lady Gregory's Abbey Theatre drama: Ireland real and ideal', in Shaun Richards (ed.), *Cambridge Companion to Twentieth-Century Irish Drama* (Cambridge: Cambridge University Press, 2004); Roy Foster, 'A troubled house', *Guardian*, 4 February 2004. • **36.** Thinking it likely her assassination of Edward VII would result in her own death, Gonne had made a cousin guardian of her daughter Iseult: *ODNB*, 'Maud Gonne'. • **37.** In reality, the main author of *Cathleen ni Houlihan* was Lady Gregory, who wrote on a manuscript of the play: 'All this mine alone'; 'Lady Gregory, unsung hero of the Irish Literary Revival', *The Economist*, 10 March 2020. • **38.** abbeytheatre. ie/about/history. • **39.** When Lady Gregory told de Valera in 1921 that he had been 'so often in my prayers I wanted to see what you looked like', she believed it was the first time they had met: Colm Tóibín, *Lady Gregory's Toothbrush* (Dublin: Lilliput Press, 2002) loc.1160. • **40.** *ODNB*, 'Isabella Augusta, Lady Gregory (*née* Persse)'. • **41.** *Selected Plays of Lady Gregory* (Gerrards Cross: Colin Smythe Ltd, 1983); Anna Pilz, 'Lady Gregory's *The Gaol Gate*, Terence MacSwiney and the Abbey Theatre', *Irish Studies Review*, 2015; George Cusack, *The Politics of Identity in Irish Drama: W. B. Yeats, Augusta Gregory and J. M. Synge* (London: Routledge, 2009), p. 102. • **42.** David Neligan, *A Spy in the Castle* (London: Macgibbon and Kee, 1968), p. 82. • **43.** First night programme at: artsandculture.google.com/asset/when-the-dawn-is-come-by-thomas-macdonagh-programme-for-the-first-production-abbey-theatre/3 QF83yD9S8Jd8w?hl=en. • **44.** Thomas MacDonagh, *When the Dawn is Come* (Dublin: Mansell & Co, 1908), p. 14. • **45.** MacDonagh complained, however, that the play was 'badly performed'. Unusually for a performance at the Abbey, according to the reviewer in the *Irish Times*: 'In many cases, [actors] forgot their words and had to wait until the prompter came to their aid, while not infrequently whole passages from the dialogue seemed to be omitted': Shane Kenna, *Thomas MacDonagh: 16 Lives* (Dublin: O'Brien Press, 2014) • **46.** *The Times*, 1 April 1912. • **47.** *ODNB*, 'John McCormack'. He did, however, spend part of the Second World War in Britain. • **48.** Kenna, *Thomas*

MacDonagh. At the time, however, as many at the Abbey Theatre regretted the Easter Rising as supported it. Yeats' first reaction, as he wrote to Gregory, was that 'all the work of years has been overturned, all the bringing together of classes, all the freeing of Irish literature and criticism from politics'. R. F. Foster, *W. B. Yeats: A Life*, vol. 2: *The Arch-poet, 1915–1939* (Oxford: Oxford University Press, 2003). • **49.** James Moran, *Staging the Easter Rising: 1916 as Theatre* (Cork: Cork University Press, 2005); Eugene McNulty & Róisín Ní Ghairbhí (eds), *Patrick Pearse and the Theatre* (Dublin: Four Courts Press, 2016). • **50.** The radical activist Francis Sheehy-Skeffington, summarily executed after the Rising, dismissed *Under Which Flag?* as 'all propag[anda]; no construction'. Nicholas Allen, 'Imagining the Rising', in Nicholas Grene and Chris Morash (eds), *The Oxford Handbook of Modern Irish Theatre* (Oxford: Oxford University Press, 2016). • **51.** Foster, *Vivid Faces*, pp. 93, 137. • **52.** John McCourt, *Roll Away the Reel World: James Joyce and Cinema* (Cork: Cork University Press, 2010) • **53.** Simon Heffer, *The Age of Decadence: Britain 1880 to 1914* (London: Random House, 2017), p. 165. • **54.** *New Statesman*, 10 January 1914; Philip Waller, *Writers, Readers, and Reputations: Literary Life in Britain 1870–1918* (Oxford: Oxford University Press, 2008), ch. 1. • **55.** Ian Christie, *Robert Paul and the Origins of British Cinema* (Chicago: University of Chicago Press, 2019), pp. 152–4. • **56.** screenonline.org.uk/film/id/1114460/index.html. • **57.** Though not responsible to the Lord Chancellor, the self-regulating British Board of Film Censors (BBFC), founded in 1912, made little attempt to push back the boundaries of censorship. • **58.** Waller, *Writers, Readers, and Reputations*, p. 9. • **59.** blog.nationalarchives.gov.uk/a-century-of-british-film-censorship. • **60.** Andrew, *Defence of the Realm*, pp. 50–51. • **61.** Gustav Steinhauer, *Steinhauer: The Kaiser's Masterspy as Told by Himself*, ed. Sidney Felstead (London: Bodley Head, 1930), p. 37. Steinhauer is scarcely likely to have fabricated such a devastating denunciation of his own incompetence. • **62.** Andrew, *Defence of the Realm*, pp. 53–4. • **63.** Ibid., pp. 54–5. • **64.** imdb.com/title/tt2184307; Waller, *Writers, Readers, and Reputations*, p. 9. • **65.** *The White Lie* (1914), *The Sons of Satan* (1915) and *Sadounah* (1915). Le Queux continued writing during the 1920s, transferring some of his alarmism from the Kaiser's Germany to the postwar 'scandal of the Moscow Bolshevik propaganda' and the Soviet use of 'secret wireless'. But he no longer attracted much interest from film studios. • **66.** screenonline.org.uk/film/id/1114339/index.html.

9: The First World War

• **1.** The film version of Guy Du Maurier's 1909 play, *An Englishman's Home*, released by the British and Colonial Kinematograph Company in September

1914, depicting a German invasion of England assisted by spies, had nothing like the impact of the original drama. • **2.** 'German suspect tried as a spy', *New York Times*, 31 October 1914; 'Spy executed in tower of London', ibid., 11 Nov. 1914. • **3.** *Daily Express*, 11 November 1914. • **4.** Leonard Sellers, *Shot in the Tower: The Story of the Spies Executed in the Tower of London during the First World War*, 2nd edn (Barnsley: Pen & Sword, 2009), ch. 2. • **5.** Andrew, *Defence of the Realm*, p.65. • **6.** Sellers, *Shot in the Tower*, pp. 21–2, 35. • **7.** Though not revealed at the time the shelling was made possible by the Admiralty's failure to make good use of available intelligence. • **8.** Andrew, *Defence of the Realm*, pp. 64–72. • **9.** A. C. Grant Duff ('late Minister Resident Dresden & Coburg') to Kell, 14 August 1914; Andrew, *Defence of the Realm*, pp. 56–8. • **10.** After the outbreak of war, Clarkson came up with his own thoroughly British greasepaint as a patriotic alternative to the high-quality German Leichner makeup, which had been used for decades throughout the theatre industry: Roger Foss, *Till the Boys Come Home: How British Theatre Fought the Great War* (London: The History Press, 2018), pp. 48–9. • **11.** MI5 Archives; cited in Andrew, *Defence of the Realm*, pp. 56–8. • **12.** Thomas Boghardt, *Spies of the Kaiser: German Covert Operations in Britain during the First World War Era* (Basingstoke: Palgrave Macmillan, 2004), p. 125. • **13.** gutenberg.org/files/15715/15715-h/15715-h.htm. • **14.** John Mullen, *The Show Must Go On: Popular Song in Britain during the First World War* (London: Routledge, 2015). Mullen calculates that in 1916 the price of the cheapest gramophone would pay for 220 tickets to the music hall. • **15.** royalarmouries.org/stories/tower-of-london/spies-in-the-tower-fernando-buschmann. • **16.** Edwin Ruis, *Spynest: British and German Espionage from Neutral Holland 1914–1918* (Stroud: History Press, 2016). Sir Basil Thomson, *Queer People* (London: Hodder and Stoughton, 1922), p.152. • **17.** TNA, ARP_HIP0246565. • **18.** Kristie Macrakis, *Prisoners, Lovers, and Spies: The Story of Invisible Ink from Herodotus to al-Qaeda* (New Haven and London: Yale University Press, 2014), pp. 139–42. • **19.** TNA, KV 2/3. • **20.** Ruis, *Spynest*, ch. 8. • **21.** TNA, KV 2/3. • **22.** This was probably a reference to Vieyra, who had formerly 'been touring as a music-hall performer with a Dutch passport' and was 'now in custody'. • **23.** Troup to chief constables, 16 July 1916; TNA, HO 45/10779/277334/15. • **24.** In 1920 Vieyra's sentence was further reduced to ten years. • **25.** Andrew, *Defence of the Realm*, pp. 76–7. • **26.** The text of Gamelin's *rapport secret* of 6 January 1956, the day after the death of Mistinguett, is published in Bruno Fuligni (ed.), *Dans les archives inédites des services secrets: Un siècle d'espionnage français (1871–1989)* (Paris: Gallimard, 2014), pp.158–60. • **27.** Clément Tibère, 'Mistinguett (Bourgeois, Jeanne, dite)', in Hugues Moutouh and Jérôme Poirot (eds), *Dictionnaire du Renseignement*, 2nd edn (Paris: Perrin, 2020). • **28.** Gamelin, *rapport secret*, 6 January 1956; Fuligni (ed.), *Dans les archives inédites*, pp. 158–60.

• **29.** Bruno Fuligni, *Mata Hari: Les vies insolentes de l'agent H21* (Paris: Gallimard, 2017); Mary W. Craig, *A Tangled Web: Mata Hari: Dancer, Courtesan, Spy* (Stroud: The History Press, 2017). Julie Wheelwright, *Mata Hari and the Myth of Women in Espionage* (London: Collins & Brown, 1992), pp 19–28. Unlike previous writers on Zelle, Fuligni and Craig had full access to her recently declassified French intelligence file. • **30.** Sturgis, *Oscar*, parts VI, VII. • **31.** Fuligni, *Mata Hari*. Craig, *A Tangled Web*. • **32.** Zelle's two-volume MI5 file is in TNA: KV 2/1–2. • **33.** Fuligni, *Mata Hari*, p. 64. • **34.** Olivier Lahaie, 'Mata Hari ou le badinage fatal'; probably the best analysis of her French intelligence file: penseemiliterre.fr/mata-hari-ou-le-badinage-fatal_78_1013077.html. • **35.** TNA, KV 2/2. • **36.** Lahaie, 'Mata Hari ou le badinage fatal'. • **37.** Ibid. • **38.** Thomson's susceptibility to such 'charm' led to his public disgrace in 1925 after he was fined £5 for 'committing an act in violation of public decency' in Hyde Park with a young woman named Thelma de Lava. Thomson claimed unsuccessfully that he was carrying out research for a book on the London vice trade. • **39.** Sir Basil Thomson, *Queer People*, pp. 182–3. • **40.** Lahaie, 'Mata Hari ou le badinage fatal'. • **41.** Ibid. • **42.** Craig, *A Tangled Web*, p. 192. • **43.** TNA, KV 2/2. • **44.** Zelle interrogation by Bouchardon, the examining magistrate, 21 February 1917; cited by Craig, *A Tangled Web*, p. 193. Zelle told Bouchardon that her wartime liaisons had included five French officers, three or four English, three Germans, one Belgian, one Dutch, one Italian, one Irish, one Montenegrin and one Russian. • **45.** For example, by Russell Warren Howe, *Mata Hari: The True Story* (New York: Dodd, Mead & Co., 1986), pp. 11–12. • **46.** H. A. Pakenham (Paris) to R. D. Waterhouse, 28 November 1917: TNA, KV 2/2 • **47.** Lahaie, 'Mata Hari ou le badinage fatal'. • **48.** George Bernard Shaw, 'The Roger Casement trial: An unpublished statement', *The Massachusetts Review*, vol. 5 (1964), no. 2; Fintan O'Toole, 'Bernard Shaw to Roger Casement: Put on the performance of your life', *Irish Times*, 26 March 2016; Dermot McEvoy, 'How two literary legends tried to save Sir Roger Casement from the gallows': irishcentral.com/roots/history/sir-roger-casement-execution. • **49.** *Augustus Does His Bit* was first performed at the Royal Court Theatre in January 1917; gutenberg.org/files/3487/3487-h/3487-h.htm. • **50.** Andrew, *Defence of the Realm*, p. 87. • **51.** Room 40 provided intelligence which should have prevented German battlecruisers shelling Scarborough, Whitby and Hartlepool in December 1914, but it was misinterpreted by the Admiralty, which had no prewar experience of SIGINT. • **52.** Andrew, *The Secret World*, pp. 508–18. • **53.** Army Security Agency, 'Historical Background of the Signal Security Agency' (unpublished), vol. 2, pp. 17–18: National Archives, Washington DC (NAW), RG 457, NC3-457-77-1. • **54.** Penelope Fitzgerald, *The Knox Brothers* (London: Macmillan, 1977), pp. 90–92, 137; Andrew, *Secret Service*, p. 94. • **55.** Fitzgerald,

Knox Brothers, p. 93. • **56.** ODNB, 'Francis Lyall [Frank] Birch'. • **57.** Ibid; bletchleypark.org.uk/roll-of-honour/786. • **58.** Mavis Batey, *The Man Who Broke Enigmas* (London: Biteback, 2009), ch. 3. • **59.** Original copy in Denniston MSS, Churchill College Cambridge Archive Centre (CCAC), DENN 3/3. The title page reveals that the verses are by Knox. Birch simultaneously wrote an official, classified history of the work of ID25, entitled 'A Contribution to the History of German naval warfare, 1914 –1918', which described its contribution to defeating the U-boats in the long-drawn-out Battle of the Atlantic. • **60.** Andrew, *The Secret World*, pp. 508–9, 516–17, 543–4. • **61.** US decrypts were produced by the military SIGINT agency, MI1b, which sent copies to Hall: Andrew, *The Secret World*, pp. 533–4; Daniel Larsen, *Plotting for Peace: American Peacemakers, British Codebreakers, and Britain at War, 1914–1917* (Cambridge: Cambridge University Press, 2021), ch. 9. • **62.** S. W. Roskill, *Hankey: Man of Secrets*, vol. 1 (London: Collins, 1970), p. 247. • **63.** Admiral John Godfrey, unpublished memoirs, vol. 5, pp. 132–7, CCAC, GDFY 1/6. • **64.** Andrew, *The Secret World*, p. 516. Though balding, Hall was not in fact bald. • **65.** Selina Hastings, *The Secret Lives of Somerset Maugham* (London: John Murray, 2010), p. 205. • **66.** Ibid., p. 203. 'I have never had such an enormous success as *Caroline*,' Maugham wrote to his brother Charles. 'We play to over £2,000 a week, which [producer] Dion Boucicault [Jr] tells me is the largest sum he has known a comedy to earn in his whole experience in the theatre.' • **67.** Andrew, *For the President's Eyes Only*, pp. 47–50. Maugham's experiences in St Petersburg did, however, inspire two short stories in his *Ashenden, or the British Agent*, one of the classics of spy fiction (see below). • **68.** Hastings, *Somerset Maugham*, p. 204 • **69.** Alan Judd, *The Quest for C: Sir Mansfield Cumming and the Founding of the Secret Service* (London: HarperCollins, 1999), pp. 420–21. • **70.** Jeffery, *MI6*, p. 730. • **71.** Judd, *Quest for Mansfield Cumming*, pp. 420–21. • **72.** ODNB, 'Edward Knoblock'. • **73.** Edward Knoblock, *Round the Room: An Autobiography* (London: Chapman & Hall, 1939), p. 209. • **74.** Ted Morgan, *Somerset Maugham* (London: Jonathan Cape, 1980), p. 231. • **75.** Before becoming head of station at the end of 1915, Mackenzie had worked for a few months under Rhys Samson: Jeffery, *MI6*, p. 126. • **76.** Andrew Linklater, *Compton Mackenzie, A Life* (London: Chatto & Windus, 1987), pp. 86–8. • **77.** Compton Mackenzie, *First Athenian Memories* (London: Cassell, 1931), p. 130. • **78.** Jeffery, *MI6*, p. 126. • **79.** The unexpurgated version of Compton Mackenzie's *Greek Memories*, banned in 1932, was republished by Biteback in 2012. The original, banned version survives in Cambridge University Library and a few other locations. • **80.** Mackenzie, *Greek Memories*. • **81.** Ibid. • **82.** Paul Dukes was the younger brother of the playwright and theatre impresario Ashley Dukes, who was the husband of Ballet Rambert's founder Marie Rambert. • **83.** ODNB, 'Sir Paul Dukes'; Sir Paul Dukes, *The*

Story of 'ST 25': Adventure and Romance in the Secret Intelligence Service in Red Russia (London: Cassell, 1938). • **84.** I. Peters, 'Vospominaniia o rabote v VChK v pervyi god revoliutsii', *Proletarskaia Revoliutsiia*, no. 10 (33), (1924), p. 9; Nick Heath, 'Bim-Bom, Bang-Bang! Chekists and clowns' (3 June 2018): libcom.org/history/bim-bom-bang-bang-chekists-clowns; George Leggett, *The Cheka: Lenin's Political Polce* (Oxford: Clarendon Press, 1981), p. 60. • **85.** In the early 1920s both moved abroad. Radunsky, however, returned in 1925 and made his peace with the Soviet one-party state. Resuming his role as Bim, he and the new Bom (Nikolai Vitsak) avoided political satire and stuck to traditional musical routines. In 1939 both were made Honoured Artists of the Soviet Union. Heath, 'Bim-Bom, Bang-Bang!' • **86.** Sir Paul Dukes, *Red Dusk and the Morrow. Adventures and Investigations in Red Russia* (London: Williams and Norgate, 1922), p. 13. Since Cumming's name was classified, Dukes refers to him only as 'the chief'. • **87.** Dukes, *Red Dusk and the Morrow.* • **88.** Ibid.; Robert Service, *Spies and Commissars: Bolshevik Russia and the West* (London: Macmillan, 2011), pp. 231–4. • **89.** Report of the All-Russia Central Executive Committee and the Council of Peoples Commissars, 5 December 1919: marxists.org/archive/lenin/works/1919/dec/05.htm. • **90.** Christopher Andrew and Vasili Mitrokhin, *The Mitrokhin Archive: The KGB in Europe and the West*, paperback edn (London: Penguin, 2000), p. 37. On the sometimes chaotic execution of counter-revolutionaries, see D. B. Pavlov, 'The tribunal phase of the Soviet judicial system, 1917–1922', *Russian Studies in History*, vol. 58, no. 4 (2019). • **91.** Dukes, *The Story of 'ST 25'*, pp. 221, 263. • **92.** Andrew, *Secret Service*, p. 173. • **93.** Phil Tomaselli, in researching his book *Tracing your Secret Service Ancestors* (Barnsley: Pen and Sword Books, 2009), identified a number of wartime MI5 recruits with entertainment industry backgrounds, and has kindly made his research available to the authors. MI5 employment records show, amongst those recruited in various capacities, the actor manager Francis Duguld, Cambridge Footlights Director and actor-manager Lawrence Grossmith, singer Richard Lambart, film actor Frederick Lloyd, Shakespearian actor William Lynton and playwright and screen actor Gilbert 'Gilly' Wakefield. • **94.** Andrew, *Defence of the Realm*, pp. 113–15. • **95.** Andrew, *Defence of the Realm*, pp. 59–63. • **96.** Tammy M. Proctor, *Female Intelligence: Women and Espionage in the First World War* (New York: NYU Press, 2003), p. 59. • **97.** Evelyn Forbes, 'My Life in Beauty' (unpublished memoir kindly made available to the authors by her son, Mike Forbes), • **98.** Andrew, *Defence of the Realm*, pp.122, 128. • **99.** 'New dresses for "Chu Chin Chow" very suitable for the sultry climate of Old Bagdad', *The Tatler*, 12 September 1917. • **100.** D. B. Scott, *From the Erotic to the Demonic: On Critical Musicology* (Oxford: Oxford University Press, 2003), p. 173; Johnston, *Lord Chamberlain's Blue Pencil*, p. 129. • **101.** After leaving

SIS, Edward Knoblock would later write the 1934 screenplay. *ODNB*, 'Edward Knoblock'. • **102.** MI5 archives, cited by Andrew, *Defence of the Realm*, p. 113. • **103.** Clarkson had also provided costumes and wigs to troops performing entertainments on the front line. 'This catering for scratch theatrical shows in Picardy and Salonika and the North Sea has grown to such a remarkable extent that it constitutes a special department of my business,' he wrote in the annual of the theatrical newspaper *The Era*. 'And while I disposed of all my old stock for free, I have been compelled to levy a nominal charge as a matter of sheer self-protection.' *The Era* Annual, 1918, p. 95. • **104.** Constance Kell, *A Secret Well Kept: The Untold Story of Sir Vernon Kell, Founder of MI5* (London: Conway, 2017) p. 170. The authors are grateful to Mike Forbes for sharing with us his mother's copy of the *Hush-Hush* revue programme, featuring a bound Vernon Kell on the front cover. • **105.** Jeffery, *MI6*, photograph facing p. 171. • **106.** Ibid., pp. 175–7. • **107.** Andrew, *Secret Service*, pp. 221–2. • **108.** Jeffery, *MI6*, p. 238. • **109.** Dukes, *Red Dusk and the Morrow*, title page. • **110.** *ODNB*, 'Sir Paul Dukes'. • **111.** Sir Paul Dukes, *Yoga for the Western World* (1958); id., *The Yoga of Health, Youth, and Joy: A Treatise on Hatha Yoga Adapted to the West* (1960). • **112.** hoover.org/news/featured-find-yoga-master-disguise.

10: Between the Wars

• **1.** Andrew, *Defence of the Realm*, pp. 119–23. • **2.** Ibid., pp. 156–9. • **3.** MI5's informant also wrongly described her father as a senator: MI5 report to the Home Secretary, August 1928, TNA HO files; text in Alan Travis, 'MI5 spied on Tallulah's romp with Eton boys', *The Guardian*, 3 March 2000. • **4.** Brendan Gill, 'Making a noise in the world: Tallulah Bankhead's rise to fame', *Vanity Fair*, 7 October 1972; Joel Lobenthal, *Tallulah!: The Life and Times of a Leading Lady* (New York: HarperCollins, 2004); Judith Mackrell, *Flappers: Six Women of a Dangerous Generation* (London: Macmillan, 2013), ch. 4. • **5.** MI5 report to the Home Secretary, August 1928: Travis, 'MI5 spied on Tallulah's romp with Eton boys.' • **6.** *ODNB*, 'William Bridgeman'; ibid., 'Cyril Alington'. • **7.** Alan Travis, 'MI5 spied on Tallulah's romp with Eton boys'; 'Hollywood star seduced Eton boys': iol.co.za/travel/world/hollywood-star-seduced-eton-boys-29940. • **8.** Gill, 'Making a noise in the world'. • **9.** Tallulah Bankhead, *Tallulah: My Autobiography* (New York: Harper & Brothers, 1952). • **10.** John Pearson, *The Life of Ian Fleming* (London: Bloomsbury Reader, 2013). • **11.** After expulsion from Eton, Bond went to Fettes College, Edinburgh. William Boyd, 'From Fettes with love': life.spectator.co.uk/articles/from-fettes-with-love. • **12.** Lawrence was an established media star by the time Fleming entered Eton in 1921. Fleming got to know his work well. During his brief period as a director of the Dropmore Press, before becoming a best-selling novelist, Fleming bought the rights to, and published, a volume of Lawrence's letters: Andrew Lycett, *Ian Fleming*, paperback edn (London: Phoenix, 1996), pp. 201–2. • **13.** Playing opposite O'Toole, as Prince Faisal, was Alec Guinness, who had himself won an *Evening Standard* Theatre Award for his portrayal of Lawrence in the 1960 premiere of Terence Rattigan's play *Ross*. • **14.** Andrew, *Secret World*, pp. 508, 528–30. • **15.** winstonchurchill.org/publications/finest-hour/finest-hour-119/churchill-and-lawrence-lawrence-of-arabia. • **16.** Joel C. Hodson, 'Lowell Thomas, T. E. Lawrence and the Creation of a Legend', *American History Magazine*, October 2000. Lowell Thomas interview, WPEN Radio, 1965, Marist Special Collections, audio file 1790–03; cliohistory.org/Thomas-lawrence/show/groundbreaking production • **17.** Dr Juliette Desplat, speaking in 'On The Record: Lawrence and Bell', TNA podcast, 9 May 2019: media.nationalarchives.gov.uk/index.php/record-lawrence-bell. • **18.** Lawrence to Sir Archibald Murray, 10 January 1920: Malcolm Brown (ed.), *Lawrence of Arabia: The Selected Letters* (London: Little Books, 2005), p. 181. • **19.** TEI studies.org, Lowell Thomas in London, 1919-20 (blog post by Jeremy Wilson, 3 April 1910), http://www.telstudies.org/discussion/diplomacy_1918-1922/lowell_thomas_in_london_1919-20.shtml. • **20.** The Irish Republican Army (IRA) emerged as a fusion of the IRB and Irish Volunteers. • **21.** Andrew, *Secret Service*, pp. 251–5; Ranelagh, *Short History of Ireland*, pp. 221–4. • **22.** Alison Martin, 'The "Big Fella" and the theatre', *Ireland's Own*, no. 5663, 6 July 2018, pp. 17–19. • **23.** Lawrence to Charlotte Shaw, 18 January 1926, in J. and N. Wilson (eds), *T. E. Lawrence, Correspondence with Bernard and Charlotte Shaw*, vol. 3: *1928* (Dublin: Castle Hill Press, 2008), pp. 15–18. • **24.** Lawrence could only have met Collins during the negotiations if he had been in London on or around 5 December 1921, but he had yet to return from a mission to the Middle East. We are very grateful to Nicole Wilson and Dr John Ranelagh for advice on this complex chronology. For other examples of Lawrence's intermittent unreliability in the later 1920s when recalling earlier episodes, see the comments of his mostly admiring first biographer, Robert Graves: Robert Graves and Basil Liddell Hart (eds), *T. E. Lawrence, Letters to His Biographers*, single-vol. edn (London: Cassell, 1963), part 1, p. 161. • **25.** Lawrence James, *The Golden Warrior: The Life and Legend of Lawrence of Arabia* (London: Weidenfeld & Nicolson, 1991). • **26.** Ibid. • **27.** Lowell Thomas, *With Lawrence in Arabia* (London: Hutchinson, 1924), illustration facing p. 251. • **28.** 'Harry Chase portraits, 1918, 1919', post by Joe Berton, USA, 3 February 1999: telstudies.org/discussion/diplomacy_1918–1922/list_harry_chase_portraits.shtml (cited with his permission). • **29.** Graves and Liddell Hart (eds), *T. E. Lawrence Letters to His Biographers*, part 1, p. 89. • **30.** A. W.

Lawrence, *T. E. Lawrence by His Friends* (London: Jonathan Cape, 1954); pp. 242–5. • **31.** Andrew Kelly, James Pepper, and Jeffrey Richards (eds), *Filming T. E. Lawrence: Korda's Lost Epics* (London & New York: I.B.Tauris Publishers, 1997), p. 3; cited in Paul Alkon, 'Churchill and Lawrence: Imagining Scenarios, Churchill's Advice for Alexander Korda's Stillborn Film, "Lawrence of Arabia"', *Finest Hours*, no. 119 (Summer 2003), p. 37: winstonchurchill.org/ publications/finest-hour/finest-hour-119/churchill-and-lawrence-imagining-scenarios. • **32.** In 1959, Korda finally sold the rights to producer Sam Spiegel, who engaged David Lean as the director of *Lawrence of Arabia* (1962), starring Peter O'Toole in the performance that would define his career. • **33.** The later US ambassador to Moscow, George Kennan, shared Maugham's assessment of Francis: '[His] taste and habits were the robust and simple ones of the American Middle West at the turn of the century. As such, they bore little affinity to the refined predilections of continental diplomatic society': George F. Kennan, *Russia Leaves the War* (Princeton: Princeton University Press, 1989), pp. 36–8. • **34.** Andrew, *Secret Service*, pp. 209–10. • **35.** W. Somerset Maugham, *Ashenden* (London: Vintage, 2000), ch. 8, p. 34. • **36.** Both published by Cassell in London, Toronto, Melbourne and Sydney. • **37.** Mark Kaufman, 'Spyography: Compton Mackenzie, modernism, and the intelligence memoir': scalar.usc.edu/works/the-space-between-literature-and-culture-1914–1945/vol13_2017_kaufman. • **38.** Mackenzie, *Greek Memories* (Biteback edition). After recovering from the accident, Cumming used a wooden scooter to propel himself with his undamaged leg along the corridors of the War Office in Whitehall – later re-enacted by Christopher Andrew when presenting a BBC2 *Timewatch* documentary on Cumming in 1985. In 1918 Cumming replaced this scooter with a motorised American Autoped; Andrew, *For the President's Eyes Only*, p. 38. • **39.** TNA, KV2/1271–2. • **40.** Mark A. Vieira, *Sin in Soft Focus: Pre-Code Hollywood* (New York: Harry N. Abrams, 1999), pp. 52–4. • **41.** *ODNB*, 'Marthe McKenna'. • **42.** Ibid. • **43.** Marthe McKenna, *I Was a Spy!* (London: Pool of London Press, 1932/2015); foreword by Winston S. Churchill, pp. 5–6. • **44.** R. P. Weston and Bert Lee, 'Olga Pulloffski, the Beautiful Spy' (Francis, Day and Hunter Ltd, 1935/EMI Music Publishing). • **45.** Post-war BBC listeners and viewers had no idea that Knight, who appeared regularly on the hugely popular radio programme *Children's Hour*, had been a senior intelligence officer. • **46.** [Maxwell Knight], 'On the subject of Sex, in connection with using women as agents', M.S. Report'; TNA, KV4/227. Knight put nothing on record about his own sexuality, but his conviction that the best male as well as female agents were not 'markedly oversexed or undersexed' probably provides a clue to the extent of his own sexual appetites. • **47.** Ibid., pp. 18, 33–4; 'The Woolwich Arsenal Case – Summary Report', 13 February 1950, TNA, KV2/1023, p. 13; 'Statement of

"X" the informant in this case', 25 January 1938, TNA, KV2/1022, p. 1. Knight's other female agents early in the Second World War included three who penetrated the antisemitic, pro-Nazi Right Club: Andrew, *Defence of the Realm*, p. 221. • **48.** Loosely based on John Buchan's *The Thirty-Nine Steps*, the film starred Robert Donat and Madeleine Carroll. • **49.** TNA, KV2/3822. • **50.** Rattigan was among the 'muzzled' playwrights: Dominic Shellard and Steve Nicholson with Miriam Handley, *The Lord Chamberlain Regrets ...: A History of British Theatre Censorship* (London: British Library, 2004), pp.119–23. • **51.** rbth.com/history/329891-5-foreign-movies-stalin-watched. • **52.** James Smith, 'Soviet films and British intelligence in the 1930s: The case of Kino Films and MI5', in Beasley and Bullock, *Russia in Britain*. • **53.** Jennifer S. Palmer, *Cedric Belfrage: Anglo-American Nonconformist* (Washington DC & London: Minerva Press, 1996). • **54.** Cedric Belfrage, 'Virginia's Real'; silentera.com/articles/motionPicture/1928/1228/pp59-87-95.html. • **55.** Palmer, *Cedric Belfrage*. • **56.** Guide to Cedric Belfrage papers: dlib.nyu.edu/findingaids/html/tamwag/tam_143/bioghist.html. • **57.** John Earl Haynes, Harvey Klehr and Alexander Vassiliev, *Spies: The Rise and Fall of the KGB in America* (New Haven: Yale University Press, 2009), pp. 445–56. • **58.** Excerpt from letter from 'Nikolay' (Peter Gutzeit, NKVD resident in New York) to C. 1934, Vassiliev Yellow Notebook #3, f. 30595 v.1: digitalarchive.wilsoncenter.org/collection/86/vassiliev-notebooks. • **59.** Report by Betty (Zarubin), 8 June 1938, Vassiliev Yellow Notebook #3 (ibid.). • **60.** Vassiliev Yellow Notebook #3 (ibid.). • **61.** David Burke, The *Lawn Road Flats: Spies, Writers and Artists*, with introduction by Christopher Andrew (Woodbridge: Boydell & Brewer, 2014); Julius Green, *Agatha Christie: A Life in Theatre*, revised edn (London: HarperCollins, 2018). It is tempting to imagine Christie and Deutsch discussing Christie's spy thriller *N or M?* while chatting over dinner at the Isobar. Alas, they did not overlap; Christie did not arrive until 1941. The longest-serving Soviet agent recruited while living at Lawn Road was Melita Sirnis (later Norwood). • **62.** MI5 file on Arnold Deutsch; TNA, KV2/4428. • **63.** Deutsch's PhD was in chemistry but he also took courses in psychology. • **64.** Andrew and Mitrokhin, *The Mitrokhin Archive*, pp. 73–4. • **65.** Though Deutsch had joined the Austrian Young Communists in 1922, in documents throughout his years at Vienna University he described himself, perhaps for cover reasons, as Jewish by religion (*mosaisch*) as well as by ethnicity (*jüdisch*): Andrew and Gordievsky, *KGB*, pp. 15–60. • **66.** We are grateful for this information to Mr Ronnie Deutsch, son of Oscar. • **67.** File entry dated 12 Jan 1937. 'Extract from Home Office file no. D.3441 for Deutsch, Arnold', TNA, KV2/4428. The original Home Office file has not survived. • **68.** Burt's critics accuse him of falsifying some of the data on which he based his work on the heritability of intelligence. *ODNB*, 'Cyril Burt'. • **69.** File entry dated 16 April 1937:

'Extract from Home Office file no. D.3441 for DEUTSCH, Arnold', TNA, KV2/4428. • **70.** Minutes dated 22 April 1937, 15 June 1937, 4 Jan 1938: ibid. • **71.** Andrew and Mitrokhin, *The Mitrokhin Archive*, p. 73. • **72.** en.wikipedia.org/wiki/List_of_highest-grossing_films_in_the_Soviet_Union. • **73.** Andrew, *Defence of the Realm*, ch. 4 • **74.** Unsigned copy of letter from MI5 to Kenneth Younger, 20 June 1940; TNA, KV2/4428. • **75.** Andrew, *The Secret World*, p. 593. • **76.** Charles E. Bohlen, *Witness to History 1929–1969* (London: Weidenfeld & Nicolson, 1973), p. 34. • **77.** Harpo Marx and Rowland Barber, *Harpo Speaks!* (New York: Limelight Editions, 1988), ch. 18. En route to Moscow, Harpo travelled through Germany where Hitler had come to power earlier in the year and was horrified to witness the increasing persecution of the Jewish population: 'I had not been so wholly conscious of being a Jew since my *bar mitzvah* ... I got across Germany as fast as I could go.' • **78.** Ibid. • **79.** Ibid. Though Harpo probably failed to realise it, the Secret Service was then a department of the Treasury, whose main responsibility was for the personal security of the president; it was not involved in foreign intelligence or, so far as is known, in Roosevelt's confidential correspondence with any of his ambassadors. • **80.** In Bullitt's confidential correspondence with Roosevelt and others over many years, there is also no sign of the use of the Secret Service to deliver any of his letters. Orville H. Bullitt (ed.) *For the President – Personal and Secret: Correspondence between Franklin D. Roosevelt and William C. Bullitt*, with an introduction by George F. Kennan (Boston: Houghton Mifflin, 1972) Use of the Secret Service would have been particularly unlikely in 1933 after its failure to prevent an almost successful assassination attempt against FDR earlier in the year. • **81.** Despite the restrictions imposed on most foreign diplomats, Kent was able to acquire a car, a gun and a studio, where he took nude photographs of his NKVD-approved Russian teacher. Andrew, *Secret World*, p. 592. • **82.** Bohlen, *Witness to History*, pp. 20–21. In 1939 the new military attaché, Ivan Yeaton, was appalled by the general state of embassy security, noted that the parties frequently organised by consular staff regularly included women guests 'generously provided by the NKVD'; unpublished 'Memoirs of Ivan D. Yeaton', US Army Military History Institute, Carlisle Barracks, PA. • **83.** Wellington A. Samouce, 'I do understand the Russians', Samouce papers, US Army Military History Institute, Carlisle Barracks, PA, pp. 52–3; Andrew, *Secret World*, p. 662. • **84.** The term 'show trial' – a translation of the Russian *pokazatel'nyi protsess* (показательный процесс) – was first used by the *New York Times* Moscow correspondent, Walter Duranty. • **85.** Elizabeth A. Wood, *Performing Justice: Agitation Trials in Early Soviet Russia* (Ithaca: Cornell University Press, 2005), ch. 6; Andrew and Gordievsky, *KGB*, pp. 131–3; Julie A. Cassiday, 'Marble columns and Jupiter lights: Theatrical and cinematic modeling of Soviet show trials in the 1920s', *Slavic and East European Journal*, vol. 42 (1998), no. 4. • **86.** Jansen and Petrov, *Stalin's Loyal Executioner*, p. 207. • **87.** R. C. Tucker and S. F. Cohen (eds), *The Great Purge Trial* (New York: Grosset and Dunlap, 1965). • **88.** Interview with Sir Fitzroy Maclean, *Timewatch*, BBC2, December 1988. The episode also appears in Maclean's memoir, *Eastern Approaches*. • **89.** *New York Times*, 1 March 1938. • **90.** Andrew and Elkner, 'Stalin and foreign intelligence', pp. 71–2. • **91.** Both security failures are fully documented in Dzerzhinsky's private archive; Andrew, *Secret World*, p. 574. • **92.** Julie Fedor, *Russia and the Cult of State Security: The Chekist Tradition from Lenin to Putin* (London: Routledge, 2011), pp. 18, 190 n. 66. • **93.** Andrew and Gordievsky, *KGB*, p. 154. • **94.** Svetlana Lokhova, *The Spy Who Changed History* (London: William Collins, 2018), ch. 10. It was not for another half-century that American and British intelligence discovered the full extent of NKVD scientific and technological intelligence (S&T) collection in the United States before the Second World War. • **95.** Shirley Temple Black, *Child Star: An Autobiography* (New York: McGraw-Hill, 1988). Just over half a century later, she was to be US ambassador in Prague during the 'Velvet Revolution', which ended communist rule, and the election as President of the formerly persecuted playwright Václav Havel. • **96.** Andrew, *For the President's Eyes Only*, pp. 457–8. • **97.** Stephanie Thames, 'Code of the Secret Service', *TCM Movie Database*. • **98.** Andrew, *For the President's Eyes Only*, pp. 457–8. In 1979 Reagan was to become both the first movie star and the first fictional secret agent to be elected US President. • **99.** Sir Dermot Turing, *Codebreakers of Bletchley Park* (London: Arcturus: 2020), ch. 2. • **100.** Stephanie Thames, 'Code of the Secret Service', *TCM Movie Database*. • **101.** In 1947 Reagan was to star with the teenage Shirley Temple in *That Hagen Girl*. Temple, though she liked Reagan personally, had no doubt that it was her own worst film: Black, *Child Star*. It may also have been Reagan's. The film was included in the popular 1978 book, *The Fifty Worst Films of All Time*.

11: The Second World War

• **1.** Asa Briggs, *The History of Broadcasting in the United Kingdom*, vol. 2: *The Golden Age of Wireless* (Oxford: Oxford University Press, 1995), p. 235. In practice, almost the whole population had some access to the BBC. • **2.** Andrew, *Defence of the Realm*, pp. 172–3. • **3.** Burgess sent Deutsch an account of the meeting with Footman; Andrew Lownie, *Stalin's Englishman: The Lives of Guy Burgess* (London: Hodder & Stoughton, 2015), p. 84. • **4.** Ibid, pp. 84–5. • **5.** Ibid, p. 89. • **6.** Ibid, pp. 97–8; Andrew and Gordievsky, *KGB*, pp. 231–2. • **7.** Andrew and Mitrokhin, *The Mitrokhin Archive*, pp. 83–4. • **8.** Lownie,

Stalin's Englishman:, p.72. • **9.** The formal introduction of 'negative vetting' involved checking MI5 files for 'adverse' information on potential recruits, but not active investigation. Though it failed to inhibit Burgess and prevent his use of communist speakers during his two periods as a producer, in the early Cold War MI5 sent the BBC 'adverse' reports on about 10 per cent of its applicants. On a number of occasions, MI5 resisted requests from the BBC for more extensive vetting of its staff. Andrew, *Defence of the Realm*, pp. 396–7. • **10.** Churchill had agreed to introduce a series of BBC talks on the Mediterranean but cancelled them because of the 1938 Czechoslovak crisis: Lownie, *Stalin's Englishman*, ch. 12; Stewart Purvis and Jeff Hulbert, *Guy Burgess: The Spy Who Knew Everyone* (London: Biteback, 2016), ch. 3. • **11.** Kim Philby, *My Silent War*, paperback edn (St Albans: Granada, 1969), p. 24. • **12.** MI5 to Ministry of Information, 24 May 1939: TNA, KV 2/3774. • **13.** John Baxendale, *J. B. Priestley and English Culture* (Manchester: University of Manchester Press, 2008), ch. 5. • **14.** *Spectator*, 13 December 1940. • **15.** Andrew, *The Secret World*, pp. 625–7. • **16.** Burgess, 'Draft Suggestions for Talks on Russia', 15 July 1941, BBC Written Archives Centre, R51/520/1. • **17.** Lownie, *Stalin's Englishman*, p. 127. • **18.** TNA, KV2/3941. After the Second World War, MI5 considered Hill, then a Fellow (later Master) of Balliol College, 'one of the leading Communists at Oxford University'. • **19.** Note by John Coatman, 7 April 1941: TNA, KV 2/2175. MI5 was far more interested in Miller than in Littlewood, partly because he deserted from the army in 1940. James Smith, *British Writers and MI5 Surveillance, 1930–1960* (Cambridge: Cambridge University Press, 2013), ch. 3. • **20.** Hyde police report, 2 September 1943; TNA, KV 2/2757. • **21.** Security Service Archives; Andrew, *Defence of the Realm*, p. 270–72. • **22.** Gabriel Gorodetsky (ed.), *The Maisky Diairies: Red Ambassador to the Court of St James, 1932–1943* (New Haven: Yale University Press, 2015), p. 394. • **23.** Ibid., p.398. • **24.** Lownie, *Stalin's Englishman*, loc. 2511. • **25.** On the centenary of his birth in 2004, Rostovsky/Henri was praised in *Pravda* as 'one of the brightest and most successful Soviet secret agents to serve in Germany and the United Kingdom'. 'Moscow soirée marks birth centenary of Soviet writer-cum-spy', *Pravda*, 18 February 2004: pravdareport.com/news/science/55551-n. • **26.** This extract from Henri's talk was rebroadcast in the Radio 4 documentary 'Christmas 1941', 25 December 1981, presenter: Christopher Andrew; producer: Peter Everett. • **27.** Andrew and Gordievsky, *KGB*, pp. 337–8; Lownie, *Stalin's Englishman*, loc. 2252. • **28.** Train was also famous for his portrayal in ITMA of the dipsomaniac Colonel Chinstrap, who interpreted much of what was said to him as the offer of a drink, to which he replied with his catchphrase, 'I don't mind if I do.' • **29.** Edward Stourton, *Auntie's War: The BBC during the Second World War* (London: Black Swan 2018), pp. 234, 237. • **30.** Andrew and Mitrokhin, *The Mitrokhin*

Archive, p. 220. • **31.** Max Hastings, *The Secret War: Spies, Codes and Guerrillas 1939–1945* (London: William Collins, 2015), p. 447. • **32.** The first major international air show, at Reims in 1909, attracted almost 500,000 spectators and set the precedent for future shows with specially built grandstands, restaurants, and press facilities: centennialofflight.net/essay/Social/airshows/SH20.htm. • **33.** Christopher Draper, *The Mad Major* (Dunstable and London: Waterlow & Sons, 1962), pp. 138–40. • **34.** Ibid., p.149. pp.; 'Major Christopher Draper', n.d., TNA, KV 2/365; 'Pre-War Espionage on behalf of Germany in Great Britain', March 1942, TNA, KV 3/47; Andrew, *Defence of the Realm*, pp. 209–10. • **35.** On the US espionage trial, see ibid., p. 210. • **36.** Draper, *The Mad Major*, p. 154. • **37.** Andrew, *Defence of the Realm*, pp. 248–9; James Hayward, *Hitler's Spy: The True Story of Arthur Owens, Double Agent Snow* (London: Simon & Schuster, 2012), chs. 1–3. • **38.** TNA, KV2/448. • **39.** Andrew, *Defence of the Realm*, p. 249. • **40.** Emily Wilson, 'The War in the Dark: The Security Service and the Abwehr 1939–1944' (PhD dissertation, University of Cambridge, 2003), p. 126. • **41.** Thaddeus Holt, *The Deceivers: Allied Military Deception in the Second World War* (London: Weidenfeld & Nicolson, 2004), p. 131. • **42.** Andrew, *Defence of the Realm*, pp. 284–5. • **43.** Minutes in TNA, KV 4/63. • **44.** Masterman was studying in Germany as a postgraduate historian in August 1914, and was interned for the remainder of the war: Andrew, *Defence of the Realm*, pp. 255–6. • **45.** In the 1920s Masterman was also reputed to be the best squash player in Oxford University: 'Times Portrait Gallery: J. C. Masterman', *The Times*, 10 October 1958. • **46.** J.C. Masterman, *Bits and Pieces* (London: Hodder, 1961), p. 9. The fifty *dramatis personae* of *Marshal Ney* would have presented significant production problems. • **47.** J. C. Masterman (with an introduction by R.C. Sherriff), *Marshal Ney: A Play in Five Acts* (London: Cobden-Sanderson, 1937), pp.6-7. Sherriff's own Napoleonic drama, *St Helena*, had been premiered at the Old Vic in 1936. • **48.** *The Spectator*, 24 December 1937. • **49.** Andrew, *Defence of the Realm*, pp. 221–4. • **50.** Guy Liddell diary, 30 September 1939: TNA, KV 4/185. • **51.** J. C. Masterman, *The Double-Cross System in the War of 1939 to 1945*, paperback edn (London: Sphere Books, 1973). The italics are Masterman's. • **52.** Captain P. E. S. Finney, 're Mills' Circus', 9 April 1941: TNA, KV 4/211, s.23a; Hotel details (subsequently amended) in 'Accommodation Plan', ibid., s.38a. Nigel West, *The A-Z of British Intelligence* (London: Scarecrow Press, 2009), p. 362. • **53.** Andrew, *Defence of the Realm*, p. 258. • **54.** Kell had retired in 1940; the DG for the next year was Brigadier Oswald Allen 'Jasper' Harker. • **55.** Andrew, *Defence of the Realm*, pp. 258–9. The legal justification was presumably that any double agent attempting to assist an invading army would have been regarded as, in effect, an enemy combatant. • **56.** Adam Shelley, 'Empire of Shadows: British Intelligence in the Middle East 1939–1946' (PhD diss.,

Cambridge, 2007); Holt, *The Deceivers*. Clarke's younger brother was the screenwriter 'Tibby' Clarke (who won an Oscar for 1951's *The Lavender Hill Mob*), and he himself was a regular cinemagoer. • **57.** Michael Howard, *British Intelligence in the Second World War*, vol. 5: *Strategic Deception* (London: HMSO, 1990), p. xi. • **58.** Nigel West and Oleg Tsarev, *Crown Jewels: The British Secrets at the Heart of the KGB Archives* (London: HarperCollins, 1998), pp. 308–9. • **59.** Ibid., pp. 317–19. • **60.** Holt, *The Deceivers*, p. 43. An enquiry by Lord Gort concluded that Clarke 'seems in all other respects to be mentally stable': Wilson, 'The War in the Dark', p. 193; Nicholas Rankin, *Churchill's Wizards: The British Genius for Deception 1914–1945* (London: Faber & Faber, 2008), p. 261. • **61.** Howard, *British Intelligence in the Second World War*, vol. 5, pp. 26–7. • **62.** Ibid., pp. 55–63. • **63.** Henry Hemming, *M: Maxwell Knight, MI5's Greatest Spy Master* (London: Penguin, 2017), p. 199. • **64.** Phil Baker, *The Devil is a Gentleman: The Life and Times of Dennis Wheatley* (Sawtry, Cambs: Daedalus Books, 2009), chs 30–32. • **65.** Ibid., ch. 32. • **66.** Nicholas Rankin, *A Genius for Deception: How Cunning Helped the British Win Two World Wars* (Oxford: Oxford University Press, 2011), p. 181. When Marlene Dietrich entertained the troops in Algiers in 1944, Clarke made sure that he got to meet her personally. • **67.** Geoffrey and Natalie Barkas, *The Camouflage Story from Aintree to Alamein* (London: Cassell, 1952), p. 196. • **68.** Jasper Maskelyne, *Magic: Top Secret* (New York: Stanley Paul, 1949); cf. the more critical assessment in Peter Forbes, *Dazzled and Deceived: Mimicry and Camouflage* (New Haven & London: Yale University Press, 2009), pp. 156–9. • **69.** M. E. Clifton James, *I Was Monty's Double* (London: Hamilton and Co., 1954); Holt, *The Deceivers*, pp. 561–62, 815 • **70.** Howard, *British Intelligence in the Second World War*, vol. 5, pp. 18–19. The fullest accounts of BOVRIL/GARBO's extraordinary career are: Juan Pujol García and Nigel West, *Operation Garbo: The Personal Story of the Most Successful Spy of World War II* (1985, repr. London: Biteback, 2011) and Mark Seaman (ed.), *GARBO: The Spy who Saved D-Day* (London, PRO publications, 2004). • **71.** TNA, KV 2/1067 • **72.** TNA, KV 2/1068. • **73.** Tony Insall, *Secret Alliances: Special Operations and Intelligence in Norway 1940–1945* (London: Biteback, 2019), pp. 133–5. Obituary, John Moe, Daily Telegraph, 7 July 2001. • **74.** Howard, *British Intelligence in the Second World War*, vol. 5, pp. 55–63. • **75.** See MUTT's MI5 file: TNA, KV 2/1067. • **76.** Andrew, *Defence of the Realm*, pp. 284–5; Miranda Carter, *Anthony Blunt: His Lives* (London: Macmillan, 2001), pp. 94–5, 257. • **77.** Pujol García and West, *Operation Garbo*, introduction. • **78.** Sir Michael Howard calls their collaboration 'one of those rare partnerships between two exceptionally gifted men whose inventive genius inspired and complemented one another': Howard, *British Intelligence in the Second World War*, vol. 5, p. 231. • **79.** mi5.gov.uk/agent-garbo. On Mills's subsequent role as MI5 liaison officer in Canada in supporting GARBO's fictitious agent network, see Pujol García and West, *Operation Garbo*. • **80.** Andrew, *The Secret World*, pp. 625, 680. • **81.** Andrew, *Defence of the Realm*, p. 280; Andrew and Mitrokhin, *Mitrokhin Archive*, pp. 157–9. • **82.** Robert Hutton, *Agent Jack: The True Story of MI5's Secret Nazi Hunter* (London: Weidenfeld & Nicolson, 2018). • **83.** TNA, KV 6/118 • **84.** Duff Cooper to Petrie, 9 March 1943, 1943: TNA, KV 4/83, s.1a. Duff Cooper was so enthused by MINCEMEAT that in 1950 he published a novel based on it, *Operation Heartbreak*. As late as 10 March 1943, Guy Liddell noted in his diary that Churchill, despite his close interest in the work of SIS, Bletchley Park and SOE, still knew nothing about Security Service operations. • **85.** There are numerous surveillance records in Ivor Montagu's MI5 file: TNA, KV 2/598–600. • **86.** Russell Campbell, *Codename Intelligentsia: The Life and Times of the Honourable Ivor Montagu, Filmmaker, Communist, Spy* (Stroud: The History Press, 2018), p. 234. • **87.** British intelligence did not obtain proof of Ivor Montagu's recruitment as Agent INTELLIGENTSIA in 1940 until GRU telegrams from London were belatedly decrypted in the early 1960s: Andrew, *Defence of the Realm*, p. 379. • **88.** Campbell, *Codename Intelligentsia*. • **89.** Bevan, 'Mincemeat', n. d.: TNA, CAB 154/67/63, cited by Holt, *The Deceivers*, p. 376. • **90.** Ben Macintyre, *Operation Mincemeat* (London: Bloomsbury, 2010), ch. 2. • **91.** Holt, *The Deceivers*, p. 374; Andrew, *Defence of the Realm*, pp. 286–7. • **92.** Holt, *The Deceivers*, p. 375. • **93.** Ibid., p.374. • **94.** Andrew, *Defence of the Realm*, p. 287; Ewen Montagu, *The Man Who Never Was* (London: Evans, 1953). • **95.** MacIntyre, *Operation Mincemeat*, p. 188; John Fisher, *What a Performance: The Life of Sid Field* (London: Seeley, 1975) p. 102. The revue also featured two young solo comedians who would later team up as Morecambe and Wise: comedy.co.uk/features/comedy_chronicles/ desperately-seeking-sid. • **96.** After the kidnapping of two SIS officers at Venlo on the Dutch border early in the war, the fragmented German intelligence system had missed a wonderful opportunity to mount a major deception against the British: Andrew, *Defence of the Realm*, p. 244. • **97.** Howard, *British Intelligence in the Second World War*, vol. 5, pp. 90–92. Ian Dear and M. R. D. Foot (eds), *The Oxford Companion to the Second World War* (Oxford: Oxford University Press, 1995), p. 751. • **98.** *ODNB*, 'Ewen Montagu'. • **99.** Cholmondeley also worked on the film, though in this case as an uncredited technical advisor rather than a performer. Nigel Balchin's screenplay won a BAFTA award. Macintyre, *Operation Mincemeat*, p. 321; imdb.com/ title/tt0049471; ok.ru/video/294338562723 (the scene featuring Montagu is at 16:40). • **100.** Andrew, *Defence of the Realm*, pp. 296–7. • **101.** Holt, *The Deceivers*, p. 577; David Stafford, *Ten Days to D-Day* (London: Little, Brown, 2003), p. 307. • **102.** According to the official history of strategic deception (usually the most authoritative account), GARBO did not get through to Madrid until 6.08 a.m; Howard, *British Intelligence in the Second World War*, vol. 5, p. 185. Some other accounts claim that GARBO did not make contact until 8 a.m. • **103.** The Abwehr case officer claimed more speciously that, because GARBO's reports had left the High Command 'completely forewarned and prepared', the arrival of his warning that the Allied invasion forces were on their way to the Normandy beaches would have had little greater impact 'had it arrived three or four hours earlier': ibid. • **104.** 'Report on the Activities of the Security Service during June, 1944', 3 July 1944: TNA, KV 4/83, s.42a. • **105.** Andrew and Mitrokhin, *The Mitrokhin Archive*, pp. 165–6. • **106.** Guy Liddell diary, 21 December 1944: TNA, KV 4/185. • **107.** TNA, CAB 154/104; Wilson, 'The War in the Dark', pp. 221–6. • **108.** Andrew, *Defence of the Realm*, pp. 317–18. • **109.** Pujol García and West, *Operation Garbo*, introduction. Tomás Harris had been killed in a car accident in Majorca in 1964. GARBO died in 1988. • **110.** youtube.com/watch?v=-oFCG2K4sFo. Cyril Mills continued to provide occasional assistance to MI5 during the early Cold War. According to Peter Wright's not always reliable memoirs, MI5 equipment was sometimes moved around London in a garishly coloured Bertram Mills Circus van: Peter Wright with Paul Greengrass, *Spycatcher: The Candid Autobiography of a Senior Intelligence Officer* (paperback edn, New York: Dell, 1988), pp. 131–2).

12: Shaken not Stirred

• **1.** Andrew, *For the President's Eyes Only*, pp. 93–4; Jeffery, *MI6*, pp. 439–41. • **2.** Jeffery, *MI6*, pp. 438–43; T. J. Naftali, 'Intrepid's last deception: Documenting the career of Sir William Stephenson', *Intelligence and National Security*, vol. 3, no. 3 (1993). • **3.** Henry Hemming, *Our Man in New York: The British Plot to Bring America into the Second World War* (London: Quercus, 2019), pp. 178–80. • **4.** Bond was assisted by a 'colleague', also armed with a Remington thirty-thirty, who shot out the consulate window: 'I shot immediately after him, through the hole he had made. I got the Jap in the mouth as he turned to gape at the broken window': Ian Fleming, *Casino Royale*, Vintage edn (London: Vintage, 2012), p. 169. • **5.** This was made public during the 1945 Congressional Pearl Harbor Attack Hearings. The main Japanese naval cipher, known to the Americans as JN25b, was not broken until after Pearl Harbor. • **6.** The authorised history of GCHQ concludes that Godfrey understood SIGINT 'as well as anyone' outside Bletchley; John Robert Ferris, *Behind the Enigma: The Authorized History of GCHQ, Britain's Secret Cyber-Intelligence Agency* (London: Bloomsbury, 2020), Kindle edn, loc. 3928. • **7.** Lycett, *Ian Fleming*, paperback edn, pp. 130–1. • **8.** Hemming, *Our Man in New York*, p. 94. • **9.** In

1927 she had become the first black woman to star in a silent movie, *Siren of the Tropics*. • **10.** Melanie Zeck (2014): blog.oup.com/2014/06/josephine-baker-sensational-woman. • **11.** A. E. Hotchner (2015): smithsonianmag.com/arts-culture/ernest-hemingway-in-love-180956617. • **12.** Ean Wood, *The Josephine Baker Story* (London: Omnibus Press, 2010). • **13.** Frédéric Guelton, 'Joséphine Baker contre les Nazis: un agent de charme pour la France libre', in Fuligni, *Dans les archives inédites*; Jacques Abtey, *La Guerre secrète de Joséphine Baker* (Paris: Éditions Siboney, 1948). • **14.** Chauncey K. Robinson (2018): peoplesworld.org/article/josephine-baker-iconic-entertainer-resistance-spy-and-american-hero. • **15.** Secret report by Abtey on his missions in November and December 1940, 24 July 1943; reproduced in Fuligni, *Dans les archives inédites*, pp. 468–70. • **16.** Jacques Abtey, *La guerre secrète*. • **17.** Ibid.; Wood, *The Josephine Baker Story*, ch. 11. • **18.** Sébastien Albertelli, 'Les services secrets de la France Libre: Le Bureau central de renseignement et d'action (BCRA), 1940–1944', *Guerres mondiales et conflits contemporains*, no. 2 (2011), p. 9. • **19.** Sébastien Albertelli, *Les services secrets du général de Gaulle: Le BCRA 1940–1944* (Paris: Perrin, 2020), p. 44. • **20.** Wood, *The Josephine Baker Story*, ch. 11. • **21.** Guelton, 'Joséphine Baker contre les Nazis', p. 467. • **22.** Secret report by Commandant Alla Dumesnil-Gillet, 3 Oct. 1946; text in Fuligni, *Dans les archives inédites*, pp. 470–1. Dumesnil-Gillet offered to provide more details of Josephine's missions to anyone entitled to know them. These details, alas, are not on record. • **23.** Wood, *The Josephine Baker Story*, ch. 12. • **24.** Olivier Wieviorka, *Histoire du débarquement en Normandie: des origines à la libération de Paris, 1941–1944* (Paris: Seuil, 2007). • **25.** Hemming, *Our Man in New York*; Bill MacDonald, *The True Intrepid: Sir William Stephenson and the Unknown Agents* (Vancouver: Raincoast Books, 1998); Nicholas Cull, *Selling War: The British Propaganda Campaign Against American 'Neutrality' in World War II* (Oxford: Oxford University Press, 1995). On the Belfrage brothers, see: vault.fbi.gov/rosenberg-case/julius rosenberg/julius-rosenberg-batch-4. • **26.** Simon Callow, 'Blithe Spirit', *The Guardian*, 15 December 2007. • **27.** Barry Day (ed.), *The Letters of Noël Coward* (London: Methuen Drama, 2008), p. 375. • **28.** Ibid., pp. 407–8. • **29.** Ibid., p. 405. • **30.** *Sunday Express*, 4 Aug 1940. • **31.** nytimes.com/1942/12/24/archives/in-which-we-serve-depicting-cruel-realities-of-this-war-is.html. • **32.** Day (ed.), *The Letters of Noël Coward*, p. 403. • **33.** Ibid., p. 404. • **34.** Noël Coward Archive, ref PC 19366 (n. d., unaddressed); noelcowardarchive.com. • **35.** William Stevenson, *Intrepid's Last Case* (London: Sphere, 1984). • **36.** MacDonald, *The True Intrepid*, p. 262 • **37.** MI5 report on de Wohl, 31 August 1940: TNA, KV 2/2821, s101a. The first volume of de Wohl's MI5 file, covering his early years in Britain, does not survive. • **38.** Ibid. • **39.** Dr Felix Jay, *Traditional Astrologer*, no. 16, March 1998: skyscript.co.uk/wohl.html. • **40.** Lycett, *Ian Fleming*, p. 134. • **41.** Paul Winter,

'Fathoming the Führer: British Intelligence, Adolf Hitler and the German High Command, 1939–1945', Cambridge University PhD thesis (2009). • **42.** TNA, KV 2/2821. • **43.** The declassified BSC official history was published in 1998, with an introduction by Nigel West, as *British Security Coordination: The Secret History of British Intelligence in the Americas* (London: St Ermin's Press). • **44.** *British Security Coordination*, pp. 102–4. • **45.** Eric Maschwitz, *No Chip on My Shoulder* (London: Herbert Jenkins, 1957), pp. 83–7; Hemming, *Our Man in New York*, pp. 170–1. • **46.** bfi.org.uk/films-tv-people/4ce2b6b0 96bdo. • **47.** *New York Times*, 8 January 1945. • **48.** Hemming, *Our Man in New York*, p. 247. In the classified official history of BSC written at the end of the war, the section on the establishment of Station M immediately follows the account of de Wohl's 'triumphant' propaganda campaign in the United States. • **49.** Maschwitz, *No Chip on My Shoulder*, pp. 144–5. • **50.** Hemming, *Our Man in New York*, pp. 247–9. • **51.** Maschwitz, *No Chip On My Shoulder*, pp. 144–5. • **52.** Naftali, 'Intrepid's Last Deception', pp. 91–2, n. 26. • **53.** Ivar Bryce, *You Only Live Once: Memories of Ian Fleming* (London: Weidenfeld and Nicolson, 1984). • **54.** Andrew, *For the President's Eyes Only*, pp. 102–3. • **55.** Thomas E. Mahl, *Desperate Deception: British Covert Operations in the United States, 1939–44* (Dulles, VA: Potomac Books, 2000), p. 15. The document, marked MOST SECRET, and at that time at TNA, HS 1/333, was supplied to Mahl by Professor Nick Cull, and the author (referenced in the document as G.106) was identified to Mahl as Maschwitz by SOE Adviser Gervase Cowell. • **56.** In retrospect, Dansey's deputy in the 'Z' organisation, Kenneth Cohen, believed that 'What it achieved was very limited.' Interview by Christopher Andrew with Commander Kenneth Cohen, 19 October 1981. • **57.** John Fleet, 'Alexander Korda: Churchill's Man in Hollywood' (2018): winstonchurchill.org/publications/ finest-hour/finest-hour-179/alexander-korda-churchills-man-hollywood; Mahl, *Desperate Deception*. • **58.** Andrew, *The Secret World*, pp. 635–6. • **59.** Rhodri Jeffreys-Jones, *The Nazi Spy Ring in America: Hitler's Agents, the FBI and the Case that Stirred the Nation* (Washington DC: Georgetown University Press, 2020). • **60.** Simon Wilmetts, *In Secrecy's Shadow: The OSS and CIA in Hollywood Cinema 1941–1979* (Edinburgh: Edinburgh University Press, 2016), pp. 102–4. • **61.** *ODNB*, 'Helen MacInnes'; Gerald Highet obituary, *New York Times*, 21 January 1978. MacInnes and Highet were an inseparable couple; both became US citizens in the 1950s • **62.** Michael Smith, *The Secrets of Station X: How Bletchley Park Helped Win the War* (London: Biteback, 2011), ch. 10; bbc.co.uk/ programmes/articles/Q3lFn2vTv9JMgxX98bRhL/the-bletchley-girls-cracking-women; historyextra.com/period/second-world-war/female-codebreakers-women-bletchley-park-tessa-dunlop. • **63.** A comparison later made by several former Bletchley staff to Christopher Andrew, who had been an under-graduate member of the *Footlights*. Bill Marchant was later ambassador to

Cuba at the beginning of the Castro era and a great admirer of Graham Greene's *Our Man in Havana*. • **64.** Michael Smith, *Debs of Bletchley Park and Other Stories* (London: Aurium Press, 2015), ch. 1. • **65.** Smith, *The Secrets of Station X*, ch. 10. To celebrate VE Day, Travis and his wife Muriel (née Fry) later gave – apparently at their own expense – a fancy-dress ball for 'many hundreds' of Bletchley staff: *ODNB*, 'Sir Edward Travis'. • **66.** Ibid., 'Francis Lyall [Frank] Birch'; Turing, *Codebreakers of Bletchley Park*; biography of Birch in Bletchley Park 'Hall of Fame': bletchleypark.org.uk/cms/record_attach ments/1877.pdf. • **67.** imdb.com/name/nm0083257. • **68.** *ODNB*, 'Sir William Stephenson'; Naftali, 'Intrepid's Last Deception'. • **69.** Though none of Belfrage's doubtless lengthy KGB file has been released in Moscow, a brief extract from it (now at CCAC) was exfiltrated by Vasili Mitrokhin: Andrew and Mitrokhin, *The Mitrokhin Archive*, pp. 146, 163. Belfrage's 9-volume MI5 file, which overlaps with his FBI file, was declassified in 2015: TNA, KV 2/4004–4012. • **70.** Belfrage's former contemporary at Corpus Christi College, Cambridge, the writer Christopher Isherwood wrote in his diary after visiting him in California late in 1939: 'Belfrage had changed very much since I knew him at Cambridge. He is no longer the adroit social circumnavigator, the man-about-Europe, *the* born columnist. He is now a cut-and-dried Stalinist, conventionally cynical, a little sour.' Christopher Isherwood, *Diaries*, vol. 1 (London: Vintage, 2011), p. 64. • **71.** John Earl Haynes and Harvey Klehr, *Venona: Decoding Soviet Espionage in America* (New Haven CT: Yale University Press, 1999, pp. 110–11. • **72.** Andrew and Mitrokhin, *The Mitrokhin Archive*, pp. 146, 163. • **73.** PWE and MI5 minutes of 22 and 24 August 1944: TNA, KV 2/4004. • **74.** Report to MI5, 19 November 1945: ibid. • **75.** FBI report 'Re Cedric Belfrage, June 1947, NY 65–14603: fbi.gov/rosenberg-case/julius-rosenberg/julius-rosenberg-batch-4. • **76.** Paterson (Washington) to DG, 2 Nov. 1950: TNA, KV 2/4004. Belfrage was deported from the US in 1955 as an undesirable alien. MI5 thought it would be difficult to disprove in court his fabricated claim to have passed classified documents to the Russians on instructions from BSC and SIS. • **77.** Mark A. Bradley, *A Very Principled Boy: The Life of Duncan Lee, Red Spy and Cold Warrior* (New York: Basic Books, 2014). • **78.** Andrew, *For the President's Eyes Only*, pp. 147–50. • **79.** Jim Worsham, 'Truman, Bacall and That Photograph' (2014); prologue.blogs.archives.gov/2014/08/14/truman-bacall-and-that-photo graph. • **80.** Truman, Memorandum for the Secretaries of State, War and the Navy, 12 September 1945, Naval Aide Files, box 10, file1, Harry S. Truman Presidential Library; Andrew, *For the President's Eyes Only*, pp. 149–62. • **81.** Executive Order 9621 gave the R&A section of OSS to the State Department and transferred what remained of the espionage and counter-espionage elements to the Army as a new Strategic Services Unit

(SSU). Neither received much of a welcome: Andrew, *For the President's Eyes Only*, pp. 160–61. • **82.** Patrick McGilligan, *Backstory: Interviews with Screenwriters of Hollywood's Golden Age* (Oakland: University of California Press, 1986), p. 380 • **83.** Simon Wilmetts, *In Secrecy's Shadow: The OSS and CIA in Hollywood Cinema 1941–1979*, p. 85. • **84.** *New York Times*, 27 May 1946. • **85.** Kevin Brianton, *Hollywood Divided: The 1950 Screen Directors Guild Meeting and the Impact of the Blacklist* (Lexington: University of Kentucky Press, 2016), pp. 12–15. • **86.** Wilmetts, *In Secrecy's Shadow*, pp. 92–9. • **87.** Ibid., pp. 104–13. • **88.** *New York Times*, 16 January 1947. • **89.** Andrew, *For the President's Eyes Only*, pp. 163–8. • **90.** Rhodri Jeffreys-Jones, 'Why was the CIA Founded in 1947?', *Intelligence and National Security*, vol. 12, no. 1 (1997), pp. 26–7.

13: Cold War Intelligence and the Entertainment Business

• **1.** British intelligence too had a global reach but only a fraction of the resources of its American allies and Soviet opponents; Jeffery, *MI6*, ch. 21. • **2.** GCHQ was not acknowledged as a SIGINT agency until 1982. Even the word SIGINT remained classified. • **3.** Jonathan Rée (ed.), *A Schoolmaster's War: Harry Rée, British Agent in the French Resistance* (New Haven/London: Yale University Press, 2020): a unique compendium of Harry Rée's writings with items from family archives, commentary and chronology edited by his son Jonathan. Further documentation on Rée's wartime career in his official file: TNA, HS9/1249/3. • **4.** historic-uk.com/HistoryUK/HistoryofBritain/The-Female-Spies-Of-SOE. • **5.** Susan Ottaway, *Sisters, Secrets and Sacrifice* (London: HarperCollins, 2013), chs 4–7, 10. • **6.** Rée, *A Schoolmaster's War*, p. 207. • **7.** imdb.com/title/tt0177204. • **8.** M. R. D. Foot, *SOE in France*, new edn (London: Routledge, 2004), pp. 255–6; Peter Dixon, *Guardians of Churchill's Secret Army: Men of the Intelligence Corps in the Special Operations Executive* (London: Cloudshill Press, 2018), pp. 135–6. • **9.** Rée, *A Schoolmaster's War*, p. 207. • **10.** Ottaway, *Sisters, Secrets and Sacrifice*, p. 275. • **11.** Ibid., p. 182. • **12.** imdb.com/title/tt0177204. • **13.** Rée, *A Schoolmaster's War*, p. 136. • **14.** Harry Rée, anonymous BBC talk, April 1945: 'I didn't enjoy it [returning to France]': Rée, *A Schoolmaster's War*, p. 142. • **15.** Jules Robert to Rée, 29 July 1945; ibid, p. 142. • **16.** Fedor, *Russia and the Cult of State Secrecy*, p. 89. • **17.** Andrew and Mitrokhin, *The Mitrokhin Archive*, pp. 466–7, 469–71, 480. • **18.** Fedor, *Russia and the Cult of State Secrecy*, pp. 90–91. • **19.** Ibid., pp. 114–15. • **20.** Daniel J. Leab, *Orwell Subverted: The CIA and the Filming of 'Animal Farm'* (University Park: Pennsylvania State University Press, 2007). • **21.** Leab, *Orwell Subverted*. • **22.** Duncan White, *Cold Warriors: Writers Who Waged the Literary*

Cold War (New York/London: Little, Brown, 2019), introduction. • **23.** Leab, *Orwell Subverted*. • **24.** Graham Greene, foreword to Kim Philby, *My Silent War*, paperback edn. Philby's eclectic reading in Moscow, ordered from a Cambridge bookseller, included novels by Greene and two other former SIS officers, Somerset Maugham and John le Carré, as well as detective stories by Agatha Christie and thrillers by Patricia Highsmith: bbc.co.uk/news/magazine-14677624. • **25.** While in Britain he had taken the name Smollett. Though there was as yet no proof that Smolka was a Soviet agent, Orwell reported to the Foreign Office in 1949 that he was 'a very slimy person' and 'almost certainly [an] agent of some kind': Leab, *Orwell Subverted*, p. 152. • **26.** Michael Shelden, *Graham Greene: The Man Within* (London: Heinemann, 1994), pp. 317–21. • **27.** Joseph McBride, *Whatever Happened to Orson Welles? A Portrait of an Independent Career* (Lexington: University of Kentucky Press, 2006). • **28.** The Hollywood Ten were two directors (Herbert J. Biberman and Edward Dmytryk) and eight screenwriters (Alvah Bessie, Lester Cole, Ring Lardner, Jr, John Howard Lawson, Albert Maltz, Samuel Ornitz, Robert Adrian Scott and Dalton Trumbo). Dmytryk later turned FBI informer. The remainder were unable to return to work in Hollywood, though a number continued in the film industry abroad. Brianton, *Hollywood Divided*. • **29.** Soviet intelligence reports in Vassiliev Yellow Notebook #3: digitalarchive.wilsoncenter.org/collection/86/vassiliev-notebooks, cited by John Earl Haynes, Harvey Klehr and Alexander Vassiliev, *Spies: The Rise and Fall of the KGB in America*, pp. 449–53. The film is nowadays less highly rated. • **30.** nytimes.com/1960/05/21/archives/screen-man-on-a-stringfilm-based-on-morros-spy-career-opens.html. • **31.** John Meroney, author of the forthcoming *Rehearsals for a Lead Role: Ronald Reagan in The Hollywood Wars*, concludes that Reagan 'told the bureau what he told others publicly about communist influences in the Hollywood he knew. He didn't seek out the FBI originally; agents came to him. Moreover, he had little to tell them that the bureau didn't already know': latimes.com/archives/la-xpm-2010-dec-12-la-oe-meroney-reagan-20101212-story.html. Declassified material from Reagan's FBI file is at vault.fbi.gov/ronald-wilson-reagan. • **32.** Reagan later disapproved of the political purposes to which he believed Robeson's concert had been put. His HUAC testimony is at reaganfoundation.org/media/51313/red-scare.pdf. • **33.** The two most recent biographies of Reagan provide balanced assessments of his years in early Cold-War Hollywood: H. W. Brands, *Ronald Reagan: The Life* (New York: Doubleday, 2015); Bob Spitz, *Reagan: An American Journey* (New York: Penguin, 2018). • **34.** Brianton, *Hollywood Divided*. • **35.** Andrew, *For the President's Eyes Only*, pp. 179–80. • **36.** Christopher Hull, *Our Man Down in Havana: The Story Behind Graham Greene's Cold War Spy Novel* (London: Pegasus Books, 2019), pp. 99–100. • **37.** Greene never explicitly mentions the CIA, referring to Pyle as an officer of the OSS 'or whatever his gang are now called'. • **38.** Willmetts, *In Secrecy's Shadow*, pp. 142–59. • **39.** TNA KV 2/3822. MI5's file on Redgrave, opened in 1940, ends in 1961. • **40.** Film censors at the time, however, allowed no nudity on screen. • **41.** Marchant to Home, 10 November 1962: TNA, FO371/162408; Hull, *Our Man Down in Havana*, p. 273. No one in the British diplomatic service was better placed than Marchant to identify satirical content in intelligence reports. • **42.** *ODNB*, 'Graham Greene'. Though Greene's personal regard for Philby seems to have been genuine, Evelyn Waugh, among others, was convinced that he 'is a secret agent on our side and all his buttering up of the Russians is "cover"'. • **43.** Norman Sherry, *The Life of Graham Greene*, vol. 2 (London: Jonathan Cape, 1994), p. xiv. • **44.** Ian Fleming, *From Russia With Love*, Penguin Decades edn (London: Penguin, 2010), 'Author's Note'. • **45.** Fleming, *From Russia With Love*, Penguin Decades edn, p. 63. • **46.** On Wildprett, see Andrew and Mitrokhin, *The Mitrokhin Archive*, p. 470. • **47.** In the film version, Klebb is equally fearsome but works for SPECTRE rather than SMERSH. • **48.** Christopher Andrew, 'Introduction' to Ian Fleming, *From Russia With Love*, Penguin Decades edn. • **49.** The Spector/Lector episode probably inspired Leo Marks, former SOE cryptographer, to write the story which became the basis for the 1968 film, *Sebastian*. The film stars Dirk Bogarde as an ex-Oxford professor who runs a large, all-female 'decoding' (SIGINT) office. It was not a critical success; Bogarde himself called it 'a non-event'. Sheridan Morley, *Dirk Bogarde: Rank Outsider*, 2nd edn (London: Bloomsbury, 1999). Leo Marks's very readable memoirs, *Between Silk and Cyanide: A Codemaker's Story 1941–1945* (London: HarperCollins, 1998) are unreliable. • **50.** Fleming, *From Russia With Love*, Penguin Decades edn, p. 62. Connery had brown, not blue, eyes and no scars. • **51.** Andrew, 'Introduction', ibid. • **52.** TNA, KV 2/3384–5. • **53.** Van Gyseghem later wrote an enthusiastic tribute to *Theatre in Soviet Russia* (London: Faber and Faber, 1943). • **54.** Special Branch report, 31 October 1937: TNA, KV 2/1829. • **55.** 'Paul Robeson, American Citizen', 24 July 1947, ibid. • **56.** The Kenyan independence leader, Jomo Kenyatta, knew better. While studying in Moscow in the 1930s, he took part in a written protest at 'the derogatory portrayal of Negroes in the cultural institutions of the Soviet Union' as 'real monkeys': Andrew, *Defence of the Realm*, p. 455. • **57.** Alex Kellar (MI5) to G. N. Jackson (FO), 1 May 1950: TNA, KV 2/1829. • **58.** There are numerous examples of the surveillance in Robeson's MI5 file: TNA, KV 2/1829. • **59.** Gilbert King, 'What Paul Robeson said', *Smithsonian Magazine*, 13 September 2011. • **60.** FBI San Francisco to Hoover, 25 January 1949; vault.fbi.gov/billie-holiday/billie-holiday-part-01-of-01/view. • **61.** Johann Hari, *Chasing the Scream: The Search for the Truth about Addiction*, paperback edn (London: Bloomsbury, 2019), ch. 1. • **62.** Tallulah Bankhead to Hoover, 9 February 1949; vault.fbi.gov/billie-holiday/billie-holiday-part-01-of-01/view. Holiday was not, as she later claimed, directly involved in the telephone call to Hoover. On the affair between Bankhead and Holiday, see Joel Lobenthal, *Tallulah! The Life and Times of a Leading Lady* (New York: HarperCollins, 2004), Kindle edn, pp.409–10; Nigel Barnes, *Willow, Weep for Me: The Life of Billie Holiday*, Kindle edn (2019), pp. 327–8. • **63.** Lilian Helman, *Pentimento: A Book of Portraits* (New York: New American Library, 1973), p. 146 • **64.** Tallulah Bankhead to Hoover, 9 February 1949; vault.fbi.gov/billie-holiday/billie-holiday-part-01-of-01/view. • **65.** Barnes, *Willow, Weep for Me* • **66.** Tallulah Bankhead to Hoover, 9 February 1949; vault.fbi.gov/billie-holiday/billie-holiday-part-01-of-01/view. • **67.** Hoover to Tallulah Bankhead, 11 February 1949: ibid. • **68.** 'Tallulah and Billie'; starsandletters.blogspot.com/2017/04/tallulah-billie.html. • **69.** Billie Holiday died on 17 July 1959, aged only forty-four, from pulmonary edema and heart failure caused by cirrhosis of the liver in a hospital bed where, a month earlier, she had been arrested for drug possession. • **70.** Tony Howard, '"My Travail's history": Perspectives on the roads to "Othello", Stratford-upon-Avon 1959', *Shakespeare Bulletin*, vol. 28, no. 1 (2010), p.104. • **71.** stpauls.co.uk/history-collections/history/history-highlights/the-samson-of-song-paul-robeson-at-st-pauls-cathedral. • **72.** Robeson's first performance as Othello had been in London at the Savoy Theatre in 1930 – the first black Othello in Britain since Ira Aldridge a century earlier: ibid., p. 95. • **73.** Plans for internment were wound down during the later 1950s: Andrew, *Defence of the Realm*, pp. 405–6. • **74.** TNA, KV 2/3106–7. • **75.** John McCourt, 'Time to take Brendan Behan out of theatrical borstal', *Irish Times*, 20 July 2019. • **76.** 'Brendan Behan', [1956,] TNA, KV 2/3181. • **77.** *ODNB*, 'Brendan Behan' (by Joan Littlewood). On the CPGB leadership's bugged discussions of Theatre Workshop productions, see Smith, *British Writers and MI5 Surveillance*, ch. 3. No record survives of the discussion of *A Quare Fellow*. • **78.** David Doyle, 'English hangmen and a Dublin jail, 1923–54' (2014): law.ox.ac.uk/centres-institutes/centre-criminology/blog/2014/12/english-hangmen-and-dublin-jail-1923–54. • **79.** *The Quare Fellow*, Act II. • **80.** 'Healey Group Finance', 27 November 1956: TNA, KV 2/3181. • **81.** Intercepted letter, Behan to Barbara Niven (CPGB), 8 November 1956: ibid. • **82.** MI5 report on Brendan Behan, 11 June 1956: ibid. • **83.** FBI memorandum, 'Subject: "The Best Man" Legitimate Play. New York City, New York', 1 April 1961: J. Pat Brown, B. C. D. Lipton and Michael Morisy (eds), *Writers under Surveillance: The FBI Files* (Cambridge, MA: MIT Press, 2018), pp. 358–9. • **84.** FBI memorandum, 'Subject: James Baldwin', 7 June 1963; ibid., p. 12. • **85.** SAC New York to Hoover, 'James Arthur Baldwin. Security Matter', 18 December 1963: vault.fbi.gov/james-baldwin/James%20Baldwin%20Part%2001%20of%2002/view. • **86.** FBI

Memorandum, 'James Arthur Baldwin, Information Concerning', 20 July 1964: Brown, Lipton and Morisy (eds), *Writers under Surveillance*, pp. 18–19. • **87.** *ODNB*, 'Sir Charles Spencer Chaplin'. • **88.** TNA, KV2/3700–1. • **89.** In 2015 Clara Saint confirmed this account of Nureyev's defection: time. com/5576070/white-crow-true-story-rudolf-nureyev; news.bbc.co.uk/ onthisday/hi/dates/stories/june/17/newsid_4461000/4461353.stm. • **90.** Rudolf Nureyev, *Nureyev: An Autobiography with Pictures*, ed. Alexander Bland (London: Hodder & Stoughton, 1962), pp. 96–7. • **91.** CCAC, GBR/0014/ MITN; Andrew and Mitrokhin, *The Mitrokhin Archive*, pp. 480–81. • **92.** Victor Sheymov, *Tower of Secrets: A Real-Life Spy Thriller* (Annapolis, MD: Naval Institute Press, 1993), pp. 92–3. • **93.** CCAC, GBR/0014/MITN; Andrew and Mitrokhin, *The Mitrokhin Archive*, pp. 481–2. • **94.** Peter Finn and Petra Couvee, *The Zhivago Affair: The Kremlin, the CIA, and the Battle Over a Forbidden Book* (New York: Pantheon, 2014); Joe McGasko, 'Inside the making of Dr Zhivago' (2015): https://www.biography.com/news/doctor-zhivago-facts-50-anniversary; Nicholas Dumovic, 'Hearts and minds: The CIA as white hats in the Cold War', *International Journal of Intelligence of Intelligence and CounterIntelligence*, vol. 29, no. 1 (2016). Though *Doctor Zhivago*, unlike *Lawrence of Arabia*, won none of the major Oscars, it almost swept the board at the Golden Globe Awards – Best Film, Best Actor, Best Director, Best Screenplay, Best Music. • **95.** Elizabeth Wilson, *Mstislav Rostropovich: Cellist, Teacher, Legend* (London: Faber, 2007). • **96.** Among those dining in Corpus Hall that evening was Christopher Andrew, Fellow of the College and at that time its Director of Studies in History. • **97.** CCAC, GBR/0014/MITN; Andrew and Mitrokhin, *The Mitrokhin Archive*, pp. 7, 27–8. • **98.** bnr.bg/en/post/100515076/1969-start-of-most-successful-bulgarian-tv-series-of-all-time-at-each-kilometer. • **99.** Andrew and Mitrokhin, *The Mitrokhin Archive*, pp. 506–8; Oleg Kalugin, *Spymaster: My 32 Years in Intelligence and Espionage against the West* (London: Smith Gryphon, 1994), pp. 178–83. • **100.** Erik Jens, 'Cold War spy fiction in Russian popular culture: From suspicion to acceptance via *Seventeen Moments of Spring*', *Studies in Intelligence*, vol. 61, no. 2 (2017); cia.gov/resources/csi/ studies-in-intelligence/volume-61-no-2/cold-war-spy-fiction-in-russian-popular-culture-from-suspicion-to-acceptance-via-seventeen-moments-of-spring. • **101.** Filip Kopacevic, 'The FSB Literati: The first prize winners of the Federal Security Service literature award competition, 2006–2018', *Intelligence and National Security*, vol. 34, no.5 (2019), p. 638. • **102.** Ibid. 'Was the Soviet James Bond Vladimir Putin's role model?', 10 May 2017: bbc.co.uk/news/magazine-39862225. • **103.** Wilmetts, *In Secrecy's Shadow*, pp. 232–5. • **104.** Ibid., pp. 232–3. • **105.** Liddy's jobs in the FBI had included working as Hoover's ghost-writer. • **106.** Andrew, *For the President's Eyes Only*, pp. 384–5. • **107.** Cast list for *All The President's Men* (based on the 1974 book of the same title by

Woodward and Bernstein): en.wikipedia.org/wiki/All_the_President%27s_ Men_(film). • **108.** Though he authorised other, equally disreputable, covert action against political opponents, it is possible that Nixon did not know in advance of the Watergate break-in. • **109.** Hence, for example, the box-office success of Oliver Stone's 1991 film *JFK* described by the *Washington Post* reviewer as 'a marvellously paranoid thriller' (20 December 1991). • **110.** Tom Brokaw, 'The story behind "Deep Throat"', *NBC News*, 6 July 2005.• **111.** Felt had been case officer for the Abwehr agent, Helmut Goldschmidt, recruited by British intelligence as a double agent, codenamed PEASANT: Holt, *The Deceivers*, pp. 452–6. • **112.** Bob Woodward, *The Secret Man: The Story of Watergate's Deep Throat* (New York: Simon & Schuster, 2005), Max Holland, *Leak: Why Mark Felt Became Deep Throat*(Lawrence: University Press of Kansas, 2012).• **113.** Andrew, *For the President's Eyes Only*, pp. 386–7. • **114.** Interview with Richard Helms by Christopher Andrew, April 1992. • **115.** The most up-to-date biography of Turing is by his nephew, Sir Dermot Turing: *Prof: Alan Turing Decoded*. • **116.** Stephenson's *ODNB* entry concludes that *A Man Called Intrepid* is 'almost entirely a work of fiction'. • **117.** The records of the Petroleum Warfare Department, which make no mention of Stephenson, are in TNA, POWE 45. • **118.** The former SOE member, Jacqueline Nearne (see above), who had never met Stephenson, dismissed *A Man Called Intrepid* as absurd; Ottaway, *Sisters, Secrets and Sacrifice*, p. 275. • **119.** David Stafford, 'A myth called Intrepid', *Saturday Night*, October 1989. • **120.** John le Carré, 'Afterword' (2014) to the fiftieth-anniversary Penguin Classics edn of *The Spy Who Came in from the Cold* (London: Penguin, 2014). • **121.** William Boyd, introduction, ibid. • **122.** Le Carré, 'Afterword', ibid. • **123.** John le Carré, *Call for the Dead*, Modern Classics edn (London: Penguin, 2011), ch. 15. • **124.** Le Carré wrote later: ' ... When I came to write *Tinker Tailor Soldier Spy*, it was Kim Philby's murky lamp that lit my path': John le Carré, *The Pigeon Tunnel: Stories of My Life* (London: Penguin, 2016), pp. 30–31. *Tinker, Tailor, Soldier, Spy* was an easy winner in an unprecedented SIS public poll organised by its chief Richard Moore on World Book Day 2021 to discover le Carré's most poular novel; tweet by @ChiefMI6 on 4 March 2020. • **125.** Adam Sisman, *John le Carré: The Biography* (London: Bloomsbury, 2015), pp. 405–13. • **126.** Le Carré, *The Pigeon Tunnel*, p. 20. • **127.** Sir Richard Dearlove, speaking at the 2018 Cliveden Literary Festival: telegraph.co.uk/news/2019/09/29/ ex-mi6-chief-says-british-spies-angry-john-lecarre-making-look. • **128.** Le Carré, *The Pigeon Tunnel*, pp. 180–81. • **129.** Sisman, *John le Carré*, p. 505. • **130.** nsarchive2.gwu.edu/NSAEBB/NSAEBB438/docs/doc_50.pdf. • **131.** Anthony Lane, 'Film within a Film', *New Yorker*, 15 October 2012. • **132.** *Argo* won Oscars for Best Picture, Best Adapted Screenplay and Best Film Editing. • **133.** CCAC, GBR/0014/MITN; Andrew and Mitrokhin, *The Mitrokhin Archive*,

p. 712. • **134.** 'Russians Denounce Michael Jackson', *New York Times*, 21 June 1984; 'Enemy from the West: Jackson-mania in the USSR': michaeljackson. ru/michael-jackson-in-ussr. • **135.** The next four groups on the Komsomol list were the B-52s, Madness, the Clash and the Stranglers. Alexei Yurchak, *Everything Was Forever, Until It Was No More* (Princeton, NJ: Princeton University Press, 2005), pp. 214–15. • **136.** snopes.com/fact-check/kgb-agent-sex-pistols. • **137.** Yurchak, *Everything Was Forever*, pp. 214–15. • **138.** Clarissa de Waal, *Albania: Portrait of a Country in Transition*, 2nd edition (London: I.B.Tauris, 2014).

14: Spies in the Limelight

• **1.** Andrew, *Secret World*, pp. 752–3. • **2.** globaltimes.cn/page/202101/1212058. shtml. • **3.** Shenshen Cai, 'Contemporary Chinese revolutionary spy-themed TV serials and their uses': chinafilminsider.com/contemporary-chinese-revolutionary-spy-themed-tv-serials-and-their-uses. • **4.** Andrew Nathan, Perry Link and Liang Zhang, *The Tiananmen Papers: The Chinese Leadership's Decision To Use Force Against Their Own People* (London: Abacus, 2002). • **5.** Louisa Lim, *The People's Republic of Amnesia: Tiananmen Revisited* (New York: Oxford University Press, 2014); Andrew, *Secret World*, pp. 753–4. • **6.** Roger Faligot and Natasha Lehrer, *Chinese Spies: From Chairman Mao to Xi Jinping* (London: Hurst, 2019), p. 138. The author of the report was Raymond Nart, deputy head of the Direction de la Surveillance du Territoire (DST), regarded on both sides of the Channel as one of the ablest French intelligence officers of his generation. Though Shi admitted working later for Chinese intelligence, he never admitted being targeted on Boursicot at the outset. Tod Hoffman, a former Chinese expert in the Canadian Security Intelligence Service, reached conclusions similar to Nart's in his book, *The Spy Within: Larry Chin and China's Penetration of the CIA* (Toronto: Bev Editions, 2008), ch. 4. • **7.** Siu Leung Li, *Cross-Dressing in Chinese Opera* (Hong Kong: Hong Kong University Press, 2003). Shi was a former pupil of Mei Lanfang (1894–1961), the most famous female impersonator in Beijing Opera Xu Wei: 'Greatest operatic roles by female impersonator', *Shanghai Daily*, 28 November 2013. • **8.** Martine Azoulai, 'La véritable histoire de M. Butterfly, chanteur d'opéra et maîtresse d'un diplomate français': vanityfair.fr/culture/ecrans/story/article-mag-la-veritable-histoire-de-mbutterfly-chanteur-dopera-et-maitresse-dun-diplomate-francais/5298. On Henri M's identity, see Clive Hamilton and Mareike Ohlberg, *Hidden Hand: Exposing How The Chinese Communist Party Is Reshaping The World* (London: One World, 2020), p. 168. • **9.** Both the original six-year jail sentences and the presidential pardons given to Boursicot and Shi Pei Pu reflected the relative unimportance of the secrets betrayed by Boursicot. • **10.** Faligot and Lehrer, *Chinese Spies*, p. 139. Hamilton and Ohlberg, *Hidden Hand*, pp. 167–8. • **11.** Over the next three years, Vassall was blackmailed into supplying the KGB with far more important classified documents than those given by Boursicot to Shi Pei Pu: John Vassall, *Vassall* (London: Sidgwick & Jackson, 1975); Andrew and Mitrokhin, *The Mitrokhin Archive*, p. 523. • **12.** lemonde.fr/societe/ article/2020/07/10/deux-ex-agents-de-la-dgse-condamnes-pour-trahison-au-profit-de-la-chine_6045884_3224.html. • **13.** Andrew and Mitrokhin, *The Mitrokhin Archive*, pp. 433–4. • **14.** 'Miss KGB and images of the past', *Washington Post*, 31 October 1990; David Remnick, 'Patriot Games', *New Yorker*, 3 March 2014. • **15.** The text of the appeal of the 'State Committee for the State of Emergency' was published in *The Times* on 19 August 1991. • **16.** Mikhail Gorbachev, *The August Coup: The Truth and the Lessons* (London: HarperCollins, 1991), p. 31. • **17.** To celebrate the fall of the Berlin Wall in November 1989, Rostropovich had played Bach cello suites all night at the frontier between West and East Berlin. • **18.** Elizabeth Wilson, *Mstislav Rostropovich: Cellist, Teacher, Legend*. Wilson was a friend and former pupil of Rostropovich at the Moscow Conservatoire. • **19.** Tully Potter, 'Mstislav Rostropovich', *The Guardian*, 28 April 2007. • **20.** Yurchak, *Everything Was Forever*, ch. 6. • **21.** Richard Bienstock, 'Scorpions' "Wind of Change": The Oral History of 1990's Epic Power Ballad' (2015): rollingstone.com/music/ music-news/scorpions-wind-of-change-the-oral-history-of-1990s-epic-power-ballad-63069; Anton Bregestovski, 'Rock group meet Gorbachev', UPI, 15 December 1991: https://www.upi.com/Archives/1991/12/15/Rock-group-meet-Gorbachev/8/12692773200. • **22.** sterlewine.substack.com/p/wind-of-change-scorpions-overshadowed. • **23.** 'A son returns to remind the Russians', *New York Times*, 27 September 1993. • **24.** The only previous DG to be publicly identified was the former police chief, Sir Percy Sillitoe, in 1946. • **25.** Stella Rimington, *Open Secret: The Autobiography of the Former Director-General on MI5* (London: Hutchinson, 2001), ch. 19; Stella Rimington interview, December 2018: bigissue.com/interviews/stella-rimington-kgb-saw-us-as-extraordi nary-creatures-from-another-world. • **26.** Andrew, *Defence of the Realm*, p. 774. • **27.** Ibid, pp. 774–5; Rimington, *Open Secret*, ch. 20. • **28.** Andrew, *Defence of the Realm*, pp. 776–8. • **29.** Richard Norton-Taylor, 'The slick spymaster', *Guardian*, 20 June 1994. • **30.** Andrew, *Defence of the Realm*, p. 778. • **31.** news. bbc.co.uk/1/hi/uk/1532221.stm • **32.** Rimington revealed her fantasy of playing Octopussy at a book festival in 2011: telegraph.co.uk/culture/books/ ways-with-words/8628803/Ways-with-Words-I-would-rather-have-been-a-Bond-girl-says-Dame-Stella-Rimington.html. The heroine of the ten spy novels written by Rimington after her retirement in 1996, MI5 officer Liz Carlyle, is far less exotic than Octopussy. A condescending *Guardian* reviewer describes

Carlyle as 'pretty, single, bright ... with no personality traits worth mentioning': theguardian.com/books/2006/aug/20/crimebooks.features. • **33.** Andrew, *Defence of the Realm*, p. 730 • **34.** Andrew and Gordievsky, *KGB: The Inside Story of its Foreign Operations from Lenin to Gorbachev*. This was followed by two volumes of the top-secret KGB documents which Gordievsky had secretly supplied to SIS: *Instructions from The Centre: Top Secret Files on KGB Foreign Operations, 1975–1985* (London: Hodder & Stoughton, 1991; published in USA as *Comrade Kryuchkov's Instructions* by Stanford UP, 1993); and *More Instructions from The Centre: Top Secret Files on KGB Global Operations 1975–1985* (London/USA: Frank Cass, 1992). • **35.** Andrew, *Defence of the Realm*, section D, ch. 6. Though Cairncross, like Blunt, had secretly confessed to MI5 in 1964 and been publicly identified as a Soviet spy by the *Sunday Times* in 1979, his importance to the KGB had been underestimated. • **36.** Andrew, *Defence of the Realm*, pp. 518–21, 706–7, 760–66. • **37.** Producer: Michael Beckham; presenter: Christopher Andrew: bfi.org.uk/films-tv-people/4ce2b830d30df. Since writing and presenting the 5-part Radio 4 series, *The Profession of Intelligence*, in the early 1980s, Andrew has presented a number of radio and TV documentaries on intelligence and historical topics. • **38.** *The Fifth Man* ended with Andrew interviewing John Cairncross briefly outside his house opposite a vineyard in the French department of the Var. A microphone in Andrew's top pocket was disguised as a pen and a blanket on the back seat of a car parked nearby concealed the sound engineer who was recording the brief interview in which Cairncross essentially admitted the importance of the intelligence he had passed to Moscow from Bletchley Park in the middle of the Second World War. • **39.** Andrew and Mitrokhin, *The Mitrokhin Archive*, pp. xxxviii, 1. • **40.** Andrew, *Defence of the Realm*, pp. 182–3, 579–82. • **41.** For several years even Russian intelligence failed to realise that Mitrokhin had left Russia and continued to pay his pension. • **42.** On the collaboration, see the introduction to the paperback edition. • **43.** David Omand, *How Spies Think: Ten Lessons in Intelligence* (London: Viking, 2010), pp.109–12. • **44.** Ben Miller, 'CIA officer who directed Iraq source "Curveball"', *Washington Post*, 7 August 2015. Presentation by Colin Powell to the UN Security Council, 5 February 2003: Andrew, *The Secret World*, pp. 739–40. Ben Macintyre, 'MI6 needs an eye for a lie and a tooth for the truth', *The Times*, 7 July 2016; bbc.co.uk/news/uk-21786506. • **45.** Andrew, *Secret World*, pp. 740–41. • **46.** Tony Blair, *A Journey* (London: Hutchinson, 2010), p. 374. • **47.** Hoffman, *The Spy Within*; Wise, *Tiger Trap: America's Secret Spy War with China* (Boston: Houghton, Mifflin, Harcourt, 2011); Peter Mattis and Matthew Brazil, *Chinese Communist Espionage: An Intelligence Primer* (Annapolis, MD: Naval Institute Press, 2019). • **48.** 'Huawei: why is it being banned from the UK's 5G network?': bbc.co.uk/news/newsbeat-47041341. • **49.** Mai Jia, *Decoded*

(London: Penguin, 2014); Mai Jia, *In The Dark* (London: Penguin, 2015). • **50.** Objections to publication were raised by only two of the committee: Eric Daly, 'Decrypting Mai Jia', *Beijing Review*, 27 March 2014. • **51.** grayhawk-agency.blogspot.com/p/mai-jia.html. • **52.** Yang Min, 'Spy, abjection, and post-socialist identity: Chinese neo-spy films since 2009', *Studies in the Humanities*, vol. 44/5, nos 1–2 (2019). • **53.** In 2019 Mai suddenly announced that, though spy novels had made him famous, he would write no more: Wang Kaihao, 'Finding a new secret to success', *China Daily*, 2 April 2019. • **54.** Both copies are now in the George W. Bush presidential library. • **55.** 'Sun Tzu and the art of soft power', *The Economist*, 17 December 2011. • **56.** by Becky Sheetz-Runkle. • **57.** by Don Wade. • **58.** suntzugames.com. • **59.** See, for example: @parishilton 29 July 2017. • **60.** hollywoodreporter.com/live-feed/game-thrones-star-narrating-art-784679. • **61.** Blake Franko, 'Russia has been reading The Art of War', *National Interest*, 22 October 2016; John Gray, 'What Sun Tzu knew', *New Statesman*, 29 January 2020. • **62.** Fedor, *Russia and the Cult of State Security*, pp. 180–81. • **63.** Andrei Soldatov and Irina Borogan, *The New Nobility: The Restoration of Russia's Security State and the Enduring Legacy of the KGB* (New York: Public Affairs, 2010), ch. 9. • **64.** Robert M. Gates, *Exercise of Power: American Failures, Successes, and a New Path Forward in the Post-Cold War World* (New York: Alfred A. Knopf, 2020), p. 55. • **65.** Christopher Andrew and Vasili Mitrokhin, *The Mitrokhin Archive II: The KGB in the World* (London: Penguin, 2005), pp. 490–91; Fedor, *Russia and the Cult of State Security*, pp. 180–81. • **66.** Those who have attended services at St Sofia in recent years include, on several occasions, a member of the Cambridge Intelligence Seminar. • **67.** In 2006 Alexi II also consecrated the Church of the Holy Protomartyr and Healer Panteleimon at the FSB Central Hospital: interfax-religion.com/?act=news&div=76. • **68.** Nancy Condee, *The Imperial Trace: Recent Russian Cinema* (Oxford: Oxford University Press, 2009), ch. 2; Robert Coalson, 'Does Putin, like Lenin, see film as "most important of the arts"?' (2008): rfcrl.org/a/Putin_To_Head_Film_Council/1361814.html. • **69.** Fedor, *Russia and the Cult of State Security*, p. 153. • **70.** Filip Kopacevic, 'The FSB Literati', pp. 639–40. • **71.** Fedor, *Russia and the Cult of State Security*, p. 153. • **72.** moscsp.ru/en/nikolai-vyacheslavovich-rastorguev-i-rastorguev-tozhe-reshil.html. • **73.** Alexander Osipovich, 'Un-Hollywood: In Russia, films promote the state', *Wall Street Journal*, 9 January 2008. • **74.** Olga Mesropova, 'The Apocalypse Code', in Birgit Beumers (ed.), *Directory of World Cinema: Russia 2* (Bristol: Intellect Books, 2015). • **75.** From, notably, the British Academy of Film and Television Arts (BAFTA), the Royal Television Society, Broadcast Awards and BBC Drama Awards. • **76.** Other guest stars included Jenny Agutter, Robert Hardy, Keeley Hawes, Hugh Laurie, Matthew Macfadyen and Simon Russell Beale. • **77.**

Ben Walsh, 'Spooks: The drama with more ghosts than most', *Independent*, 8 October 2010. • **78.** Tara Conlan, 'BBC's Spooks to end after a decade', *Guardian*, 11 August 2011. • **79.** MI5 'War on Terry' (WOT) revue in June 2007; the pirates drew some inspiration from a sketch by Andy Hamilton; Andrew, *Defence of the Realm*, p. 819. • **80.** Many years after the Boer War, Kell and Baden-Powell recall some (fictitious) medical memories:

> LORD BADEN-POWELL: You remember those pills they gave us?
> SIR VERNON KELL: ... What pills?
> BADEN-POWELL: Those pills they gave us to stop us wanting women.
> KELL: ... What about them?
> BADEN-POWELL: ... I think they're beginning to work.

The part of Kell was played by Christopher Andrew. • **81.** Also very successful was the US TV *Homeland* series, based on an Israeli TV drama, running from 2011 to 2020. • **82.** Having served two terms as President, then the legal maximum, Putin was in the middle of a four-year-term as prime minister before returning to the presidency. • **83.** Shaun Walker, 'And now, viewers, it's the Anna Chapman Show', *Independent*, 23 January 2011. • **84.** abcnews.go.com/Blotter/anna-chapman-nude-playboy-nabs-political-post/story?id=12459384. • **85.** theguardian.com/world/2016/may/07/discovered-our-parents-were-russian-spies-tim-alex-foley. • **86.** Laura M. Holson, 'The Dark Stuff, Distilled', *New York Times*, 29 March 2013. • **87.** theguardian.com/tv-and-radio/2017/may/30/secrets-lies-new-cold-war-how-the-americans-became-topical. • **88.** Among the many awards won by *The Americans* was the 2018 Golden Globe for best TV drama series. In the same year, Matthew Rhys won the Emmy for outstanding lead actor in a drama series; Joe Weisberg and his collaborator, Joel Fields, won the Emmy for outstanding writing in a drama series. • **89.** Marti Peterson's recollections were placed on the CIA website in 2018, but have since been removed. • **90.** 'Bernard Émié: "Nous voulons diffuser en France l'indispensable culture du renseignement"' (2019): emilemagazine.fr/article/2019/6/25/bernard-emie-nous-voulons-diffuser-en-france-lindispensable-culture-du-renseignement; Bruno Fuligni, Le Bureau des légendes *décrypté* (Paris: L'Iconoclaste, 2018). • **91.** Ibid.; 'Ce que "Le bureau des légendes" doit à la réalité', *Vanity Fair* (France), October 2018. • **92.** Yves Trotignon, *Politique du secret: regards sur "Le Bureau des légendes"* (Paris: PUF, 2018). • **93.** Abram Belkaid, 'La gloire de l'espionnage français': monde-diplomatique.fr/mav/154/BELKAID/57758. • **94.** hollywoodreporter.com/live-feed/homeland-producers-obamas-favorite-show-327282. • **95.** Belkaid, 'La gloire de l'espionnage français'; David Smith, 'Clare Danes on the end of Homeland: "It was so nice to play such a badass"', *The Observer*, 5 April 2020. • **96.** In 2019 the Museum moved to a larger site in Washington's L'Enfant Plaza. • **97.** Maltz provided about half the total $40-million capital cost. City loans and private investors supplied the remainder. • **98.** youtube. com/watch?v=wrOtRz5E_OM. • **99.** After his five-year term, Christopher Andrew was succeeded as British board member by Stella Rimington. Now Emeritus board member, he continues to give occasional presentations in the museum. • **100.** On Kalugin's KGB operations in the United States, see Andrew, *The Secret World*, pp. 684–6. • **101.** Spyscape, a large interactive museum in New York, which gives all visitors an assessment of their espionage skills, has also proved very popular with both adults and children since opening in 2018. See reports on tripadvisor.com. • **102.** When Andrew's 'authorised' but independent history, *The Defence of the Realm*, was published in 2009, the Director-General, Jonathan Evans, wrote in a foreword: 'Writing a history for publication which covers the work of the [Security] Service up to the present day is ... one which I do not believe that any other major intelligence service anywhere in the world has attempted.' The SIS official history (Jeffery, *MI6*), published in 2010, stops in 1949. • **103.** MI5 began releasing some its oldest files in 1997. SIS policy remains not to declassify any past files. • **104.** *Daily Mail*, 3 March 2009. • **105.** TNA, KV 2/3496 • **106.** James Smith. 'The MacDonald Discussion Group: A communist conspiracy in Britain's cold war film and theatre industry – Or MI5's honey-pot?', *Historical Journal of Film, Radio and Television*, vol. 35, no. 3 (2015). • **107.** TNA, KV 2/2994. • **108.** Brian Viner, 'Herbert Lom: The odd fellow', *The Independent*, 18 December 2004. • **109.** Herbert Lom, *Enter a Spy: The Double Life of Christopher Marlowe* (London: Merlin Press, 1978). • **110.** Alan Judd, *A Fine Madness: A novel inspired by the life and death of Christopher Marlowe* (London: Simon & Schuster, 2021). This remarkable novel uses the reliable historical evidence on Marlowe's career as the basis for an imaginative reconstruction of some of what will probably never be discovered about his life and death as a spy. Judd's Thoroughgood novels (in the latest of which Thoroughgood becomes C) are the best so far published on SIS today. • **111.** Information to Christopher Andrew from one of those in the royal box. • **112.** Though the award was given for the Queen's long-term patronage of British film and TV, it was prompted by what BAFTA chairman John Willis called her performance as 'the most memorable Bond girl yet'. Julie Miller, 'Queen Elizabeth Accepts BAFTA Award for Being "the Most Memorable Bond Girl Yet"', *Vanity Fair*, 5 April 2013. • **113.** 'Why have an international movie star and filmmaker visit the CIA? ... The Agency is held accountable by Congress and scrutinized by the American people. While secrets must be kept and the clandestine nature of the CIA's work held sacred, the CIA works, where appropriate, with the film industry to combat misrep-resentations and assist in balanced and accurate portrayals.' Statement placed on CIA website in 2018 but since removed; see also: express.co.uk/entertain ment/films/983720/James-Bond-25-Daniel-Craig-CIA-visit-Central-Intelligence-Agency. • **114.** A sign over the entrance to the CIA's classified museum at Langley quotes from *The Tempest*, Act II, Scene 1: 'What's past is prologue'. Five months after Craig's visit to CIA headquarters, Christopher Andrew was invited to lecture in its main auditorium on 'The Secret History of Secret Intelligence'. • **115.** themarlowesociety.com/history. In 2013, to mark the 450th anniversary of Marlowe's birth, the Marlowe Society staged performances of all his plays and readings of his poetry. • **116.** *Spy Kids*, produced by Dimension Films, New York, was the first US film series featuring child spies. The director, Robert Rodriguez, described the first of the four films, premiered in 2001, as 'Willy Wonka meets James Bond'. Promoted as comedy family films, they feature two children who get drawn into their parents' espionage. *Guardian*, 11 April 2001. • **117.** Horowitz's other TV dramas include *Foyle's War*. The first six series, featuring Chief Superintendent Christopher Foyle, are set in Hastings during the Second World War. In the seventh and final series, Foyle works for MI5 during the Cold War. • **118.** Lucy Mangan, 'Alex Rider review – slick, silly fun with the teenage James Bond', *Guardian*, 4 June 2020. Sony production of a second Rider series began early in 2021. • **119.** In 2000 the British Film Institute put *Blue Peter* sixth in its list of the '100 Greatest British Television Programmes'. • **120.** The chair of the three judges was TV presenter Sonali Shah. • **121.** One appalling twentieth-century precedent for the use of child spies did not influence Project PETRA. During Stalin's Terror, children had been used as informers against their own families. Some developed adult levels of paranoia: Orlando Figes, *Whisperers: Private Life In Stalin's Russia* (London: Allen Lane, 2007). • **122.** The *Blue Peter* team visited Corpus Christi College, Cambridge, to see and discuss the Marlowe portrait with Christopher Andrew. • **123.** theguardian.com/media/2015/apr/09/mi5-allows-tv-cameras-inside-blue-peter-special. • **124.** cia.gov/spy-kids. • **125.** defense.gouv.fr/dgse/tout-le-site/concours-alkindi2. • **126.** francetvinfo.fr/economie/emploi/metiers/armee-et-securite/les-soldats-de-lombre-reportage-sur-les-agents-secrets-francais_4013231.html. • **127.** Syed Ali Zafar, 'The cultural industry', 30 September 2020; thenews.com.pk/print/722204-the-cultural-industry. • **128.** zingoy.com/blog/watch-uri-the-surgical-strike-full-hd-movie-online-on-zee5; Sohini Chattopadhaya, 'Bollywood's love affair with the intelligence forces', *The Hindu*, 27 April 2019. • **129.** Rebecca Ratcliffe, 'Bollywood film awards: Kashmiri spy thriller Raazi wins best picture', *Guardian*, 19 September 2019. The film was banned in Pakistan even before a general ban on Bollywood movies was introduced in 2019. There is some confusion in the film on Indian intelligence organisation. • **130.** Samrudhi Ghosh, 'London Confidential review: Mouni Roy and Purab Kohli race against time to prevent Chinese virus outbreak', *Hindustan Times*, 19 September 2020; zee5.com/global/movies/details/london-confidential/0–0-227385. • **131.** spycraftentertainment. com. • **132.** Interviewed by Christopher Andrew. • **133.** @ChiefMI6, 31 October 2020. • **134.** @ChiefMI6, 7 March 2021. Interview with Richard Moore by Tom Newton Dunn, *Sunday Times*, 25 April 2021. • **135.** @ASDGovAu, 16 March 2021. • **136.** @GCHQ, 13 August 2020. • **137.** @CIA, 14 February 2021. The tweet produced 9,454 'likes' and 3,135 retweets. • **138.** @GCHQ, 14 February 2021. • **139.** @ChiefMI6, 14 December 2020. • **140.** @ChiefMI6, 4 March 2021. • **141.** sis.gov.uk/explore-careers.html. • **142.** @ChiefMI6, 19 February 2021. McKellen, who at the age of 81 was in rehearsals for his ground-breaking 'age blind' performance as Hamlet, retweeted the video. At the time of writing he has four million followers on Twitter; Richard Moore has 107,300. • **143.** @GCHQ, 23 March 2021. https://www.gchq.gov.uk/news/the-turing-challenge. • **144.** @ChiefMI6, 28 February 2021. • **145.** https://www.imdb.com/title/tt0113189/characters/nm0001132 • **146.** Ewen MacAskill, 'James Bond would not get job with real MI6, says spy chief', *Guardian*, 8 December 2016. • **147.** Interview with Sir Alex Younger by Roula Khalaf, *Financial Times*, 30 September 2020. • **148.** Sir Richard Dearlove, 'What MI6 really thought of John le Carré', *Daily Telegraph*, 14 December 2020. • **149.** @ChiefMI6, 1 October 2020.

Bibliography of Publications

All archival and most internet sources (as of January 2021) are identified in the Notes

Addison, Joseph, *Delphi Complete Works of Joseph Addison* (Hastings: Delphi Classics, 2017)

Akkerman, Nadine, *Invisible Agents: Women and Espionage in Seventeenth-Century Britain* (Oxford: Oxford University Press, 2018)

Albertelli, Sébastien, 'Les services secrets de la France Libre: Le Bureau central de renseignement et d'action (BCRA), 1940–1944', *Guerres mondiales et conflits contemporains*, no. 2 (2011)

—, *Les services secrets du général de Gaulle: Le BCRA 1940–1944* (Paris: Perrin, 2020)

Aldgate, Anthony and Richards, Jeffrey, *Britain Can Take It: British Cinema in the Second World War* (London, Basil Blackwell, 1986)

Aldrich, Richard J. and Cormac, Rory, *The Black Door: Spies, Secret Intelligence and British Prime Ministers* (London: William Collins, 2016)

Alford, Stephen, *The Watchers: A Secret History of the Reign of Elizabeth I* (London: Allen Lane, 2012)

Allen, Nicholas, 'Imagining the Rising', in Nicholas Grene and Chris Morash (eds), *The Oxford Handbook of Modern Irish Theatre* (Oxford: Oxford University Press, 2016)

Anderson, Emily (ed. & trans.), *The Letters of Beethoven* (London: Macmillan, 1961), vol. 2

Anderson, Nancy K. (ed.), *Pushkin: The Little Tragedies* (New Haven and London: Yale University Press, 2000)

Andrew, Christopher, *Théophile Delcassé and the Making of the Entente Cordiale* (London: Macmillan, 1968)

—, 'Déchiffrement et diplomatie: Le cabinet noir du Quai d'Orsay sous la Troisième République', *Relations Internationales*, no. 5 (1976)

—, 'Codebreakers and Foreign Offices: The French, British and American experience', in Christopher Andrew and David Dilks (eds), *The Missing*

Dimension: Governments and Intelligence Communities in the Twentieth Century (London: Palgrave, 1984)

—, *Secret Service: The Making of the British Intelligence Community*, 3rd edn (London: Sceptre, 1991)

—, *For the President's Eyes Only: Secret Intelligence and the American Presidency from Washington to Bush* (London: HarperCollins, 1995)

—, 'Casement and British Intelligence', in Mary E. Daly (ed.), *Roger Casement in Irish and World History* (Dublin: Royal Irish Academy, 2005)

—, *The Defence of the Realm: The Authorized History of MI5*, rev. paperback edn (London: Penguin Books, 2010)

—, *The Secret World: A History of Intelligence* (London: Allen Lane, 2018)

— and Julie Elkner, 'Stalin and foreign intelligence', in Harold Shukman (ed.), *Redefining Stalinism* (London: Frank Cass, 2003)

— and Oleg Gordievsky, *KGB: The Inside Story of Its Foreign Operations from Lenin to Gorbachev* (London: Sceptre, 1991)

— and Oleg Gordievsky (eds), *Instructions from the Centre: Top Secret Files on KGB Foreign Operations, 1975–1985* (London: Hodder & Stoughton, 1991); slightly revised US edition published as *Comrade Kryuchkov's Instructions: Top Secret Files on KGB Foreign Operations, 1975–1985* (Stanford, Calif.: Stanford University Press, 1993)

— and Vasili Mitrokhin, *The Mitrokhin Archive: The KGB in Europe and the West* (London: Allen Lane, 1999)

—, *The Mitrokhin Archive II: The KGB and the World* (London: Allen Lane, 2005)

Andrieux, Louis, *Souvenirs d'un préfet de police* (Paris: J. Rouff, 1885)

Atkinson, Rick, *The British are Coming: The War For America, 1775–1777* (London: William Collins, 2019)

Aubrey, Philip, *Mr Secretary Thurloe: Cromwell's Secretary of State* (London: Athlone Press, 1990)

Backscheider, Paula A., *Daniel Defoe: His Life* (Baltimore: Johns Hopkins University Press, 1989)

Baden-Powell, Sir Robert [later Baron], *My Adventures as a Spy* (London: C. Arthur Pearson, 1925)

Baker, Nicholson, 'The greatest liar?', *Columbia Journalism Review*, July–Aug. 2009

Baker, Phil, *The Devil is a Gentleman: The Life and Times of Dennis Wheatley* (Sawtry: Daedalus Books, 2009)

Bankhead, Tallulah, *Tallulah: My Autobiography* (New York: Harper & Brothers, 1952)

Barkas, Geoffrey and Natalie, *The Camouflage Story from Aintree to Alamein* (London: Cassell, 1952)

Barnes, Nigel, *Willow, Weep for Me: The Life of Billie Holiday*, Kindle edn (2019)

Bate, Jonathan, *Radical Wordsworth: The Poet who Changed the World* (London: William Collins, 2020)

Battestin, M.C. and R. R., *Henry Fielding: A Life*, new edn (London: Routledge, 1993)

Baxendale, John, *J. B. Priestley and English Culture* (Manchester: University of Manchester Press, 2008)

Bazeries, Étienne, and Burgaud E., *Le Masque de fer: Révélations de la correspondance chiffrée de Louis XIV* (Paris: Firmin, Didot, 1893)

Beasley, Rebecca and Bullock, Philip Ross (eds), *Russia in Britain, 1880–1940: From Melodrama to Modernism* (Oxford: Oxford University Press, 2013)

Beeley, Philip and Scriba, Christoph J. (eds), *The Correspondence of John Wallis (1616–1703)*, 6 vols (Oxford: Oxford University Press, 2003–)

Bellos, David, *The Novel of the Century: The Extraordinary Adventure of 'Les Misérables'* (London: Particular Books, 2017)

Bély, Lucien, *Espions et ambassadeurs au temps de Louis XIV* (Paris: Fayard, 1990)

—, *Les Secrets de Louis XIV: Mystères d'État et pouvoir absolu* (Paris: Tallandier, 2013)

Berry, Herbert, 'Playhouses', in Arthur F. Kinney (ed.), *A Companion to Renaissance Drama* (Oxford: Blackwell, 2000)

Bevington, David and Rasmussen, Eric (eds), *Christopher Marlowe, Dr Faustus: The A and B Texts (1604, 1616)*, parallel text edition (Manchester: Manchester University Press, 2014)

Bezio, Kristin M. S., '"Munday I sweare shalbee a hollidaye": The politics of Anthony Munday, from anti-Catholic spy to civic pageanteer (1579–1630)', *Études Anglaises*, vol. 71, no. 4 (2018)

Birch, Frank: *This Freedom of Ours* (Cambridge: Cambridge University Press, 1937)

—, Knox, Dilly and Mackeson, G. P., with introductions by Mavis Batey and Edward Wakeling, *Alice in I.D.25: A Codebreaking Parody of Alice's Adventures in Wonderland* (Stroud: Pitkin Publishing for the Bletchley Park Trust, 2015)

Birch, Thomas (ed.), *A Collection of the State Papers of John Thurloe* (London: Printed for the executor of F. Gyles, 1742): british-history.ac.uk/search/series/thurloe-papers

Black, Joseph L. (ed.) *The Martin Marprelate Tracts* (Cambridge: Cambridge University Press, 2008)

—, 'The Marprelate controversy', in Andrew Hadfield (ed.), *The Oxford Handbook of English Prose 1500–1640* (Oxford: Oxford University Press, 2013)

Black, Shirley Temple, *Child Star: An Autobiography* (New York: McGraw Hill, 1988)

Blair, Tony, *A Journey* (London: Hutchinson, 2010)

Blanc, André, *F. C. Dancourt, 1661–1725: la Comédie française à l'heure du soleil couchant* (Paris: Editions Jean-Michel Place, 1984)

Bloom, Harold (ed.), *William Shakespeare's As You Like It* (Philadelphia: Chelsea House, 2004)

Bogar, Thomas A., *American Presidents Attend the Theatre: The Playgoing Experiences of Each Chief Executive* (Jefferson, NC: McFarland & Co., 2006)

—, *Backstage at the Lincoln Assassination: The Untold Story of the Actors and Stagehands at Ford's Theatre* (Washington, DC: Regnery History, 2013)

Boghardt, Thomas, *Spies of the Kaiser: German Covert Operations in Britain during the First World War Era* (Basingstoke: Palgrave Macmillan, 2004)

Bohlen, Charles E., *Witness to History, 1929–1969* (London: Weidenfeld & Nicolson, 1973)

Botica, Allan Richard, 'Audience, Playhouse and Play in Restoration Theatre, 1660–1710', DPhil thesis, Oxford University (1986)

Boyd, Belle, *Belle Boyd, in Camp and Prison*, 2 vols (London: Saunders, Otley and Co., 1865)

Boyle, David, *Blondel's Song: The Capture, Imprisonment and Ransom of Richard the Lionheart* (London: Penguin, 2006)

Brands, H. W., *Ronald Reagan: The Life* (New York: Doubleday, 2015)

Brendon, Piers, *Eminent Edwardians* (London: Andre Deutsch, 1979)

Brianton, Kevin, *Hollywood Divided: The 1950 Screen Directors Guild Meeting and the Impact of the Blacklist* (Lexington: University of Kentucky Press, 2016)

Briggs, Asa, *The History of Broadcasting in the United Kingdom*, vol. 2: *The Golden Age of Wireless* (Oxford: Oxford University Press, 1995)

Britland, Karen, *Drama at the Courts of Queen Henrietta Maria* (Cambridge: Cambridge University Press, 2006)

British Security Coordination: The Secret History of British Intelligence in the Americas, with introduction by Nigel West (London: St Ermin's Press, 1998)

Brown, J. Pat; Lipton, B. C. D.; and Morisy, Michael (eds), *Writers under Surveillance: The FBI Files* (Cambridge, Mass.: MIT Press, 2018),

Brown, Malcolm (ed.), *Lawrence of Arabia: The Selected Letters* (London: Little Books, 2005)

Bryce, Ivar, *You Only Live Once: Memories of Ian Fleming* (London: Weidenfeld and Nicolson, 1984)

Bullitt, Orville H. (ed.) *For the President – Personal and Secret: Correspondence between Franklin D. Roosevelt and William C. Bullitt*, with an introduction by George F. Kennan (Boston: Houghton Mifflin, 1972)

Burke, David, *The Lawn Road Flats: Spies, Writers and Artists*, with introduction by Christopher Andrew (Woodbridge: Boydell & Brewer, 2014)

Burns, Edward (ed.), *King Henry VI, Part 1*, The Arden Shakespeare, Series 3 (London: Bloomsbury, 2000)

Burrows, Simon, 'The Chevalier d'Eon, media manipulation and the making of an eighteenth-century celebrity', in Simon Burrows, Jonathan Conlin, Russell Goulbourne and Valerie Mainz (eds), *The Chevalier d'Eon and His Worlds: Gender, Espionage and Politics in the Eighteenth Century* (London: Continuum, 2010)

Burwick, Frederick, *Romanticism: Keywords* (Hoboken, NJ: Wiley-Blackwell, 2015)

—, 'The Borderers (1796–1842)', in Richard Gravil and Daniel Robinson (eds), *The Oxford Handbook of William Wordworth* (Oxford: Oxford University Press, 2015)

Cairncross, John, *The Enigma Spy: An Autobiography* (London: Century, 2007)

Cameron, W. J. (ed.), *New Light on Aphra Behn* (Auckland: Wakefield Press, 1961)

Campbell, Russell, *Codename Intelligentsia: The Life and Times of the Honourable Ivor Montagu, Filmmaker, Communist, Spy* (Stroud: The History Press, 2018)

Carlyle, Thomas (ed.), *Oliver Cromwell's Letters and Speeches*, 4 vols (Leipzig: Bernhard Tauchnitz, 1861)

Carter, Miranda, *Anthony Blunt: His Lives* (London: Macmillan, 2001)

Casanova, Jacques (trans. Arthur Machen) *Memoirs of Jacques Casanova de Seingalt, 1725–1798* [Reproduction of the unabridged 1894 London edition] (Frankfurt: Outlook Verlag, 2018)

Cassiday, Julie A., 'Marble columns and Jupiter lights: Theatrical and cinematic modeling of Soviet show trials in the 1920s', *Slavic and East European Journal*, vol. 42, no. 4 (1998)

—, *The Enemy on Trial: Early Soviet Courts on Stage and Screen* (DeKalb, Ill.: Northern Illinois University Press, 2000)

Central Intelligence Agency, *Intelligence in the Civil War* (Washington, DC: Central Intelligence Agency, 2007)

Chambers, David Ian, 'The past and present state of Chinese intelligence historiography', *Studies in Intelligence*, vol. 56, no. 3 (2012)

Chambers, E. K., *The Elizabethan Stage*, 4 vols (Oxford: Clarendon Press, 1923),

Chance, J. F., 'The "Swedish Plot" of 1716–17', *English Historical Review*, vol. 18 (1903)

Chase, Philander D. (ed.), *Papers of George Washington: Revolutionary War Series*, vol. 1 (Charlottesville and London: University Press of Virginia, 1985)

Choudhury, Mita, *Interculturalism and Resistance in the London Theater, 1660–1800: Identity, Performance, Empire* (Lewisburg, Pa.: Bucknell University Press, 2000)

Christen, William J., *Pauline Cushman: Spy of the Cumberland* (Edinburgh: Edinburgh University Press, 2006)

Christie, Ian, *Robert Paul and the Origins of British Cinema* (Chicago: University of Chicago Press, 2019)

Churchill, W. S., *The World Crisis*, 5 vols, vol. 1: *1911–1914*; vol. 2: *1915* (London: Thornton Butterworth, 1923)

—, *My Early Life* (London: Eland, 2000 [first publ. 1930])

—, *The Second World War*, 6 vols, vol. 2: *Their Finest Hour*; vol. 5: *Closing the Ring* (London: Penguin Books, 2005 [first publ. 1949; 1951])

Clarendon, Edward Hyde, Earl of, *The History of the Rebellion and Civil Wars in England* (Oxford: Oxford University Press, 1843 [first publ. 1702–4])

Clark, D. M., *The Rise of the British Treasury* (New Haven: Yale University Press, 1960)

Claydon, Tony, *William III and the Godly Revolution* (Cambridge: Cambridge University Press, 2004)

Clinton, Bill, *My Life* (London: Arrow Books, 2005)

Cobban, Alfred, *A History of Modern France*, 2 vols (Harmondsworth: Penguin Books, 1961)

Combe, Kirk, 'Making monkeys of important men: Performance satire and Rochester's "Alexander Bendo's Brochure"', *Journal for Early Modern Cultural Studies*, vol. 12, no. 2 (2012)

Comentale, Edward P.; Watt, Stephen; and Willman, Skip (eds), *Ian Fleming and James Bond: The Cultural Politics of 007* (Bloomington: Indiana University Press, 2005)

Condee, Nancy, *The Imperial Trace: Recent Russian Cinema* (Oxford: Oxford University Press, 2009)

Conley, John, *The Suspicion of Virtue: Women Philosophers in Neoclassical France* (Ithaca, NY: Cornell University Press, 2002)

Conlin, Jonathan, 'Wilkes, the Chevalier d'Eon and "the dregs of liberty": An Anglo-French Perspective on Ministerial Despotism', *English Historical Review*, vol. 120 (2005)

—, 'The strange case of the Chevalier d'Eon', *History Today*, vol. 60, no. 4 (2010)

Cook, Andrew, *M: MI5's First Spymaster* (London: Tempus, 2002)

Coste, Maurice, *Souvenirs d'avant le déluge, 1870–1914* (Paris: Perrin, 1927)

Coward, Noël, *Autobiography* [a combination of *Present Indicative* (1937), *Future Indefinite* (1954) and the uncompleted *Past Conditional*] (London: Methuen, 1986)

Craig, Mary W., *A Tangled Web: Mata Hari: Dancer, Courtesan, Spy* (Stroud: The History Press, 2017)

Cressy, David, *Dangerous Talk: Scandalous, Seditious and Treasonable Speech in Pre-Modern England* (Oxford: Oxford University Press, 2010)

Cruikshanks, Eveline (ed.), *Ideology and Conspiracy: Aspects of Jacobitism, 1689–1759* (Edinburgh: John Donald, 1982)

— and Erskine-Hill, Howard, *The Atterbury Plot* (Basingstoke: Palgrave Macmillan, 2004)

Cull, Nicholas, *Selling War: The British Propaganda Campaign Against American 'Neutrality' in World War II* (Oxford: Oxford University Press, 1995)

Cusack, George, *The Politics of Identity in Irish Drama: W. B. Yeats, Augusta Gregory and J. M. Synge* (London: Routledge, 2009)

Daly, Raymond, *Celtic and Ireland in Song and Story* (Kilcock: Studio Print, 2008)

Daudet, Ernest, *Police politique: Chronique des temps de la restauration, d'après les rapports d'agents secrets et les papiers du cabinet noir, 1815–20* (Paris: Plon-Nourrit, 1912)

Davidson, Ian, *Voltaire: A Life* (London: Profile Books, 2010)

Day, Barry (ed.), *The Letters of Noël Coward* (London: Methuen Drama, 2008)

Dear, I. C. B., and Foot, M. R. D. (eds.), *The Oxford Companion to the Second World War* (Oxford: Oxford University Press, 1995)

De La Hodde [Delahodde], Lucien, *The Cradle of Rebellions: A History of the Secret Societies of France*, facsimile edn (Charleston, SC: Nabu Press, 2012)

Denniston, A. G., 'The Government Code and Cypher School between the wars', in Christopher Andrew (ed.), *Codebreaking and Signals Intelligence* (London: Frank Cass, 1986)

Dickie, Simon, 'Fielding's rape jokes', *The Review of English Studies*, vol. 61, no. 251 (2010).

Dictionnaire de biographie française, sous la direction de J. Balteau, A. Rastoul et M. Prévost, avec le concours de nombreux collaborateurs (Paris: Letouzey et Ané, 1929–)

Dillon, Matthew, *Omens and Oracles: Divination in Ancient Greece* (London: Routledge, 2017)

Dixon, Peter, *Guardians of Churchill's Secret Army: Men of the Intelligence Corps in the Special Operations Executive* (London: Cloudshill Press, 2018)

Donaldson, Ian, *Ben Jonson: A Life* (Oxford: Oxford University Press, 2011)

Donohue, Joseph (ed.), *The Cambridge History of British Theatre*, vol. 2 (Cambridge: Cambridge University Press, 2004)

Downer, Martyn, *The Sultan of Zanzibar: The Bizarre World and Spectacular Hoaxes of Horace de Vere Cole* (London: Black Spring Press, 2010)

Downes, Kerry, *Sir John Vanbrugh: A Biography* (London: Sidgwick & Jackson, 1987)

Downie, J. A., 'Secret Service payments to Daniel Defoe, 1710–1714', *The Review of English Studies*, vol. 30 (1979)

—, *A Political Biography of Henry Fielding* (London: Routledge, 2009)

Draper, Christopher, *The Mad Major* (Dunstable and London: Waterlow & Sons, 1962)

Dugdale, Blanche E. C., *Balfour: A Life of Arthur James Balfour*, 2 vols. (London: Hutchinson, 1936–7)

Dukes, Paul, *Red Dusk and the Morrow. Adventures and Investigations in Red Russia* (London: Williams and Norgate, 1922)

—, *The Story of 'ST 25': Adventure and Romance in the Secret Intelligence Service in Red Russia* (London: Cassell, 1938)

—, *The Yoga of Health, Youth, and Joy: A Treatise on Hatha Yoga Adapted to the West* (London: Cassell, 1960)

Dulles, Allen W., *The Craft of Intelligence* (London: Weidenfeld & Nicolson, 1963)

Dumas, Alexandre, *Histoire de la vie politique et privée de Louis-Philippe* (Paris: Dufour et Mulat, 1852)

Dumovic, Nicholas, 'Hearts and minds: The CIA as white hats in the Cold War', *International Journal of Intelligence and CounterIntelligence*, vol. 29, no. 1 (2016)

Dunlap, William, *A History of the American Theatre During the Revolution and After* (Champagne: University of Illinois Press, 2005 [first publ. 1832])

Dunn, Dennis J., *Caught between Roosevelt and Stalin: America's Ambassadors to Moscow* (Lexington: University Press of Kentucky, 1998)

Dunning, Chester, 'The tragic fate of Pushkin's comedy', in Alexander Dolinin (ed.), *The Uncensored Boris Godunov : The Case for Pushkin's Original Comedy, with Annotated Text and Translation* (Madison: University of Wisconsin Press, 2006)

—, 'The Tsar's red pencil: Nicholas I and censorship of Pushkin's "Boris Godunov"', *Slavic and East European Journal*, vol. 54, no. 2 (2010)

— et al., *The Uncensored Boris Godunov: The Case for Pushkin's Original Comedy* (Madison: University of Wisconsin Press, 2006)

Dutton, Richard, *Shakespeare's Theatre: A History* (Hoboken, NJ: Wiley-Blackwell, 2018),

Eisenhower, Dwight D., *Crusade in Europe* (New York: Doubleday, 1948)

Ekberg, Carl J., 'From Dutch to European War: Louis XIV and Louvois are tested', *French Historical Studies*, vol. 8, no. 3 (1974)

Elkner, Julie, *Russia and the Cult of State Security: The Chekist Tradition, from Lenin to Putin* (London: Routledge, 2011)

Ellis, Frank H. (ed.), *John Wilmot, Earl of Rochester: Selected Works* (London: Penguin, 2004)

Ellis, Kenneth, *The Post Office in the Eighteenth Century: A Study in Administrative History* (London: Oxford University Press, 1958)

Émile-Zola, Brigitte and Pagès, Alain, *Lettres à Jeanne Rozerot: 1892–1902* (Paris: Gallimard, 2004)

Emsley, Clive, 'The Home Office and its sources of information and investigation 1791–1801', *English Historical Review*, vol. 94 (1979)

Escholier, Raymond, *Un amant de génie, Victor Hugo: Lettres d'amour et carnets inédits* (Paris: Fayard, 1979)

Faligot, Roger and Lehrer, Natasha, *Chinese Spies: From Chairman Mao to Xi Jinping* (London: Hurst, 2019)

Feingold, Mordechai, 'The reluctant martyr: John Hart's English mission', *Journal of Jesuit Studies*, vol. 6 (2019)

Ferris, John Robert, *Behind the Enigma: The Authorized History of GCHQ, Britain's Secret Cyber-Intelligence Agency* (London: Bloomsbury, 2020)

Figes, Orlando, *Whisperers: Private Life in Stalin's Russia* (London: Allen Lane, 2007)

Finberg, A. J. (ed.), *Vertue Note Books, I*, Walpole Society, vol. 18 (Oxford: Oxford University Press, 1930)

Finn, Peter and Couvee, Petra, *The Zhivago Affair: The Kremlin, the CIA, and the Battle over a Forbidden Book* (New York: Pantheon, 2014)

Fisher, John, *What a Performance: The Life of Sid Field* (London: Seeley, 1975)

Fitzgerald, Penelope, *The Knox Brothers* (London: Macmillan, 1977)

Fitzpatrick, John C. (ed.), *The Writings of George Washington* (Washington, DC: US Government Printing Office, 1931–44)

Fleming, Ian, *From Russia With Love*, Penguin Decades edn (London: Penguin, 2010)

Flexner, James T., *George Washington: The Forge of Experience (1732–1775)* (London: Leo Cooper, 1973)

Flower, Michael Attyah, *The Seer in Ancient Greece*, Kindle edn (Berkeley and Los Angeles: University of California Press, 2008)

Foakes, R. A. and Bickett, R. T., *Henslowe's Diary* (Cambridge: Cambridge University Press, 1961)

Foot, M. R. D., *SOE in France*, new edn (London: Routledge, 2004)

Forbes, Peter, *Dazzled and Deceived: Mimicry and Camouflage* (New Haven and London: Yale University Press, 2009)

Foss, Roger, *Till the Boys Come Home: How British Theatre Fought the Great War* (London: The History Press, 2018)

Foster, R. F. W. *B.Yeats: A Life*, vol. 2: *The Arch-Poet, 1915–1939* (Oxford: Oxford University Press, 2003

—, *Vivid Faces: The Revolutionary Generation in Ireland 1890–1923*, paperback edn (London: Penguin, 2015)

Fowler, Robert (ed.), *The Cambridge Companion to Homer* (Cambridge: Cambridge University Press, 2004)

Franko, Blake, 'Russia has been reading The Art of War', *National Interest*, 22 October 2016

Fraser, Antonia, *King Charles II* (London: Weidenfeld and Nicolson, 1979)

Fraser, Peter, *The Intelligence of the Secretaries of State and Their Monopoly of Licensed News, 1660–1688* (Cambridge: Cambridge University Press, 1956)

Freedman, David, *The Last Days of Alfred Hitchcock. A Memoir Featuring the Screenplay of 'Alfred Hitchcock's The Short Night'* (New York: The Overlook Press, 1999)

Fuligni, Bruno, *La Police des écrivains*, 2nd edn (Paris: Editions Horay, 2011)

—, (ed.), *Dans les archives inédites des services secrets: Un siècle d'espionnage français (1871–1989)* (Paris: Gallimard, 2014)

—, *Mata Hari: Les vies insolentes de l'agent H21* (Paris: Gallimard, 2017)

—, *Le Bureau des légendes décrypté* (Paris: L'Iconoclaste, 2018)

Gates, Robert M., *Exercise of Power: American Failures, Successes, and a New Path Forward in the Post-Cold War World* (New York: Alfred A. Knopf, 2020)

Gatrell, Vic, *City of Laughter: Sex and Satire in Eighteenth-Century London* (London: Atlantic Books, 2006)

Genêt, Stéphane, *Les Espions des lumières: Actions secrètes et espionnage militaire au temps de Louis XV* (Paris: Ministère de la Défense, 2013)

George, M. Dorothy, *Catalogue of Political and Personal Satires in the British Museum*, vol. 7 (1942), vol. 9 (1949)

Getty, J. Arch, and Naumov, Oleg V. (eds), *The Road to Terror: Stalin and the Self-Destruction of the Bolsheviks, 1932–1939* (New Haven, Conn.: Yale University Press, 2002)

Gilbert, Martin, *Winston S. Churchill*, 8 vols (London: Heinemann, 1966–88); vol. 3: *The Challenge of War, 1914–1916* (1971); vol. 6: *Finest Hour, 1939–1941* (1983)

Gillespie, David, *Early Soviet Cinema: Innovation, Ideology and Propaganda* (London: Wallflower, 2000)

Gioe, David, 'The Anglo-American Special Intelligence Relationship: Wartime Causes and Cold War Consequences, 1940–63', PhD thesis (University of Cambridge, 2014)

Goldstein, Robert Justin, 'Introduction' and 'France', in Robert Justin Goldstein (ed.), *The Frightful Stage: Political Censorship of the Stage in Nineteenth-Century Europe* (New York: Berghahn Books, 2009)

Gorbachev, Mikhail, *The August Coup: The Truth and the Lessons* (London: HarperCollins, 1991)

Gordievsky, Oleg, *Next Stop Execution* (London: Macmillan, 1995)

Gorodetsky, Gabriel (ed.), *The Maisky Diaries: Red Ambassador to the Court of St James's 1932–1943* (New Haven: Yale University Press, 2015)

Graham, Winston, *The Spanish Armadas* (London: Pan Macmillan, 2003)

Graves, Robert and Liddell Hart, Basil (eds), *T. E. Lawrence, Letters to His Biographers*, single-vol. edn (London: Cassell, 1963)

Green, Julius, *Agatha Christie: A Life in Theatre* (London: HarperCollins, 2018)

Greenblatt, Stephen, *Will in the World: How Shakespeare Became Shakespeare* (London: Bodley Head, 2016)

Greenwall, Harry J., *The Strange Life of Willy Clarkson: An Experiment in Biography* (London: J. Long, 1936)

Gregory, Lady, *Selected Plays of Lady Gregory* (Gerrards Cross: Colin Smythe Ltd, 1983)

Griffith, Samuel B. (ed. and trans.), *Sun Tzu: The Art of War*, rev. edn (Oxford: Oxford University Press, 1971)

— (ed. and trans.), *The Illustrated Art of War* (Oxford: Oxford University Press, 2005)

Guillemin, Henri, *Hugo et la sexualité* (Paris: Gallimard, 1954).

Guillot, Catherine, 'Richelieu et le théâtre', *Transversalités*, no. 1 (2011)

Hadfield, Andrew, *Lying in Early Modern English Culture: From the Oath of Supremacy to the Oath of Allegiance* (Oxford: Oxford University Press, 2017)

Haines, Robin, *Charles Trevelyan and the Great Irish Famine* (Dublin: Four Courts Press, 2004)

Hall, Edith, *Greek Tragedy: Suffering Under the Sun* (Oxford: Oxford University Press, 2013)

Hamilton, Clive and Ohlberg, Mareike, *Hidden Hand: Exposing How the Chinese Communist Party is Reshaping The World* (London: One World, 2020)

Hamilton, Donna B., *Anthony Munday and the Catholics, 1560–1633* (London: Routledge, 2005)

Hari, Johann, *Chasing the Scream: The Search for the Truth about Addiction*, paperback edn (London: Bloomsbury, 2019)

Hastings, Max, *The Secret War: Spies, Codes and Guerrillas 1939–1945* (London: William Collins, 2015)

Hastings, Selina, *The Secret Lives of Somerset Maugham* (London: John Murray, 2010)

Hauge, Peter, 'Dowland and his time in Copenhagen, 1598–1606', *Early Music*, vol. 41, no. 2 (2013)

—, 'John Dowland's employment at the royal Danish court: Musician, agent – and spy?', in M. Keblusek and B. V. Noldus (eds) *Double Agents: Cultural and Political Brokerage in Early Modern Europe* (Leyden: Brill, 2011)

Hauterive, Ernest d', *La Police secrète du Premier Empire. Bulletins quotidiens adressés par Fouché à l'Empereur*, 5 vols (Paris: Perrin et Clavreuil, 1908–64)

Haynes, John Earl and Klehr, Harvey, *Venona: Decoding Soviet Espionage in America* (New Haven: Yale University Press, 1999)

— and Vassiliev, Alexander, *Spies: The Rise and Fall of the KGB in America* (New Haven: Yale University Press, 2009)

Hayward, James, *Hitler's Spy: The True Story of Arthur Owens, Double Agent Snow* (London: Simon & Schuster, 2012)

Healey, George Harris (ed.), *The Letters of Daniel Defoe* (Oxford: Oxford University Press, 2016)

Heartz, Daniel, 'Mozart and Da Ponte', *The Musical Quarterly*, vol. 79, no. 4 (1995)

Heffer, Simon, *The Age of Decadence: Britain 1880 to 1914* (London: Random House, 2017)

Helman, Lilian, *Pentimento: A Book of Portraits* (New York: New American Library, 1973)

Hemming, Henry, *M: Maxwell Knight, MI5's Greatest Spy Master* (London: Penguin, 2017)

—, *Our Man in New York: The British Plot to Bring America into the Second World War* (London: Quercus, 2019)

Hinsley, Sir F. H., *British Intelligence in the Second World War*, abridged edn (London: HMSO, 1993)

— and Alan Stripp (eds.), *Codebreakers: The Inside Story of Bletchley Park* (Oxford: Oxford University Press, 1993)

— et al., *British Intelligence in the Second World War: Its Influence on Strategy and Operations*, vols 1, 2, 3i, 3ii, 4 (London: HMSO, 1979–90)

Hoare, Philip, *Noël Coward: A Biography* (London: Mandarin, 1995)

Hodson, Joel, 'Lowell Thomas, T. E. Lawrence and the creation of a legend', *American History Magazine*, October 2000

Hoffman, Tod, *The Spy Within: Larry Chin and China's Penetration of the CIA* (Toronto: Bev Editions, 2008)

Holland, Max, *Leak: Why Mark Felt Became Deep Throat* (Lawrence: University Press of Kansas, 2012)

Holland, Merlin (ed.), *Oscar Wilde: A Life in Letters* (London: Fourth Estate, 2003)

Holman, Peter, *Four and Twenty Fiddlers: The Violin at the English Court, 1540–1690* (Oxford: Clarendon Press, 1993)

Holmes, Richard, *Marlborough: England's Fragile Genius* (London: HarperPress, 2008)

Holt, Thaddeus, *The Deceivers: Allied Military Deception in the Second World War* (London: Weidenfeld & Nicolson, 2004)

Homer, *The Iliad*, trans. E. V. Rieu, ed. Peter Jones (London: Penguin Books, 2014)

Honan, Park, *Christopher Marlowe: Poet and Spy* (Oxford: Oxford University Press, 2005)

Hopkins, Lisa, *A Christopher Marlowe Chronology* (Basingstoke: Palgrave Macmillan, 2005)

Hopkins, Paul, 'Sham plots and real plots in the 1690s', in Eveline Cruikshanks (ed.), *Ideology and Conspiracy: Aspects of Jacobitism, 1689–1759* (Edinburgh: John Donald, 1982)

Howard, Christopher, *Sir John Yorke of Nidderdale, 1565–1634* (London: Sheed & Ward, 1939)

Howard, Michael, *British Intelligence in the Second World War*, vol. 5: *Strategic Deception* (London: HMSO, 1990)

Howard, Tony, '"My Travail's history": Perspectives on the roads to "Othello", Stratford-upon-Avon 1959', *Shakespeare Bulletin*, vol. 28, no. 1 (2010)

Howarth, William D., *Beaumarchais and the Theatre* (London: Routledge, 1995)

Huggins, Michael, 'The "Nation" and Giuseppe Mazzini, 1842–48', *New Hibernia Review*, vol. 17, no. 3 (2013)

Hughes, Charles (ed.), 'Nicholas Faunt's Discourse Touching the Office of Principal Secretary of State &c., 1592', *English Historical Review*, vol. 50, no. 79 (1905)

Hugo, Victor, *Choses vues 1870–1885*, ed. Hubert Juin (Paris: Gallimard, 1972)

Hull, Christopher, *Our Man Down in Havana: The Story Behind Graham Greene's Cold War Spy Novel* (London: Pegasus Books, 2019)

Hutton, Robert, *Agent Jack: The True Story of MI5's Secret Nazi Hunter* (London: Weidenfeld & Nicolson, 2018)

Insall, Tony, *Secret Alliances: Special Operations and Intelligence in Norway 1940–1945* (London: Biteback, 2019)

Isherwood, Christopher, *Diaries*, vol. 1 (London: Vintage, 2011)

Jackson, David (ed.), *The Diaries of George Washington* (Charlottesville: University Press of Virginia, 1976)

James, Lawrence, *The Golden Warrior: The Life and Legend of Lawrence of Arabia* (London: Weidenfeld & Nicolson, 1991).

James, W. M., *The Eyes of the Navy: A Biographical Study of Admiral Sir Reginald Hall* (London: Methuen, 1955)

Jansen, Marc and Petrov, Nikita, *Stalin's Loyal Executioner: People's Commissar Nikolai Ezhov, 1895–1940* (Stanford, Calif.: Hoover Institution Press, 2002)

Jasanoff, Maya, *The Dawn Watch: Joseph Conrad in a Global World* (London: William Collins, 2017)

Jeffery, Keith, *MI6: The History of the Secret Intelligence Service, 1909–1949* (London: Bloomsbury, 2010)

Jeffreys-Jones, Rhodri, *The Nazi Spy Ring in America: Hitler's Agents, the FBI and the Case that Stirred the Nation* (Washington, DC, Georgetown University Press, 2020)

—, 'Why was the CIA founded in 1947?', in Rhodri Jeffreys-Jones and Christopher Andrew (eds), *Eternal Vigilance? 50 Years of the CIA* (London: Frank Cass, 1997)

Jenkins, Tricia, *The CIA in Hollywood: How the Agency Shapes Film and Television* (Austin, Tex.: University of Texas Press, 2012)

Jens, Erik, 'Cold War spy fiction in Russian popular culture: From suspicion to acceptance via *Seventeen Moments of Spring*', *Studies in Intelligence*, vol. 61, no. 2 (2017)

Jia, Mai, *Decoded* (London: Penguin, 2014)

—, *In The Dark* (London: Penguin, 2015)

—, *L'Enfer des codes* (Paris: Robert Laffont, 2015)

Johnston, John, *The Lord Chancellor's Blue Pencil* (London: Hodder & Stoughton, 1990)

Jones, Clyve, 'Robert Harley and the myth of the golden thread: Family piety, journalism and the history of the assassination attempt of 8 March 1711', *British Library Journal*, 2010

Jones, Peter, 'Antoine de Guiscard, "Abbé de la Bourlie", "Marquis de Guiscard"', *British Library Journal*, 1982

Jordan, Don and Walsh, Michael, *The King's Revenge: Charles II and the Greatest Manhunt in British History* (London: Little, Brown, 2012)

Judd, Alan, *The Quest for C: Sir Mansfield Cumming and the Founding of the British Secret Service* (London: HarperCollins, 1999)

—, *A Fine Madness: A Novel Inspired by the Life and Death of Christopher Marlowe* (London: Simon & Schuster, 2021)

Kahn, David, *The Codebreakers: The Story of Secret Writing* (New York: Macmillan, 1967)

—, *The Reader of Gentlemen's Mail: Herbert O. Yardley and American Intelligence* (New Haven, Conn.: Yale University Press, 2004)

—, 'The Man in the Iron Mask – encore et enfin, cryptologically', *Cryptologia*, vol. 29, no. 1 (2005)

—, 'Intelligence lessons in *Macbeth*', *Intelligence and National Security*, vol. 24, no. 2 (2009)

Kalugin, Oleg, *Spymaster: My 32 Years in Intelligence and Espionage against the West* (London: Smyth Gryphon, 1994)

Kanes, Martin, '"Germinal": Drama and dramatic structure', *Modern Philology*, vol. 61, no. 1 (1963)

Kautilya, *The Arthashastra*, ed. and trans. L. J. Rangarajan (Haryana, India: Penguin, 1992)

Keblusek, Marika, 'Artists as cultural and political agents', in Marika Keblusek and Badeloch Noldus (eds), *Double Agents: Cultural and Political Brokerage in Early Modern Europe* (Leiden: Brill, 2011)

Keenan, Siobhan, *Travelling Players in Shakespeare's England* (Basingstoke: Palgrave Macmillan, 2002)

—, 'The Simpson Players of Jacobean Yorkshire and the professional stage', *Theatre Notebook*, vol. 67, no. 1 (2013)

Kelly, Andrew; Pepper, James; and Richards, Jeffrey (eds), *Filming T. E. Lawrence: Korda's Lost Epics* (London & New York: I.B.Tauris Publishers, 1997),

Kelly, Ian, *Casanova: Actor, Lover, Priest, Spy* (London: Hodder & Stoughton, 2008)

Kelly, Michael, *Reminiscences of Michael Kelly of the King's Theatre and Theatre Royal Drury Lane* (London: H. Colburn, 1826)

Kendall, Roy, *Christopher Marlowe and Richard Baines: Journeys Through the Elizabethan Underworld* (Madison, NJ: Fairleigh Dickinson University Press, 2003)

Kenna, Shane, *War in the Shadows: The Irish-Americans Who Bombed Victorian Britain* (Dublin: Irish Academic Press, 2013)

—, *Thomas MacDonagh: 16 Lives* (Dublin: O'Brien Press, 2014)

Kennan, George F., *Russia Leaves the War* (Princeton: Princeton University Press, 1989)

Kilmeade, Brian and Yaeger, Don, *George Washington's Secret Six: The Spy Ring that Saved the American Revolution* (New York: Sentinel, 2013)

King, Gilbert, 'What Paul Robeson said', *Smithsonian Magazine*, 13 September 2011

Kirkman, Francis, *The Wits; or sport upon sport: in selected pieces of drollery, digested into scenes by way of dialogue* (London: Printed by E.C. for Fancis [sic] Kirkman, 1672)

Kishlansky, Mark, *A Monarchy Transformed: Britain 1630–1714* (London: Penguin Books, 1997)

Knoblock, Edward, *Round the Room: An Autobiography* (London: Chapman & Hall, 1939)

Kopacevic, Filip, 'The FSB Literati: The first prize winners of the Federal Security Service literature award competition, 2006–2018', *Intelligence and National Security*, vol. 34, no. 5 (2019)

Krakovitch, Odile, *Hugo censuré: La liberté au théâtre au XIXe siècle* (Paris: Calmann-Lévy, 1985)

Lahaie, Olivier, 'Mata Hari ou le badinage fatal', *Cahiers de la pensée mili-Terre*, December 2018

Lane, Anthony, 'Film within a film', *New Yorker*, 15 October 2012

Larsen, Daniel, *Plotting for Peace: American Peacemakers, British Codebreakers, and Britain at War, 1914–1917* (Cambridge: Cambridge University Press, 2021)

Latham, Robert (ed.), *Samuel Pepys and the Second Dutch War: Pepys's Navy White Book and Brooke House Papers* (Aldershot: Scolar Press, 1995)

Lawrence, A. W., *T. E. Lawrence by His Friends* (London: Jonathan Cape, 1954)

Lawrence, T. E., *Seven Pillars of Wisdom* (London: Random House, 2008 [first publ. 1922])

Leab, Daniel J., *Orwell Subverted: The CIA and the Filming of 'Animal Farm'* (University Park: Pennsylvania State University Press, 2007)

Le Carré, John, *Call for the Dead*, Modern Classics edn (London: Penguin, 2011)

—, *The Pigeon Tunnel: Stories of My Life* (London: Penguin, 2016)

Leggett, George, *The Cheka: Lenin's Political Police* (London: Clarendon Press, 1981)

Le Queux, William, *The Invasion of 1910* (London: R. Nash, 1906)

—, *Spies of the Kaiser: Plotting the Downfall of England* (London: Hurst & Blackett, 1909); reissued with introduction by Nicholas Hiley (London: Frank Cass, 1996)

Levi, Anthony, *Cardinal Richelieu and the Making of France* (London: Constable, 2000)

Lewcock, Dawn, *Sir William Davenant, the Court Masque, and the English Seventeenth Century Scenic Stage, c1605–c1700* (Amherst, NY: Cambria Press, 2008)

Li, Siu Leung, *Cross-Dressing in Chinese Opera* (Hong Kong: Hong Kong University Press, 2003)

Liang, Hsi-huey, *The Rise of Modern Police and the European State System from Metternich to the Second World War* (Cambridge: Cambridge University Press, 1992)

Lim, Louisa, *The People's Republic of Amnesia: Tiananmen Revisited* (New York: Oxford University Press, 2014)

Linklater, Andrew, *Compton Mackenzie: A Life* (London: Chatto & Windus, 1987)

Lobenthal, Joel, *Tallulah! The Life and Times of a Leading Lady* (New York: HarperCollins, 2004)

Lokhova, Svetlana, *The Spy Who Changed History* (London: William Collins, 2018)

Lom, Herbert, *Enter a Spy: The Double Life of Christopher Marlowe* (London: Merlin Press, 1978).

Lord, John, 'Sir John Vanbrugh and the 1st Duke of Ancaster: Newly discovered documents', *Architectural History*, vol. 34 (2016)

Lownie, Andrew, *Stalin's Englishman: The Lives of Guy Burgess* (London: Hodder & Stoughton, 2015)

Lycett, Andrew, *Ian Fleming*, paperback edn (London: Phoenix, 1996)

McBride, Ian (ed.), *History and Memory in Modern Ireland* (Cambridge: Cambridge University Press, 2001)

McBride, Joseph, *Whatever Happened to Orson Welles? A Portrait of an Independent Career* (Lexington: University of Kentucky Press, 2006)

McCourt, John, *Roll Away the Reel World: James Joyce and Cinema* (Cork: Cork University Press, 2010)

MacDonagh, Thomas, *When the Dawn is Come* (Dublin: Mansell & Co, 1908)

MacDonald, Bill, *The True Intrepid: Sir William Stephenson and the Unknown Agents* (Vancouver: Raincoast Books, 1998)

McFeely, Deirdre, *Dion Boucicault : Irish Identity on Stage* (Cambridge: Cambridge University Press, 2012)

McGilligan, Patrick, *Backstory: Interviews with Screenwriters of Hollywood's Golden Age* (Oakland: University of California Press, 1986)

MacGregor, Neil, *Shakespeare's Restless World* (London: Allen Lane, 2012)

Macintyre, Ben, *Double Cross: The True Story of the D-Day Spies* (London: Bloomsbury, 2012)

—, *Operation Mincemeat* (London: Bloomsbury, 2016)

McKenna, Marthe, *I Was a Spy!* (London: Pool of London Press, [1932] 2015)

Mackenzie, Compton, *First Athenian Memories* (London: Cassell, 1931)

—, *Greek Memories* (London: Biteback, 2017)

Mackrell, Judith, *Flappers: Six Women of a Dangerous Generation* (London: Macmillan, 2013)

McLaren, Angus, 'Smoke and mirrors: Willy Clarkson and the role of disguises in inter war England,' *Journal of Social History*, vol. 40, no. 3 (2007)

McMillin, Scott and Maclean, Sally-Beth, *The Queen's Men and Their Plays* (Cambridge: Cambridge University Press, 1998)

McMinn, Joseph, *Jonathan Swift and the Arts* (Newark: University of Delaware Press, 2010)

McNulty, Eugene and Ní Ghairbhí, Róisín (eds), *Patrick Pearse and the Theatre* (Dublin: Four Courts Press, 2016)

McRae, Andrew, 'Farting in the House of Commons: Popular humour and political discourse in Early Modern England', in Mark Knights and Adam Morton (eds), *The Power of Laughter and Satire in Early Modern Britain: Political and Religious Culture, 1500–1820* (Martlesham: Boydell & Brewer, 2017)

Macrakis, Kristie, *Prisoners, Lovers, and Spies: The Story of Invisible Ink from Herodotus to Al-Qaeda* (New Haven, Conn.: Yale University Press, 2014)

Mahl, Thomas E., *Desperate Deception: British Covert Operations in the United States, 1939–44* (Stirling VA: Potomac Books, 1999)

Marks, Leo, *Between Silk and Cyanide: A Codemaker's War 1941–1945* (London: HarperCollins, 1998)

Marlowe, Christopher, *The Complete Plays*, rev. edn (London: Penguin Classics, 2003)

Marquis, Hugues, *Les Agents de l'ennemi. Les Espions à la solde de l'Angleterre dans une France en révolution* (Paris: Vendémiaire, 2014)

Marsh, Moira, 'Bunga-bunga on the Dreadnought: Hoax, race and Woolf', *Comedy Studies,* vol. 9, no. 2 (2018)

Marshall, Alan, *Intelligence and Espionage in the Reign of Charles II, 1660–1685* (Cambridge: Cambridge University Press, 1994)

—, '"Memorialls for Mrs Affora"*: Aphra Behn and the Restoration intelligence world', *Women's Writing,* vol. 22, no.1 (2015).

Martin, Allison, 'The "Big Fella" and the theatre', *Ireland's Own,* no. 5663, 6 July 2018

Martin, Patrick H., *Elizabethan Espionage: Plotters and Spies in the Struggle between Catholicism and the Crown* (Jefferson, North Carolina: McFarland & Co., 2016)

Marx, Harpo and Barber, Rowland, *Harpo Speaks!* (New York: Limelight Editions, 1988)

Maschwitz, Eric, *No Chip on My Shoulder* (London: Herbert Jenkins, 1957)

Maskelyne, Jasper, *Magic. Top Secret* (New York: Stanley Paul, 1949)

Masterman, J. C., *Marshal Ney: A Play in Five Acts with a Preface by R. C. Sherriff* (London: Cobden-Sanderson, 1937)

—, *Bits and Pieces* (London: Hodder & Stoughton, 1962)

—, *The Double-Cross System* (London: Sphere, 1973)

Mattis, Peter and Brazil, Matthew, *Chinese Communist Espionage: An Intelligence Primer* (Annapolis, Md.: Naval Institute Press, 2019)

Maugham, W. Somerset, *Ashenden: Or, The British Agent* (London: Mandarin, 1991)

Mehta, Usha and Thakkar, Usha, *Kautilya and His Arthashastra* (New Delhi: S. Chand, 1980)

Melby, Christian K., 'Empire and nation in British future-war and invasion-scare fiction, 1871–1914', *Historical Journal,* vol. 63, no. 2 (2020)

Melgounov, Sergey Petrovich, *The Red Terror in Russia* (London: J. M. Dent, 1925)

Mendez, Antonio J., *The Master of Disguise: My Secret Life in the CIA* (New York: HarperCollins, 2009)

Merriam, Thomas, 'The misunderstanding of Munday as author of Sir Thomas More', *The Review of English Studies,* no. 204 (2000)

Mesropova, Olga, 'The Apocalypse Code', in Birgit Beumers (ed.), *Directory of World Cinema: Russia 2* (Bristol: Intellect Books, 2015)

Miller, Julie, 'Queen Elizabeth accepts BAFTA award for being "the most memorable Bond girl yet"', *Vanity Fair,* 5 April 2013

Milling, Jane and Thomson, Peter, *The Cambridge History of British Theatre* (Cambridge: Cambridge University Press, 2004)

Min, Yang, 'Spy, abjection, and post-socialist identity: Chinese neo-spy films since 2009', *Studies in the Humanities*, vol. 44/5, nos 1–2 (2019)

Miola, Robert S., 'Ben Jonson, Catholic poet', *Renaissance and Reformation / Renaissance et Réforme*, vol. 25, no. 4 (2001)

Mitrokhin, Vasili (ed.), *KGB Lexicon: The Soviet Intelligence Officer's Handbook* (London: Frank Cass, 2002)

Mitterand, Henri, *Zola*, 3 vols (Paris: Fayard, 1999–2002)

Mohs, Polly A., *Military Intelligence and the Arab Revolt: The First Modern Intelligence War* (London: Routledge, 2008)

Montagu, Ewen, *The Man Who Never Was* (London: Evans, 1953).

Moody, Joanna, *Traces of Nidderdale in 40 Years and 40 Objects: Stories of the Museum* (Pateley Bridge: Nidderdale History Museum, 2014)

Moran, James, *Staging the Easter Rising: 1916 as Theatre* (Cork: Cork University Press, 2005)

Moran, Richard, *Knowing Right from Wrong: The Insanity Defense of Daniel McNaughtan* (New York: Simon and Schuster, 2000)

Morgan, Ted, *Somerset Maugham* (London: Jonathan Cape, 1980)

Morley, Sheridan, *Dirk Bogarde: Rank Outsider*, 2nd edn (London: Bloomsbury, 1999)

Muggeridge, Malcolm, *Chronicles of Wasted Time*, vol. 2: *The Infernal Grove* (London: Fontana, 1973)

Mullen, John, *The Show Must Go On: Popular Song in Britain during the First World War* (London: Routledge, 2015)

Munday, Anthony, *A Discoverie of Edmund Campion and his Confederates ...* (1582)

Munday, Anthony, *A breefe and true reporte of the execution of certaine traytours at Tiborne, the xxviii, and xxx days of Maye* (1582)

Munday, Anthony, *The English Roman Life*, ed. Philip J. Ayres (Oxford: Clarendon Press, 1980)

Munro, Lucy, 'The queen and the cockpit: Henrietta Maria's theatrical patronage revisited', *Shakespeare Bulletin*, vol. 37, no. 1 (2019)

Murphy, Maura, 'The ballad singer and the role of the seditious ballad in nineteenth-century Ireland: Dublin Castle's view', *Ulster Folklife Magazine*, vol. 25 (1979).

Murphy, Neil, 'Spies, informers and Thomas Howard's defence of England's northern frontier in 1523', *Historical Research*, vol. 93, no. 260 (2020)

Naftali, Timothy J., 'Intrepid's last deception: Documenting the career of Sir William Stephenson', *Intelligence and National Security*, vol. 8, no. 3 (1993)

Nagy, John A., *George Washington's Secret Spy War: The Making of America's First Spymaster* (New York: St. Martin's Press, 2016)

Nance, John V., '"We, John Cade": Shakespeare, Marlowe, and the authorship of. 4.2.33–189 *2 Henry VI*', *Shakespeare*, vol. 13, no. 1 (2017)

Nathan, Andrew; Link, Perry; and Zhang, Liang, *The Tiananmen Papers: The Chinese Leadership's Decision to Use Force against Their Own People* (London: Abacus, 2002)

Nelligan, David, *A Spy in the Castle* (London: MacGibbon and Kee, 1968)

Néraudau, Jean-Pierre, *L'Olympe du Roi-Soleil* (Paris: Les Belles-Lettres, 1986)

Newton, Michael, '"Nihilists of Castlebar!": Exporting Russian Nihilism in the 1880s and the case of Oscar Wilde's *Vera; or the Nihilists*', in Beasley and Bullock, *Russia in Britain, 1880–1940* (q.v.)

Nicholl, Charles, *The Reckoning: The Murder of Christopher Marlowe*, 2nd edn (London: Vintage, 2002)

Nichols, Stephen G., 'The early troubadours: Guilhem IX to Bernart de Ventadorn', in Simon Gaunt and Sarah Kay (eds), *The Troubadours: An Introduction* (Cambridge: Cambridge University Press, 1999)

Nicolai, Walter, *The German Secret Service*, trans. George Renwick (London: S. Paul, 1924)

Novak, Maximilian E., *Daniel Defoe, Master of Fictions: His Life and Ideas* (Oxford: Oxford University Press, 2001)

Nureyev, Rudolf, *Nureyev: An Autobiography with Pictures*, ed. Alexander Bland (London: Hodder & Stoughton, 1962)

Omand, Sir David, *How Spies Think: 10 Lessons in Intelligence* (London: Viking, 2020)

O Meara, Liam, *Zozimus: The Life and Works of Michael Moran* (Dublin: Riposte Books, 2011)

Ostovich, Helen; Syme, Holger Schott; and Griffin, Andrew (eds), *Locating the Queen's Men, 1583–1603: Material Practices and Conditions of Playing* (Farnham and Burlington, Vt.: Ashgate, 2009)

Ottaway, Susan, *Sisters, Secrets and Sacrifice* (London: HarperCollins, 2013)

Otto, Beatrice K., *Fools are Everywhere: The Court Jester Around the World* (Chicago: University of Chicago Press, 2001)

Ozanam, Didier and Antoine, Michel, *Correspondance secrète du Comte de Broglie avec Louis XV*, 2 vols (Paris: Librarie C. Klinksieck, 1956–61)

Palmer, Jennifer S., *Cedric Belfrage: Anglo-American Nonconformist* (Washington DC & London: Minerva Press, 1996)

Parfitt, Richard, '"Oh, what matter when for Erin dear we fall?" Music and Irish Nationalism, 1848–1913', *Irish Studies Review*, vol. 23, no. 4 (2015)

—, *Musical Culture and the Spirit of Irish Nationalism, 1848–1972* (London: Routledge, 2020)

Parolin, Christina, *Radical Spaces: Venues of Popular Politics in London, 1790–c.1845* (Canberra: ANU E Press, 2010)

Parry, Glyn, *The Arch-Conjuror of England: John Dee and Magic at the Courts of Renaissance Europe* (New Haven and London: Yale University Press, 2012)

Pavlov, D. B., 'The tribunal phase of the Soviet judicial system, 1917–1922', *Russian Studies in History*, vol. 58, no. 4 (2019)

Pearce, Edward, *The Great Man: Sir Robert Walpole – Scoundrel, Genius and Britain's First Prime Minister* (London: Jonathan Cape, 2007)

Pearson, John, *The Life of Ian Fleming* (London: Bloomsbury Reader, 2013)

Peel, A., *Tracts Ascribed to Richard Bancroft* (Cambridge: Cambridge University Press, 1953)

Perrault, Charles, *Les Hommes illustres qui ont paru en France pendant ce siècle avec leurs portraits au naturel* (Paris: Antoine Dezallier, 1696)

Perrotet, Tony, 'When Casanova met Mozart', *Smithsonian Magazine*, 21 March 2012

Peters, I., 'Vospominaniya o rabote v VChK v pervyi god revolyutsii', *Proletarskaia Revolyutsiya*, no. 10 (33) (1924)

Pethica, James, 'Lady Gregory's Abbey Theatre drama: Ireland real and ideal', in Shaun Richards (ed.), *Cambridge Companion to Twentieth-Century Irish Drama* (Cambridge: Cambridge University Press, 2004)

Petrov, Kristian, '"Strike out, right and left!": A conceptual-historical analysis of 1860s Russian nihilism and its notion of negation', *Studies in Eastern European Thought*, vol. 71, no. 2 (2019)

Philby, Kim, *My Silent War* (St Albans: Granada, 1969)

Phythian, Mark, 'Profiles in intelligence: An interview with Michael Herman', *Intelligence and National Security*, vol. 31, no. 2 (2016)

—, 'Profiles in intelligence: An interview with Professor Christopher Andrew', *Intelligence and National Security*, vol. 32, no. 4 (2017)

Pickering, Michael, *Blackface Minstrelsy in Britain* (Burlington, Vt.: Ashgate, 2008)

Pierre, Benoist, *Le Père Joseph. L'Éminence grise de Richelieu* (Paris: Éditions Perrin, 2007)

Pilz, Anna, 'Lady Gregory's *The Gaol Gate*, Terence MacSwiney and the Abbey Theatre', *Irish Studies Review*, 2015

Pinto, V. de S. (ed.), *The Famous Pathologist, or, The Noble Mountebank, by Thomas Alcock and John Wilmot, Earl of Rochester* (Nottingham: Sisson & Parker, 1961)

Porter, Linda, *Mistresses: Sex and Scandal at the Court of Charles II* (London: Picador, 2020)

Posnanski, Joe, *The Life and Afterlife of Harry Houdini* (London: Avid Reader, 2019}

Poynting, Sarah, '"The rare and excellent partes of Mr Walter Montague": Henrietta Maria and her playwright', in Erin Grifley (ed.), *Henrietta Maria: Piety, Politics and Patronage* (Aldershot: Ashgate, 2008)

— (ed.), *The Shepherds' Paradise, by Walter Montagu*, Malone Society Reprint, vol. 159 (Oxford: Oxford University Press, 1998)

Preto, Paolo, 'Giacomo Casanova and the Venetian inquisitors: A domestic espionage system in eighteenth-century Europe', in Daniel Szechi (ed.), *The Dangerous Trade: Spies, Spymasters and the Making of Europe* (Dundee: Dundee University Press, 2010)

Price, Cecil, *The Dramatic Works of Richard Brinsley Sheridan* (Oxford: Clarendon Press, 1973), vol. 2

Proctor, Tammy M., *Female Intelligence: Women and Espionage in the First World War* (New York: NYU Press, 2003)

Pujol García, Juan and West, Nigel, *Operation Garbo: The Personal Story of the Most Successful Spy of World War II* (1985, repr. London: Biteback, 2011)

Purinton, Marjean D., 'Wordsworth's "The Borderers" and the ideology of revolution', *The Wordsworth Circle*, vol. 23, no. 2 (1992)

Purvis, Stewart and Hulbert, Jeff, *Guy Burgess: The Spy Who Knew Everyone* (London: Biteback, 2016)

Ranelagh, John, *A Short History of Ireland*, 3rd edn (Cambridge: Cambridge University Press, 2012)

Rankin, Nicholas, *Churchill's Wizards: The British Genius for Deception, 1914–1945* (London: Faber & Faber, 2008)

—, *A Genius for Deception: How Cunning Helped the British Win Two World Wars* (Oxford: Oxford University Press, 2011)

Read, Charles, 'British Economic Policy and Ireland, *c.*1841–53', University of Cambridge, PhD thesis (2016)

—, 'Laissez-faire, the Irish famine, and British financial crisis', *Economic History Review*, vol. 69, no. 2 (2016)

Read, Conyers, *Mr Secretary Walsingham and the Policy of Queen Elizabeth*, 3 vols (Oxford: Clarendon Press, 1925)

Read, Piers Paul, *The Dreyfus Affair* (London: Bloomsbury, 2012)

Rée, Jonathan (ed.), *A Schoolmaster's War: Harry Rée, British Agent in the French Resistance* (New Haven/London: Yale University Press, 2020)

Remnick, David, 'Patriot Games', *New Yorker*, 3 March 2014.

Riggs, David, *The World of Christopher Marlowe* (London: Faber & Faber, 2004)

Rimington, Stella, *Open Secret: The Autobiography of the Former Director-General of MI5* (London: Hutchinson, 2001)

Robb, Graham, *Victor Hugo* (London: Picador, 1997)

Root-Bernstein, Michèle, *Boulevard Theater and Revolution in Eighteenth-Century Paris* (Ann Arbor: UMI Research Press, 1981)

Rose, P. K., *The Founding Fathers of American Intelligence* (Langley, Va.: CIA Center for the Study of Intelligence, 1999)

Rosen, Michael, *The Disappearance of Zola: Love, Literature and the Dreyfus Case* (London: Faber & Faber, 2017)

Roskill, S. W., *Hankey: Man of Secrets*, vol. 1 (London: Collins, 1970)

Rosten, Leo, *Hollywood: The Movie Colony, the Movie Makers* (New York: Harcourt, Brace, 1941)

Ruff, Lillian M. and Wilson, D. Arnold, 'The madrigal, the lute song and Elizabethan politics', *Past & Present*, no. 44 (August 1969)

Ruis, Edwin, *Spynest: British and German Espionage from Neutral Holland 1914–1918* (Stroud: History Press, 2016)

Russell, Gillian, *Women, Sociability and Theatre in Georgian London* (Cambridge: Cambridge University Press, 2007)

Ruud, Charles A., and Stepanov, Sergei A., *Fontanka 16: The Tsars' Secret Police* (Montreal and Kingston, Ont.: McGill–Queen's University Press, 1999)

Sarmiento, F. L., *Life of Pauline Cushman, The Celebrated Union Spy and Scout* (Philadelphia: John E. Potter & Co., 1890)

Schiff, Stacy, *A Great Improvisation: Franklin in France* (New York: Henry Holt, 2005)

Schuyler, Susan, 'Crowds, Fenianism and the Victorian stage', *Journal of Victorian Culture*, vol. 16, no. 2 (2011)

Scott, D. B., *From the Erotic to the Demonic: On Critical Musicology* (Oxford: Oxford University Press, 2003)

Scott, H. M., *The Birth of a Great Power System, 1740–1815* (Harlow: Longman, 2005)

Seaman, Mark (ed.), *GARBO: The Spy who Saved D-Day* (London, PRO publications, 2004)

Searle, Alison, 'Ben Jonson and religion', in Eugene Giddens (ed.), *The Oxford Handbook of Ben Jonson* (Oxford: Oxford University Press, 2015)

Sebag-Montefiore, Simon, *The Romanovs: 1613–1917* (London: Weidenfeld & Nicolson, 2016)

Seilhamer, George O., *History of the American Theatre*, vol. 2: *During the Revolution and After* (London: Ardent Media, 1968)

Sellers, Leonard, *Shot in the Tower: The Story of the Spies Executed in the Tower of London during the First World War*, 2nd edn (Barnsley: Pen & Sword, 2009)

Senelick, Laurence, '"For God, for Czar, for Fatherland": Russians on the British stage from Napoleon to the Great War', in Beasley and Bullock, *Russia in Britain, 1880–1940* (q.v.)

Service, Robert, *Spies and Commissars: Bolshevik Russia and the West* (London: Macmillan, 2011)

Shapiro, James, *1606: Shakespeare and the Year of Lear* (London: Faber & Faber, 2015)

Shaw, George Bernard, *The Doctor's Dilemma, Getting Married and The Shewing-Up of Blanco Posnet* (London: Constable, 1924)

Shelden, Michael, *Graham Greene: The Man Within* (London: Heinemann, 1994)

Shellard, Dominic and Nicholson, Steve, with Handley, Miriam, *The Lord Chamberlain Regrets … : A History of British Theatre Censorship* (London: British Library, 2004)

Shelley, Adam, 'Empire of Shadows: British Intelligence in the Middle East 1939–1946' (PhD dissertation, Cambridge, 2007)

Sherry, Norman, *The Life of Graham Greene*, vol. 2 (London: Jonathan Cape, 1994)

Sheymov, Victor, *Tower of Secrets: A Real-Life Spy Thriller* (Annapolis, Md.: Naval Institute Press, 1993)

Sisman, Adam, *John le Carré: The Biography* (London: Bloomsbury, 2015)

Skinnider, Margaret, *Doing my Bit for Ireland* (New York: Century, 1917)

Smith, James, *British Writers and MI5 Surveillance, 1930–1960* (Cambridge: Cambridge University Press, 2013)

—, 'Soviet films and British intelligence in the 1930s: The case of Kino Films and MI5', in Beasley and Bullock, *Russia in Britain, 1880–1940* (q.v.)

—, 'The MacDonald Discussion Group: A communist conspiracy in Britain's cold war film and theatre industry – Or MI5's honey-pot?', *Historical Journal of Film, Radio and Television*, vol. 35, no. 3 (2015)

Smith, Michael, *The Secrets of Station X: How Bletchley Park Helped Win the War* (London: Biteback, 2011)

—, *Debs of Bletchley Park and Other Stories* (London: Aurium Press, 2015)

Smith, Richard Angus, 'Spying and Surveillance in Shakespeare's Dramatic Courts', PhD thesis, University of Sydney (2014)

Smithers, Peter, *The Life of Joseph Addison* (Oxford: Clarendon Press, 1954)

Snook, Edith, '"Soveraigne Receipts" and the politics of beauty in *The Queens Closet Opened*', *Early Modern Literary Studies*, Special Issue 15 (August 2007)

Sohmer, Steve, *Reading Shakespeare's Mind* (Manchester: Manchester University Press, 2017)

Soldatov, Andrei and Borogan, Irina, *The New Nobility: The Restoration of Russia's Security State and the Enduring Legacy of the KGB* (New York: Public Affairs, 2010)

Somerset, Anne, *Queen Anne: The Politics of Passion* (London: HarperPress, 2012)

Sparrow, Elizabeth, 'The Alien Office, 1792–1806', *The Historical Journal*, vol. 33, no. 2 (1990)

Spiller, Elizabeth, 'Printed recipe books in medical, political, and scientific contexts', in Laura Lunger Knoppers (ed.), *The Oxford Handbook of Literature and the English Revolution* (Oxford: Oxford University Press, 2012)

Spink, Ian, *Cavalier Songwriter: Henry Lawes* (Oxford: Oxford University Press, 2000)

Spitz, Bob, *Reagan: An American Journey* (New York: Penguin, 2018)

Stafford, David, 'A myth called Intrepid', *Saturday Night*, October 1989

—, *The Silent Game: The Real World of Imaginary Spies* (Toronto: Lester & Orpen Dennys, 1989)

—, *Ten Days to D-Day* (London: Little, Brown, 2003)

Stark, Gary D., 'Germany', in Goldstein (ed.), *The Frightful Stage* (q.v.)

Staves, Susan, 'Tragedy', in Jane Moody and Daniel O'Quinn (eds), *The Cambridge Companion to British Theatre, 1730–1830* (Cambridge: Cambridge University Press, 2007)

Steinhauer, Gustav, *Steinhauer: The Kaiser's Masterspy as Told by Himself*, ed. Sidney Felstead (London: The Bodley Head, 1930)

Stepniak, S., *Underground Russia: Revolutionary Profiles and Sketches from Life* (London: Smith Elder, 1883; Kindle edn)

Stevenson, William, *A Man Called Intrepid* (New York: Harcourt Brace Jovanovich, 1976)

—, *Intrepid's Last Case* (London: Sphere, 1984).

Stewart, Ann Marie, *The Ravishing Restoration: Aphra Behn, Violence and Comedy* (Selinsgrove, Pa.: Susquehanna University Press, 2010)

Stourton, Edward, *Auntie's War: The BBC during the Second World War* (London: Black Swan 2018)

Streitberger, W. R., *The Masters of the Revels and Elizabeth I's Court Theatre* (Oxford: Oxford University Press, 2016)

Stubbs, John, *Reprobates: The Cavaliers of the English Civil War* (London: Viking, 2011)

Sturgis, Matthew, *Oscar* (London: Head of Zeus, 2018)

Sun Tzu, *The Art of War: Bilingual Chinese and English Text*, trans. Lionel Giles with an introduction by John Minford (Hong Kong: Tuttle Publishing, 2016)

Swanson, James L., *Manhunt: The 12-Day Chase for Lincoln's Killer* (New York: William Morrow, 2006)

Swift, Anthony, 'Russia', in Goldstein (ed.), *The Frightful Stage* (q.v.)

Szechi, D., *Jacobitism and Tory Politics 1710–14* (Edinburgh: John Donald, 2012)

Tabachnick, Stephen E. (ed.), *The T.E. Lawrence Puzzle* (Athens, Ga.: The University of Georgia Press, 1984)

Taylor, David Francis, *Theatres of Opposition: Empire, Revolution and Richard Brinsley Sheridan* (Oxford: Oxford University Press, 2012)

—, 'Rochester, the theatre and Restoration theatricality', in Matthew C. Augustine (ed.), *Lord Rochester in the Restoration World* (Cambridge: Cambridge University Press, 2015)

Taylor, Gary; Jowett, John; Bourrus, Terri; and Egan, Gabriel (eds), *The New Oxford Shakespeare: Modern Critical Edition: The Complete Works* (Oxford: Oxford University Press, 2016)

Taylor, Richard, *Film Propaganda: Soviet Russia and Nazi Germany*, revised edn, (London, I.B.Tauris, 1988)

Thale, Mary (ed.), *Selections from the Papers of the London Corresponding Society 1792–1799* (Cambridge: Cambridge University Press, 1983)

Thames, Stephanie, 'Code of the Secret Service', *TCM Movie Database*

Thomas, Marcel, *L'Affaire sans Dreyfus* (Paris: A. Fayard, 1961)

Thomas, David; Carlton, David; and Etienne, Anne, *Theatre Censorship from Walpole to Wilson* (Oxford: Oxford University Press, 2007)

Thomas, Lowell, *With Lawrence in Arabia* (London: Hutchinson, 1924)

Thomas, Vivian, *Shakespeare's Political and Economic Language*, Arden Shakespeare Dictionaries (London: Bloomsbury, 2008)

Thomson, Sir Basil, *Queer People* (London: Hodder and Stoughton, 1922)

Tibère, Clément, 'Mistinguett (Bourgeois, Jeanne, dite)', in Hugues Moutouh and Jérôme Poirot (eds), *Dictionnaire du Renseignement*, 2nd edn (Paris: Perrin, 2020).

Todd, Janet, *The Secret Life of Aphra Behn* (London: Bloomsbury Reader, 2017)

Tóibín, Colm, *Lady Gregory's Toothbrush* (Dublin: Lilliput Press, 2002)

Tomaselli, Phil, *Tracing your Secret Service Ancestors* (Barnsley: Pen and Sword Books, 2009)

Tombs, Robert, *The English and Their History* (London: Allen Lane, 2014)

—, and Tombs, Isabelle, *That Sweet Enemy: The French and the British from the Sun King to the Present* (London: William Heinemann, 2006)

Toomey, Emily, 'The actress who left the stage to become a Civil War spy', *Smithsonian Magazine*, 12 August 2019

Trotignon, Yves, *Politique du secret: regards sur 'Le Bureau des légendes'* (Paris: PUF 2018).

Tucker, R. C. and Cohen, S. F. (eds), *The Great Purge Trial* (New York: Grosset and Dunlap, 1965)

Turing, Sir Dermot, *Prof: Alan Turing Decoded* (Stroud: The History Press, 2016)

—, *Codebreakers of Bletchley Park* (London: Arcturus, 2020)

Uglow, Jenny, *A Gambling Man: Charles II and the Restoration, 1660–1670* (London: Faber & Faber, 2009)

Urban, Mark, *The Man Who Broke Napoleon's Codes: The Story of George Scovell* (London: Faber & Faber, 2002)

Urstad, Tone Sundt, *Sir Robert Walpole's Poets: The Use of Literature as Pro-Government Propaganda, 1721–1742* (Newark: University of Delaware Press, 1999)

Vaillé, Eugène, *Le Cabinet noir* (Paris: Presses Universitaires de France, 1950)

Van Gyseghem, André, *Theatre in Soviet Russia* (London: Faber & Faber, 1943).

Vaninskaya, Anna, '"Truth about Russia": Russia in Britain at the Fin de Siècle', in Josephine M. Guy (ed.), *Edinburgh Companion to Fin de Siècle Literature, Culture and the Arts* (Edinburgh: Edinburgh University Press, 2017)

Vargo, Gregory, 'Chartist drama: The performance of revolt', *Victorian Studies*, vol. 61, no. 1 (2018)

— (ed.), *Chartist Drama* (Manchester: Manchester University Press, 2020)

Vassall, John, *Vassall* (London: Sidgwick & Jackson, 1975)

Verhoeven, Claudia, 'Adventures in terrorism: Sergei Stepniak-Kravchinsky and the literary lives of the Russian revolutionary community', in J. Coy, B. Marschke, I. Poley and C. Verhoeven (eds), *Kinship, Community, and Self: Essays in Honor of David Warren Sabean* (New York: Berghahn Books, 2015)

Vieira, Mark A., *Sin in Soft Focus: Pre-Code Hollywood* (New York: Harry N. Abrams, 1999)

Viry, Auriane de, '16 mai 1717: Le jeune Voltaire est embastillé', *Revue des Deux Mondes*, 16 May 2017

Vizetelly, Ernest, *With Zola in England: A Story of Exile* (London: Chatto & Windus, 1899)

Waal, Clarissa de, *Albania: Portrait of a Country in Transition*, 2nd edition (London: I.B.Tauris, 2014)

Walkling, Andrew R., 'Masque and politics at the Restoration court: John Crowne's "Calisto"', *Early Music*, vol. 24, no. 1 (1996)

Waller, Douglas, *Lincoln's Spies: Their Secret War to Save a Nation* (New York: Simon & Schuster, 2019)

Walpole, Horace, *Letters from the Hon. Horace Walpole to George Montagu, Esq. from the Year 1736 to the Year 1770* (London: Rodwell & Martin, 1818)

Walton, Calder, *Empire of Secrets: British Intelligence, the Cold War and the Twilight of Empire* (London: HarperPress, 2013)

— and Andrew, Christopher, 'Traitorous Blake motivated by Cold War convictions', *Engelsberg Ideas*, 15 January 2021

Wark, Wesley K. (ed.), *Spy Fiction, Spy Films, and Real Intelligence* (London: Frank Cass, 1991)

Watkins, Stephen, 'The protectorate playhouse: William Davenant's cockpit in the 1650s', *Shakespeare Bulletin*, vol. 37, no. 1 (2019)

Weil, M.-H. (ed.), *Les Dessous du Congrès de Vienne, d'après les documents originaux du ministère impérial et royal de l'Intérieur à Vienne*, 2 vols (Paris: Librairie Payot, 1917)

Weis, René, *Shakespeare Revealed: A Biography* (London: John Murray, 2007)

Wells, Stanley, *Shakespeare and Co.* (London: Allen Lane, 2006)

West, Nigel, *The A-Z of British Intelligence* (London: Scarecrow Press, 2009)

— and Tsarev, Oleg, *Crown Jewels: The British Secrets at the Heart of the KGB Archives* (London: HarperCollins, 1998)

Weston, R. P. and Lee, Bert, 'Olga Pulloffski, the Beautiful Spy' (Francis, Day and Hunter Ltd, 1935/EMI Music Publishing)

Westrate, Bruce, *The Arab Bureau: British Policy in the Middle East, 1916–1920* (University Park: University of Pennsylvania Press, 1992)

Wheelwright, Julie, *Mata Hari and the Myth of Women in Espionage* (London: Collins & Brown, 1992)

Wheen, Francis, *Karl Marx* (London: Fourth Estate, 2000)

White, Duncan, *Cold Warriors: Writers Who Waged the Literary Cold War* (New York and London: Little, Brown, 2019)

White, Rosie, *Violent Femmes: Women as Spies in Popular Culture* (London: Routledge, 2007)

Wiel, Jérôme aan de, 'German invasion and spy scares in Ireland, 1890s–1914: Between fiction and fact', *Études irlandaises*, vol. 37, no. 1 (2012)

Wieviorka, Olivier, *Histoire du débarquement en Normandie: Des origines à la libération de Paris, 1941–1944* (Paris: Seuil, 2007)

Wilkes, Sue, *Regency Spies: Secret History of Britain's Rebels and Revolutionaries* (Barnsley: Pen & Sword, 2015)

Williams, Abigail and O'Connor, Kate, 'Aphra Behn and the Restoration theatre'; writersinspire.org/content/aphra-behn-restoration-theatre

Williamson, G. S., 'What killed August von Kotzebue? The temptations of virtue and the political theology of German nationalism, 1789–1819', *Journal of Modern History*, vol. 72, no. 4 (2000)

Wilmetts, Simon, *In Secrecy's Shadow: The OSS and CIA in Hollywood Cinema 1941–1979* (Edinburgh: Edinburgh University Press, 2016)

Wilson, Elizabeth, *Mstislav Rostropovich: Cellist, Teacher, Legend* (London: Faber, 2007)

Wilson, Emily, 'The War in the Dark: The Security Service and the Abwehr 1939–1944' (PhD dissertation, University of Cambridge, 2003)

Wilson, Frances, 'The lost art of table talk', *Literary Review*, February 2014

Wilson, Jennifer, 'When Oscar Wilde colluded with the Russians', *The Paris Review*, 18 October 2017

Wilson, J. and N. (eds), *T. E. Lawrence, Correspondence with Bernard and Charlotte Shaw*, vol. 3: *1928* (Dublin: Castle Hill Press, 2008)

Winton, Calhoun, *John Gay and the London Theatre* (Lexington: University of Kentucky Press, 1993)

Wise, David, *Tiger Trap: America's Secret Spy War with China* (Boston: Houghton, Mifflin, Harcourt, 2011)

Wood, Andy, 'Subordination, solidarity and the limits of popular agency in a Yorkshire valley *c.* 1596–1615', *Past & Present*, no. 193 (November 2006)

Wood, Ean, *The Josephine Baker Story* (London: Omnibus Press, 2010)

Wood, Elizabeth A., *Performing Justice: Agitation Trials in Early Soviet Russia* (Ithaca: Cornell University Press, 2005)

Wood, Harry, '"The play all London is discussing": The great success of Guy du Maurier's *An Englishman's Home*, 1909', *Theatre Notebook*, vol. 70, no. 3 (2016)

Woodward, Bob, *The Secret Man: The Story of Watergate's Deep Throat* (New York: Simon & Schuster, 2005)

Worrall, David, *Theatric Revolution: Drama, Censorship, and the Romantic Period Subcultures 1773–1832* (Oxford: Oxford University Press, 2006)

Wright, Peter, with Greengrass, Paul, *Spycatcher: The Candid Autobiography of a Senior Intelligence Officer* (paperback edition, New York: Dell, 1988)

Yardley, Herbert O., *The American Black Chamber* (Boston: Houghton Mifflin, 1931)

Young, Kevin, *Bunk: The Rise of Hoaxes, Humbug, Plagiarists, Phonies, Post-Facts, and Fake News* (Minneapolis: Graywolf Press, 2017)

Yurchak, Alexei, *Everything Was Forever, Until It Was No More* (Princeton, NJ: Princeton University Press, 2005)

Zamoyski, Adam, *Phantom Terror: The Threat of Revolution and the Repression of Liberty, 1789–1848* (London: William Collins, 2014)

Zimmermann, G. D., *Songs of Irish Rebellion: Political Street Ballads and Rebel Songs, 1780–1900* (Dublin: Allen Figgis, 1967)

Zola, Émile, 'Naturalism on the stage' (1881), in Cole, Toby (ed.), *Playwrights on Playwriting: From Ibsen to Ionescu* (New York: Cooper Square Press, 2001)

Picture credits

Grateful acknowledgement is made to the following for permission to reproduce images: AA Film Archive/Alamy Stock Photo (pp. 4, 355); Allstar Picture Library/Alamy Stock Photo (p. 366); The Arthur Lloyd Archive (p. 164); BBC Photo Library (pp. 284, 372, 376); Bettmann via Getty Images (pp. 293, 311); Bletchley Park Trust (p. 290); Olivier Boitet/AP/Shutterstock (p. 342); bpk/Staatsbibliothek zu Berlin/Ruth Schacht (p. 116); The British Library (p. 151); The Trustees of the British Museum (pp. 7, 81, 108, 110, 113); Churchill Archives Centre (p. 191); P. F. Debert/Centre des Archives diplomatiques du ministère des Affaires étrangères de la Courneuve (p. 92); The Dennis Wheatley Museum (p. 257 top and bottom left); dpa picture alliance/Alamy Stock Photo (p. 357); Everett Collection/Alamy Stock Photo (pp. 232, 239, 240, 296); Fenimore Art Museum (p. 123); Folger Shakespeare Library/LUNA Folger Digital Image Collection (pp. 31, 34); Commander Mike Forbes (p. 205); History and Art Collection/Alamy Stock Photo (p. 163); Hoover Institution Library & Archives, Sir Paul Dukes papers, Box 3, Folder (p. 207); Hulton Archive/Stringer via Getty Images (p. 260); Nick Jones (p. 218); Keystone-France/Gamma-Rapho via Getty Images (p. 157); LA Times (p. 282); The Lawbook Exchange (p. 128); David Levenson via Getty Images (p. 351); Library of Congress (pp. 125, 138, 139 left); LMPC via Getty Images (p. 222); The Marist Archives & Special Collections/Marist Library (p. 213); The Master and Fellows of Corpus Christi College, Cambridge (pp. 18, 19); The Mitrokhin Estate (p. 353); Moviestore Collection Ltd/Alamy Stock Photo (p. 310); National Archives (pp. 38, 62, 181, 229, 255, 261, 316); National Portrait Gallery, London (pp. 53, 63, 165); PA Images/Alamy Stock Photo (p. 348); Peter Newark Military Pictures/Bridgeman Images (p. 139 right); PhotoQuest via Getty Images (p. 304); PictureLux/The Hollywood Archive/Alamy Stock Photo (p. 287); Eugene Robert

Richee via Getty Images (p. 211); The Roosevelt Library, NARA (p. 285); Royal Shakespeare Company (p. 320); SilverScreen/Alamy Stock Photo (p. 279); SHONE via Getty Images (p. 343); Sotheby's (p. 52); SPUTNIK/Alamy Stock Photo (pp. 328, 359); Théâtre des Champs-Elysées (p. 302); Times Newspapers/Shutterstock (p. 352); Harry S. Truman Presidential Library & Museum (p. 294); Victoria and Albert Museum, London (pp. 29, 71); Keith Waldegrave/Mail on Sunday/Shutterstock (p. 268); Andy Walmsley (p. 247); The Wellcome Collection (p. 89); Westminster Abbey Library (pp. 59, 65); Alexander Zemlianichenko/AP/Shutterstock (p. 345).

Every effort has been made to trace and contact copyright holders. The publishers will be pleased to correct any mistakes or omissions in future editions.

Acknowledgements

Much of the original inspiration for *Stars and Spies* came from Corpus Christi College, Cambridge, where, over twenty years apart, both its authors read history. Corpus is the college of Britain's first dramatist-spy, Christopher Marlowe. During their careers as, respectively, Cambridge historian and theatre producer, Christopher Andrew and Julius Green became intrigued by some more recent Corpus spies who also worked in the entertainment business. While working with Vasili Mitrokhin on top-secret material he had exfiltrated from KGB files in Moscow, Andrew was struck by evidence that the leading Hollywood film critic, Cedric Belfrage, had worked for Soviet as well as British intelligence. As a circus director himself, Green was impressed by the key role in MI5 of the circus impresario, Cyril Bertram Mills, during the Second World War.

Before the weekly meetings of the Cambridge Intelligence Seminar, the convenors and speakers meet in Corpus Old Combination Room beneath a painting dated 1585 which is believed to be the only contemporary portrait of Marlowe. During research for both the text and illustrations of *Stars and Spies*, Seminar presentations and discussions at Corpus have been a constant source of inspiration.

There is no space, alas, to thank by name all those who have offered helpful comments and suggestions at presentations of some of our research on both sides of the Atlantic, on cruises visiting some of the locations in this book, and after our broadcast documentaries over many years. We are particularly grateful, however, to all the following for responding to research queries and/or for commenting on various parts of the text and illustrations: Professor Haroon Ahmed, John Barker, Louisa Barker, Ian and Sandy Bell, Gill Bennett, Professor Tim Blanning, Dr Piers Brendon, Vyvyen Brendon, Alan Brodie, Gerry Cottle, Professor Katherine Ellis, Dr Mel Evans, Professor Mirjam

Foot, Professor Vic Gatrell, Oleg Gordievsky, Professor Hyman Gross, Nicholas Howard, Professor Peter Jackson, Alan Judd, Tarun Krishnakumar, Professor Neil Kent, Dr Dan Larsen, Dr Thomas Maguire, Keith Melton, Professor Eunan O'Halpin, Sir David Omand, Dr Allen Packwood, Professor Glyn Parry, Hayden Peake, Dr John Ranelagh, Dr Gabriela Richterova, Dr Tim Schmaltz, Dr David Smith, Professor Norio Suzuki, Dr John Thompson, Dr Isabelle Tombs, Professor Robert Tombs, Henrietta Twycross-Martin, Dr Jackie Ui Chionna, Dr Calder Walton, Dr Stephen Whalley, Baron Wilson of Dinton, Nicole Wilson, J. D. Work and Dr Patrick Zutshi.

The expertise and support of our literary agent, Bill Hamilton, and our editor, Jörg Hensgen, have been indispensable. Our warm thanks to both. By remarkable serendipity, our copy-editor, Dr Henry Howard, worked on our text at a desk in Johnby Hall next to a priest's hole which over 400 years ago sheltered a Catholic priest briefly mentioned in our book. We owe him a great debt for his exceptional expertise and insights on topics ranging from early English music to the history of GCHQ. We are also most grateful to our picture researcher, Piers Haslam, for tracking down our chosen illustrations from a wide variety of international sources.

Errors that remain are, of course, our responsibility. We shall be grateful to readers kind enough to point them out to us.

Christopher Andrew and Julius Green

Index

Abbey Theatre, Dublin, 169, 170, 215
Above Suspicion (1943 film), 288–9
Abtey, Maurice, 273, 274, 275
Abwehr, 248–52, 259–63, 266–7, 311
Abyssinia, 164–6
Aces of the Air (Draper), 248
Act for Regulating Theatres (1843), 132, 224
Act of Union (1707), 76–8
active measures, 45, 88, 325, 358
Adams, John, 236
Adcock, Frank, 191, *192*
Addison, Joseph, 79–83, 98, 101
Adelphi Theatre, London, 150
Adler, Larry, 371
Administration of Special Tasks, 304
Admiralty, 190–94, 263
Affleck, Ben, *337*
Afghanistan, 338
Agar, Augustus, 201–2, 206
Ageloff, Sylvia, 3
Air Ministry, 263
Al Din and a Wonderful Ramp (Clarke), 255
Aladdin (pantomime), 191, 276
Alamire, Petrus, 8–9
Albania, A Fish and A Motorcar (Footman), 241
Alchemist, The (Jonson) 45
Alex Rider novels, 374
Alexander I, Emperor of Russia, 116, 118
Alexander II, Emperor of Russia, 121, 136, 148–9, 150
Alexander Nevsky (Prokofiev), 346
Alexandra Palace, London, 250
Alexy II, Patriarch, 359
Alfield, Thomas, 15
Alfonso XIII, King of Spain, 184
Alfred, King of the Anglo-Saxons, 7–8, *7*
Algeria, 275
Algonquin Hotel, New York, 209
Alhambra, London, 154
Alice in Blunderland (Clarke), 255
Alice's Adventures in Wonderland (Carroll), 191
Alien Office, 108, 110

Aliens Act (1793), 108
Alington, Cyril, 210
All Souls College, Oxford, 244, 245
All the President's Men (1976 film), 330
Allen, William, 141
Allenby, Edmund, 212
Alliluyeva, Svetlana, 225
Alsop, Carleton, 305
Amateur Dramatic Club (ADC), 300
Amazon, 358
American Ballet Theatre, New York, 324
American Civil War (1861–5), 136–40
American Legion, 278
American Revolution (1765–83), 2, 96–102
Americans, The (TV series), 366–8, *366*
Amman, Jordan, 216
André, John, 124
Andrew, Christopher, 349, 352, 370, 374–5
Andrieux, Louis, 143–4
Andropov, Yuri, 326, 327–8, 343, 360
Anglo-Boer War (1899–1902), 169, 172–3
Anglo-Dutch Wars
   1652–4, 54
   1665–7, 61, 62, 63
Anglo-Russian Commission, 198
Anglo-Saxons, 7
Anglo-Spanish War
   1585–1604, 13–14, 30, 166
   1625–1630, 46
Animal Farm (Orwell), 305–6, 329
Annan, Noel, 90
Anne of Austria, Queen consort, 93
Anne of Denmark, Queen consort, 35, 40–41
Anne, Queen of Great Britain, 76, 79, 80, 82
Anslinger, Harry, 317
d'Anthès, Georges, 122
Antwerp, 60, 61, 62, 63, 301
Apocalypse Code (2007 film), 361–2, *361*
Aqaba, Jordan, 212, 214
Arab Revolt (1916–18), 211–12, 214, 215
Arabian Nights, 204

Arbuthnott, James, *257*
Argentina, 284
Argo (2012 film), 337
Arlington, Henry Bennet, 1st Earl, 61, 62,
    63, 64, 68–9
armigers, 42
Arnold, Benedict, 123
d'Arouet, François-Marie, 83
Art of War, The (Sun Tzu), 5, 6, 358
Arthashastra (Kautilya), 5–6, 8
As You Like It (Shakespeare), 23
Asche, Oscar, 204–5, 214
Ashenden (Maugham), 217–18
Asquith, Herbert Henry, 162, 167
Association of Former Intelligence Officers
    (AFIO), 370
astrology, 281–3, *282*
At Every Kilometre (TV series), 326
Athenian Memories (Mackenzie), 219
Athens, Greece, 197
Atkyns, Charlotte, 101, 107, *108*, 222
Atlantic Charter (1941), 287
Attack on a Picquet (1899 film), 173
Atterbury, Francis, 85, 86
Auden, W. H., 225
Augustus Does His Bit (Shaw), 189–90
Australia, 380
Austria, 91–2, 116, 229–30
Aztec Empire (1428–1521), 43

B1a, 250–55, 259, 263–5, 268, 269
Babington, Anthony, 12, 20, 25, 35
Bacall, Lauren, 294–5, *294*
Baden-Powell, Robert, 179, *180*
Badge of Military Merit, 123
Baines, Richard, 22
Baird, Edward 'Teddy', 301
Bajolet, Bernard, 368
Baker, Josephine, 272–6, *273*
Baldwin, James, 322
Baldwin, Stanley, 210
Balkan Holiday (Footman), 241
ballet, 323–4
Balliol College, Oxford, 166
Baltzar, Thomas, 56
Banister, John, 56
Bank of England, 111
Bankhead, Tallulah, 208–10, *211*, 317–18, *319*
Barbier de Séville, Le (Beaumarchais), 94,
    96–7
Bardem, Javier, 374
Barkas, Geoffrey, 258
Barnum, Phineas Taylor, 139
Barras, Jacques-Melchior Saint-Laurent,
    comte de, 101
Bastille House, Greenwich Park, 74
Bastille Prison, Paris, 83, 106, 107, 109

Bate, Jonathan, 28
Battle of Blenheim (1704), 76, 82
Battle of El Alamein (1942), 258
Battle of Saratoga (1777), 100
Battle of the Boyne (1690), 75
Battleship Potemkin (1925 film), 226
Bazeries, Etienne, 93
Bazhenov, Sergei, 361–2
de Beaumarchais, Pierre-Augustin, 2, 94–7,
    100–103, 120
Beaumont Society, 102
Beaumont, Francis, 45
van Beethoven, Ludwig, 115
Beggar's Opera, The (Gay), 87–8
Behan, Brendan, 320–21
Behn, Aphra, 60–65, *61*, *65*, 68
Belfrage, Bruce, 277
Belfrage, Cedric, 226–7, 277, 291–2
Belgium, 178, 186, 187, 221
von Benckendorff, Alexander, 117, 118, 119,
    121, 122
Bendo, Alexander, 66–8
Bennet, Henry, 1st Earl of Arlington, 61–2,
    63, 64, 68–9
Bennett, Alan, 24, 310
Bentley, Elizabeth, 292
Bermuda, 332, *333*
Bernal, J. D., 226
Bernard, Pierre Arnold, 207
Bernhardt, Sarah, 146, 163, 184
Bernstein, Carl, 330
Berry, Herbert, 12
Best Man, The (Vidal), 321–2
Bevan, Aneurin, 226
Bevan, John Henry, 255, *257*, 260
Bhatt, Alia, 378
Bianchi, Daniela, 314
Bijou Picture Theatre, Finchley Road, 2, 181
Billotte, Pierre, 276
Bim-Bom, 199–200, 206
Birch, Frank, 191, 243, 289, 290, 291
Birmingham, Ernest Barnes, Bishop, 226
Bissell, Daniel, 123
Black August (Wheatley), 256
Black Panther (2018 film), 5
Black Tom Pier, New Jersey, 182
blackface, 164–6
Blair, Tony, 356
Blake, William, 126
blasphemy, 128
Bletchley Park, 125, 240, 247–8, 374
    Birch and, 191
    Churchill and, 262, 314
    declassification, 331–2
    Fleming and, 272, 314
    Gibson and, 289

Philby and, 243
Pujol and, 259
Soviet infiltration, 291, 350
Stephenson and, 291
Truman and, 295
Blockade of Boston, The (Burgoyne), 100
Blondel de Nesle, 8
Bloody Sunday (1920), 214
Bloomsbury group, 163
Blue Angel, The (1935 film), 194
Blue Peter, 374–6
Blunt, Anthony, 24, 231, 244, 245, 261, 262, 264, 291, 335, 349
van Blyenberch, Abraham, 36
Boddington, Herbert 'Con', 208
'Bodenstown Churchyard' (Davis), 131
Boer War (1899–1902), 169, 172–3
Bohlen, Charles 'Chip', 234
de Boisdeffre, Raoul, 156
Bolingbroke, Henry St John, 1st Viscount, 84, 85–6
Bollywood, 377–8
Bond Street, London, 262
Bond, Anne, 86
book reading, 172
Booth, John Wilkes, 3, 136–8, 137, 138
Borderers, The (Wordsworth), 112
Borgnine, Ernest, 308
Boris Godunov (Pushkin), 117
Boshnyak, Alexander, 118–19
Boston, Massachusetts, 98–100
Boucicault, Dion, 142–3, 150
Bourgeois, Jeanne, 182–4, 183, 273
Boursicot, Bernard, 340–42, 342
Boutell, Elizabeth, 65
Bow Street Runners, 90
Boy Scouts, 179, 199
Boyd, Isabella 'Belle', 139–40, 139, 222
Boyer, Charles, 295
Boyle, David, 8
Bracken, Brendan, 332
Bradford Grammar School, 300, 303
Brando, Marlon, 250
Brazil, 274
Breaking the Code (Whitemore), 332
Breeckow, Georg, 180
Brezhnev, Leonid, 327, 337, 338
Bristol, England, 111, 112
British Board of Film Censors (BBFC), 173, 225, 245
British Broadcasting Corporation (BBC), 2, 131, 223–4, 284, 291, 326, 347
  Blue Peter Project Petra (2015), 374–6
  MI5 and, 242, 244
  Soviet infiltration, 241–7
British Deciphering Branch, 85
British Postal Censorship, 180, 181

British Security Coordination (BSC), 271–2, 276–93, 332, 333
British Union of Fascists, 263
British Workers' Theatre Movement, 225
Bronson Canyon, Los Angeles, 297
Brothers of the Aryan World Order, 262
Bruce, Henry, 148
Brutus (Voltaire), 86
Bryce, Ivar, 276, 284
Buchanan, George, 218
Buckingham, George Villiers, 1st Duke, 45–6
Buckingham, George Villiers, 2nd Duke, 68
Bulgaria, 325–7
Bullitt, William Christian, 232, 233, 234
de Bulonde, Vivien, 93
Bundesnachrichtendienst (BND), 354
Bureau central de renseignements et d'action (BCRA), 274
Bureau des légendes, Le (TV series), 368–9
Burgess, Guy, 24, 231, 241–6, 242, 262, 267, 310, 349
Burghley, William Cecil, 1st Baron, 28–9
Burgoyne, John, 99–102, 100
Burke, Edmund Michael, 296
Burnet, Gilbert, 66
Burschenschaften, 115–16
Burt, Cyril, 231
Bury St Edmunds, Suffolk, 260
Buschmann, Fernando, 179
Bush, George H. W., 370
Bush, George W., 354
de Bussy, François, 91, 92
Buxton, Edward, 293
Byron, George Gordon, 126

'Ça Ira', 109
Café Grangier, Sochaux, 303
Cage, Nicholas, 355
Cagney, James, 297
Cairncross, John, 231, 350–51
Calisto (Crowne), 66
Call from the Dead (Le Carré), 335
Callaghan, James, 349
Callow, Simon, 277
Cambodia, 24
Cambridge University, 18, 20, 23, 42, 46, 50, 190, 191, 226, 228, 289
  Footlights revues, 289
  Mai Jia at, 356–7
  Soviet spy ring, 228, 230, 231, 241–7, 261–2, 264, 267, 291, 310, 349–51
Camp X, Ontario, 276, 333
Camp, The (Sheridan), 101, 107, 108
Campion, Edmund, 15, 16
Canada, 276, 284
Cánovas del Castillo, Antonio, 136

Captain Swing, 127
Carlile, Richard, 126–9
Carlsbad decrees (1819), 116
Carlyle, Thomas, 134
Carnegie Hall, New York, 319
Carnot, Sadi, 136
Caroline (Maugham), 194–5
Carr, Robert, 1st Earl of Somerset, 45
Carroll, Lewis, 191
Carroll, Madeleine, 221, 223
Carte, Thomas, 85
Carton, Florent 'Dancourt', 74–5
Caruso, Enrico, 171
Casanova, Giacomo, 103–5, *104*
Case is Altered, The (Jonson), 40
Casement, Roger, 189
Casino de Paris, Paris, 183
Casino Royale (Fleming), 271, 312
Castle, John, 125
Castlereagh, Robert Stewart, Viscount, 125
Castro, Fidel, *311*
Catesby, Robert, 37, 39
Catherine of Braganza, Queen consort,
    57, 68
Cathleen ni Houlihan (Gregory and
    Yeats), 169
Catholicism
    Caroline era (1625–49), 47, 49
    Civil War era (1642–51), 50, 53
    Cold War era (1947–91), 307, 312
    Elizabethan era (1558–1603), 11, 13–17,
        19, 20, 26, 28–30, 32
    Jacobean era (1603–1625), 32, 35–41,
        44, 46
    Restoration era (1660–88), 61, 68, 70
Catiline His Conspiracy (Jonson), 44
Cato (Addison), 79, 98, 101
Cavalcanti, Alberto, 226
Cecil, Robert, 28–9, 31–2, 37–9, 46
Cecil, William, 28–9
Central Intelligence Agency (CIA), 77, 299,
    366–8
    Canadian Caper (1979–80), 2, 336–7
    Center for the Study of Intelligence, 97
    covert actions, 45
    film industry and, 305–6, 309, 328–9
    Hale statue, 98
    Indochina War, First (1946–54), 309
    Khokhlov defection (1954), 304, 313
    Langley HQ, 98, 329, 373
    Mitrokhin exfiltration (1992), 352, 367
    Nixon, relations with, 24
    Pasternak, promotion of, 324
    Reel vs Real initiatives, 367, 373
    Spy Kids programme, 376–7
    television depictions, 366–8, 369
    Twitter account, 5, 380

Watergate scandal (1972–4), 329–31
Weisberg's training, 366
Central Intelligence Group (CIG), 298
Central Office of Information, 300
Chapel Royal, 56
Chaplin, Charles, 322–3
Chapman, Anna, 363–5, *365*
Chapman, George, 36
Charles I, King of England and Scotland,
    35, 41, 46–53, 57, 58, 59
Charles II, King of England and Scotland,
    56, 57–60, 62, 64, 66, 68–70, 79
Charteris, Francis, 86
Chartist movement (1838–57), 132–3
Chase, Harry, 212, 213, 216, *216*
Château de la Source, France, 84
Château de Vincennes, France, 188
Châtiments, Les (Hugo), 135
Cheka, 199–202, 206, 226, 237
Chekists, The (1939 play), 237
Cheltenham Ladies' College, 203
Chesapeake Bay, 101
Chétardie, Jacques-Joachim Trotti, marquis
    de, 92
Chevalier d'Éon, 94–5, *95*, 102, *103*, 106
Chevalier, Maurice, 184
Childers, Erskine, 159
China Syndrome, The (1979 film), 336
China, 339–43, 356–8
    Art of War, The, 5, 6
    Boursicot–Shi case (1983–6), 340
    COVID-19 pandemic (2019–21), 378
    India, relations with, 378
    S&T operations, 356
    Tiananmen Square massacre (1989), 340
Chips (Pelissier), 168
Chitty Chitty Bang Bang (1968 film), 276
Cholmley, Richard, 42
Cholmondeley, Charles, 264, *265*
Chopin, Frédéric, 168
Christian IV, King of Denmark, 30, 35
Christie, Agatha, 23–4, 229
Chu Chin Chow (Asche), 204–5, 214
Churchill, Winston, *332*
    Atlantic Charter (1941), 287
    BSC and, 286–7, 292
    Burgess, relationship with, 242
    Cairncross and, 350
    deception operations, 262, 263–4, 266,
        267, 270
    Korda, relationship with, 217
    Lawrence, relationship with, 214
    Maugham, relationship with, 218
    McKenna, relationship with, 222
    Paris Peace Conference (1919), 212
    Reith, relationship with, 242
    Russian Civil War (1917–23), 206

SIGINT, 242, 262, 314
That Hamilton Woman! (1941 film), 286–7
Pearl Harbor attack (1941), 288
ULTRA decrypts, 262, 314
cigarette packet gun, 304, *305*
Cinema Research and Development
  Ltd, 231
cinemas, 172
Civil War (1642–51), 48–51, 52, 57, 58, 64
Clan na Gael, 169
Clare College, Cambridge, 20
Clark, Neil Gordon, *257*
Clarke, Dudley, 254–5, *255*, 258
Clarkson, William, 163–6, *164*, 179, 206,
  258, *351*
Clemenceau, Georges, 158
Clifford, Thomas, 68
Clifton James, Meyrick Edward, 258
Clinch, Charles Powell, 124
Clinton, Bill, 370
Cloak and Dagger (1946 film), 296–7
Coatman, John, 245
cocaine, 254, 317
Cockpit Theatre, Drury Lane, 56, 57
Code of the Secret Service (1939 film), 240
codebreaking
  Elizabethan England (1558–1603), 11, 25,
    32, 49
  English Civil War (1642–51), 50
  Georgian Britain (1714–1837), 85, 86, 91
  Louis XIII's France (1610–1643), 49–50
  Louis XIV's France (1643–1715), 71–2
  Louis XV's France (1715–1774), 91–3
  Napoleonic Wars (1803–1815), 124–5
  Nicholas II's Russia (1894–1917), 167
  Soviet Union (1922–91), 234
  World War I (1914–18), 134, 186,
    190–94
  World War II (1939–45), 248, 259, 262,
    265, 271–2, 290, 291, 295
  see also Bletchley Park
Cold War (1947–91), 124, 268, 299, 300–38
  Afghanistan War (1979–89), 338
  Cuban Missile Crisis (1962), 311
  Hungarian uprising (1956), 315, 321
  Markov assassination (1978), 327
  nuclear weapons, 311, 332, 349
Coleman, Catherine, 56
Coleman, Edward, 55, 56
Coleridge, Samuel Taylor, 112
Collegium Anglorum, Rome, 14
Collins, Michael, 214–15
Colman, Ronald, 251
Colonial Office, 214, 316
Columbia, 336
Columbia University, 289
Comédie-Française, 73, 74, 84, 105

Committee of Imperial Defence (CID),
  161, 166
Common Sense, 88
communism, 148, 208, 224, 225–7, 229, 242,
  244–6, 278, 292
  First Red Scare (1917–20), 208
  Second Red Scare (1947–57), 305–9, 317,
    319, 322, 371–2
Communist Party
  of Britain, 208, 223, 245, 309, 310,
    315, 321
  of Soviet Union, 201, 226, 227, 237,
    338, 345
  of United States, 227, 307, 369, 371
Condon, Edward O'Meagher, 141
Confidential Agent (1945 film), 294–5
Connery, Sean, 314–15, 347, *355*, 381, 382
Connolly, James, 171
Connolly, Sean, 171
Conrad, Joseph, 160
Cooke, Henry, 56
Cooper, Alfred Duff, 263, 266, 286
Cooper, Gary, 297
Cooper, James Fenimore, 123–4, *123*, 161
Cooper, Thomas, 26
Cornwallis, Charles, 1st Marquess, 101
Cornwell, David, 218, 334
Corpus Christi College, Cambridge, 18, 23,
  226, *325*
Coste, Maurice, 146
Counter-Espionage Bureau, 174, 176
Country House, The (Vanbrugh), 75
courtesans, 7
Covent Garden, London, 90, 102, 126, 132,
  213, *324*
COVID-19 pandemic (2019–21), 339, 378
Coward, Noël, 3, 276, 277–80, *279*, 311
Cowes Regatta, 166
Craft of Intelligence, The (Dulles), 77
Craftsman, The, 89
Craig, Daniel, *4*, *372*, 373–4, *373*
Craig, Douglas, 289
Crawford, Joan, 289
Cripplegate Institute, London, 202
Cripps, Richard Stafford 226
de Croissy, Colbert, 68–70
Cromwell, Oliver, 53–6, 75, 99
Cromwell, Richard, 56
Cronenberg, David, 342
Crowley, Aleister, 256
Crowne, John, 66
Crowther, Bosley, 296, 298
Cruel Brother, The (Davenant), 48
Cruikshank, George, 90, 125
Crusade, Third (1189–1192), 8
Cuban Missile Crisis (1962), 311
Cumberbatch, Benedict, 332

Cumming, Homer Stille, 240
Cumming, Mansfield, 1, 162–6, *163*,
      194–200, 206–7, 217, 220
CURVEBALL, 354–6
Curzon, George, 1st Marquess, 206
Cushman, Pauline, 138–9, *139*, 222
Czech Republic, 105

D-Day (1944), 258, 266, 267, 268, 297
Da Ponte, Lorenzo, 103
Dahl, Roald, 276, 280
Daily Express, 176
Daily Mail, 160, 231, 372
Daily Worker, 226
'Dance of the Seven Veils', 214
Dance, Eric, 252
Dancourt, 74–5
Danes, Claire, 369
Danilin, Sergei, 238
Dansey, Claude, 286
Danton, Georges, 106
Darzhavna Sigurnost (DS), 325
Davenant, William, 48, 52–6, *53*, 57, 59, *59*,
      64, 73
Davies, Tom, 87
Davis, Jefferson, 138
Davis, Thomas Osborne, 131
Dawson, Douglas, 168
De Gaulle, Charles, 274–6
De Havilland, *248*, *249*, 253
De la Pole, Richard, 8–9
De La Thorillière, Thérèse, 74
De Valera, Eamon, 170
Deane, Silas, 96, 97
Dearlove, Richard, 1, 336, 382
Decembrist Revolt (1825), 118
Deciphering Branch, 134
Declaration of the Rights of Man (1789),
      106, 144
Decoded (Mai), 356
Dee, John, 43
Defoe, Daniel, 24, 77–83
Dehn, Paul, 276
Dekker, Thomas, 250
Delalande, Michel-Richard, 71
Delon, Alain, 329
Dench, Judy, 4–5, *4*, 348
Denmark, 30–32
Derry Opera House, 142
Desmarets, Jean, 49
Desperate Journey (1942 film), 240
Deutsch, Arnold, 228–31, *229*, *230*, 241
Deutsch, Oscar, 229, 230, 231
Deuxième Bureau, 156, 273–4
DGSE (Direction générale de la sécurité
      extérieure), 368
Diamonds Are Forever (Fleming), 284

Dickens, Charles, 133
Dietrich, Marlene, 194, 221, 223
Dillon, Stephen, 186
Dimbleby Lecture, 347–8
Director of Central Intelligence (DCI),
      298, 370
Director of Naval Intelligence (DNI),
      190, 192
Dishonored (1931 film), 221
Disney, 306
Disraeli, Benjamin, 143
Dnepropetrovsk Oblast, Russia, 337
Dobb, Maurice, 226
Doctor Faustus (Marlowe), 19–20
Doctor Zhivago (Pasternak), 324
Don Giovanni (Mozart), 105
Donovan, William 'Big Bill', 270, 272, 284,
      293–4, *293*, 295, 296–9, 334
Dorset Garden Theatre, London, 60
Dorset, John Sackville, 3rd Duke, 102, 106
double agents, 2, 248–55, 258–63, 266–9,
      330, 331
Douglas, Michael, 336
Doval, Ajit, 378
Dowland, John, 28–30, *29*
Dr No (Fleming), 315, 379
Drake, Francis, 13–14
Draper, Christopher, 248–50, *249*
Dreadnought, HMS, 164–6
Dreyfus Affair (1894–1906), 144, 155–8
Drouet, Juliette, 146
Drury Lane theatre, London
      1663–1674 first theatre, 60
      1674–1791 second theatre, 79, 83, 90, 99,
            101, 102, 108, 126
      1794–1809 third theatre, 109, 111, 113
      1812–present fourth theatre, 112, 126,
            132, 143
Dryden, John, 64, 66, 67
Du Maurier, Gerald, 167
Du Maurier, Guy, 167–9
Dublin, Ireland
      Abbey Theatre, 169, 170, 215
      Bloody Sunday (1920), 214
      Castle, 129, 130, 131, 170
      Easter Rising (1916), 170, 171, 172
      Englishman's Home performance
            (1909), 169
      Home Rule demonstration (1912), 170
      Mountjoy Prison, 320
      Rebellion (1803), 132
      Under Which Flag? performance
            (1916), 171
Dudley, Robert, 1st Earl of Leicester, 13
Duggan, Larry, 232
Duke's Men, 60, 73
Dukes, Paul, 198–202, *201*, 206–7, *207*

Dulles, Allen, 77, 309
Dumas, Alexandre, 93, 144
Dunkirk evacuation (1940), 244, 256
'Dunlavin Green' (ballad), 130
Dutch Republic (1588–1795), 54, 61, 62, 63
Dynamite War (1881–85), 152–3, 155
Dzerzhinsky, Felix, 236–7, 327, 344, 345

Earnest, Peter, 370
East Germany (1949–90), 306, 327, 334, 335
Easter Rising (1916), 170, 171, 172, 189, 190
Eastward Ho! (Chapman, Jonson and
    Marston), 36
Economist, The, 357
Eden, Anthony, 322
Edinburgh, Philip Mountbatten, Duke, 268
Edinburgh, Scotland, 172, 176, 197
Edmonds, James, 161, 168
Edward VII, King of the United Kingdom,
    142, 167
Eiffel Tower, Paris, 187
1812 Overture (Tchaikovsky), 346
Eisenhower, Dwight, 264
Eisenstein, Sergei, 226
Elisabeth, Empress of Austria, 136
Elizabeth I, Queen of England, 2, 9, 11–12,
    30–32, 32, 35, 40, 98, 166, 307, 372
    assassination plots, 11–12
    death (1603), 35
    Rainbow Portrait (c.1600), 31, 372
Elizabeth II, Queen of the United Kingdom,
    247, 339, 372–3, 372
Elizabeth, Empress of Russia, 92
Ellis, Havelock, 226
Embassy Theatre, London, 315
Émié, Bernard, 368, 377
Emmet, Robert, 132
England
    Caroline era (1625–1649), 47–8
    Civil War era (1642–1651), 48–51, 52, 57,
        58, 64
    Elizabethan era (1558–1603), 2, 9, 11–35,
        40, 98, 166
    Interregnum era (1649–1660), 51–6, 75
    Jacobean era (1603–1625), 32, 35–47
    Restoration era (1660–1715), 56,
        57–75, 76
Englishman Abroad, An (1983 TV drama), 310
Englishman's Home, An (Du Maurier), 167–9
Enigma machine, 125, 248, 314
Enter a Spy (Lom), 372
Erskine-Hill, Evelyn, 203
Esterhazy, Ferdinand, 156
Estonia, 115
Eton College, Berkshire, 209, 210, 211, 241,
    242, 284
Eugene Onegin (Pushkin), 117

Eugénie, Empress consort, 135
Euston Hall, Suffolk, 69
Evans, Thomas, 111
Evelyn, John, 59, 69
Ewing, Alfred, 190, 191
Extremes Meet (Mackenzie), 219

F.B.I. Front (1942 film), 288
Faisal I, King of Iraq, 212
Faneuil Hall, Boston, 99
Farr, Finis, 305
Fars Fausselandry, vicomtesse de, 95
Fast's Hotel, Jerusalem, 214
Faunt, Nicholas, 22
Fawkes, Guy, 37
Featherstone, Jane, 362
Fedele and Fortunio (Munday), 17, 26
Federal Bureau of Investigation (FBI), 234,
    238–9, 321–2
    Belfrage, liaison with, 291–2
    Chaplin, surveillance of, 322, 323
    Coward, surveillance of, 278
    film industry and, 288, 297, 298
    Holiday, surveillance of, 317–18
    Hollywood informants, 308
    Moscow embassy sweep (1944), 234
    Operation GHOST STORIES (c.2000–2010),
        363–8
    Robeson, surveillance of, 317, 319
    Watergate scandal (1972–4), 330–31
Federal Narcotics Bureau, 317
Feign'd Courtesans, The (Behn), 64, 65
Felt, Mark, 330
Fenian movement, 141–3, 152–3, 155,
    171, 214
Ferrabosco, Alfonso, 56
Festival of the Golden Rump, The, 88–90, 89
Fetterlein, Ernst, 167
Fianna Éireann, 169
Field, Sidney, 265–6
Fielding, Henry, 86, 88, 90, 91
Fifteen-Minute Hamlet, The (Stoppard), 348
Fifth Man, The (1990 documentary), 350–51
film/TV industry
    China, 357, 377
    France, 238–9
    India, 377–9
    Russian Federation, 360–62
    Soviet Union, 225–7, 236, 303–5, 327–8
    United Kingdom, 172–5, 225–6, 228–31,
        300–303, 305–7, 362
    United States, 224, 227–8, 231–4, 286–9,
        294–8, 305–11, 328–9, 360, 363–8
Fine Madness, A (Judd), 372
Finney, Philip Edmund Stanley, 253
Finter, Alec, 257
Five Eyes, 3, 380

Five Graves to Cairo (1943 film), 258
Fleming, Ian, 210–11, 264, 271–2, 276, 281,
    284, 306, 312–15, 347
Fleming, Jeremy, 382
de Fleury, André-Hercule, 91
Flying Deuces, The (1939 film), 227–8
Flynn, Errol, 240
von Fock, Maxim, 117
Folie du Jour, La (Baker), 273
Folies Bergère, Paris, 183
Follow My Leader (Maurice and Rattigan), 225
Fonteyn, Margot, 324
Foot, M. R. D., 303
Footlights revues, 289
Footman, David, 241
Forbes, Evelyn, 203
Forc'd Marriage, The (Behn), 64
Ford, Corey, 296
Ford, John, 225
Foreign Legion, 228
Foreign Office, 198, 214, 224, 350
Forever and a Day (Horowitz), 374
Foster, Roy, 172
Fotheringhay Castle, Northamptonshire, 25
Fox, Charles James, 109, *110*
Fradkov, Mikhail, 359
Frederick II, King of Prussia, 91
Free France (1940–44), 274–6
Freud, Sigmund, 229
France
    American Revolutionary War (1775–83),
        2, 96–7, 101
    assassinations of kings, 11, 41
    Boursicot–Shi case (1983–6), 340
    censorship in, 90–91, 94, 146
    CURVEBALL defection (1999), 354
    DGSE, 368–9, 377
    Dreyfus Affair (1894–1906), 144,
        155–8, 159
    First Empire era (1804–1815), 124–5
    First Republic era (1792–1804), 107–112
    Foreign Legion, 228
    Indochina War (1946–54), 309, 312
    Liberation of Paris (1944), 276
    Louis XIII era (1610–1643), 46–7, 48, 49,
        50, 71
    Louis XIV era (1643–1715), 50, *55*, 68,
        70–73, 76, 90, 92–3
    Louis XV era (1715–1774), 83, 91–3, 94
    Louis XVI era (1774–1792), 94–7, 101,
        106–7
    Medici's Flying Squadron, 7
    Napoleonic Wars (1803–1815), 124–5
    Nine Years War (1688–97), 74
    Paris Commune (1871), 136, 148
    Revolution (1789–99), 90, 102,
        106–112, 144
    Revolution (1830), 90
    Revolution (1848), 90
    Second Empire era (1852–70), 90,
        135, 146
    Richelieu's intelligence system, 49–50
    Terror (1793–4), 106, 107
    Third Republic era (1870–1940), 136,
        143–8, 155–8, 159
    Treaty of Dover (1670), 68
    War of the Spanish Succession (1702–14),
        76, 78, 82
    World War I (1914–18), 178, 182–8
    World War II (1939–45), 255, 258, 260,
        266–8, 273–6, 297, 300–303
Frizer, Ingram, 23, 374
From Russia, with Love (Fleming), 312–15
FSB (Federalnaya Sluzhba Bezopasnosti),
    358–62, 363, 370
Fuller, Thomas, 12
Furibond (Powell), 114

Gable, Clark, 305
Gaelic American, 169
Gaelic League, 214
Game of Thrones (TV series), 5, 358
Gamelin, Maurice, 183–4
Gandhi, Indira, 378
Ganibal, Abram, 119
Gaol Gate, The (Gregory), 170
Garbo, Greta, 221, *222*, 223, 261
GARBO *see* Pujol García, Juan
Garfield, James, 136
Garibaldi's restaurant, London, 262
Garland, Judy, 317
Garrick, David, 99, 108
Gates, Robert, 359
Gaumont Cinematograph Company, 173
Gay, John, 86, 87–8
Geheime Kabinets-Kanzlei, 92
Geneva, Switzerland, 194
Gentleman in Grey, The (Mackenzie), 197
George I, King of Great Britain, 79, 82
George II, King of Great Britain, 89
George III, King of Great Britain, 112,
    124, *236*
George IV, King of the United
    Kingdom, *103*
George V, King of the United Kingdom, 106
George VI, King of the United Kingdom,
    256, 267, 270
German Confederation (1815–66), 116
German nationalism, 115–16
German Spy Peril, The (1914 film), 175
Germany
    Confederation era (1815–66), 116
    East Germany (1949–90), 306, 327,
        334, *335*

Federal Republic (1990–present), 354
Imperial era (1871–1918), 2, 154, 159–62, 166, 167–9, 172–98, 202, 222
Nazi era (1933–45) *see* Nazi Germany
West Germany (1949–90), 304, 305, 306
World War I (1914–18), 174–5, 176–98, 202, 222, 283
World War II (1939–45) *see under* Nazi Germany
Germinal (Zola), 14
Gestapo, 246, 263, 295, 298
Gibbons, Christopher, 56
Gibson, Pamela, 289
Giffard, Henry, 90
Gilbert, W. S., 159–60
Gillen, Aidan, 358
Gillray, James, 90
Girl Guides, 203
Giselle (ballet), 324
Glad, Tor, 259–61, 261
Glasgow, Scotland, 259
glasnost/perestroika (1985–91), 345–6
Globe Theatre, London, 23, 23, 39
Glorious Revolution (1688), 73, 75
'God Save Ireland', 141–2
'God Save the King/Queen', 109, 113, 142, 169
Godfrey, John, 271, 272
Goethe, Johann Wolfgang von, 115
Gogol, Nikolai, 120–21
Golden Rump, The, 88–90, 89
Goldeneye, Jamaica, 284
Goldfinger (1964 film), 276
Goldsmith, Oliver, 90
Gollancz, Victor, 226
Golos, Jacob, 292
Goncharova, Natalya, 119–20, 121, 122
Gone with the Wind (1939 film), 286
Gonse, Charles Arthur, 156
Goodbye, Mr Chips (1939 film), 283
Goodman's Fields Theatre, London, 90
Gorbachev, Mikhail, 343, 344, 345
Gordievsky, Oleg, 349–51, 350, 351, 352
Gordon-Tombe, Eric, 256
Gordon, Avril, 265
Gordon, Thomas, 87
Göring, Hermann, 283
Gouthwaite Hall, Yorkshire, 42
Government Communications Headquarters (GCHQ), 290, 303, 380, 382
Government Inspector, The (Gogol), 120–21
Granada, 349, 350–51
Grangier, Hélène, 303
Grant Duff, Arthur Cuninghame, 178
Grant, Duncan, 163
Grant, Ulysses S., 138
Grasse, François-Joseph-Paul, comte de, 101

Graves, Robert, 216
Gray, Olga, 223
Great Britain (1707–1801), 76–91, 94–114
American Revolution (1765–83), 2, 95–102, 123, 124
French Revolution (1789–99), 106–9
George III assassination attempt (1800), 112
Jacobite movement, 80, 85, 91
Greece, 196–8, 264, 265
Greek Memories (Mackenzie), 197–8, 219
Greenblatt, Stephen, 21
Greene, Graham, 244, 295, 306–7, 309–12, 329, 335
Greenwich Park, London, 74
Greenwood, John, 301
Gregory XIII, Pope, 14–15
Gregory, Isabella Augusta, Lady, 169–70
Grey, Edward, 167, 168
Gromov, Mikhail, 238
GRU (Glavnoje Razvedyvatel'noje Upravlenije), 313
Guardian, 348, 367
de Guerchy, Claude Louis François, 94–5
Guinness, Alec, 310, 311, 335, 347
de Guiscard, Antoine, 79–80, 81
Gulliver's Travels (Swift), 85
Gunpowder Plot (1605), 32, 36–7, 41, 175
Guthrum, King of East Anglia, 7
Gutzeit, Peter, 227
Gwatkin, Norman, 225
Gwyn, Nell, 60, 64, 65, 70
van Gyseghem, André, 315

Hadfield, James, 112, 113
Haldane, Richard, 1st Viscount, 161–2, 167–8
Hale, Nathan, 97, 98, 122
Halifax, George Montagu, 1st Earl, 79
Hall, Abel, 128
Hall, Henry, 223
Hall, Reginald 'Blinker', 190, 192, 193–4, 283
Hamilton, Alexander, 236
Hamlet (Shakespeare), 13, 23–4, 25, 34, 83, 118, 310
Hammersmith, London, 191, 224, 276
Hampstead, London, 228
Hampstead Everyman Theatre, London, 191
Hampton Court Palace, Richmond, 54
Handley, Tommy, 246, 247
Hankey, Maurice, 193
Hanley, Michael, 349
Hardy, Oliver, 227–8, 228
Hardy, Thomas, 160
Harley, Robert, 1st Earl of Oxford, 77–82, 81

Harmer, Christopher, 269
Harmony Week, 380
Harriman, Averell, 288
Harris, Tomás, 259, 261, 266, 267
Harrow School, Middlesex, 289
Hastings, Selina, 195
Hastings, William, 1st Baron, 22
Haymarket, London, 82, 109, 154, 204
Hays, Will, 240
Heartbreak House (Shaw), 215
Heiress, The (Burgoyne), 102
Helms, Richard, 331
Hemingway, Ernest, 273
Henri, Ernst, 246
Henriade, La (Voltaire), 84, 85–6
Henrietta Anne, Duchess of Orleans, 68
Henrietta Maria, Queen consort, 46, 47–8,
        49, 50–52, 52, 57–8
Henry III, King of France, 11
Henry IV (Shakespeare), 21
Henry IV, King of France, 11, 41
Henry V (Shakespeare), 21, 25
Henry VI (Shakespeare), 22
Henry VIII, King of England, 8–9
Henry, Prince of Wales, 35, 41
High, Nathaniel, 140
Highet, Gilbert, 289
Hill, Aaron, 99
Hill, Christopher, 244, 245
Hilton, Paris, 358
Hinchley Cooke, Edward, 178–9
Hiss, Alger, 232
Historical Register for 1736, The (Fielding), 88
Hitchcock, Alfred, 224, 264
Hitler, Adolf, 224, 225, 248, 249, 249, 274,
        281, 287
Hoffman, Dustin, 330
Hohenlohe-Bartenstein, Johannes, Prince,
        183–4
Holden Agreement (1942), 290
Holiday, Billie, 317–18, 319
Holland, Hugh, 40
Holles, Denzil, 1st Baron, 71
Hollis, Roger, 350
Holloway, Joseph, 172
Hollywood *see* film industry, United States
Hollywood Ten, 307, 309
Home Office
     Bankhead, surveillance of, 208–9
     Deutsch and, 229, 230, 231
     Paris Commune (1871), 148
     radical movement infiltration (1800s),
        125–9
     World War I (1914–18), 174, 179, 182
Homeland (TV series), 369
homosexuality, 209, 342, 381–2
honey-traps, 6, 60–61, 68–9, 342

Hoover Institution, 207
Hoover, Herbert, 280
Hoover, J. Edgar, 238–9, 239, 297–8, 305,
        317–19, 321–2, 330, 379
Horowitz, Anthony, 374, 375
Hortalez et Compagnie, 96–7
Hotel Angleterre, Geneva, 194
Hotel Paradiso (play), 348
Houdini, Harry, 154–5
House on 92nd Street (1945 film), 288
House Un-American Activities Committee,
        296, 307
Household Words (Dickens), 133
How, John, 83
Howard, Michael, 251, 254
Howe, William, 97
Hu Jintao, 358
Huawei, 356
Hudson, George, 56
Hugo, Victor, 135–6, 144–7, 145, 158
Huguenots, 50
HUMINT, 49, 193, 272, 289, 293
Hungarian Rising (1956), 315, 321
Hunt, Everette Howard, 305, 306, 329, 330
Hush-Hush revue (1919), 5, 202–6, 203, 205,
        362–3
Hussein Ibn Ali, Sharif of Mecca, 212
Hussein, Saddam, 354–6
Hwang, David Henry, 341

I Was a Spy (McKenna), 221
Ibsen, Henrik, 150
ID25, 190–94
If England were Invaded (1914 film), 175
Imitation Game, The (2014 film), 332
immersive theatre, 236
In The Dark (Mai), 357
In Which We Serve (1942 film), 278, 279
Independent, 362
India
     Bollywood, 377–8
     Maurya Empire (322–184 BC), 5–6
     RAW, 378
Indochina War (1946–54), 309, 312
influence operations, 15
International Spy Museum, Washington
        DC, 369–71
'Internationale', 246
Invasion of 1910, The (Le Queux), 160, 173
Iran, 2, 336–7
Iraq, 339, 354–6
Ireland, 129–31, 169–72, 214–15
     ballads in, 129–31
     Behan, 320–21
     Bloody Sunday (1920), 214
     Casement trial (1916), 189–90
     English Civil War (1642–51), 50

Englishman's Home performance (1909), 169
Fenian movement, 141–3, 152–3, 155, 171, 214
film industry, 172
Free State (1922–37), 215, 321
French Revolutionary Wars (1792–1802), 111
Great Famine (1845–52), 130
Home Rule demonstration (1912), 170
National Theatre Society, 169
'Nation Once Again, A', 131, 170–71
Rebellion (1798), 130, 131
Rebellion (1803), 132
Rebellion (1867), 141, 152, 171
Rebellion (1917), 170, 171, 172, 189, 190
War of Independence (1919–21), 214–15
Wilde and, 150
Williamite War (1688–91), 75
World War I (1914–18), 189–90
World War II (1939–45), 254
Young Ireland, 131, 134
Irish Republican Army (IRA), 170, 221, 320–21
Irish Republican Brotherhood (IRB), 141, 170, 171, 214
Irons, Jeremy, 342
Isherwood, Christopher, 225
Isle of Dogs, The (Jonson and Nashe), 33–4
Israel, 354
It's That Man Again, 246–7, 247
Italy, 225, 248, 264, 273, 274

J'Accuse … ! (Zola), 156–8
Jackanory (TV series), 221
Jackson, Michael, 337
Jackson, Thomas 'Stonewall', 139–40
Jacobi, Derek, 332
Jacobites, 80, 85, 91
Jamaica, 284
James Bond franchise, 4, 162, 211, 256, 271, 276, 284, 295, 300, 312–15, 372–3, 379–80, 382
    Casino Royale, 271, 312
    Dr No, 315, 379
    Forever and a Day, 374
    From Russia, with Love, 312–15
    Goldfinger, 276
    International Spy Museum and, 371
    Le Carré and, 334
    No Time to Die, 373, 379
    Octopussy, 349
    Olympic opening ceremony (2012), 372–3
    Rimington and, 5, 346, 348–9
    Skyfall, 4, 4, 374

Thunderball, 276
Trigger Mortis, 374
James VI and I, King of England, Ireland and Scotland, 32, 35, 36, 43, 45–7
    Gunpowder Plot (1605), 36–7, 41
    Tempest performance (1611), 43
James VII and II, King of Scotland and England, 59–60, 73, 74, 75
James, Lawrence, 215
al-Janabi, Ahmed Alwan, 354–6
Japan, 236, 248, 271–2, 273, 294, 295
    Pearl Harbor attack (1941), 278, 281, 286, 287–8, 291, 299
Jay, Felix, 281
Jay, John, 236
Jefferson, Thomas, 236
Jena University, 116
Jericho, Palestine, 212
Jerusalem, 214
Jew of Malta, The (Marlowe), 22
Jiang Benhu, 356–7, 357
Joffre, Joseph, 183
Johnson, Helen, 205
Joint Planning Staff (JPS), 256
Jones, Douglas, 289
Jones, Ernest, 132
Jones, Martin Furnival, 268
Jonson, Ashton, 167–8
Jonson, Ben, 3, 18, 33–41, 36, 44–5, 48, 59
Jordan, 216
Joseph, Solomon 'Sol', 231
Journey's End (Sherriff), 252
Joyce, James, 172
Joynson-Hicks, William, 209
Judd, Alan, 372
Julius Caesar (Shakespeare), 137, 138
Junior Secret Service Club, 239–40
Juvisy-sur-Orge, France, 71, 71, 72

Kalle, Arnold, 187
Kalugin, Oleg, 327, 370
Kapital, Das (Marx), 148
Kautilya, 5–6, 8
Keating, Fred, 208
Keats, John, 126
Kell, Vernon, 5, 162, 174, 176, 178–9, 205, 206, 208, 221, 363
Kelley, Edward, 43
Kelly, Michael, 113
Kemp, William, 13, 27, 234
Kennedy, John F., 312, 330
Kent, Tyler, 234
Kerensky, Alexander, 195, 218
de Kéroualle, Louise, 68–70, 69
Kerrigan, John, 78
Ketteringham, Norfolk, 107
Keystone comedies, 181

KGB (Komitet gosudarstvennoy bezopasnosti), 45, 231, 304–5, 323–5, 327–8
   ABEL, 298
   active measures, 45, 88, 325, 358
   entertainment and, 323–5, 327–8, 337–8
   female officers, 314
   Gordievsky exfiltration (1985), 349
   honey-traps, 342
   Kalugin, 370
   Khokhlov defection (1954), 304, 313
   Lubyanka HQ, 327, 344, *345*
   Markov assassination (1978), 327
   Miss KGB (1990), 343–4
   public image, 327–8, 343, 360
   Stashinsky defection (1961), 305, 313
KGB: The Inside Story (Andrew and Gordievsky), 349
Khokhlov, Nikolai, 304–4, 313
Killigrew, Thomas, 57–60
al-Kindi, Yaqub ibn Ishaq, 377
King John (Shakespeare), 24
King Lear (Shakespeare), 48, 300
King, Tom, 322
King's Bench Prison, London, 49
King's College, Cambridge, 190, 191
King's Men, 35, 60
King's Theatre, Hammersmith, 224
Kings Cabinet Opened, The (1645), 50–51
Kino, 225–6
Kipps (Wells), 197
Kirby, Luke, 14, 16
Kirov Ballet, 323–4
Kirwan, Barney, 320–21
Kismet (Knoblock), 195, 204, 214
Klingender, Francis 'Fred', 244, 245
Knight, Mary, 66
Knight, Maxwell, 223, 256
Knoblock, Edward, 195–7, *196*, 204, 214
Knole, Kent, 102
Knox, Alfred Dillwyn, 191
Kohout, Hans, 263
Komsomol, *338*, 345
Königsberg, Prussia, 115
Korda, Alexander, 217, 286, 287
Korean War (1950–53), 369
Korotkov, Alexander, 308
von Kotzebue, August, 115–16
Krämer, Carl, 186
Kravchinsky, Sergei, 148, 149, 151–2, *152*
Kropotkin, Sasha, 195, 218
Krupskaya, Nadezhda, 237
Kryuchkov, Vladimir, 344
Kupferle, Anton, *177*

Labourer, 132
Ladd, Alan, *295*, *296*
'Ladder of Love, The', 180, *181*

Ladoux, Georges, 187
Lady Sings the Blues (Holiday), 318
Lady Vanishes, The (1938 film), 224
Lancaster, Burt, 329
Lang, Fritz, 297
Langley, Noel, 276
Larissa, Greece, 198
Larkin, Michael, 141
Last of the Crusaders, The, 213, 215
Last of the Mohicans, The (Cooper), 124
Laurel, Stan, 227–8
Lavrov, Pyotr, 151
Lawes, Henry, 55, 56
Lawn Road Flats, Hampstead, 228
Lawrence of Arabia (1962), 211, 212
Lawrence, T. E., 211–17, *213*, *216*
Le Carré, John, 218, 334–6, 347, 357, 381, 382
Le Nôtre, André, 72
Le Queux, William, 160–61, 173, 174, 176
Leahy, William, 298
Lean, David, 211, 278, 324
Leather, Edwin 'Ted', 333
Leatherstocking Tales, The (Cooper), 124
Leclerc du Tremblay, François, 49
Lee, Bert, 223
Lee, Duncan Chaplin, 232, 293
Lee, Henry, 97
Leicester, Robert Dudley, 1st Earl, 13
Leigh, Vivien, 286, *287*
Lely, Peter, 60, *61*
Lenin, Vladimir Ilyich, 200, 201, 236, 237
Lesieur, Stephen, 30
Leslie, Jean Gerard, 265
Levy, Benn, 276
Levy, Paul, 317
Li Peng, 340
Lichfield, Richard, *34*
Liddell, Guy, 267
Liddy, George Gordon, 329
Light a Candle, Mamma (Stavitsky), 358
Limelight (1952 film), 322
Lincoln, Abraham, 3, 136–7, *137*, 139
Littlewood, Joan, 245, 321
Litvinov, Maxim, 233
Liverpool, Merseyside, 259
Lloyd George, David, 193, 215
Lockroy, Édouard, 146
Lockwood, Margaret, 224
Lody, Carl Hans, 176–8, *177*
Lom, Herbert, 372
London, England
   Adelphi Theatre, 150
   Alexandra Palace, 250
   Alhambra, 154
   Blitz (1940–41), 277
   Bond Street art dealers, 262

Clarkson's shop, 163, *164*
Covent Garden, 90, 102, 126, 132, 213, 324
Cripplegate Institute, 202
Dorset Garden Theatre, 60
Drury Lane *see* Drury Lane
Dynamite War (1881–85), 152–3, 155
Embassy Theatre, 315
Garibaldi's restaurant, 262
Globe Theatre, 23, 25, 39
Goodman's Fields Theatre, 90
Greenwich Park, 74
Hammersmith, 191, 224, 276
Hampstead, 191, 228
Haymarket, 82, 109, 154, 204
King's Bench Prison, 49
Madame Tussaud's, 157
Milton Street Theatre, 132
Muswell Hill, 172
Newgate Prison, 37, 80
Olympic Games (2012), 372
Royal Albert Hall, 213
Royal Arsenal, 258
Royal Ballet, 324
Royal Festival Hall, 324
Royal Opera House, 90, 126, 213
Royal Tournament, 258
Rutland House, 54, 56
Rotunda, 126–7, 128
Savoy Hotel, 206
Savoy Theatre, 246
Simpson's Grand Cigar Divan, 154
St Paul's Cathedral, 319
Thames House, *375*, 376
Tower of London, 179
Westminster Abbey, 59, 65, *65*, 124
Westminster Hall, 15, 39
Wyndham's Theatre, 167, *168*
London Cinematograph Company, 173
London Confidential (2020 film), 378, *379*
London Controlling Section (LCS), 255–8, 264
London Corresponding Society (LCS), 107, 109, 110
London Symphony Orchestra, 301
London University, 228
Lord Arthur Savile's Crime (Wilde), 153
Lord Chamberlain, 90, 109, 132, 142–3, 167–8, 184, 205, *225*
Lord Chamberlain's Men, *35*
Lost Patrol (1934 film), 225
Louis XIII, King of France, 46, 49, 50, 71
Louis XIV, King of France, 50, 68, 70–73, *71*, 90
Louis XV, King of France, 83, 91, 94
Louis XVI, King of France, 96, 106, 107
de Loutherbourg, Philippe, 101

Love's Labour's Lost (Shakespeare), 28
Lubyanka, Moscow, 327, 344, *345*
Lully, Jean-Baptiste, 71
Lycett, Andrew, 314
Lyly, John, 27, 28
Lynam, George, 110
Lyric Hammersmith, London, 191, 276

M. Butterfly (Hwang), 341–2
de Mably, Gabriel Bonnot, 106
MacBain, Alastair, 296
Macbeth (Shakespeare), 24, 25–6, *43*, 376
MacColl, Ewan, 245
MacDonagh, Thomas, 170–71
MacInnes, Helen, 288
Mackenzie, Compton, 163, 197–8, 217, 219–21
Mackeson, G. P., *191*
Maclean, Donald, 231, 241, 267, 349
Maclean, Fitzroy, 236
MacMurray, Fred, 289
Madame Butterfly (Puccini), 341
Madame Tussaud's, London, 157
Madison, James, 236
Madrid, Spain, 184, 187, 254, 267
Magdalen College, Oxford, 54
Magnificent Seven, The (1960 film), 231
Mai Jia, 356–7, *357*
Maibaum, Richard, 295
Maid of the Oaks, The (Burgoyne), 99
Maintenon, Françoise d'Aubigné, marquise de, 73, 90
Maisky, Ivan, 245–6
Makarova, Natalia, 324
Maklyarsky, Mikhail, 304
Malloy, Christopher, 42
Maltz, Milton, 369
'Man and the Echo' (Yeats), 169
Man Called Intrepid, A (Stevenson), 332–4
Man in the Iron Mask, 92–3
Man of Destiny (Shaw), 214
Man on a String (1960 film), 308
Man Who Never Was, The (1956 film), 266
Manasco, Carter, 299
Manchester, England, 141
Manioc, Henri, 342–3
Mankiewicz, Joseph, 309
Mankowitz, Wolf, *315*, *316*
Mann, Wilfred, 350
Marais, Marin, 72
Marchant, Herbert 'Bill', 289, 311
Maria Anna, Spanish Infanta, 46
Mariage de Figaro, Le (Beaumarchais), 94, 102, 103, 120
Marie-Antoinette, Queen consort, 95, 107, *108*

Marie-Thérèse, Queen consort of France, 73
Mariinsky Ballet, 323
Mariinsky Imperial Opera, 198
Markov, Georgi, 325–7, *326*
Marlborough, John Churchill, 1st Duke, 76, 78, 82
Marlowe, Christopher, 3, 17–20, *19*, 21–3, 335, 372, 374, 375
Marprelate Controversy (1588–9), 26, 27
Marshal Ney (Masterman), 251
Marston, John, 36
Martin, Pierre-Denis, *71*
Marvell, Andrew, 64
Marx, Harpo, 232–5, *232*
Marx, Karl, 133, 147–8, 151, 229
Mary II, King of England and Scotland, 74
Mary, Queen of Scots, 11, 20, 25, 49
Maschwitz, Eric, 276, 277, 283–4, 286, 291
Mason, James, 250
Masque of Blacknesse (Jonson), 40–41
Massachusetts General Court, 99
Massachusetts Institute of Technology (MIT), 238
Masterman, John Cecil, 251, 258, 268
Mata Hari, 2, 184–8, *185*, 214, 219, 221, 223, 261, 311, 357
Matveev, Oleg, 360
Maugham, William Somerset, 194–5, 197, 217–19, 221
Maurice, Anthony, 225
Maurya Empire (322–184 BC), 5
Maxse, Marjorie, 243
May, Thomas, 59
Mayorova, Katya, 343–4, *343*
Mazarin, Jules, 93
Mazzini, Giuseppe, 134
McCarthy, Joseph, 309, 319
McCormack, John, 171
McFeely, Deirdre, 143
McGranery, James, 322
McKellen, Ian, 381–2, *381*
McKenna, John 'Jock', 222
McKenna, Marthe, 221–2
McKenna, Reginald, 174
McKinley, William, 136
McMurrough, Dermot, 129
de' Medici, Catherine, 7
Medvedev, Dmitry, 365
Medway, Jill, 289
Meine, Klaus, 345
meiren ji, 342–3
Melfort, John Drummond, 1st Earl, 75
Melville, William, 154–5
'Memory of the Dead, The' (ballad), 131
Men of the F.B.I. (1941 film), 288
Mendes, Samuel, 374
Mendez, Tony, 2, 336, 370

Mendez, Jonna, 367, 370
Menzies, Stewart, 262, 270
Mercader, Ramón, 3
Mercury Vindicated (Jonson), 45
Meres, Francis, 28, 40
Mérope (Voltaire), 91
Merry Wives of Windsor, The (Shakespeare), 30–31, *31*
Message, The (2009 film), 357
Messerschmitt, 253
Metropolitan Police Force, 133, 143, 179
von Metternich, Klemens, 116, 134
Mexico, 2, 43, 192, 283
Mezentsev, Nikolai, 148, 149
MI1c, 194–8, 206–7, 217–21
MI5
    B1a, 250–55, 259, 263–5, 268
    Bankhead, surveillance of, 208–10
    BBC, supervision of, 242, 244
    Behan, surveillance of, 320–21
    British Security Coordination (BSC), 271
    Chaplin, surveillance of, 322–3
    communists, surveillance of, 226, 245, 292, 310, 315, 320, 321, 371
    declassification of files, 371
    double agents, 248–55, 258–63, 266–9
    female recruits, 4–5, 203, 223
    film industry and, 303
    foundation (1909), 162
    Gordievsky exfiltration (1985), 349
    Hollis' directorship (1956–65), 350
    Hush-Hush revue (1919), 5, 202–6, *203*, *205*, 362–3
    Le Carré's service, 335
    Lody, capture of (1914), 176
    Mackenzie, surveillance of, 221
    Mata Hari, surveillance of, 186, 187, 188
    MI6, relations with, 208, 259, 291
    Nachrichten-Abteilung, surveillance of, 174
    official histories, 371
    Operation GARBO (1942–4), 262, 266–9, 306, 311
    Operation MINCEMEAT (1943), 2, 263–6
    Redgrave, surveillance of, 224
    Rimington's directorship (1992–6), 5, 346–9
    role play, use of, 1
    Soviet infiltration, 244, 261–2, 264, 291
    Thames House HQ, *375*, 376
    Twenty Committee, 251–5
    World War I (1914–18), 174, 176, 178–9, 186–8, 202–6
    World War II (1939–45), 248–55, 258–69
MI6
    British Security Coordination (BSC), 270, 271–2, 276–93, 332, 333

CURVEBALL affair (1999–2002), 354, 356
film industry and, 303
foundation (1909), 162
Gordievsky exfiltration (1985), 349
Greene's service, 306, 310, 312, 335
Indochina War (1946–54), 312
James Bond and, 4, 379–80
Le Carré's service, 335
MI5, relations with, 208, 259, 291
official histories, 371
Operation PIMLICO (1985), 349
Queen's Speech (1992), 339
role play, use of, 1
Russian Civil War (1917–23), 198–202
Soviet infiltration, 241, 242–3, 291, 306
Twenty Committee, 251
Twitter accounts, 380–82
World War I (1914–18), 194–8, 206–7, 217–21
World War II (1939–45), 251, 259, 270, 271–2, 276–93
Z organisation, 286
Michael, Glyndwr, 264, 265
Mickiewicz, Adam, 118
Mihailović, Draža, 292
Mikado, The (Gilbert and Sullivan), 159–60
Miller, James, 245
Mills, Bertram, 253, 258
Mills, Cyril Bertram, 253, 259, 261, 268–9, 268
Milton Street Theatre, London, 132
Milton, John, 14
Ministry of State Security (MSS), 339 40, 356, 378
Mirame (Desmarets), 49
Misérables, Les (Hugo), 135, 144
Mistinguett, 182–4, 183, 273
Mitrokhin Archive, The (Andrew and Mitrokhin), 352
Mitrokhin, Vasili, 352–4, 353, 354, 367
Modi, Narendra, 378
Moe, John 'Helge', 259–61, 261
Molière, 72–3
Monde diplomatique, Le, 369
Monde, Le, 343
Montagu, Ewen, 264, 265, 266
Montagu, George, 1st Earl of Halifax, 79
Montagu, Ralph, 1st Duke, 72
Montagu, Walter, 46–8, 50, 58
Montbéliard, France, 301
Monteagle, William Parker, 4th Baron, 37, 39
Montgomery, Bernard, 1st Viscount, 258
Moore, Richard, 379–82
Moran, Michael, 130–31
More, Thomas, 28
Morley, Derrick, 257

Morros, Boris, 227–8, 228, 307–8
Mosley, Oswald, 263
Mosquito fighter-bombers, 263
Moulin Rouge, Paris, 183, 185
Mountbatten, Louis, 1st Earl, 278
Mountjoy Prison, Dublin, 320
Mousetrap, The (Christie), 23–4
Mozart and Salieri (Pushkin), 117
Mozart, Wolfgang Amadeus, 94, 103, 105
MR MILLS' CIRCUS operation (1941), 253–4
Mr. Emmanuel (1944 film), 283
Munday, Anthony, 14–17, 18, 26–8, 40
Munich crisis (1938), 225
Münster Verlag, 230
Murphy, Audie, 310
Mussolini, Benito, 225, 274
Mussorgsky, Modest, 245
Muswell Hill, London, 172
Mutch, Walter, 231
Mutt and Jeff show (1920), 260
My 10 Years as a Counterspy (Morros), 308
My Adventures as a Spy (Baden-Powell), 179, 180

N or M? (Christie), 229
Nachrichten-Abteilung, 162, 174
Napier, Diana, 314
Napoleon I, Emperor of the French, 124, 214, 287
Napoleon III, Emperor of the French, 135
Napoleonic Wars (1803–1815), 124
Nashe, Thomas, 12, 27–8, 33–4, 34
'Nation Once Again, A' (Davis), 131, 170 71
Nation, 131, 134
National Geographic Society, 213
National Intelligence Authority (NIA), 298
National Security Agency, 369, 380
National Symphony Orchestra, Washington DC, 325
National Theatre Society, 169
naturalism, 147
Nazi Germany (1933–45)
astrology in, 281
deception operations against, 2, 247–69
Duquesne spy ring, 288
Enigma machine, 125, 248, 314
France, occupation of (1940–44), 274, 300–303
Gestapo, 246, 263, 295
Munich crisis (1938), 225
Operation SEALION (1940, planned), 274
South America plan hoax, 284–5, 285, 291
Soviet agents in, 227, 236, 246
Soviet Union, invasion of (1941), 244
theatre and, 224
US, war declared on (1941), 288

Nearne, Jacqueline, 300–302, 333, *333*
Neligan, David, 170
Nepean, Evan, 108
Netherdale, Yorkshire, 41
Netherlands, 180–82, 186, 187
New Park Theater, New York, 124
New Statesman, 172
New York Daily News, 150
New York Sun, 281
New York Times, 138–9, 176, 236, 278, 298
New York, United States, 99, 124, 209, 250,
    270, 271, 306
Newgate Prison, London, 37, 80
Newton, Isaac, 357
Nicholas I, Emperor of Russia, 117, 119–22,
    148, 359
Nicholas II, Emperor of Russia, 166–7, 306
Nicolai, Walter, 186
'Nightingale Sang in Berkeley, A'
    (Maschwitz), 283
Nihilists, 148–52, 153
Nine Years War (1688–97), 74
Nisbett, Louisa, 132
Niven, Barbara, 321
Niven, David, 332
Nixon, Richard, 24, 329–31
NKVD (Naródnyy komissariát vnútrennikh
    dyél), 2, 226–9, 234, 236
  BBC, infiltration of, 241–7
  Belfrage, 226–7, 277, 291–2
  Bletchley Park, infiltration of, 291
  BSC, infiltration of, 291–2
  Cambridge spy ring, 228, 230, 231, 241–7,
    261–2, 264, 267, 291, 310, 349–51
  Deutsch, 228–31, 241
  Great Terror (1936–8), 235, 237
  Hollywood, infiltration of, 227–8, 295,
    307–8
  Ivy League spy rings, 232
  MI5, infiltration of, 244, 261–2, 264, 291
  MI6, infiltration of, 241, 242–3, 291
  OSS, infiltration of, 293
  PAX Association, 312
  show trials, 236
  Tupolev ANT-25 flight (1937), 237–8
  US embassy surveillance, 234
  Woolwich spy ring, 223
No Time to Die (2021 film), 373, 379
Normandy landings (1944), 258, 266, 267,
    268, 297
Norris, Hermione, 362
North Atlantic Treaty Organization
    (NATO), 349
North, Frederick, 2nd Earl of Guilford, 102
Northern Star, 133
Norway, 255, 259–60
Norwood, Melita 'Letty', 351–4, *352*

Notre-Dame de Paris (Hugo), 146
Now It Can Be Told (1947 film), 301–2, *302*,
    333, *333*
Nozze de Figaro, Le (Mozart), 94
Nureyev, Rudolf, 323–4
Nyack, New York, 207

O.S.S. (1946 film), 295–6, *296*
O'Brien, Michael, 141
O'Casey, Seán, 171–2
O'Connell, Daniel, 131
O'Connor, Feargus, 132
O'Toole, Peter, 211, 212
Obama, Barack, 369
October (1928 film), 226
Octopussy (1983 film), 349
Ode to Liberty (Pushkin), 118
OEdipe (Voltaire), 83–4
Office of Strategic Services (OSS), 272, 292,
    293–8
Official Secrets Act (1920), 218, 219,
    220, 292
Okhrana, 149
Okolovich, Georgy Sergeyevich, 304–5, 313
Oldfield, Maurice, 335
'Olga Pulloffski, the Beautiful Spy' (Lee and
    Weston), 223
Oliver, Isaac, 31
Oliver, William, 125
Olivier, Laurence, 252, 286–7, *287*, 310
Olympic Games, 372
Omnipotent Oom, 207
On the Frontier (Auden and Isherwood), 225
OP-20-G, 290
Operation BARBAROSSA (1941), 244
Operation COPPERHEAD (1944), 258
Operation FRIEDENSTURM (1918), 184
Operation GARBO (1942–4), 262, 266–9,
    306, 311
Operation GHOST STORIES (c. 2000–2010),
    363–8
Operation Heartbreak (Cooper), 266
Operation HUSKY (1943), 264, 265
Operation MINCEMEAT (1943), 2, 263–6
Operation MR MILLS' CIRCUS (1941), 253–4
Operation OVERLORD (1944), 258, 266, 267,
    268, 297
Operation PIMLICO (1985), 349
Operation SEALION (1940, planned), 274
Operation TORCH (1942), 255, 260, 275
Operation TROJAN SHIELD (2018–21), 2
Order of St Anne, 118
Oroonoko (Behn), 60
Orton, Henry, 14
Orwell, George, 305–6, 329
Orwell, Sonia, 305
Osorio (Coleridge), 112

Ostertag, Major, 167
Othello (Shakespeare), 319–20
Ottoman Empire (1299–1922), 121, 212
Our Man in Havana (Greene), 280, 310–12, 355
Owens, Arthur, 250, *251*, 253, 254
Owens, Patricia, 250, *251*
Oxford Playhouse, 252
Oxford Tragedy, An (Masterman), 251
Oxford University, 54, 166, 203, 244, 245
Oxford, Robert Harley, 1st Earl, 77–82, *81*

Page, Walter Hines, 192, 194
Pagnol, Marcel, 93
Paisiello, Giovanni, 94
Pakenham, Hercules, 188
Pakistan, 378
Palestine, 212, 216
Palmer, Barbara, 57
Panama, 285
Paramount Pictures, 227, 295, 307
Paris, France
    Commune (1871), 136, 148
    Liberation (1944), 276
    Peace Conference (1919), 212
    Robeson's visit (1949), 317
    World War I (1914–18), 182–8
    World War II (1939–45), 273
Parker, Andrew, *376*, 376
Parker, John, 136
Parrot, Henry, 34
Pasternak, Boris, 324
patent theatres, 90, 125–7, 132
Patrushev, Nikolai, 359–60
Paul, Robert, 172
PAX Association, 312
Pearl Harbor attack (1941), 278, 281, 286, 287–8, 292, 299
Peel, Robert, 130, 133, 134
Peierls, Rudolf, 350
Pelissier, Harry, 168
Penguin Modern Classics, 357
Peninsular War (1807–14), 124
Penry-Jones, Rupert, 362
People's Vigilance Committee, 310
Pepys, Samuel, 56, 57, 58, 61, 64
Père Joseph, 49
Pericles (Shakespeare), 41
Peril of the Fleet, The (1909 film), 173
Perrault, Charles, 49, 72
Perse School, Cambridge, 289
Pétain, Henri Philippe, 274
Peter I, Emperor of Russia, 119
Peterson, Marti, 367–8
Peteval, Harold, *257*
Petrie, David, 253, 262, 267
Petty, Alan, 372

Peugeot family, 301
Phelippes, Thomas, 11, 25, 32, 49, 50, 71, 166
Philadelphia, Pennsylvania, 99
Philby, Kim, 231, 243, 262, 267, 381
    BBC, work at, 241
    Bletchley Park application, 243
    Clarke, reports on, 254
    cricket, love of, 381
    D-Day, reporting on, 267
    Deutsch, recruitment by, 230
    Greene, relationship with, 306–7, 312
    MI6, work at, 243, 291, 306–7
    Moscow, defection to (1951), 349
    postage stamp, 332
    SOE, work at, 243
Philip II, King of France, 8
Philip II, King of Spain, 11, 13, 30
Philip IV, King of Spain, 46
Philippe, Duke of Orleans, 84
Pichel, Irving, 296
Pickford, Mary, *230*
Picquart, Georges, 155
Pierrepoint, Albert, 321
Pigott, Edward, 150, 159
Pinewood Studios, 301
Pink Floyd, 338
Pink Panther films, 372
Pitt, William, 106, 107, 108, 109
Playboy, 365
Playfair, Giles, 276
Playfair, Nigel, 276
Pleydall-Bouverie, Jane, *257*
Plough and the Stars, The (O'Casey), 171
Poley, Robert, 20, 23, 34
Political Warfare Executive, 292
Pollitt, Harry, 223
Pope, Alexander, 84
Poquelin, Jean-Baptiste 72–3
Portsmouth, Louise de Kéroualle, Duchess, 68–70, *69*
Portugal, 274
Powell, Colin, 355, 356
Powell, James, 111, 114
Prague, 105
Preto, Paolo, 105
Priestley, J. B., 243
Primakov, Yevgeny, 336
Prince of Wales, HMS, 287
Project Petra (2015), 375–6
Prokofiev, Sergei, 346
Provok'd Wife, The (Vanbrugh), 74
Prussia (1701–1918), 91, 115, 116, 133, 160
Puccini, Giacomo, 341
Pujol García, Juan, 258–9, 261–2, 266–9, 306, 311
Punch, 173

Purcell, Henry, 56
Puritanism, 26, 48, 54, 98–9
Pushkin, Alexander, 117–22, *119*
Putin, Vladimir, 328, 358–60, *359*, 365

Quare Fellow, The (Behan), 321
Queen's Men, 12, 13, 21, 24
Queen's Players, 21
Queens Closet Opened, The (1655), 51–2, *52*
Queens' College, Cambridge, 357
Queer People (Thomson), *177*
Quiet American, The (Greene), 309–10, 329

Raazi (2018 film), 378
Radio Free Europe, 326
Radunsky, Ivan, 199–200, 206
Raid of 1915, The (1913 film), 173, 175
Rape upon Rape (Fielding), 86
Rastorguev, Nikolai, 360
Rattigan, Terence, 225
Ravaillac, François, 41
Razvedchik's Feat, The (1947), 303–4
Reagan, Ronald, 239–40, *240*, 308–9, 334, 349, *350*
Red Lamp, The (Tristram), 153, 154
Redford, George, 159, 168
Redford, Robert, 330
Redgrave, Michael, 224, 309–10, *310*
Rée, Harry, 300–303
Reed, Carol, 307
Reed, Michael, 77
Reed, Ronnie, 265
Reel vs Real initiatives, 367, 373
Reich, Wilhelm, 229–30
Reims, France, 8, 15, 19
Reith, John, 242
Relapse, The (Vanbrugh), 75
Renaudot, Eusèbe, 75
Research and Analysis Wing (RAW), 378
Review, The, 82
Revolt in the Desert (Lawrence), 216
Rhode Island, 102
Rhys, Matthew, *366*, 367
Richard I, King of England, 8
Richard III (Shakespeare), 21, 22
Richardson, Ian, 335
Richelieu, Armand Jean du Plessis, duc de, 49, 98
Richmond, Virginia, 138
Riddle of the Sands, The (Childers), 159
Rifkind, Malcolm, 336
Rimbaud, Arthur, 147
Rimington, Stella, *5*, 346–9, *348*
Ring, Denis, 129
Rivals, The (Sheridan), 197
Robb, Graham, 146
Robert, Jules, 303

Roberts, Eric, 263
Robertson, Thomas Argyll 'Tar', 250–51, 253, 268–9
Robeson, Paul, 308, 315–16, 318–20, *320*
Robespierre, Maximilien, 106
Robinson Crusoe (Defoe), 82, 83, 224
Rochant, Éric, 368
de Rochemont, Louis, 288, 297–8, 305–6, 308
Rochester, Francis Atterbury, Bishop of, 85, 86
Rochester, John Wilmot, 2nd Earl, 65–8, *67*
Rock, The (1996 film), *355*, 356
Rockefeller Center, New York, 271
Roderigue Hortalez et Compagnie, 96–7
Roman Republic (510–27 BC), 44
Room 40, Admiralty, 190–94
Rooney, Anne, 129
Roosevelt, Franklin Delano, 193, 238, 240, 270, 280, 284–8, 291, 332
Rose Theatre, Bankside, 21–2, 28
Rosenthal, Robert, *177*
Rossignol, Antoine, 49–50, 71–2
Rossignol, Bonaventure, 71, 72
Rossini, Gioachino Antonio, 94, 116
Rosten, Leo, 6
Rostovsky, Semyon, 246
Rostropovich, Mstislav, 325, 344, 346
Rothschild, Victor, 3rd Baron, 350
Rousseau, Jean-Jacques, 106
Rover, The (Behn), 64
Roy, Mouni, 378
Royal Air Force (RAF), 215, 248, 249, 263, 300, 301
Royal Albert Hall, London, 213
Royal Arsenal, Woolwich, 258
Royal Artillery Officers' Dramatic Club, 258
Royal Ballet, London, 324
Royal Charles, 58
Royal Festival Hall, London, 324
Royal Fusiliers, 167
Royal Holloway College, 203
Royal Navy, 63, 112, 159, 162, 167, 173, 189, 244
Royal Opera House, London, 90, 126, 213
Royal Tournament, Olympia, 258
Royaume de Lilliput, 181
Rozerot, Jeanne, 156, *157*
Russell, John, 1st Earl, 130
Russell, Keri, *366*
Russian Civil War (1917–23), 198–202, 237
Russian Empire (1721–1917), 117–22
    censorship in, 117–18, 121
    Decembrist Revolt (1825), 118
    Elizabeth's coup (1741), 92
    Kotzebue in, 115–16
    Nicholas II's UK visit (1909), 166–7

'Nihilist' revolutionaries, 148–52, 153
People's Will, 148–9
Revolution (1917), 195, 217–18, 316
Third Section, 117–22, 148–9
World War I (1914–18), 182, 195, 217–18
Russian Federation (1991–present), 346–7, 358–62
  film industry, 360–62
  prisoner exchange (2010), 364–5
  religion in, 358–60
  Skripal poisonings (2018), 364
Russian Orthodox Church, 358–60
Russian Revolution (1917), 195, 217–18, 316
Russian Soviet Republic (1917–22), 199–202
  see also Soviet Union
Rutland House, London, 54, 56
de Rysbach, Courtenay, 177, 180, 181

S&T, 354–5
Saint Sofia Church, Moscow, 359–60
Saint-Germain-en-Laye, France, 53, 74, 75
Saint-Simon, Louis de Rouvroy, duc de, 70
Sakharov, Andrei, 343
Salisbury poisonings (2018), 364
Salisbury, James Cecil, 1st Marquess, 109
Salisbury, Robert Cecil, 1st Earl, 28–9, 31–2, 37–9, 46
Salome (Wilde), 184
Sand, Karl, 116
Sandherr, Jean Conrad, 155
Sandhurst, Berkshire, 211
Savoy Hotel, London, 206
Savoy Theatre, London, 246
Sawyers, Frank, 288
Scapa Flow, 190
Schiller, Friedrich, 115, 116
von Schleich, Eduard Ritter, 248
Schlesinger, John, 310
School for Danger (1944 film), 300, 302
School for Scandal (Sheridan), 101, 197
Scorpio (1973 film), 328–9
Scorpions (band), 345–6
Scotland
  Act of Union (1707), 76–8
  World War I (1914–18), 176
Scotland Yard, 147, 148, 152, 153, 174, 208
Scott, Thomas, 59, 60
Scott, William, 60–62, 75
Scout Movement, 179, 199, 203
Screen Actors Guild, 308
Secret Agent, The (Conrad), 160
Secret du roi, 94, 102
Secret Intelligence Service (SIS) see MI6
Secret Mission, The (1950 film), 304
Secret Office, 134
Secret Service Bureau, 162, 166
Secret Service Fund, 78–80, 82–3, 87

Secret Service of the Sky (de Wohl), 281
Secrets of the Soul, Constellation of Love (Stavitsky), 358
Sejanus His Fall (Jonson), 36, 40
Sektion P, 182
Seligmann, Ann, 315
Sellers, Peter, 372
Sells, William, 220
Semashko, Michael, 202
Semyonov, Yulian, 327, 328
September 11 attacks (2001), 339
Seraph, HMS, 265
Seven Pillars of Wisdom (Lawrence), 216
Seventeen Moments of Spring (TV series), 327–8, 328
Sévigné, Marie de Rabutin-Chantal, marquise de, 73
Sex Pistols, 338
Shaftesbury, Anthony Ashley Cooper, 1st Earl, 68
Shakespeare, John, 20–21
Shakespeare, William, 9, 13, 20–26, 28, 33, 35, 43–4, 45, 48, 118, 137
  As You Like It, 23
  Hamlet, 13, 23–4, 25, 34, 83, 118, 310
  Henry IV, 21
  Henry V, 21, 25, 167
  Henry VI, 22
  Julius Caesar, 137, 138
  King John, 24
  King Lear, 48, 300
  Love's Labour's Lost, 28
  Macbeth, 24, 25–6, 43, 376
  Merry Wives of Windsor, The, 30–31, 31
  Othello, 319–20
  Pericles, 41
  Richard III, 21, 22
  Tempest, The, 43–4, 45
  Titus Andronicus, 22
  Troilus and Cressida, 191
Shakespeare Memorial Theatre, Stratford-upon-Avon, 310, 319–20
Shakhty trial (1928), 235
Sharples, Eliza, 128–9
Shashkova, Eleonora, 327
Shaughraun, The (Boursicault), 142–3
Shaw, George Bernard, 168, 189–90, 214, 215, 216
Shaw, Robert, 313
Shelley, Mary, 126
Shelley, Percy Bysshe, 126
Shepherd's Paradise, The (Montagu), 47
Sheridan, Richard, 90, 101, 107–114, 197
Sherriff, Robert Cedric, 252
Sherry, Norman, 312
Sherwood, Robert, 293
Shi Pei Pu, 340–42, 341, 342

Shirley, James, 55
Shmelev, I. I., 305
Shoemaker's Holiday, The (Dekker), 250
Shooting the Spy (1899 film), 173
Shumovsky, Stanislav, 238
Sicily, 264, 265, 266
Sidmouth, Henry Addington, 1st
    Viscount, 125
Sidney Sussex College, Cambridge, 46
Sidney, Philip, 13
Siege of Rhodes, The (Davenant), 55–6
SIGINT
    Elizabethan England (1558–1603),
      24–5, 166
    Georgian Britain (1714–1837), 85, 86, 91
    Interregnum England (1649–1660), 54
    Louis XIII's France (1610–1643), 49, 50
    Louis XIV's France (1643–1715), 71
    Louis XV's France (1715–1774), 91–3
    Napoleonic Wars (1803–1815), 124–5
    Nicholas II's Russia (1894–1917), 167
    People's Republic of China (1949–present),
      356
    Restoration England (1660–1688), 75, 76
    Second Empire France (1852–1870), 135
    Soviet Union (1922–91), 232, 234
    World War I (1914–18), 134, 186,
      190–94, 212
    World War II (1939–45), 191, 240, 243,
      247–8, 289–91, 295, 314
    see also Bletchley Park
Simpson, Christopher, 41–2
Simpson, Robert, 41–2
Simpson's Grand Cigar Divan, London, 154
Sinclair, Hugh, 220
Single Spies (Bennett), 24
Sinn Féin, 129–30
Sir Thomas More (Munday), 28
Sissmore, Jane, 204, 223
Skeres, Nicholas, 23
Skripal, Sergei, 364
Skyfall (2012 film), 4, *4*, 374
slavery, 60
Sleeping Beauty (Vsevolozhsky), 323
SMERSH, 313
Smiley's People (Le Carré), 336
Smilg, Benjamin, 238
Smith, Thomas and John, 46
Smolka, Peter, 307
Soble, Jack, 307–8
Sochaux, France, 301, 303
Society of United Englishmen, 111
SOE in France (Foot), 303
Somerset, Robert Carr, 1st Earl, 45
Sorochintsy Fair (Cui and Mussorgsky), 245
Sotheby's, 262
Souers, Sidney, 298

South Africa, 169, 172–3
Soviet Union (1922–91), 2, 45, 208, 223,
    225–39, 241–7, 323–8
    active measures, 45, 88, 325, 358
    Afghanistan War (1979–89), 338
    ballet in, 323–4
    BBC, infiltration of, 241–7
    Belfrage, 226–7
    Bletchley Park, infiltration of, 291, 350
    BSC, infiltration of, 291–2
    Cambridge spy ring, 228, 230, 231, 241–7,
      261–2, 264, 267, 291, 310, 349–51
    Cold War era (1947–91), 303–5, 307–8,
      311, 315, 323–8, 337–8, 349–54
    coup d'état attempt (1991), 344–5
    Cuban Missile Crisis (1962), 311
    Deutsch, 228–31, 241
    dissolution (1991), 344–6
    film industry, 225–7, 236, 327–8
    German invasion (1941), 244
    glasnost/*perestroika* (1985–91), 345–6
    Great Terror (1936–8), 235, 237
    GRU, 313
    Hollywood, infiltration of, 227–8, 295,
      307–8
    Hungarian Rising (1956), 315, 321
    Ivy League spy rings, 232
    Marx's tour (1933–4), 232–4
    MI5, infiltration of, 244, 261–2, 264, 291
    MI6, infiltration of, 241, 242–3, 291, 306
    Miss KGB (1990), 343–4
    OSS, infiltration of, 293
    Poland, hegemony over (1947–89), 312
    pop music in, 337–8, 345–6
    show trials, 235–6, 264
    SIGINT, 232, 234
    SMERSH, 313
    Trotsky assassination (1940), 3, 304
    Tupolev ANT-25 flight (1937), 237–8
    US embassy, 232–5
    Woolwich spy ring, 223
    World War II (1939–45), 244–7, 254,
      261–2, 264
Spain
    American Revolutionary War
      (1775–83), 97
    Aztec Empire, conquest of (1519–21), 43
    Civil War (1936–9), 259
    Elizabethan England, relations with, 11,
      13–14, 30, 166, 307
    Jacobean England, relations with, 46
    War of the Succession (1702–14), 76,
      78, 82
    World War I (1914–18), 184, 187
    World War II (1939–45), 254, 263, 264,
      267, 274, 306
Special Branch, 143, 154, 174, 208, 210, 316

Special Operations Executive (SOE), 243, 271, 281, 300, 301
Spectator, The, 79, 133
Sperling, Milton, 297
Spielberg, Steven, 337
Spies of the Kaiser (Le Queux), 160–61
Spinoza, Baruch, 112
Spooks (TV series), 362, 367
Spy Kids programme, 376–7
Spy Who Came in from the Cold, The (1965 film), 276, 334–5
Spy, The (Cooper), 123–4, 161
Spy's Choirbook, The, 9
Spycatcher (Wright), 350
Spycraft Entertainment, 378–9
St Augustine's, Canterbury, 47
St Christopher (play), 41–2
St John's College, Cambridge, 289
St John's Eve (Jones), 132
St Paul's Cathedral, London, 319
St Peter's Church, Ketteringham, 107
Stafford, David, 333
Stalin Prize, 304
Stalin, Joseph, 3, 225, 233, 235, 236, 246, 262, 306
Standart, 167
Standen, Anthony, 13
Stanevsky, Mechislav, 199–200, 206
Star Chamber, 23, 42
Stashinsky, Bogdan, 305, 313
Station M, 284–5
Stavitsky, Vasily, 358–9
Steinhauer, Gustav, 154, 174
Stephen, Adrian, 165
Stephenson, Mary, 293
Stephenson, William, 270–72, 271, 276–7, 283–5, 284, 291–3, 293, 332–4
Stepniak, Sergei, 148, 149, 151–2, 152
von Sternberg, Josef, 221
Stevenson, William, 332
Stone Guest, The (Pushkin), 122
Stonewall, 382
Stoppard, Tom, 348
Stoyanov, Dimitar, 326, 327
Strike (1925 film), 226
Strike a New Note (1943 revue), 265–6
Strindberg, August, 147
Strong, George Veazey, 271
Stuart, Charles Edward, 91
Stuart, Frances, 61–2
Stubbes, William, 41
Sudoplatov, Pavel, 304
Suez Crisis (1956), 322
Sullivan, Timothy Daniel, 141
Summer, Donna, 338
Sun Tzu, 5, 358
Sunday Express, 278

Sunday Pictorial, 231
Sûreté, 121, 135–6, 143–6, 147, 155–8, 186
Surinam, 60
SVR (Sluzhba Vneshney Razvedki), 358, 364, 370
Swan Theatre, Bankside, 33
Swift, Jonathan, 76, 77, 84, 85
Swing (Taylor), 127
Switzerland, 116, 228
Sylt, 193
syphilis, 48, 53

Tamburlaine (Marlowe), 17–18, 21
Tarlton, Richard, 12–13, 27
Tartuffe (Molière), 72–3
Tate, William, 111
Taylor, Robert, 127–9, 128
Tchaikovsky, Pyotr, 323, 346
Tempest, The (Shakespeare), 43–4, 45
Temple of Love, The (Davenant), 48
Temple, Shirley, 237–8, 238, 239
Territorial Force, 167, 168
Thames House, London, 375, 376
Thames Television, 269
That Hamilton Woman! (1941 film), 286–7, 287
Thatcher, Margaret, 335, 349
Théâtre du Château-d'Eau, Paris, 144
Théâtre du Palais-Royal, Paris, 49
Theatre Royal, Covent Garden, 90, 102, 126
Theatre Royal, Drury Lane *see under* Drury Lane
Theatre Royal, Dublin, 169
Theatre, Shoreditch, 12
Theatres Act (1843), 132, 224
Theatrical Licensing Act (1737), 90, 126
Thérèse Raquin (Zola), 147
'These Foolish Things Remind Me of You' (Maschwitz), 283
Third Crusade (1189–1192), 8
Third Man, The (Greene), 307
Third Section, 117–22, 148–9
13 Rue Madeleine (1947 film), 297–8
39 Steps, The (1935 film), 224
Thirty Years War (1618–48), 46
This is Your Life (TV series), 269
Thomas, Lowell, 212–13, 214, 213, 216
Thomson, Basil, 174, 177, 180, 187, 208
'Through the Tall Grass' (Lyube), 360
Thunderball (1965 film), 276
Thurloe, John, 54–6, 61, 75
Thwaites, William, 168
Tiananmen Square massacre (1989), 340
Tiberius, Roman Emperor, 36
Tikhonov, Vyacheslav, 327, 328
Tilney, Edmund, 12, 28
Time magazine, 323

Times, The, 109, 129, 134, 152, 174, 307, 352–3
Tinker, Tailor, Soldier, Spy (Le Carré), 335, 381
Titus Andronicus (Shakespeare), 22
Todd, Janet, 60, 66
'Tone's Grave' (Davis), 131
Too True to be Good (Shaw), 217
Topcliffe, Richard, 17, 26, 33
Totonto, Ontario, 284
Tower of London, 179
Towne, Rosella, 240
Train, Jack, 246
Travis, Edward, 290
Treasury, 350
Treaty of Dover (1670), 68
Tresham, Francis, 37
Trevelyan, Charles, 130
Trieste, 104
Trigger Mortis (Horowitz), 374
Trinity College, Cambridge, 42, 241, 242
Tristram, William Outram, 153, 154
Troilus and Cressida (Shakespeare), 191
Trotignon, Yves, 368
Trotsky, Leon, 3, 200, 235, 262–3, 306
Trotskyism, 3, 236, 262–3
troubadours, 8
Troup, Edward, 179, 182
Truman, Elizabeth 'Bess', 294
Truman, Harry S., 294–9, 294, 309, 322
Trumbull, John, 100
Tube Alloys (1941–5), 352
Tupolev ANT-25 flight (1937), 237–8
Turing, Alan, 331–2, 356, 382
Turner, Tina, 338
Twenty Committee, 251–5, 264
Twitter, 5, 380

Ukraine, 304, 305, 313
ULTRA *see* Bletchley Park
Under Which Flag? (Connolly), 171–2
Underground Russia (Stepniak), 149, 151
Union of Soviet Writers, 315
Union Square Theatre, New York, 150
United Artists, 328
United Irishmen, 111
United Kingdom (1801–present)
    BBC spy ring, 241–7
    British Security Coordination (BSC), 271–2, 276–93, 332, 333
    Chartist movement (1838–57), 132–3
    Cold War era (1947–91), 300–303, 305–7, 309–17, 319–21, 331–6, 349–54
    CURVEBALL affair (1999–2002), 354–6
    Dreadnought hoax (1910), 164–6
    Edwardian era (1901–14), 159–74
    Gordievsky exfiltration (1985), 349
    Holden Agreement (1942), 290
    Interwar era (1919–39), 202–7, 208–32, 236
    Irish conflict *see* Ireland; Northern Ireland
    Marx in, 147–8
    Mitrokhin exfiltration (1992), 352
    Moscow embassy, 236
    Munich crisis (1938), 225
    Napoleonic Wars (1803–1815), 124–5
    Project Petra (2015), 375–6
    radical movements (1800s), 125–9
    Robeson in, 315–16, 319
    rural riots (1830–31), 127
    Russian revolutionaries in, 148
    Russian Civil War (1917–23), 198–202
    Skripal poisonings (2018), 364
    Secret Service, foundation of (1909), 162
    Spycatcher affair (1985–8), 350
    Suez Crisis (1956), 322
    Tube Alloys (1941–5), 352
    Victorian era (1837–1901), 125–34, 147–55
    World War I (1914–18), 134, 162–3, 166, 174–5, 176–98, 202
    World War II (1939–45), 2, 125, 191, 240, 243, 244–69, 270–95, 300–303
    see also England; Great Britain
United Nations, 306
United Russia, 360, 365
Unity Theatre Communist Group, 310
University College, London, 231
Uri: The Surgical Strike (2019 film), 378

Valley Forge, Pennsylvania, 101
Van Dyck, Anthony, 58
Van Lew, Elizabeth, 138
Vanbrugh, John, 74–5, 76, 82–3
Vaninskaya, Anna, 148
Vansittart, Robert, 1st Baron, 215
Vassall, John, 342
Venetian Outlaw, The (Powell), 111
Venetian Republic (697–1797), 58, 103–5
Venezuela, 262
Vera; or, The Nihilists (Wilde), 149–51
Vergennes, Charles Gravier, comte de, 96
Verlaine, Paul, 147
Versailles, France, 70–71, 72
Vichy France (1940–44), 274, 275
Victoria and Albert, 167
Victoria, Queen of the United Kingdom, 130, 152–3, 172
Vidal, Gore, 321
Vidocq, Eugène-François, 135
Vienna University, 229
Vietnam, 309, 312
Vieyra, Leopold, 180–82
Villiers, George, 1st Duke of Buckingham, 45–6

Villiers, George, 2nd Duke of Buckingham, 68
Vinnicombe, Ewan, 375
Vishnevskaya, Galina, 325
Viskovatov, Stepan, 118–19
Vogue, 203
Völkischer Beobachter, 249
Vollmoeller, Karl Gustav, 194
Volpone (Jonson), 39
Voltaire, 83–6, 91–93, 94, 99

'Wacht am Rhein, Die', 169
Wade, Ida, 260
Wales, 253
Wallis, John, 50, 71, 75
Walpole, Robert, 84–90, 95
Walsh, James, 112
Walsh, Richard, 39
Walsingham, Francis, 11–20, 22–3, 26, 32, 37, 47, 61, 372, 374
Wanamaker, Samuel, 319–20, *320*
Wang Zhen, 340
War of the Spanish Succession (1702–14), 76, 78, 82
War Office, 161, 162, 168, 212, 214, 251
Warner Brothers, 239–40, 294
Warsaw Pact, 328
Washington National Symphony Orchestra, 346
Washington Post, 325, 344
Washington, George, 97, 99, 101, 123, 124, 236
Water on the Brain (Mackenzie), 220
Watergate scandal (1972–4), 305, 329–31
Watford Grammar School, 303
Wavell, Archibald, 254
Webb, Beatrice, 189
Webb, Clifton, 266
Webb, William, 56
Week in Westminster, The, 246
Weisberg, Joseph, 366, *367*
Welles, Orson, 307
Wellington, Arthur Wellesley, 1st Duke, 124
Wells, H. G., 197
Wells, William 'Dicky', *319*
West Germany (1949–90), 304, 305, 306
Westminster Abbey, London, 59, 65, *65*, 124
Westminster Hall, London, 15, 39
Weston, Robert Patrick, 223
Wheatley, Dennis, 256–8, *257*
When the Dawn is Come (MacDonagh), 170, 171
'Where Does the Motherland Begin?', 365
Whisky Galore (Mackenzie), 221
White, Harry Dexter, 232
Whitelocke, Bulstrode, 54
Whitemore, Hugh, 331–2
Whitgift, John, 26, 27

Whitty, May, 224
Wickham, Glynne, 90
Wilde, Oscar, 149–51, *151*, 184
Wilhelm II, German Kaiser, 154, 174
Wilkes, John, 102, *110*
Willes, Edward, 85
William III, King of England and Scotland, 73–4, 75
William of Malmesbury, 7
William Tell (Schiller), 116
Williams, Anthony, 370
Williamson, Joseph, 61, 63
Willis, Robert, 21
Wills, Frank, 330
Wilmot, John, 65–8, 67
Wilson, Duncan, 325
Wilson, Elizabeth, 325
Wilson, Tony, 209
Wilson, Trevor, 312
Wilson, Woodrow, 192, 194, 195
Winant, John, 288
'Wind of Change' (Scorpions), 345–6
Wind Talk (Mai), 357
Window (anti-radar technology), 362
Windsor Castle, Berkshire, 247
Wingate, Ronald, *157*
Winner, Michael, *329*
With Lawrence in Arabia (Thomas), 210
Wizard of Oz (1939 film), 276
de Wohl, Louis, 281–3, *282*
Wolfe Tone, Theobald, 131
Wolfe Tones, The, 131
Wolsey, Thomas, 8–9
Woodstock, Oxfordshire, 76
Woodward, Bob, 330
Woolf, Virginia, 64, 163–5, *165*
Woolsey, James, 370
Woolwich Arsenal spy ring, 223
Wordsworth, William, 106, 112, 126
World in Action (TV series), 350
World War I (1914–18), 134, 162–3, 172, 174–5, 176–98, 202
   Arab Revolt (1916–18), 211–12, 214, 215
   Armistice (1918), 202
   Black Tom Pier sabotage (1916), 182
   Casement trial (1916), 189–90
   Easter Rising (1916), 170, 171, 172, 189, 190
   fighter aces, 247–8, 270
   film and, 174–5
   ID25, 190–94
   Lody trial (1914), 176–8
   Mata Hari, 2, 184–8, 214, 219, 221, 223
   MI1c, 194–8, 206–7, 217–21
   Operation FRIEDENSTURM (1918), 184
   SIGINT, 134, 186, 190–94, 212
   trench warfare, 178
   Vieyra trial (1916), 180–82

World War II (1939–45), 243–69, 270–95
 Bletchley Park *see* Bletchley Park
 Blitz (1940–41), 277
 disinformation, 2, 247–69
 Dunkirk evacuation (1940), 244, 256
 Middle East theatre, 254, 255
 North African campaign (1940–43), 254,
  255, 258
 Office of Strategic Services (OSS), 272,
  292, 293–8
 Operation BARBAROSSA (1941), 244
 Operation COPPERHEAD (1944), 258
 Operation GARBO (1942–4), 262, 266–9,
  306, 311
 Operation HUSKY (1943), 264, 265
 Operation MINCEMEAT (1943), 2,
  263–6
 Operation OVERLORD (1944), 258, 266,
  267, 268, 297
 Operation SEALION (1940, planned), 274
 Operation TORCH (1942), 255,
  260, 275
 Pearl Harbor attack (1941), 278, 281, 286,
  287–8, 292, 299
 Special Operations Executive (SOE), 243,
  271, 281, 300–303
 Tube Alloys (1941–5), 352
Worrall, David, 126
Wright, Peter, 350
Wright, Thomas, 35, 37
Wyndham's Theatre, London, 167, 168

Xi Jinping, 357

Yagoda, Genrikh, 236
Yeats, W. B., 169
Yeltsin, Boris, 344, 346, 358
Yezhov, Nikolai, 235, 236
yoga, 207
York University, 303
Yorke, John, 42
Yorktown campaign (1781), 101–2
You Only Live Twice (1967 film), 276
Young Ireland, 131, 134
Younger, Alexander, 382
Yugoslavia (1918–2003), 292
Yumashev, Andrei, 238

Z organisation, 286
Zadok the Priest (Lawes), 56
Zaïre (Voltaire), 99
Zarubin, Vasily, 227
Zasulich, Vera, 149
Zavorotnyuk, Anastasia, 361–2
Zelle, Margaretha, 2, 184–8, *185*, 214, 219,
  221, 223, 261, 311, 357
Zetterling, Mai, 371
Zhivkov, Todor, 325, 326
Zimmermann telegram (1917), 192
Zola, Alexandrine, 156, 157
Zola, Émile, 146–7, 155–8, *157*
Zouzou (1934 film), 273
Zozimus, 130–31